MARLENE DIETRICH

MARLENE DIETRICH

by her daughter

MARIA RIVA

BLOOMSBURY

First published in Great Britain 1992
Bloomsbury Publishing Limited, 2 Soho Square, London W1V 5DE

Published in the United States by Alfred A. Knopf, Inc., New York,
and simultaneously in Canada by Random House of Canada Limited, Toronto

A CIP catalogue record for this book
is available from the British Library

ISBN 0 7475 1375 9

Typeset by Hewer Text Composition Services, Edinburgh
Printed by Clays Limited, St Ives plc

To all who verified my memory, amended it, jogged it, challenged it, refined it, my deepest gratitude.

To all who lived with the results of it and loved me still, my eternal devotion.

This book is for the Rivas, big and small and yet to be –

and

Tami

CONTENTS

SCHÖNEBERG   3

BERLIN   43

HOLLYWOOD – THE BEGINNING   89

PARIS–VIENNA   203

HOLLYWOOD – THE MAGIC YEARS   261

LONDON AND BEYOND   407

BOX OFFICE POISON   433

WARTIME   495

GONE A' SOLDIERING   543

SHOWTIME   589

THE WORLD   693

PARIS   767

INDEX   797

PICTURE SOURCES

Lucien Angier: page 416 *bottom*

Daily Express: page 719 *bottom*

Dietrich Archive/Kobal Collection: pages 38, 72 *top & bottom*, 73 *top left, top right & bottom*, 94 *top*, 95 *top & bottom*, 96 *top left, top right & bottom*, 98 *top left & bottom*, 99, 144 *bottom*, 145 *top & bottom*, 149 *top & bottom*, 150 *bottom*, 151 *top*, 273 *top & bottom*, 274, 275, 276, 322 *top & bottom*, 323, 368 *top*, 370 *top*, 380 *top & bottom*, 381 *top & bottom*, 382, 383, 399 *top left, top right & bottom*, 400 *bottom*, 415 *top & bottom*, 439 *top, middle & bottom*, 440 *top*, 510 *top & bottom*, 511 *top & bottom*, 512 *top & middle*, 513 *top*, 523 *top & bottom*, 524 *bottom*, 525 *top right and bottom*, 537 *top & bottom*, 538, 585 *top & bottom*, 586, 609 *top*, 611 *top & bottom*, 612 *top*, 623 *bottom*, 625 *top & bottom*, 626 *top & bottom*, 663 *top & bottom*, 664 *top*, 665 *top & bottom*, 687 *top left, top right and bottom*, 668–9, 699 *top & bottom*, 700 *top*, 717

Milton Greene: page 745 *top*

Milton Greene/*Life* magazine: page 624

Kobal Collection: page 98 *top right*

Alexander Liberman: page 666

Life magazine: page 609 *bottom*

Arnold Newman/*Life* magazine: page 610 *top*

Paris Match: page 716 *bottom*

Photo Giocomelli, Venice: page 461 *top & bottom*

Photo Star, Cannes: page 474 *bottom*

Photo Werhard, Salzburg: page 418 *top*

UPI/Bettmann Archive: pages 610 *bottom*, 745 *bottom*

US Army: pages 525 *top left*, 548 *top & bottom*, 550 *bottom left & bottom right*, 551, 569 *top & bottom*, 570 *top & bottom*, 571 *top*, 572

Ginette Vachon: page 746 *top*

All other illustrations from the Dietrich Archive

MARLENE DIETRICH

SCHÖNEBERG

HE MUST HAVE BEEN GORGEOUS! Ramrod straight, the deep blue of his perfectly tailored cavalry uniform taut across the muscles of his fencer's back, elegant face, its high cheekbones emphasizing eyes glinting clear blue behind hooded lids. "Bedroom eyes" had not been invented yet, but it would have suited Louis Otto Dietrich perfectly. He looked exactly what he was: a Prussian officer, born to class and privilege. He had removed his spiked helmet, his red-blond hair – the world would one day report its color as being "Titian" when describing his daughter's – caught the glint of the afternoon sun as it filtered through the Victorian lace curtains of his father's library. An acknowledged rake, Louis Dietrich was used to tongue-lashings from his long-suffering parent.

"Once and for all, if you don't stop with these whores of yours, you will be sent across the sea to be scalped by Indians!"

Louis had been threatened with banishment to far-off America and its Indian hordes so often, he remained silent, at attention in front of his father's desk, waiting for the usual lecture to run its course. It was a well-known threat that neither man took seriously. As only the second son of an aristocratic family, Louis knew he had little to look forward to, even less to lose. An automatic military commission assured him the elegance of a suitable uniform and a steady supply of drinking and gambling companions. Courtesans belonged to this life as much as the shiny dueling sword at his slender hip. Having recently distinguished himself in all regimental protocols required, he felt his military credentials were henceforth ones that the Fatherland could be justly proud of; his duty done, he now deserved to resume his favorite sport. Louis loved the game of love; the hunt, the chase, the capture, the inevitable surrender. Like a blue-eyed falcon, he swooped, and girls swooned in anticipation.

"God damn it, Louis! Don't you have anything to say?" Calmly, as though reciting his catechism, the son promised his father once again, he would mend his wild ways, protect the noble name of Dietrich from the slightest hint of scandal, strive diligently to present the family with what it seemed to want so fervently, a son they could be justly proud of. Louis could charm the larks off the linden trees. This monthly ritual of "making Louis see the error of his ways" always ended with a formal handshake, a deferential clicking of heels by the son, a gallant toast to the Kaiser in the excellent champagne his father's cellar was known for. Unrepentant, Louis kept right on making German maidenhood happy.

But when he brought his talents into the ancestral home, seducing one of the parlor maids, his outraged mother took charge – no lengthy discussions, certainly no champagne! She announced to one and all: "Louis is getting married!"

The Dietrichs were summoned to a family council. The brothers, sisters, uncles, aunts, cousins, the whole imposing clan. They arrived in sumptuous landaus, on prancing horseback, some in their Daimler "Strength Wagons" that frightened the sleek harness horses. Amidst much shaking of bonneted heads, stroking of mustaches, clinking of Meissen china and Bavarian crystal, the eligibility and availability of Berlin's virgins were discussed, scrutinized as precisely as a military objective. The campaign to find a suitable bride "to keep Louis in line" had begun. It soon floundered. It seemed the Golden Falcon's reputation had filtered into an amazing number of the best homes. Proud Prussian mamas closed ranks, refusing to allow their innocent daughters even to be considered likely candidates for marriage to such a "shocking bounder." While the family searched, Louis rode his horses and his amours with equal gusto.

The list of available brides dwindled. There *was* that rather quiet, nearly pretty, jeweler's daughter. The one whose father made those beautiful timepieces, perfect craftsmanship, really works of art. Her dowry would be substantial, the family honored to have their daughter marry above her station.

Wilhelmina Elisabeth Josephine Felsing was a good girl. She obeyed her mother, respected her father, asked nothing more of life than to do her duty, properly. Not really pretty, she looked capable and trustworthy. Her dark brown eyes could hold a hint of mischief, but rarely did she permit herself such frivolity of inner spirit. It wasn't that she lacked warmth or a sense of emotion. Actually, she would later discover that she was capable of tumultuous passion, but even then, if confronted by choice, duty always took preference over anything else. Being German, this suited her. Being a Victorian female, her future was known to her, which also suited her. Being of marriageable age, her father would soon transfer his responsibility for her existence to a suitable husband. She knew her place in Berlin society, that of a successful tradesman's daughter. Josephine, as she was called, had been schooled well. She knew the duties of a good wife: to oversee the servants, personally inspect the folding of linen, the weekly polishing of silver, beating of carpets, seasonal exchange of draperies, itemizing of the larder, selecting daily menus with the cook, stitching her husband's monograms on his personal linen, bearing him heirs.

She was just twenty-one when Louis Dietrich, resigned to his fate, came to her parents' house to pay his respects. Properly chaperoned by her proud mother, Josephine watched him as he approached. His male beauty shocked her so, instead of lowering her eyes as she curtsied to him, her startled gaze remained fixed on his face.

"Fräulein Felsing," he murmured softly, brushing his mouth across the back of her cool hand, and, for this sensible, lackluster girl, time stood still. She loved him! A timeless passion, unquestioned, unexplained, sometimes unwanted, through betrayal, carnage of war, even beyond death, till the end of her days.

She wore white lace, a matching capelet of cashmere against the winter cold. The traditional band of myrtle holding her bridal veil, its circle securely closed, denoting her virginity; a Victorian girl in new Edwardian finery. Louis, having resigned his military officer's elegance for the equally dashing uniform of a lieutenant in the elite imperial police, towered beside her in deep plum and opulent gold braid. They said their vows in an Anglican ceremony. It was December of 1898; she was twenty-two, he, thirty.

They moved into their new home in Schöneberg, a fashionable town near Berlin where Louis was stationed. Schöneberg was aptly named. It was indeed a pretty place, full of tall poplar trees, flowered gardens, intimate squares, careful architecture. The gracefully curved streetlamps were newly electrified; dark green trolley cars, with their small exterior platforms, no longer needed horses to pull them along their tracks – now boasted tall electric antennae with which to join the new century. Josephine ran her small establishment with an efficiency far beyond her years. Everything shone, sparkled, functioned properly. Louis was enchanted by this so-serious young bride wanting only to please. Being married might prove a pleasing diversion after all.

WHEN THE MIDWIFE ANNOUNCED the birth of his daughter, Louis acknowledged the news with a shrug of his beautifully tailored shoulders and ordered his horse, his duty done. His father would be disappointed that it was not a son, but as no child of his could inherit, be it male or female, it really made very little difference. He felt he needed a change of scene. His latest mistress was becoming tiresome, and now that Josephine would be suckling the child, he resolved to lock the connecting door between their bedrooms; while breeding women discomforted him, there was something about making love to a mother that he found somehow distasteful.

Josephine named her first child Elisabeth. A potato-dumpling baby, brown-eyed, quiet, undemanding, a being aiming to please as unobtrusively as possible. Deep down, hidden inside her, she would cry "Love me," but no one ever heard her. Her birth created a loneliness in her mother for which she was never forgiven, nor knew the cause.

Josephine went about her daily duties as efficient housekeeper and mother, living for the rare sound of a turning key in the night that brought the end of yearning.

Three weeks after her twenty-fifth birthday, the morning of December 27, 1901, after a particularly difficult labor, Josephine gave birth to a second daughter. An incandescent creature, the top of her perfect head covered in fine down the color of a summer sunset. Her skin held the luminosity of oriental pearls, a glint of clear blue behind hooded lids, the Golden Falcon in miniature. Josephine looked down at this perfect being at her breast, and the passion she felt for the man who had created it transferred itself to his child. She felt it like a raging force leaving her body. With this new love, twin to the old, came a terrible fear, an inexplicable haunting: Could the child have inherited the father's appetites? Would she, too, find facility in hurting those who loved her? She vowed to guard her, if necessary even from herself. Josephine named her new daughter Maria Magdalena. Was it to implore God's protection that she chose this name, or clairvoyance?

BY THE AGE OF TWENTY-NINE, Josephine was old. Frustration had worked its corrosion. The early blossoming, so callously terminated, had withered a young girl into a cold woman, set in her ways, stoic, given to commands, dictums, and ponderous truisms. In her dark skirt, severe high-necked bodice, sensible shoes, a stranger coming to call would have taken her for the dour housekeeper, not the young mistress of the house in Schöneberg. Josephine ran her home, reared her daughters with an iron hand. They feared her. But parental fear being such a normal prerequisite in a good Prussian home, the two little girls accepted it as normal and thrived.

Elisabeth, known as Liesel, was an intelligent child. Like the small brown sparrow she resembled, she picked up any crumbs of affection that fell her way. She loved books, taught herself to read before the age of five and, whenever her younger sister didn't need her, escaped to the attic and its treasure of books. She adored her beautiful sister. Liesel was one of those rare people incapable of envy. Still, it would be nice to be beautiful and then be loved for it, but Liesel was a sensible child and accepted her plainness at a very early age.

Maria Magdalena was special – everyone knew it without reasoning, accepting its truth. Lena, as she was known, knew it too. She felt different from those around her. She was sure all the beautiful things in the world had been created just to please her. She kept this knowledge inside, knowing her mother would not approve her thinking of herself as something special. Her sister knew it though. Furtively, she permitted Liesel to pick up her dolls for her, make her bed, be her happy handmaiden. After all, as it made Liesel so happy to do things for her, it was really a kindness that she offered her older sister to enjoy. She did wish, though, that Liesel would stop calling her by that silly nickname she had invented and made her very own. Lena did not like being called Pussy Cat. It was not dignified for a Dietrich of nearly four. Besides, Liesel knew how much she disliked pets. Mutti didn't allow any animals in the house. For once, Lena could wholeheartedly agree with one of her mother's strict rules. Lena liked her father. Vati never made rules. He left all that to Mutti. He did engage the ladies of good class who came to tutor them in foreign languages. He always made very sure they were attractive, besides speaking impeccable French and English. Liesel preferred English. Lena adored French, because it made everything sound so romantic.

Louis was so rarely at home, to his daughters he remained a nebulous figure of male authority throughout their youth. Soon war would erase him completely from their young lives.

For now, Europe was at peace. It was a time of plenty; the Victorian era ended, the elegance of Edwardian England reached across the Channel. Berlin had become the largest industrial city in Europe, the prized jewel in its Kaiser's crown. Many believed the city rivaled Paris in everything, including its beautiful women in the latest fashions, strolling along the linden-treed avenues.

Through the years of watching her cope, the women of the Dietrich family had become genuinely fond of Louis's wife. To show their affection and approval of Josephine's exemplary behavior, they often came to take tea with the young matron, bringing some of the city's sparkle into her lackluster life. The poor child never went anywhere. Well – she *couldn't* very well, could she, without a husband to escort her! Over creamy mocha and vanilla crescents they chatted, gossiped, had a lovely visit, while Josephine listened politely and saw to their needs.

"Only yesterday," said a buxom lady in dark russet and precious cameo, "I simply had to find some beige embroidery wool. The tapestry, you know, the one that hangs in our music room? I discovered a slight tear, right on the forearm of one of the muses! Immediately, I ordered the carriage brought around and rushed off to Wertheim Department Store. It is owned by Jews; nevertheless, I believe it is one of the great wonders of Berlin. Everywhere those opulent floral arrangements! And those chandeliers! Must be as many as Versailles. The food halls had just received a new shipment of salmon from the Caspian Sea – and great tubs of caviar. I immediately purchased some for my husband. The Czar could not have better at his table. I also purchased some of that delicious nougat – just arrived from Florence – for the children, and a weightless paisley shawl for Max's mother – it is her seventieth birthday next week. Then I enjoyed a delectable tea, accompanied by a Hungarian babka bursting with sultanas. Of course, I returned home absolutely exhausted, but quite content."

"Ingeborg, did you find the beige tapestry wool?" a very thin lady in deep purple inquired.

"Yes, of course! You know as well as I, Sophia, that Wertheim's emporium carries absolutely everything!"

"My husband read in this morning's paper and then told me," announced a mousy lady in pale gray alpaca, "there has been an earthquake in an important city somewhere in North America. 'A *real* catastrophe,' my husband said."

"I believe the city is named San Francisco, after Saint Francis of Assisi." The lady in purple liked to set things straight.

"Oh, yes. I believe that *is* the name of it. My husband said many lives have been lost."

A stern lady, in strict navy blue – when standing she must have been extremely tall for, even seated, she loomed over the rest – intoned in a voice used to command:

"The Kaiser has met with the Czar of All the Russias – in Swinemünde. Yes, you heard me. I said Swinemünde. I have often taken my husband and children there. I always have said there is nothing so invigorating as north sea air. Our Kaiser undoubtedly is of the same mind."

A fat dachshund sat up, begged, received a sugared reward, then resumed his snooze beneath the laden tea table.

The new memorial church the Kaiser had commissioned, to be built in memory of his grandfather, was a topic they all found interesting. Had someone heard that its main spire was to be 113 meters high? It would be glorious! But why the planned star on its pinnacle? Like for the top of a Christmas tree! Not proper for a religious edifice of such importance.

"The Kaiser Wilhelm Memorial Church will be a triumph of ecclesiastical architecture for centuries to come, even if they do insist on that Christmas ornament!" intoned the lady in navy, and that ended the discussion.

"My cook tells me that on the north side, some women – she used the term 'ladies,' but of course I cannot believe that; over there they are all of the working class, but my cook insisted it was 'ladies' – marched there with banners, advocating that women should be given 'rights'. What rights? What some will do to draw attention to themselves! Shameful! 'Look after your husbands, homes, and children, and get off the streets,' they should be told." This, they all could agree with.

"We have taken a box for the opening of the new operetta. Is your husband taking you?" the mouse-gray lady inquired of the deep purple, who answered haughtily: "No, my dear. My husband and I are giving a musical soirée of Schumann lieder that evening."

"My husband told me the palace has announced there is to be another parade this week. The Kaiser does so love his parades! Do you suppose the Kaiserin will again be attired in that unattractive pale shade of lavender she is so partial to?" This led them all into a politely heated discussion of the latest fashions, which, of course, took up the rest of the afternoon.

Before the ladies took their leave, the daughters of the house were summoned down from their nursery floor to pay their respects, recite a Goethe poem, and receive a pat on their shiny heads from their approving aunts. They suffered this with the resigned patience of well-brought-up children.

But when their Tante Valli came to call, that was different!

Tante Valli was a beauty. A vibrant Lorelei! Having married well, she could afford to indulge her superb sense of luxury. She flung her doting husband's money about without a moment's concern. Her hunting stallions were the best horseflesh England could breed. Her riding habits were visions of broadcloth and velvet, usually jet black, her favorite color; the shiny top hat, secured by its attractive face veil, was a marvel of efficiency and inspired seduction. She ran her many estates with skillful panache, was known for her elaborate banquets and her tall footmen, whom she chose personally to her private specifications of uniform height and good looks.

When Tante Valli materialized, laden with exotic fruits and Paris

bonbons, even Josephine lost her stern expression and smiled. The whole
house seemed to wake from its somber sleep. Tante Valli sparkled. Both
girls adored her. She made such a pretty picture. Her little muff of real
otter from North America, her tightly fitted jacket trimmed with the same
rare fur, her hat a concoction of velvet bows and birds' wings. A vision in
forest green. While Liesel listened intently to her aunt's stories of the latest
voyages to far-off places, Lena feasted her eyes on her handmade shoes –
dark green and pearl, the delicate hand-stitching of her matching leather
gloves, the perfection of the Brussels lace at her throat. She resolved
someday she too would dress like a fine lady, look ravishingly beautiful
– just like her Tante Valli.

If Louis happened to be at home, Tante Valli shocked the girls by
accepting a glass of cognac from him, downing it like a man, chortling
at her own audacity and Josephine's horrified expression. She had always
been able to match Louis drink for drink and delighted in challenging his
masculine prowess – the only woman to whom he allowed this privilege.
Tante Valli had been the only one in the family who had sided with him
against a forced marriage. Nevertheless, now she had adopted "that poor
child," as the family referred to Josephine, brightening her lonely life
whenever she found the time, and reprimanding Louis for his negligent
behavior.

In the spring of 1906, when Lena was nearly five, the family had their
portrait taken by the royal court photographer. Tante Valli arranged
for the sitting, chose their finery, laughed at Louis's pompous expression, delighted in the effect of the straw hats she had chosen for the
little girls.

The time was fast approaching when the girls would be old enough for
school. Josephine's training of her young daughters to be good German
wives now went hand in hand with their formal education.

"You can't know when servants have performed their tasks incorrectly
unless you have learned to do such tasks yourself – correctly" was one
of the edicts the girls heard repeatedly. So they learned to mend, scrub,
polish, beat, brush, rub, and scour, while an ever-changing series of
ladies taught them French, English, piano, violin, and deportment. By
the time the Dietrich girls were old enough to begin school, both could
easily have skipped the first two grades, but, of course, this was not
permitted. The discipline of following the established curriculum was
diligently adhered to.

So, one dark cold morning, two little girls in braids and black wool
stockings marched off to school. Strapped to their backs, a large leather
briefcase heavy with books – the obligatory harness for all European
schoolchildren. The Augusta Victoria School for Girls loomed dark and

foreboding in the early morning light. Liesel pushed against the heavy iron gate for her little sister to enter. Taking her mittened hand, she led them both to their day's duty.

Liesel was happy in school. Everything that contributed to learning suited her. Her sister didn't like it, but, equally conditioned to taking orders, Lena too had no problem fitting into the strict structure of the school. Both girls delivered the excellent marks expected of them. On their return home each day, the girls first removed their street shoes, placed them neatly in the box provided in the entrance hall. After lacing up their indoor shoes, they washed their hands, changed from their school dress into their study pinafores. A minimum of two hours' homework preceded French conversation and composition with a private tutor. Then an hour's piano and violin practice, followed by a nourishing supper, eaten in strictest silence, as chatter was considered a hindrance to proper digestion. After their meal, English conversation and composition with another lady tutor ended their long day. Only after their mother had rebraided their hair for the night were the girls permitted a precious half hour to do with as they wished. Liesel always chose to read, while her sister smoothed the long satin ribbons of many colors she was collecting to tie to her mandolin. Somehow, somewhere, Lena had found the time to learn to play this Italian instrument. She thought it romantic and planned to tie her pretty collection to its neck. In a book, she had discovered a drawing of a wandering gypsy boy, and wanted to be one, playing a mandolin, trailing ribbons.

IN 1912, FOR EASTER, Tante Valli gave Lena a secret gift, a small red morocco-bound diary, embossed in gold. Its elegance appealed to the young girl immediately.

"Write in this your feelings," her aunt whispered. "You are old enough now to have them. Remember, it is always good to have a secret friend whom you can confide in."

In the years to come, Lena would pour her heart out in books of many colors, but this first one, the one she nicknamed Red, was her favorite. Sometimes she wrote in Berlin slang, unique in its sardonic, street-smart flippancy, so very different from the aristocratic High German that was spoken at home, that one has to wonder where she could have picked it up. Although its cutting tone left her whenever she waxed romantic, throughout her life the Berlinese of the streets could be instantly recalled. Now, at the age of ten and a half, a lifelong habit was about to begin.

LEFT: Louis Otto Dietrich and his bride, Wilhelmina Elisabeth Josephine Felsing. Berlin, 1898.

BELOW: The first portrait of the Dietrich family: Liese, age six, her mother, father, and little sister, Lena (who so loved her beribboned hat she wore it for the rest of the day), age five.

ABOVE, LEFT: The Dietrich sisters in their schoolroom smocks—ready to be "good girls."

ABOVE, RIGHT: With their Mutti at the seashore.

BELOW: Lena's class picture taken in 1909, when she was seven and a half. She wore a special bow that day and always thought she should have been placed in the front row.

The sinking of the *Titanic* in April of that year did not stir Lena's emotions, so she felt no need to record this tragedy. Two months later, during a summer outing, something did happen in her life that she finally considered was important enough to set down:

8 June 1912
Dear Little Red. Yesterday it was wonderful! We went on an excursion to Saatwinken with H. Schultz. I sat on his lap. Dear diary, you just can't imagine how nice it was. A thousand kisses,

Your Leni

One of the favorite places for young people to congregate was Berlin's large ice-skating rink. It boasted twinkling lights and a brass band that played Strauss waltzes and the latest sentimental tunes of love, loss, yearning, and suffering – Lena's favorite music.

26 February 1913
On the skating rink it was wonderful. I fell down and right away a lot of boys rushed to help me. Good-bye for now, sweet Red. Lots of kisses.

Your Leni

17 January 1914
At the ice rink, they play all the time the song "All Men Are Rogues." That's certainly true except for certain special people like Losch, Vati, and Uncle Willi and maybe someone with initials – S. F.? I don't want to write the name. Somebody may peek. I have to stop. Have my violin lesson. Adieu my Red.

Your Leni

19 January 1914
Today at the skating rink it was really nice. Liesel just asked if I was writing all that rubbish about boys again. Well, really! Is it rubbish, my sweet Red? Certainly not! *We* know what stuff *she* writes about, don't we. Liesel is so goody-good.

Kisses
Your Leni

Despite Lena's exemplary behavior at school and at home, Josephine recognized in her younger daughter an inner rebellion that alarmed her. It bore watching, closely. Liesel was instructed to accompany her younger sister everywhere, watch, report immediately any unladylike behavior, should there ever be any. Always dependable, ever obliging, Liesel now had her work cut out for her. She, who hated ice skating – it made her weak ankles ache so – skated with dogged determination. Head down, her little chunky body braced for balance, she plowed the ice, intent on keeping Lena and her latest conquest in constant sight. Instead of reading her beloved books, she trudged for what seemed miles, back and forth, keeping an eagle eye on Leni while she "bummeled," Berlin slang for the custom of visiting with one's friends while strolling up and down along the avenue at twilight. Wherever her Pussy Cat went, so did Liesel, the trusty watchdog.

30 January 1914

In school today I got a black mark because someone tickled me and I laughed. So of course Mutti had to give me a lecture about "friends." I can't help it if I don't have any girlfriends. Today I tried it with Anne Marie Richter in Composition Class, but she is so silly and she is already thirteen years old. So how to make friends in class? As I sit only with the Jews it's not easy. Mutti says I should ask for an isolated seat. . . . I already am expecting the worst from the children in Braunschweig this summer – but I hope they'll be nice. I am now taking myself very strongly in hand. Today Stephi Berliner pulled my cap off at least 6 times. Well! Was I mad! Now I have 4 black marks and 4 reproaches, one in attention, one in deportment, one in tidiness and 4 reproaches in behavior! Holy cow!

Now I have to go to bed. I have a toothache. Adieu.

Leni was considering changing the look of her name. While the schoolmaster's back was turned, she used the back pages of her copybook to try out the different effects. "Marie Magdalene" – that looked nice, with the two e's at either end, instead of two a's. Vati's name, Louis, was after a French king, so hers should have been French, too. But, as all maids were called Marie, perhaps that was the reason hers had that a on the end instead? In her much studied and labored-over German script, she wrote her full name. What a long time it took! She tried to shorten it: "Marialena," "Marlena" – she liked the sound of that one. Maybe now, the last e she liked would look right: "Marlene." She wrote it again: "MARLENE." She wrote it again: "MARLENE" – "Marlene Dietrich" – yes! That looked right. That she really liked! She rehearsed it a few more times, then closed the light blue copybook, very satisfied with herself. At the age of thirteen, she had invented the name *Marlene*.

1 February 1914

Yesterday Otti Raush was here. I think she will become my friend. In school they'll make fun maybe. Today I was at a real cinema. Chic. "Good-bye," Sweet Red.

Leni

From the Ural mountains to the lush green hills of Ireland, everyone felt the special magic of that summer of 1914. It was a golden time, not seen too often. Everywhere, vacations to seashores and mountain resorts were under way. Berlin's many sidewalk cafés, always full, overflowed as patrons basked in the soft sunshine, taking their time over their chilled Rhine wines and frosted lemonades. In the parks, acacia trees bloomed, children in white sailor suits rolled their wooden hoops, the long navy ribbons of their straw hats fluttering out behind them. In the famous gardens of Berlin's illustrious zoo, English nannies paraded their lace-adorned charges in tall-wheeled carriages. Parasoled ladies in sprigged muslin promenaded their little dogs. Young men rowed pretty girls on the calm waters of the River Spree, believing they had a glorious future, that life would be forever beautiful.

In a town called Sarajevo, on the borders of Serbia and the Austro-Hungarian Empire, the Austrian Crown Prince Francis Ferdinand, on a state visit, handed his wife, Sophie, into the open touring car, seated himself beside her, and gave the command for the cortège to begin. A band played. The royal car moved slowly down the imposing avenue. A flock of white doves circled above, like sudden snowflakes against the clear blue of the summer sky.

Suddenly, a moving shadow! A young man jumped onto the running board of the car and fired two shots.

History would record that at 11:15, on a beautiful summer morning, on the 28th of June, in the year 1914, by this one act of political murder, entire generations of young men would be condemned to death.

While the populations of Europe still enjoyed their summer vacations, their governments decided their fate.

On the 28th of July, Austria-Hungary declared war on Serbia. In quick succession, old alliances, as well as secret ones, were invoked. Germany declared war on Russia; Germany declared war on France; Britain declared war on Germany; Serbia declared war on Germany; France declared war on Austria–Hungary; Britain declared war on Austria–Hungary; Japan declared war on Germany; Austria–Hungary declared war on Japan; Austria–Hungary declared war on Belgium; Russia declared war on Turkey; France and Britain declared war on Turkey. Later, Italy would declare war on Germany, Turkey, and Austria–Hungary. Etc., etc. The United States would follow. The first global war had begun.

15 August 1914
Now it is war! Awful. Vati left on the 6th of August to the Western Front. Mutti cries all the time. In Harzburg it was nice. The dance instructor – was he sweet!

I think our school will be closed. No French girls anymore. Still some English ones. Yesterday I had my violin class and I played for Germany.

Your Leni

No one believed the war would last out the summer. In the cafés and coffeehouses, the Berliners referred to it as "that cute little war." By September, this flippant attitude had disappeared.

26 September 1914
War! Vati was wounded. Shrapnel wound in his right arm. He was sent to Braunschweig. Mutti took us there. He lay in the military hospital. We stayed in Pension Müller-Bartenstein, Jerusalem Street, No. 2. Very nice. 180 marks for just three weeks. A lot of money. Vati was sweet. After 4 weeks, he went away on Saturday in a car, like a prince. Uncle Otto and George have the Iron Cross.

9 October 1914
Uncle Willi has the Iron Cross too, that's fantastic! I am now in Class 3M. Hats off to me. Auf wiedersehen.

Leni

9 December 1914
The story is funny and sad at the same time. Vati's whole battalion has lice! We are knitting pulse warmers with two needles in all our classes in school. I don't want to go to that upper school. I am so scared of those girls. Sweet Red, I miss my Vati so much.

Your Leni

In that first terrible winter of the Great War, soldiers dug trenches along both the western and eastern fronts. In the German and French languages, the word for *trench* derives from the word meaning "to dig a grave," an appropriate name for what was to come.

15 December 1914
Uncle Otto has been killed. Shot in the neck on the fourth of December. Everybody's crying. Uncle Otto had the front of his skull shot away. Kisses.

Leni

3 February 1915
Liesel is completely head over heels "in love" with Hanni. There exist animals called monkeys – my sister belongs to them. Oh! I am so furious about Liesel being *so* in love. Beloved . . . betrothed . . . be married . . . I am in love too . . . ?? R. is sweet!!

Leni

6 March 1915
Today we learned dry painting. Violets on silk and paper, and sunflowers
on wood. Violets for my sweet golden Tante Valli for her birthday.
Terrible about our beautiful ship Togoland! – really mean! I just hope
the English will get a really good beating today.

Ever chemists of diabolical genius, the Germans launched their first
poison-gas attack on the 22nd of April, 1915. The rest of the world
condemned it as an act of barbarism, then set about developing their
own lethal substances. The gas mask was invented, became standard
issue on both sides. Finally the Germans surpassed even themselves –
they perfected a new gas, an oily mixture that did not hover in the
air but dropped, clung to what it fell on, then ate its way through
it: cloth, leather, living flesh, muscle, lung tissue – anything. In order
for poison gas to reach its correct targets, it was essential to calculate
temperature, wind velocity, and direction. This made the firing of gas
canisters time-consuming and hazardous. A sudden shift of the wind
could turn the lethal cloud back onto its masters. This, probably more
than conscience, kept chemical warfare from dominating the next years
of the war.

29 April 1915
They have gone to get Uncle Otto. Soon we are going on vacation to Dessau – finally! I could stay there forever. I think maybe
Uncle Otto was not killed. Maybe it's not sure. Why did he have to
die?

NOW THE LADIES CAME to the house in Schöneberg not to gossip – to
weep. Always calm, sensible, dependable, Josephine would know what
to do, what to say, ease their grief, give them comfort when none seemed
possible. Like silent crows, they gathered. Their black garments against
the parquet floors, sounding like the faint rustle of autumn leaves. More
and more, Josephine assumed the role of family matriarch. They all
believed Josephine Dietrich to be the strongest one among them. Perhaps
they were right. The girls, concealed on the landing, would watch their
mother bring loaded trays of liverwurst sandwiches and steaming coffee.
They knew she believed in feeding the bereaved, that physical stamina
was essential for coping with grief. True, the ladies always did feel a
little better on leaving Josephine's house. Watching, Liesel would cry in
sympathy for those black figures bent in sorrow. Lena, never a lover of

stark reality, continued to see life from her own perspective. When Tante
Valli, newly widowed, came to stay, Lena was overjoyed.

4 February 1916
Tante Valli is here. It's wonderful! Just now I put a branch of pine with
paper roses on her bed, with a poem I wrote for her.

> If I had beautiful roses,
> I would pick them for you,
> but since we are in wintertime,
> this I couldn't do.
> Just look at these flowers
> and think of me.
> I love you.

6 February 1916
Tante Valli is so heavenly sweet! Yesterday she wore a black dress with
white collar and white cuffs. She looked completely divine. Chic. She also
had black patent shoes. Last night I kissed her a lot but still I feel something
is missing – the one kiss she gives me is not enough. I am so happy when
she gives me a kiss – like with Grete in Dessau, but she is *my aunt*. Liesel
also gives her kisses. Yesterday when I played the Nostalgia Waltz from
Beethoven to her, she cried. I wanted to throw away my violin and run
to her and kiss away her tears.

10 February 1916
Now Tante Valli has gone. It is terrible. She gave me a silver bracelet,
which I am not allowed to wear at school. Luckily, I got a few of her
cigarette ends she smoked at Tante Eimini's, they have silken tips. When
she was gone, I sat before her bed and cried my eyes out. Just now, doing
my mathematics, I started crying again because I suddenly thought how
quiet everything is again.

15 June 1916
Vati is being sent toward the Eastern Front. Mutti traveled to Westphalia
to try to meet him. But his train had already left and Mutti tried to
follow the train but couldn't. She missed him by being five minutes
late. She is terribly sad. Yesterday, as Mutti was away, we went to
see a revue at the Variety. We fell about with laughter. Vati sent us
some real photographs. In one of them he is with a gorgeous pilot
officer whose name is Lackner. Upstairs we now play "Nurse." Of
course, I am in charge of nursing Lackner, more precisely Hans-Heinz
von Lackner, Lieutenant Colonel of 92nd Infantry Regiment, age 23,
born in Braunschweig. My black scarf makes me look like a real nurse
and I look good in it. By the way, I am not so crazy about Tante Valli

anymore. At the moment I'm not crazy about anybody! In a few weeks
we will be in Harzburg – then I will probably be crazy about someone
again there.

Of all the new breed of daring young men who, in 1914, first took
warfare into the sky, the German ace Baron Manfred von Richthofen was
probably the most glamorous. Idolized by his countrymen, respected by
his enemies, he embodied that "white silk scarf fluttering in the wind"
image of the truly romantic pilot. In typical daredevil fashion, he painted
his special Fokker triplane bright red, so as to be instantly visible to his
English counterparts. His enemies rewarded this arrogant bravery by
naming him the Red Baron. These very young men, who in their little
planes swooped like fragile kites above the earth while killing and being
killed, were the real glamour boys of this first modern war, as they would
be in the next and the next and the next. As with knights of old, single
combat always seems to be accorded an extra dose of gallant heroism.
Only the fact that young ladies of good family did not read newspapers,
that radio and television were nonexistent, can account for the omission of
this dashing hero figure from Lena's girlish diaries. With him, she would
really have had something to swoon about, as she did twenty-eight years
later for anyone sporting a winged insignia on his uniform.

It was Tante Valli, her pale face a mask of grief, who brought the news
of Louis's death to Josephine. It was she who held the stricken woman
in her arms, murmured the well-worn phrases of comfort and solace,
hoping to reach her through the icy shock, led her to her room, made her
lie down, covered her with the big feather bed, knowing soon the cold
of sorrow would invade her soul. Then she waited in the silent house for
the children's return.
    That night, Liesel cried herself to sleep, a photograph of her father
clutched in her hand. Lena refused to believe any of it. Tante Valli had
no right to make up such terrible lies about something so serious. She
curtsied to her aunt and marched off to her room. Lena did not cry.
Daughters of brave soldiers never cried.
    Behind the closed door of her room, Josephine mourned alone. When
she finally emerged, her widow's weeds enfolded her like bat's wings.
She plaited the traditional black ribbons tightly into her daughters' braids,
sewed the black armbands onto their school clothes, hung black crepe on
the big front door of the house in Schöneberg. Life in wartime Germany
resumed its dance of death.

June 1916
Now everybody is dead. Today Vati will be buried. This morning we did
not go to school but to the Memorial Cemetery to be by Vati. His grave
was just being dug. It is terribly boring here now – the only interesting
boy on the bummel is Schmidt.

Leni

NOW A WOMAN ALONE with two children to raise, Josephine was
frantic. She knew her widow's pension would not be enough. Soon
the girls would outgrow their shoes – what then? Where could she
find leather in wartime? Even if she cut up Louis's riding boots, where
would she find the money to pay the cobbler? Even food was becoming
scarce. Her ration certificate became her most valuable possession. Her
days were spent in long queues waiting, hoping that when her turn
finally came, someone still had something left to sell. By the winter
of 1916, the bread was made of turnips, the meat rations bones and
offal; milk and cheese nonexistent; potatoes had been replaced by yellow
turnips. Coffee, such an integral part of Berlin's social structure, was
made from the ground nut of the beech tree. "Ersatz" in everything
had become a way of daily life. In the working-class sections of the
city, women pooled whatever precious rations they could find, set up
communal kitchens where, for forty pfennigs, everyone could buy a
liter of thin soup with which to feed their families. In the fashionable
section of Berlin, black-market restaurants flourished. There, embossed
menus offered pheasant, succulent goose, crackling pork roasts, a choice
of vegetables, chocolate cakes, and assorted ices. As always, in any
war, the very rich could feast, while the poor scavenged to feed their
children.

When influenza swept through the beleaguered city, Josephine knew
the time had come to take her children and leave Berlin. Having to say
good-bye to the house in Schöneberg was like losing Louis all over again,
now he would truly be gone. She, who rarely allowed herself tears, cried
for all the young dreams lost; then turning her back on the past, she walked
away. She had her duty to do.

Josephine settled her small family in a rented apartment sixty-five miles
southwest of Berlin, in a town called Dessau.

Dessau
9 November 1916
I got to the bummel at 6:15. They told me that Fritz was there at 6.

Wouldn't you know it with my luck! So I waited, hoping he would come but of course he never showed. If he had come up to me it would have been great – because Mutti was away in town. I saw him later at violin lessons. I always get to my lesson before he is finished. If Herbert Hirsh only knew *that*. He swooned over me in Hartsbad. He was sort of interesting. What was especially interesting was his hot kissing in the dark hallway, for which I got real angry at him. He is 14 years old but behaves like 17. His father is an ugly old Jew that Mutti thought might be dangerous. Herbert was a nice distraction for me in Berlin but uncomfortable because he always stood in front of the door, waiting to accompany me everywhere and, of course, I didn't want to be seen with him in front of the others. Before we left Berlin, I saw him the last time. The day we were leaving, he rode by on his bicycle. I had some roses from Tante Elsa, so I pretended I had gotten them from an admirer and told him they should have been from him. After that, he bicycled away in a hurry. I think I'll write to him and reawaken his ardor again. Here every girl has her own admirer, otherwise Dessau would be a bore.

Dessau
6 December 1916
Today I bummeled and a gang of boys pulled my cap and bothered me. That always happens when a new one comes who isn't known yet. I can't go tomorrow because 3 days in a row I am not allowed to stroll. Now I am even supposed to be in bed by quarter to nine! At fifteen?! Liese is so "virtuous" – she never goes past Cavaliere Street because she is afraid someone might think she is bummeling. Tante Eimini has Spanish influenza – Mutti has gone there to nurse her. I had to go over to Tante Agnes, when I got there she had nothing better to do than reproach me all my sins. "Why was I on the bummel yesterday?" "Who did I see?" "How many times did I go up and down?"! My only fun, if you can call it that, is to stroll for half an hour with a girlfriend in the evening after my homework. And now, even this is not allowed! Well, I don't care! I am going anyway!

10 December 1916
Today he smiled so cutely. He was wounded, so wears civilian clothes. His name is F. Schuricke and he always looks at me in a bold way. In the morning, I see him on the trolley car, and in the evening when he comes back again, when we stroll. Now *this* I will not allow anybody to take away from me! (By the way, with Tante Valli it is over.)

Dessau
13 January 1917
Maybe I am a bit overexcited, but I can't help it, I love him. With all my love. And what is so beautiful about the whole thing is that he likes me!

Doesn't he look up to my window every time he passes my house, to see if I'm standing there waiting for him? Dumb to be like that, but nice too, to know for who one does a new hairstyle, gets dressed up, even though he hardly notices it. He is, after all, my first love. Before, I knew nothing of love. Tomorrow, I will see you on the promenade, Fritzi. I will see you, you, you, you angel – you, you wonderful you! About my old loves, I always laughed. About my first love, I will never laugh! I hope Mutti doesn't spoil it all for me.

16 January 1917
Now it's all over. The whole thing didn't mean a thing to him. And I let myself go and showed him how much I liked him. I'll never give myself to somebody like I did to him, somebody who doesn't care, somebody who was only interested to hear what a young "schoolgirl" thought about him. No, I am too good for that! I'll remember all the feeling but with F. S., it's over!

After months of continuous carnage, the Battle of Verdun had ended. It had cost the French 542,000 men. The German casualties stood at 434,000.

4 February 1917
I had a very big fight with Mutti. She said that as I "hang around" with all those schoolboys, that I must be boy crazy. First of all, I don't "hang around with boys," and, second, they are all just good friends. One doesn't have to fall in love with them all the time and, even so, this doesn't have to mean that one is "man crazy"! Some people always see something bad in the most harmless things. She said, "If you become obsessed with men, you will be sent to a boarding school." PUH! That is so stupid! She is always trying to find fault for nothing and I really do think: "What a boring life!" When one talks with a schoolboy on the skating rink, one is "man crazy"? No, no! That's really too much for me to have to take!

19 February 1917
I am crazy about Ulle Bülow. Detley Ernst-Ulrich Erich Otto Wilhelm von Bülow. He is so divinely good-looking. His mother is, or was, Jewish, and so, of course, he has something special about him – a special race beauty, cute and so thoroughbred! Besides, he is terribly chic! He is 16, he used to ignore me but now he doesn't.

Even in Dessau, the "turnip winter" was becoming a stark reality. Slowly, the skin of women, children, and old men took on the yellow-orange hue of the lowly rutabaga. That is, everyone's but Lena's. Hers retained its porcelain pallor. Throughout her life, she often referred to this time of her youth: "During the war, all we had to eat was turnips, just turnips, nothing else. After a while, everyone's skin turned yellow – but not mine. Mine didn't. Funny? I was only six years old at that time." She was actually sixteen. Marlene could toss years about like confetti.

That winter, when Eduard von Losch proposed marriage to the young widow Dietrich, Josephine accepted with gratitude and affection. Eduard had been Louis's best friend. She had known and respected him since her husband had first brought him to the house to meet his new bride. Later, he had been the only one of Louis's friends who she felt had not condoned her husband's irresponsible behavior.

Eduard was a kind man, willing to care for the ready-made family of his friend, asking nothing more than to protect them during these hard times. He did not expect Josephine to love him. For him, loving her was enough.

The von Losch family was outraged. They informed Eduard he would be marrying beneath his station, that they considered Josephine Dietrich to be nothing more than an ambitious social climber, and, if he insisted on this foolishness, the family would not only refuse to receive his wife, they would henceforth wash their hands of the whole distasteful affair.

She wore black. Eduard and Josephine were married in a simple ceremony, as befitted the bride's recent widowhood and wartime. Her young daughters were not present. Although Liesel continued to mourn her real father, she accepted her new stepfather with genuine affection. Lena ignored the marriage entirely, behaved as though it never happened. Her mother's name might now be von Losch, hers would remain forever – Dietrich. In later years, her real father and von Losch would superimpose on her memory, each man losing his own identity, becoming one.

Eduard installed his new family in his lovely house situated in one of the most fashionable residential districts of Berlin. Now, each day was like a little Christmas. For a while, the war seemed far away. Some mornings there was real milk, even a whole piece of cheese. Little brown paper parcels of precious coffee beans miraculously appeared. Two, sometimes even three, whole lumps of sugar, and bread – real flour bread! The joy of seeing Josephine smile was so irresistible Eduard searched the city for precious luxuries, grateful he had the means to pay the exorbitant black-market prices. One night, Josephine found a fresh flower on her pillow. A perfect yellow rose! A rose in wartime Berlin? Where could Eduard ever have found it! It must have cost a fortune! Eduard just beamed; to see his wife happy was wonderful! Soon he would have to leave her. He had so little time left to give her joy.

Berlin
2 April 1917
Finally, I've got a place where I can be alone. They've fixed up the small
attic above the bathroom for me. I have a big rug, pink curtains, and electric
light. It's very cozy in the evening. I pine so for spring, for summer. Even
though we have this large house, here one only goes out to see what other
people are wearing and always worries if one is dressed well enough – and
modern! Oh, it would be so nice to lie in a meadow, wearing a dirndl dress,
just dreaming. I asked Mutti if I could go to Tante Touton. "No." If I were
a mother, I would be happy to have my child have fun, eat well, instead
of sitting in Berlin studying. It's sad that I am not in love with Ulle von
Bülow anymore. I mean, the way I was before – it really was nice to feel
that way.

Kisses
Your Leni

German submarines hunted the North Atlantic for enemy and neutrals
alike. After holding off as long as possible, Woodrow Wilson declared that
the United States was at war with Germany. Soon American doughboys
were massed in France, ready to march to the lilting tunes of Irving Berlin
and George M. Cohan, off to save the world. Why was not the issue. It
was going to be one glorious adventure!
    Across the rolling hills of Château-Thierry, an endless sea of small
white crosses marks their passage.

13 April 1917
I am not crazy about anyone. Today we got a photograph of Uncle
Max. Sweet, sweet Uncle Max. Now that his Zeppelin was shot down
and he is dead, one thinks of how sweet he was. I think the war will
never end. Now even America! I think I better stop and write again
when I have something interesting to write about. I'm waiting for a
new love.

17 May 1917
Spring is here now, with a summer heat. Yesterday, after my violin lesson,
two boys followed me on the Kurfürstendamm.

2 June 1917
Yesterday and today I gathered money for the U-boat donations. Tomorrow I am going to try to get out of it. Here we live such a boring life.
Mutti keeps telling us how well we live but she doesn't understand that
we miss a *little* fun.

The western front now extended about three hundred miles, from the coast of Flanders, near Dunkirk, to the Swiss border, near the town of Basel. The eastern front stretched a thousand miles, from the Baltic Sea down to the Black Sea.

18 June 1917
I am starting to love Margaret Rosendorf from Liesel's class – otherwise my heart is very empty. It's so much nicer if one has someone – it makes you feel so pretty. We did an excursion to Faulbaummern. There an elderly gentleman kept following me. His name was Wiebett. I went to see the Henny Porten film. I love her. I finally convinced Mutti to change Liesel's hairstyle. Until now, she wore her braids like snails at the back of her head. Now she wears a bun with a special bow. Now I wear my hair up, and when something special is happening, I let a curl fall. After all, for a braid I am now too old.

28 June 1917
I love Henny Porten so. I sent off a picture postcard for her to autograph but she doesn't know whom she sends them back to. Just signs it, sticks it in an envelope, and off it goes. Must be easy. There are new pictures of her with her child – the poor thing; she is still so young and gets put on a picture postcard. Princess Eduard is in a sanitarium for hysteria. I hope she gets out. She was nice when I met her at Tante Valli's. I just got a violin that cost 2,000 marks. The violin's sound is pure. This means *they* want to train me? Well, practicing will be awfully pleasant, I'm sure! I wrote a poem about "brave U-boats."

The day came for Eduard to rejoin his infantry regiment. He held Josephine close. He loved to see the change in her. She looked so sweet in her new summer dress. Pale yellow suited her. He did not want to remember her in black. He had made all the necessary arrangements. Should he be killed, she was provided for, she would have to beg no one. He kissed her. She clung to him. . . . Don't go – don't leave me – Please – her heart cried. She knew she mustn't say it, mustn't burden him with her need.

"I'll be back. Yes! I will! By Christmas. The war will be over by then. I must go – write to me. Every day! I love you!"

She stood there all alone long after his train had gone. Then she turned and went home.

Bad Liebenstein
7 July 1917
We are in Liebenstein. I was looking forward to it, but it is nothing! In the morning we go to take the waters and the rest of the time one hangs around bored stiff. All kinds of poor people live here in fancy surroundings. People

don't come here to have a good time. Wherever one looks, all kinds of children, either who have the eyes completely closed or big blisters on the lids. Nothing better than a spa to have fun!

Yesterday we saw the moon come into the shadow of the earth. Very beautiful.

Henny Porten sent me back my picture cards. Big cold letters – her signature.

Next to our hotel, they are building – the workmen are French prisoners of war.

That summer, corpses rotted in the golden sun. Men trapped in the trenches by constant heavy mortar fire were unable to reach them to drag them off the battlefields. Rats feasted on the flesh of horses and men alike.

17 July 1917
Countess Gersdorf, your feet are pink my heart is set on fire for you!

I am dying of love for her, she is beautiful like an angel, she is my angel. I would like to hold her hand and kiss it wildly until I die. She does not know how great my love is. She thinks I only like her a lot, as Liese does. But this time it's really passion, deep, deep love. My sweet Countess. She is so beautiful.

Yesterday I was with her in the park. Sometimes I feel that she presses my arm slightly. Today I could not even eat my breakfast, I was so excited, but Liese said I should eat. My sweet beloved Countess said, "You go with her now and get your breakfast." She knows that Mutti wants me to have my breakfast and I obey her like a dog. I kissed her hand, she had sweet gray leather gloves on, and said, "Little Leni, you are not going to kiss that dirty glove, are you?" She calls me "You" the familiar way and also "Marlenchen," as I asked her to. She said, "You want us to be girlfriends, don't you?" I was in Eisenach with her, it was divine. For her husband's birthday, she bought a silver medallion on a long chain and had them engrave on it: Knight, Count Harry von Gersdorf. She gave me a clover leaf she had picked herself, she is having it framed in silver under glass. On the way to Eisenach on the train, we passed inside a tunnel, she took my arm and put her head on my shoulder. I immediately kissed her arm and hands. When we came out of the tunnel, she was smiling. On the way back, there was a young officer sitting next to us. She said, "It is Count Wiser, isn't it?" He wanted to introduce himself to me but the Countess did it: "Count Wiser, Fräulein von Losch."

In the next tunnel, I kissed her hands again – she became very merry. Later on, the train stopped for half an hour and she ordered three beers. We drank a lot and made fun about people we knew. She said, "Marlenchen, don't you dare to get drunk." Afterwards, they told me to go home with the vicar's wife to get rid of me. Later on, I told her: "My dear

Countess, you don't need me anymore, do you?" She said, "No," but
I'm sure it's so.

We went to see the musical comedy *The Poor Student*. I sat next to her.
She wore black velvet. As soon as it was dark, I whispered to her, "My dear
Countess, you are absolutely ravishing." She answered, "Shush . . . when
we go to see *Fledermaus*, I will be even prettier." On the 24th it will be the
Countess's birthday. I hope I will be allowed to wear my white dress.

Although Josephine had booked rooms for the whole month of July, she
suddenly changed her mind and returned to Berlin. The aunts wondered
what could possibly have happened to alter her summer plans so abruptly,
but, of course, were much too well brought up to inquire.

Berlin
14 August 1917
Parting was short and hurtful. Besides the clover leaf, she gave me an
amethyst mounted in silver. I wrote a poem for her. What she thought
of it, I don't know. I told her I loved her and signed it "Marlene." If
she weren't married, I would do anything to win her heart and get her
before her Count Gersdorf. Even now, I'd like to be him. I long for her.
She does not know it. She comes here in September and maybe she'll ask
me to accompany her to the races to pass the time and have me as her
"boy." Really, that's all I was when we were in Liebenstein. She refuses
to admit that she treats Liesel and me in the same way. It's not fair, since
I have a crush on her and Liesel doesn't. She said that Liesel was only
allowed to kiss her hand but not her shoulder and this was only allowed
to me. But when the Countess gave a pendant to Liese as a present, Liese
did kiss her shoulder, and when I reminded the Countess, she answered,
"But what could I do?" So, in fact, she does treat us both the same. How
indulgent love is. Love suffers, tolerates, hopes. Her picture is in my locket.
Sometimes my love is like a baby's, although it is serious, like a grown-up.
It is the kind of love I could feel for a man. What a shame, really, that she
doesn't understand me, she only thinks it's a simple crush. I call it a crush
myself, but in reality, it's not that easy. The whole situation! A crush one
can forget easily, but one's love not.

Berlin
30 August 1917
She wrote a postcard two days ago, and since – nothing. Of course, this is
what always happens with those people you meet during the summer, but,
I am still disappointed. Did I ever really have a pure happy love? When we
parted, she said: "Marlenchen, don't cry!" What can I do but cry when I
know that she is beginning to forget me?

THIS TIME, a regimental outrider brought Josephine the news of her husband's death. At the age of forty, she was a widow for the second time.

With infinite care, she lay the withered rose between the layers of precious tissue paper enfolding the yellow dress, and closed the box. Leaving it on the bed, she turned and left the room. Her black veil brushed her cheek. From the ring at her waist, she selected a key and locked the door. She never entered that room again, nor wore a pale yellow dress. Liesel cried, prayed for Eduard's soul to enter heaven. Lena's diary ignores his death completely.

17 September 1917
My soul is filled with Henny Porten. Yesterday Hanne, Hein, and I went to see her film *The Captive Soul*, at the Mozart Theater. I just can't describe how beautiful it was, because of her, naturally. She takes her robe off to go bathing – naked. You see only to her shoulders, but on the sides, you can see more. She's wonderful.

It rained, as though it would never stop. Shell craters, trenches filled with water. Battlefields oozed mud! Exhausted men, loaded down with heavy equipment, fell, were sucked down into the slime, and drowned before anyone could reach them.

19 October 1917
I went to her house with flowers but she had moved. The porter's wife told me her new address because she took pity on me, seeing me with my flowers, but it was late and suddenly I didn't like the flowers anymore. I must study my part a lot, since at school we are going to stage *The Governess*, by Kohner. I am Franziska. I am sure I will go on the stage.

In Vincennes, the German spy Mata Hari was executed by a French firing squad. Thirteen years later, Lena would play this dramatic moment beautifully on film. In 1917, when no one claimed this ravishing lady's corpse, it ended up on the table of a pathology class, but that was not in the film *Dishonored*.

27 October 1917
Sunday we have the first dress rehearsal. I have stage fright. I am playing the part of a man and am wearing my black sports trousers, Mutti's riding coat and white lace shirt. When I play Franziska, I hope she'll lend me her pink evening dress, because it's so well cut and suits me and I must have a long dress.

4 November 1917
Yesterday, at a party, instead of place cards there were cards with
quotations on them and we had to find our places according to the
quotation. I found mine immediately: "What is life without the glow
of love?"

Three days later, the Russian Revolution, which had been in progress
for years, became official: The Bolsheviks had seized power. Soon civil
war and famine would send Russia into further turmoil.

15 November 1917
Countess Gersdorf and her husband Harry are visiting with us. She pretends
she can't get over that I don't have a crush on her anymore. She looks at me
really dismayed and plays "the young lover." *Now* I have Henny Porten's
picture in my locket and everywhere around my room – now the shoe is
on the other foot. She keeps kissing me when she sees me. Her husband
is lovely to her. Today she was sick and he cared for her. It was really
touching. I hope I have one like that one day.

On the 20th of November, iron-plated "landships" attacked the German lines near Cambrai, and the word *tank* entered into the language
of war.

22 November 1917
On Sunday there was a big celebration in the Mozart Theater, two films
featuring Henny Porten. I waited for her and gave her four wine-colored
carnations that cost me four marks. She looked absolutely divine and gave
me the most beautiful handshake in the world. Sometimes my yearning
for her overwhelms me so, I have to rush into a store and buy one of her
picture postcards just to look at her beautiful face.

That winter, the temperature fell to minus twenty-two degrees cen-
tigrade. Typhus swept through the working-class sections of the city.
Corpses, left outside houses to be collected in the morning by horse-
drawn death wagons, froze on the doorsteps.

14 January 1918
I love you! How nice to be able to say that, how nice it is to hear that.
It is a small, small word, but in that word there is all the happiness and
suffering in the world.

19 January 1918
I am happy. Yesterday I still cried, today I laugh. I had bought a bunch
of wild violets and lily of the valley. I stood in front of her house and

saw a carriage parked there. I thought it must be hers, so I waited. Suddenly, an angel that looked like Henny Porten came out. I handed the flowers over to her and she smiled! She's much more beautiful in life than in films.

The German army issued "licenses to kill" to front-line soldiers suspected of shell shock. If in a fit of unbalanced rage they happened to shoot one of their own, they could not be court-martialed, leaving them free to remain on active duty. In England, men on short leave from the front were considered too unstable to be permitted to take their army rifles home with them.

17 April 1918
In a week from now I will be confirmed. It does not impress me very much. The Dietrich family will get together for the event. That will be nice.

The French forces on the western front were being ravaged by a new enemy, Spanish influenza. More than two thousand serious cases per day were being evacuated. The Germans used this as an opportunity for maximum effort. The Second Battle of the Marne was about to begin. The Germans had fifty-two divisions in the field; the Allies stood ready with thirty-six.

1 June 1918
Erna Schonbach visited me and I was so dumb, I gave her my diary to read. Of course, with all my crushes. I never did that before. She said that she could see by reading it that my love is superficial because my heart is so big. I felt like crying when she said that to me. Superficial?

11 June 1918
I went to Hilde Sperling's birthday. With my first glass of punch, one of her friends said: "A toast to the one we love," and they all raised their glasses and knew to whom. Only I didn't. I didn't know who I loved. Yesterday I was upset and was so stupid to confide in Mutti about it. Most of the time she is wrong about me. She even makes Liesel watch me getting on the streetcar! That sort of thing makes one want to misbehave on purpose. Well, I can't change her and she can't change me.

The German offensive had inflicted some 447,921 casualties on the British, 490,000 on the French. The Germans, double that! Both sides were literally running out of men. Only the Americans were still able to replace their dead and wounded. Germany was on the defensive.

During this time, Lena's diary records that she is ill. At first it sounds as
though it might be a slight case of rheumatic fever, but what seems much
more likely, considering her exaggerated romantic character, is that she
was suffering from depression, brought on by sexual frustration. Freud's
theories were still much too new to have reached an elderly resident
physician of a minor watering place in Bavaria, and so the good doctor
handed down a diagnosis reminiscent of Elizabeth Barrett Browning.

Herzbad Altheide
7 July 1918
I am in bed feeling sad. The doctor said I have a heart condition, that the
muscle of my heart has slackened. I am not allowed to walk more than 60
minutes a day, and this, slowly. In the morning I take special sulphur baths.
After, I must lie down until midday, and later on, another two hours more.
In between, I may go and take the waters. This is my fantastic vacation
I yearned so much for! I am not allowed to dance anymore. I've begun to
sing pretty Bavarian and Austrian songs, using chords to make up for my
weak and breathy voice. I spend a lot of time playing my mandolin and
dreaming. Mutti says, "You can dream, but don't be empty-headed."
    Today the weather is wonderful, the sun is shining, and I am lying here.
Of course, tomorrow when I can get up, it'll pour! I just mustn't allow
myself to look forward to anything.

Facing stunning defeat, Germany was in turmoil. By the 8th of
November, a full-scale revolution had begun. Riots swept every major
city. At the front, soldiers on all sides were deserting in huge numbers.
They could take no more.

Berlin
9 November 1918
Why must I experience these terrible times? I did so want a golden youth
and now it turned out like this! I am sorry about the Kaiser and all the
others. They say bad things will happen tonight. The mob was after
people with carriages. We had some ladies invited for tea but none of
them could get through to our house. Only Countess Gersdorf did.
On Kurfürstendamm, her husband got his epaulets torn off by armed
soldiers, and everywhere one looks, there are red flags. What does the
nation want? They have what they wanted, haven't they? Oh, if I were
a little bit happy, things wouldn't be so difficult to bear. Maybe soon a
time will come when I will be able to tell about happiness again – only
happiness.

On the 11th of November, Armistice was declared. The Great War was
officially over, its cost staggering. The victorious nations had mobilized

42 million men – their killed, wounded, and missing stood at 22 million. The vanquished, having put 23 million men in the field, had lost 15 million. Germany alone sacrificed 7 million of her youth. The civilian body count from disease and starvation was never tabulated.

Granted the world had lost a generation of its young men, but by this very sacrifice, it had been made "safe – forever." "Forever" lasted about as long as it took the Treaty of Versailles to be drawn up and signed seven months later, laying the convenient groundwork for Hitler and his Nazi doctrines. Still, it took determined propagation and twenty years of insidious gestation to produce, once again, enough willing cannon fodder to supply another war of glorified killing. Defeated Germans are a dangerous race.

Berlin
12 April 1919
Why am I so different from Liesel and Mutti? Both of them are so dry and calculating, I am like a black sheep of the family to them. Yesterday there was a première at the Mozart Theater. I was looking forward to everything – the music, Henny – but Liesel, who after her exams is bored, nagged so long that I let her come with me. To make things "perfect," Mutti came too! Well, that's what happens when one is happy about something special. I was so looking forward to going alone. I'm sure I had made myself too pretty, so both of them were anxious because of my good looks. Somebody told me I looked so pretty, and like a doll one wants to keep on kissing. I'm sure that's what a few other gentlemen thought too, who accompanied me to my box. An elderly gentleman asked me if I was a film actress. When Mutti arrived, I immediately made myself well behaved and coy. It is really terrible not to have at least one person to confide in, to tell that person what one feels and not have a lecture right away, like Mutti gives. Still she always says she wants to be her children's best friend. I wonder what I would have left if I ever told her everything. I long so much for so many unreachable things, like a teenager longing for her first love at school. It's not nice to always have those very sad moods.

2 May 1919
I'm in love. I have known it for a few days, but whether I am really happy, this I don't know. That's where I am dumb. I always think about what may happen, I can't even be glad about a few lovely moments because I always say to myself: Why even start loving – it won't last, and then my heart will be even sadder.

I wish I were more superficial. It would be wonderful to enjoy the moment without thinking about the future. But I just can't, and so, I just make his life difficult instead of making him happy for those few minutes. Why can't I once be loved by someone I'm allowed to love who loves me back? I was told I do not show enough pride, enough restraint when loving somebody. This book is a real sentimental tome, only when I am sad I write in it. But that's not so. Maybe this book will talk about happiness again some day, but I don't believe it. Then again, one never knows.

Josephine, now alarmed by the postwar madness sweeping Berlin, rented a small house in the country, in case it should become necessary, once again, to evacuate her daughters from the city.

16 June 1919
Well, it seems like happiness is about to come back into my arms like a good child. Once again, I am in love, but this time it is different – an old sweetheart of my youth – that "word" says it all! I don't think about anything, as is usually the case when I am in love – this makes me so happy, so calm.

   I know exactly that he won't try anything more and so, I don't have to be afraid. We are like children – happy just to see each other when we meet. I look at him and it is enough for him. At least, I love again. I needed that. After him, there will probably be someone else.

Berlin
19 August 1919
We came back from Bad Pyrmont. I left my heart there. I don't think I will ever find somebody I will like for both his looks and personality, as much as he, who has my heart. His name is D. Strohman, and comes from Westphalia. We met at a party and danced from 1 to 4 – every dance. The next day, he invited me to another party but I wasn't allowed to go, I was very sad. He must have been very bored with me – because all I ever said was "I have to ask my mother first."

   Three days before we had to leave, we went together again and we had fun and suddenly, in fun, he starts declaring his love. For me, it was awful to make fun of things that were so important to me. We parted laughing; he asked: "Will you dream about me?" After that I didn't see him again. Out of sight, out of mind! He probably has received my letter inviting him, but probably won't come. I don't want him to, really. At a spa, things are loose. Here I am constantly under Mutti's surveillance and he would be bored. With him, for the first time I felt like marrying somebody. I never thought about that with other men, but I must get this out of my mind as soon as possible. The fortune-teller told me I would get to know a man during my next trip. Yes? In Springeberg, we had 70 Americans who rented a whole restaurant. The Springebergers were shocked that we wanted to speak to them. Mutti forbade us to dance with them but one of them was an officer and wouldn't leave me alone until he could dance with me. I was dancing when Mutti arrived. She started to talk to them and met a colonel who knows Uncle Willi, and so in no time at all, I was sitting at a table with three nice officers and ate ices and chocolate biscuits that they had brought. They asked for my address and wanted to know if they could come and visit. Unfortunately, their steamship left at 8 o'clock in the morning. I'm curious if they will keep their promise and write.

Beggars everywhere. Young men with deadened faces, eyes emptied of all further feeling. Bent forms with vacant trouser legs and flapping sleeves, oversized safety pins their badge of courage. On every street corner of every nation, they swing their crutches, tap their canes to the rhythm of a private despair. In England, they sell pencils. In France, shoelaces. In Berlin, organ grinders let a monkey beg for them.

17 September 1919
Springeberg satisfies us completely. We go out there on Sundays and come back on Mondays. During the week we talk about "out there." I am loved there because I am still new, still fashionable. For the moment, they are all crazy about me. Erich Schupp, who in his youth really loved me, Paul Botchen, who is older and more manly. I am nice to Erich, more out of pity, and I can't decide between them. Saturdays and Sundays I kiss enough for the whole week. I really should be very ashamed. All those who know me confirm this if I ask them what they think of me: I am all right for kissing and having fun, but to marry – God forbid! This is the result of my behavior, for example, that I allow myself to be kissed so easily. Of course, I can't expect respect. I can't help it. It is not my fault if my romantic nature has no limits. Who knows where I will end up. Hopefully, somebody will come, have the kindness to marry me soon. There is a film in town called *Demi-Vierges*. They say it is a typical case of young ladies from the so-called upper class who-mature-sooner, want to experience the tickling thrill of erotic adventures. They seduce the man, then give him *almost* everything – "*Tout* except *ça*." Playing with fire, until one day they get burned, then laugh. This describes me exactly. Till now I still have had the strength to say No as it got to the very moment. But that is getting hopeless. They are all alike: He "can't control himself anymore," and, as my feelings arouse his, it is no longer a love of youth. It is too late for that. Anyway, it wouldn't be enough for me anymore. It would be so beautiful to just let go and love. But, of course, that can't be.

Josephine knew that she had waited much too long. She now made good her threat and packed her daughter off to boarding school. Her mistake was choosing one in Weimar, a most romantic town, famous for being the home of one of Lena's gods, the poet Goethe. At first, Lena's forced exile seemed to work its control.

Weimar
7 October 1920
How long I haven't written. I have been away from home for six
months now.

Now I am here in Weimar in this boarding school for "upper-class girls"
and feel so lonely. Liesel is not with me and all those I loved so much have
forgotten me. I could just cry. The only things I have here are the violin
lessons with Prof. Reitz that give me a little joy. But is that enough for me,
who was so used to being loved? – and suddenly now here, nothing?

Weimar
8 October 1920
If only someone would come to take away my longing and lock it inside
a gilded cage. I wish someone would come and, with his love, make me
happy and so content that I would forget all the tears shed for other
past loves.

Weimar
10 October 1920
I am so unhappy because I don't have anybody who loves me. I am so
used to being loved.

Miss Arnoldi, the headmistress, wants to change me according to her
standards and Mutti seems to agree with that and be happy about it. As
everyone is working so hard to change me, I hope something will come
out of it that will please Mutti.

It had taken no time at all before Lena's violin teacher was completely
under her spell. During their private lessons the urge to touch his lovely
pupil was so overwhelming, the good professor had to keep his hands in
the pockets of his frock coat.

On one of her monthly visits, Josephine, sensing something strange in
the attitude of her daughter's music teacher, suggested that perhaps she
should be moved from Professor Reitz's class to that of another professor
of the violin. Though greatly disturbed, the headmistress decided a little
talk with the smitten professor would suffice.

Weimar
21 October 1920
Just now I had my violin lesson. It seems to me that Professor Reitz
is somewhat disappointed in me. In everything? At the beginning, as I
always played what I knew, he was very happy and wrote to Mutti about
it. Now, confronted with new material, I don't progress as quickly as I
did. Mutti thinks that he can't teach me anything further and that I should
go on to Professor Fleisch. She doesn't understand anything about it. If I

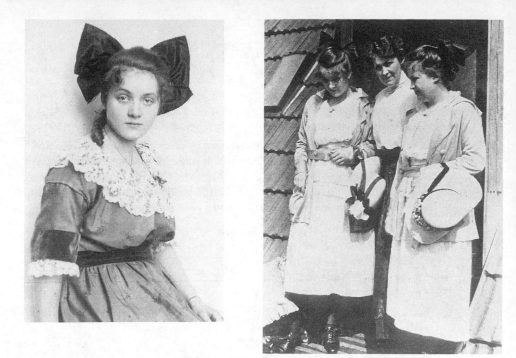

ABOVE, LEFT: By the time she was seventeen, she had invented the name Marlene and let a curl fall to her shoulder on special occasions.

ABOVE, RIGHT: The Dietrich sisters and their mother, the widow von Losch. I love this picture. Why my mother hid it, I'll never know. Look at those beautiful ankles in those handmade shoes.

BELOW, LEFT: Lovely Weimar, where the poet Goethe—my mother's most adored god—lived and where her mother sent her to boarding school, hoping it would tame her, which it didn't.

BELOW, RIGHT: Marlene at twenty-one, the buxom bathing beauty.

The young Berlin actress draped in panne velvet, looking properly lyrical.

were different, or if I weren't so pleasure-seeking, or if I could do what I wanted, maybe I would be somebody someday. But the way I do it, just practicing a lot, with chores, visits, taking my mind off it, makes it all impossible! Maybe someone will have the kindness to marry me and then my career as an artist can end – but practice for years just to play at home? How could one have the strength to pursue such a thing?

Weimar
14 November 1920
Mutti was here and Miss Arnoldi told her all about my sins (flirting) during concerts. I don't do that! But what can I do about it if I am noticed everywhere I go? I am now playing Handel sonatas. Reitz is playing with me. If I just had somebody who loved me, I would be so grateful to him. I would be so happy if he spoke sweet, sweet words to me. We would go out together into the autumn, hand in hand, into the golden season. Leaves would glow golden but – they are cold and gray and I walk all alone.

 I long so much for Christmas. Four weeks left. If I were happy, those four weeks would fly. I wouldn't want to be the Kaiser. I wish I could stop time when I want – but this even the Kaiser can't do.

 For some reason, Lena did not fall in love over the Christmas vacation. On her return to Weimar, her last semester at boarding school, her smitten professor awaited her.

 Why are male music teachers such staples of romantic fiction? It can't only be the making of beautiful music together that sets those inevitable scenes of seduction. The proximity of a respected older man in a private room, whose door can be firmly closed, must have a great deal to do with it. So, the moment came, as it was destined to, when beautiful girl with violin offered up her virginity on the altar of a Handel sonata. It wasn't out of fear of discovery that Lena left this momentous occurrence out of her diary – it was disappointment!

 "He groaned, heaved, panted. Didn't even take his trousers off. I just lay there on that old settee, the red plush scratching my behind, my skirts over my head. The whole thing, *very* uncomfortable," is how she would describe her very first sexual encounter to her daughter some forty years later. To top it off, the Academy of Music did not accept Fräulein Dietrich as a pupil.

 Disillusioned, Lena returned to Berlin, boredom, and rampant postwar inflation. Liesel, having received her university certification, broke with the tradition of her class, and went to work. Her substantial pay as a full teacher was a godsend. Against her mother's wishes, using Liesel's action as an excuse, Lena applied for entrance to the celebrated Max

Reinhardt Acting Academy. She had decided that if she couldn't be a famous violinist, she would become a "famous actress of the theater" instead. For her entrance audition, she chose a highly dramatic piece from Goethe's *Faust* – Margarete's prayer to the Virgin. It became one of Marlene's most repeated and believed stories: that after completing this lengthy soliloquy, her knees were so red and swollen she had trouble rising to her feet, when a male voice drifted toward her out of the vast darkness of the auditorium of the Deutsches Theater. This disembodied voice is supposed to have intoned: "Fräulein Dietrich, raise your skirt. We want to see your legs," thereby breaking a young thespian's heart by its crass callousness. It was automatically assumed, of course, that this voice belonged to the Master himself. In reality, the great Reinhardt did not attend tryouts of mere aspiring students. Although legend has it that Marlene Dietrich was a famous graduate of the illustrious professor, she was not. That she managed to appear in numerous small parts in many of the Reinhardt-owned theaters and productions, especially at his Deutsches Theater, was true. This gave her the association with the Master she longed for, and conveniently allowed the world press to assume her more respectable status, that of student of the Reinhardt Academy, instead of the lesser one of ambitious would-be actress.

In later years, Herr Doktor Reinhardt saw no reason to set the record straight, for by that time, his self-proclaimed one-time pupil was even more famous than he or his Berlin school. By his public silence, Lena's tale entered into her legend.

She worked hard, auditioned for everything, played anything, never tired, could do a walk-on maid in Act I of one play, dash across town, and appear as one of many "elegant ladies" at a cocktail party in Act II of yet another play. Her childhood training in ballet and Isadora Duncan-type dancing made her able to join the chorus line in Act III of a revue down the street. Her extraordinary discipline, so ingrained by her upbringing, got her work that her inexperience and youth might have lost her. Soon smitten stage managers wrote "Marlene Dietrich" at the top of their casting sheets.

Her talent for appropriating the clothes she wore in her various parts developed at this time. If Marlene Dietrich thought she looked ravishing in an evening dress, playing the tiny part of a dinner guest, it somehow was sure to end up hanging in her closet, instead of back at the theatrical costumers. In this nonchalant larceny, she was way ahead of her time. Hollywood kleptomania, the keeping for oneself anything and everything that is not nailed down during the making of a film, was still many years off. She stockpiled everything. Gloves to suit any role: for "starving matchgirl on street corner," she had a perfect pair, all holes and missing

fingers; whores? red net up to the elbow, just a little torn; white kid
gloves for ladies; black kid for middle class. Scarves and boas of all
shades, textures, and lengths. Dozens of handbags, essential props for
giving instant recognition of the status and character of their owner. And
hats? Did she have hats!

BERLIN

BY 1922, Marlene could sprint across the length and breadth of Berlin, appear as any woman called for. She had the energy, dedication, discipline, and the greatest private prop shop in town. It was just a matter of time before this inventive supply sergeant with a magical face would drift into the still young moving-picture business. Around Berlin, movie companies were sprouting like mushrooms. Any abandoned warehouse could become an automatic dream factory. Not having the luxury of California sunlight, any large structure with a glass roof was a treasure to acquire. Companies like Ufa had built enormous glass sheds that let in the precious light so essential to film. Without the restrictions of sound, one of these sheds could crank out eight movies simultaneously. In one cubicle, a comic does an exaggerated pratfall, dropping a tall stack of dishes. Next to him, a woman tears her hair, wailing – her lover has gone, her ten children are screaming. Next to her, a string quartet is setting the actors' mood for an intimate scene of lyrical passion. Next to the mooning lovebirds, a snowstorm rages, wet huskies are howling, while around the corner, a crowd roars as Marie Antoinette is being carted off to the guillotine, and Bavarian peasants are dancing around a Maypole, accompanied by eight accordions that will never be heard. In this glass icehouse, in the German winter, a hundred freezing, frantic people scurry, creating out of an insane bedlam the magic that people will go to see to escape their realities for a nickel a seat.

The first time Lena went on an "extra" casting call, she wore a pirate's hat, a pheasant's tail feather stuck through its crown, a panne velvet coat, complete with dangling four-legged fur piece of a very long-dead red fox, and, stuck in her eye, her father's monocle. She got the part. In that outfit,

what casting director could have missed her! Although they took away her
hat and dangling animal, they left the monocle and stuck her and it in the
spectators' gallery of a courtroom scene. On her second try, she already
felt quite disdainful of the new medium, considered it rather vulgar, in
comparison to the real "theater." Marlene always pronounced this word
as though it was part of the Papal High Mass at Saint Peter's on Easter
Sunday.

Having heard they were looking for a woman to play a small part
of a "girlfriend" in a film, she assumed she must certainly be a
demi-mondaine, as a lady not too virginally pure was known, and
so, adorned her well-endowed body with a slightly revealing flapper
dress, long, absinthe green gloves, and matching high-heeled shoes.
Just in case the "girlfriend" turned out to be nothing more than
"a girl of the streets," she brought along one of her collection of
ratty feather boas. Decked out in this "girlfriend" finery, she stood
with other hopefuls, waiting for the assistant director to make his
choice.

Rudolph Sieber always maintained that it was those garish green
gloves that first drew his eyes to the girl who was to become his
wife.

"She looked so ridiculous in that contrived getup! Like a child
playing grown-up! I wanted to laugh. Of course, I didn't. I gave
her the job. Even under all that junk, she looked right for the part of
Lucie."

"He looked at me and I couldn't believe it! He was so beautiful!
His blond hair shone. He was dressed like an English lord on his
country estate. A little assistant director in films in *real* tweeds? Right
away, I knew I loved him! I played that part of the girl in a chiffon
dress – she was not at all vulgar. Jannings was in the film, but
we never met – my part was much too small to be in the film
that long."

When Rudi proposed to Marlene, she accepted him without hesitation,
fully convinced she had finally found the one she had been longing for,
the one to "enter the fall together, hand in hand, in the midst of a golden
season."

Her mother was not pleased. Josephine had so hoped for a really fine
marriage for her beautiful daughter, but runaway postwar inflation had
done away with dowries, and arranged liaisons between aristocratic
families were now as much a part of the past as the Kaiser. Marriage,
even to a Czechoslovakian-Austrian Catholic, might be better than
leaving Lena to roam free among those "Gypsies." Josephine equated
all actors with tribes of shiftless, tambourine-playing thieves. If this man

really loved Lena, God give him the strength to curb her wild romantic nature. Josephine resolved to help this stranger whom her daughter had chosen.

Lena wanted to drive to her wedding, at the resplendent Kaiser Wilhelm Memorial Church, in an open, horse-drawn carriage. She thought it would look so romantic to have her white veil billowing out behind her for all to see – she was a bride! Josephine said that would be too theatrical and hired a large Packard instead to drive the couple to the church.

She placed the band of myrtle on her daughter's head, with long hairpins securing its unbroken circle to the bridal veil. She kissed the child she loved the best, but did not let it show. How beautiful she looked – in her modern wedding dress, with her white-stockinged ankles showing. Louis would have liked the picture she made. She looked so very much like him. For a moment, longing and memory overwhelmed her, then she gathered her coldness about her heart and sent Louis's daughter off to become a wife.

In the safe darkness of the motorcar, Lena quickly removed the myrtle band, tearing at it until its circle lay open. Then she repositioned it onto her head. She could not enter a church with her myrtle intact; she had lost that virginal right on a settee in Weimar. Smiling, Rudi helped her resecure her wedding veil. Throughout his life, it is what he did best: served this incandescent creature it was his tragedy to love. Lena became Frau Rudolph Sieber on the 17th of May, 1923. She was twenty-one and a half. He was twenty-seven.

Berlin
2 July 1923
How long is it since I last wrote in here? What could I have written about the most happy last year in Weimar? I will be eternally grateful for those times, especially to those who made it so nice for me.

Now I am married and didn't even take his picture with me! But it doesn't matter, there are things one NEVER forgets. The time after Weimar was quite dull. I gave up playing the violin and then started my other profession – one year with the Deutsches Theater and others. And now, tranquillity, as much as that is possible in love.

Since the wedding, I have been able to live only for my husband, since I didn't have any film and only have to play in the theater in the winter. I am very satisfied because I know that he is happy and I am longing for a child. Since we rent a furnished apartment and there is no immediate possibility to get a bigger one, I know it is not possible for the moment. One thing is certain, nothing is a

ABOVE, LEFT: In virginal white, Marlene Dietrich becomes the wife of
Rudolf Sieber, May 17, 1923.

ABOVE, RIGHT: Old Berlin and its famous Kaiser Wilhelm Memorial
Church, which Marlene loved and where she was married.

BELOW, LEFT: In August 1924, at twenty–three, four months pregnant.

BELOW, RIGHT: With her child, Maria Elizabeth, age four months.

ABOVE, LEFT: Two bathing beauties on the sands of Swinemünde.
ABOVE, RIGHT: Rudi and his demure wife, the summer of 1926.
LEFT: By 1927, Marlene Dietrich, wife and mother, was back working full time.

Films, theater, and revues—
she did them all, 1926–27.

LEFT: While filming in Vienna, my mother learned to play the musical saw. She was very proud of this accomplishment—besides, playing it showed off her legs.

BELOW: More important roles in moving pictures in Germany, 1928.

ABOVE: A rare picture of my mother being coy—very un-Dietrich. This one, too, she had hidden away.

RIGHT: Handsome Rudi Sieber and his beautiful wife. At times my parents resembled each other so, they could have been taken for brother and sister.

In 1928, the Sieber family before the hurricane of world fame.

substitute for a child. But, if I had a child, I would then have to live with Mutti.

BERLIN, IN THE ROARING TWENTIES, really roared. Chicago might have its speakeasies, flappers, gangsters' molls, and wild-wild women, but Sodom and Gomorrah was Berlin. Prostitutes languished on every street corner. Their distinctive white makeup a perfect complement to their erotic getups. Feathers, chains, tassels, and whips, they possessed the streets like birds of promised paradise. Marlene and her friends, crammed into Rudi's small roadster, loved to cruise the streets any hour of the day, admiring the free show. Marlene was particularly skilled in identifying who were the transvestites on parade. She insisted that only *they* knew how to wear the obligatory garter belt with style. Her favorite was a blond, whose trademark of white satin top hat and ruffled panties she particularly admired.

"Only pansies know how to look like a sexy woman" was one of Marlene's famous remarks. She was becoming known for her sharp wit, her sensual freedom, her bisexual appreciation. All this, without seeming vulgarity. A tall order in postwar Berlin, where everything and anything was permitted. The more erotic, bawdy, and amoral, the more acceptable. Rudi's taste was always impeccable. His instinct for what was right, what would work for his wife's professional image, was amazingly astute. He knew it was all right for her to play at vulgarity, but not become it. To startle and intrigue the world was his aim for her, without her losing the aloofness of the true aristocrat. Without really understanding these subtleties, Marlene adored this concept and did what he told her. She and Rudi frequented the many cabarets where transvestites congregated and performed. They accepted her as a loving sister, often turning to her for advice: "Marlenchen – is this rouge right for me?" . . . "What do you think – more mascara?" . . . "Are these gloves too, too garish green for this dress?" . . . "What *shall* I do with this damn boa? Throw it when I come on – or trail it?"

"Trail it! Darling . . . trail it! . . . Black appliquéd satin swans? No, no. Not for you, dearie, too cheap. You should only wear red, make it *your* color – lipstick red! Everything . . . shoes, stockings, garter belt. Everything! Oh, and tell Stefan, no use having a dress slit up to his navel if he then forgets to shave his legs!"

She had Rudi's tailor make her a man's evening suit. Stunning, in top hat, white tie, and tails, she would arrive to dance with her fine-feathered pals. They adored her. She embodied all they yearned to be, the ultimate gender crossover blend of perfection.

Josephine watched and worried. A child, yes, that's what Lena needed. A child would settle her down to be a proper wife, forget this acting madness. So Josephine searched, and found a large apartment on the fashionable Kaiserallee, just a few blocks from the house that Eduard had left her. What Lena wanted, she was about to get!

Marlene Sieber loved being pregnant. Once was enough, but while it lasted, she delighted in its intimacy and convenient benefits.

"No more love-making," her husband was told. Marlene always preferred glowing romance to actual sex, enduring it with her husband only out of a sense of wifely duty. Now, under the sweeping excuse that the act might harm their unborn child, she eliminated sex from their marriage altogether. Her husband, loving her, agreed to whatever she thought best. By the time he realized what she had done and why, it was too late for him to change her course. Although they stayed married for over fifty years, sometimes even lived together, their physical relationship stopped the day Marlene knew she was "with child." By the time she gave birth, she had convinced herself that her child was her own creation. Nothing so vulgar as male sperm had anything to do with it. She and she alone had made her child in her own image. The child was hers, by right of immaculate conception.

No customary at-home birth for Marlene. Her daughter was born in Berlin's foremost private clinic, assisted into the world by the skill of a famous professor of obstetrics.

"Oh, how I suffered! He had to cut a little down *there* to get you out – that's why you had such a beautiful head," I was told from the age of two. The memory of her ordeal of childbirth, the beauty of a new mother's delicate exhaustion, she used to perfection ten years later in *The Scarlet Empress*.

There are as many versions of my birth as there are of the actual date on which it occurred. Actually, Dietrich's only child was born on December 13, 1924. The month and the day were kept, but as she changed her birth year, so did her daughter's. Not until my father died in 1976 and I found my birth certificate among his papers did I know for sure how old I really was. Such minor uncertainties were part of my childhood. Until I was twelve, I wasn't sure who my real father was either; granted the one I called "Papi" seemed to be the best candidate, but . . . who knew for sure? Did I resemble him? That didn't help much either, for except for his brown eyes, he looked enough like my mother to be her handsome brother. I didn't churn about all this confusion. My mother had told me so often that I was hers and hers alone, that whoever was my biological father wouldn't have had a chance in my life anyway.

With my birth, Marlene and Rudi became Mutti and Papi to each other, their daughter, and most of their intimate friends. Motherhood was now her central role. A sober dedication laced with a constant fear that I might sicken and die at any moment, or, worse, be less than perfect. She breastfed me with such constancy that for the rest of my life I was told I was solely responsible for my mother's sagging breasts, that she had sacrificed their youthful tautness to my childish greed. As I was first told of my culpability at the age of two, I felt guilty for years whenever I saw all the trouble my mother's breasts caused her.

BY THE FALL OF 1925, Greta Garbo had arrived in Hollywood, old Field Marshal von Hindenburg was president of Germany, Adolf Hitler had published the first volume of *Mein Kampf*, Charlie Chaplin's *The Gold Rush* was acclaimed, and Marlene Dietrich was more than ready to go back to work.

By 1926, Ernst Lubitsch had left the studios of Berlin, deciding Hollywood, and he, would profit from his multiple skills; Ernest Hemingway's first novel, *The Sun Also Rises*, was published; Dr. Joseph Goebbels was appointed district leader of Berlin for the Nazi party; and Marlene Dietrich was back at work full-time. She appeared in two films that year, numerous plays and revues, small parts, some even walk-ons, but whenever she appeared no audience could take its eyes off her. Hardly realizing it, she was becoming a Berlin celebrity.

18 October 1926
It is impossible to fill the time gap here. There is too much that has happened in between. My child will soon be 2 years old. I want to write the most important things so that later I will know what I have been through. The child is the only thing I have – nothing else. Mutti is still so nice to me and the child makes her happy. I am slowly beginning to pay her back for all her love – otherwise there is nothing. I play in the theater and in

films and earn money. I have just reread this diary – oh God, where is all that wonderful exuberance, that being carried away by feelings? All gone! Nobody understands that I am so attached to the child because nobody knows that apart from that, I have nothing. I, myself, experience nothing as a woman – nothing as a person. The child is incredible, strangers who don't even belong to the family love her and miss her. The child is the essence of my life. I think I will die young. I hope to at least rear the child and would like to stay alive as long as Mutti lives. And Liesel – (Things are not going well with her. One can't help her. I love her dearly.)

Liesel had married a "low-class rotter," as her husband was always referred to within the family, had borne a son, whom no one ever mentioned. Her life would take a very different course than that of her lovely Pussy Cat.

I was nearly three when my father started keeping pigeons on the roof. I knew that Tata Losch, as I called my mother's mother, had found and was helping with the rent of our comfortable apartment in one of Berlin's better neighborhoods. That's why I had a room of my own, with a window that looked onto a little park. My father had a study, where he slept, my mother occupied the big bedroom at the end of the dark hall. The dining room, with its massive china cabinet and twelve high-backed chairs, was used on Sundays when my mother was home for dinner. I was still too young to really know where she went or what she did, but when my mother was home, her presence was so overwhelming, her passionate love for me so all-enveloping, its force was sufficient to fill her absences in between.

A young girl from the country had been hired to look after my physical needs. She was kind and caring. She scrubbed me, the floors, was polite to my father, but took orders only from my mother, whom she adored. Her name was Becky and I liked her. She didn't kiss me all over, hug me breathless, tell everyone in the park to look at how beautiful I was, stuff food down my throat, turn white if I sneezed, gasp in horror at a cough, or take my temperature continually. Above all, she didn't tell my mother about my being on the roof with my father to feed the pigeons. I loved it up there – in all kinds of weather, it was a special place. Sky and clouds and the coo of the birds. My father, a very methodical man, had his seeds all organized in marked jars and small wooden boxes. I didn't know why some birds got one kind and others got another, but I knew he knew – he was an authority on so many things. I would sit very still on my special box and watch my father feed his friends. I remember the color of the sky was just

like the blue-gray of the pigeons' feathers. Berlin skies have a look
of steel.

Why did I never rush to tell my mother of those special moments? It
would have been such a natural thing to do for a three year old, to wish
to share a joy – at least, proclaim it. I have often wondered what made
me choose not to, at such an early age. Maybe I knew, even then, that my
mother would resent my receiving joy from anyone but herself. So I kept
quiet and never questioned why my father never mentioned it either, just
felt somehow relieved that he didn't.

My father had lots of things that fascinated me. He owned a four-door
motorcar with a canvas top that folded, its dashboard inlaid wood, and
soft leather seats. This chef d'oeuvre boasted a gadget that absolutely
entranced me: Attached to the dashboard was a box that, whenever my
father pushed its lever, dispensed a single cigarette *already* lit! My father
never needed to take his eyes off the road to grope for a lighter to light
a cigarette, his arrived glowing to his fingertips! How this was done
was a mystery to me then as now. How in inflation-ridden Germany
he could afford such a marvel – not to mention the elegant car that came
with it – is another riddle. But then, how could my mother, playing bit
parts for the ridiculously low pay of those days, own the mink coat she
wore? Long before Hollywood stardom, in the Dietrich-Sieber family,
such incongruities were quite run of the mill. As a very young child, I
saw luxuries come and go, be replaced by more luxuries, without any
fanfare or particular excitement. No "Look, everyone – I got it! The coat
I have been saving for, the one I wanted for so long. . . . It's mine! Isn't
it wonderful? Let's celebrate!" My mother just appeared one day with a
mink coat, threw it on a chair, from where it slipped to the floor, lying
there forgotten while she strode off to the kitchen to cook dinner.

I always knew my mother was special. Why had nothing to do with it
– she just was – like winter was cold and summer warm. She commanded
the emotions one felt for her. In the park, I often saw little girls hug their
mothers, take their hand – touch them spontaneously. One just didn't do
that with mine. It wasn't that she would have pulled away or been angry if
I had. One just didn't dare, until she indicated you could. My mother was
like royalty. When she spoke, people listened. When she moved, people
watched. At the age of three, I knew quite definitely that I did not have
a mother, that I belonged to a queen. Once that was settled in my head,
I was quite content with my lot. Not until much later did I yearn for a
real mother, like real people had.

I was allowed to stay up late when my mother entertained. Perched
on top of my father's huge dictionary, I sat at the big dining table as I
had been taught, quietly listening. My mother's colorful friends would

tell stories of the plays they were in, the cabarets, revues, even sing their numbers from the shows, discuss the extra work in moving pictures, the latest books and music, whom they liked, whom they didn't, and why. Later, in my bed, I would go over everything I had heard, trying to understand it all and remember. My mother was very pleased with me when I remembered everything that in any way involved her. When she questioned me, if I could come up with an exact account of any conversation, I gained her approval. Everyone sought my mother's approval – it meant smooth sailing ahead. Why so many were afraid of her displeasure, I never understood. I just knew that I was one of them.

In the fall of 1927, my mother left for Vienna. She stayed away a long time. She worked in two moving pictures in the daytime and in a play with music and dancing in a theater at night. My father added some carrier pigeons to his collection. He showed me how to attach little message capsules onto their thin legs and told me how bravely they had flown during the war. When I was older, he promised to show me his medals. I was fascinated. Some people loved to talk about "the Great War" – others, like my mother's mother, refused to have it even mentioned in her presence.

During the time my mother was in Vienna, a friend of hers came often to keep us company. Her name was Tamara. My father and mother called her Tami, until they were angry with her for something, then it was back to "Tamara!" with a special sharp emphasis on the *a*'s. She looked exactly as I imagined a White Russian refugee should. High Slavic cheekbones, lithe dancer's body, long dark hair, deep brown eyes like those of a frightened doe. I visualized her pursued by savage wolves across Siberian ice floes, the beautiful Russian aristocrat in desperate flight. I wasn't my mother's daughter for nothing! When my mother first introduced us, Tami squatted down to my level, shook my hand, smiled, and said, "Hello, Mariachen." Her soft German, with its Russian cadence, sounded like the purr of a contented kitten! I thought she was wonderful, and even more than wonderful – she was real. Tami never pretended, never lied, never faked, never deceived. In those early years, laughter still bubbled from her as though she had a hidden spring of happiness tucked deep down inside her. During my entire youth, Tami was my friend, the one person I loved the most. I knew my father loved her too. Why not, she was so lovable. That Tami loved him, I also knew. That this would cause her death, that I could not know. If I had, perhaps I could have saved her. That thought haunts me still.

WHEN MY MOTHER finally came home, she brought with her a big saw that she had learned to play clamped between her knees, and a new friend, her costar Willi Forst. He patted me on the head when I curtsied, shook hands with my father, whom he seemed to know, and stayed for dinner, often.

The fascinating evenings in our dining room resumed. Now my mother was sometimes too busy to cook, so her mother took expensive taxis to bring whole meals from her home only a few blocks away. She never stayed, just delivered her stuffed cabbage rolls that were almost as good as the ones my mother made. The evenings my father went to the famous Kempinski were my favorites. He would bring home a banquet of all sorts of sausages, smoked salmon, caviar, marinated herring, dill pickles, Russian black bread, and a whole smoked eel. Before cutting me a piece, he would grab its head and tail, pretend to play it like a long black flute. It made me laugh so hard, I had to quickly scramble down off my perch to get to the bathroom in time! This always made my mother laugh.

That year I had a lot of news to digest and remember. It seemed an American gentleman, with a German name, had gotten into a little airplane and, all alone, had flown it from America all the way across the ocean to Paris, without stopping even once. Then there was the one about a "Jewish" singer, one who painted his face black and had actually been heard making sounds in a moving picture. That news *really* stirred up a big discussion at the dinner table. Some argued that hearing what actors said would ruin the dramatic impact of moving pictures; others, like my father, thought it was a "technical marvel," that now everything would be different. My mother's comment, which of course everyone agreed with, was: "Well, if sound comes, that will be the end of acting with the eyes – no more faces, only stupid talk."

By the time I was four, I knew a lot of grown-ups. My mother always presented me as "the only love of my life," which, I noticed, made some of the gentlemen, even some of the ladies, very uncomfortable, but my father – not at all. Being a German child, I knew never to ask leading questions about anything; but it was not easy keeping track of all the different grown-ups my mother adored one week who disappeared the next.

Richard Tauber sang so beautifully – he stayed around quite a long time. For some reason, Mr. Forst didn't like Mr. Tauber at all. That's when my mother decided to fall in love with a song instead. She went around with her trusty gramophone, playing the latest phonograph record from America, humming, "You're the Cream in My Coffee," until we all wished she'd find another favorite. That year, she had a big success in a revue, *It's in the Air*, composed by Mischa Spoliansky. One number that stopped the show every night was sung by the star Margo Lion and

Marlene Dietrich. A very sophisticated fox trot, the song made fun of the exaggerated, effusive friendships women have for each other. The way it was performed left no doubt of its lesbian overtones.

Just to make quite sure no one missed this point, both ladies wore a big bunch of violets, the acknowledged flower of "the girls." Of course, I didn't know why everyone hooted with laughter when my mother and her friend sang it for us at our dinner table, but after hearing it for the hundredth time, I could do a very professional rendering of it myself, which was received with even more hoots and hollers than my mother's. It became one of my best party pieces.

Our dinners were full of fascinating news that year. *The Threepenny Opera*, by a Bertolt Brecht and a Kurt Weill, had premièred in Berlin. My mother adored it. She sang me some of the songs. I couldn't understand them at all. She loved them – as much as she disliked the latest hits arriving from across the sea. "Sonny Boy," by the same Jewish gentleman of the year before, she called ridiculous, and another song, from yet another Jewish gentleman, who sometimes sang with a black face, "Makin' Whoopee," *that* she thought was "just too vulgar for words." That night, in bed, I had to think it all through. First, what was meant by "vulgar"? Second, why did everyone in America have to sing with black paint on their face?

Being a December baby, I was never a year older until the *end* of a year. I found that very confusing. As 1929 began, I kept telling everyone who asked that I was now five.

"No, sweetheart. You are only *four*. Your birthday was only last month." As numbers always confused me, I took her word for it. My mother was very strict about my age. That was the year of the Big Crash and the discovery of my "only imperfection," as my mother called it.

She announced both tragedies in the same breath:

"Papi, have you *heard*? It's all over the studios – Wall Street has collapsed, whatever that means. In America there are *millionaires* jumping out of windows . . . and the doctor says the child has crooked legs! I told you I saw something not right there!"

My father already knew of the first drama but not the second one. I quickly looked down at my legs: They looked perfectly straight to *me*. But my mother was convinced I was doomed to "ugliness"! So, for the next two years, I slept with corrective braces on my legs. They were very Germanic-looking, burnished steel and leather, with bolts that had to be tightened or released with a wrench of awesome proportion. Their weight kept me from turning in my sleep. Only later, after my mother returned from becoming a "real movie star in Hollywood," were my legs finally allowed to emerge from their nightly prisons, looking absolutely normal, just as they had two years earlier!

But back in 1929, it was still braces time. My mother would screw them on in the evening before rushing to the theater to make an 8:15 curtain, remove them at the crack of dawn before rushing off to the Studio. She made three films the beginning of that year, still silents, appearing in a leading role at night at the Berliner Theater in a highly successful revue entitled *Two Neckties*. The songs again by her friend Spoliansky, the story was based on the simple comic premise of two bow ties. The black one denoting a lowly waiter, the white one a gentleman of "class."

IN A HURRY AS ALWAYS, my mother was wolfing down her dinner. Her mouth full of frankfurters and potato salad, she mumbled something about having to get to the theater especially early that evening because . . . the rest was muffled by the potato salad. My father and I waited for her to wash it all down with her beer.

"What were you *trying* to say, Mutti?" my father asked in that polite tone he used when slightly annoyed. She pushed half a heel of rye bread into her mouth, mumbled something that sounded like the name of someone.

"I, and the child, will wait – until you have finished chewing."

"I said," my mother spoke, choosing each word distinctly, with exaggerated emphasis, "that-a-very-important-American-director-who-is-going-to-do the Emil Jannings talking picture at Ufa is supposed to be in the audience tonight."

My father disliked embroidery – he wanted information given with precision and clarity:

"Why?"

My mother was clearing the plates.

"How would *I* know? They say he has been looking all over Berlin for the whore in the film . . . maybe he thinks . . ."

"You?" my father smiled, helping himself to more cheese. Annoyed that he was still eating, my mother handed him back his bread and butter plate.

"Don't be stupid. Can you see me playing a cheap whore in a . . ."

"Yes."

My mother gave him a look, lifted me down off my chair, time for bed and leg irons. My father finished his Liptauer and wine, calmly by himself.

"When Tami comes, have her check the child, she's in bed," I heard my mother say in the hall as she was putting on her evening coat. Tami? Wonderful! Now I had something to stay awake for. My father's voice drifted out from the dining room.

"Mutti, have you read Heinrich Mann's book lately?"

"What do you mean?" My mother sounded really annoyed now. "*Professor Unrat*? – a terrible book. How this von Sternberg – how can you be a Jew and have a *von*? Anyway – Jannings will overact like he always does, and with sound, even more! No! It's all going to be *so* depressing! Like a Fritz Lang film . . . I'm late – kiss you – are you and Tami picking me up after?" She was nearly out of our building, her voice echoed from the stairs. My father shouted after her:

"Yes . . . Mutti! Be especially aloof in your big scene tonight. All the others will be bidding for attention with a famous American director out front. If you seem unconcerned, it will make you stand out."

"Why should I want to do that?"

The door of our building slammed. She was on her way.

THE FIRST MEETING of those two titans of film history has been dissected, invented, manipulated, embellished by so many – so often – that no one can find their way through the maze of words back to the absolute truth. Even the two stars of this piece, in their separate autobiographies, when recounting their first propitious encounters, have embroidered a bit. I cannot swear to Josef von Sternberg having done so, but I know for a fact that over sixty years, Marlene Dietrich's accounts changed with each telling – that at the end of her life, she was still editing, tightening their two first meetings, to make these scenes play better. I heard it as it happened, before it was all restaged by journalists, gossip columnists, studio publicity departments, university scholars, and all the others who aspired to be part of the legend.

The argument that went on over what my mother should wear for her first interview with the Big American Director took up a whole dinner. She was determined to wear her best "waterfront whore" outfit. My father insisted she dress like a lady.

"You want me to look like 'fresh out of a high-class girls' finishing school'?" my mother jeered.

"Yes!" my father said ever so quietly. That meant he was really angry.

"You must be nuts! Lulu-Lulu or Lola-Lola or Hupsi-Poopsi, or whatever they say he is going to call her, is a cheap tart! Margo told me she heard, someone at Ufa said I was right for the part because I have a 'juicy' behind. For *that* I am supposed to wear my beautiful suit with the white cuffs? Ridiculous!"

Marlene Dietrich arrived for her first appointment with Josef von Sternberg at the Ufa studios wearing her best suit and white kid gloves, having only added two dangling silver foxes to give her a little confidence. She returned, furious.

"Papi! Wait till you hear what happened today at the studio! Emil Jannings, and some other man, came in to see who was in the office with the Herr Direktor. Looked at me, then said: 'Get up, walk up and down' . . . like some horse! This Josef von Sternberg" – she stressed the *von*, underlining it with a fast laugh – "*he* is a *very* intelligent man, quite different from the usual type. After those two well-poisoners left, he nearly apologized. . . . Nice? *And* he *still* wants to make a test. Even after I told him how terribly I photograph, how my nose sticks up like a duck's behind and he should have them show him some of those terrible films I'm in . . ."

"You told him . . ." My father was shaking his head in disbelief.

"Yes, why not? Let him see right away what they do to me on film . . . then he will know!"

Von Sternberg already knew; he had found the woman he had been searching for. Nevertheless, he arranged for a test. *That* day, she returned from the Studio absolutely enthralled:

"That man is brilliant! Absolutely brilliant! . . . And *sweet*! . . . You know what he did today? He pinned that awful dress they put on me in Wardrobe for the test. He did it, himself. A BIG director! Then he told them what to do with my terrible hair. I told him that it always looks like a cat had just licked it, but he wouldn't listen. You know, Papi, he knows about everything! He can tell everyone how to do their job . . . right! He is amazing. Not just *big important* talk like all the others . . . He *really knows*. Of course, you were right, as usual – I had to sing for the test. He said, 'What do you know in English?' Papi – in English! So . . . I did 'Cream in My Coffee.' But that's not a *vulgar* song, so I tried to do it à la *very* cheap soubrette. The piano player didn't know all the music, and so I got angry – but this is what this von Sternberg wanted! He told me to keep on singing, stop and really yell when he played it all wrong. So I did. Then later, I climbed up on the piano, crossed my legs, and sang 'Wenn Man Auseinander Geht!' That was easy, but the first one – terrible! . . . But we got through it. And, listen to *this*: This von Sternberg says he is going to make *The Blue Angel* in *English*! At the same time as *German*! They haven't even made a talking picture at Ufa yet and now they are going to do it in *two* languages at once? It's a good thing I am not going to be in it!"

She had the part before the test, but she didn't know it.

Overriding all opposition to his choice, von Sternberg forced Ufa to sign Marlene Dietrich to play the supporting female lead in *The Blue Angel*, Germany's first full-length talking picture. Her salary for the film: five thousand dollars. My father and her friends were jubilant. Champagne flowed, my mother kept looking at them all as though they were demented.

"You – you all think this is going to be easy? Hah! Nebbish! [Her favorite Yiddish expression of sarcasm, she used it to mean everything from "big deal" "so what?" to "oh sure," "you bet," and "tell it to the marines."] She's a waterfront *whore*! I'll never be able to show my face again! What if this Sternberg suddenly decides he wants naked tits? What do I do then? Huh? Of course, none of you thought of *that* possibility!" She stormed off to the kitchen to get my father's mustard and more cucumber salad.

I was a little worried at her outburst. She seemed really annoyed with everyone, but my father just smiled and kept eating his juicy knackwurst as though nothing was wrong. I had learned that he was usually right in gauging my mother's moods, so I followed his lead and went on with my dinner. By the time our "resistant" star returned, someone at the table had mentioned a new book, *A Farewell to Arms*, and someone else said that Vicki Baum had written one called *Grand Hotel*. That launched my mother into how she hated Baum, but that this Hemingway must be a dream of a man to write like that, and so the subject had changed. I thought the latest news of a lot of gangsters being mowed down on some Saint's Day in a town called Chicago the most exciting subject of that whole evening – besides my mother becoming a "waterfront whore," of course.

By the time Josef von Sternberg first came to dinner, I had heard so much about him, I couldn't wait to meet the "Big American Director who shouldn't have a *von*." When a stocky little man with a big droopy mustache and the saddest eyes I had ever seen appeared, I was rather disappointed. Except for a long camel-hair coat, spats, and elegant walking cane, he didn't look so important at all. His voice was wonderful, though. Deep and soft – like silky velvet. He spoke perfect German, with the lilt of an Austrian accent.

I was introduced, curtsied, waited, as I had been taught, for him to hold out his hand first, giving me permission to shake it. Nothing happened! I was sort of stuck there, waiting, wondering what to do.

My father said: "Jo, remember you are in Germany. The child is waiting to shake hands."

That seemed to embarrass the little man. Quickly, he shook my hand and smiled. I decided any grown-up who could feel embarrassed about not knowing something in front of a child had to be nice.

I always thought of von Sternberg in that context, a man easily embarrassed, vulnerable, unsure. He spent so much energy pretending just the opposite, always trying to hide what he believed to be his weaknesses. So many people ended up hating this lonely, gifted little man, utterly convinced that he was a monster; they just couldn't see anything beyond their own selfish antagonism. But back in 1929, I was still a child who sensed, but could not yet analyze why, I felt this man was nice, not to be feared, no matter what anyone had to say about him.

Now, our dinner group consisted of immediate family only: my mother, her director, my father, Tami, and the listening sponge, me. Our only subject: the film, their film. At first, von Sternberg seemed surprised, a little ill at ease, with a four year old in constant attendance, but when he realized I wouldn't disturb anyone with childish prattle, he accepted it, and, like everyone else, after a while forgot I was there. As my mother and von Sternberg always spoke German to each other, there was never any language barrier for me.

In that still new time of their relationship, my mother behaved as though he was a god. As though his overcoat had magic powers, she fondled it before hanging it up herself in the hall closet. She cooked only what she had found out he liked, serving him first, even before my father, who seemed to agree entirely with this deferential treatment. While Tami cleared, and generally saw to the comfort of everyone at the table, my mother sat without moving, entranced, listening. Von Sternberg was so serious, so intense, so passionate about this film he was making.

"I want immediate *sound. Swamp* the audience immediately. *Envelop* them with raw sound. . . . early morning sounds . . . hard heels on cobblestone streets, the slap of water thrown on a storefront from a metal bucket . . . dogs barking . . . rattle of thick breakfast dishes. A canary sings. The professor has a canary? Yes! The professor has a canary! Yes! Sound! Sound! It's so correct, the German word for sound, *klang*! That says it so much better than our word – a *klang* film! 'KLANG,'" he bellowed the word. "You feel how it vibrates? That's what we must do! From the first moment the audience must be *deluged* with sound, conditioned instantly, it must learn to concentrate on hearing, to *listen* to dialogue *above* the *klang*."

I didn't know about the rest of the group, but I had goose pimples. What a wonderful little man! Suddenly calm, he turned to my mother:

"Be at the studio at eleven, tomorrow. The designer wants to meet you. I have seen some of the sketches for the costumes and have okayed them."

My mother, eyes adoring, nodded silently. The word *okay* was now an accepted part of our daily vocabulary. I liked it, it sounded cheerful!

The front door slammed. "No!" My mother stormed into the kitchen. "Papi, where are you?"

I knew where he was, but she was so mad I didn't dare tell her that he was on the roof. I knew how she hated those pigeons of his, so I kept silent.

"Papi-e-e! Where the devil are you? *Not again* on the roof . . ."

She was so angry, she was mumbling to herself. She shoved her purse and gloves at me. I ran to put them in their proper place. Chores like that I was good at, I always did them right, exactly the way my mother wanted it done. By the time I got back, she was standing on the kitchen chair, yelling up through the transom:

"Papi? If you are up there, come down immediately! I have trouble!"

My father's cool voice descended from above:

"Mutti, the neighbors can hear you – you sound like a fishwife, screaming like that!"

"Oh, Papi – Please – please come down . . ." Her voice had dropped two octaves. "I need you. Everything is wrong. I don't know what to do – Papi, please, come," she pleaded.

My father, having made his point, arrived, ready to help.

"You can't imagine what they want me to wear. I can't even describe it – it's so – so – Awful! And certainly not in front of the child!"

Was I going to be told to leave, just when it was going to be exciting? I hoped not!

"Is it *that* vulgar?" my father asked as he went to the hall bathroom, my mother following him, I close behind.

"No, that's not it, Papi! Of course it is vulgar – it *has to be*! But it is *stupid*! The look is so *stupid*! – uninteresting, boring – nothing to catch the eye. Blank! Bo-o-o-oring!"

Like a surgeon about to operate, my father washed his hands, using the

special glycerine soap from England that he preferred. Still silent, he dried
them, turned down the French cuffs of his broadcloth shirt, refastened his
gold cuff links, took another pregnant pause, and said:

"I'll talk to Jo. He doesn't know you yet. Don't worry."

My mother heaved a sigh of relief, threw her fur coat on the toilet seat,
and went off to chop onions for dinner.

Tami made her wonderful beef stroganoff that night. Mister von
Sternberg loved it. After the red currant pudding and vanilla sauce, my
mother put her arm around Tami's thin shoulders and led her out of the
dining room, closing the sliding oak doors behind them. Overlooked, I
was left behind with the two gentlemen. My father flicked open his gold
case, offered von Sternberg a cigarette, took one himself, lit both with
his matching Dunhill lighter and said:

"Jo, have you had any time to see something of the city?"

"Not much, but enough to know not to waste my energy. Rudi, thank
God for Erich Pommer. Without him, nothing would be possible. . . .
If we had more producers like him – what films we could make! He
has taste *and* understanding of the creative process. Such a rarity in our
business."

"Jo," my father tapped the end of his cigarette against the edge of the
big glass ashtray, "*that* is what I wanted to mention – the process, the
creative process – the visual impact, even with sound, it is still the core
of our profession – "

"Core? It's the life's blood! Without the image, there is nothing. The
eye sees long before the ear hears."

"Jo, have you thought of giving Marlene the chance to *create*," he
stressed the word ever so lightly, "her own costumes?" Von Sternberg
raised a dubious eyebrow, but didn't comment. "She has an uncanny
knack for what looks right. An instinct. I have never seen it to fail, once
she knows the character. Try it – see what she comes up with. Let her
put it together."

Von Sternberg smoked in silence, then nodded. I couldn't wait to see
what my mother would concoct. I hoped it wouldn't be considered too
"vulgar for the child to see."

She was ecstatic. Day after day, Tami, Becky, and I were given
directions where to search – closets, chests of drawers, old forgotten hat
boxes, dilapidated suitcases, dusty trunks – for long-forgotten treasures.
Our apartment began to look like an enormous rummage sale. She
found a tacky belt with a big rhinestone buckle and screamed with glee.
A threadbare kimono threw her into absolute raptures. "Wonderful!
Wonderful!" she kept muttering while wading through tons of what
looked to us like Salvation Army rejects.

"I need a collar – old satin if possible, and *dirty* white. Everyone look for old collars! . . . In that terrible revue, remember, Tami? In that awful chorus line, didn't we have to wear things on our arms – like cuffs? In lamé . . . remember? – those ugly things? I kept them, but *where*? Maybe in that hatbox I had in the theater during *Broadway*?"

My father just managed to push his way through the front door when she grabbed his arm.

"Don't take your hat off! We have to go out right away, drive around the streets and look for *whores*! Remember that one who always wore a garter belt with a white satin top hat? We have to find him – I want his *panties*." She was dragging him down the stairs, not a moment to lose – "Naughty Lola" was about to get her look!

Oh, how I wish I could have been there to see von Sternberg's expression when Dietrich first presented him with her concept of his Lola. He must have been startled, perhaps even slightly apprehensive, but he knew what looked right. He always did. Good thing Jannings wasn't present, he might have guessed sooner than he did that *The Blue Angel* would no longer be his starring vehicle and have done something about it then. As it was, my mother returned from seeing von Sternberg and said:

"He just looked at me with those baroque eyes of his, then – what do you think he said?"

We all waited with bated breath. She let us hang, building suspense, then grinning triumphantly, announced:

"He said: 'Marlenchen' – he called me Marlenchen! – 'Wonderful – wonderful – Simply wonderful!'" We all hugged each other – she had won! That night my father had to take her to every dive in Berlin to look for more items of whore clothing.

Another new god emerged – another little man. This time without a mustache, or a *von*, whose eyes were never sad. I didn't see him too often that year, my mother worked with him mostly at the Studio, but I heard about him and his music constantly.

"Papi – no one, not even Spoli could have written these songs. Every day, another double entendre thing for me to sing! The words! How he does it! Amazing!"

She sang a song about being Lola, the darling of the season, whose many men loved her, who had a pianola she wouldn't let anyone touch. It was a real snappy number – I loved it.

"Papi, *you* know what is meant by 'pi-a-no-la,'" my mother chortled. "So vulgar – and so *right*. Papi, he is a genius, that Hollander. For *The*

Blue Angel, he is a genius! Listen to this one – today, he doodle-doodled on the piano, tried this, then that – it's my favorite in the film!"

Again, the tune was full of brass and snap. Legs spread, hands on hips, she sang: She was going to go and find herself a man, a man who could kiss and wanted to. A man with fire, who knew what to do with it.

"But the song, the one that *everybody* loves, something about 'moths and flames' and 'I can't help it that all men want me' – that one is terrible! Thank God, once *The Blue Angel* is finally finished, I will never have to sing *that* awful song again!"

Now mornings came really early. It was still dark outside when my mother switched on the lights, pulled back the covers, unscrewed my braces, hurried me into my clothes, pushed a woolen cap on my head, marched us double-time down the stairs, out the big glass door, into the frosty air, down the silent street to my grandmother's house. The deep sound of the bell echoed. My grandmother opened the massive door, dim light outlining her imposing figure, at that predawn hour fully dressed, everything in place.

"Good morning, Lena – you are late!" My mother pushed me toward her, as her mother reached for me. With a look that was both censure and resigned patience, she said: "Go, Lena . . . to your . . . work." She hesitated slightly over the last word, as though searching for a better one to describe my mother's activity. "Your child will be taken care of," and, with a nod of dismissal, closed the door.

I didn't know why my grandmother sounded so annoyed – or why my mother always left cowed, without saying a single word. I did know, though, not to mention it.

First, I stuffed my hat and mittens into the pockets of my winter coat, then hung it carefully on the special hook provided for me. After that, shoes had to come off. "Shoes bring in the dirt off the streets" was one of my grandmother's favorite sayings. This took a little time, as I had to really tug hard to loosen the long laces. "Aristocrats have thin ankles, only peasants have thick ones" was one of my mother's favorite sayings. Each time she put on my high-topped shoes, I figured I must have the peasant kind – she pulled so hard on the laces. Next, my grandmother helped me into my gray pinafore, buttoning it up the back where I couldn't reach. As silent as a creeping cat, in my thick felt house shoes, I padded behind the lady of the house to "the thorough washing of my street hands" before going to the warm kitchen, where, on the big iron stove, my breakfast was steaming – waiting for me.

My mother's mother was strict about so many things, but if you did exactly what she told you, correctly, her way, she was always fair, sometimes even nice. While my mother was being marvelous on a chair in frilly panties and garter belt, I, perched on a tall kitchen stool, learned to peel potatoes, properly; rinse glass in vinegar to make it sparkle; plunge chicken into boiling water to make plucking its feathers easier; mothproof Turkish carpets by scrubbing them with fresh sauerkraut, which also cleaned and brought up their deep colors beautifully. This was one of my favorite "learning to be a wife" chores. On my knees, clutching the heavy brush, I would sneak some of the spicy, fresh kraut from the barrel, munching happily while I scrubbed.

That house was so dark, so empty, it could get really spooky there. One day, I took all my courage and went exploring through its cavernous upper floors. At the top of the house, I found a long, low cupboard, just big enough to crawl into, and at its farthest end, under a small leaded window – a doll's house! A minute, bejeweled world, with chandeliers that actually tinkled when touched, delicate gilt chairs, red velvet betasseled draperies, a fireplace, its carved fruitwood mantel laden with tiny porcelain shepherdesses and pewter candelabra. My knees tucked under my chin, I sat in wonder, drinking in this lilliputian miracle, until my grandmother's voice, calling me, echoing below, broke the spell. From then on, I prayed my mother's film would take forever, did everything and anything exactly as my grandmother wanted, lickety-split, then escaped to the magic world I had discovered. How did that little house get there? Who did it belong to? Who played there before me? All questions I never dared ask, was never told the secrets of. My grandmother must have known where I disappeared to each day, but she never said a word to me or my mother. I have often wondered why.

AS THE WORK on the film progressed, my mother was home less and less. Some mornings it was my father who woke me, then delivered me to my grandmother. When my mother did appear, she kissed me, fed me, changed her clothes, and talked.

"That von Sternberg – absolutely *mad*! This film is a *disaster*! It will never work! What do you think he has done? He has built big wooden boxes for the cameras to sit in – something about blocking out the noise when they are cranking. He creeps in there with them and *disappears*! How can anybody direct a film locked up in a *wooden box*?" She kissed me and ran.

As *The Blue Angel* was shot in sequence, my mother kept us informed of all her daily troubles:

"Today, Jannings did the scene in the schoolroom – where he has to say 'the' in English. He had trouble with the *th*. Funny? He made a whole picture in English in America with von Sternberg, and he can't say 'the'? I can say 'the' perfectly," and to demonstrate, she put her tongue between her front teeth, said the English word, and blew face powder all over her dressing table.

I was never allowed on the set of *The Blue Angel*. My mother considered it a vulgar film, unfit for her innocent child. But at home, she talked of nothing else.

"Papi, *you* made me do this *abortion*. It's all so *ugly*! Fat women – He has big fat women sitting all over on the nightclub stage. You've seen it – it's a *tiny* stage! Any day now it's going to collapse under all that blubber . . . and I am going to break my neck. And the smoke! You should see the smoke! Thick, like fog! Why bother with all the work on the costumes when all you will be able to see is those big, fat shapes behind fog!"

"You think I am having trouble with the English? I'm having trouble with the *German*! Von Sternberg keeps telling me to stop being the 'fine lady.' He keeps yelling at me. 'You are supposed to be a *slut*! Do you understand that, Madame of the Weimar finishing school? We need to do a little *acting* here!' This is all *your* fault, Papi!"

There were times when she cried, when my father held her, telling her not to be discouraged, that in the end it would all work out and be wonderful. She had such trouble with the low-class Berlin slang. Knowing it was not her problem. Acknowledging that she knew it so well and then doing it in front of the crew and von Sternberg was the real hurdle for the "girl from a good family," as she liked to define herself. The English version never gave her as much trouble as getting over this inhibition of speaking in low-class Berlin slang. In English, my mother always felt like a foreigner, disguise was therefore easier. Later, rarely did the real Dietrich emerge when performing in English. Mostly, that language called forth the acquired persona, not the Leni of the youthful diaries.

"There is no real script. Everyone, even Pommer, is worried – but von Sternberg will not allow anyone to interfere with him. He has it all written in his head. How wonderful to work with a man who knows what he wants and then knows exactly how to *get* it – but I wish he would tell something to someone!"

One cold dawn, she rushed into my room, snapped on the light, handed me the wrench, said, "You do it!" and started rummaging frantically through my toy chest. A stuffed rabbit flew out one way, a clown puppet followed, blocks, balls, the place was a mess. She turned, giving me a "you did it" look:

"Where is it? Did you take it?"

Hardly awake, completely confused, I stammered, "What?" which probably sounded very guilty.

"*You* know what! My black doll! Where did you have it?"

"Mutti, I *never* play with *him*. I am not allowed to. But Papi had him."

She whirled.

"*Papi!* You have my nigger!" and off she ran. Now my father was going to get it! I didn't mean to make trouble for him, but I had seen him fixing the grass skirt of my mother's black felt savage. Later, running down the dark street on the way to dropping me off, she had her black doll clutched securely under her arm. Wherever Dietrich went, her black savage was sure to go. He was her good-luck charm throughout her life – her professional one. In her real life, astrology took his place.

"Herr Direktor told me today I am finally to be permitted to see – they call it 'rushes' – what was shot two days ago. He also informed me that I was to keep my mouth shut! – until they were over! I *may* comment only *after* the lights come back on in the projection room. Such la-di-da, these Americans – really!"

She returned the next day, full of wonder:

"Papi, it is still a vulgar film – but *Mister* von Sternberg is a . . . god! A god! A Master! No wonder they all hate him . . . they *know* they can't touch him. He paints, like Rembrandt, with his lights. That face, up there on the screen, a real seafront harbor tart – she is *right*! She is absolutely wonderful!"

This is the first time I heard my mother refer to herself in the third person. It was the beginning of her thinking of Dietrich as a product, quite removed from her own reality.

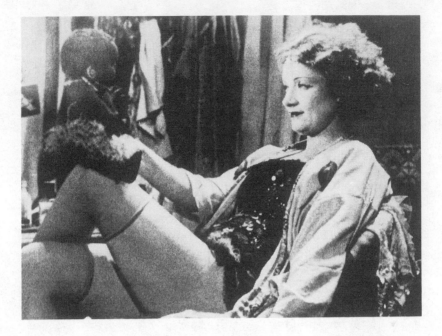

ABOVE: In 1930, Marlene Dietrich
creates a sensation as Lola in *The
Blue Angel*, Germany's first talkie.
RIGHT: Josef von Sternberg, the
genius who made this great film and
Dietrich's fame possible.

ABOVE, LEFT: Lola, the water-front tart, astride her famous chair. My mother's favorite pose from *The Blue Angel*, although her fat thighs made her shudder each time she looked at it.

ABOVE, RIGHT: Von Sternberg directing his star, Emil Jannings, while his "discovery" tries to smile beguilingly, hoping for a response. By now the great Jannings knew she was stealing the film from him. He ignores her.

LEFT: With her mascot, her black felt doll, in *The Blue Angel*. Throughout her life he went wherever she did.

"And remember those terrible fat women I didn't like, that Jo put behind me in the scene? They're *so* fat, they make *me* look *thin*! Jo knew why he put them there *that* early in the film – he already knew what would look right!"

"Now, that one awful song I told you about has English lyrics. What do you think it is called? 'Falling in Love Again'! That's not English for 'I'm from Head to Foot Made for Love.' It's bad enough I have to sing that awful song also in English without all the words being changed and now making no sense *whatsoever*!"

"Today, I said, 'Why don't you let me sit on something else? How many times can one be erotic with a chair? What about trying a barrel – a barrel at least has a different look and I maybe can stretch out one leg and pull up the other one.' So you know what he'll do? He'll focus his boxes up my crotch anyway. . . . This whole thing is *impossible*. I am ashamed to walk on the set!"

"JO HAS A WONDERFUL IDEA. Papi, you know the picture postcards that the schoolboys have, secretly of the whore – the one Jannings gets so furious about in the scene? Well! Jo had the Studio glue little wispy feathers just on the top of the panties. Then, in the scene he shows them all blowing on the card to lift the feathers up and show – you know what. Brilliant idea? Now, *that's* erotic!"

My mother was now important enough to even have her own studio dresser, who turned out to be a thin, angular spinster by the name of Resi. Within weeks, she became my mother's personal maid, on constant call, day or night. Resi was to remain with us throughout most of the Sternberg films, the model of servitude and petrified devotion.

Sometime during the filming of *The Blue Angel*, I decided to rename myself. No one ever called me by my real name anyway, unless they were angry with me; "Maria! Come here!" meant *big* trouble. Some children invent a friend, an imaginary playmate; I suppose I was simply looking for my own identity, so, one day I announced that henceforth I was to be known as Heidede. God only knows where I got *that* from, probably something to do with *Heidi* – I was deep into an idyllic Alpine period. Everyone took my proclamation very seriously. From then on, my mother called me "The Child," "Sweetheart," "Angel," "Love of my Life"; my father, "the child," or "Kater"; and the rest of the world:

Heidede Daughter of Marlene Dietrich!

One evening, my mother had a little time left, so she joined us at the dinner table.

"Today, in the choking scene, he really tried to choke me! Jo saw it, made some excuse, and stopped the scene. What is *wrong* with Jannings? He is so brilliant in this film. What an actor! Sometimes, he gets *too* much . . . but then Jo always has one of those long talks with him, while we all wait and relax, but then, when he comes back, he is again – wonderful! So why, suddenly, can't he *act* choking?!, instead of really trying to do it?"

My father poured them both a beer.

"Mutti, if I were Jannings, I would choke you and *not* stop when the director calls 'Cut!' "

"What do you mean?" My mother was outraged. "It's all *my* fault again?"

"You have taken the film away from him – *The Blue Angel* now belongs to Marlene Dietrich, not to Emil Jannings, its star. He must know it!"

"Well, if that is true, then it is Jo's fault, not mine! I only do what he tells me to do. Jannings should choke Jo, not *me*!" and went out to get her coat and go to work at the theater.

The Berlin film industry was quite aware that in its midst, a phenomenon was in the making. Hollywood knew it just as quickly. Being the American distributors of *The Blue Angel*, as well as von Sternberg's home studio, Paramount decided it would be a good idea to sign up the English-speaking German sex bomb with the good-looking gams that everyone was talking about.

MARLENE DIETRICH SIEBER
KAISERALLEE 54 BERLIN   29 JAN 1930
HAVE PLEASURE TO INVITE YOU TO JOIN BRILLIANT ROSTER OF PLAYERS AT PARAMOUNT PUBLIX STOP OFFER YOU SEVEN YEAR CONTRACT BEGINNING AT FIVE HUNDRED DOLLARS PER WEEK ESCALATING TO THREE THOUSAND FIVE HUNDRED PER WEEK IN SEVENTH YEAR. CONGRATULATIONS. PLEASE CONFIRM BY CABLE. BERLIN OFFICE WILL ARRANGE FIRST CLASS TRAVEL AND IS AT YOUR DISPOSAL FOR ANY HELP REQUIRED.
                              BP SCHULBERG
                              VICE PRESIDENT
                              PARAMOUNT PUBLIX CORPORATION

Reading the cable out loud, my mother was more outraged by the superiority of its tone than by the low salary offered: "What vain people. They just assume I couldn't possibly say no. They congratulate me, even!" and threw it across the table to my father, and left to bring von Sternberg's lunch to the Studio where he was editing *The Blue Angel*.

THE BLUE ANGEL was finished, the revue had closed. My mother was out of work. Von Sternberg would soon be returning to America; she now rarely left his side. He kept trying to persuade her to accept the Paramount offer. Her excuses not to were, first, my welfare; second, as Ufa still held an option on her services, she was not free to sign with anyone else. When they finally decided not to pick up her contract, she was convinced she was no good, that everyone had been wrong about how "wonderful" she was, that her so-called great career in films was finished.

"You see? What did I tell you? Ufa also thinks I am so bad in the film they don't even want me under contract!"

"Don't be ridiculous. They are just too stupid to know what they've got, which is to your advantage," said my father.

"Yes! Wonderful! Now you are free to sign with Paramount." Von Sternberg was ecstatic.

"I will not go to America, I have told you. How do I know what will happen there? Any country that can make a dog a film star is not to be taken seriously. And The Child? Schlep The Child all the way across the ocean? And how do you know, now that Ufa has said no, that those big bosses at Paramount still want me?"

"They want you, believe me, they want you, and when I show them the film, they'll *beg* you. As for The Child, nothing but sunshine all day and her own swimming pool – what's bad about that?"

It sounded terrific! The sunshine part. The pool I wasn't so sure of, I would have to learn to swim first.

"If you insist I go, Jo, then I would have to come first – alone. To see if it is all as 'wonderful' as you say. Then I could come back here and maybe get the child. But, if I don't like it? If I have signed a contract – what do I do then? And how can I be sure you, only YOU, will direct me? – No! No! It is all *much* too complicated. Here, I can work without all these terrible problems!"

"I will not stay here and be subjected to this utter stupidity!" said von

Sternberg, and walked out of the room. My mother cried: "JO," and ran after him into the hall. My father lit a cigarette. We waited. Her arm locked in von Sternberg's, my mother reentered them both into our dining room, looked at my father beseechingly:

"Papi – *you* tell him. Tell Jo I can't leave The Child!"

Von Sternberg turned to go. She clutched at him:

"Sweetheart!" I knew *this* time that didn't mean me.

"Mutti, you are asking me to decide?" my father said, ever so softly.

"Yes, *you* tell Jo . . . I can't . . ." She let it hang.

"If you really want *my* opinion, I personally think there is absolutely no reason for you *not* to go." My mother gave him a furious look. "Let me finish, please. As for the child, you have left her before – for much lesser things. So this wouldn't be the first time. My advice is: Go to America. Trust Jo. Listen to him. Do exactly what he tells you to do. With Jo there to protect and guide you, you have a once-in-a-lifetime opportunity. You would be a fool to throw it all away. The child will stay here. Here she has me, Tami, and Becky. When you get back, we will all still be here, waiting for you."

Von Sternberg could have kissed him. It sounded to me as though my mother would be going to America.

THE EVENING THAT VON STERNBERG was ready to leave, we all kissed him good-bye, except my mother. She was going back to his apartment to help him pack, then say her good-byes properly at the boat train.

The next day, I courageously ventured to ask: "Mutti, if you go away to America like Papi says, may I have a dog then, please?" and lo and behold, she answered, "Yes – but not a mongrel," before rushing to the Studio to record the songs from *The Blue Angel* onto phonograph records. From then on, I didn't notice much of anything, I was much too busy looking through my picture books for my heart's desire. When the time came for my mother to leave, I wanted to be ready with my choice of breed. Whatever it turned out to be, it had to be huggable.

While my mother packed her trunks, carefully wrapped her black doll, filled out shopping lists, and kissed me with the sadness of a soldier about to go into battle, back at Paramount von Sternberg had negotiated new terms for his protégée. Miss Dietrich was now bound contractually to make two films only. If she then decided to

return to her native land, forsaking Hollywood stardom, she would
be permitted to do so, provided she signed a legal document stating
that once having been released by Paramount, she would not sign
with any other American studio. If, on the other hand, Miss Dietrich
decided to pursue an American career, her Paramount contract would
automatically be reactivated, her salary raised substantially. A clause
giving Marlene Dietrich choice of director was added to the contract
– an unheard-of concession by a studio to a yet unknown, untried
performer.

As early as April of 1929, an article had appeared in a Berlin tabloid
that mentioned Marlene Dietrich in connection with a Swedish actress,
already a star in Hollywood. It could be that this was the very first time
that Dietrich was ever linked to Greta Garbo, and it is more than likely
that this item had been brought to the attention of Paramount. The
vicious rivalry between studios was true and justified. Their earning
power and prestige depended entirely on the talents they controlled.
As the Metro group owned Garbo, every other major studio was
searching frantically for another such sublime creature – loaded with
foreign mystery, European sophistication, hypnotic accented voice, and,
if at all possible, high cheekbones and hooded eyes – with which to
give the mighty MGM a run for box-office revenues. It is possible
that even more than von Sternberg's effusive recommendations, those
gorgeous legs, and sexy garter belt of *The Blue Angel*, it was the
uncanny resemblance to Garbo that decided Paramount to play along
with Dietrich's demands. It was this very need to best the competition
that was to turn a very saucy, honest talent into that mysterious
enigma that became "Marlene Dietrich." What she might have become,
had her raw talent been allowed to develop in the direction of her
absolutely superb performance in *The Blue Angel*, makes for heady
speculation.

But this was not to be. The adoration of a brilliant image-maker,
the greed of the studio system, and, most of all, her own narcissism
turned what could have been to what had to be: the breathtaking endless
close-ups, the veils, the clothes, the legs, the genderless sex, that amazing
beauty – always that astounding beauty – until manufactured imagery
became her reality. At rare moments throughout her professional life,
the spark that had ignited *The Blue Angel* would flare, but never
again catch true fire. After a while, Dietrich didn't even bother to
recognize its presence. Legends don't need to search for things lost –
they *are*.

Only one thing worried me about my mother journeying to far-off America. Might the Indians there try to scalp her? As carefully as I could, I brought this subject up. My mother was packing hat boxes. She said that although Americans were still very uneducated, scalping was no longer a daily occurrence and for me not to be so dramatic. I wasn't completely convinced. On one of her rare visits, my Aunt Liesel had read to me from *The Last of the Mohicans*, and so I knew something my mother obviously didn't – that America could be a very dangerous place. Then again, I knew if my mother made up her mind not to give up her hair, no poor redskin in the whole world would have a chance of getting it away from her. So, when the time finally came to say good-bye to her, I did so without any qualms. With the little man there to protect her, I knew she would be "okay."

In the early evening of the 31st of March, 1930, looking like a real queen in white chiffon and full-length ermine coat, my mother held me close and cried. I had a cold and she couldn't tear herself away, didn't want to leave me for fear I would die without her there to comfort me. But she had to go – it was the night of the gala opening of *The Blue Angel* at the big Gloriapalast Theater, where members of the cast were scheduled to take a bow with the star of the film, Emil Jannings. Directly after the performance, my mother was to take the boat train to Bremerhaven, there to board the SS *Bremen*, bound for New York.

"The second you hear the telephone ring, answer it!" she said to Becky, as she checked my braces. "The moment I can, I will telephone to hear how The Child is. In two hours, take her temperature again so you can tell me. If I can sneak out during the film, I will come back. If the boat wasn't sailing tonight, I wouldn't go to this damned thing at all."

My father and Willi Forst, both resplendent in their tails, called from the hall: "Mutti, it's time to go. You have to be there before the lights go down."

I hugged her carefully, not to mess up anything.

"Don't forget me," she whispered, and was gone.

Three hours later, she was a "star." An instant triumph. The name she had invented, "Marlene," "Marlene," shouted in rapture and adulation for the first time. She hardly heard it – her mind was on my temperature.

She wouldn't allow my father to accompany her to Bremerhaven. She sent him back to wake me, take my temperature himself, make sure I was all right, tell me how much she missed me already.

He looked very handsome that night. I always thought my father looked as wonderful in tails as my mother did.

"Papi, is Mutti really gone?" I asked. Not waiting for an answer, "Is Mutti coming back?"

"Yes, Kater, but not right away. First she will make another film with Mr. von Sternberg."

"Was it a real big night? A big success for her tonight?"

"Yes . . . a great success," this said quietly with a hollow sound. He seemed tired. He sat down on the edge of the bed. I got very courageous.

"Will you get me a dog tomorrow, like she promised? Will you – please?"

"Yes, I already picked one out." He bent down and I saw the wrench. The moment the braces were off, I hugged him – hard. He asked me if I had said my prayers. He was the only one who ever asked me that. He tucked me in, turned off the light – left, leaving the door ajar. The hall light made a cozy glow on my linoleum floor. I wondered how the audience had liked the pianola song, and if the lamé cuffs we found had looked right with the white satin top hat costume. . . . I fell asleep and dreamt of a puppy of my very own to love.

The very first thing my mother must have done on boarding the ship that night was to write us a radiogram. Of course, as always, in German. In those days, the word *stop* was used as punctuation in any language.

R SIEBER
KAISERALLEE, 54 BERLIN   I APRIL 1930   03:16 AM
PAPILEIN MISS YOU LONELY REGRET TRIP ALREADY STOP TELL MY ANGEL THAT
I NEVER SAW THE FILM THAT I WAS ONLY THINKING OF HER ADORABLE SELF
STOP GOOD NIGHT KISSES =

                                                             MUTTI

R SIEBER
KAISERALLEE, 54 BERLIN   I APRIL 1930   II:48 AM
GOOD MORNING STOP BOAT ROLLS BAD WEATHER STRONG WINDS STOP ALONE
IN MID OCEAN WHEN I COULD BE AT HOME AND HAPPY KISSES =

                                                             MUTTI

MARLENE DIETRICH SIEBER
SS BREMEN   I APRIL 1930   13:17 PM
MISSING YOU MUTTI STOP CRITICS AT YOUR FEET STOP JANNINGS GETS GOOD
MENTIONS BUT IT IS NOT AN EMIL JANNINGS FILM ANYMORE STOP MARLENE
DIETRICH RUNS AWAY WITH IT STOP THE CHILD IS WELL STOP LONGING
KISSES =

                                                             PAPI

MARLENE DIETRICH
SS BREMEN   2 APRIL 1930   12:15 PM
CONGRATULATIONS TO US BOTH STOP NEW FILM WILL BE CALLED MOROCCO
BASED ON STORY AMY JOLLY FROM BOOK YOU SLIPPED INTO MY LUGGAGE
STOP YOU WILL BE AT LEAST FABULOUS =

JO

JOSEF VON STERNBERG
PARAMOUNT STUDIOS HOLLYWOOD CALIF   2 APRIL 30   15:01 PM
WHO WILL PLAY OPPOSITE ME =

MARLENE

MARLENE DIETRICH
SS BREMEN   3 APRIL 30   12:45 PM
GARY COOPER WILL PLAY OPPOSITE YOU STOP MANY THANKS YOUR EFFU-
SIVE CABLE EXPRESSING YOUR PROFOUND GRATITUDE TO ME FOR LIFT-
ING YOU INTO THE STRATOSPHERE DESPITE YOUR TEDIOUS RESISTANCE
STOP DO NOT KISS MY HAND MADAME STOP YOU HAVE PERMITTED
MY CAMERA TO WORSHIP YOU AND IN TURN YOU HAVE WORSHIPPED
YOURSELF =

JO

R SIEBER
KAISERALLEE, 54 BERLIN   3 APR 30   14:51 PM
BE SURE SEND JO CABLE CONGRATULATIONS STOP VERY TOUCHY STOP I HUG
THE CHILD =

MUTTI

J VON STERNBERG
PARAMOUNT STUDIO HOLLYWOOD CALIF   3 APRIL 30   14:53 PM
YOU KNOW I ADORE YOU =

MARLENE

MARLENE DIETRICH
SS BREMEN   4 APRIL 1930   09:15 AM
YOUR APOLOGY IS ACCEPTED =

JO

R SIEBER
KAISERALLEE, 54 BERLIN   4 APR 30   13:16 PM
RESI SEASICK SINCE FIRST DAY LIKE ALL MAIDS ON BOARD STOP TODAY SHE
LOST HER TEETH OVER THE SIDE STOP I HAVE TO SEND FOR MUSH BECAUSE SHE
WONT LEAVE THE ROOM STOP CALL MUTTI TELL HER I AM WELL AND MISSING
HER STOP AND YOU KISSES =

MUTTI

MARLENE DIETRICH
SS BREMEN   5 APR 1930   14:29 PM
REICHSFILMBLATT QUOTE ONE IS ALMOST STUNNED BY MISS DIETRICHS
PERFORMANCE STOP HER ABILITY TO TAKE OVER SCENES EFFORTLESSLY BUT
WITH SIMPLE AND TOTAL COMMAND IS SOMETHING WE HAVE UNTIL NOW
NEVER EXPERIENCED END QUOTE CONGRATULATIONS MUTTI STOP HEAR THAT
EMIL JANNINGS IS KILLING HIMSELF STOP LONGING KISSES =
                                                                    PAPI

R SIEBER
KAISERALLEE, 54 BERLIN   5 APR 1930   20:32 PM
AM REMEMBERING JANNINGS WARNING AGAINST JO QUOTE FOR MY OWN
GOOD END QUOTE BY THE WAY THANKS FOR YOUR ADVICE STOP KISSES =
                                                                    MUTTI

MARLENE DIETRICH
SS BREMEN
UNRESTRAINED RAVE FROM KRACAUER QUOTE DIETRICHS LOLA-LOLA IS A
NEW INCARNATION OF SEX THIS PETTY BOURGEOIS BERLIN TART WITH HER
PROVOCATIVE LEGS AND EASY MANNERS SHOWS AN IMPASSIVITY WHICH
INCITES ONE TO GROPE FOR THE SECRET BEHIND HER CALLOUS EGOTISM AND
COOL INSOLENCE END QUOTE KISSES =
                                                                    PAPI

R SIEBER
KAISERALLEE, 54 BERLIN
SEND CLIPPING TO JO WHO IS THE SECRET STOP KISSES =
                                                                    MUTTI

JOSEF VON STERNBERG
PARAMOUNT STUDIOS HOLLYWOOD
I AM SORRY YOU THOUGHT I TAKE YOU FOR GRANTED STOP DONT YOU
KNOW THAT FROM THE SECOND DAY OF SHOOTING I HAVE UNDERSTOOD
THAT WITHOUT YOU I AM NOTHING =
                                                                    MARLENE

MARLENE DIETRICH
SS BREMEN
PLEASE FORGIVE MY TERRIBLE AND INEXCUSABLE PERSONALITY STOP IT IS THE
WAY I AM NO MATTER HOW I TRY TO BE BETTER STOP I WILL TRY HARDER =
                                                                    JO

R SIEBER
KAISERALLEE, 54 BERLIN   7 APRIL 30   16:00 PM
ARRIVING NEW YORK TWO DAYS LATE DUE TO TREMENDOUS GALES BLOWING
US BACK STOP I DONT MIND STOP I DREAD HAVING TO GET OFF THIS GERMAN

SHIP THE LAST LINK WITH MY NATIVE LANGUAGE MY HOMELAND THE CUSTOMS
I UNDERSTAND STOP LOVE KISSES =

MUTTI

I got a squirming ball of white fluff with shoe-button eyes and ears that flopped. My first four-legged friend! I was sublimely happy. When my mother's letters began arriving, each new installment was read aloud at the dinner table, like an exciting serial.

The Ambassador
New York City

9 April 1930

Papilein,

I'll need time to get accustomed to America. This morning on the boat I was told that my beige suit was wrong for arrival photographs. They wanted me in a black dress and mink coat sitting on top of my suitcases. You know that I take orders, but sitting on top of luggage? Wearing a fur coat in the hot sun? At four o'clock there is a press conference here at the hotel and I am supposed to be dressed for "cocktail hour." Whatever *that* is.

Tonight I am going out with Walter Wanger, Paramount's East Coast head of production, and his wife. He was one of a group from the Studio who came out to the boat on a Coast Guard launch to greet me. He said, "I am instructed to take you out to dinner and show you around New York with my wife." Instructed! Gracious, eh?

I can use the change from Resi, who never left the stateroom because she wouldn't walk on deck without her teeth. By the way, she's at the dentist and will have new ones today. The Studio arranged that. Nice to have powerful connections.

I am looking forward to these four days in New York.

Tell the child how I long for her and I kiss her picture.

Mutti

ON THE PENNSYLVANIA RAILROAD

10 April 1930

Papilein,

I'm not going to be four days in New York. I'm on the train to Chicago. When Walter Wanger called for me last night, there was an "indisposed" wife. I went with him to a dark restaurant which they call a "speakeasy." He explained that they call them that because when they first opened the customers were supposed to "speak easy," meaning softly, not to attract the police. Mr. Wanger was charming and explained that he had brought me there because I had said in the press conference that I adore Harry Richman and this was where he sings in person. And soon Mr. Richman was on stage and singing "On the Sunny Side of the Street," which I've played I don't know how many times on my gramophone and hearing it there from him in person was very exciting. Then my handsome escort asked me to dance and when he had me in his arms he whispered, "von Sternberg's right, you *are* the find of the century," and then he had me in his hands as well as in his arms and I thought of asking if this was also in his instructions, but the way it happened was not amusing and rather embarrassing. So I excused myself to go to the powder room, left the speakeasy, found a taxi, and got back to the hotel. I telephoned Jo. Luckily I got him at home and told him what happened. As you know, I wasn't so angry because a man had given me a little squeeze on the behind, that's what it is there for. What I disliked was that it seemed to be taken for granted, that this was in my contract, a sort of *derecho del señor.* They had the same attitude on the dock and at the press conference: "Sit on that trunk. Pull up your skirt. Higher. Give us more leg." I explained that I also disliked being placed in a position for journalists to ask stupid questions like "How do you like America?" when I had only been here for 10 minutes and not yet left the dock. There is no scintillating answer to that, unless nasty, and so I sounded dull.

Jo said, "Take the next train out here. I'll have the hotel change your reservations. Don't speak to anyone! Just get out of New York. I'll take care of everything."

Tell my angel I love her. Kisses and love,

Mutti

On Board the Santa Fe
CHIEF

Chicago, 11 April 1930

Dearest Papi,

I spoke to Jo from Chicago. He said he would join us on this train at a station called Albuquerque (you should *hear* the way that's pronounced), which is a day from Hollywood, in order to shield me from more surprises. The train is comfortable, we take our meals in our drawing room. Resi is happy with her new teeth. *The Last Day!!* Jo got on in Albuquerque. I didn't know what a sacrifice that was until now we are going through the desert and the heat is unbelievable. We have to keep the windows wide open, but the air that comes in is like flames, and filthy. We spread sheets on seats because the velvet plush burns the legs. Get off at each station to have a walk but the heat drives us back. And Jo made this trip yesterday and now again today!

He has everything organized. We get off at Pasadena, a station before

Los Angeles, to avoid journalists. There will be a few there, but they are a "Studio-controlled press" who use only the stories the Studio writes, and they submit their photos to Publicity for approval and touching up before they publish them. What comfort to have Jo here in command.

Tomorrow: Hollywood.

Love. Kisses. Missing you.

Mutti

Beverly Hills
14 April 1930

Papilein,

Well, the "Great Find of the Century" is in Hollywood. I am in a pretty little house that Jo rented for me in Beverly Hills, a residential section not far from the Studio. Arrival in Pasadena went well. Flowers, and a green Rolls-Royce, a gift from the studio. I have 2 maids, so Resi will have companionship if she will learn a few words of English.

Jo opened a bank account for me with 10,000 dollars from the Studio. He showed me how to write a check. I enclose a sample for $1,000. My first check. Don't frame it. Spend it. It hardly feels like money this way.

Here there are blue skies, and the weather is unbelievably mild after Berlin. Tomorrow we start work on the costumes. One of them will be my own top hat, white tie, and tails that Jo saw me wear in Berlin at that party. I will be told my lines day by day, in fact, line by line. So, with nothing to learn, I have little to do. I cut flowers and I read.

I try to eat nothing. I look good in Berlin but what was right for a buxom tart from Lübeck isn't right for *Morocco*. Amy Jolly is supposed to be sleek and mysterious.

I am glad to be making all this money and I am looking forward to making another film with Jo, but homesickness nags me.

Love, kisses,
M.

I remember the time my mother was far away in America with a sense of calm, sectional memories – the day my father brought home a small trick figure of Felix the Cat, whose tail grew as if by magic when a lit match was held to his bottom; being allowed to really get acquainted with my father's room. If I had known what the Spanish Inquisition was, I would have known what my father's room looked like. Dark monastery wood, blood-red moiré walls, and everywhere, massive religious artifacts. Even without knowing, I felt its ominous secular spookiness. Around his alcoved bed ran a shelf on which stood transparent glass apothecary jars that contained gelatinous masses illuminated from behind. My father, really a frustrated surgeon, had acquired his specimens from a medical student friend of his youth. He instructed me as to what each of them was, plus their assigned functions in the human body. It was fascinating. He had a heart swimming around in formaldehyde, a pretty good-looking liver, a bit of cerebellum and – half a kidney. My mother made a wonderful kidney dish with a Dijon mustard sauce, but my father's illuminated one was much more exciting and interesting. When the tall wax tapers were burning on their wrought-iron stands, the frankincense spiraled from the silver thurible, and the organs glowed, I would sit, fingering a huge ivory rosary – feeling ever so specially good and holy. Sometimes I expected a whole human being to materialize out of those organs on the shelf, like some resurrected saint, but although I waited, that never happened. My father took me to visit his parents, who lived in a little house in Czechoslovakia. That made me very happy. I loved them, loved being there; Tami looked after us, loved us, cooked wonderful Russian food, filled the rooms with her happy laughter. My father didn't get angry as often, my dog was allowed to sleep with me, and my Aunt Liesel taught me to read. All in all, it was a wonderful time.

Papilein,

The costume work is good and I enjoy it. The designer, Travis Banton, is talented. Jo tells us what he wants and Travis and I discuss what the clothes should be. He has the same respect for Jo that I have and is willing to do the sketches over and over until they are right. We have the same kind of endurance, we never tire.

What is tiring is keeping up long conversations in English. Travis is American and Jo refuses to speak a word of German to me. If I tell him I need to have a rest, he says, "No, what you *need* is to speak English more easily. Continue in English, please." He corrects my grammar, plus my pronunciation. And I learn new words, new expressions every day. That's good, but you can imagine the joy when I can speak to you. So, stop worrying that it's so expensive. I'll have plenty of money and I can spend it on hearing you and The Child.

Resi and I go to the new films. We saw *All Quiet on the Western Front*. It's a tremendous success here. Fascinating that it's the same Remarque I used to see at Mutzbauer's. Please send me the book. I want to read it in the German the way he wrote it.

I wait outside the house for the postman to come. Please write. Kisses, love,

Mutti

My father told me that my mother was sending us photographs that Mr. von Sternberg had taken of her. Big ones, beautiful ones for something called Publicity, and they arrived in big, gray, cardboard-lined envelopes bearing the Paramount crest. Even to a child's eye, they were something luminous, like a Madonna, not quite real. It's a funny sensation, looking at a face you know, or think you know, is your mother's, who has been made into a deity.

When she telephoned, I yelled over the crackling noises, hoping she could hear me so very far away:

"Mutti, did you see any Indians? Are there cowboys? Does the sun shine *all* the time? Can you send me a real Indian suit, with a bow and arrow, real feathers and everything – please? Are there palm trees? Oh, and yesterday Papi played his eel and we all laughed and missed you."

Sometimes, instead of writing letters or telephoning, my mother sent her voice, recorded on thin celluloid records that my father put on our gramophone and played for me.

"Sweetheart . . . are you listening? . . . my angel." I nodded at the machine. "Do you know what I have in my mouth? Your tooth, the one you lost that Papi sent me. That's how I can keep you close inside of me. A part of you. Sweetheart . . . I walk around this beautiful house and you are nowhere to be found. Are you all right? Are you eating? I cry because I can't cook for you, and smell your wonderful smell and brush your hair and see your sleeping face. I miss you, miss you . . . miss you. My life is empty without you. I will come back to you soon . . . soon . . . my love."

I didn't like those records; that disembodied voice – so sad, so full of yearning – disturbed me. Although my father insisted I listen to them twice over, I had a feeling he didn't like them either.

Beverly Hills

Papilein,

Jo was asked to make a trailer to introduce me to the Sales Department, so we made a short scene in which I wore my white tie and tails. The Studio roof blew off. "Slacks" (the word used here for trousers). It seems that "slacks" are not worn by women in America. The feeling is that no man looks at a woman in trousers.

Jo told them, "I'm responsible for directing Miss Dietrich and she will wear what I choose!" (I also wear shorts, revealing dress, etc., in the film.) All in black, by the way. I begged Jo to let me wear black. I eat nothing, but I still look fat. He doesn't think I am, and nothing is more difficult to photograph well than black, but to please me, he agreed.

We were both invited to a party at the Schulbergs' house, the last thing either of us feels like doing now. Jo said that I didn't have to go. But, he said, "It would be wise to create goodwill," he rolled those baroque eyes, "an absurd waste of effort as it is not possible to create 'goodwill' with anything but a money-making picture." To be courteous, we went.

I wore my navy blazer, white flannel *trousers*, and a yachting cap (to create just a *little* "ill" will).

Kisses, Mutti

She enclosed a photograph taken by von Sternberg of her in "yachting" outfit. She and it had been such a sensation with the ladies of the elite Malibu Beach community that, she wrote on the back, "The Studio plans to issue thousands of these with the caption – 'The Woman Even Women Can Adore.'" My father laughed, framed it, and placed it among the other images of our queen that were beginning to crowd the long narrow table that stood in our living room. Whenever you were in that room, that magnetic gaze from all those beautiful eyes seemed to follow you about. My mother's pictured face always affected me with a feeling of eerie discomfort, as though she was actually there, waiting, ready to emerge, breathing, from out of the paper images.

HOLLYWOOD – THE BEGINNING

Papilein,

Tomorrow we begin shooting. It's been amusing, all this "the new thing from Germany" and "Paramount's answer to Garbo" and "The Great Find of the Century," but now I feel a responsibility to Jo to *be* just that, and though I'm sure that with his help I can be, still I am nervous and apprehensive.

M.

Sea mist envelops the deck of a small steamer, somewhere off the coast of North Africa. A woman appears. Evening light just touching shadows the cheekbones; the small, close-fitting hat outlines the perfectly shaped head; only her eyes, those eyes that have seen too much of the world, carry their disillusion to the silent watchers. Just below the line of veil, her mouth, its perfect curve suggests a lingering vulnerability left over from some forgotten past when she still trusted, still believed in love. Her sleepy lids rise, languidly she gazes, evaluates the stranger come to her assistance, and says: "I won't need any help." Like a bursting balloon, the *lp* explodes in the earphones of the sound man; he tears them off his head and looks at the director, aghast. Von Sternberg calls, "cut"; everything on the giant soundstage comes to a dead stop.

She had been nervous for days. She knew that for her first American starring role, the guttural, uncultured English that had worked for her in *The Blue Angel* would be wrong for the woman of illusion and mystery von Sternberg and she had been busy creating for weeks in the Studio portrait gallery. Long before principal photography began on *Morocco*, she had already become the ultimate face that all portrait photographers dream of. Hundreds of images of the new Dietrich, as von Sternberg saw her, had been circulated throughout the Paramount lot; the excitement they created everywhere was topped only by the jubilant hysteria of the studio's Publicity Department. Now, for the first time, this magical face had spoken, and with a single sound, had shattered its illusion.

Going over to von Sternberg, the sound man suggested drowning out the entire word with the blare from the ship's foghorn. The cameraman, not wanting to interfere with that breathtaking close-up, suggested dubbing the word in later when Miss Dietrich had learned the correct English pronunciation. Clustered around the director, their voices low, they conferred. Like a child about to be punished, the star remained standing on her mark, in silent apprehension.

"Thank you for your logical suggestions. We will now take a ten-minute break. Clear the set. Only Miss Dietrich will remain." Alone with her on the darkened, empty stage, von Sternberg lit her cigarette and spoke to her in German. Yes, they could block out any mispronounced words with a foghorn, just as they had disguised the German-sounding *th* in the word *moths* while she sang "Falling in Love Again" in Berlin, and if, in the upcoming nightclub scene in *Morocco* she had another problem, they could cover that with simple applause. Then, in some future scenes, maybe a pistol shot, traffic noises, horses' hooves – everything was possible, but he and she were in the process of creating a star, a luminous being. Such a creature had to have her own unique sound, her own song of the Lorelei, not relying on cheap mechanical tricks. She had to seduce the audiences of the world with her voice, as she would their eyes, and they had to start this process from the very beginning.

She knew he was right, took a deep breath, nodded; the crew was called back in. Again, she tried and failed. Over and over she tried, but shame, the prospect of ridicule, rattled her. She panicked, trying too hard to correct her pronunciation – she only exaggerated it more! It began to border on the comic. But no one dared laugh, nor wanted to. By the twentieth take, they felt sorry for her, angry at von Sternberg for refusing to alter the word, doggedly insisting she do it, correctly. By the thirtieth take, the crew thought him cruel, hating him for badgering this beautiful, distraught woman.

Von Sternberg refused to let it go. Killing the lights, he walked up to her once again, said to her softly in German:

"Now, listen to me carefully. Make your mind a blank. Forget everything! Now, I want you to say the word in German: H-E-L-P. Each letter of this word has the exact sound that it has in the German alphabet. Understand?" She nodded, numb with fear of another failure. "Say the word in *German*! Now, *do* it!" She did what he had told her – it worked! And was perfect! The crew nearly cheered but didn't dare.

She wrote:

It was the worst day of my life. I think finally after 49 takes, maybe 48. I don't want to remember. By the end of the day I was shaking from humiliation and plain exhaustion. But Jo was right. At least I don't have to dread the rushes tomorrow.

Von Sternberg had sent her a peace offering to the dressing room, signing his card The Villain. She enclosed it in the letter to my father, without any further comment.

Papilein,
    Today they said my hair appears dark on the screen, and Hair-Dressing said they had to bleach it. I refused. When Jo came in he told them, "Ridiculous." The head of Hair-Dressing said, "It's necessary. It's impossible – " Jo cut him off. "Everything is possible and nothing is necessary." He carries me in the palm of his hand, making everything work, protecting me in every way. On the set he permits nobody near me. Today the sound man told me to speak louder. Jo said, "You are forbidden to speak to Miss Dietrich. Speak to me and I will tell her – if I choose to." And his patience with me in my black clothes and how I hide myself behind large chairs, while saying "longing words."
    Gary Cooper is pleasant and good-looking. The newspapers have said that Lupe Velez (his girlfriend) has threatened to scratch my eyes out if I come near him. How can I? She sits on his lap between scenes. I don't go close enough, God knows, to see what they're doing, but it looks like they are doing something that is usually done in private.
    Nellie Manley is the girl who comes from Hair-Dressing. She's supposed to be my hairdresser, but you know I do my own hair. But she's good and takes orders. I was walking past Bing Crosby's dressing room and I heard Tauber's voice. It was "Warum." I stopped and listened. Nellie kept saying: "Ya better get outa 'ere. Tomorrow, the *Reporter*'ll have: 'Dietrich in Bing's dressing room!'" She meant *The Hollywood Reporter*, a little newspaper that everyone here reads and worries about.
    So I listened from my dressing room with the door open. Now I know why Bing Crosby is such a big star and why I love his records so. He learned it all from Tauber. I am filled with melancholy and I find myself pressing The Child's photograph to my heart, longing to feel her again. . . .

"MISS DIETRICH, do exactly as I say: Look at him, count one-two, say: 'You better go now . . .' Move to the door, count one-two-three-four, *slowly*! Turn, don't look at him, say: "I'm . . ." *stop*. Count one-two-three-four. Keep your eyes on his face. Don't blink. *Then* say – *slowly* – 'Beginning to *like* you.' "

> He shot it in a close-up, the longest one I have ever seen, and around the Studio they are saying it is the sexiest come-hither look that's ever been filmed. Jo knew so well how the face would photograph, how those long eyelids would look. When I saw it in the rushes, I thought that it was the ultimate of sex. But if while you are seeing it, you know that I'm counting one, two, three – it can be very funny!

When the postman brought my Indian suit, it had everything! Even a tomahawk, painted green and blue, with leather thongs that dangled. That night I was allowed to wear it at the dinner table. Even if I hadn't been given permission, I doubt if anyone could have gotten it off me!

> "Miss Dietrich. What did I just tell you to do?"
> "You told me to take a cigarette from the box."
> "I believe I also told you that you are terrified?"
> "But you told me to conceal it!"
> "Not from *me*, from Menjou."
> His anger, as usual, unnerved her. She paused for breath:
> "Mister . . . von . . . Sternberg . . . I . . . don't know what else you want me to do."
> *"Do it! . . . Sound! . . . Roll 'em . . . action!"*
> Inwardly trembling, under pressure, humiliated, unwilling to show it, she did the scene. Fighting for control, her face set, she reached into the box, removed a cigarette; the camera recorded her frightened rigidity and that her hand trembled.
> *"Cut* . . . print that!"
> It was the trembling of the hand he had wanted.

> Papilein,
>   Jo is more capable of bringing out of me the emotion I feel inside than I am. Mutti made acting very difficult for me. It was always, "Mask your feelings. . . . You must not show your feelings. . . . Bad manners . . ." Jo tells me what to do and I do it. I am his soldier, he is my leader, and he carries me over every inch of film: "Turn your head to the left, now to the right, slowly. . . ." And it is comfortable to take orders, but at times exhausting. . . . The grips call me the Pink Angel because they find me courteous, not temperamental. With Jo von Sternberg on the set, there is little room for more temperament. But, to be fair, most of it is simply his tool to extract emotions.

And visually he has accomplished what Hair-Dressing said was impossible without bleach. He has changed the tone of my hair with light, using a backlight so skillfully that it touches only the tips of my hair, causing a glow like a halo. He is a poet who writes with images rather than words, and instead of a pencil, he uses light and a camera.

I am his product, all of his making. He hollows my cheeks with shadows, widens the look of my eyes, and I am fascinated by that face up there on the screen and look forward to the rushes each day to see what I, his creature, will look like.

THE FILM FINISHED, von Sternberg began his private odyssey: cutting, splicing, forming *Morocco* into the magical whole he had envisioned. He screened the finished film for my mother – just the two of them in one of the Studio's private projection rooms. Throughout, she held his hand, never said a word, squeezing it each time she found something wonderful. He loved to recount that after it was over, his hand was bruised and swelling rapidly. That night, driving home together, she slipped a note into his trouser pocket:

> You – Only you – the Master – the Giver – Reason for my existence – the Teacher – the Love my heart and brain must follow.

She liked what she had written so much, she sent my father a copy. Almost immediately, their next film was put into production. A loosely based story, written by von Sternberg, of a beautiful female spy, executed in the last scene by a handsome firing squad, entitled *X-27*. For the American market, the studio renamed it *Dishonored*. At MGM, *Mata Hari* was being hastily prepared as Garbo's next film.

Paramount had not released *The Blue Angel* until after their new foreign property had been transformed into a threat to Garbo and acclaimed in an American-made film. So by the time the German-made film hit the American market, in December 1930, the public had already been hypnotized by the mysterious woman of *Morocco*, released a month before. Although *The Blue Angel*'s Lola was acclaimed, that wonderful, brassy waterfront tart didn't have a chance to break the still-smoldering mold of the world-weary woman of *Morocco*. By the time Marlene Dietrich's second American film was released, three months after the first two, her name already stood in the stellar position, above the title, where it would remain for years to come.

ABOVE: March 31, 1930, still dressed in the finery she wore at the gala premiere of *The Blue Angel*, a new German star leaves Berlin by train for Bremerhaven to catch the ship that will take her across the seas to America.

LEFT: Aboard the SS *Bremen*. Dietrich's mannish attire was not at all unusual in the Berlin culture of the 1920s.

BELOW: In Hollywood, my mother phoned us every day, wishing she were back home.

LEFT: Von Sternberg's and Dietrich's "shocking surprise." Instead of immediately showing her legs in her first American film, *Morocco*, she made her initial appearance in white tie and tails—and America went wild.
BELOW: During this film no love was lost between Dietrich and her costar, Gary Cooper. She was in love with her director, and Cooper liked to have the Mexican actress Lupe Velez sit on his lap between takes.

ABOVE, LEFT: For *Dishonored,* von Sternberg gave Dietrich a
Chinese coolie doll to keep her black "Savage" company. She took
them with her throughout her professional life.

ABOVE, RIGHT: The famous *Blue Angel* fan card that was distributed in the United States after the release of *Morocco.*

BELOW: Von Sternberg, Dietrich, and Charlie Chaplin in 1930.
Famous stars were often made to visit each other's sets for publicity
stills. Dietrich did not like Chaplin. She considered most comedians
of the silent era "low-class circus performers."

ABOVE, LEFT: Leaving Germany in 1931, on the *Bremen*. Me, very grown-up, in my new white rabbit coat, and my mother in her spotted leopard that my father disliked.

ABOVE, RIGHT: In California, we posed by the Art Deco pool of our first rented "Palace" in sunny Beverly Hills.

LEFT: The 1930s movie star in all her splendor. Feathers and jewels, Rolls-Royce and liveried chauffeur—the works.

ABOVE, LEFT: Dietrich watching herself in her full-length mirror on the set of *Shanghai Express*.

ABOVE, RIGHT: The gate of Paramount Studio, my real home.

RIGHT: On the set, in my usual place off camera, watching my mother be Marlene Dietrich.

BELOW: The Dietrich dressing room on Paramount's Stars Dressing Room Row.

Shanghai Express, 1931. Shanghai Lily, in her fabulous black cock-feather costume and venetian-blind veil. Its creation was my first introduction to film design at its awesome best.

Always quite unaware of the business end of the industry, my mother did what she was told, satisfied all of von Sternberg's dreams, packed up her little house, charged him with finding a bigger one with a "swimming pool for The Child," and kissed him good-bye. She would be back in Berlin in time for my sixth birthday.

1930 was about to end. She was almost twenty-nine. She had made three films that would live forever, two of them remembered primarily because of her presence in them. Achieved world stardom. What a year that was for the romantic young girl from Schöneberg.

Seeing her off at the California station, von Sternberg slipped his farewell note into her trouser pocket:

> Beloved – of all beloved – I thank you for my lovely note and for everything good or bad – it was beautiful. Forgive me for being as I am – I would not, could not, be otherwise.
>
> Good-bye, my love – May your days be beautiful,
>
> > Your
> > Jo.

My mother's return was heralded by the arrival of her new steamer trunks, made to order for her in America: two-toned gray, brass-buttoned, emblazoned with large black *M*'s and *D*'s. There were six of them, the size of closets. They filled our hall, like a monogrammed Stonehenge. Once unlocked, their gray silk damask-padded interiors became my favorite playhouses.

For a second, I did not recognize the thin, elegant lady who strode into our apartment – then I was being kissed all over and knew my mother had returned. Still, there was a difference. A new authority, a self-assurance, as though a queen had been turned into a king. Of course, I was wearing my Indian suit for the big occasion. She fell to her knees, hugging me, squeezing me so hard, I coughed.

"What? You have a cold? Papi! The child coughed! I leave you sick – I return to you sick? Take off that ridiculous getup and get into bed right away. . . ." Life was back to normal.

All her Berlin friends rushed over to welcome her home. We all listened, enraptured, to her many stories of Hollywood and the making of her first American films.

"Wait till you see *Morocco*. It is breathtaking – all von Sternberg's work. I look wonderful, the close-ups are unbelievable. But wait till you see my arms! The fattest things in the film. I had the same trouble with my big thighs. Of course we had to show the legs, but Jo didn't want to do it again with the garter belt; besides, in America they have a real *thing* about garter belts. They get *shocked* – sort of a Marquis de Sade thing with them. So we designed box-cut shorts in black velvet to hide the hips, but again I had trouble. The black line of the shorts made my white thighs look ENORMOUS, but *that* I fixed with a long fringed boa. I let it sort of hang on top of whatever thigh was nearest to the camera!"

She loaded her plate with another helping of stuffed cabbage. She seemed half-starved. Just before dinner, I had seen her munching on a hunk of pumpernickel, loaded with goose fat.

"The best part of *Morocco* is when I am in my own tails. They look unbelievably beautiful! Von Sternberg uses that look *first*. The audience, of course, is expecting the *legs* – so you see her in trousers *first*! Good idea? Jo's, of course. He knew how wonderful the top hat and tails would look and . . . You know, for some reason Garbo looks terrible in men's clothes – which is strange, because everyone says she's one of "the girls." You know what *I* do in the tails? I go over to a pretty woman at a table and kiss her – on the mouth – then I take the gardenia she is wearing, put it under my nose, and in-ha-le it! Well . . . you *know* how *and* why I do it . . . like *that*. Good? Then I flick the flower to Cooper. The audiences go wild. Can you imagine if even Americans get that scene, what will happen once the film opens in Europe?

"You know," she took another dill pickle, "just because they are intelligent with some things, they can also be very stupid. They get just as excited about me walking after Cooper into the desert. Now, really! Jo *made* me walk after the camp followers – into the desert, in my *high-heeled shoes*! We had such a fight about that. Finally, he let me take those stupid shoes off, halfway through the shot. Of course, the burning sand scorched the soles of my feet, but in the film, *first* with the shoes *on* looks right. He knew. He saw that in his mind's eye, and now everyone loves it. Jo says, sometimes I can be very wrong – and he is right. And you should hear the questions American reporters ask. Intimate things like, 'What is your shoe size? What do you weigh? How tall are you?' Amazing . . . such rudeness. That's private! Okay for wardrobe people to know . . . but Americans are obsessed with things like that. Finally I had to ask Travis Banton, 'So what *am* I?' He said, 'Five feet and six inches' – whatever *that* is. Do you know what that means in *real* measurements, Papi?"

My father answered, "One meter sixty-seven and one-half centimeters."

"Now that's *really* confusing!"

"Mutti," very daring, I asked, "Was your savage in *Morocco*?"

She attacked the apple strudel. "Of course, my angel . . . and now I have another one. Mister von Sternberg gave me one made by the same Lancie people – a coolie, also in felt, with real black hair, a pointed straw hat and wooden Chinese shoes. Both dolls sit on my makeup table in the dressing-room scene, and also in *Dishonored*."

That Christmas we had the biggest tree ever, loaded down with so many twinkling red wax candles their heat warmed the whole room. I got a grocery store with a waist-high counter, complete with brass scales, little weights, and trays of assorted sausages made of marzipan. They looked so real you thought you could smell the smoked pork. With a small knife, I spent hours cutting slices, weighing, selling my wares, making change from a little silvered cash register. Tami and Becky were my best customers. My last Christmas in Germany was very special.

Now that I was "officially" six, I knew I was old enough to go to school. I wanted so to go – learn things, meet real children, have friends, thick schoolbooks, a briefcase to strap to my back, maybe even a wooden pencil box with a felt pen wiper and a squishy eraser. But there wasn't time for all that; we were scheduled to leave on a ship for a new life in a place called Hollywood. Maybe children went to school there too. Maybe I would be allowed to go. I asked my father.

"No, Kater. There they all speak English and you can only speak German. First you will have to learn the language. Only then will you be allowed to go to school."

I already knew "okay"; I resolved to learn the rest quickly.

"Do American children get wooden pencil boxes with pen wipers?"

"Probably." I could see my father, busy making out shipping lists, was getting annoyed with this questioning. It was time to make myself scarce.

While my mother was in London for the premiere of *Morocco*, my puppy got sick. My father took him away to the doctor. He returned, told me that it had died, "which was just as well, as he had been born with a growth in his lower intestines, which would have caused his death eventually anyway." He was very precise and informative, as when explaining his jars of organs. He patted my shoulder, told me not to be emotional, and went to cancel the reservation he had made on the SS *Bremen* for one dog in Miss Dietrich's party. I could talk to Tami, even cry. She never preached bravery; she believed in feeling things, not pretending. So I told her of my sorrow, and she held me, comforted me, let me mourn without rhetoric.

Just before we were scheduled to leave Berlin, my mother took me to the doctor to have him reexamine my "crooked" legs. He now declared them fully cured. First, my mother kissed him, then she kissed my legs. On returning home, she called to Resi: "Unpack the child's braces – she is cured!" My father just smiled, had no further comment to add to this "miracle" of modern medicine.

Becky was coming with us. "As none of you knows how to speak English, you can all learn it together," my mother announced. I went around saying my good-byes. I made a special visit to my grandmother. She looked at me as though I was doomed – told me to be good, always obey my mother, remember I was a German no matter what happened, then gave me the nicest kiss she had ever given me and said: "Until we meet again!" Before leaving her house, I said a private good-bye to the little glowing house in the attic.

I got a white rabbit-fur coat, with matching hat and muff that hung on a silken cord around my neck. White leggings and fur-trimmed boots completed my sumptuous departure outfit. I looked ready for a very elegant expedition to the North Pole. My mother wore an original Art Deco-printed wool from Patou in Paris, and her leopard coat, the one from *The Blue Angel* that had, somehow, found its way into her collection. My father did not approve of her ensemble.

"You can't wear a patterned dress with a patterned fur like leopard," he said. My mother, surprised, looked at herself in the mirror, would have changed, but there wasn't time.

The SS *Bremen* loomed so big! Even bending backward I could hardly see to the top of her huge smokestacks. How could anything that was *so big* and heavy float on water all the way to America? Leaving my mother and the Paramount Studio representatives to cope with the pack of reporters snapping at her heels, my father led Becky, Resi, and me up the covered gangplank into the ship. The smell of rubber and metal polish hit my stomach like a fist – and we weren't even moving yet! But I swallowed, and trotted along the gleaming corridors until we arrived at our suite of staterooms. Everything was huge, square, sharp-edged, bare: shining chrome, chalk white, coal-black luxury, cold as ice. Amidst all this vastness stood lonely pieces of necessary furniture. Our suite was so big everyone had their own stateroom, even the trunks. The rest of the luggage not needed for our seven days at sea was secured in the hold of the big ship. Very blond, blue-eyed young men in crisp mess jackets began playing a catchy little tune on hand-held chimes, singing out, "All Ashore Who's Going Ashore." Everyone got very flustered, busy, and weepy.

My mother kissed my father; my mother kissed Willi Forst; my mother kissed Tami; my mother kissed numerous others; they all kissed her. I kissed my father, clung to Tami. Tami kissed me hard, holding me as though it hurt her, slipped me a little package wrapped in Russian decorated paper. Last-minute instructions were issued by my mother. The *Bremen* sounded its horn!

My mother, already too recognizable to appear in public without creating a commotion, remained in our suite, while Becky and I went on top amidst waving, shouting people, trying to pick out my father and Tami amidst the throngs of well-wishers crowding the pier below. I stood by the rail, waving frantically, hoping they could see me. Tucked inside the deep pocket of my rabbit coat was Tami's going-away present – a wooden pencil box, complete with felt pen-wiper and squishy eraser. Though I never got to use it in a real school, I kept it for years, like a talisman!

I returned to our staterooms just in time to witness Operation Sterilization. This was my first introduction to what would become a well-known ritual throughout my life with Dietrich. Her absolute mania, bordering on phobia, for disinfecting any bathroom, particularly toilets, we happened to come in contact with. No matter where we alighted, be it palace, castle, luxury ship, train, or hotel, the moment we arrived, out came the bottles of surgical alcohol: Operation Toilet Seat was under way. It was a mania that even the discovery of penicillin did not affect. After "the *filth* that men have and then leave on toilet seats" had been annihilated, I followed Resi around, watching her take cards from the many floral arrangements, place them in a big brown envelope marked "Bremen – April 1931." I didn't realize it at the time but I was learning the rules of a job that would later become mine. As she harvested the little white cards, Resi explained to me that Madame did not keep cards to see who had sent flowers. Madame did not write thank-you notes to people who were *supposed* to send flowers. The only reason one had to save the cards was in case any time in the future, Madame might question if someone in particular had *not* sent flowers. There was no fear that friends' flowers would go unnoticed, as anyone close enough to Madame *would know* not to send "personal flowers" on such occasions, when Madame would already be overrun with *compulsory* flowers. Anything to do with flowers was always very complicated with my mother.

The next day, I was seasick for the first time, but, unfortunately, not the last time in my life. My mother was very nice about it, held my head over her decontaminated toilet, let me brush my teeth with her special pink tooth powder from London. It was I who felt I had let her down somehow, had been less than a perfect traveling companion.

I knew how she liked everything to be beautiful – music, poems, places, people. What people thought wasn't so important, as long as they looked beautiful thinking it. Whatever it was, I was sure throwing up could not be considered lovely to look at! I decided I better learn to fix my stomach, but I was doomed to failure: undulating limousines and winding canyon roads awaited me in Hollywood.

The *Bremen* had a playroom where first-class passengers could park their underfoot offspring. I, who had never been exposed to children, let alone to group activities involving them, thought it was all very exciting and new. A big-busted Brünnhilde, in starched uniform complete with navy cape and nautical braid, meticulously supervised the laid-out sequences of our enjoyment. During "rocking horse," we rocked; "story time," we listened to tales of lost children in very dark forests about to be pounced on by hungry witches; "Punch and Judy time," we watched a puppet with a very big club hit a puppet with a very big hooked nose repeatedly over the head; "coloring time," we colored! Each one was given a tin box full of pretty colored pencils, a book of animal pictures, and told which of them was to be the subject of that day. My first time in the playroom was a "donkey day." Wanting to be really a part of this strange new children's world, I concentrated on doing a proper job on my donkey, deciding that purple was just the right color for its perky ears. Hard at work, I felt a sharp tap on my shoulder:

"What *are* you doing?" said a very annoyed voice in ominous German.

"I am coloring my donkey's ears, Madame."

"Purple?" The outraged lady turned to the rest of the group. "Who here has ever seen a donkey with purple ears?"

I saw some hands quickly covering *their* donkeys. There were a lot of giggles and some nasty snickering. Brünnhilde removed the offending page from my coloring book, with a long forefinger tapping another picture of a naked donkey, instructed me in no uncertain terms to get it right *this* time or forfeit my coloring box for the rest of the trans-Atlantic crossing. I was also informed that if I strayed beyond the black outlines, I would get another unpleasant surprise. From then on, my donkeys were one hundred percent gray, *all over*. Many years later, I had my revenge against Teutonic Artistic Suppression by eliminating illustrated coloring books from my children's formative years.

I didn't get to swim in the *Bremen* pool because I didn't know how. Neither did Becky nor Resi, and my mother hated swimming. Besides, she would never have shown herself in a bathing suit for strangers to ogle at. So I sat, watching the ladies and gentlemen in their thick navy wool bathing costumes, rubber caps, and decorated rubber bathing shoes, cavorting amongst the tiles.. Ships' swimming pools, no matter how luxuriously Roman, always smelled of disinfectants and artificial heat, the high-pitched screams of gaiety and splashing reverberating off the tiled walls made one feel one was in a subterranean sanitarium for the deranged.

I knew my mother expected reports on what I was doing while away from her, so one day I launched into my donkey experience:

". . . and the nurse said, 'Purple?' Then she asked the other children – "

My mother sat down at the makeup table, saying: "Sweetheart, don't just talk for the sake of talking. When you speak, have something interesting and intelligent to say. At seven, actually you're really just still six, you are not too young to learn that!"

"Oh," I said, "I thought I *was* being interesting."

My mother spat on her mascara, rubbing the black cake vigorously with the little brush.

"No. What children do is usually not very interesting. Just be quiet and listen to what intelligent people around you are saying. Learn from them and remember, as I have taught you." She brushed her lashes with gooey black.

"I will listen to what *you* say, then, Mutti." I wasn't being sarcastic or ingratiating. I truly meant it. I knew my mother was very intelligent – everyone always said so. She looked at me in the mirror and smiled her approval. My answer had pleased her. I planned to remember that.

Finally, the Big Day arrived! All the trunks, hat boxes, suitcases were packed and ready. The long "tip list" had been taken care of, our arrival outfits laid out and waiting. While my mother was busy setting her hair, I escaped, stood on the very top deck of the ship looking for "America." Enveloped in sea mist, I saw a huge lady, a torch held high, as though lighting our way to a safe harbor – and suddenly I knew, my heart told me, I WAS HOME!

Becky, Resi, and I – by now I thought of us as "the troops" – were sent on ahead to disembark. One of the many Paramount representatives, who seemed to materialize out of nowhere no matter where in the world we happened to appear – they all looked so alike they must have been cloned on the Paramount lot – led us quickly and expertly to an enormous enclosure and placed us under a big sign with the letter S. I was about to ask Resi what it meant, when suddenly my mother appeared, her face chalk white, grabbed my wrist pulling me after her, we ran. The reporters, sensing a scoop, took up the scent, followed at our heels. A Paramount clone shouted "Here!" – pushed us into a big black car, and off the pier we roared to the safety of the Hotel Ambassador, way station for our stopover in New York City before boarding the train for Chicago. Until we entered our hotel suite, my mother never uttered a sound nor released the viselike grip on my wrist. Without removing her hat or coat, she placed a transcontinental call to von Sternberg in Hollywood, then lit a cigarette and waited, her face a mask. The telephone rang. She snapped up the earpiece, grabbed the pedestal, shouted into the mouthpiece in rapid German:

"Jo? There will be no train for you to meet. Do you hear me? I am returning to Berlin on the next ship. How dare you allow that woman to do this to me and my child. An alienation of affection suit? You, who so love to control everything and everybody! Your own wife you can't control! I am taking my child back to Europe, where people have manners."

She slammed the earpiece back onto its cradle, then picked it up again, placed a trans-Atlantic call to my father in Berlin. Again, we waited. Again, she smoked. Silence. I in my arrival outfit sat on the apricot satin chair, wondering in which direction I was going to go and who had alienated whom – and why. My mother smoked, waited. The phone rang:

"Papi?"

Now came a precise account of the sequence of events as they had happened to her: "Yes! A process server, right on the gangplank! That ugly wife of his is suing *me*! Yes . . . I know. . . . It is *unbelievable*! She says I stole her husband away from her? She never had him in the first place! She makes his life a misery! We are leaving America!"

In the many rooms of our suite, telephones began ringing in unison. Becky and Resi had arrived and the three of us scurried around, falling over each other answering calls from the different heads of Paramount, von Sternberg, Studio lawyers, and others. As our English reached to "Hello" and "Vait Pleez," we kept up a hectic round-robin, handing over telephones to my mother, our only English-speaker. She sprinted from room to room, telling everyone that she was on her way back to *dignified* Berlin. I was getting hungry and wondered where in this palace a bathroom might be hidden. My mother put in another call to my father, then ordered breakfast from something called "room service." Within seconds, a rolling table appeared, laden with the most gorgeous china I had ever seen. There were tall glasses of shimmering water, in which floated what looked like real ice in the shape of little cubes – American magic! And the food – amazing. Something called "bacon" that looked funny but tasted wonderful! A big pitcher held juice from real oranges and something called "red currant jelly" that my mother said was terrible but I thought was beautiful, the way it first quivered, then dissolved on the warm buttery bread called "toast." The second call to my father finally came through:

"Yes, Papi! Yes. I know! Schulberg, Lasky, Edington said all that. I am throwing away a *great* career, out of anger. More like *outrage*! They all tell me I am now such a valuable member of the 'Great Paramount Family,' the Studio will protect me from anything! All I can say is nebbish! So, then why didn't they stop the process server on the gangplank? . . . I know . . . I know . . . yes . . . I know . . . I kiss you, The Child also. If the Berlin papers pick it up, call Mutti – tell her it is not true . . . and call Liesel too."

Deep in thought, she picked up a strip of bacon from my plate, munched it, took a sip of her coffee, then, squaring her shoulders, announced to the "troops" that we were continuing on to Chicago and Hollywood. The Paramount brigade smuggled us safely out of the hotel, past the waiting press.

"My God! Another flower shop!" my mother exclaimed on entering our drawing room on the 20th Century Limited. I was becoming aware that wherever my mother alighted, a greenhouse materialized! She told Resi to first ring for the Pullman porter – before disinfecting.

A discreet knock, a polite "Yes, ma'am," and there stood a man with a black face! I knew it was rude to stare, but I couldn't help it. My mother said something to him in English, which I couldn't understand but was obvious, as after numerous trips all the baskets of flowers had been removed. Satisfied, she surveyed our stripped drawing room:

"Now we can breathe! Why people insist on choking off oxygen with flowers I can never understand. Don't they *know* it's a compartment on a *train*?"

I just had to ask. "Mutti, that man – he had a black face! Just like your savage!"

"Oh, sweetheart! In this country you will see a lot of them – they are everywhere, most of them are maids and tap dancers, and in Beverly Hills, all the gardeners are Chinamen! This is a *very* mixed-up country."

My new home sounded more fascinating every minute!

The next morning, we arrived in Chicago. I looked for gangsters, but only the Paramount clones were there to whisk us off to the Blackstone Hotel, to another luxurious suite of red plush and gold leaf, where we bathed before we boarded the Santa Fe Chief that would take us to California. After the removal of the "choking" flowers and "dirty men's" disease, we settled into our drawing rooms for the four days still left to reach our destination. The lower and upper berths of one compartment were made up immediately. It would be our bedroom; the other became our living room. My mother remained in her traveling pajamas for the entire trip, writing, answering telegrams, reading. All our meals were served by our friendly Pullman porter. Becky and Resi were allowed to eat theirs in what was called a "dining car." I wished I could go with them and see what it was like!

In Albuquerque (I had been practicing how to say that), I saw my first American Indian. A big, rotund lady covered in colored beads, sitting by the side of the tracks, selling trinkets and tightly woven baskets. I ran along the platform to her side, clutching the dollar bill my mother had given me, hoping I could buy something before the train pulled out and left me in the American desert! My mother shouted out of the window for me to hurry; she was getting very nervous. I pointed to a small polished stone whose color I had never seen. The woman picked it up and held it out; it looked so bright against the brown callused hand. I nodded vigorously. Holding out my money, we exchanged treasures. I curtsied and ran back inside the train clutching my first turquoise, still warm from the desert sun.

A blond woman had boarded and entered our compartment. My mother allowed her to kiss her cheek, introduced her to me as "Miss Nellie Manley from the Studio, who had come to do her hair." She reached out and hugged me, said, "Hiya, hon." I didn't understand the English, but the hug I did. I liked her immediately.

THE TANGY SMELL of citrus woke me. Quickly, I climbed down off my bunk onto my mother's empty one. On my knees, my arms resting along the edge of the open window, I watched as row upon row of chubby, dark green trees skipped along to the rhythm of our passing train. They were so laden with fruit, they looked as though covered in orange-colored polka dots. In Berlin, an orange was so precious it was given as a gift at Christmas, and here there were thousands and thousands of them! Some more of that magic I was beginning to accept as being "special-to-America."

When the train stopped, I knew that now we must finally be in Pasadena, because Mr. von Sternberg entered our compartment and took my mother in his arms. She pulled away, saying coldly: "Well? Is everything fixed? Do we get off this train or not?" He answered her in English. Whatever he said must have satisfied her, because she adjusted her man's slouch hat, straightened her tie, took my hand, and marched us off the train.

Quite a large group of gentlemen were waiting for us, their big square cameras held ready to record our arrival, but when they saw me, they stopped – turned to von Sternberg, obviously confused. In German, he explained to my mother that children were not considered an appropriate companion for Mysterious Stars and I should stand aside, out of frame.

"Oh? First I am called a 'home-wrecker,' now I am not supposed to be a mother? This is MY child. She BELONGS to me. No STUDIO is going to dictate to me WHAT I can or cannot do with my own child. They don't want her? Then they don't get me!" and taking my hand, she marched us to a dark green touring car, its winged finial sparkling in the bright sun.

Von Sternberg joined us and off we went. My mother was so angry, she kept repeating her threat to leave for Germany on the next boat. I was beginning to feel sorry for the little man. He kept trying to tell her he would fix this problem too, that "motherhood" was a completely new concept for a Hollywood glamour star. That was why the press had acted as they had, but that this attitude could be changed – that he had an idea if she would only trust him.

"Oh, trust you? Like this thing with your wife and the process server?"

"You must know that I knew nothing about that until *after* it all happened. Beloved, I would never allow anyone to hurt you!"

Her steely look stopped him.

"Hurt? No, Jo – Embarrassed! Degraded! Shamed! Humiliated!"

We drove the rest of the way in stony silence. Hills and curves, everywhere big eucalyptus trees, tall spindly palms, tall fat palms, small chunky palms, lush grass, flower-covered bushes. Now emerald carpets bordered onto immaculate sidewalks, low white houses with terra-cotta roofs, black ornate iron gates, everywhere flowers in wild profusion: they clung, dripped, cascaded, covered every surface available to them. Breathless with wonder, I asked if this was Hollywood and was told "No!" It was Beverly Hills, where we were going to live. So, we were going to live in Paradise!

The car curved into a driveway where a house nestled amongst tall cyprus and banana trees that looked so stark and out of place I thought we were about to board the *Bremen* again. Von Sternberg was eager to show my mother the house he had picked out for her. Our new home was real 1930s Art Deco. Elegant, cold, like an Erté illustration, all fluid detachment – to exist in, not to live in. I was too young to know why I felt so intimidated by all that cool perfection, then it just made me feel uncomfortable. There were so many rooms and all had designated names and functions. Holding my hand, my mother followed von Sternberg around, smoking her cigarette, rather bored by his enthusiasm. Flinging open enormous glass-paneled doors, we exited an equally enormous reception room into *my* garden. I took possession of this wonder immediately, even before von Sternberg announced: "And here is the garden for the child, with her own swimming pool." The Olympic pool had so many mosaic tiles, it looked like the *Bremen* one, but its surface sparkled in the strong sunlight like a million diamonds, and that made all the difference. My mother was welcome to the elegant house; I claimed this sun-drenched domain and was happy. My real life had begun. As I always mentally filed my childhood memories by the places we inhabited, my mother's films, her lovers, and special events; this first Hollywood house became the one of *Shanghai Express, Blonde Venus*, Maurice Chevalier, the Lindbergh kidnapping, and our own kidnapping threat.

The next day was full of "firsts." The thick inventory book, where everything in our rented mansion was recorded, itemized, valued, down to the minutest doily. My mother hated inventories. She figured living in a house made it hers – everything in it, her personal property. In those days, fully furnished houses meant fully stocked households. Our inventory lists never had fewer than eight complete dinner services for fifty, six separate lunch and tea services, all of bone china, dozens and dozens of crystal goblets, and linen enough to stock Buckingham Palace. This house also boasted fourteen-karat gold cutlery; the sterling silver was for lunch. Such luxuries never impressed my mother. She accepted all trappings of wealth as the normal accompaniments to fame. So when I ate my soup with a solid gold spoon, following my mother's lead I thought nothing of it.

The very first time I was taken to Paramount Studio, I didn't notice its famous wrought-iron gate, I was too excited. Our big American director was going to take my picture! First, I had my hair washed and set by "Nellie from Hair-Dressing"; then a dream of a dress materialized – all flowered organdy and tiny puffed sleeves. I was worried that my arms would look too fat, but trusted Mister von Sternberg to know what to do about that. My mother was shrouded in black velvet, her only adornment a demure collar of Venetian lace. Von Sternberg created in that first portrait sitting that included me, the Eternal Madonna, Luminous Woman with luminous child. My mother was so enchanted with the results she ordered dozens and dozens, then sent the photographs to everyone she knew or had ever known. Von Sternberg was so happy that she wasn't angry with him anymore.

The Studio bosses, at first so reticent to accept the new mother image, were also very pleased. They realized that they'd been handed a bonus: Dietrich not only had "Sex," "Mystery," "European Sophistication," and those LEGS, but now had acquired "Madonnahood." Let MGM top that one! Where was Garbo going to find herself a kid in a hurry? The Publicity Department was ordered to print thousands of postcards of "Dietrich and child" and distribute them to the clamoring fans. A memo was attached to the order to crop negatives at waist level to hide my size. As von Sternberg had only shot our faces, the Publicity Department needn't have worried. Over the years, no official portrait was ever taken of me standing. If one was absolutely necessary, the camera was placed high, to foreshorten my body. This was a satisfactory solution for Paramount as well as my mother. It kept me a "little girl" so much longer. There exist pictures of me at the age of ten that anyone would swear were those of a six or seven year old.

Overnight, Hollywood motherhood, even for "femmes fatales," became fashionable, a child a necessary adornment to acquire. Adoption agencies were flooded with requests for "cute little girls." Not little boys; boys were still thought to be more suited to the image of male stars. My mother was triumphant, von Sternberg relieved, content he had finally done something that really pleased her. Paramount gloated. Their biggest female star could now be marketed in many directions, even attract the paying public in the Bible Belt, a section of the country that had been unreachable before.

WE SETTLED INTO OUR BEVERLY HILLS "pre-film preparation" life. Most mornings, von Sternberg, in spanking white flannel trousers, silk shirt, and ascot, appeared for breakfast in the garden. My mother served him her famous scrambled eggs under our big, navy blue, white-fringed umbrella that matched the ornate set of wrought-iron cushioned arm-chairs and glass-top table. The sterling glistened, the porcelain shone, the crystal sparkled; my mother wore cream silk lounging pajamas with a wide organza hat; the breeze rustled the banana leaves, the pool reflected the brilliant blue of the cloudless sky . . . a simple Hollywood breakfast.

Some mornings, Maurice Chevalier took von Sternberg's place, also attired in white flannels but sporting a jaunty beret. I rather liked this new friend of my mother's. He laughed a lot, made her laugh, had a wicked wink that he used continually, like punctuation, and, of course, he loved my mother's eggs. That really was a prerequisite for being one of Dietrich's intimate admirers. They had to adore her scrambled eggs or be considered perhaps too dumb to appreciate all the other finer things of life. This could have very revealing consequences, for my mother worked on the premise that if one of the senses could be out of kilter, *all* were suspect! When Chevalier was making my mother happy, I usually disappeared. As they chatted away in their private French, I couldn't understand what was being said, although between his cute winks, saucy smirks, rolling of the eyes, and Gallic expressive waving of hands, most meanings were pretty obvious. Still, Chevalier somehow never intrigued me. He knew you knew – everyone knew that Chevalier adored Monsieur Chevalier and that was all that was really important *to* know.

Our evenings were spent sitting in our cavernous – I never knew *what* to call that room – my mother called it Our Drawing Room, von Sternberg Our Living Room, the inventory book had it down as The Reception Room. We would sit there, my mother doing ladylike needlepoint, her canvas stretched taut on a wooden frame in front of her, von Sternberg with a tall stack of movie scripts piled high on the floor by his chair, reading them simultaneously, shaking his head in disapproval. I, watching the flames, hoping one of them would decide to turn on the big wooden radio that had so many exciting things coming out of it.

Sometime before the beginning of work for my mother's film, von Sternberg gave me a present of a full-grown parrot. It arrived complete with a five-foot perch, metal feeding cups, and dangling retaining chain around one ugly clawed foot. Von Sternberg must have had a thing about birds, because the next year he had the Studio build an aviary in our garden, then stocked it with every exotic feathered specimen available. A zoo would have been proud to own it! The only trouble was the different species were either allergic to each other or avowed enemies, because one fine morning, my aviary was strewn with brightly colored corpses. While I cried and dug tiny graves around the regal flower beds, driving our Japanese gardeners to the edge of committing hara-kiri, a Paramount crew arrived, dismantled the domed structure, removed it and its depressing contents from our premises. The first bird was no joy either! Although he looked splendid, all hussar blue and crimson, tail feathers hanging nearly to the ground, his curved beak could kill. His piercing eyes told you he would love to. His vulturelike talons were ready for anything that moved within his range. I hated that parrot! He sat on that perch by the glass doors to the garden, just waiting. It was worth one's life trying to get in or out of the house. My mother was forced to walk out of the front door, around the house to the back, and enter our garden from the alley – just to avoid confronting that red-and-blue vulture. Why his position was never moved or he gotten rid of, I never knew. Must have had something to do with not wanting to "hurt Jo's feelings," although his feelings were being hurt repeatedly by much more important things; getting rid of the mean parrot was not one of them. I knew how much my mother hated pets. In this fine house, with all the valuable carpets, I hadn't dared to ask if I could have another dog. Now, with this parrot making a mess with his droppings and pumpkin seeds, I knew I couldn't possibly get a yes out of her.

"I'M FAT!" my mother said and stopped eating. Dietrich never "went on diets." Didn't even know what a calorie was. Just as she never put cold cream, that revered facial grease of the thirties, on her face, she ignored all maintenance of herself until the very last moment. Now, as was her custom during her entire professional life, she got ready for work – drank coffee, tea, tumblers of hot water loaded with epsom salts, smoked, and nibbled. It was her choice of finger foods that always astounded me. Dill pickles, raw sauerkraut, uncooked frankfurters, pickled herring, and salami. As she did this long before the advent of vitamin pills, how my mother didn't succumb to malnutrition, beriberi, or at least acute gastroenteritis, is a medical mystery.

Every afternoon, I had to report to von Sternberg for an hour's conversation in "everyday" English. He was appalled at my mother's refusing to teach me, saying to her that it bordered on neglect, expecting a child to live in a strange new country with strange new people and customs, isolated by the barrier of language. When she replied that there was no reason for me to speak English because everyone in our house spoke German, he refused further comment and set up his own program to help me. He taught me what I would need to know. No "the crayon of my aunt is on the table" kind of stuff, but useful words like "soundstage," "makeup," "Wardrobe Department," "Commissary," "preproduction," "dressing room," "back lot," "designer," "director," "print that," and all such really important stuff. I was so grateful. In between our lessons, I listened to "Lum and Abner" on the radio and developed a country twang, conversed with the gardeners, picked up a little Japanese whine, and rounded it all off with the singing ends of sentences I learned from one of the maids, who was Irish. My mother, appalled by all this variety, told me to *stop*, listen *only* to Crosby sing "like Tauber," which smoothed out all pronunciations in my speech, until it flowed like warm oil. Exasperated, von Sternberg bought a metronome and, with its help, got me back onto a sensible rhythm. Turning to my mother, he remarked, "You know, beloved, you could use this. It wouldn't be a bad idea for you to practice a little, to achieve a more effective cadence."

That night, in bed, I heard them arguing down the hall in my mother's room. I hoped it wouldn't mean the end of my learning English – but my lessons continued and the metronome stayed.

By the time we drove through the Studio gate to our first "Wardrobe Department" "preproduction" costume meeting with Paramount's head "designer," I knew where, why, and to whom we were going in *English*. That was a very comforting feeling.

After being introduced and curtseying to a gentleman who looked as though he had stepped off a yacht, my mother indicated a wing chair and told me to sit. Travis Banton's private domain in Paramount's Wardrobe Department looked very British, exuded elegant masculinity. He had embraced my mother with such warmth and effusive affection, I knew immediately they must be real pals.

"Travis, sweetheart." Aha, another "sweetheart." I had been right – he *was* special. They spoke in rapid English, lots of chuckles and easy laughter. They were having such fun, I wished I could understand all they were saying.

That evening, my mother told her director about her morning with her designer.

"Jo, today Travis asked me, 'Does anyone know what she does in this film? Why she is there in the first place? How many costumes we have to make?' and I said, 'Don't ask *me*. All *I* know is that it plays inside a train going somewhere Oriental. Jo hasn't even given her a name yet!'" Von Sternberg stopped writing, lifted his eyes off his yellow pad:

"Her name is Shanghai Lily and it doesn't only play inside a train."

"Whatever. Then Travis asked me if I knew who the man was, and again, I had to say no. But *he* knew. He said it's someone called Clive Brook, who is ever so British, has a jawline that never ends, but nothing else."

"Travis, as usual, is astute and basically correct," said von Sternberg without raising his eyes or pencil off his pad.

"So . . . I have to be . . . *again* mysterious?" My mother gave it her best Yiddish cadence. Von Sternberg replied in kind:

"Yes . . . again . . . beautifully mysterious, Mammale. Aren't you lucky!"

I hoped I would be allowed to watch "mysterious". being created. The very next day, I got my wish. Driving to the Studio, my mother talked – not to me, we hadn't reached that professional collaborative relationship we would have later. Now she spoke to herself, using my physical presence as an excuse to speak her thoughts out loud:

"I'm fat! much fatter than *Morocco*. Even if I eat absolutely nothing, can't get thin enough by the time shooting starts. Black – it all has to be again – *black*. – But not flat . . . learned that in *Morocco* – Must find something to break up the flatness. Black – what breaks up black on black? Impossible! . . . Must take more laxatives – drink coffee – from now on, just smoke. . . . Train – China – Heat – Dust – Jo says everything very oriental – like opium-den feeling. So . . . maybe, she should be . . . different. . . . Like some rare, strange bird . . . feathers?"

She leaned forward, rolled down the glass partition between us and our chauffeur.

"Harry, when we get to the Studio, don't go to the dressing room. Drive directly to the Wardrobe Department, and you can go a little faster!"

My mother hated cars, never learned to drive, was always apprehensive when riding in a car. Accelerated speed was strictly forbidden. For her, to permit anyone to go over forty miles an hour meant that she was either in love with the driver or, if in her own car, an emergency.

The moment Harry pulled up in front of Wardrobe, she jumped out, sprinted up the stairs, burst into Banton's off-limits office, crying, "FEATHERS! Travis – feathers! What do you think? . . . *Black feathers!* Now, what bird has black feathers that will photograph?" As the word has the same sound in German, I figured we were about to look for the adornment of exotic black birds.

They lay in big square boxes, big long boxes, big deep boxes, big flat boxes. I didn't know there were so many black-feathered birds in the whole world! Some curled, some rippled, some spiked, some swooped, some quivered, some dripped, some floated, some just lay there – black, ominous, and junglelike. My mother walked among the containers, cupping, dipping her hands into the contents, letting this bounty waft between her fingers, testing weight, shape, color, and ability to refract the intense light streaming down from the ceiling of the big fitting room. Ostrich? . . . too thick, but stripped, not bad for . . . maybe a negligee in another scene? Egret? . . . Too difficult to shape, but some was ordered in white to put on a hat later in the film when they might need a little relief from the too-black look. . . . Bird of paradise? Dyed badly. . . . Heron? Too thin and wispy. . . . Black swan? Too lightweight and dull. . . . Crow? Too stiff. Eagle? Too wide, and anyway impossible except for Indian films. Marabou? Too fluffy. Close at her heels, Travis Banton kept asking his assistant where the latest shipment from the Amazon jungle was. Suddenly he stopped, pivoted on his heels:

"Charlie! Get me fighting cocks – the tail feathers from real Mexican fighting cocks! And if their condition isn't iridescent enough, we can give them a green wash!"

The cocks who finally sacrificed their plumage for the famous look of *Shanghai Express* must have been in superb condition, for when the feathers arrived, their black-green iridescence was so intense it shimmered through the tissue paper they were wrapped in. My mother was pleased – kissed Travis on both cheeks, called to me in my assigned corner:

"Sweetheart, come! Look! A Dream! *Black*, with its own light! Narrow, naturally curved! *Now*, Travis can design the first costume, that will be THE look of the film."

He did and it was.

For weeks, I sat and watched a masterpiece in the making. I can't ever remember being bored witnessing this astounding dedication to perfection. Even as a child, I considered it a privilege being a part of it. Day in and day out, they worked, sometimes for twelve-hour stretches. My mother never tired, had a bladder of astounding capacity, could fit for hours without moving a muscle, and, as she was perpetually starving herself, such normal things as breaking for food, bathroom, and rest did not exist while Dietrich prepared clothes for a film, or in later years, her stage dresses. Travis Banton knew my mother very well.

I liked him. No matter what time of day, and that could mean anywhere from six a.m. to two a.m., Travis looked like one of his sketches – elegant, with a kind of razzmatazz. He dressed the head designer of Paramount as carefully as one of his stars, usually in cashmere blazer, immaculate white flannels, paisley ascot tucked into the open neck of a cream silk French-cuffed shirt. He had the Ronald Colman look long before Ronald Colman *had* a look. He was particularly proud of his shoes, rumored around the Studio as being handmade for him in London. His favorite pair boasted a design of black scrolls on a white background – like fancy golf shoes without cleats and tongue. He crossed his legs continually to show them off. He seemed permanently ready for an afternoon of cricket and high tea. Only his poor nose didn't fit his image; his bloomed à la W. C. Fields. But, as I never saw him take a drink or behave as though he had had a few too many, its bulbous magenta must have been caused by the high blood pressure that usually struck people when working with Dietrich.

Travis must have come to the conclusion during their first two films together that although most people belonged to the human species, my mother did not. So, with her he had devised a rotation system to relieve his fitters and personnel, as well as a food delivery schedule for himself and his assistants, to which he now added a new human being – me. Except for the arrival of our lunches from the Studio Commissary, I don't think my mother ever noticed the changeover of the swarm of neat little ladies, their wrists adorned with their trademark, the pincushion. It was kindness that made Travis Banton look out for his people, not union laws. During the Depression, jobs were so precious that anyone lucky enough to have one would do almost anything to keep it. The apparent subservience that the Depression created in those fortunate enough to have work, perfectly suited my mother's attitude toward all those who served her for pay. In her day, no one quit, walked out, because of personal differences or ill treatment. They took everything, all types of abuse, swallowed whatever little pride left them, did as they were told, knowing that if they were fired, starvation awaited them.

Always quite unaware of what existed outside of her immediate world, this attitude of "the little people" suited Dietrich, for she functioned on this plane. She truly believed that once she had paid someone a wage, she had bought their life as well as their labor. She did not employ people, she owned them. As a big Hollywood movie star during the depth of the Depression, this attitude found no opposition. Later, "legend reverence," especially in Europe, fostered the same subservient results.

Because of Travis Banton's feeding system, I was exposed to some very special things. One day, he ordered me something he called Egg Salad on White. My first sandwich arrived, wrapped in waxy paper, accompanied by a heavy glass bottle containing a fizzy brown liquid he called "Coca-Cola." AMBROSIA!

Through the mirror, my mother gave him a very critical look, but was too busy creating the cock-feather cloche to get involved with my unorthodox menu. While I ate my heavenly lunch, being careful not to let the paper rustle and disturb, I watched my mother flip bolts. It was veil day. She was determined to repeat the impact of the "veiled look" used so effectively in both *Morocco* and *Dishonored* and was looking for the right veil for the molded cock-feather hat waiting for completion. Numbered bolts were strewn about the gray-carpeted floor. She picked up one, marked "Black 3," tossed it forward, unrolling a gossamer mesh with tiny puffs of black, held a piece across her eyes, let it fall; flipped "Black 10," scrutinized its diamond shapes against her skin, let the piece slip to the floor; kicked "Black 5" off to the side, recognizing it as being the one used in *Morocco*. Three hours later, the fitting room floor looked as though every spider in the whole world had spun its web upon it. Nothing had been found, everything rejected. It was beginning to get dark outside. The funny Victorian streetlamps along the landscaped street of Paramount were lit. In those days, everyone worked until someone gave them permission to go home. There had been four changeovers and still Travis hadn't yawned once! I yawned secretly when I went to the bathroom but never stayed away too long, rushing back for fear that the right veiling might have been found without me there to witness the great moment of its discovery.

"Marlene, my pet, are you absolutely set on adding a veil? The feathers may look busy enough. The way we have them placed now is so perfect, just outlining the one cheek onto the jawline. A veil might possibly distract."

"No, Travis, something is missing. Maybe these are all too delicate? Thicker patterns, maybe?" Black 39, 40, 41, 42 were carried in by exhausted assistants. 39 had big polka dots, made her face look like she had black chicken pox. 40 had up-and-down squiggles. 41 had horizontal lines, like shadows cast by Venetian blinds, absolutely impossible with the diagonally laid pattern of the feathers on the hat form. Still, she held a piece of it across her eyes and something amazing happened! Her face sprang to life. Travis let out a wild whoop (I found out later he was from Texas, where they made such startling noises), clapped his hands in ecstasy, the little ladies nearly sank to their knees in grateful relief. My mother just smiled, carefully slipped off the pinned hat form, handed it and 41 to Travis, kissed his cheek, took my hand, and walked us rapidly out of the darkened Wardrobe Department. Time to go home and cook our director's dinner!

The day came when everything was finally ready. Von Sternberg was called over to Wardrobe to view Shanghai Lily for the first time. He entered the fitting room, saw my mother, stopped perfectly still, feasting his eyes. She stood on a raised platform, reflected forever in the tall bank of mirrors in back of her. Eyes languid behind the striped veil, head glistening smooth of close-laid clinging black. The dress was long, its three-quarter loose coat of fluid crepe bordered in feathers. Like ocean waves of incandescent black, they crested onto her neck, tumbled along her shoulders down her arms, stopping only where they met the duller black of tightly fitted gloves of thinnest kid. A perfect strand of large crystal beads coaxed the eye to travel downward. Her handbag, its black and white Art Deco pattern, stopped the eye at waist level. The rarest black bird imaginable. We all held our breath. Would he storm out? Announce that it was impossible to photograph, which everyone knew it was, even my mother? Still without saying a word, he moved slowly toward her, reached up his hand, helped her step down; bending low before her, he kissed her gloved hand, and said softly in German:

"If *you* believe I am skilled enough to know how to photograph this, then all I can offer you is – to *do* the impossible." Turning to an apprehensive Travis, he nodded, saying in English:

"A superb execution of an impossible design. I congratulate you all," and left. The sighs of relief could have propelled a ten-masted schooner across the seas. Then we celebrated. Travis served forbidden champagne in little paper cups, even the little ladies had a sip. This repeated challenging of each other's talents was the true genius of the Sternberg-Dietrich collaboration. She set him and his camera impossible tasks to overcome. He demanded of her things beyond the range of her talent. They flung down these artist's gauntlets like duelists, fully expecting to kill or be killed, and loved it when they both survived each supreme test.

The next day, we started work on the black chiffon negligee with the stripped, clipped ostrich feathers, and Travis ordered me what he called a "chocolate malted." After that, I gave up being surprised. I knew I had reached the zenith – the high point of American culinary perfection! (Until I had my first peanut butter and jelly sandwich, of course.)

Sundays, we stayed home and worked at "relaxing." My mother washed her hair and let it just hang, wore no makeup, and cooked. Von Sternberg set up his easel in the garden, opened a big wooden case filled with row upon row of silver tubes, unfolded his little canvas stool, and, palette hooked securely on thumb and forefinger, painted bursting hibiscus under azure skies. I could watch him for hours. He seemed really happy. So unlike his usual self – all intense, somber, and moody. Even his choice of colors showed it: no blacks, no dark shadows, all was bright and airy, full of scarlet and brilliant hues. I would spread the funny papers on the grass by his chair, next to him. I learned to read my first English following the adventures of Orphan Annie and Dagwood. The Katzenjammer Kids I didn't like – they were much too German for me, the new All-American Kid.

Sunday was also the day our special little old lady delivered. By this time I knew all about Prohibition, gangsters, and shootouts over Demon Drink. So when the interior of her rickety baby carriage emitted sounds of clinking glass instead of a baby's cry, I knew our friendly neighborhood bootlegger had come to call. She was something! She had a toothless leer, liked to be addressed as Mrs. Gladys-Marie, treated her bottles with infinite care, unfolding their flannelette blankets, lifting them gently, handing them over as tenderly as though they were real babies. I always wanted to ask her why the gin was wrapped in a pink blanket and the scotch in a blue one, but never dared. She was just weird enough to take offense at such an intimate question and decide to cut off our supply of hooch.

The problems with von Sternberg's wife had not been resolved as quickly as everyone had hoped. Apparently she now wanted money to comfort her injured pride and made this fact known to the press. The morals clause that every Hollywood contract contained, to keep the sexual excesses of actors in some sort of check, worried my mother. Although she was convinced that no studio would dare to invoke such a clause against her, still, the image of the Spotless Lady Aristocrat who might act Fallen Woman but wasn't one could be tarnished after all. Suddenly, the announcement was made that my father would soon be arriving to pay us all a visit, but that Tami would not be accompanying him. I was so disappointed. I wanted to show her all the wonderful things in my new kingdom. I did not realize yet that the time had come when she must be kept hidden from the press.

"Don't eat the liverwurst, sweetheart – that's the special one for Papi." Neither was I allowed near the smoked salmon, Genoese salami, or the Camembert direct from Paris, France, that Chevalier had brought as a welcome gift. Every corner of the house was scrubbed, polished, waxed, and beflowered. A range of cashmere sweaters appeared. "Papi may not remember, I told him in the evenings it gets cool here." V–neck, turtleneck, polo – "Who knows what type Papi will like for America," and just in case these didn't suit, a selection of cardigans in his favorite shade gradations of brown, green, beige, and gray. Dark green heavy silk pajamas were a must, as were elegant dressing gowns, Italian slippers, "California" slacks, bathing trunks, and terry-cloth pool robes. In those days, the clothes were easy to buy, *if* you had money. Not so the special food items. Foreign imports were rare, international food stores as yet unknown. Gladys–Marie found and delivered something guaranteed to be lager that my father later called bottled piss! His assigned room looked onto the garden, was bigger than either my mother's or the one our director kept his things in. We all worked to make everything especially comfortable for our visitor. My mother thought the Tiffany lamps by his bed were not good enough, too "la-di-da delicate," and the bentwood armchair not fit for reading in, so the Paramount Prop Department sent over a Studio truck with wrought-iron lamps with authentic parchment shades and a high-backed, carved mahogany throne used in some movie about Queen Isabella of Spain, which we all knew my father would absolutely adore. Von Sternberg contributed a magnificent crucifix, which was hung over Papi's bed. By the time he arrived, you could have gone to confession in that room and felt comfortable about it.

Paramount was willing to go along with the many facets of their star. "Wifehood" might work, just as Madonnahood had, without damaging the primary image of the Woman of Mystery. It was Dietrich's greatest strength that whatever role she decided to play in life, at any given time, somehow never interfered with the established one of glamorous Femme Fatale, a feat never equaled by Garbo, actually not even attempted. This amazing chameleon quality for becoming many women, which practically bordered on schizophrenia, really set Dietrich apart from her arch-rival. Garbo's range was refined to only one splendid category – "Divine" – whereas Dietrich's bag was full of tricks.

We all drove to Pasadena to greet my father. He stepped down off the train wearing a white linen suit, looking every inch the sleek European come to call, kissed my mother, who was, as usual, in her man's outfit of sports jacket, slouch hat, and tie, her only concession to The Welcoming Wife a white skirt instead of her usual trousers. My father picked me up, without groaning, flung his arm around von Sternberg's shoulders, and we all posed for the press for what was to become the famous photograph printed and reprinted around the world of "Marlene Dietrich and family." Paramount's directive of cropping me worked. For no one ever saw how my legs dangled halfway down my father's body, nor the desperate clutch of his hand trying to support my weight on his hip – nor the fact that our director and his star were wearing the same shoes.

Now our dinners again centered around food and news. My father told us that all sorts of German millionaires were supporting something called the Nazi party, especially Mr. Hugenberg, who was the boss of Ufa and a chairman of Krupp, and someone called Thyssen. There were heated discussions over a German film about girls in a boarding school who did things to each other that couldn't be described in front of "The Child," and had my mother read the new Pearl Buck book called *The Good Earth*?, to which my mother replied: "Is that the one about China?" When my father answered that it was, she gave an exasperated snort. "China here! China there! China . . . what is this obsession with China? The whole lot is swarming with slant-eyed people! If I see one more yellow face, I am going to throw up!" and left to get my father more cabbage rolls.

Von Sternberg looked rather crestfallen after this attack, but my father gave him a broad, knowing wink, which made our little man smile, and by the time my mother returned they were having a lovely discussion about light diffusion and someone who got a Nobel Prize for it.

Chevalier came, was told that his Camembert was sheer perfection, and became my father's new pal. I never knew why those two liked each other so, but they did for years. As usual, when Chevalier appeared, everyone automatically switched to French, so I asked to be excused and went to listen to "real American" on the radio.

I WAS COMING OUT from behind the wisteria. I had been burying something again – I was always conducting funerals among the gardenias – probably another lizard or a worm. This penchant for burials actually proved that I must be my father's daughter. I heard them talking on the patio. The name Maurice stopped me. I thought he was about to join them for lunch and all the French would begin; then I heard my mother say:

"But Papi, he loves me. But, you know he had gonorrhea when he was seventeen, that's why he's impotent." Oh, dear. Why did my mother have to tell my father that Chevalier loved her? A husband didn't like to hear such things from his wife. But my father threw back his blond head and laughed. I stood rooted to my spot, intrigued!

"Oh, Mutti! They can't ALL have had gonorrhea!" he spluttered. What that word meant must be funny.

"You would be surprised how many! Of course, Jo, being a Jew, never stops – they always want to do it, all the time! Especially if they are small and have a thing for tall, blue-eyed Christians." Now my mother was laughing.

"Margo sends you her undying love, and Bergner. They all miss you."

"And how I miss them! Here no women have brains. Certainly not at the Studio and, with Jo, that's the only place one sees. There is that vulgar Bankhead, awful, chases the bit players. There is that ugly Claudette Colbert, so 'shopgirl French.' Lombard is pretty but too 'palsy' American, and tries to look like me, and Crosby's chorines, and . . . who else is there? Now, at Garbo's Studio, there they have women – beautiful ones. I don't mean that Norma Shearer – she's a dead fish, and that new one, Harlow, too low-class. But they have some that are very interesting, but with Jo, of course, impossible!"

"Mutti, are you happy here?" my father asked, very seriously.

"Happy? What is happy?"

I turned and walked back down to the pool. I had thought she was happy. I wondered, with so many people loving her, why wasn't she?

Then came the memorable morning when my father observed me enjoying myself ensconced within the safety of my trusty life-ring. Walking to the edge of the deep end of the swimming pool, he called:
"Maria, come!"
Frantically trying to think of what I could possibly have done wrong to deserve my real name, I paddled over to him. He bent, reached down, plucked me from my ring, and threw me back into the water. Spluttering, I bobbed up to the surface, scared out of my wits. My father shouted: "Swim!" I took one desperate look at him and knew I better do what he said. I learned to swim that day, swam like a fish all my life, and never lost that fear of drowning.
Before we even had to buy a second liverwurst or the Roget Gallet sandalwood soap wore out, my father's beige cowhide steamer trunk, with its R.S. initials, appeared and was packed with his new treasures. The day he left, he handed me a terrier puppy, whom he had christened Teddy, told me to make sure this one didn't die, to take care of my mother, to behave myself, to finish reading all the books he had brought from Berlin, to do all the arithmetic pages he had made up for me, to write him a letter on every Monday of every week, to be polite, quiet. . . . I am afraid I stopped listening the moment the dog was in my arms. My mother cried. Von Sternberg came to take him to Union Station in downtown Los Angeles, not Pasadena. The departure of Rudolph Sieber, husband of Marlene Dietrich, was not being publicized. I hugged my little dog, praying my mother would allow me to keep him. Gloriosky! She did!

NO BEING DROPPED OFF at my grandmother's house, not even winter cold. Still predawn, the air a little chilly but now soft with the hint of mock orange and the smell of desert sands and the cozy soft leather interior of a Rolls to whisk us to work. The guard at the Studio gate saluted: "Good morning, Miss Dietrich. Good morning, little Heidede." Thanks to von Sternberg, I chimed: "Good morning, Mr. Mac," proud of my perfect cadence. The streetlamps on dressing-room row were lit: in Carole Lombard's room, the lights were on, so were Claudette Colbert and Bing Crosby's. That didn't mean that the stars were there, their entourage sometimes came ahead of the star to prepare and organize. As my mother never trusted anyone's ability to do things for her correctly without her supervision, she and her entourage moved as an inseparable unit.

This, my very first day of the beginning of shooting a film, remains a kaleidoscope of firsts that would become such an integral part of my life. The smell of greasepaint, fresh coffee, and Danish pastry, the big Make-Up Department all garish light, famous faces naked, devoid of adornment, some tired, half awake, all imperfections showing – terribly human, somehow vulnerable – awaiting the application of their masks of painted perfection. Hair-Dressing, equally lit, equally exposing the normalcy of flat-haired goddesses and some slightly balding gods, the sweet, sticky smell of setting lotion and hair glue replacing the linseed oil of greasepaint, the perfume of coffee and Danish. My mother becoming one of the crowd, an astounding revelation to me, who believed she was unique, the only one of her kind. Watching as she pushed skilled hands away, took over the task of doing her own face, drawing a fine line of lighter shade than her base, down the center of her nose, dipping the rounded end of a thin hairpin into white greasepaint, lining the inside of her lower eyelid. Looking at her in the big bulb-festooned mirror, seeing that suddenly straightened nose, those now oversized eyes, and coming all the way back to my original concept: that yes . . . she was, after all, truly unique.

Back in her private room, the dressing: the rapidity of all those helping hands, the precision of those movements that never seemed to lose their way or interfere with each other's tasks. The final look of her that caught your breath between a gasp and soundless wonder. The crisp command: "LET'S GO!" that galvanized everyone into individual action, us into the waiting limousine. My mother's suspended state. The first time I witnessed this, it frightened me. Once I realized the reason for it, I understood; accepting such abnormal things became automatic. Once made-up, hair in place, hat, veil, cock feathers positioned; never a blink, swallow, shift, pull, twitch, cough, sneeze, or word; weight balanced on one buttock, shoulder, and thigh; fingertips braced against the car seat to decrease body pressure from all wrinkleable surfaces; eyes open, locked into nonmovement; painted lips ajar, frozen. Sometimes, with a particularly intricate costume, I swear my mother actually stopped breathing until we reached the door of the soundstage, then came back to life – every single part of her intact, untarnished perfection.

The car rounded a corner, slowly. Harry was trained in driving a work of art to her destination. A dreary railroad yard, deserted except for a few lonely Pullman wagons and . . . suddenly, CHINA! Bustling, frantic, hot, dusty, crowded, milling, scurrying, overpopulated China. Chickens, goats, paper lanterns, straw-hatted coolies, ragged urchins, scrawny dogs, bags, trunks, baskets, crates, and boxes, roped parcels in all shapes and sizes. Above, a sea of banners, long, narrow white cloth panels painted with Chinese letters.

In the midst of all this dramatic confusion, a train, a *real* one, its huge black locomotive belching steam, and high on top, our little man, busily painting shadows onto its back. As nature had refused von Sternberg clouds that day, undaunted, he was painting his own. He always loathed being bested by anything – so usually found a way to overcome such "personal affronts" of nature. Only with my mother did he ever willfully capitulate to a force greater than him.

Resurrected, my mother carefully exited her car, and that frenzied bit of fake Orient froze. Chickens forgot to squawk, dogs stopped in midbark; carpenters, electricians, extras, some two hundred beings stared, enchanted. Von Sternberg, hearing sudden silence, looked down to see what had gotten in the way of everyone's work, spied his star giving off her black iridescence, waved to her, smiled his agreement of the homage paid her, then shouted: "Let's get back to work, boys," and went back to painting his white shadows.

I got to join the crew. Travis made me a special "attendant to Miss Marlene Dietrich" uniform, a white wraparound coat, like barbers wore. Properly attired, it was my job to stand outside the lit parameter of a set – my mother's hand mirror, poised, ready for her summons. I had my instructions down pat! If she called "Wardrobe," I was not to stir – that meant she had discovered a tiny wrinkle and her wardrobe attendant would run, black cushion in one hand, hot iron in the other, slip cushion under cloth, eliminate the offending bubble, then retreat back into the shadows, her work done. But, if the call was "Make-up," that meant *run* – brought me and her Make-up girl, Dot Pondel, to my mother's side. I handed her the precious mirror, Dot the even more precious lip brush, already dipped in gooey red. If the call was "Hair," I also got to run – this time Nellie and comb would join me. In those days, before Pan-Cake and hair spray, these calls were continual, and with Dietrich's perfectionism, even more so. Not only did she have a sixth sense about anything out of line, she also had her own constant watchdog, her full-length mirror. Framed, on its own rolling platform, it boasted three high-wattage bulbs along each side, was so positioned that whatever von Sternberg's camera saw, so did Dietrich's peripheral eye. She used it constantly, adjusting, correcting anything and everything she considered imperfect in any way. Von Sternberg never interfered, never lost patience with this maniacal perfection.

I learned some big lessons during this, my first film. When that shout came – "QUIET ON THE SET!" "ROLL 'EM!" "SOUND!"

"ACTION!" – that's when a tickle started in your throat, made you just *have* to cough. But you mustn't ever, *ever* let it happen! If you were so weak and stupid that you made even the tiniest noise of any kind, someone enraged would yell: "CUT!" and two hundred pairs of eyes would search for the traitor who had dared to ruin a take! Before a take *don't* ever eat a cracker without drinking afterward, carefully! Swallow – make quite sure nothing's stuck. Breathe in – make sure nothing is in there to tickle. If you *must* "go," cross your legs tight, you can't until the next "set-up." Best "stand easy": tensed muscles make "wind." And don't ever, *ever* move, not even a hair. The second you hear the director yell "CUT," cough, sneeze, jiggle, and fart, life is your oyster. How movie stars, under the added strain and awesome responsibility of having to also act, ever accomplish these Herculean feats of control always astounded me.

I also learned that sometimes Nellie from Hair-Dressing stood in front of the locked door of my mother's dressing room while she was still inside it. At such times, I was told that a screening of a film had been arranged for me in one of the Studio's many private projection rooms. Fantastic! I would run, hoping it would turn out to be the Marx Brothers' latest, or Carole Lombard's. If, during my sprint across the Studio lot, I happened to meet von Sternberg, those times he never noticed me, just walked by, his head bent, shoulders hunched, sort of angry, deep in thought.

Anna May Wong and my mother became chummy. Between takes, they talked, not rehearsing their scenes, just soft conversation, smoked, sipped cool coffee through their straws. My mother fussed over Miss Wong's square bangs and had Travis redesign one of her kimonos so it would be more flattering. She liked Miss Wong much better than her leading man, who turned out exactly as Travis had described him – a photogenic jaw, British, and little else. By the third week of filming *Shanghai Express*, I experienced my first clearing of the set. I didn't know what had triggered it, but when "Clear the set" was called that morning, I hesitated – looked at my mother for direction. When she nodded, mouthing "Go," I joined the hundred-odd men and sprinkling of women outside. The crew seemed quite used to this ominous exodus. I didn't know then that crews usually stayed together from one Sternberg film to another, and that clearing the set was a procedure they had become used to – even welcomed. It meant getting out into the bright sunshine, having a smoke, leaning against the wall improving their California tans, while Dietrich was inside being taught how to act. After one of these upheavals, we finally broke for lunch. As my mother never ate while working, her stomach bloated with even the tiniest intake of food, our lunches consisted of me eating, while she redid her face and hair.

That day, in complete silence, each movement slow and deliberate, she removed the long black velvet dress, handed it to the waiting Wardrobe girl; it would be freshened, checked, and steamed during the time allotted; unhooked the special brassière, handed it to Nellie, who gave her another, more comfortable one; put on her cotton makeup coat, knotted its belt tightly; wound up her gramophone, put a Tauber record on, and sat down at her table, scrutinizing her face in the brightly lit mirror.

Von Sternberg knocked on the screen door, got a "Come," and entered, carrying his sandwich. She straightened, hurried to get him a proper plate and linen napkin. I poured him his Coca-Cola – he liked it too!

"Beloved, did I exhaust you?"

"No, never. I just try not to fail you!"

He finished his ham on rye, wiped his mustache, kissed the back of her neck, smiled at her in the mirror, and went back to work.

Small "special" dressing-room jobs were assigned to me. I became good at blowing feathers, I shook fur very well to my mother's specifications. I also became expert at eyelash thinning. In those days, false eyelashes were terribly thick. For Dietrich's face, they had to be thinned by half. My mother stood over me as I slid lashes off the gossamer band. "Yes . . . more. . . . Otherwise the eyes look like Garbo's. She puts so many on, they look like feather dusters. They say those are her own. Nebbish!" I was also allowed to realign the dozens of black wax eyebrow pencils that Dot sharpened with her trusty penknife. I hoped someday to be considered old enough to do that job myself.

Because of von Sternberg's truly magical lighting, my mother's limp, wispy hair took on thickness, life, and incredible sheen. So much, in fact, that a rumor began to circulate that it wasn't von Sternberg's lights, that Dietrich was actually putting real gold dust in her hair to get that special sparkle. For once, a rumor was left to flourish. My mother refused to comment, the heads of Hair-Dressing smiled secretly, Nellie's lips were sealed, Publicity had a field day. While the song "Brother Can You Spare a Dime?" was sweeping the country, the gossip columns announced: "Marlene Dietrich grinds a fifty-dollar gold piece into dust every day and sprinkles it on her hair."

Paramount also insured her legs, for one million dollars; Publicity was on the ball. Years later, when my mother broke her leg, she bemoaned that lost Paramount policy. Oh, to be a cosseted, protected contract player again!

We had just arrived back from the set on our lunch break when a gentleman in a wrinkled linen suit swung open the door, entered the dressing room without knocking.

"Hi, Heid-e-ede. Never can get my tongue around that. . . . 'Cute' name . . . you sure are growing – better watch it, eh? Don't get *too* big, girlie. . . . We don't want to have to take pictures of you sitting down all the time!"

A booming laugh, a twinkling eye, a saucy wink, checked quickly as my mother slowly turned from her dressing table.

"Good morning, Marleen-n! Ah – yeah – ah, *Miss* Dietrich. I know you're busy . . . But this won't take more than a second, I swear. You see, we came up with this really GREAT idea for this li'l gal of yours – for her *birthday*! Now, just listen – please! You'll LOVE IT! . . . You know the back lot, where von Sternberg has built his China? Well – now get this: with that train, the crazy chickens, all those extras doing the Chinese coolie bit, we got this terrific idea. How about a CHINESE BIRTHDAY PARTY – FOR MARLENE'S KID! . . . Right there on the set! We'll get all the stars' kids, dress *them* up like little coolies! *Photoplay, Silver Screen* – everybody'll come to cover *that*! Chinese firecrackers . . . the WORKS! We'll get national coverage, and to top it off – are you ready for this? – *you and Clive Brook bring in the cake*, in the shape of a *train*, with 'Happy Birthday, Heid-e-ede' . . . boy, that name . . . 'from the cast and crew of *Shanghai Express*' in big, frosted Chinese letters! GET THE PICTURE?"

I was riveted. Fabulous! Great! Wonderful! I wanted my birthday right away!

My mother had not moved a muscle throughout the entire presentation. Now she slowly rose, registered my excitement, fixed me with her famous hooded look that could control a charging rhino at twenty paces, turned this same glacial stare toward the anticipatory impresario. One black-sheathed elegant arm rose slightly toward him. White slender index finger pointing to the dressing-room door, she intoned the word "OUT." He stumbled over his own feet getting out of there. It was one of my mother's better performances of Lady Macbeth!

I wasn't heartbroken, it was fun just hearing about such a party. This was not the last time Paramount tried to give me one. All were rejected, of course, and she was right. The outrageous birthday extravaganzas that Joan Crawford later staged for her precious darlings proved once again my mother's innate good taste – sometimes.

My seventh birthday dawned on another perfect day of perpetual sunshine. I wondered when the cold of winter would come and when I would finally be allowed to go to school. The sun continued to shine, my pencil box remained wrapped in its pretty paper. My father, now working in Paris dubbing films into foreign languages for Paramount, thanked my mother for my existence:

CABLE=PARIS 12 13 1931 DEC 13 AM 11 11
DIETRICH
HOLLYWOOD
CONGRATULATE YOU ON THIS DAY I THANK YOU MUTTI LOVE
KISSES

PAPI

Bullock's Wilshire was our only emporium. Beverly Hills had no department stores then, Rodeo Drive was a just a lazy street in a pretty palm-treed village that Laurel and Hardy used as a backdrop. So one ventured forth by chauffeured car to Hollywood on Wilshire Boulevard, not quite as far as downtown Los Angeles, but nearly, and there it was – our version of the Chrysler Building! Not as tall, not as majestic; you really couldn't visualize King Kong clinging to its sides, but in a town of one-storied haciendas, clapboard bungalows, and fruit-juice stands in the shape of oranges, it was your eight-story skyscraper, all Art Deco, carved concrete, and triangular glass.

My mother must have needed something that the Studio could not supply, because she decided to go to Bullock's one morning and to take me with her. As she was the only adult who spoke fluent English in our house, she was forced to go herself. She was not pleased. I was excited – it was the first time we were going somewhere other than the Studio. Telephone poles, gas stations with red flying horses, chunky palms, hot-dog stands shaped like dachshunds – the Wilshire Boulevard of 1931 not so different from today, except that the little houses are now black-glass banks and the crystal cleanness is not constant. That day, the sun shone hot, a bright yellow in a postcard-blue sky. I knew all this was quite impossible, as it was nearly Christmas, so it had to be some more magic. That, I could accept easily! That was part of my new life!

The doorman, resplendent in the Bullock's colors of bitter chocolate and beige, ushered us through the ornate glass doors. Harry and the green Rolls remained parked directly in front of the store; then, the streets were always empty. The vaulted main floor looked like a French cathedral – they could have used it for *The Hunchback of Notre Dame*. It was awesome.

And there, in the very center, there it stood. A GIANT Christmas tree. I nearly fell over backward, trying to see the huge silver star on its top. But the wonder of it – the tree was *white*! How was that possible? A snow-covered tree INSIDE, while the sun shone OUTSIDE? . . . But the most marvelous sight of all was the lights. Not candles, as we had in Berlin, but electric lights, and they were *blue*! Every garland, every ornament, and glass ball . . . Madonna Blue! I just stood there, mesmerized. I don't remember what we did or where we went that day, I was in a sapphire daze. When I got home, I talked of nothing else.

As we always kept our German customs, Christmas was in the evening of the 24th. The 25th was just for eating. Santa Claus never came to our house. Santa belonged to "the type of people who buy those stupid greeting cards." Anyway, my mother did not like being upstaged, especially in generosity. In her entire life, she never made an anonymous gift, either to person or organization. She considered gratitude too important a tool to relinquish it. In Dietrich's family, she was the giver of gifts and no one else. Even in Germany, I knew who gave me my presents and exactly what degree of gratitude each one required. This – my first American Christmas – I was a little older, but the same rules applied. First, one waited patiently in new dress and shoes before the closed living-room doors. "Silent Night" would begin to play on the gramophone, the doors would open, and there would be the little green tree, lighting up the darkened room with all its tiny candles, the air filled with the perfume of pine and chocolate. It was this very first moment of Christmas that I loved most – the special time, the welcome of the shining tree, the music, and the smell of home.

This year, my dress was silk, my American Mary Janes, white kid. As the music started, von Sternberg and my mother opened the heavy double doors to our reception room and the world turned a brilliant blue. There, in all its twenty-foot splendor, stood my department-store tree! The only thing missing was the ping of the elevator bells in the background.

My mother had such fun with her fabulous surprise. Everyone at the studio heard about "The Child's blue Christmas tree" and how she had managed to buy it complete from Bullock's department store! It really did look fantastic – I wished I could tell everyone about my tree, but they had already heard all about it.

In order to take Christmas pictures in proper light, carpenters arrived from the Studio, sawed the tree into sections, then reassembled it in the garden, where the sun cooked the thick white oil paint that gave off fumes that made my stomach heave, while I posed cutely among the nailed-back-together branches. No color film (yet) in those days, so when I turned green, and the tree, "singed-oil-yellow," it didn't show in the pictures. I always wished I had had someone besides the staff to show it to. It was a great Hollywood tree.

Rudolph Sieber

Paris, Sunday, 14 February 1932

Muttilein,

I was so happy to see that your Christmas was nice and that you did not suffer too much for not having me with you. It did help to be at my parents. With them there were not such big presents: I gave them something they really wanted, a radio, not a big one. They are overjoyed.

But what you got, that is a distinctly different matter – four bracelets with diamonds! You promised me you would send pictures of them, I am waiting impatiently, I am curious to see them. I did not know that Jo also paid for the sapphire ring.

I also did not realize there were such terrible arguments with him. I know that he is not easy but this must somehow get better in time. He loves you and tortures you because he loves you, because he feels somehow helpless in front of you and therefore that is his way of compensating for his weakness. I just remembered this: I sent you before Christmas a picture of the three of us, it is a photo from some newspaper that an accountant of ours here would like autographed by you and Kater and which I asked you to send directly to him. He still hasn't received it, sign it and send it!! Do it, please, you know how that type of person is.

I hope you liked the hats and stockings I bought for you in Berlin. Do not forget me.

Papi

Shanghai Express opened to rave reviews. Von Sternberg had already written my mother's next film. He had told us the story. In this one, she would be a devoted, dedicated mother, a perfect wife, a sacrificial wife, a down-and-out streetwalker, a rowdy nightclub singer, an elegant "kept" woman, an acclaimed cabaret entertainer, and all the way back to beloved "once-only-unfaithful" wife. I thought von Sternberg was being just a little too generous, but my mother loved it, absolutely adored it – even bestowed on him one of her best kisses. Our director beamed; Paramount accepted the story line of *Blonde Venus*.

Herbert Marshall would be cast as the long-suffering husband, and a discovery of Mae West's, a bit player named Cary Grant, would do as the "swanky lover." But the Studio balked at the ending. I never knew what ending was whose finally – only that the first one, written by von Sternberg, was refused; that, insulted, he walked off the picture; that another director was assigned to the film; that my mother refused categorically to work for anyone but von Sternberg; that he was secretly very happy at her taking this stand; and that the Studio was furious.

On April 26th, 1932, Paramount announced that Marlene Dietrich had been put on suspension for refusing to obey contractual conditions and would be replaced in *Blonde Venus* by Tallulah Bankhead. Tallulah was quoted as saying: "I always did want to get into Dietrich's pants," which did not endear her to Paramount or the Hay's Office, the mighty censor of film morals, but got a laugh out of Dietrich. Next Paramount announced that the Studio was suing Josef von Sternberg for one hundred thousand dollars in damages. His answer was typical: "Only a hundred thousand? How insulting!"

Most stars put on suspension panicked. Their livelihood cut off, their careers "on hold," their future stardom threatened. Not my mother. She slept, cleaned the house, baked, cooked for an unseen army, tasted everything, nibbled all day – then got all dolled up and went dancing with Chevalier all night. She was just a little miffed at him though; she had seen him making eyes at Jeanette MacDonald at the Studio, but forgave him because he danced so well, and, as she put it, "It's too stupid to really get angry about." Of course, they were seen; of course, they were photographed cheek to cheek; of course, Chevalier gloried in all this attention; of course, von Sternberg was jealous. One night, he waited up for her and their verbal combat was so loud, it woke me – even Teddy, who had crept upstairs to find me from his basket in the pantry. Oh, dear – couldn't my mother have snuck in by the garden door, not upset our little man so? Especially after he worked so hard, gave her that wonderful sapphire ring, so blue, so like my Christmas tree! After all, he loved her – couldn't she be just a little kinder?

Although I was never close to Chevalier, I understood that his main attraction for my mother was his being so un-American. Even my father had been drawn to him. In the midst of all this "American-ism," these foreigners sought each other out in their homesickness. Even if I recognized that, I couldn't sympathize with this constant yearning of my mother's for far-off European shores. As both were Paramount stars, the Studio of course released the photograph of Dietrich in the arms of Chevalier. The wire services picked it up and printed it all over the world. My father cabled for permission to use the picture for a promotional postcard for my mother's European recording company, Polydor. My mother wrote back, explaining the sensitive situation:

Papilein,
   I can authorize the postcard that Polydor wants, but I can't provide prints because Jo went to the Studio at night, took the negatives out of the files and destroyed them. He accused me of infidelity, of deliberately

trying to embarrass him. He called me a whore, then asked if I had slept with Maurice. I just can't stand jealousy. . . .

She enclosed von Sternberg's apology as proof of what she had to suffer through:

My love, woman I truly love,
  I already regret what I said. You do not deserve such accusations, and my attitude was, as usual, unpleasant and incomprehensible. Somehow, sometime, I slipped out of the right way, got lost and can't find the way back to myself again. I have done nothing to deserve your respect and little to keep it. One cannot erase words and one must pay the penalty for each ugly word. That I do.

                                                                      Jo

Because of my mother's nonworking schedule, suddenly "family" excursions were possible. We actually went out to see movies, like real people did – in movie houses – instead of ordering them to be shown at the Studio. Of course, we never had to pay, and the managers snuck us in through the side doors after the lights went down so my mother wouldn't be recognized, and we never really saw the very end of a film because we had to sneak out before the lights came back on. Still, it was fun pretending we were going "to the movies," like *real* people! We also drove down to the ocean. That was one of my favorite jaunts, seeing the sea gulls, the huge breakers, the endless horizon. My mother never exposed herself to the sun, not only because of her profession; in those days she disliked tans in general. She thought they only suited men, and then only handsome ones, so when we drove to the ocean, we usually went late in the day, at sunset.

I first heard it on the radio in the butler's pantry, then one of the maids burst into tears. Someone had stolen a baby from that man with the German name who had flown all alone across the ocean. I thought it was terrible and wondered why anyone would do such a cruel thing. I had to ask our chauffeur what *ransom* meant. When he told me, I hoped Mr. Lindbergh was very rich so he could buy back his baby. Days passed. Even with those famous men of the Federal Bureau of Investigation looking everywhere, the baby was not found. I thought maybe my father's method might work, and said a really nice prayer. Rumors mushroomed. There wasn't a state where someone didn't report that the kidnappers had been seen. Across America, everyone looked for the Lindbergh baby. When it was announced that it might have been brought into southern California, we began looking too. Now, on those excursions down to the beach, Harry was told to drive into every dark alley, down every back street, while we, our heads sticking out of our Rolls, investigated every shadow, looked for dimly lit rooms among the shacks, searched for those terrible kidnappers. The ransom was paid, and, on the 12th of May, the Lindbergh baby was found – dead.

Three days later, our first ransom note arrived, postmarked "Arcade Station Los Angeles, May 15, 1932."

WE WANT $10,000 ELEVEN P.M. MAY 16. HAVE YOUR CAR JUST IN FRONT OF YOUR HOME. PUT MONEY PACKAGES ABOUT SIX INCHES FROM STREET ON REAR BUMPER. DON'T CALL POLICE. WANTED ONLY $5 AND $10 BILLS. QUICK SERVICE. LINDBERGH BUSINESS. KEEP SILENT. DON'T BE CRAZY.

My mother called my father in Paris, told him to get on the next boat: "Hurry, Papi!" Even if he made every single connection, it would still take him at least ten days to get to us. I wondered if he would make it in time to see me before I was whisked off! My mother became completely unhinged. Von Sternberg and Chevalier were summoned and ordered to bring guns "ready to shoot." The Paramount Prop Department must have outfitted them, for they arrived in bulging shoulder holsters, toting fully loaded carbines. Von Sternberg insisted on calling in the FBI and, to muzzle the press, Paramount's head of Publicity. By now the house was overrun by local, county, and state police, Studio representatives, security guards, Paramount Publicity, sundry marcelled secretaries, and their sidekicks. My mother's hand was like a vise around my wrist, gluing me to her side; eyes glazed, she kept telling me, "As long as you are with your mother, you are safe. With your mother you are safe. No one can take you away from me," over and over again. She scared the hell out of me! When the FBI arrived, I knew I was a goner – only Edward G. Robinson could save me now! The garden and all accessible rooms were declared "off limits" – I was moved into one of the maids' rooms in the back and told to "stay." Waking up one night, I found von Sternberg on the floor by my bed, revolver ready, fast asleep. Another night, Chevalier, equally armed and ready, snoring musically.

Another ransom note arrived, postmarked May 17th. And another on May 25th.

MAMA, LISTEN DON'T BE A FOOL. OTHERS PAID ALL AND
SO WILL YOU.

I turned on the maid's radio and heard that "Marlene Dietrich's little girl
Heidede was about to be kidnapped." Gee! I had made the radio – even
if it was with that stupid name. I hoped I would still be around to hear
the next bulletin.

I can't have been an easy child to live with during this terrible time for
my mother. The whole drama was such a great script, I felt I was in my
own exciting movie and enjoyed the thrill of stardom.

Another ransom note arrived on May 30:

YOU CAN DECIDE FOR YOURSELF. YOUR MONEY OR DEATH
NOTICE. WHAT ABOUT IT? LINDBERGH BUSINESS!

Newspapers were sliced carefully into the size of bills, then formed into
neat bundles, each received a marked five-dollar bill on either side that
would "fool" the kidnappers. When there were the right number of
phony stacks, they were put in two big brown-paper grocery bags,
placed on the bumper of a special "prop" car parked in front of our
house. Then some fifty pairs of sharp eyes watched that bumper from
the many hidden lookout points around and inside the house. For hours
and hours, they staked out that bumper, my mother serving everybody
coffee and sandwiches to keep up their "watching" strength. But no one
ever came to pick up that newspaper money, and suddenly the ransom
notes stopped coming!

By the time my father made it, all was over, but, of course, never
forgotten. Still, he took charge, sent my mother to bed – she dragged
herself upstairs, slept for the first time in weeks – told me to go back to
my old room and read a book, instructed the nervous servants to clean
the messy house and to prepare a decent lunch for Mister von Sternberg,
Mister Chevalier, and himself, which he expected to be served in the
garden promptly within the hour, and followed by his pals, went off to
check on our supply of bootleg wines. The next day, bodyguards were
hired to guard me. For the first weeks, there were four daytime, four
nighttime guards on constant duty. These were reduced to two and two
when no further ransom notes appeared. As added security, a handler,
in padded attire, delivered a massive German shepherd trained by the
police to attack, guaranteed to sink his razor-sharp fangs into anything
that looked my way. This beast had a passionate attachment to balls.
Throw him anything that rolled and he was off at full sprint. He was
a great example of a ferocious killer. All he did all day was wag that

long bushy tail of his, begging to chase the love of his life across the lawn. Our parrot would have made a better guard dog.

Despite all these precautions, my mother still insisted we were leaving for "safe" Berlin. Any remark about forsaking her stardom was answered by an icy look, accompanied by, "If I wasn't a *famous movie star*, there wouldn't have been any kidnapping." Such truth no one could argue with. Everyone had their own reasons for trying to come up with a solution that would keep her in Hollywood. Von Sternberg feared if she left now, he would lose her. I feared I would lose America; my father, his comfortable life in Paris. Chevalier had nothing to lose, so waited around to see what everyone else would come up with. Knowing that only the discipline of work would be able to break through her terror, von Sternberg capitulated, accepted all of Paramount's script changes, and *Blonde Venus* was, once again, a Dietrich-Sternberg vehicle.

Still, it took the combined persuasion of the police, the FBI, and my sacred vow never ever to stray beyond the confines of our house and walled-in garden, before my mother agreed to remain in America and return to work. On learning that the film had never been put into actual production with her so-called replacement, she said: "Aha! So it was all a Studio trick to get me worried! Stupid people. The only thing now is that Tallulah won't be able to say she got into Dietrich's pants," and burst out laughing. Like a flock of birds, we were all startled at that sudden sound coming from her. She had laughed! Von Sternberg had done it! Our "soldier" was once more ready to go forth and do her magic duty.

On every window, every door, iron bars were installed. The front door got an electrified gate. At night, with the curtains drawn, it wasn't so bad, but in the daytime, it could feel a little like you were doing time in Alcatraz. My bodyguards were nice, though, like caring fathers, who knew what they did was for my own good, but wished they didn't have to. They smuggled me lollipops and my favorite, forbidden chewing gum, talked to me, became my friends. So we spent our sunlit days. My father took on the role of exasperated professor to overindulged, undereducated, movie star's treasure, stood over me as I did sums, read German books, practiced forming the intricate letters of ancient Germanic script, then attempted an even more impossible task: trying to balance my mother's checkbooks without notated stubs.

After my labors, I swam, dressed Teddy in baby clothes, stuck him into my splendid doll carriage, wheeled it and him around the garden, while my killer dog searched for the many round objects he kept hidden and always forgot where. The "vulture" waited for someone – anyone – to attempt to get past him. The maids maided, the guards guarded. Life was quiet and "boo-o-oring," as my mother pronounced it. I knew enough English to finally be allowed to go to school, but that dream was now definitely over. No learning new exciting things together with other children, no friends, no sleepovers, no real parents to meet, no metal lunch box, no proper place to use my pencil box. Those would-be kidnappers really did my mother a big favor, they supplied her with the accepted, even laudable excuse, for keeping her child constantly by her side, isolated from the normal world that just might have had some influence on me, possibly have become more important to me than the one she inhabited and controlled. The outside world sympathized with her devoted efforts, believed she only shielded me from danger, while actually keeping me for herself.

I felt I had lost something. I was just too young to know the scope of it.

While my father was still in residence, our dinners resumed. My mother began to think of other things than my being snatched from her. She asked my father, anxiously:

"Papi, before all this, did you talk to Mutti? Did you tell her about coming here? What did you say?" My father hesitated, as though he didn't really want to discuss my grandmother.

"Well?" My mother stood facing him, holding the serving bowl, looking at him intently.

"Mutti, you must try to understand how your mother feels – how she thinks. Berlin is her home. All her friends are there . . . her house. No one believes that this political situation will last – "

" 'No one believes!' Then why did you have Paramount give you that job dubbing films in Paris? Why are you now packing up everything, leaving Berlin and moving there?"

"Because I believe that what is developing in Germany is extremely dangerous, that it may get even worse . . . may eventually lead us into another war!"

"You see! So why won't Mutti come?" She banged down the bowl of mashed potatoes, making the gravy jump.

"Because . . ." my father started patiently.

My mother interrupted him: "War! That's *too* dramatic. Going off, leaving one's country – that's too big a to-do. I'm not talking about that! I'm talking about *living* here with me and The Child, in the sunshine, while I make pictures. You can't tell me that this life here with palm trees, servants, chauffeurs, even now with the bodyguards, is not still better than that old house in the Berlin cold and streetcars! Liesel, I can understand – it's that terrible husband of hers, he probably wouldn't let her have that boy she is so gaga about – but Mutti? She is all alone, with no one! What's the difference if I send her money for there or she lives here for nothing?"

I could see my father was about to answer that but decided not to. I got the distinct feeling that my grandmother did not want to live with us and that my father knew why, sort of agreed with her – up to a point.

Teddy chewed up one of my father's elegant new slippers and got us into real trouble. My father was very angry at Teddy's lack of proper training. My mother, when confronted, shrugged her shoulders, indicated "what else could one expect from a dog" and went off to cook dinner for her men. I promised and promised Teddy would learn to be good, but no use. When my father left, he would take my dog with him. Teddy was about to be "trained" by Rudolph Sieber – an awesome destiny!

When von Sternberg came to drive my father to the station, I held Teddy close. He was still so young. I whispered in his furry ear not to be afraid, just to obey without question, do everything he was told immediately – then things would be okay – kissed him, and handed him over to his new master. I prayed I would see him again. My mother and I accompanied them just up to the electrified front door, too dangerous to go any further – kidnappers might still be lurking in the banana trees ready to pounce. With our arms stuck through the bars, we waved until the car made the turn onto Sunset Boulevard.

I think Buddy the Killer missed his new friend as much as I. For days, we both drooped around the garden being sad. One of the guards brought me a green frog in a mason jar – that was nice of him – and Paramount delivered a purebred spitz. Its ruff was so bushy, Sir Walter Raleigh would have been proud to wear it. His pedigree looked like a legal brief. That dog was so "pure," it twitched, yapped constantly, drove Buddy's already sensitive nerves to breaking point. I thought, seriously, of offering him to the Vulture! In my world, one was not allowed to have cozy mongrels. Anything that could win best of show at Westminster was acceptable, but nothing less. During the years of my Hollywood childhood, I had a blue-black Scottie, with one of those ridiculous names like Sir McDuff of Aberdeen, an Irish setter, Colleen of Shaughnessy O'Day, a chow chow, with the blackest tongue imaginable, who bore the title of Chin Ming Soo Woo, bit the maid, and lasted only a week . . . and many, many more. At one time, I think I must have gone through the entire elegant canine kingdom. Whatever happened to all those dogs? I really don't know, just that as the gardeners put down their little green jars of potent ant poison, my dogs seemed to disappear along with the ants. I have visions of four-legged corpses continually being discovered by distraught Japanese, my mother calling Paramount to immediately deliver another dog before The Child discovered "the cruelty of life." Actually, my mother disliking pets the way she did, this rapid canine turnover must have stretched her "for The Child" generosity a great deal, but she kept ordering pedigreed replacements nevertheless. My friends suddenly disappearing like that at first frightened me a little. Why had they left me? By the time I got up the courage to ask somebody, a new dog arrived and my mother told me to play with it and be "happy." I did as I was told.

I remained at home behind bars, dogs and bodyguards alert to the slightest rustle in the bougainvillea. For a while, my mother went to the Studio without me. Each parting might be forever, each return a heart-rending relief that I was still there! In the evenings, she kept me up to date on the costumes in preparation. Although I hoped, she never did bring me back an "egg salad on white."

"You know what we did today? Decided to put her in tails! But this time, all in white. Good idea? Even the top hat – white."

I asked, "Like *The Blue Angel* one?"

"No – no. Much more elegant. . . . The only thing I don't like is the lapels, white on white . . . too plain next to the dickey."

I ventured: "Maybe you could sparkle them up a little?"

My mother stopped changing her shoes, looked at me, and our collaborative relationship was born! It was to last through the rest of her professional life. It was perhaps the only plane on which we ever functioned as "professional" friends – nearly equals. Now she just stared at me.

"What did you say?"

Thinking I might have overstepped my position, I hesitated.

"Repeat it!" she commanded.

"Well, Mutti . . . I just thought . . . if you say the white lapels next to the white shirtfront will photograph flat, couldn't you put some sparkle on the lapels – maybe?" The last came out a hushed croak. My spit had dried up!

"That's it! RHINESTONES! Come here!" she picked up the telephone, dialed: "Travis! The Child knew! What to do with the lapels – yes. She knew! Make the surface in rhinestones! Brilliant? Now we can do the hatband too and also outline the slits of the pockets to continue the sparkle down. I know, difficult for Jo, but he always knows what to do. Here – tell The Child yourself how wonderful . . . ," and handed me the receiver. Travis Banton told me I was a "genius"; I thanked him.

Over dinner that night, von Sternberg was told all about my "designer" brilliance. He smiled benignly, threw me a look like, "Thanks, kid. That's all I needed – reflected shadows bouncing all over my goddess's face!" and went on eating his favorite Hungarian goulash.

"Sweetheart, we are making a hat, for the flophouse scene. Very cheap, poor looking, dipped brim for shadows, with, maybe, a small bunch of shiny cherries to pick up the light in the front. A lace blouse, with some holes on the shoulder to look vulgar and poor . . ."

I could just see it – my mother, all downtrodden, sad. I wondered, though, what a flophouse was. Whatever, I knew von Sternberg would fill it with his lovely shadows.

My father, back in Paris, had rendezvoused with his pal Chevalier. They cabled together:

CABLE=PARIS
NLT MARLENE
HOLLYWOOD (CALIF)=
WE HAD A NICE DINNER AT BELLE AURORE THE CRAWFISH NOT AS GOOD AS YOURS STOP HAVE DRUNK TO YOUR HEALTH AND TO MARIA STOP WE MISS YOU PAINFULLY

MAURICE RUDI

My mother was pleased. She always liked it when her admirers became friends, when those who worshiped her became congenial members of the congregation.

Still locked into my territory, *Blonde Venus* began filming without my valuable presence.

My mother was gulping down her epsom salts and hot water, standing on her bathroom scales, checking.

"Sweetheart, today we did the bath scene. The little boy who plays the child is sweet. You remember the way I used to wash you in Berlin? Well, that's how I did it, in a big white apron, just like I used to do with you when you were small." Her voice got a little weepy, remembering "the good old days." "Mister von Sternberg liked how I did it, so it was all easy today, but then, after the scene, I cried because you weren't there to see it and we had to break early for lunch – to redo my eyes. Herbert Marshall plays the part of the husband. Nice man, again British, but a better actor . . . but this one can't walk – he has a wooden leg. He has all sorts of

tricks to distract the eye away from the way he can't move. Interesting
– on the rushes you hardly notice the limp. Why would anybody with a
wooden leg want to become an actor? Funny. Nellie and Dot send their
love, everyone asks where you are. I tell them . . . 'Safe.'"

I missed the Studio. I hoped my mother would soon break down,
decide she couldn't stand it anymore, call me back to take up my mirror
and my position watching her be the distraught wife who had sacrificed
all. But it took a while before she capitulated, and so I wasn't there to
see the big Voodoo number, nor the fuzzy-wuzzy wig, so like Harpo's,
that she wore coming out of her gorilla.

"Sweetheart, you should have been there! The drums beat, I sway as a
gorilla . . . slowly slip off one paw – one beautiful hand appears, like the
neck of a white swan – then more jungle swaying, then the other beautiful
hand appears . . . more of that swaying. I nearly got carsick! Then I slowly
take off the big monkey head and you see my face, hair completely pulled
back – a Nefertiti face – on the fat gorilla body. Good?"

We were having Sunday lunch on the patio, lots and lots of cold cuts,
potato salad, black bread, and cheese. My mother, her eyes yearning,
stared at the bologna, smoke in resentful puffs as we gorged. Von
Sternberg took a sip of Gladys-Marie's "piss":

"Beloved, did you hear Garmes will be nominated for best cinemato-
graphy by the Academy for *Shanghai Express*?"

"I don't believe it! For *your* superb work, they are going to give *him*
an award?"

"As he is a very fine cameraman, he deserves it."

"Those idiots. Look how they started, with that – that – 'matchgirl,'
that Janet Gaynor. Now, really! For sighing on painted rooftops of Paris,
you get an award for *acting*? Look at Garbo. Didn't they want to give her
one for that terrible *Grand Hotel*? Now, I have seen her be wonderful, but
in *that* abortion, slinking around mooning à la fake Russian all over that
awful ham, Barrymore – that was just *too* much. . . . That hoity-toity
Academy giving its prizes – for what? Like children, they have to reward
each other? Don't they *know* when they're good? Do they have to be given
a prize to know it? . . . And over lunch! They actually go to that depressing
Cocoanut Grove, with the fake nuts up in those cardboard palm trees . . .
and have themselves applauded? Terrible – the vanity of actors."

And that finished the Academy Awards in our household.

THE MORNING OUR MILKMAN got inside the house was my lucky day. My mother decided that if he could get by the attack dog, armed guards, not to mention the parrot, I was safer behind the gates of Paramount Studio. So, at least I did get to see the costume of the "Hot Voodoo" number, unfortunately the swaying gorilla already hung back in Wardrobe, waiting for a jungle picture. I was "home" again. In no time it seemed as though I had never been away, except that now my bodyguard had to follow me wherever I went. That wasn't so bad, everyone thought he was just a wandering extra from a gangster movie looking for his set.

My mother really liking anyone, without romantic passionate over-tones, was so rare that I never forgot them. Mae West, her dressing-room neighbor, was such a one. She was permitted her free-and-easy American ways without ever being given the "Dietrich Freeze." She would open the screen door of my mother's dressing room, knocking on its wood frame as she entered, the only person who ever got away with that!

"Hi, ducky!" She stood back, hands on those famous hips, rolling her eyes, doing her own best imitation of herself as she took in my mother's revealing costume for the Voodoo scenes. Mae let out a low appreciative whistle:

"Not bad, honey – not bad AT ALL!"

"But look, Mae – the legs again! Always the same thing, they *want* the *legs*!"

"Yeah! You give 'em the bottom and I'll give 'em the top!" She cupped her small hands under her ample bosom, pushing it even further out of the tight corset she always wore, even under her dressing gown. My mother laughed. Mae West could always make her laugh. "Ducks – we have to go for the women too. Not just the men. Remember that. If it were just the men, all I'd have to do is take 'em out . . ." With that, she lifted one breast out of the corset.

It was truly gorgeous! It took very little to shock my mother. Mae West, knowing this, loved to tease her. Now, with her famous naughty smirk, she gathered up her alabaster treasure, placed it carefully back into its whalebone cage, patted the inside of Dietrich's naked thigh, and sashayed out! My mother threw back her head and roared with laughter. She was always a great audience to a perfect performance. I had not fully understood this scene, but I always remembered it because of the fun they had together. I often wondered why their friendship never flourished beyond the Paramount lot. They had so much in common, professionally at least. Their superb self-mockery, their ability to think of their film-image in the third person, their instinctive intelligence of always knowing what could or couldn't work for them, and their amazing

ABOVE: Sundays at home. When von Sternberg
painted in the garden, I liked to keep him company.
BELOW: A new addition to our California family—
my father.

ABOVE: My mother loved *Blonde Venus*. In it, she
got to play a hausfrau, a mother, a fallen angel, a
whore, and a successful nightclub entertainer—all
in one film. She thought a newcomer, Cary Grant,
could become a star someday.

BELOW: At 6 a.m., dressed in her usual attire, ready
to be driven to work in her green Rolls-Royce.

ABOVE: The husband, the director, the star, and one organdied daughter watching polo on Sunday, our day off.

BELOW: The famous custom-built, mile-long Cadillac that took the place of our regal Rolls-Royce.

RIGHT: In 1932, kidnappers had a lot of imagination. Some of the ransom notes sent to Dietrich threatening her child.

BELOW, LEFT: Dietrich on the balcony of the Hearst beach mansion she rented in 1933.

BELOW, RIGHT: The Child, with her friends. My daytime bodyguards and Buddy, the Killer Dog, on the Santa Monica beach.

BOTTOM, LEFT: The Child, with her father's lover, Tami. I loved her, too.

BOTTOM, RIGHT: The Child, with her mother's lover, Mercedes. I thought *she* was creepy!

LEFT: My mother in love with her first Frenchman, Maurice Chevalier.
ABOVE: Our favorite tennis champion, Fred Perry, with Dietrich, Tami, and Rudi—a happy family in Santa Monica.
BELOW: The Mistress, the Wife, the Husband.

ABOVE: At the Studio Commissary, lunching with her new director Rouben Mamoulian, her old lover Maurice Chevalier, her child, and her husband. Judging by the boutonnieres, it must have been "Poppy Day."

BELOW: On the set of *Song of Songs*, the first American film without von Sternberg. By this time, her costar, Brian Aherne, had fallen in love, and it shows.

ABOVE: Before there were transatlantic passenger flights, one "reclined"
while crossing the Atlantic on the way to France.
BELOW: My father, who hated being driven by chauffeurs only slightly
more than he hated a touring car with its canvas top down, sulks, while my
mother looks patient in a mannish slouch hat.

ABOVE: The family out to dinner in Paris. Brian Aherne, who had expected to dine with his love alone, found himself part of this intimate foursome and was, naturally, very shocked. This evening my mother wore her new gilt bib necklace but wasn't sure she liked the effect.

BELOW: A few weeks later, with von Sternberg in tow, Dietrich's golden bib had been handed down to Tami. My mother had decided that it looked cheap.

achievement of being accepted by men and women alike. But Mae never came to our house, or was cooked a special dinner. Their adjoining dressing rooms were the only setting for their friendship – these two world-famous women, who played the vamp so very well. I always wanted to see them together in a film. What fun that would have been, and then again, maybe not; they might have canceled each other out.

My mother wrote to my father:

> . . . and she really took one out, Papi, shaking it as she spoke, the way someone would punctuate with a finger! There's a young, handsome cockney Englishman by the name of Cary Grant, that Jo cast as the lover. Mae found him. What do you think he does? To make more money, he sells SHIRTS on the set and he's so charming that people come from all over the lot to buy them from him!

September 8, 1932

Papilein,

I have begun to pack. The *Bremen* sails October 10th. I've let the house go after this month. It will be good for The Child to see Germany again. She is already two hundred percent American, and I long to stand on my own soil, to see Mutti.

The studio is again talking about giving me another director. Again they are so stupid! Jo describes our industry's bosses as "men who know what they want but not how to spell it." I wait for the wonderful day when we leave this house behind. Jo's secretary will find us a new one when we have to return. The bars and electric gates would always remind us of the fear and unhappiness for The Child and me.

Kisses
M.

Of course I hated the thought of leaving. Berlin had become a memory of winter cold and stone houses; and if I was far away, how would I know if that nice Mr. Roosevelt from the radio would get to be president?

SI 83 CABLE=PARIS   1932 SEP 15, pm 4 07
NLT MARLENE
HOLLYWOOD CALIFORNIA
YOU SHOULDN'T GO GERMANY NOW POLITICAL SITUATION DANGEROUS STOP
NEW ELECTIONS HAVE RAISED DANGER OF CIVIL WAR STOP MILLION KISSES
PAPI

I almost cheered when my mother read the cable, but caught myself in time. That evening, she showed it to von Sternberg.

"Beloved, Rudi must be right. Even here at the Studio I hear about some strange things going on at Ufa. I know how much you want to get away from here, but I caution you to think before you decide to rush off – simply because you want to get away from me."

He softened the last remark with one of his most tender smiles. My mother was about to retort when Chevalier sauntered in, which usually meant von Sternberg left, which he did.

BLONDE VENUS opened and was a resounding flop. Dietrich as a hausfrau was definitely not to their liking. The gorilla number with those legs, and the white tails, that was okay, but the rest the American public rejected. Completely unconcerned, my mother was just furious that some ridiculous political upheaval could keep her from returning to Berlin. Nevertheless, she decided to heed my father's warning. Von Sternberg's office was instructed to cancel our reservations on the *Bremen*, but we would keep the ones for the train. At least, we could escape the "intellectual void" of Hollywood by going to New York City. My bodyguards were told to pack for winter and to bring extra bullets.

Except for the day when I packed a few of my belongings and left my mother's house for that sad and foolish teenage marriage, I do not remember ever physically moving out of one Hollywood house into another. The only packing we ever did was clothes into trunks and suitcases. No moving-van arrival day for us. We simply walked out the front door and others changed our location for us. So it was this time. My mother always believed in the healing power of sea air. As she had done in Germany, whenever I was sick, she would again take her child to the sea, this time to recuperate from the fear of kidnapping instead of a head cold. She gave orders to find her "a house on the ocean and not in that terrible place, Malibu, where all the nouveaux riches like the Schulbergs live," and we left for New York.

We returned to a white colonial structure with overtones of ancient Greece, the guest house of the William Randolph Hearst estate, built for his mistress, Marion Davies. The main house, equally Athenian but four times the size of ours, lay to our left; a little Wimbledon separated the owners from the tenants. As the Hearsts never used their beach mansion during the time the Dietrich contingent lived next door, I never met this famous couple. My mother used to tell me, later, of banquets at the

Hearst private Taj Mahal, San Simeon, but no bacchanalian soirées in Santa Monica Athens during our stay.

Our guest house boasted a Parthenon temple entrance, a Tudor spiral staircase complete with a Versailles-type chandelier hung low from a vaulted ceiling on a chain thick enough to hold an aircraft carrier's anchor. The portico, at the back of the house, overlooking the Pacific Ocean, was pure Cape Cod, the columns supporting its roof – Hollywood Corinthian. Below, a swimming pool covered the space where a garden would have been. It and the house were surrounded by a high white wall. In the front, it shielded one from the traffic of the Pacific Coast Highway and the fifteen-story bank of earth opposite our front door, in the back, from the ocean eighteen feet away at low tide. Between the roar of twenty-foot breakers and trucks speeding toward San Diego, this house was wonderfully crazy. It became the one of *Song of Songs*, Mercedes de Acosta, Fred Perry, Brian Aherne, my father's third visit, this time special because he brought Tami, which made me happy, and a special distinction: the big earthquake of 1933.

Mercedes de Acosta looked like a Spanish Dracula. The body of a young boy, jet-black hair cut like a toreador's close to the head, chalk-white face, deep-set black eyes permanently shadowed. Her air of mystery or imminent death by consumption appealed to my mother's romantic nature. She was known not so much for her skill as a screenwriter, as for being the lover of Greta Garbo. She also laid claim to having serviced Duse. My mother told me she found her sobbing in the kitchen during a party at the Thalbergs' house. Garbo had once again been cruel to this suffering Latin lady and so, what could Dietrich do but comfort and console. This kitchen meeting had many versions but always ended with the "cruel Swede" being replaced by the "luminous German aristocrat." My mother mentions their first meeting in a letter to my father:

> Thalberg had one of those very grand parties. I met a writer, Spanish, very attractive, named Mercedes de Acosta. They say Garbo's crazy about her. For me, she was a relief from this narrow Hollywood mentality. Here they should build all the churches in the shape of a box office.
> Kisses

and again, a day later:

> Papilein,
>   I saw Mercedes de Acosta again. Apparently Garbo gives her a hard time, not just by playing around – which by the way is why she is in the hospital with gonorrhea – also she is the kind of person who counts every

cube of sugar to make sure the maid isn't stealing, or eating too well. I am sorry for Mercedes. Her face was white and thin and she seemed sad and lonely – as I am – and not well. I was attracted to her and brought an armful of tuberoses to her house. I told her I would cook marvelous things for her and get her well and strong.

De Acosta was getting stronger by the minute. Messengers arrived at our temple door, sometimes four or five times a day, bearing thick parchment envelopes from "the smitten Latin," whose stationery proclaimed, in raised letters, MERCEDES DE ACOSTA. She also assigned herself highly romantic pseudonyms, such as "White Prince" or "Raphael." My mother was also treated to this exaggerated fantasy: she became "Golden One," "Wonderful One," "Darling One" ad nauseam. I have to admit that after a few weeks of this, not all of the "White Prince's" letters were read. Some were stuffed into odd drawers, forgotten. The ones read, my mother kept for a while, then sent them on to my father.

MERCEDES DE ACOSTA

Wonderful one,
It is one week today since your beautiful Naughty hand opened a white rose. Last night was even more wonderful and each time I see you it grows more wonderful and exciting. You with your exquisite white pansy face – and before you go to bed will you ring me so that I can just hear your voice.

Your "Raphael"

It was after she stayed at our house that I came to a decision about our "Latin lover." She was so "smitten," she was boring! Maybe this suited Greta Garbo, but I knew my mother would soon find it suffocating. But she was between pictures and it helped to fill the time "being adored." So my mother played the Golden One to the hilt, and, as always with any of her roles, the costume had to match the characterization. I got to play along.

It had become a fashionable pastime in Hollywood to attend tennis matches. The great Bill Tilden was a sought-after dinner guest by the Hollywood party-givers, who always vied for any famous new blood that might come their way. The practically incestuous guest lists have always been a recurrent nightmare to would-be "hostesses with the mostest" within the industry. Fred Perry, another tennis champion, was also a courted dinner partner. Even better than Tilden, who was just brilliant on the courts, Fred Perry was a charmer both on and off. Jet-black hair, slicked down close to the head, an aquiline, handsome face, an athlete's body. I wondered if de Acosta noticed the similarity. In those days, the tennis uniform for men was immaculate white flannel trousers pleated and cuffed, creamy white silk shirt, exchanged after a match for an equally creamy polo-neck sweater. The starring cast of "Santa Monica Beach House" wore creamy white flannel trousers, shirts, and polo necks with an added Dietrich touch: an equally creamy white beret, a little Chevalier touch! De Acosta, who usually wore this exact costume, was, of course, ecstatic. It never occurred to her that our outfits could have been inspired by anyone but herself. She also took credit for my new boyish haircut – didn't she know that Dietrich never approved of female hair with masculine attire? I had worn trousers before and loved them, but now they were the uniform of the day. Fred Perry taught my mother to play tennis with great patience and lots of little passionate hugs, punctuated with rapid kissing between flying balls. I sort of hoped the smitten Spaniard might arrive and witness the smitten Englishman at work, but my mother was very skillful at keeping her admirers from overlapping.

FINALLY, VON STERNBERG returned from one of those long voyages he undertook even then, always to strange and distant places, as though looking for an impossible cure. His love for my mother left him drained and angry, usually more at himself than at her. Later, I think he hated what he considered a degrading weakness in himself that kept him passionately in love with a woman he had come to despise. He was too intelligent not to realize that his talent was forfeit.

It may not have been a conscious decision but an inner need that prompted him to once more agreeing, go along with Studio orders to change Dietrich's director, for it was not at all like von Sternberg to counsel my mother to follow any orders but his own. If he and my mother had decided not to separate professionally, no studio in the world could have forced them to do so. Together, they had been and were invincible. So, when he had that sad and stormy meeting with her that day, I think he had decided its outcome long before arriving at our house. I had seen them arguing so often, each as stubborn as the other, professional heels dug in, neither ready to give an inch. But this time was different. He was depressed but firm. She, frozen, closed in, as she always got when frightened or apprehensive. They spoke, but were so controlled, explosive emotion so contained, the air almost crackled! He told her to make her next film, *Song of Songs*, without him, and to use her contractual right of choosing her director – to be Rouben Mamoulian.

"This way, you will be in the hands of a gentleman who is also a very talented and successful director." Still no word from my mother, just that incredulous stare riveted on his face.

"He won't be strong enough to fight you, to make you understand what is needed from you to make a scene important. But, if you behave yourself, you may get away with an acceptable performance. Besides, you will enjoy designing the period costumes. No doubt that you will be beautiful, as you will have my lighting." With one last look at her stricken face, von Sternberg turned and left the room. I followed him. He looked so tired.

"Kater, I have done all I can! Take care of your mother!" As he left our house, I noticed he too was wearing white flannels. Poor Jo!

Slowly, my mother climbed the curved staircase, head down, her anger showed only in the whiteness of her knuckles as she gripped the black-lacquered banister. I knew enough to leave her be. She entered her bedroom and slowly closed her door. I had not yet been exposed to Shakespeare's plays, but when, years later, I saw my mother repeat a similar exit, I remembered this first time and knew immediately it belonged in a performance of Lady Macbeth. All was silent inside our house, only my mother's gramophone seemed alive, Tauber singing her favorite Austrian schmaltz. This was the first time I experienced this type of withdrawal, a form of mourning that was to be such a well-known behavior of Dietrich for the rest of her life. In the final years, she remained in her bedroom permanently, but in 1932, she emerged after only twenty-four hours. In her hand she held one of my notes. I had written her one of my little love notes. She treasured them, and as they seemed to lift her moods, I wrote them often, slipping my crayoned epistles under her bedroom door. I had felt that, after von Sternberg's departure, one of my notes was definitely needed. It read:

Oh Mutti! You are so sad, I miss you and I love you.

Kater

Now she kissed it, pushed it into her trouser pocket, reached out for my hand, and marched us to the library and her desk. We began opening her mail.

MERCEDES DE ACOSTA

My Wonderful One,
   . . . I am angered that anyone can hurt or wound you. . . I only know

that I would like to keep my arms around you to protect you from any pain.

I pray that I was no way the cause of this thing – that Mr. von Sternberg did not know about me. To lose such a friend as Mr. von Sternberg and harm your work just for loving me would indeed be paying too large a price. Beautiful, thrilling Firebird – Do not forget your wings that belong only to you that do not need anyone else to carry you high, up high!

Something in this letter angered my mother, for she pushed the parchment tome to one side, exclaiming, "Really, she is getting too vain – that woman!," and with that, dismissed the White Prince for the rest of the day. Years later, when I found the de Acosta letters while packing up my father's house, I realized what had prompted my mother's remark so many years ago. The ego that de Acosta displayed in thinking that she, or anyone else, was important enough in my mother's life to have been the cause of a separation between von Sternberg and Dietrich, had astounded her. No one could ever have done that, except von Sternberg himself.

A bit of comic relief was about to lighten my mother's next few days. An odd couple had recently joined the Dietrich entourage. They were always around. They tasted the many dishes and bakings, always exclaiming, "Divine," at the right moment. Clucked and listened rapt to any outpourings, were very clever in never letting it be seen that they were absorbing every juicy tidbit with which to shine in their own circles; were always available, on call, day or night, to deliver steaming chicken soup to anyone in speeding jalopy, privately noting name and address for their future use; shopped, ran errands, making themselves ingratiatingly useful to become indispensable, and thereby, permanent fixtures in Dietrich's coveted inner circle.

My mother, unfortunately, attracted their kind – we had so many of them over the years. Fame begets scavengers, whose only importance lies in the leavings they forage. My mother always fell for it. Dietrich was terribly naive about homosexual cons. Later, Clifton Webb called these two "Dietrich's private Rosencrantz and Guildenstern." She didn't get what he meant then either, she just thought it was one of his usual witty remarks.

That day, when "the boys" fluttered in aghast, I was sent out to swim. Thirty years later, my mother told it to me like this:

"Those two came to the beach house and said, 'The most terrible thing has happened!' Garbo was supposed to go north, where I don't know, and they had bought all the warm clothes for her she told them to get at the Army and Navy store. You know Garbo, never spent a cent! The car was packed and standing in front of Mercedes de Acosta's house and they waited and waited. Finally, de Acosta went to Garbo's house and there she found out that Garbo had gone away with Mamoulian instead of her. de Acosta was crying, so, of course, I took her in and fed her. In those days, they had borders between the states" (here I did not question that, as I did not want to stop her flow), "and when the border guards stopped the car to look in, they of course recognized Garbo, so naturally she had to turn around, and came back to Hollywood!"

"And de Acosta was still crying?" I asked.

"Oh, she was always dramatic – real Span-e-e-sh! Later, when I had a strep throat and the doctor said you might catch it, I went into a hospital – not a big one – some little one, near Santa Monica. There I had this nurse, who said to me, 'Guess who is here in this hospital? Greta Garbo! She's got gonorrhea!'" My mother paused for effect. "She got it from Mamoulian!"

"From Mamoulian? Really?" I gasped.

"You have to get it from *somewhere!*"

THE DAY CAME when my mother had to face what was now referred to as "Jo's desertion." The possibility of lawsuits by Paramount, as well as another suspension, and, worse, the sly rumor that Dietrich was "finished," unable to remain a star without her creator, did more to snap her into action than all her other worries. For the first time since *The Blue Angel*, she was without her private champion. She called my father at his apartment in Paris, acted out the full scene of Jo's betrayal, adding a bit of dialogue here and there to convey the drama of the situation. He listened quietly, let her play the scene to its dramatic conclusion, agreed with all the injustices done her, then calmly set her back onto the path she could logically follow. He knew that this German loved being given orders, but it was the way one gave them that got results. It went something like this:

"Mutti, you have been through so much – first with The Child, then the difficult film, and now, this! I cannot forgive Jo this thoughtlessness at this time! To desert you! He really is a cruel and selfish man!"

"No, Papi. I think he really means it for my own good."

By that remark, I knew my father was on the right track – he had gotten her to actually defend von Sternberg.

"But, you are right! I must force myself to meet this Mamoulian. They say he is Garbo's boyfriend, did you know that? Cute? Another thing I don't need! With de Acosta and now him – I'm surrounded by Garbo's lovers! Yes, I will telephone him." I was put on the phone to say good-bye to my father and took the opportunity of sending a kiss to Tami.

My mother did not telephone Mamoulian directly. Dietrich never made the first move in business, only romance. She considered it bad manners for a "lady" to involve herself in negotiations. What she did was to call her agent. She had never established a professional relationship with him because everything had always been in von Sternberg's commanding hands. But now, she needed a new buffer, a go-between, a loyal aide-de-camp.

Harry Edington arrived at our Greek temple, a slight man with one of those obligatory cashmere polo coats, complete with trailing belt. He was sharp, quick-witted, with a sense of humor and New York savvy. My mother, with a pregnant look, handed him the newly delivered shooting script of *Song of Songs*.

"Have you read . . . this 'thing'?"

Edington was much too astute an agent to admit that, despite having read it, he had once advised her to do it. So he settled himself into one of the giant black-and-silver Art Deco armchairs, his feet just reaching the floor, and under her watchful eye proceeded to reread what the first time around had already been a concentrated effort. No emotion crossed his face. Nothing, either positive or negative, for her to pounce on and confront him with. I sat in my usual observation post, the corner of the mile-long black-and-silver couch. She smoked, we waited. After a long time, he sighed, placed the thick script on the glass-and-chrome table, and looked her straight in the eye.

"It really is the worst script I have ever read! You are right! We'll have to do something about it. In the meantime, put it somewhere – where it can't smell up the house!" My mother loved it! She had a professional with taste who agreed with her and was ready to do battle for her. He left quickly with a "Leave it to me."

What he came up against at Paramount shook even him. Dietrich was to report for work on *Song of Songs* when ordered, regardless of what she thought of the script. If Dietrich did not, she would be put on suspension, forfeit her $300,000 salary, and be sued for the $185,000 it had cost the Studio to turn this property into a Dietrich vehicle. The top brass at Paramount had decided to bring Dietrich, now without von Sternberg, finally to heel. Edington was too good an agent to confront his client with this type of dictum. He knew that somehow, he had to achieve the near impossible, get her to conform, agree to do the picture – without creating any more antagonism. Privately, he was appalled at the harsh attitude against Dietrich. He also knew that, had he been allowed to function as her agent in the past, this situation would never have developed.

I always admired the way he now handled my mother. He did not know her well, but instinctively approached her correctly. He reentered our living room like a general concerned for the lives of his troops. He laid the enemy's strength before her. It seemed obvious to me – again in my corner on the couch – that he had done some added research on my mother, for he seemed to know that Dietrich spent whatever she made and never saved or invested a cent, for he stressed the loss of income – not only this time, but that she risked having monies deducted from any future salaries. That "the Studio was legally in the right" he slipped in, but immediately went on to say that that was not the most important problem. What was, was that any legal action would keep her in California and, without any money coming in for perhaps a *very* long time. With that he knew he had her, but a little insurance of success never hurt, so he added a slight suggestion: Why not meet with Mamoulian, see what he had to contribute? Maybe between the two of them something could be salvaged. Get this picture over with, then she could have that *nice long* rest in Europe. Edington was a great agent. His troops, my mother and I, were ready to do battle his way and save him, the Studio, and Dietrich a lot of grief. My mother consented to a meeting with Mamoulian, with Edington as chaperon. Dietrich always saw to it that, whenever possible, adversaries were outnumbered at first encounter.

Rouben Mamoulian was not your Hollywood-type director. No von Stroheim boots and riding crop, not even Cecil B. De Mille pomposity. What he was was East Coast Ivy League Gray Flannel Suit. His jacket actually matched his pants, complete with Brooks Brothers shirt and understated tie. And was he quiet! Mamoulian wasn't just calm, he seemed becalmed. No storms in this man's sails; even later when working with a Dietrich who was fighting him all the way, he remained unruffled. *Song of Songs* was the only film they ever made together. It always seemed to me to have a claustrophobic slowness, as though it had been made underwater.

Mamoulian agreed that the script was far from perfect, but one never knew what could be done during production. Being primarily a theater director, he thought in terms of development of approach and character within the process of the work, always risky in a technical media, and certainly impossible with Dietrich. But that he was to find out later. Now he told her how grateful he was that a Studio was willing to pay him at all for what he considered a privilege, and why not make life easy and simple by going along with what Paramount wanted?

"*Josef von Sternberg* would never agree to direct anything he did not approve of," my mother proclaimed imperiously. She got no rise out of Mamoulian, though I noticed that Edington winced. Mamoulian conceded that he was certainly not von Sternberg and that he really couldn't do much about that, but he intended to do his very best by her; after all, he was a great admirer of her beauty and her talent – now he was pleased to observe that she was also very intelligent! With that statement, I knew we were going to do *Song of Songs*. Poor Mamoulian, he didn't know what he was getting into.

Dietrich was not yet ready to "forgive" and return to the "enemy lot." Her loyalty had never been to her Studio, only to von Sternberg. But costume discussions had to begin, and for the first time, the design meetings were held at our house.

Song of Songs, being a period film, necessitated research in order to know what one could get away with without being too obviously incorrect. Whole generations have learned their history from the movies, an awesome responsibility for the industry – for the most part taken very seriously, or completely ignored. In those days, more than today, Hollywood's way of interpreting history, even everyday life, was much more flamboyant, wonderfully exciting. During the Depression, no one wanted to pay to see reality – that was there for nothing! Travis came to Santa Monica, laden down with huge books from the Costume Research Department. I was always fascinated by those exhaustive collections of drawings, illustrations, reproductions of any given period in human history. There were books on *Foot Attire through the Ages, Hats and Head Covering, Gloves, Bags and Reticules, Jewelry and Adornments, Wigs and Hair, Infant Swaddling Clothes, Aprons, Shawls and Fichus*, and much more. I remember one subtitle, "Viking Leg-Bindings," had a chapter all their own! With De Mille on the lot, of course the Egyptian and Early Christian sections took up a whole room in the Research Department. I would sit for hours, looking through these wonderful treasure troves of information. I too learned my history the Hollywood way. I discovered that at the court of Louis XVI, the ladies' elaborate wigs had little traps hidden inside to catch the mice that infested those tall concoctions of filthy, powdered horsehair. Now, with such unique knowledge, who needed school? As my mother still did not consider schooling a necessity for her "brilliant" eight year old, I was left undisturbed amidst the swaddling clothes of Celtic peasants. Later, when I finally was given some proper instruction, I was already too old to ever absorb the basic structure of grammar, spelling, and arithmetic. But in swaddling clothes, I could have gotten an A-plus anywhere!

Now we were geared to muffs and ermine tails and flounces on the bottom of Edwardian skirts. Of all the beautiful costumes in *Song of*

Songs, my mother loved her version of the principal evening dress the best. She knew she looked magnificent in it. The fact that, historically, this costume was a bit off was completely ignored. After all, if you look that breathtaking in off-the-shoulder black velvet and fabulous picture hat adorned with black egret, who cares about authenticity! Years later, when Cecil Beaton recreated this look for *My Fair Lady*, he could not use those magnificent feathers – they had been outlawed by then. But in the twenties and thirties, the slaughter of the beautiful for human adornment was rampant. Later, my mother took conservation laws very personally. She hated them. If Dietrich wanted to wear baby seal, how dare anyone tell her she couldn't? For years she smuggled bird of paradise feathers from one country to another, later storing them carefully in shrouds of acid-free tissue paper in old trunks. Animal skins, torn and mostly moth-eaten, left over from old fur coats and costumes, received the same archival treatment and rotted peacefully away, never used, but never relinquished and never forgotten.

The first part of *Song of Songs* did not interest my mother's inventive talent. She just repeated, with a few embellishments, her "sweet young peasant girl" look from *Dishonored* and went on from there.

WE WERE STILL in this preproduction period, the hair designs had not been agreed on, nor the all-important "wedding dress," nothing definitely decided and "set in work," the Studio term for when cloth was finally cut and given on to the many seamstresses, when suddenly, there was a private crisis in our house. It concerned my nurse Becky, who had fallen in love! I am not sure, but I think it was with the grocer. Now, not only was it an outrage within my mother's household to dare to fall in love with anyone but her, but to want to marry and then leave? That was the ultimate crime. My mother, who was such a fanatic about her personal privacy, had absolutely no respect for the private life of others. So big, frightened sobbing from poor Becky and strident Prussian accusations of desertion and ingratitude from my mother filled our house. Finally, like Little Eva, Becky fled across the Pacific Coast Highway and was seen no more. I must have been sad and lonely without her, but somehow, that is not a memory of that time, probably because of what happened as a direct result of Becky's leaving. My mother, as always when in trouble, phoned my father. This trans-Atlantic cry for help with The Child resulted in my father making yet another long journey to America, this time bringing

Tami with him to look after me. I was so happy that Becky and her devotion were forgotten, I am ashamed to say.

While we waited for the replacements to arrive, "the boys" were commandeered to watch The Child while she played in the ocean or swam in the Olympic-sized pool. Although I was half a fish by now, they trembled lest an accident occur and they be held responsible. As we disliked each other intensely, I am sure I made these times particularly harrowing for them. I probably dove off the deep end and then stayed under as long as I possibly could, driving them frantic. When the two could "bear no more," de Acosta volunteered for duty. Anything to get inside the house and into her "Golden One's" aura. Actually, I was much too old by this time to require such concentrated supervision, but it kept everyone busy and my mother calmed.

The time had finally come for Dietrich to meet her new leading man. Brian Aherne didn't know it, but he was halfway to being accepted before she ever spoke to him. He was English, therefore automatically "cultured," in the theater, therefore instantly far above the level of "film actor." The only thing against him was his possible stupidity for having accepted such a "stupid part in such a bad script."

Sweet Brian didn't disappoint her in any category. The day I met him, I did my curtsey, shook his hand, and instantly loved this very nice man. We became and stayed friends forever. He called me Kater, and what a father he was to me! He became my mother's lover almost immediately, and so de Acosta began to annoy. Frantic signals of denial were made to whoever answered the phone and announced the Spanish Lothario. Dietrich, who was rarely ill and considered "not feeling well" a stupid lack of self-discipline, began using this excuse with de Acosta, who was too much in love with my mother, as well as with herself, to think it could be a lie.

I could never figure out how my mother managed all those affairs without ever having a lover actually move into our house. When I was in my teens, she moved me out to different hotels and houses, supervised by governess-companions, some of them slightly unorthodox and unsavory. But when I was still a "child," no strangers ever suddenly appeared at breakfast in their dressing gowns, not even von Sternberg. Although we had so many different customers for my mother's famous scrambled eggs, they rang the front doorbell, fully clothed. Although years later, Sinatra and Gabin could lay claim to the distinction of having Dietrich come to them, she rarely left the comfort of her own environment, expecting all those who worshiped at her bed to stay there with her. It must have been so exhausting and uncomfortable for everyone, those predawn maneuvers of getting up, dressing, and driving home, only to return a few hours later as though nothing had "transpired." I am certain my mother was the one who insisted on these scenarios, Because of The Child.

It also gave her time for her manic ritual of the Ice Water and Vinegar Douche. My mother's most guarded and precious possession, besides her foundation, was her pink rubber douche bag. She was never without one in use, and had at least four backups in case one sprung a leak. Heinz white vinegar was bought by the case. Even when, in 1944, she discovered the diaphragm and bought a dozen of them before going off to war, they joined her trusted rubber bag as the first essentials packed for overseas duty. How my mother was able to escape multiple pregnancies during all those many years always amazed me. Only once did her foolproof method of vinegar and ice water fail, and she never forgave her costar for that! He was the culprit – not her trusty douche bag. It was blameless! It could do no wrong. She was sixty-four and madly in love with someone new, when, in 1965, my mother asked me on the telephone from Australia:

"Sweetheart, what is a – I'll spell it. It's a strange name – C for Charlie, O for Ocean, N for Nancy, D, Denver, O, Ocean, M, Marlene." At moments like these, I used to wonder if operators do sometimes listen in. I carefully described and explained the character and function of our subject. She exclaimed:

"Oh! THAT thing. That, I never let them use! So stupid. They have to fuss around in the dark with it. Anyway, it makes them nice and so grateful when you tell them they don't have to wear it!"

Back in those early days, all that game-playing and intrigue, seemingly for my benefit, was really unnecessary. I was accustomed to my mother always having someone around. I never questioned their gender or what they were actually there for. If they brought me expensive dolls and made a fuss over "the beautiful child," I didn't like them and stayed out of their way. If they saw no reason for courting the child simply because they were "busy" with the mother, I respected them, as I did von Sternberg and Gabin, years later.

If they treated me as an entity all on my own and judged me accordingly, as Brian Aherne did, I loved them. Some of my best friends emerged from the ranks of my mother's lovers. My life was so crazy, it is difficult to explain and equally difficult to accept, I know, but only if one compares it by normal standards. I knew no family to draw comparisons from. Also, except for my father's rather theatrical but frustrated Catholicism, I had no religious training that might at least have offered some basis of morals. After all, if you don't know what a "normal" family is, how can you recognize that yours is abnormal? My mother was either in love or out of love or in the process of falling in love – continually. Wasn't every mother? When finally I did meet my

first real family, the husband was sleeping with my mother, the wife
would have liked to do the same, and, although their daughter became
a friend, I certainly could not readjust my concept of "normalcy" from
observing her home life.

I have never judged my mother for her emotional gluttony, only for
the way she treated those who loved her. Occasionally, the rapidity of
her turnover of bed partners became embarrassing, but that one learned
to ignore over the years. I would have hated her habits more had she
been motivated by sexual appetite. But all Dietrich ever wanted, needed,
desired, was Romance with every capital *R* available, declarations of
utter devotion, lyrical passion. She accepted the accompanying sex as the
inescapable burden women had to endure. She would earnestly explain
this to me. I was a grown woman, with a family of my own, but she
felt I needed some sex education nevertheless:

"They always want to put their 'thing' in – that's all they want. If you
don't let them do it right away, they say you don't love them and get
angry with you and leave!" She preferred fellatio, it put into her hand
the power to direct the scene. Besides, European women were expected
to have great skill in that department.

Dietrich also adored impotent men. "They are nice. You can sleep and
it's cozy!" Adopted American expressions were always pronounced in
italics. Those "cozy" men naturally worshiped her. Her lack of concern,
her obvious enjoyment despite their affliction, usually brought about
miraculous cures. It was only when they regained their sexual equilibrium
that she had enough and left them . . . flat!

For a few days, all work on the preparations for *Song of Songs* was
shelved. Even our charming Englishman was temporarily put aside.
We were in full swing, getting the rooms ready, preparing for my
father's and Tami's arrival. All the things Papi might conceivably need,
want, and like were thought of and stocked. Now we also had Tami's
possible needs to anticipate. My mother's bathroom shelves and cabinets
were raided for those creams and lotions she never used. Anything that
Dietrich did not want, and Tami could be grateful for, was moved
to her room. That was the first dress rehearsal of what from then
on became the accepted procedure whenever Tami lived with us *en
famille*. She was always installed in the room next to my mother and
across from my father. Even in the many hotels we stayed in together,
this arrangement persisted. Did they really think that by putting Tami
across or down the hall from my father that I would remain innocently
unaware of the sleeping arrangements? All these elaborate, dramatically

staged maneuvers to camouflage what was so blatantly obvious? All done because "The Child mustn't know"? Perhaps there was also another reason – to repeatedly and continually remind that sweet, sensitive woman of her true position of "mistress" to the husband within the domain of his wife? How frightened Tami was of being discovered crossing the hall to my father's bedroom, for all those years in all those elegant houses and fashionable hotels we all inhabited. Why did she allow this to be done to her, I used to wonder. I was still too young to understand the destructive power of obsessive love and how easily it can be manipulated by others for their own purposes. Although by 1933 I was "a hundred years wise" in relationships between woman and man, woman and woman, effeminate men, greed, hypocrisy, and consuming mother love, I knew absolutely nothing about sex, either its biological function or emotional association. Nor that an actual physical act had anything to do with the relationships surrounding me. Even later, when I was much older and knew what was happening in my father's bedroom, I still felt the same as I had when still so innocent – just so sorry that sweet woman was made to steal across the hall and be shamed. This charade of Tami's position in the Dietrich-Sieber marriage continued even after I was a grown woman with a family and one could safely assume that The Child now knew! In 1944, when my mother joined the USO and left for war and glory, I lived for a while in my father's New York apartment. With my mother gone, Tami moved back into my father's bedroom. After all those years of subterfuge, both Tami and I loved the relief of such sudden luxurious honesty. My father didn't understand our reaction at all. Sure enough, when our "war hero" returned, back went Tami into her own little room down the hall. My father was then forty-seven, Dietrich was forty-two, and I was twenty. Nevertheless, the cruel little game of musical bedrooms continued whenever my mother was in residence, yet never, even from my earliest childhood memory, did my father and mother ever sleep together in the same room. *That* would have been just too much to ask, I supposed, even for The Child's sake. That abnormal behavior she was left to sort out for herself.

At last, the big day arrived. I was actually allowed to drive alone to the Pasadena station to meet my father and Tami. Years later I realized that Dietrich did not, at this precarious time in her career, want another "happy family" photo to hit the front pages – this time with Tami taking the place of von Sternberg. But that day I was just happy to be alone with my bodyguard going to meet Tami. I had not seen her for so long – we hugged each other with tears and happy laughter.

Soon everyone was installed and functioning. My mother's fittings began, but now, instead of accompanying her to the Studio, I stayed home. Dietrich told everyone:

"Rudi loves the beach, why ask him to give it up! Fittings would only bore him. Let them all be happy!" and she smiled, sighing bravely – the Eternal Provider for those who dozed in the sunshine. Rudi was actually quite occupied – making new friends. With his usual Austrian charm, he discussed the history of tennis rackets with Fred Perry, listened consolingly to de Acosta, gossiped with "the boys," searched for illegal spirits with his old pal Chevalier, and wondered why his wife's new English interest stayed away. The thought of meeting the husband of the woman he was in love with was a bit too much for Brian's proper concept of things. Tami cleaned, cooked her wonderful Russian dishes, and loved me without fuss or pretension. When my mother returned from work, the table was laid, the dinner deliciously ready, the house sparkling, The Child content. Naturally, as Tami was only doing what she had been brought over for, no acknowledgment or appreciation was forthcoming.

Tami swam, as my mother did, like a pregnant frog, but unlike my mother, was not afraid of water and willing to let me teach her the "American" crawl. As my father's strictness made us both nervous, we snuck our lesson whenever he worked inside on the accounts, trying to save my mother from ruin. This job awaited him on every visit. He behaved as though he resented this charge, but secretly loved the challenge of unraveling the financial mess my mother was perpetually in. Now I even had someone to disappear with whenever "the boys" materialized or Dracula, chalk-faced and forever "dying of love", appeared. As Tami thought them all as creepy as I did, we would take long walks along the beach to avoid my mother's motley crew. With Tami beside me, it wasn't so bad having my constant shadows, in full business suits, following behind. I built her sand castles, assuring her that American sand was far superior to the one we used in Swinemünde. She loved ice cream sodas, thick malteds, hamburgers with all the fixings, all of America, and me! On top of everything else so nice about her, I had forgotten how thoroughly un-German Tami was; she even thought that Goethe was rather morbid. That did it! I knew why I loved her so!

Our White Prince appeared less and less. Although her written outpourings continued to be delivered, my mother seemed irritated by their regularity. It was obvious that de Acosta's cloying emotionalism had finally begun to pall. As always with my mother, the time had come when even the most "in" person became the most "out." One just had to sit back and wait. It was inevitable. Sometime, somewhere, somehow, the lover, the friend, the one-time courted, the adored, the essential being, would overstep, make that fatal mistake, whatever it might be, at any given time, and *bang*! that private door to Dietrich slammed shut. Everyone faced this future eventually. Now the White Prince's time was near. My mother had had enough of "Greta this" and "Greta that," and de Acosta's need to tell her so.

Golden One,
   . . . To try and explain my real feeling for Greta would be impossible since I really do not understand myself. I do know that I have built up in my emotions a person that does not exist. My mind sees the real person – a Swedish servant girl with a face touched by God – only interested in money, her health, sex, food and sleep. And yet her face tricks my mind and my spirit builds her up into something that fights with my brain. I do love her but I only love the person I have created and not the person who is real. . . .
   Until I was seventeen I was a real religious fanatic. Then I met Duse and until I met Greta, gave her the same fanaticism until I transferred it to Greta. And during those periods of fanaticism they have not prevented me from being in love with other people – which seems to take another side of my nature. It was so with you. I was passionately in love with you. I could still be if I allowed myself.

My mother looked up and said to my father:
"Wait till you read this! She is going to 'allow' herself? Really! de Acosta is too vain for words!" She went back to her letter:

   Many times when I am away from you I desire you terribly and always when I am with you. I know you have felt my desire because I have known you when you felt it.
   I only am as I am, and God knows I would give anything in my life to be different. You will see I shall get over this "insanity" and then perhaps you will love me a little again. But if I do get over it what then shall I pray to? And what will then turn this gray life into starlight?
   I would like to correct a point in your mind by telling you that I never pretended to the studio to be friends with Greta when I was not! Greta for three years and a half has told me that she longed to do "Jeanne d'Arc" and wanted me to write it. When we were in Carmel, she again said she would rather do it than anything and lamented the fact that Hepburn was going to do it.

My mother was frowning! Shaking her head, lighting cigarettes – this letter seemed to never end:
"Papi, she is on again about Garbo doing 'Joan of Arc.' What stupidity!

Can't you just see Garbo – hearing voices? Being ever so religious à la
Swede? That girl Hepburn will also be awful, but at least very 'intense'
and terribly *elegant* while burning at the stake!"

My father laughed, my mother frowned over her letter:

> When I returned to the studio, they assigned me *Camille*. I told them I
> was sure Greta would not do it. Thalberg then asked if I knew what she
> would like. I suggested "Jeanne d'Arc" and spoke the truth in saying she
> has many times told me she wished to do it.
>
> Perhaps this letter will mean nothing to you. But I shall always
> cherish the days and nights that you did love me and your beauti-
> ful efforts to drag me out of my "indigo" moods. Perhaps after all
> they were not so in vain as you think as now I look back upon
> them as something marvelous and extraordinary and they give me
> strength.
>
> Darling One, I kiss you all over – everywhere. And I kiss your spirit
> as well as your beautiful body.

My mother let the White Prince flounder. She had much more important things to cope with. The Studio had come up with another demand.
They announced that they expected her to pose for the nude statue that
played an important part in *Song of Songs*. By now my mother concluded
she had "prostituted" herself enough for this film. Always one of her pet
sayings whenever finances forced her to do what she knew beforehand
would be mediocre. So she refused, informed the Studio they could use
anybody's beautiful body, put Dietrich's head on it, release the news that
Dietrich had posed nude for the statue in the film, and the tabloids would
take it from there!

"The gullible fans believe everything they read, anyway," was her
final comment. But there was another, much more important reason for
her refusal to pose nude. Her breasts. Although she maintained that she
had sacrificed a perfect pair of alabaster domes to my baby greed, I had
discovered that I was innocent of such destruction. Dietrich, young or
old, had terrible breasts – they hung, drooped, and sagged. Brassières
and, finally, her secret "foundation" were the most important items of
clothing in all our lives, for she expected those of her real inner circle to
suffer this affliction with her.

Dietrich bought every make and model of every brassiere ever designed.
If she thought she might have found the perfect one, dozens were
immediately ordered, only to end up in storage boxes when they didn't
work out after all. The first thing we did on arriving in a new town or
country was to look for lingerie shops. Maybe this time we might find the
magic cut that could transform her, as she called them, "ugly" breasts into

the pert, upstanding young glands she so desired. She agonized over each fitting. Each blouse, dress, and sweater had its own style of bra – never interchanged, always carried with us in marked envelopes, "for Fittings." For some low-cut dresses, when nothing would do the uplifting effect correctly, wide strips of adhesive would pull and fold the flesh into the aesthetic shape of a young and perfect woman. Not until later, when her amazing foundation was conceived, the best-kept secret of the Dietrich Legend, could she relax and appear perfect, as well as "naked" whenever she chose.

But even she could not invent anything for those moments when lovers waited in anticipation of perfection finally revealed. She collected thin silk dressing gowns and perfected a slithering exit from robe to under the bed sheet that was like quicksilver. She was just as expert at doing this maneuver in reverse. Sex was always in total darkness. For longer liaisons, or those that were particularly romantic, she would describe those as, "You know, when you don't have to do it right away, where they let you sleep together – nice and comfortable, not all that work!" For those preferred men, she designed flowing chiffon nightgowns with flesh-colored gossamer brassières built in. Unheard of in those days.

"In life" is a wonderful saying that I was brought up with. It means: anything that is real, as opposed to anything that is "movie star" work associated and, therefore, unreal. For those who live in a world of make-believe, it is important to maintain this distinction. So "in life" and alone, Dietrich wore severe pajama jackets and let her breasts hang down as they wished.

Every lover played a role within my mother's romanticizing, usually without ever being aware of having been cast in a role in the first place. Even if they lived with her, they never became really "in life" people. She invented the scripts that lovers unconsciously followed, believing that they alone knew her because they loved her. Yet none of them ever did. Reality and romance were not allowed to overlap in Dietrich's life.

Dietrich also believed that her hands and feet were unattractive, and therefore camouflaged them. Another saying I grew up with was "after the Russian Revolution." A common and accepted theory in the thirties was that Bolshevik hordes, once arrived, would identify and then kill aristocrats – recognizing them just by looking at their delicate white hands. My mother, therefore, always assured me to have no fear of the Cossacks. On seeing *her* hands, any good Russian would automatically accept her as a fellow peasant. One of the few times she associated herself with what she considered "lowly stock." Dietrich's photographed hands were always the first thing she retouched. Fingers were lengthened, slimmed, and smoothed. "In life," she kept them in expressive movement, posed in smoking attitudes, inside trousers pockets, or sheathed in the thinnest gloves.

It was no accident that Dietrich's shoes were superb, always handmade; the fittings took forever, but the results were ultimately worthy of the perfection of the legs they belonged to. For those hated occasions when she had to show her feet, she hid them with gossamer stockings, jewelry, dirt, and makeup, as in *A Foreign Affair* and *Golden Earrings*, or gold paint and bangles, as in *Kismet*.

Actually, it was not that she thought only *her* feet were unattractive; she believed the human foot was ugly. Noses she was not in love with either! As a matter of fact, Dietrich thought human beings, as a whole, quite unattractive. She was always amazed when seeing normal people in crowded places such as airports or hotel lobbies.

"Look at how many ugly people there are in the world! No wonder they pay *us* so much money!"

That nice Mr. Roosevelt became My President and Gladys-Marie and her baby carriage were seen no more. Everyone sang "Happy Days Are Here Again" and, for her thirty-first birthday, my mother bought herself a present. Of course, she did not think of it in that light. To her, it was simply a necessity. The chunky green Rolls no longer fitted her image. Just as Dietrich had progressed from a nightclub tart to a sleek femme fatale, it was high time for her car to do the same. For once, we were not scrutinizing glossies of her face, but equally shimmering images of cars.

With her usual perfectionism and inspired help from the famous body designer, Fisher, the Dietrich Cadillac was custom-designed and built, then delivered to our door. Long before stretch limousines existed, our new car was so long that no garage, either in America or later in Europe, was deep enough to house it. Its exceptional length was due to the specially constructed trunk, a sort of metal-encased chest of drawers, that hung on the back, and the separated driver's section that stuck out in the front. What a car! A glorified hearse, with pizazz! I loved its gray flannel interior that muffled the sound of traffic like a tomb. The recessed triple mirrors on either side of the rear seat that with just a flick of the finger unfolded, appeared like magic, their individual lights aglow, and, marvel to end all marvels, a radio that played – even when the car was in motion! For days I kept looking for its plug; my mother couldn't understand how it could play without one. The floor was carpeted in Tibetan goat. It looked so glamorous that my mother never had it changed, even though she came to hate it, for it constantly tangled its long hairs around her high heels, making her trip, catapult into the backseat whenever she entered. With this new chariot came a new chauffeur. Gone was chunky Harry of the massive green Rolls. In came Bridges, tall and sexy, of the sleek black Cadillac. Not quite as gorgeous as the car, but close. The big difference was that, whereas the car did not know it was sexy, our new chauffeur did. His livery, chosen by my mother, suited him: a cross between the costume worn by Fairbanks in *The Prisoner of Zenda* and Rudolf Hapsburg of Mayerling fame. All black, everything fitted his muscular frame perfectly, from his tall English boots that shone like ebony to his driving gloves of softest Italian leather. All he needed to complete the picture was a sword. He made do with a classy derringer for my protection instead.

I always knew when principal photography was about to begin. Long white boxes, like miniature coffins, would arrive from the only elegant florist in Beverly Hills, from director and costar. This time the longest stemmed red roses I had ever seen, from Mamoulian, who didn't know her taste in flowers – yet – and tuberoses from Brian, who was a fast learner and did.

The drive from Santa Monica to Paramount took longer than from Beverly Hills. She was tense in the car – like a soldier going into battle. I tucked the black-and-white colobus monkey car-rug closer around her. It was always cold in this desert town so early in the morning. As usual, she didn't speak. Only once, when she rolled down the partition to ask Bridges if he had all the thermos bottles in front. It was her custom to carry five tall thermoses filled with an assortment of her soups, broths, and European-type coffee when going to work. As we drove through the Paramount gate, it felt as if it was the first time. Nellie and Dot were there – waiting on the sidewalk in front of the dressing room. Some lights were already on along the street. Nellie, balancing two wig blocks, opened the screen door and unlocked the dressing room. My mother, as usual, entered ahead of us, switching on the lights as she marched to her makeup table in the back room. We followed, with our individual responsibilities: Nellie, with the two crowns of braids perfectly matched to my mother's hair; Dot, with her large special suitcase filled with makeup, all organized in individual trays that pulled out like a concertina; I, with my mother's makeup coats and mine, on hangers, draped over my arms; and, finally, Bridges, with the deep leather bag holding the thermoses. No word had been spoken. Not unusual. We were all highly trained and knew our duties. My mother took off her trousers and sweater, Dot hung them on their special hangers in the closet. I handed my mother her makeup coat; she tied the attached cloth belt tightly around her waist, pushed the sleeves up on her arms. Dot knelt, unlaced the men's oxfords and replaced them with the beige, open-back slippers. I placed the green tin of Lucky Strikes with the gold Dunhill lighter by the large glass ashtray, next to the dish with the marabou powder puffs. Dot poured coffee into the Meissen cup, added the cream. Nellie had begun to set the hair. First the waves, put in with fingers, then pushing spirals of hair onto the scalp in perfect circles, securing them with the hairpins my mother handed her. What skill it took in those days before bobby pins and rollers.

Under the hair dryer, my mother began to study her lines. I had never seen her do that before. With von Sternberg, the presence of a typed script was more a placebo to keep the Studio bosses at bay. My mother had always just listened to him tell the story, then discussed the costumes, never even asked about the dialogue. She knew, when the time came, her director would tell her what to say, how to say it, what expression he wanted in her eyes. It was not only her incredible discipline that achieved such breathtaking results on that giant screen, it was also her complete trust in the genius of her mentor.

But she had decided that Rouben Mamoulian was not genius material and so saw no reason to trust him without reading the day's scene first. I watched her. Dietrich had an interesting way of memorizing. She never spoke the lines out loud or asked to be cued. She would just read the scene over and over again without making a sound. Only when she was certain that she knew it, would she allow herself to be cued, and then only if it was a long scene. Short ones shouldn't require double-checking of her memory. She considered it her duty to know what she was expected to know. She had no interest in anyone in the scene with her. They had their duty, she had hers. They would do theirs, she hers, and the director would edit the results into a scene. In some later films, she was forced to adapt herself to more conventional procedures of creating a scene with other actors; she complied, but always with inner annoyance and impatience. She believed motion pictures were a technical process – let the machines and the inspired men working them do their magic; actors should be quiet and do as they were told. Those who wanted to "act" belonged in the theater.

The last cigarette was smoked before the mouth was put on. In those days, lip color was so thick, cigarettes glued fast in the guck. Hair combed out, test stills checked for position of waves, braids placed and secured with that famous Westmore twist – a sort of half-hitch with a straight hairpin that just missed penetrating the skull. The pain was really terrible! After days of shooting, the scalp was raw, but the hairpieces never moved an inch and that was the top priority. The Wardrobe girls arrived with the scheduled costume. They were always called "girls," no matter what their age. The Hair and Make-Up girls never touched Wardrobe. As everyone was a skilled specialist in their field, the lines were meticulously drawn and kept by all departments within the industry. Now, everything was ready. Dietrich looked perfect, not breathtaking, just perfect, and she knew it. She stood quietly waiting while we assembled our paraphernalia needed for our duties on the set.

"Let's Go!"

Lights were turned off, the door locked. Most of the stars left their dressing-room doors open, unless they wanted privacy. Dietrich locked hers, even when she wasn't there. I got into the car first. One always preceded Dietrich into a car, it made it easier for her to protect her wardrobe from creasing; even "in life," this became a rule. In the 1950s, when the pain in her legs, which she hid from the press, was so bad, this rule helped her tremendously to pretend agility. Everyone in her service was required to be trained in this procedure of allowing Dietrich to enter last and exit first from any vehicle. Nellie sat in front with Bridges. Dot walked the short distance and met us at the entrance to the soundstage. I think it was No. 5 that morning. It was precisely eight-thirty when she swung open the thickly padded door for Dietrich and her entourage to enter.

It is always dark in the vast perimeter of a lit set, and your eyes have to adjust from the bright sunlight you left outside. We looked for our allotted space. Nowadays, stars have their palaces on wheels, the mighty Winnebagos. In the thirties, stars made do with wooden rooms on little wheels, like gypsy wagons, right on the set. We found the dressing table already plugged in and lit, and that world-famous Hollywood symbol, the director's chair – the "MISS DIETRICH" stenciled in big black letters across its canvas back – the symbol of privilege, the personalized chair that no one else was permitted to sit in. Another rule accepted and adhered to by everyone.

This first morning of *Song of Songs*, we found one vital item was missing – my mother's mirror. Mamoulian had come up to her quietly, to say good morning. I think he just managed to get out "Good – "

"Mister Mamoulian. Where is my mirror?"

Mamoulian pivoted on his highly shined shoes; his assistant scurried to his side.

"Miss Dietrich's mirror – where is it?"

"Miss Dietrich's mirror? I'm afraid I don't know – Sir!"

"FIND IT immediately – please."

My mother's eyebrows arched a little at the so-unusual "please," but said nothing.

Suddenly there was a loud clatter and Dietrich's huge full-length mirror, bolted to its own trolley, rumbled into view. I looked at Mamoulian's face and realized he had thought we were looking for a normal hand mirror, not this mastodon trailing its own junction box and thick cables.

The electricians plugged it in, the grips, under my mother's directions, positioned it until she, standing on her marks within the shooting set, could see herself exactly as the camera would. Mamoulian and Victor Milner, the cameraman, watched with dawning respect, fascinated. It had taken her only seconds to know the exact angle and position of the first shot. We lived through some memorable moments that day. By the fifth take that morning, she knew she was in trouble. Mamoulian had not given her a single line reading. On the sixth take, she waited just long enough for the clap-board sound, reached her hand up to the suspended mike, tugged the boom down to her mouth, and with full amplification, whispered her misery, "Jo – where are you?" Her cry reached the remotest corners of that vast soundstage. The shocked crew held their breath; Nellie, Dot, and I weren't breathing at all. All eyes were focused on Mamoulian. The camera was still rolling.

Calmly, our director called, "Cut." Then, "Let's try it again – shall we?"

Everyone resumed breathing. Later, the sound man, instead of approaching her director, as she was accustomed to, came directly to her.

"Marlene, can I have more voice on that last sentence? A little more volume?"

She was momentarily stunned. Without von Sternberg, Dietrich had suddenly become approachable. First, she resented it, but later on, she rather enjoyed this new feeling of camaraderie. In later films, she even became the ultimate "buddy," fraternizing with the crew, mothering individual favorites, but always as a somewhat superior "lady of the manor." She never could quite manage the ease and naturalness of an American.

She did the scene again and increased her volume – slightly. When Mamoulian called "Cut – print that," her astonished expression spoke volumes. She stepped out of the set and spoke to him softly in the shadows.

"Mr. Mamoulian – I can do that better."

"Why, Marlene? It was perfect. Let's break for lunch."

We drove back to the dressing room in silence, no one daring to say a word. The Publicity man assigned to Song of Songs was waiting in front of the door, and without asking for permission, followed us inside. He announced that he had just switched a call from Louella Parsons directly through to my mother's private line. As he was informing Dietrich of this heresy, the phone rang, he answered it, acknowledged the gossip columnist, assured her that "Marleeen" was right here and just dying to talk to her, and thrust the receiver into my mother's shocked face.

She was trapped. One did not hang up on the most powerful Hollywood columnist. Years later she had her revenge and did it regularly, but not yet. Her German phrasing became more pronounced, as she tried to speak over her rage:

"Yes, it was this first day very pleasant. Yes, Mr. Mamoulian was charming, very talented also. Yes, I shall look forward to working with Mr. Aherne. Yes, it should be an interesting film. Now, I have only the lunch hour to redo the makeup, please excuse me. I must now say good-bye and hang up."

She just missed slamming down the receiver.

"Well – good – Marleen. Short – but great! Now at five p.m. we have an interview set here with photographs. It's with *Photoplay*, great – huh? Just wear a gorgeous robe – you know, as if they just caught you relaxing. Show a little leg!"

"Mister Mamoulian will never permit this," she said, as though to herself. She was wrong, Mamoulian had already cleared it, she was told. Carefully, she selected a cigarette from the mirrored box, using the crystal table lighter, ignoring the flame extended by affable "Publicity," exhaled; then, *very* carefully and distinctly, spelled it all out to him, his department, the Paramount Studio, and God!

"*Miss* Dietrich will be available at six o'clock, *not* before. Miss Dietrich will wear what *she* knows is suitable. Miss Dietrich will not discuss Mister von Sternberg. Miss Dietrich will answer only questions related to this picture. Miss Dietrich will continue the interview only as long as *she* believes it to be of any value to the film. No questions about her private life will be permitted. You will end the interview, *politely*, at six-thirty precisely!"

"But . . . Miss . . ."

She gave him one of her glacier looks. She hadn't finished with him and the world – yet.

"After this . . . *nothing!* . . . will ever again be arranged, scheduled, or decided without my permission *first!* . . . now . . . *go* . . . and have your lunch!" Nellie practically had to lead him out of the dressing room. Von Sternberg had thrown her to the wolves? So be it! Dietrich decided, on that first day of the first film without his protection, to protect Marlene Dietrich – herself! No one could or ever did do it better.

During this time, von Sternberg was in Berlin, negotiating a possible coproduction deal with Ufa. The fear and hatred of Jews, which had festered in German society much longer than any outsider realized, was about to erupt, become a convenient tool, change forever the conscience of the world. My father, ever apprehensive, called von Sternberg in Berlin, trying to instill in him some sense of the danger he was in, warning him that neither his acquired Aryan "von" nor his American passport would protect him if he insisted on staying too long in Germany. Stubbornly, Jo refused to worry about the Nazis, instead reacted to my mother's glowing comments about the filming of *Song of Songs* that had appeared in the German press.

S56 CABLE=WP BERLIN 69 5
NLT MARLENE
 HOLLYWOOD
GLAD TO SEE THAT YOU LIKE FILMING SO MUCH STOP SHAME THAT I WAS NEVER ABLE TO MAKE THE WORK PLEASANT FOR YOU STOP I KEEP MY FINGERS CROSSED FOR YOUR NEW WORK STOP HOPE IT WILL BE YOUR BEST STOP LAY IN HOTEL WITH FLU BUT WILL SOON BE ON MY FEET AGAIN SINCE FEVER DECREASED STOP KISS KATER AND THANKS FOR BEAUTIFUL PICTURES KISSES HAVE A GOOD TIME

My mother immediately telephoned Berlin. How could he – of *all* people – believe what was said in newspapers? Didn't he know she was *hating* every second of the film? That she *only* loved him? That without him, everything was misery and mediocrity?

"There is no face there! I saw the rushes – I look pretty, like a starlet! No mystery! And sometimes I even look fat! They just don't know . . . What should I tell them to do??"

Von Sternberg cabled his answer immediately. Happy that she still needed him, he used "kisses" to designate the full stop. He addressed it as usual to my mother's special cable address, "MARLENE HOLLYWOOD." As there was only one Marlene in the United States, this had been registered as her official cable address without the possibility of duplication. In 1933, anyone else named Marlene could only be three years old.

S65 CABLE=BERLIN 118 15
NLT MARLENE
HOLLYWOOD
THANK YOU FOR YOUR VOICE KISSES YOU SHOULD CALL ME MORE OFTEN SINCE OTHERWISE I AM COMPLETELY DAZED KISSES I KNOW EXACTLY WHAT YOU ARE GOING THROUGH AT THE MOMENT AND COULD HAVE TOLD IT TO YOU IN ADVANCE OUT OF A POWERFUL CLAIRVOYANCE BUT IT WAS UNAVOIDABLE SINCE WHEN I LEFT I WAS SO SHATTERED AND DOWN THAT I COULD NOT HAVE MADE A FILM KISSES DO SHOW YOUR CAMERAMAN

OUR OLD FILMS THEY WILL HELP HIM FIGURE OUT THE LIGHTING
BUT NOBODY WILL EVER PICTURE YOU AS I DID BECAUSE NOBODY
LOVES YOU AS MUCH AS I DO=

My mother was intelligent enough to realize that what von Sternberg
might autocratically get away with, Dietrich could not. One did not
take an established and respected cameraman by the scruff of his neck,
haul him into a projection room, and teach him his own profession by
viewing another man's talent. What she did do, quietly, was book one of
the Studio's private projection rooms for herself and set up a screening of
Morocco and *Shanghai Express*. Those in charge of the release order for films
to be viewed must have thought Dietrich was indulging in a narcissistic
orgy. So few ever understood my mother's ability to view herself in the
third person – a Thing, a Superior Product to be continuously scrutinized
for the slightest imperfection, instantly recognized, corrected, improved,
polished; a superb creation. Von Sternberg and she, the inventors and
guardians of the shrine for more than fifty years.

She took me with her. This was the first time I saw *Morocco*. Also, my
first experience of seeing a film from the viewpoint of a professional –
not as a spectator. My mother ran *Morocco* twice and *Shanghai Express*
for the rest of the day. She was about to become the gifted light man
and cameraman she was to be for the rest of her life. She had a true
instinct for black and white, light and shade imagery. Years later,
when color was developed, it bored her. "No mystery anymore," she
would say.

It was dark outside when we left the projection room. We had studied
all day and never taken a note. That was pure Dietrich. She never made
notes to remind herself, only other people "too dumb to remember."
We went home. De Acosta came over for dinner, we all ate Tami's beef
stroganoff. As my mother went through every scene of the films we had
seen that day, describing each shot, each look, everyone listened in their
own way.

The next morning we left at four-thirty and arrived on the set by eight
a.m. They were still setting the lights for the first shot of the day. My
mother walked into the set, shielding her eyes against the glare, looked
up to the grid, calculating the light sources and positions. Again the crew
stopped breathing – something was up. This time Dietrich was going
too far, overstepping boundaries held sacred and inviolate within the
industry. She glanced over her shoulder at her reflection in her mirror,
today waiting and positioned on its marks. She glanced quickly at the
group standing together by the camera dolly, then at Mamoulian, who
had risen from his chair.

"With your permission, gentlemen," and without waiting for anyone's consent, she began to issue instructions to the various electricians manning the lights up above.

"There – you – on the left – Come down a little – Not so fast! Slowly – More – Slowly – More – STOP. SET IT!" She had seen the second when to lock in that lamp by watching her mirror. Now she attacked the jungle of smaller wattage lamps that hung on individual stands, and then on to the all-important key lights. She washed out with light, then filled it in again, slowly. Shadows began to appear, molding and highlighting. The respect for her knowledge and skill could actually be felt in the atmosphere of the set. She glanced once more at her reflection, then straightened her shoulders, positioned her head, settled that amazing stillness onto her face, and looked directly into the lens of the camera. Mamoulian lifted the view-finder and Shanghai Lily, in all her luminous beauty, looked right back at him. Reverently he lowered the lens, glanced at his cameraman's awed expression, and, being the honest man he was, said without rancor for her outrageous behavior:

"Beautiful! Marlene! Utterly beautiful!"

She looked up and beyond the lights to the men in the shadows. One hand raised in salute, she said, quite gently, "Thank you, gentlemen!" and all those burly, tough guys stripped off their huge electrician's gloves, and applauded.

She had done it! All by herself, she had achieved what she had set out to do! I was so proud of her – I could have kissed her! Of course I couldn't because of the makeup, but I felt like it anyway.

Many things changed after this. My mother had taken command of Marlene Dietrich, the Movie Star. Other categories of her life became less important to her. Also, *Song of Songs* was the first film where the director did not come home with her after work to continue his role as taskmaster-lover. She was suddenly free to choose her activities and partners without a suspicious "husband figure" looking to discover and accuse. The real husband never spied or condemned, but the minions of ersatz ones did, an irritating trait that always infuriated her.

"Why can't they learn to be like Papi?" she would say. "Why must they all make everything so complicated?"

This overlapping of romances did get intricate at times, but my mother was a superb scriptwriter of cover stories and could juggle her invented innocence with consummate skill. For whatever reasons, most lovers fell for them. Their gullibility amazed me, but then again, most people in the throes of falling madly in love have their brains turned to mush.

Chevalier was still around and "Gallicly" adoring. He presented her with a magnificent square-cut emerald ring. It was the only perfect stone she ever received from a swain and started her love of all emeralds. Von Sternberg's beautiful sapphires paled in comparison. The fact that this rare jewel came from "the biggest miser that ever was – even for a Frenchman" always amused her. When Chevalier died in 1972, my mother immediately took to drinking huge quantities of Contrexeville, a diuretic mineral water, saying:

"He couldn't pee – that's why he died! I'm not going to die of that! But Chevalier was *so* stingy – he probably didn't even want to give his pee away for nothing!"

De Acosta, getting desperate, was offering my mother all sorts of services, wrote her:

I will bring anyone you want to your bed! And that is not because I love you little but because I love you so much! My Beautiful One!

I wonder what would have happened had my mother taken her up on her offer and said . . . "Bring me Garbo!"

My father must have arranged the running of the house and me to his satisfaction, for his cowhide steamer trunks were being packed and ready for the Paramount truck. Tami now had an extra trunk for all the outfits my mother had given her. If she had bleached her hair, she could have passed for a poor man's version of Dietrich; I suppose, even without the peroxide, she was that anyway. I wanted her to stay with me, but, of course, did not voice such a crazy wish; I knew she belonged to my father. So, they left for the station, train, ship, and Paris. Tami and I cried, my mother and father didn't. I have no memory of who or what took over the job of watching me inside the house. Outside, the bodyguards remained, patrolling me and the hot Pacific beach in full business suits with obvious bulges under their armpits. Subtle disguises were never their forte. They were sweet, though, and tried to melt into the scenery, but on a deserted beach that was hard to do.

Fred Perry got lost somewhere. I think it was in the direction of Constance Bennett, who collected tennis players at the time. Brian returned, was romantically in love, with a bit of British Empire flourish for good measure. Years later, when he portrayed Robert Browning in *The Barretts of Wimpole Street*, his performance took me back to those days of *Song of Songs* and the Santa Monica house. His joy was so apparent, the memories of his affair with my mother are of happy days. That is, until the time came for him, too, to be hurt and confused – not knowing what hit him. But in the early months of 1933, Brian had no inkling of what awaited him and was, therefore, still sublimely happy.

Brian became a fixture and the usual groupies took flight. I loved him for that as well. But then, he was so easy to love. He was such a kind man. He gave me my first book of Shakespeare's plays and taught me not only to read it in English but to understand some of it. He even took me, just the two of us, to the Biltmore Theatre in downtown L.A. – one never went that far, ever – to see my first Gilbert and Sullivan operetta, *H.M.S. Pinafore.* He took this child of celluloid and introduced her to the enchantment of the theater. I couldn't believe it. Something actually existed that was magical – without my mother being a part of it? Amazing! I had a giant crush on Brian Aherne when I was eight that never wavered, only matured into devoted friendship. Always I have been grateful for what he did for me.

I had two real friends during my childhood from whom I learned. Tami taught me what tragedy was, and Brian showed me that I existed, that the umbilical cord with which my mother tethered me was her doing, not nature's. I was still too young to understand it all, but I felt that these two good people loved me, just me, and for no special thing I had done to earn it. Therefore, was I perhaps lovable without my mother being the cause or result of it? I did not share this heady discovery with anyone. As with most precious possessions, one protects them from human vandalism. As I grew, I hoarded what was important to me, watched, listened, spoke only in reply, and then, usually, only what adults wanted to hear. My training in hypocrisy was phenomenal. My mother had the "perfect" child. She took great pride and full responsibility for my impeccable manners, my straight-backed, ankles-crossed, hands-in-lap stillness. Always obedient, automatically willing to obey commands, yet alert and intelligent, proving her excellent training when spoken to by coworkers or other professionals. My table manners were flawless – five forks and five different-sized wine glasses did not fluster me, just boring and tiring. It meant a long meal! But you restraightened your already rigid spine, smiled politely, waited until your gorgeous mother began eating, before you selected the correct utensil and took your first bite of Mousse de Canard à l'Orange.

I am always suspicious of perfectly behaved children and their self-satisfied parents. I search: Somewhere behind that ideal exterior, there may be a real child, crying to get out.

Thanks to my father, I now had a tutor who came to the house in the mornings, gave me lessons in German literature, with orders from my mother that "really only Goethe was essential," with penmanship a close second. The fact that this calligraphy was done in the ancient German script taught me nothing except a certain skill in the care and use of quill tips. I am still very handy at making felt pen wipers. After such arduous and productive schooling, the chauffeur would pick me up at noon and whisk me off to fantasy land, my preferred reality. It's a good thing my mother did not let me go to school after all. At the age of "just" eight, I would probably have flunked kindergarten.

On the days I had my tap dancing lessons, I did not go to the Studio. I had seen Ruby Keeler in 42nd Street and instantly knew that a short, pleated skirt above flashing tap shoes was my true destiny. Immediately, a portable wooden dance floor and appropriate costume were ordered from the Studio. A bicepted, jaunty tap dancer, who believed he was Busby Berkeley but wasn't, arrived with the floor, clicked his taps, and presented me with huge, white satin tap shoes. With me looking like Minnie Mouse, we struggled valiantly to make my dream come true. I got as far as "Shuffle Off to Buffalo" and a ludicrous version of the "Suzy-Q" before we both agreed that my destiny must lie somewhere else. But he needed the money, and to keep in with the Studio Dance Department, and I was expected to do what I was told, especially if I had asked for it in the first place; so we compromised – I cranked the handle of the gramophone, while he danced.

When my mother came home, she would tell me what had happened at the Studio:

"Sweetheart, you should have been there today. Brian was too funny. You know the scene where we have to run romantically up the hill together, hand in hand? Well, we are on that real hill on the back lot and they covered it with extra fake grass to make it look more real. So, we do the scene over and over again, like working for Mister von Sternberg. Brian could not run right – even with those long English legs of his. They don't learn to run up hills in the theater. After each take, we had to get cleaned off – the fake grass sticks to everything – redo the makeup, the hair. Between the sun, the lights, the reflectors, the wind, and the bugs, who liked the glue they used for the grass, Brian and I look like a disaster – not romantic at all! Then, we are crouching in the fake grass again, waiting for 'Action,' so we can come up into frame and start running. Right? Suddenly Brian looks down and sees a teensy-weensy grass snake, turns white, grabs my hand, and starts racing up the hill – dragging me behind him! He is so scared stiff, he doesn't stop! Mamoulian is screaming, 'CUT,' I'm screaming, 'We have passed our marks!' but he just keeps on running. We would have been in Pasadena by now if a grip hadn't caught Brian and held him – physically! Mamoulian was still yelling 'CUT.' I had lost one of my beautiful shoes somewhere along the mad dash, and of course, *that's* the take they printed! Mamoulian was so happy that Brian *finally* got it right. If they only knew – it was the *snake* that did it!"

So the sunny days came and went. *Song of Songs* was nearing completion. My mother still cooked, but now only those days when she was not on call – or Brian stayed for dinner. Of course, our Sunday baking extravaganzas continued. No matter how hot the day, my mother's oven produced! And always the same recipe! If you made the best Gugelhopf in the world, why bake anything else? A little like her career – don't try to change perfection, just repeat it!

MY MOTHER WAS SHOOTING the velvet evening dress scene that afternoon. I was laboring over my German penmanship, when suddenly my copybook scooted off in one direction while my hand flew the other way. My desk moved toward the opposite wall, my chair buckled, dumping me onto the blue linoleum. My teacher screamed, grabbed my arm, and we ran toward the main staircase. As we were trying to go down, it was coming up toward us. The huge chandelier was swinging from its cupola ceiling, hundreds of crystals jingling.

"We must get down the stairs and stand in the door frame – it's the only safe place!" my teacher shouted. She must have been a true Californian and earthquake-trained. We made it to the front door just as the chandelier crashed behind us, spraying glass everywhere. We wrenched open the heavy door just as, with a tremendous roar, the embankment slid down onto the Pacific Coast Highway, blocking it completely with earth and uprooted palm trees. The noise was incredible. Then, suddenly, everything stopped – utter silence! The palm trees seemed to quiver as they settled into the dirt, a limbo moment – then people shouting, and from everywhere, sirens. We were safe, but my mother had no way of knowing that.

When the earthquake hit, she was on the set. As the first tremor shook the soundstage, the grips on the catwalks, always the most vulnerable, grabbed their safety railings with one hand, their giant arc lights with the other. The huge set cleared in seconds. My mother, her long skirt clutched around her waist, ran toward her dressing room, her only thought to get to a telephone and call me. With the sidewalk swaying under her, she was sprinting along, nearly at her door, when Chevalier ran out in front of her, arms open to receive her, crying, "*Mon amour* – at least we can die *together*!" The "at least" was explained by my mother, whenever telling this story, as referring to their inability to make love owing to Chevalier's impotence – but "dying"? That they could do together, "at least." She didn't even stop, just ran around him, but before she could reach her door, she collided with a well-known actress, whose name always eluded her. This nameless star is supposed to have exclaimed:

"What are you running for, Marlene?"

To which my mother says she replied – gasping for breath:

"My child! I must reach my child! She is in Santa Monica!"

"Don't be so upset. She'll be okay – my children are there too and I am not worried!"

My mother screamed at her:

"Yes, but *your* children are adopted!"

To be fair, my mother told this story on herself, adding, "Wasn't that terrible of me to say that? But it is *true*. How *could* she know – she never had a child of her *own*."

As all phone lines were down, I also did not know what might have happened to my mother in the earthquake. Long Beach, just a few miles down the coast, was leveled, but our Grecian temple stood, except that now our swimming pool was in the playroom and the hall was full of powdered glass.

My mother arranged to move us into the Beverly Wilshire Hotel for the night. After the phones were repaired, we spoke, and as she could not get through the earth and roadblocks, we rendezvoused at the hotel. In the car, driving there, my mother's maid kept crying and muttering, "In Germany, we don't have earthquakes! Ever!" Of course, all this drama was very exciting, besides, I loved the Beverly Wilshire – their drugstore fountain made the best black-and-white ice cream sodas in Hollywood! My mother and I shared a double room. Before going to bed that night, we placed our tooth glasses, their rims nearly touching, on our night table. When and *if* any aftershocks occurred, the glasses would move together, making a clinking sound, enough to wake two nervous sleepers and alert them to further danger.

Our glass trick woke us often during the night. Each time we would dash down the stairs to the lobby, six floors below – meeting up with the other petrified hotel squatters in their resplendent dressing gowns. The elevators were too dangerous, and therefore forbidden. So, after each ominous rumble, we climbed back up to our suite to sleep, only to be awakened again a short time later and do our escape act all over again. After about the fifth or sixth time of this Marx Brothers routine, I remember moving our glasses apart and telling my mother that earthquake or no earthquake, she had an early call in the morning and needed to sleep. She agreed, besides, if anything disastrous were to happen, we would die "*together.*" My mother was always content with the possibility of those she loved dying *with* her. Poor Chevalier would have been shattered that he didn't qualify! Those my mother chose as being the privileged few for this honor of dying with her were never asked their preference – it was, of course, assumed that we would welcome the final end – if in her company.

In the morning, the Beverly Wilshire Hotel was still standing and the switchboard called to announce that Miss Dietrich's car and chauffeur were ready and waiting. It was work as usual. Paramount sent men and hoses to pump our pool out of the house and the Prop Department hung another crystal chandelier. As they were using all the Versailles ones on a picture, we got a Franz Josef model instead. It looked very pretty. Austrian Empire went very well with Hollywood Greek. But we never could get rid of the chlorine smell. When my wooden tap floor developed damp rot, stank of mildew, my dance lessons were canceled and Ruby Keeler was safe forever.

Mamoulian, looking gaunt but happy, intoned those always somehow moving words – "Okay, boys, that's a wrap!" *Song of Songs* was in the "can." He kissed my mother gently on the cheek, actually blushing, still her fan even after all those weeks of strain and dissension.

Always, after a film is finally completed, the company gives itself a farewell party. An enormous family shindig – everyone loving everyone, all hatchets buried, and not in each other for once. The "bigwigs" always gave presents to each other and to members of the crew. My mother was duly famous for hers. Twenty-dollar gold pieces that had been sliced open in order to implant paper-thin watches within, one half functioning as the lid that flicked open when a tiny spring was pressed along its edge; gold Patek Philippe wrist watches, with either black or brown crocodile straps. She had a thing about watches for men, and always gave them with personal messages engraved on the back, with her unique signature below. Gold cigarette cases, precious cuff links were her third choice; then came crocodile leather wallets, with or without gold corners, gold lighters, and so on down the luxury scale. For the few women, there were clips from Cartier. The special ones got them with diamonds, the others rubies, then sapphires, then patterned gold, followed by handbags, scarves, and perfume.

Brian had a stage commitment in London. His contract stipulated that he would be free to return to England without having to wait around after the completion of the film, as was the rule in case of possible retakes. His

farewell was not too depressing; we would see him soon, somewhere in
Europe. So we both kissed our favorite Englishman and said good-bye.
He left an order at the florist for a dozen tuberoses to be delivered to
my mother every day and exited with panache. My mother was like the
proverbial horse chafing at the bit, knowing the stable is near. Soon she
too could get out of Hollywood.

S4 CABLE=PARIS 38 18
NLT MARLENE
HOLLYWOOD, CALIF=
WOULD NOT GO GERMANY WITHOUT NEW AMERICAN CONTRACT IN HANDS
THEN NOBODY CAN PREVENT YOU FROM LEAVING GERMANY STOP LOVE
KISSES

PAPI

Of course, she was furious. It meant another delay. But she knew
that my father was probably right. Edington had been negotiating a
new contract for her ever since the beginning of *Song of Songs*. Now
she finally allowed him to present it to her. When he told her that
she would retain her right of approval on both script and director,
she signed the new contract without any further discussions. The
clauses relating to the number of films agreed to a year and the
sizable increase in salary were secondary to her. Control, particularly
contractual proof of control, she always considered the most important
part of any agreement.

Again my father, ever the cautious watchdog and informed travel
adviser, having made a fast reconnaissance trip to National Socialist
Germany, cabled from his regained safety of Paris:

S98 CABLE=PARIS 44 2
NLT MARLENE
      SANTAMONICA CALIF
SITUATION BERLIN TERRIBLE EVERYBODY ADVISES AGAINST YOU GOING STOP
MOST BARS AND THEATERS ARE CLOSED STOP CINEMAS IMPOSSIBLE STREET
EMPTY ALL JEWS FROM PARAMOUNT BERLIN HAVE BEEN MOVED TO PARIS
VIA VIENNA PRAGUE STOP I EXPECT YOU CHERBOURG CABLE WHEN AND HOW
MANY ROOMS AND FOR HOW LONG STOP RECEIVED FIVE PACKAGES PHOTOS
FANTASTIC MAGNIFICENT I WAIT FOR YOU
LONGING KISSES

PAPI

My mother was not too upset; as long as she could leave America, Paris
would do fine. It was decided that our booking on the *Europa* could stay as

is, as she stopped in Cherbourg before docking in her German home port of Bremerhaven. Packing lists were begun, my father started hunting for the perfect hotel for the Perfect Woman, who was going to pay for the entire lavish trip, with a contract to record six new songs for Polydor – the company that had issued her *Blue Angel* and *Morocco* records.

The rumor that the governing council of Paris would not permit Dietrich within the limits of its city while wearing male attire made headlines around the world. If this was true, or just a brilliant and very successful publicity stunt, was never proven to my satisfaction. Years later, the Connaught Hotel in London used the same tactic against Dietrich's pants; that time she was joined in her "deluxe hotel exile" by Katharine Hepburn, and again, the world press lapped it up. A gimmick that works for thirty years can't be all bad! What I do know is that the story of my mother being denied access to the boulevards of Paris while wearing trousers was always discussed as though it was a funny story and never on the basis of a personal outrage. I believe that if any city had the temerity to actually refuse Dietrich entry because of improper attire, it would warrant from her such fury that Dante's Inferno would have paled in comparison, not just a smirk and a chuckle.

Still, my father searched for hotels outside the city of Paris for whatever reason, while my mother began the long and exhausting grind of publicity portrait sittings at the Studio, for the first time without von Sternberg's loving and magical eye beneath the black cloth of the view camera. Days of preparing and assembling the private, professional outfits, their accessories, the jewels, the hair, the backdrops, and the Studio portrait-gallery props. Not only were orders from the front office filled for "private" Dietrich material, but fan portraits were needed in *Song of Songs* clothes, especially her favorite black velvet off-the-shoulder gown.

Eugene Richee had learned his lessons well. He took some of the most beautiful of Dietrich's portraits during this sitting in 1933. She, as usual, had to be part of every process. As long as the subject was Dietrich, my mother regarded all photographs as her property. She never understood "the audacity," as she referred to it, of a photographer owning any image of her face. The Dietrich face belonged to Dietrich and no one else. In the later years, it drove her crazy whenever Hurrell or Horst sold a special photograph of Dietrich without giving her the money, or Milton Greene complained when she used his work for any project of hers, whenever she wished, never asking his permission.

After this particular sitting, as with all the sessions, she presided over the contact prints, chose those she might okay, rejecting those that in her opinion did not come up to the Dietrich standard, and then it was retouching time. She shaped the nose, the hands, the knees, though rarely in those days were cheesecake shots tak.n of her. The hair, the corners of the mouth, the shoulder and bust line, were perfected by her merciless wax pencil. As she always did when the finished product pleased her particularly, she would order copies for herself, always by the dozens, in eight-by-ten- to sixteen-by-twenty-inch sizes, in glossy, matte, and quality papers impossible to find today. As soon as the Still Department delivered the heavy cartons, it was "mail time." Special cardboard-filled photo mailers, elephant gray with the Studio logo, were always at hand, crates of them, at home as well as in the dressing room. Every acquaintance, friend, and family member received samples of the latest proof of her beauty. When that was done, she took the stacks of pictures and lugged them around the Studio; wherever she could find anyone she knew, she sat them down to look. She would arrive at a dinner party laden with twelve-by-twenty-sized examples of beauty and photographic perfection. Many dinners waited and wives fumed while my mother displayed her sublime images. The photographer was never given a moment's thought. After all, without her – he wouldn't have had anything to photograph. She had even retouched his mistakes for him.

Von Sternberg returned, took one look at the rough cut of *Song of Songs*, saw how much she needed him, and decided he would agree to direct Dietrich's next film, saw the way Brian had gazed into her eyes in the close-ups, walked into our beach temple, met the smitten Spaniard, saw the framed pictures of Brian and Chevalier all over the place, and slunk home to lick his wounds in private.

Between packing her trunks, my mother decided to "forgive" von Sternberg for having deserted her, adored him, cooked for him, let him love her, wrote him warm letters hand-delivered by our sexy chauffeur, whom Jo didn't like either.

By the time the trunks were packed and ready, von Sternberg had been convinced once again that he was, had always been, the *only* one. If one loves that deeply, accepting lies as truth becomes a desperate necessity.

My mother gave von Sternberg orders to find her a house, up high somewhere, away from the sea. The salt air had rusted her special French sewing needles inside her travel case and that finished the Pacific Ocean forever! The gray coffins stood in line – waiting for the Paramount truck. I had a new navy coat, with matching silk braid, and held my white cotton gloves, carefully. I watched my mother descending the staircase. There was a subtle change in her. She had made her first American film without von Sternberg and survived. The world had not come to an end. She was not completely convinced, but it might just be possible that Marlene Dietrich was a powerful star in her own right without the necessary presence of her creator. This dawning realization was a

turning point in my mother's life. Never again would she be quite as
dependent, nor as pliable, where he was concerned. All future work
with von Sternberg was motivated out of respect and genuine gratitude,
but never again from total professional dependency. She was mistress of
herself and had the money to back it up. We boarded the Chief that day
with emotional banners flying.

Even before we pulled out of the station, my mother began her usual
train routine. The moment we entered our compartments, all shades
were pulled down and secured. There might be faces staring through
the windows – hoping to catch sight of a Movie Star. Now hidden
from the curious, with all the doors locked, she took off her departure
outfit, and, as it would not be needed again, proceeded to pack it into
a specially tagged and waiting suitcase. The next set of clothes, marked
"Chicago arrival," assembled weeks before, was already hanging in one of
the closets of our drawing room. When she had tissue-papered and folded
everything to her satisfaction, the now redundant suitcase was sent to the
baggage car to join its matching brothers of about forty pieces. As the
"coffins" had been shipped ahead, we were traveling "light."

Next, she removed the hated garter belt that always left a red welt
around her waist, then the expensive silk stockings. She rinsed them out,
carefully hung them over the towels to dry. As her brassière was packed
away with the shirt it belonged to, she put on her favorite model, the
one with the wider straps. As Dietrich would not be seen for the next
few days, she could afford to let her visual guard down.

She washed her face, as usual with only soap and water, and brushed
every curl out of her hair. A navy blue pajama with its matching man's
silk dressing gown completed the transformation. With her scrubbed face
and slicked-back hair, she looked like a young boy. A very sexy young
boy, straight out of a Noël Coward play.

My mother preferred traveling east. It meant Hollywood was behind
her and the intense heat of the desert states could be endured at the
beginning of a trip, instead of at the end, when she would be preparing
herself for an arrival. Why she disliked heat so much when she never
perspired, always intrigued me. This possible misfunction of her sweat
glands was a phenomenon one just had to accept. Dietrich was immensely
proud of never needing dress shields in any of her clothes or costumes.
After deodorants and antiperspirants were developed, she enjoyed telling
how she never needed such things.

"But why do people *get* so hot? And it looks so *ugly*! – and terrible for
the clothes!"

I often wondered if my mother just made up her mind one day that
she would not sweat and thereafter remained dry for the rest of her life. I

wouldn't put it past her. Whatever the reason, when others drooped and glistened, Dietrich marveled at the discrepancy between the Chosen and the rest of humanity and – remained dry.

This was the first trip I was allowed to become my mother's Private Attendant. To set up my mother's desk was akin to laying out an instrument table for open-heart surgery. Each item had its exact place and function. Baccarat ashtray on her right – slightly up and off center. Stemmed water glass directly above it. As European mineral waters were unavailable in America then, we brought our own spring water with us. The glass was filled, three-quarters full, and the bottle removed. A narrow, red-lacquered Chinese tray – an acquired prop from *Shanghai Express* – contained her red and blue pencils and Waterman pens, positioned dead center, directly above the large desk blotter from Hermès. Off center and slightly to the left, a bottle of blue ink. Next to it, two boxes, one containing large-size blue monogrammed paper, the other, envelopes. Below that, her woven gold cigarette case and lighter. Slightly to the left of them, the stack of Western Union forms – with their bits of carbon paper cut to size. The final item: a saucer filled with fifty-cent pieces for tips. They jingled and bounced, especially when we went around curves.

In Albuquerque, von Sternberg's first telegram caught our train, telling his beloved goddess he was lost without her; by Kansas City, he had discovered he really couldn't stand being without her:

KZ 142 51=LOSANGELES CALIF 11 523P
MARLENE SIEBER, SANTAFE CHIEF DRAWING ROOM B CAR 202 = DUE KANSASCITY 945 PM=

BELOVED GODDESS
EVERYTHING IS SO EMPTY AGAIN AND I BURN BECAUSE OF LONGING FOR YOU AND LOVE. PLEASE EXCUSE MY STUPIDITIES. ALL MY THOUGHTS ARE WITH YOU.

                                                              JO

In Chillicothe, Illinois, our Spanish Lover mooned her loneliness and Chevalier wired he was impatiently waiting, longing for her in New York. Across America, my mother's loves kept telling her how much she meant to them. She thoroughly enjoyed the trip.

While my mother wrote her coded telegrams in various languages, I curled up on the bed in the other compartment and watched the endless desert become endless cornfields. But when you heard, "Sweetheart!" you had to move, and fast. It meant we were approaching a scheduled stop and that Dietrich had a sheaf of telegrams ready to be delivered to our porter. I would run down the Pullman car, stand back as the porter swung open the heavy door, pulled up the iron trap that concealed the steps and, grabbing his special stepstool, jumped onto the station platform, all in one continuous action before the train had come to a full stop. With the stepstool beneath the Pullman car's steps, I could quickly descend without having to leap a chasm. I handed over the forms. While he sprinted to the station house and telegraph operators, I waited and breathed in Kansas City.

Back he came, handing me the usual bundle of beige Western Union envelopes for my mother. I scampered up. With one white-gloved hand clutching his stool and the other the handrail, he reversed his earlier exit maneuver – just like running a film backwards, this time shouting, "All ABOOOARD!" as he hung there in midair. We did this trapeze act at every whistle stop across America and, in the process, became great friends. My porter friends would tell me stories – of real families, with real children, and places called farms. From them I first learned that we were living in the Great Depression, that bread lines existed, that the color of a person's skin could cause great suffering and preordain their life.

My mother never fraternized with the help. She did not like the color black, except in clothes. When questioned about my long absences, I explained that I had been in the observation car. In those days, it had a platform with a railing, like a small balcony, outside at the very end of the train. It was a magic place, and I did spend a lot of time there. In the daytime, you could see where you had been only seconds before; at night, the stars traveled along with you and the air smelled of honeysuckle.

I kept my friendships to myself and thereby saved them. Years later, I discovered just how deeply rooted my mother's racism was. Although a common failing with her generation, especially with those brought up in exclusively Caucasian environments, still, it was very un-Dietrich as far as the legend went. Once, when confronted very lightly by me, she gasped:

"But Nat King Cole was a friend of mine! I *loved* him! He was so brilliant in Las Vegas!" deeply hurt and shocked. "How can you say I don't like them? I had maids that were black! It's only those that think they can be nurses that I can't stand! And those frightful wigs they insist on wearing. How can *they* be allowed to be nurses? Their hands always look dirty!" Lena Horne, of course, would have been acceptable as a member of the nursing profession; not only does she wash, but my mother thought she looked so beautiful in white.

Our arrival in Chicago went without a hitch. First, my mother endured the waiting reporters and their papers' photographers, as Resi, Nellie, and I were whisked off to the Blackstone Hotel by my bodyguard. She followed, entering the hotel as I had, through the kitchens and our suite via the service elevator. This subterranean escape from the press and fans became so regular, in some hotels I never knew what their lobbies looked like, or even where they were, but I knew what the soup of the day was going to be, and, if the seafood salad smelled funny as we dashed by it, not to order it for lunch!

As always, the Blackstone meant bath time. Everyone washed all over, for the first time since leaving California. When we were traveling west, we washed there anyway, although we had just done so only one day before. It was just a set habit to get clean at the Blackstone in Chicago. Of course, this included the hair. When making a reservation for Dietrich, one always requested a professional hair dryer, usually sent up from the hotel's beauty parlor. My mother sat under the huge metal dome, reading, while room-service waiters set up our breakfast table.

What makes room-service breakfast so distinctive? Is it because it is brought to you with a slim silver vase and delicate fresh flowers? Linen, slippery with ironed starch, bright-colored juice nestled in sparkling igloo, little chrome racks of perfect toast, glistening jams with tiny fluted spoons, and all the china matches? The secret must be that it is such a pretty way to start a day. My mother missed all the fun of those times of luxury and elegant abundance. She drank her coffee, remarking that soon she would be able to have "real" coffee in Paris, took a bite of toast and mumbled "lukewarm Kotex." I couldn't think what she meant by that, although her disapproval was obvious. I often wished my mother would enjoy something – just for the fun of it! But, for her, there had to be a good reason for pleasure, otherwise it might be frivolous and, therefore, suspect. She was so very German. Years later, she would say to me with longing, "Remember how we used to laugh?" and I would say yes, to make her feel good, but rarely do I remember my mother laughing out of pure joy.

It was time! Out we rushed, past the foggy steam stables, boarded the 20th Century Limited as it was about to leave. We were squeaky clean and ready for New York. As the Ambassador was less public than the newer hotels, it had been chosen for the rendezvous that I later learned was planned between my mother and Chevalier. We only had two days in New York before the *Europa* sailed, and she usually did not like "matinees," her term for assignations that fell into an earlier time slot than the usual *cinq-à-sept* period accepted in Europe as proper for sexual encounters. I was asked if I wanted to go to a movie! Like asking an alcoholic if he wants a drink! I immediately knew I was being evacuated and pressed my advantage by asking if I could go to the new Radio City Music Hall and be allowed to stay and see everything! Wurlitzer organ recital and all. How I loved that hymn to Art Deco. Radio City always reminded me of our first Beverly Hills house, and I felt at home there. And later when I begged Nellie to "just let me see the stage show over again – *please*!" I was allowed to stay and see the whole program, movie and all, from start to finish! Chevalier must have had a wonderful afternoon and evening – I know I did!

When I got back, bleary-eyed but happy, my mother was sitting at the desk, calm, perfectly groomed – not a hair out of place, as though nothing had happened. I don't know how she always achieved that celibate look of hers.

I washed my hands and changed my "dirty from the filthy street outside" shoes, then she read me my father's latest cable:

RCD AT 40 BROAD ST
CABLE=PARIS
NLT MARLENE DIETRICH
AMBASSADOR HOTEL PARK AVE 51ST NYC

EX WIFE OF MAURICE CHEVALIER UNFORTUNATELY AT CHATEAU MADRID WHICH IS ONLY HOTEL OUT OF TOWN STOP ON SUNDAY WILL LOOK AT FANTASTIC HOTEL VERSAILLES LITTLE BIT FURTHER BUT WONDERFULLY UNDISTURBED STOP CITY IMPOSSIBLE STOP WILL BE WAITING FOR YOU CHERBOURG STOP BUY THE TICKETS FOR THE SPECIAL TRAIN ON BOARD SHIP LOVE MISSING YOU ETERNALLY YOURS

                                                            PAPI

I was sure he would come up with the perfect hotel. My father was an inspired travel agent.

We kissed Nellie good-bye; she had come east only to do the hair, was returning to Hollywood. We exited the Ambassador in convoy. Resi, my bodyguard, I, and our clone from the New York office of Paramount, left the hotel by the lobby and into the waiting limousine. I wondered what the kitchen was offering today. My mother, who was scheduled to leave later and certainly would take the subterranean route, would be able to tell me.

My group arrived at the North German Lloyd pier where our ship, the SS *Europa*, loomed above us, gangplanks protruded from her hull like harpoons from the side of an overkilled whale. Everywhere the frenzy of scheduled departure, porters dashing about, trunks and baggage everywhere creating crazy mazes for hundreds of people to get lost in, everyone shouting to someone, who shouted to someone else, who disappeared or reappeared as they searched for friends, lovers, family, stateroom, A Deck, B Deck, Promenade Deck, purser, stewards, Aunt Emily, and the porter who had all their hand luggage and had disappeared "perhaps in that direction?" On the pier, the brass band played, unruffled, as though it was a quiet Sunday concert in the park. Like the orchestral selections at the Academy Awards, where the music matches the winner, the music always reflected the nationality of the ship. I can't recall what we got for the *Bremen* or that evening for the *Europa*, but it must have been some dirge with a Teutonic lilt. Probably something Wagnerian, done with a lot of tuba. Thank God that Austria did not have an ocean liner. My mother would certainly have traveled on it and then we would have been smothered in weeping violins and accordions. The French, forever typical, played their national anthem. Trust them to be frugal and know when they're onto a good thing. The British were the showmen. Their Cunard Line had a repertoire that included "Pack Up Your Troubles in Your Old Kitbag and Smile, Smile, Smile," "It's a Long Way to Tipperary," "Rule, Britannia!" and their pièce de résistance, as the tugboats gently "tugged" the ship out into the harbor, a lilting chorus of "Auld Lang Syne!" A few tears amidst all that gaiety never missed. The effect was so stirring that it became the custom to play this haunting tune for all departures, regardless of a ship's nationality. The United States line had Sousa and no one could really top that, although the British came close. We never traveled on an American ship. My mother, the eternal European, wanted to get away from all things American and not prolong the mediocrity by an "American" crossing.

"They probably serve Coca-Cola with dinner," or "I'm sure American stewards say 'Hi!,'" and "All the china probably has an American flag on it, the whole ship, nouveau riche like the Waldorf-Astoria," were some of my mother's comments.

Music followed one on board. No brass, but the dedication to continuous "soothing of the savage passenger" continued. In those days, Muzak à la human! Every ship had its Palm Court, where ladies in long black skirts and limp white blouses kept busy on stringed instruments of various sizes. They must have come from central casting, for they all looked like genteel music teachers from a fashionable girls' boarding school who had been denied reemployment after being apprehended doing naughty things in the gazebo with the gym teacher. As the German line had a thing for tangos, the ladies of the Palm Court Ensemble were working away at one of Valentino's favorites as I was brought aboard, incognito and safe from kidnappers. My bodyguard squeezed my shoulder, "See you soon, kid, have a great trip," and was gone.

Our staterooms, as usual, were the best, so far above the waterline we could keep our portholes open as we wished. It would have taken three-hundred-foot waves to reach them and dampen our plush carpeting. The rich are always allotted the safest section, be it ship, plane, or train. It seems they are regarded as too precious to put at risk. This troubled me as a child; it troubles me still.

It was always difficult to get into and around our staterooms. First, you had to push your way through the botanical gardens that materialized in anticipation of my mother's arrival, then you faced the mountain of suitcases and hatboxes that had still to be allotted their correct rooms and unpacked. In those days, every great hotel, ship, and train had their distinctive labels that were automatically applied to every piece of luggage by conscientious personnel wielding long-handled paintbrushes thick with amber-colored glue. My mother's dark gray bags were so strewn with these colorful stickers they looked like confetti-covered baby elephants. Both my father and my mother liked these labels so, we always traveled with spares complete with thick brush and glue pot in case any were torn in transit and had to be replaced.

Traveling was still a dramatic adventure, full of excitement. The most blasé traveler, and there were not many of them then, felt a tingle of anticipation as a ship prepared for a crossing. In the luxury class, it was party time. Even the privileged responded to this atmosphere, their only worry that if we hit rough weather, their champagne glasses might slide off the bridge table into their laps. But even that was not such a catastrophe, for everyone had at least two tuxedos and, in a pinch, white tie and tails would do. Ladies traveled with at least six different evening gowns in their cabin luggage, while dozens hung in steamer trunks stored below in the hold of the ship. Such things never worried my mother. She hated all card games and never played them, kept her hand securely around the stem of any glass that contained alcohol, and her tuxedos and her evening dresses hung ready for whatever action might arise.

Resi, with her huge leather folder of keys, all individually tagged as to bag and contents, had unlocked the "elephants" and was now submerged in an avalanche of white tissue paper. The great unpacking, "before Frau Dietrich arrives," had begun! This was my chance to escape before I was conscripted to handing her the padded hangers.

I still remember the feeling of excitement when reconnoitering a new ship. Oh, I knew I wasn't permitted beyond the first-class borders. The grand tour, especially arranged for me by the captain and conducted by the first officer, resplendent in full costume, gold braid and all, that included such special treats as the engine room, that would come later during the crossing, as it had on the *Bremen*.

Now I was on my own, and those were the best times. First, I would go down to the main lobby. The *Europa*, the pride of the German fleet, the sister ship of the *Bremen* that had first brought me to America, was another hymn to what would later be considered the architectural style of Nazi Germany. Actually, it was Prussian to the core, existing long before the Führer chose it as his favorite. Massive and somber, with lots of Roman garlands entwined with clawed eagles carved in oak. The entire Niebelunger Ring could have been staged in the first-class dining room and not seemed out of place. The crew reflected their ship's aura. In the forties, when Warner Brothers turned out those great anti-Nazi propaganda films, the actors portraying the various Gestapo, storm troopers, and U-boat officers, always reminded me of the personnel of the *Bremen* and the *Europa* in the thirties. I am sure they probably all ended up on the *Graf Spee* fighting for the Fatherland. Here again, patterned rubber covering the halls and stairs made the ship smell like a tire factory. It and the slight but constant vibration were the only reminders that you lived on a ship and not in a hotel. The main deck lobby was jammed with people. Stewards, in white mess jackets and little black bow ties à la Chaplin, scurried about delivering huge baskets of flowers as tall as chairs, their scalloped fan-shaped backs and bowed handles festooned in satin ribbons, a Jeanette MacDonald in *Maytime* prop. The German stewards carried these a little critically, as though they censured all this frivolous extravagance.

This was my first departure from an American dock, and I wanted to see it all. I took one of the elevators to the promenade deck, then ran up the remaining stairs to the open top deck, directly beneath the giant funnels. It was my favorite perch; one could see everything from there. The other berths, the different pennants of the shipping lines next to their countries' flags, curling with the early evening breeze, the bright yellow taxis endlessly coming and going, the darkened iron sculpture of the elevated subway, high above the street beyond, and far below me all those people in constant motion, like the water out in the harbor and its night tide we were scheduled to leave on. I leaned further over the railing. My mother was about to arrive. Long before she actually appeared, one could feel a tensing, a current of excitement suffuse a crowd, the way animals sense a storm long before it thunders. There she was and the clutch of frenetic men, press cards stuck in wide hat bands, who seemed forever to be walking backwards as they fired questions at her while others tore exploded flashbulbs out of their reflectors, licked the tips of new ones, screwing them in with one quicksilver motion.

My mother was dressed all in white and if she had had a pretty woman on her arm, they would have made a stunning couple. I was never really confused by my mother's masculinity or lack of femininity. It never occurred to me to wonder. "Dietrich" was neither man nor woman – "Dietrich" was just Dietrich and that was the beginning and the end of it. The imagery of "mother = woman" never entered my mind in relationship to her.

As I watched her make her way up the special gangplank, the crowd moving with her as though they belonged to her, I knew I had to get back to our stateroom, and fast. I was expected to be there, to greet her with joy. If I got into trouble before the trip had even begun, her anger would last all the way across the Atlantic Ocean and then be handed on to my father, a form of parental relay of censure. Also, I had not removed and catalogued the cards from the mass of flowers. This job, now mine, enabled my mother to throw out those flowers she hated, without bothering with who sent what. As I had seen a lot of irises, gladiolas, and delphiniums, she would be doing a lot of throwing the moment she arrived. I flew and, luckily, made it – just in time!

She seemed at ease, not furious, as she usually was after a bout with reporters. She rang for our steward, our maid, and our waiter, who all materialized immediately. She even chatted with them between issuing her orders; this was not like her at all. Then, suddenly I knew! Everyone was speaking German. My mother was home! She was happy. When she read the menu, she licked her lips and ordered everything – frankfurters, sauerkraut, liver dumplings, red cabbage, fried potatoes, liverwurst on black bread. If the *Europa* had stocked goose fat on rye, she would have ordered that too.

As I had predicted, the irises, etc., were expelled from her presence, then she attacked the usual stack of cables.

MARLENE DIETRICH
SS EUROPA

YOU WERE RIGHT MARINOU OUR MEETING WAS GRAND YESTERDAY STOP
BON VOYAGE AND GOOD LUCK
                                                    MAURICE

N213=PKY HOLLYWOOD CALIF 453P MAY 13 1933
MARLENE DIETRICH
    SS EUROPA NY

I SAY ARE YOU GOING AWAY ON PURPOSE THERE IS A SLIGHT BLUE
EVERYWHERE I LOOK BON VOYAGE DONT FORGET TO COME BACK
ROUBEN 812P

SA54 138 NI=LOS ANGELES CALIF
MARLENE DIETRICH
SS EUROPA

MY DEAR FRAULEIN VON LOSCH THERE IS NO FUN WITHOUT YOU WHAT
SHALL WE DO ON SUNDAY STOP HE CRIED ON LEAVING YOUR HOUSE STOP
I TRIED TO BE VERY MASCULINE STOP SAW S YESTERDAY UNBELIEVABLY
CHARMING YOU HIS ONLY THOUGHT OURS TOO BUT THAT MIGHT NOT
BE SO INTERESTING STOP WAS THE TRAIN BORING BRENTWOOD DOESNT
SLEEP AT ALL HAS TERRIBLE NIGHTMARES HAVE A GOOD TIME DONT FOR-
GET YOUR OLD VIOLETS OUR LOVE TO YOU AND YOUR LITTLE CAT=NOT
SIGNED

"Violets," the symbolic flower of lesbian relationships, was cutely
chosen by "the boys" for their ID. "S," of course, signified von
Sternberg. "Brentwood" meant de Acosta. A very mundane moniker,
I thought, for a "White Prince." "Little Cat" referred to me and was an
ill-disguised innuendo, completely wasted on my mother. She was never
skilled at recognizing sarcasm's double meanings. Deciphering cables was
one of the few games I played as a child.
    "All ashore who's going ashore!" – the Siegfrieds were singing their
little song again. I took my chances and asked for permission to go on
deck, to watch us leave the slip. I got a yes! – this was certainly a special
day. As usual, I exited sedately, closed the door quietly, and then . . .
sprinted! Now *everything* was lit. Paper streamers fluttered everywhere,
New Year's Eve in May. The brass band had gotten its second wind,
everyone waved, some cried, shouting last instructions that never were
understood but acknowledged anyway, children being held high to be
seen and see. I stood in my spot and felt the ship move. The tugboats,
streaming light, had begun their herculean job of guiding our giant into a
safe depth. My first departure from America and the beginning of a vigil
I kept from then on, whenever we crossed the sea. I waited for the Lady.
She was so beautiful, telling all the world that she would take care of them
and keep them safe in this wonderful country. Whenever we left, I said
good-bye to her, and when we returned, I thanked her for welcoming
me home. I must have let my affection show one day, for I remember
my mother saying: "The Statue of Liberty? Ridiculous. It is French. The
Americans can't even make their own statues, they need the French to
give them one!"
    Of course, my mother never attended the compulsory lifeboat drill,

but I loved getting into those huge vests, so heavy you wondered if they would really float, then standing in line being given instructions in "serious" tones – while taking stock of who would be in "your" lifeboat when the Tragic Moment came. At these times, as I qualified for the "women and children first" group, I felt very important.

The *Europa* that had seemed so crowded was, actually, half full in first class. Americans were already apprehensive of placing themselves on what was legally considered German soil. My mother's relaxed mood lasted quite a while, until we saw *Mein Kampf* being sold in the ship's bookstore. That shocked her, but not completely. It was still "Fatherland" time for her on the *Europa*. We did not know this was to be our last journey, ever, on a German ship.

When the metal borders that kept the dishes from scooting off were being secured around the edges of the dining tables, I knew my stomach and I were in for trouble. The ship was being battened down – rough seas ahead.

RADIO TELEGRAM P PARIS
MARLENE DIETRICH SS EUROPA
REGRET SHIP IS EMPTY SORRY HOPE AT LEAST POLITICALLY QUIET STOP
UNHAPPY KATER SEASICK POOR YOU HOPE WEATHER BETTER STOP YOU
WILL BE REWARDED FOR EVERYTHING WONDERFUL HOTEL TRIANON PALACE
VERSAILLES BEAUTIFUL PARK STOP KISS YOU AND LONGING=PAPI

The Ladies of the Palms had retired. The ship was doing its own tango. The pickled herring in sour cream was definitely *not* being ordered. Waiters rocked back and forth on their heels in time with the roll of the ship, waiting bravely in the empty dining room. My mother drank champagne, wrote cables, and read them.

RADIO TELEGRAM
3 WEST LOS ANGELES CALIF
MARLENE DIETRICH SS EUROPA
GOLDEN ONE THE SCANDINAVIAN CHILD SAW YOUR PICTURE AND THOUGHT
YOU AND YOUR ACTING BEAUTIFUL . . . STOP IT WILL MAKE YOU SMILE TO
KNOW SHE HAS DECIDED ON THE SAME DIRECTOR AND SO LIFE GOES ON STOP
I AM MISSING YOU AND WORRIED ABOUT EUROPEAN SITUATION YOU MUST
RETURN HOME SOON MY LOVE=

Finally, land! Our first port of call was Southampton, and real mail was taken aboard. Brian had his timing down pat. There was a letter from him, sent from London:

Upper Porchester Street
Cambridge Square, W.2
Telephone Ambassador 1873

Monday – Oh my sweetheart, your darling cable came this morning and I have been all day thinking of something nice that I could wireless back. I couldn't think of anything but "I love you." Now I am wondering if you will realize who it comes from! After all, everybody loves you and I have noticed that no one signs their telegrams to you, so you may think this comes from Miss de Acosta or Mr. von Sternberg or Maurice or Rouben or Gary Cooper. (Perhaps you would not suspect Bing Crosby.)

Well, it comes from me! Oh, my darling love, it was a heavenly time wasn't it? I remember you looking at your stills on the floor, so eager and excited and Maria reading the Sunday comics, so rapt and silent. I can see you walking to the set in that full gray skirt and the little blue blouse with the puffed sleeves, and your hair red golden in the sun. I can see you too in your red trousers, sitting on top of the hill under an umbrella waiting for me to come, with a carefully filled picnic basket by your side. I hear you on the telephone saying, "Here is Miss Dietrich," and I see you coming in, like a mischievous child, with a present for me held behind your back.

I have other memories too, of bright red flowers and a mirror and red quilt with you lying like a flower upon it. I have memories that rise and stifle me with desire –

It was an extraordinary time, and so unexpected, a bonne bouche thrown in by the Gods just as a surprise. Maybe it was just a dream, but even if that is so we still have had it: for that brief time we have been safe and happy and content, and for my own part I realized the value of those hours even as they passed by. So now whatever the future may hold for us we shall have dreamed the dream and shall have the memory of it to hold.

Beware of the cold. One's blood runs thin (although sometimes very fast) in California, and I have caught a most dreadful chill and feel rotten. Be sure to tell me about Maria, and give her my love if you think she can stand it. I am really devoted to her.

Alas I am also devoted to her mother and that is a complicated thing.

A bientôt mon amour

Another letter from those I found in my father's house after his death. He had saved it for nearly fifty years. I am glad that he did.

People like Dietrich never stood in line – for anything. Not even passport control. The purser came to our stateroom to personally collect our papers, before our arrival in Cherbourg. As my mother handed him our passports, I saw that mine was like hers, beige – the cover full of German typescript and those eternally stoic-looking eagles. I had a German passport! That meant I was German? I remember a terrible feeling of loss, a panic, like falling a long, long way. Until that moment I believed that I belonged to America, and now, suddenly, I found out that I didn't! But Germany was my mother's country, not mine! Never – then where *did* I belong? My mother had always told me that I was hers, now I began to really believe her and it frightened me.

PARIS–VIENNA

THE TRIANON PALACE HOTEL deserved its name. Cinderella could have
left her slipper there any time. All mirrors, French doors, and gilt. Our
suite needed only Madame de Pompadour reclining on the baby blue
chaise longue to complete the setting. As Dietrich never reclined "in
life," our chaise was never used, but it looked good, all silk brocade
and gold leaf. From the moment we had set foot on French soil, my
mother had spoken nothing but French. She spoke it with a proficiency
that always conjured up images of court dandies bowing low, flourishing
their lace handkerchiefs over pale satin knee-breeches. Paris so suited her
love of the aristocratic without restrictions. The Louis's were her kind
of fellas and "Let them eat cake" not too far removed from her own
sympathies. Her love affair with Paris was the longest liaison of her life,
and as with all of her amours, what she loved became hers by right of
expended emotion. Whenever my mother waxed romantic about places
or things, they became suspect to me. Either it meant that a new swain
was on the horizon, or that, as no one was around, she had fallen in love
with a town, a poem, a book, a song, while treading emotional waters.
The passion expended, for instance, on white lilac was just as intense as
for a lover and usually just as fleeting. Paris and everything French was
it, that late spring of '33.

"Taste the *fraises des bois*, sweetheart. That is the taste of France! Wild
strawberries in the sun – picked by young girls in white dresses!"

She spoke in capitals and exclamation points. Her wording lyrical.
Images of dappled poppy fields à la Monet became the order of the day.
The Tauber records disappeared and Chevalier sang his heart out instead.
Croissants were accorded their own scene each morning. She took off her
trousers and drifted about in pale chiffon. Everything was sweetness and
Gallic delight. We all heaved a sigh of relief. Especially my father, who

had really gone out on a limb, choosing a place that she had not okayed beforehand.

The first morning, probably to emphasize the safety of Europe, I was told I could go out alone, to play in the gardens. As one was expected to respond immediately to any permission given, off I skipped. Playing outside proved to be a bit more difficult than I had expected, for the hotel grounds had been designed to live up to the architecture. Very formal, manicured white gravel paths, bordered by precise flower beds resembling petit-point tapestry footstool patterns, and trees, clipped to resemble shapes that no decent California tree would be seen as.

So I wandered in and out of little bowers in my pleated organdy, until I felt that "playtime" would be considered over and my return accepted. Lunch was about to be served in our dining room, with its hand-painted wallpaper of ribbons and rosebuds, the fragile gilt chairs in place, my mother already seated. I had just time to change my shoes and pretend that I had washed my hands. Fortunately no one noticed, so I didn't get into trouble and helped myself to the white asparagus vinaigrette. The dishes, ordered by my father, looked as decorative as our surroundings. Only the French can paint pictures with aspic and truffles on poached chicken breasts. There I had to agree with my mother, and nothing sparkles like Baccarat crystal and Sèvres porcelain on a white linen tablecloth edged with Chantilly lace. The whole meal looked like a painting in the Louvre, and if anyone had offered me a hamburger with ketchup, I would have been ecstatic! I was really a most ungrateful child, but homesickness intrudes even into palaces.

Relaxed, my mother ate everything with the intensity of a truck driver refueling himself during a transcontinental haul. She did this her entire life. She either devoured food or starved herself. She never ate daintily, she consumed with gusto and let the "lady" image slip a little.

Everyone spoke French, even Tami. Now that I was older, my mother and father spoke this language whenever "The Child should not know," but if now *French* was going to be the *everyday* language, I decided I had better learn it quickly – it was always dangerous not to know what people were saying or thinking.

We had destroyed the perfection of the pink salmon nestled amongst the carved lemons and dark green tufts of parsley, the lavender-tipped artichokes, the pewterlike sheen of the beluga caviar, the silver filigree bucket that had spilled over with little yeast loaves, still warm from their baking, was empty; the white Burgundy that had been oohed and aahed over, its bottle empty, now stuck upside down in the silver bucket on the tripod stand; and not a single sweet crumb was left from all those raspberry tarts. My mother rose; in private I was not required to rise immediately whenever she stood, neither was my father. Tami jumped up regardless. She always functioned on the premise of "better safe than sorry." Usually she was told to "Sit!" which she did instantly, whispering a self-conscious apology for having been so "stupid." I never did manage to teach her to gauge my mother's moods correctly, although I tried each time we were together. We were all, in some way, frightened of my mother, but Tami was petrified, and all my careful coaching did not penetrate. Already, in Santa Monica, I had begun to shield her, joining her mistakes – letting such commands as "Sit!" wash over both of us. It is easier to "heel" when one is not all alone. But Tami and I were not together enough, and when we were, I was not constantly so kind or sacrificial and then she had to take it all by herself, the hard way. It took nearly thirty years to break her spirit, then destroy her mind. My mother and father were very thorough people.

This time we both sat back down. My mother left the room, my father rang for the waiters to clear the table. My mother returned, having changed into flannels and striped silk shirt. We were ready for work! Tami was sent out to walk Teddy, who was now my father's dog by right of training, although I could have sworn he winked at me when we first arrived.

My father had a special surprise to show his wife. There it stood, in the garden, like some huge aviary – a miniature Versailles ballroom, and in the center of it, a baby grand, its fruitwood patina as glowing as the parquet floor it stood on.

"For you, Mutti, to work on the songs. The sound is better than in a hotel room and here you won't be disturbed."

My mother strode over to the piano, sat, lifted the lid of the keyboard, played a series of chords, then looked at my father and smiled.

"It is perfectly tuned! That too you remembered!"

No greater praise could be given by Dietrich than that a piano was tuned – correctly! My father had his reward and now he too smiled! Right then I decided that Paris must be a lucky place – and it always was.

Our days took on their familiar working pattern. We got up to go to work in our ballroom, broke for lunch, instead of washing hair coworkers talked shop between mouthfuls, then back to the piano. It was assumed that the process of creating a song for Dietrich would interest me, and it did. Each morning I was given my Louis XV side chair and allowed to listen. My mother stood, never sat – as usual. The piano was covered in long music sheets, sharp pencils, and ashtrays. The Taittinger stood cooling in its bucket on a low table nearby. It would be years yet before the author of *All Quiet on the Western Front* introduced her to Moët & Chandon's Dom Pérignon, which the world would proclaim had been

Dietrich's champagne – forever. Everything my mother knew about wines – and the legend had it that she was an expert – she learned from Erich Maria Remarque, the true connoisseur.

Although the power of my mother's fame made negotiating deals for her far easier than might appear, still, my father had achieved quite a coup in persuading a German record company to allow a German star to record in France. What phony excuse he used to get my mother out of having to go to Berlin to work, I never knew. It must have been a very tricky situation. Hitler was chancellor of Germany, refugees were making their presence felt, and rumors of personal tragedies were everywhere, but no one appeared to be too deeply concerned yet, except those directly threatened and those, too few, actually aware of the doctrine of *Mein Kampf* and the horrific possibility of its succeeding. Thank God, my father was one of those enlightened few. Without his counsel, Dietrich's life and mine might have been quite different. It is to her credit that she recognized the truth in what he was telling her and did not argue against his determination to keep her out of Germany at all costs! But her political expertise, always lauded by the world as having been practically clairvoyant so early in the thirties, was a tutored accomplishment and not an intuitive one. Then, as usual, once Dietrich had accepted an idea, she made it her very own, with a passionate fervor that Joan of Arc might have envied.

She now became house mother to the artists fleeing Germany. The part suited her and she played it superbly. The fact that she was a Prussian added to her stature and humanity. With my Austrian-Czech father as her majordomo, Dietrich reigned over her refugee court, and a little Berlin flourished in our hotel in Versailles. Her old friend Spoliansky, Hollander, our genius of *The Blue Angel* songs, the composer Peter Kreuder, and Waxman, his arranger, who was working with her on the new songs – they and many more came, were taken over, given emotional sanctuary, fed, counseled, and consoled.

The croissants and painted chicken breasts disappeared and, thanks to my father's superb shopping know-how, bagels, chicken livers, and smoked whitefish took their place on the fancy flowered china. While the Trianon Palace Hotel chef tore his hair, my mother ran the best Jewish delicatessen in France. Now I listened to the newly homeless, sensed fear and terror, homesickness and longing, but mostly it seemed to me, even as an eight year old, stunning disbelief. They spoke strange new words, "Nazi," "S.S.," "Gestapo," but later, when I tried to find them in my dictionary, they were not there. When I asked Tami what they meant, she looked so worried I didn't insist. But when I was parked, one afternoon, in my father's apartment by myself, I went to his study to look for the book that was always being referred to. Finding it, I settled myself in my father's high-backed bishop's chair, determined to read *Mein Kampf*. Of course it was much too difficult, but I found some words I knew: "Jew," *that* I had heard often, always said with a certain disdain; like that time in Berlin, when my mother first made fun of von Sternberg having a *von*. Some words I had never heard before, like "Aryan." I was looking for others when I heard my father's voice in the hall. As no one was allowed into his study without permission, I quickly put the heavy book back exactly as I had found it and ran.

Back at the hotel that evening, feeling very courageous from my foray into such grown-up reading matter, I asked my mother what the word "Aryan" meant. I was told, "You are one, sweetheart! But you can't understand it – you are much too young. Now, go to bed. We have to work tomorrow!" I was used to this maneuver – seldom did I receive an informative answer to an inquiry of mine. Probably the reason why I was a child that scavenged information, rarely asking direct questions.

So, now I was not only a German instead of an American, I was also an Aryan? I had already decided not to be a German. Now I had better find out what this new word meant, so I could stop being that too!

Our ballroom sessions continued. My mother was always a good lyricist. The poet in her, though terribly sentimental and self-consciously world-weary, lent itself to ballads that suited her style. Some famous lyrics attributed to others were written by Dietrich, but although she would fume when certain gentlemen accepted accolades for words not entirely written by them, she never rocked their insecure boat. The fact that the gentlemen in question also knew some embarrassing truths about her might have had something to do with her sudden lack of vindictiveness.

One of my favorite songs was written that summer, "Allein in Einer Grossen Stadt," a very modern composition in the style of Brecht, and my least favorite, "Mein Blondes Baby." My mother adored it, the lyrics could have been from one of her letters. The day this song was finished, she sat me by the piano and sang it just for me, her eyes full of tears, her voice, in its three-note range, sobbing away about her blond baby who must never leave her.

It was a perfect example of how my mother perceived motherhood. This song, and the ghastly poem of Jean Richepin that she insisted on reciting at the drop of a hat, sent to everyone she had an interest in, including later to my children, are both based on the "martyrdom" of motherhood – Dietrich's most treasured image of herself.

There was a poor fool who loved a young girl
Long long ago
But she pushed him away and said to him,
Bring me, I tell you, your mother's heart
And give it to my dog.
He went and slayed his mother
Long long ago
And took the heart, it was burning red
He carried it and he stumbled and fell
And the heart rolled in the sand.
He saw the heart roll in the dust
Long long ago
A cry was heard
The heart began to speak
"Did you hurt yourself, my son?"

My mother simply adored this ghoulish concept. Now, while she sang her "Blond Baby," I sat very still, desperately searching for the proper words of praise expected from me. After all, I was being "immortalized in song," and joyful gratitude was mandatory. But it was such an awful song, words stuck in my throat. I think I opted for jumping up and throwing my arms around her neck, for I remember her exclaiming:

"The Child understands! She knows what I was telling her! Without her – there is nothing!"

She was happy and satisfied – I had done it right!

When we were not writing songs in Versailles, we worked at choosing clothes in Paris. The French press had been critical of Dietrich's insistence on wearing male attire. They editorialized that "ladies" do not flout convention. The French fashion industry, then exclusively for women, was, after all, an important part of the country's economy, so one can understand their panic at the prospect of the female population casting off their restrictive frills for the comfort of a pair of trousers. Although Hermès was showing trousers for women as early as 1930, the wire services had picked up this "new" controversy, and with the gleeful assistance of the Paramount Publicity Department, mushroomed the story into an international mini-scandal. This did not stop Dietrich from wearing her pinstriped suits as she walked up the Champs-Elysées!

Shop girls left their customers in mid-sales pitch and rushed out to catch a glimpse of her passing; in the sidewalk cafés, all service stopped, food got cold, sherbets melted, the customers didn't mind, they too stared, some men following her progress up the boulevard, unconscious of the napkin still clutched in their hand or tucked in the top of their vest. Cars braked in midtraffic, others moved along the curb, keeping pace with her stride. People forgot to cross at intersections, gendarmes forgot to blow their whistles. The following admirers grew until a huge crowd moved with us. And it wasn't the mannish suit; this happened every time Dietrich appeared, no matter what she wore!

The first time this happened, it was really scary. This had never happened in America. They were so silent! Just like that lynch mob in the movie I had seen. But these faces were not angry and the stillness was due to a sort of reverence, not menace. I knew how fans behaved, but what was happening here did not belong to the category of Movie Star Adulation at all. No one tried to touch her, or even get too close. They just seemed to want to be in her aura and feast their eyes. This extraordinary gift for generating respect from large masses of people was my mother's special inexplicable magic. It lasted her whole life. Those of us in attendance, who expected her to be torn apart any second, were constantly amazed by her assured statement – as she looked at the hordes of avid fans pushing toward her.

"Don't worry! They won't touch me. They never do." And, by god, she was right! They never did! No screaming frenzy for Dietrich, she inspired Breathless Awe. Let the papers print their lies, the people of Paris adored her.

Brian, always the protective cavalier, was worried about the "trouser" items that appeared in the British press, and in one of his letters, gave her his unsolicited advice. Never an intelligent move, where Dietrich was concerned. She considered anyone who did not agree with her the devil's advocate.

My mother commented: "Really, Brian goes on and on. He thinks I invented trousers. Hasn't he ever heard of George Sand? I thought he was an educated man! Really, such a to-do!" and continued reading.

> Might go away for a short holiday – the country is so exquisite now. Oh dear! I wish you were not so famous! I would say to you, "Come on!" and we would motor down to the Italian lakes and stay in Como, and go to the opera at the Scala in Milan, and then on to Venice. It would be so very lovely at this time of the year, and we should be very happy. Alas . . .

My mother looked up.

"Alas? How la-di-da can one get? Too much Shakespeare?"

Brian was definitely doing something wrong in that letter. Of all the people who were in love with my mother, he was my favorite, and I didn't want her to get rid of him. I watched her face – anxiously.

Alas, I do not know how I can see you at all. If I come to Versailles every boot boy in the hotel will know instantly and every paper in the world will have it the next day. It all looks very difficult for me, and many is the evening that I wish I could get out my old Chrysler again and rush off down to Santa Monica. Oh, my darling, perhaps I dreamed it all and none of it really happened.

How is Maria? I don't like children as a rule, they embarrass me. She is the only one in the world whom I really adore.

This is a dull letter. I want to put my arms around you, and words seem so lifeless and useless until I can do that.

My dearest love to you, Dietrich.

Aherne

But it was all right, when she had finished, she was not angry.

"Brian sends you his love, sweetheart. As soon as the work is finished, he is coming to Paris."

As my father entered the room, my mother handed him Brian's letter, saying:

"A sweet letter from Brian. Read what he says about the trousers. It's very funny!" and she left to get dressed.

My father selected a cigarette from his gold cigarette case, snapped the lid shut, slipped the case into the pocket of his cashmere sports jacket, lit the cigarette with his beautiful Cartier lighter, settled himself into the brocade chair by the French windows, and began to read. I stood and watched his face. I did not like my father seeing what Brian had written to her. I had no real reason for this resentment, but still, I felt funny about it. One thing for sure, when I saw Brian the next time, I would have to tell him not to use "Alas!" when he wrote to her.

My mother's whole attitude toward mail was interesting. When my father was in residence, it was his job to open and sort the mail, as it was now mine when he was not around. Bills belonged in a brown accordion-type folder, invitations to the left of the desk blotter, letters referring to work subjects in the center, and private ones to the right. Cables, of course, were opened, unfolded, and handed to her immediately. Fan letters were usually sent to her in care of her Studio. Those that did get through to her directly were left unopened and thrown away. Dietrich never concerned herself with fan mail, until she was in her late seventies and needed this constant assurance of adulation to reinforce her image of herself, sending it on to me to make certain that I was aware of how universally she was adored by strangers. My mother had no sense of privacy where letters were concerned. An astounding paradox in one so fanatically private. At first, as a child, I thought that just my father and I were trusted, then I realized that she left intimate letters about for all to read. Later, it made trying to protect her against blackmail a continuous nightmare.

If one tried to warn her against this negligent habit of hers, one would be coldly stared at and told:

"Ridiculous! No one would dare! Besides, servants don't know how to *read*! If they did, they wouldn't have to be servants!"

The only private letters she kept and protected under lock and key were those from the very famous, and then more as one might guard trophies, not memories of human relationships. Probably why my father saved all her cast-offs, while Dietrich kept the letters of Hemingway and Cocteau. My mother, an immortal in the making, knew instinctively which flock of rare birds to fly with.

Elaborate, embossed invitations arrived from the great couturier houses to the openings of their fall and winter collections. They were delivered by young messengers who looked like redesigned versions of the Philip Morris bellhop, or by primly dressed and scrubbed apprentices who had taken off their thimbles just long enough to scurry to Versailles to present their master's salutations to Madame. Dietrich was very selective. She did not shop around. She knew which designer suited the image and which would detract from it. So, we only went to see the collections of Patou, Lanvin, Molineux, and Mme. Alix Grès. Not Chanel. My mother called her "the little black suit woman"; never wore one until the fifties and never realized how much Dietrich had influenced this great designer; even to inventing the beige shoes with their black front for the cock-feather costume in *Shanghai Express*!

The four of us, plus the Sieber super-trained-canine, would sweep into whatever hallowed establishment had been chosen for that afternoon's viewing of the fall collection. The *directrice*, the "guardian at the gate" and buffer for the creative genius, always an imposing figure of authority, greeted us. These ladies were the generals of an army of skilled laborers, the drill sergeants of magnificent clotheshorses and fitters alike. Shop Steward, Mother Superior, Diplomat, Confidante, and Trusted Friend of Royalty, and the next best thing, the Very Rich. Everything concerned them, from the head beader's menstrual cramps to the late delivery of the silk organza from Italy. These select women would have been an asset to any government. Besides their brilliance as administrators, they had other things in common – they all wore dignified pearls and had numerous lieutenants for greeting the lesser mortals.

Having voiced the house's pleasure and honor at Mme. Dietrich's presence, Mme. La Directrice now moved aside, and there appeared a clutch of little ladies dressed in lint-free black with immaculate white collars and cuffs. They scurried to perform what seemed to be their one goal in life: to place the spindly gold chairs at the correct angle to the runway, seat Mme. Dietrich and her entourage, and hand out small blocks of paper like dance cards, with narrow pencils hung from a silken cord. These dedicated ladies never varied – every fashion house had them. I often wondered if, like buttons, they were acquired in sets of a dozen at a time.

Tami and I loved these outings. We would sit on our gilt chairs, pencils poised, tense with excitement and anticipation. Teddy too – he had an eye for mannequins. Suddenly, all conversation ceased and a very elegant voice announced:

"*Mesdames et Messieurs*, Ladies and Gentlemen – *Numéro Un*, Number One: '*Rêve du Matin*,' 'Morning's Dream,'" and there came a vision!

Mannequins in those days didn't prance, skip, bounce, or giggle, they slid – very slowly along narrow dove-gray runways – turned by rotating their pelvis, held this pose, allowing the audience ample time to inspect the cut and drape of the back of the creation that was theirs solely to display, then would slide back, to disappear the split second that the next number appeared from the opposite side. Great mannequins have an incredible of timing and the muscle coordination of an Olympic gymnast. I never got tired of watching them work.

"Morning's Dream" turned out to be a deeply pleated, heavy silk georgette in a shade of mother-of-pearl, a matching cloche with just a breath of veil across the eyes, long gray kid gloves, and a very large muff of milky gray fox skins, the tips of their tails sweeping the floor.

Silk and satin, velvet and wool, georgette and crepe, feathers, beads, fringes, and braids. Dresses for luncheons, for shopping, for afternoon teas, for rendezvous, for "little" dinners. Evening dresses for intimate parties, restaurant dining, night clubs, and informal weekends. Ball gowns for the opera and those oh-so-frequent banquets in châteaux. With great concentration, Tami and I wrote down all the code numbers of the gorgeous outfits we just couldn't live without and had to buy! While we dreamed our dreams and played our wishful-thinking game, my father was at work explaining to my mother that what she had chosen was either too ornate, too colorful, or too extreme for her. I think she was a little like us and wanted everything, even to the silver lamé with the five-foot train edged in black fox. Only during this first buying trip to Paris did they argue over the collections. The next year, she was far more discerning. Also, she became adept at escaping him. My father, who had relinquished his position of lover, marriage partner, functioning husband, and father with such apparent ease, held on to his title as Adviser to the Queen with a tenacity that was often startling. That this was the only role left to him to fight for, I did not realize as a child.

Clothes were never bought in those days by Dietrich for real-life wear. "In life" was so rare. A bathrobe, a cooking uniform, a "going to the Studio" outfit could last for months, without replacements. The Paris clothes were handled as we would any other costumes at the Studio, each outfit had to have its own accessories. So we went to millinery fashion shows, shoes were specially designed, handbags and gloves made to order. The "glove" artist arrived at our hotel with suitcases full of tissue-thin leather from every animal known to man, and, it seemed, even some not known. He fluttered and fussed, his spidery fingers trembled, dropping the thinnest pins I had ever seen all over the Aubusson. The tiniest bubble did not escape my mother's eagle eyes. Over and over again, the buttery leather was pinned, smoothed, repinned, until her hands looked to me as though colored honey had been poured over them. But she was still not satisfied. Using her "patient" tone, she told him, finally:

"Now you go home and tomorrow you come back and bring that white powder that sculptors and doctors use. Then we will make a cast of my hands – and then you can pin away on them, until you get it *right*!"

She had always been intrigued by the shoe designers taking castings of her feet and now, with the prospect of having to fit fifty pairs of gloves, she had come up with the brilliant solution of giving her hands to the nervous French glover as she had given her feet to the temperamental – but brilliant – Italian cobbler. She even flirted with the idea of having Paramount send her the statue from *Song of Songs*.

"Then I wouldn't have to be at the clothes fittings either! They could all pin away like crazy – and we could all go and eat!" She would have, too, except that the breasts of the statue were the ones she wished she had but didn't. For weeks, thereafter, we all came up with more and more variations on the theme, of sending plaster parts of Dietrich as stand-ins for the real thing.

When the famous gloves were finally delivered, it took twenty minutes to pull them onto her hands. Once on, my mother tried to move a finger and couldn't! It was the tightest fit of the century. They had been shaped on rigid hands and all movement was utterly impossible. Whenever my mother really laughed, she wet her pants. Now, she was running, trying to make it to the bathroom, hooting with laughter.

"I'm not going to make it! Sweetheart – quick – unbutton my fly! I can't even get them off to pee – they are so tight!"

Finally, she was sitting on the toilet, still laughing, looking at her gloved hands.

"You know, they are really perfect! Even Tante Valli would have worn these. They will be just right for stills. I won't have to retouch my hands – finally!"

From then on, each time my mother had to go to the bathroom, we would all yell: "Got your special gloves on, Mutti? Need some help?" After she had changed her pants, she packed the fifty pairs of perfection, in black tissue paper for the black, white tissue paper for the white, beige, pearl, gray and tan.

> STUDIO STILLS – GLOVES – BLACK *KID*
> ¾ LENGTH
> STUDIO STILLS – GLOVES – BLACK *KID*
> WRIST LENGTH
> 2 BUTTON

When they were all properly labeled, my father recorded the contents into the traveling inventory book and put the boxes into one of the extra large bedrooms – reserved for and already filling up with "things to go back to Hollywood."

AS MY MOTHER'S CONTRACT called for six songs, two of them in French, we now switched from German Weltschmerz to Gallic drama. One, "Assez," fascinated me. I couldn't understand the lyrics, and for once my mother seemed to avoid translating them for me. The rhythm was again very new, excitingly stark. I sat on my chair and listened to her speak the song. Dietrich had great difficulty singing lyrics, unless the melody was lilting schmaltz – à la Tauber. That, she adored and flung herself into with complete abandon. But with a more sophisticated melody, her lack of range and formal training forced her to act out the lyric within a speech pattern, a handicap that worked for her magnificently. After all, Dietrich wouldn't be Dietrich if she had ever really learned to sing. It was her pattern to unconsciously turn her professional shortcomings into magnificent accomplishment. While stars went to voice coaches and sweated over scales, Dietrich croaked and spoke and the world swooned. She was also a better actress with a lyric than she ever was with a part. The musical structure of a song left her no leeway to embroider the central theme. This restriction forced her to remain simple – tell the story of a song, interpret one main feeling, and get on to the next number. Ever the German, this suited her, and ever Dietrich, this worked for her sublimely, as though she had always planned it that way.

Our days changed when the first fittings began. We drove into Paris en masse, arriving at ten, fitting until twelve, lunching until three, fitting until five, returning to Versailles to wash and set the hair in time for the evening performance of going out to dinner at nine. Mostly, lunches were fun, even if they lasted three hours. But dinners were even longer, on show and always uncomfortable, and not just because I had to wear organdy with puffed sleeves that scratched. In Hollywood, nine o'clock was bedtime. With an alarm set to go off before dawn and a close-up lens just waiting to destroy you, no one took stupid chances except, possibly, the character actors who could always use an extra wrinkle or two, and the alcoholics, who would self-destruct anyway. But Europe meant interminable evenings and late nights.

The first fittings were a disaster. This was my mother's first Paris buying trip as a star, and nothing had prepared her for the "civilian" method of making clothes. In our world, a first fitting could be on a Monday – an elaborate costume, perfect from every conceivable camera angle, both still and in movement, completely ready two days later. But these so-expensive dress houses of the thirties catered to women who used their appointments at their "couturier" as they did those at their "coiffeur," as a daily activity around which to structure their indolent days.

Dietrich considered all who did not have to work for a living the "idle rich." When in that special tone of scorn, my mother said, "The Idle Rich!" one had instant visions of Vanderbilts and Rockefellers writhing in the flames of hell stoked by gaunt and vengeful hordes. The "nouveaux riches" were simply dismissed – beneath contempt – but the wealthy, they got it every time, unless she fancied one of them; then the rules changed. But then they always did, whenever it suited her. After all, she made the rules, therefore she had the right to alter them. So you learned to trust only those dictates in force at the moment, and never to rely on those that had been set down as gospel the day before. After getting into trouble a few times by having my ins and outs in the wrong sequence, I got the hang of it fast! One rule never changed: Dietrich was always right.

She stood in the fitting room and just looked in the mirror. I knew exactly what she was thinking. Dietrich expected all workers to be utterly dedicated to the perfection of their craft. She was! I think we spent that first week ripping seams. At first, the Lady Generals, having been called in to rescue their front-line troops, tried their charm, persuasion, and then assumed authority. It had worked when the Queen of Rumania got a little out of hand, why not with a famous Movie Star? They soon found out why not! Real royalty did not possess the hawk eyes that Hollywood royalty did. I could understand my mother's objections, the workmanship *was* shocking. The designs were wonderful; the execution – as though everything would only be seen in long-shot; but then, "in life" *was* mostly in long-shot. My mother did not think of these clothes as private attire, although the distraught French ladies couldn't know that. Dietrich never suffered fools generously, so the art of making clothes was meticulously explained, with many demonstrations to frightened women in white seamstress smocks, their tape measures hanging like necklaces around their necks. Fortunately, my mother was never as cutting in French as she could be in other languages, so our Ladies of the Pins were only stringently taught – not destroyed. In Hollywood, we had worked out a system whereby I could make my mother conscious of a fault without showing her up by actually, physically, pointing to the offending spot. She would look at me in the mirror. If I had something to show her that she or Travis had somehow overlooked, I would first lock our reflected eyes, then move mine to the place on the costume that I thought needed her attention. All she had to do was follow my eyes. I knew nothing else was necessary. Once she located the fault, she would have it corrected. We played this private game of "spot the bubble – wrinkle – crooked line" all our lives. I always knew how she hated to be touched and did my best to keep my hands off her whenever possible. Only later did I wonder how she managed all those physical liaisons despite this aversion of hers.

While hands and pins flew and nerves crackled, we, the supportive audience, sat on those ever-present fragile chairs, watching, discerning – and waiting to eat. First, my father, in his heather-toned tweeds, all muted greens and browns, then Tami, pretty in the suit my mother had worn the day before, in which *she* had looked divine, I, in my daytime navy blue with matching coat and small hat, white cotton gloves held loosely, white bobby-socked ankles crossed, also loosely, as required, and next to me, Teddy, ramrod straight, patent-leather leash held between his jaws, loosely. All in a row, like those hollow Russian dolls that capsule into one another. Finally the arguments, that always sounded so overly agitated in French, were finished and we broke for lunch.

We either ate at the Little Hungary, that served the best goulash in Europe, or at the Belle Aurore, that offered an Aladdin's treasure of hors d'oeuvres. You could eat there every day for a week, and we did often, and never repeat a dish. In both establishments, my father's preferred table was always ready, always waiting. As our routine never varied, it was really like going home to eat. One never looked at the elaborate menus. Special dishes of that day were announced with pride by the proprietor.

My father then evaluated these against his encyclopedic knowledge of the ability of the chef, then advised us what he would order for our meal. We rarely disagreed with any of his culinary decisions. Even if we might have wanted to switch the roast veal *aux romarin et truffes Lombardie* to the lamb *provençal et sauce du Midi*, it wasn't worth the hassle of the rearranging then required of appetizer, soup, vegetables, salad, cheese, and dessert. Everything would have to be rebalanced to complement the change of the main course.

"Mutti, if you insist on the veal, instead of what you should order today, the lamb, you must change the celery *à la grecque* to the artichoke vinaigrette, the spring pea soup to the cucumber, the cream one, the soufflé potatoes to *duchesse*, the string beans to leaf spinach, the endive salad to tomatoes, and the caramelized pear will be impossible! But you could have the crème brûlée."

Now it was my turn: "Kater, the asparagus have arrived from the Midi, you will have those *nature*, then the sole *bonne femme*, grilled tomatoes, new potatoes, assorted soft cheeses, and the raspberries with cream. Tami, you will have what I have."

I learned to ask for liver immediately. Automatically and without any further discussion, it demanded: fried onions, mashed potatoes, red cabbage, and cucumber salad. Don't ask me why this was a cardinal rule for liver, but at Little Hungary, it was. It made my lunchtime so much easier. Liver became known as "The Child's favorite dish." "The Child loves it so! At least she doesn't talk about those awful hamburgers of hers anymore!" Again, I was referred to as though I was not sitting there beside her. I didn't love liver that much, it just eliminated my meal from the Summit Meeting of Gastronomy. Teddy always had his dish ready and waiting for him, every restaurant knew his preferred menu of boiled beef and vegetables. I envied him.

The ordering of the wine was the next great decision of the century. Depending on my mother's stubbornness in straying from the set-forth path of consumption, this could take forever, and we only had three hours for lunch! As most everything was cooked to order, one usually waited and waited between the first courses and the entrées. During this hiatus, I ate all the bread and butter on the table, although my mother came a close second. When all the bread was gone and before ten waiters rushed to restock the supply, I was allowed to leave the table and walk Teddy. He didn't really want to move, but like me, he had learned to never even contemplate the possible joys of disobedience. So, we went out into the Paris spring and looked at life together. We returned to a "tense moment." My mother was smoking energetically – she only did that when annoyed – short, staccato puffs in the manner not yet made famous by Bette Davis. Tami looked apprehensive. Apparently, my father, on being presented the cork from the wine chosen for the veal, had detected the faintest whiff of mildew. This had, of course, necessitated a scathing reprimand of the sommelier, in perfect French for all to hear, and immediate banishment to dungeons as damp and foul as his cork. My father did get so enraged over external things, like food, wine, and service, another reason why we ate what we were told and limited our restaurant list. Like many ineffectual men, he was a tyrant in those categories in which he could get away with it. I sort of knew that, even as a child. Restaurants were his favorite arena to play Nero in, his famous wife, the type-cast Christian. With her he always chose a public place for his tantrums and toward people who couldn't talk back. Employees feared for their jobs, establishments the loss of Dietrich's patronage, Tami, I, and Teddy just feared – period! But with one of those very strange contradictions in her character, Dietrich really believed that women should not talk back to their men, that males were superior beings, whose authority must be endured with resignation.

"Papilein, I don't really need that special wine – the one I had for the soup will be fine with the veal – really!"

Tami nodded, up and down, in fast agreement. Not that her opinion counted for anything, but she tried for harmony continually. I squeezed quickly into the velour banquette. Ignoring his difficult womenfolk, my father turned to me:

"Kater, I ordered you a fresh lemonade," said in that tone that challenged my daring to ask for anything different.

"Thank you, Papi."

I prayed it would be made with just-squeezed lemons. He was uncanny how he could tell exactly when juice had been squeezed – that morning or just when ordered. If, when it arrived, he tasted my lemonade and found that it was this morning's juice, we would have a *real* upheaval. Our eating language was German. My mother and father discussed the latest Berlin arrivals, while Tami and I waited for the sword of Damocles – otherwise known as "Please, let it be – really fresh lemonade" – to make its appearance. There it was! Tall cut glass resting on a silver coaster. Before I could grab it and drink it down fast, my father got his hand on it and, sure enough, did his taste-check. We all held our breath. My father licked his lip, set the glass in front of me, saying, "You may drink that, Kater. It is fresh," and picked up the conversation at the exact point where his lemon vendetta had interrupted it. The relief was overwhelming! Another reason I loved Coca-Cola. It was so safe, it just sat there, the same wonderful stuff, unchanging the world over. We had quite a pleasant meal that day, but toward the end, we had to hurry, three hours just wasn't enough time for lunch – in Europe. My lifelong passion for fast food must have been born that summer of '33.

Our other haunt made lunch a little easier, in some ways. Immediately on being seated, by the forever "honored" proprietor and his courtly head waiter, the carts were summoned! Their mahogany frames aglow, their recessed silver trays filled with row upon row of oblong glass dishes brimming with the treasures of many gardens, seas, and farms. They rolled toward us in procession, pushed by proud waiters like nannies parading their English prams in the Bois de Boulogne. We didn't eat at the Belle Aurore – we gorged there! Each time we went, we would find some dish that we had not tasted and must add to all the others we already knew we wanted again. Skirts that had been finished and approved had to be opened and refitted, waistbands remeasured and enlarged. My mother was gaining weight! Usually a real crisis, but as she did not have to shoot the next days, the usual starving and purging with epsom salts was not necessary, yet. But something had to be done for the fittings and so, a new member joined our little group, the "girdle!" The very latest thing, it was made of flesh-colored rubber and smelled a little like a bicycle tire. We bought dozens.

My mother, who hated even her garter belts, loathed these rubbery things, especially the line they made beneath her narrow skirts. The garter belt at least allowed the line from thigh to crotch to show unhampered while moving, but this thing cut the line and created its own – right across at midthigh.

"They make you look as though you have short legs and an old behind, all flat!" she said, but tried wearing one for almost two weeks, then she gave some to Tami and the rest to our chambermaid and that was that. But, while our rubber friend lasted, he played a starring part in what might be titled "The Little Girls' Room Caper." Why my mother referred to a toilet as a room for a little girl I never knew. She probably learned it that way when she first came to Hollywood, and it stuck. In her entire life, she never asked directions to the "powder room," "ladies' room," or just plain everyday "bathroom." That is, when she needed one, which was practically never! Dietrich considered it extreme bad taste to rise from a table in order to relieve one's bladder. This, as well as the incredible discipline required in her profession, plus her pathological fear of all unknown toilet seats, created the most regimented kidneys I have ever known. Of course, those of us within her immediate circle were expected to do the same.

So, when suddenly in the middle of one of our luncheon feasts, my mother took Tami by the hand and, rising, announced that they were going to "the little girls' room," I was amazed. As no one told me to go, I sat and looked at my father. He had not liked them leaving the table like that, I was sure. We didn't speak. We sat and waited. The room buzzed, as it always did when Dietrich moved among the mortals. They returned, giggling like two naughty schoolgirls. My mother wriggled into the banquette, clutching her crocodile handbag to her chest like some secret treasure. My father smiled; her look of fun was so infectious!

"Mutti, what have you been up to? If you keep laughing like that, you will have to go back to the bathroom!" My mother was really laughing this time, even Tami had joined in.

"But Papi! We didn't go to the toilet to pee! We didn't have to. You know what we did? We took off our girdles, so we can eat more!" With that, she motioned us to duck under the table with her and there showed us her rubber hate tucked inside her handbag. As we came up for air, my father, in his best professor voice, asked,

"But what did you do with your stockings?"

"We rolled the tops round our finger and made a knot – like whores do!"

Now they were all laughing. I wondered if I could find that word in my dictionary. The way it had been said, I somehow doubted it.

The Belle Aurore's "little girls' room" was really over-honored by Dietrich's presence. Another ploy to escape gaining weight was practiced within its mirrored splendor – "the finger down the throat to induce vomiting" trick. After all, we were indulging in bacchanalian feasts, why not go the Roman way – heave, in order to eat again! I hated that. I hated the giggling, the sounds of their retching. It was my job to stand guard to make sure that no one entered until they were finished. I felt this was wrong, a bad thing for Tami, not for my mother – she could get away with anything. Nothing touched her, she wasn't real! But Tami was and could get hurt. They did this all through Europe and thought it was a lark. I worried, but didn't know what to do to stop it. This was a long time before bulimia would be recognized, but I felt its ominous shadow over someone I loved. I just didn't know its name.

My mother came up with a perfect solution for those uncomfortable after-lunch fittings. From then on, we fitted the clothes in the mornings and hats in the afternoons.

"My head doesn't get fat," she would say. "And if we still have time, after hats we can buy veiling to put away when we need it in Hollywood. Also, I want to get those wonderful silk carnations. The Studio doesn't have any of those and you never know . . ."

Uncanny woman! A year later, she would build the opening costume around those flowers for *The Devil Is a Woman*. We also went "leather shopping."

To watch my father inspect a piece of luggage at Hermès was a production. First, he would put on his gloves. Anyone's finger marks on the leather's high gloss was a sacrilege. Each hand-sewn seam was scrutinized for the tiniest flaw, the grain of the leather viewed both in daylight and in the artificial light of the showroom. Absolutely nothing escaped his connoisseur's eyes. Salesmen stood aside and trembled! He took his time. I have seen my father inspect a dozen pieces of glowing perfection, or what looked like to us poor mortals as perfection, before he was satisfied. We, the three females, were often sent out to sit at one of the cafés near Hermès. My mother, annoyed but resigned, would have coffee and smoke her cigarettes. Tami and I loved these "inspection" breaks and would choose raspberry water-ice in heavy silver goblets, surrounded by tiny fan-shaped cookies. We knew to eat fast – Dietrich wasn't all that obedient to her husband's idiosyncrasies.

Usually, we arrived back just as he found the one unique suitcase worthy of her and could counsel my mother to buy it without hesitation. There wasn't a store in Europe whose staff didn't shudder on seeing Rudolph Sieber enter their hallowed portals. But, despite their inner groans, they respected his amazing knowledge and taste. Never, in all the glamour years, was my father ever shown inferior merchandise. They wouldn't have dared! Many have written about Dietrich's husband as though he used her money negligently. It may have looked that way from the outside, but no. My mother adored his elegance, his instinct for what was correct and dignified, his exquisite sense of luxury, and catered to all this by buying anything he approved of and then giving it to him. He, on the other hand, was forever trying to teach her not to squander her money. When that finally became an impossible task, he settled for the only way left open to him – to show her what was junk and what was truly worthy of her money. She was going to buy everything for everyone anyway, might at least make sure she wasn't cheated.

We all knew my mother never tired, that she was surprised and scathing of those who fell by the wayside, so in preparation for our late dinners at Maxim's and other lush nighttime forays, my father scheduled some important accounts that *had* to be done in his apartment in Paris, and went home to take a nap. Tami, under the guise of seeing to his needs, also escaped to rest, furtively. I was left to guard and chaperon our hallowed personage, which was all right. I was trained to keep up with my mother's astounding lack of peace. I did worry about Teddy, though. I hoped the dog could stand the pace, he still had Vienna and Salzburg ahead of him.

Maxim's – all "Belle Epoque," tassels, scarlet velvet, mirrors, and gold. Candles and cut-glass lamps, the light so soft that every woman looked an untouched maiden and every man a soft-focus mystery. The whole place glowed! And I was not impressed! Wasn't that awful? I knew I should be, but when you come from a world where they can build you an exact duplicate, it is difficult to have the right respectful perspective toward reality. I was not unique in this, it's the profession. You live a life of visual illusions made to seem real. Ancient Rome is in your backyard and the Red Sea parts around the corner. The history of your universe laid out for you to walk around in, all you have to do is move from one soundstage to another. Everything is there – but nothing lives until some god shouts, "LIGHTS, CAMERA, ACTION!" and suddenly, all is vibrant and alive, and even that is mimicry. It does something to one's attitude toward life. This is not bad, not always, just different. I think it may be the reason that show people stay with their own kind – they need to be with people who react as they do. They seek the safety and familiarity to be found within their own species. But my mother never did. Actors were Gypsies after all, while she was a "born aristocrat." She put up with actors with a very small *a* and "movie people," as she referred to them, when she had to or was in love with one. But very soon would leave them behind in her quest for "writers of important books," incandescent statesmen, flamboyant generals, sublime musicians, recognized people – the revered famous. After all, *her* species was Living Legends.

My mother looked particularly beautiful that evening. She wore one of the new evening dresses that finally fit, the slinky black velvet, with all the bird of paradise feathers dyed to match, from Patou. They fanned out from her naked shoulders, throwing their mysterious pattern across that luminous skin. Long evening gloves, of the same material as the dress, her Mae West-type diamond-and-ruby bracelet, magnificent square-cut diamond brooch – and you had one gorgeous movie star! My father, in white tie and superbly cut tails, understated Lalique and diamond studs, his blond hair only slightly darker than hers, looked more than ever like her equally gorgeous brother. They made a stunning picture in black and white. Tami and I were no slouches, she in that long black silk with the rhinestone-buckled belt that von Sternberg always liked so on my mother, I, in my new sapphire-blue velvet with wide lace collar à la Three Musketeers. Our group usually stopped traffic. It could also stop conversations in midsentence. The much more famous, powerful, and wealthy would stop whatever they were doing just to feast their eyes and senses, according Dietrich a moment of homage, as though she had really done something very special to deserve it. What she had done was a few very good films, with dedicated skill and hard work, polished and honed her image, and been born incredibly beautiful. This seemed to be sufficient to rank among the angels. I didn't question this – it just always confused me.

"Sweetheart, don't worry about your dress. You can sit on silk velvet. It doesn't crush. But only real French velvet. All other velvets give you big flat marks that don't fall out, right on your behind." She held her champagne glass against her lower lip and surveyed Maxim's across its thin edge. Dietrich had a way of setting up a perfect close-up, whether there was a camera there to shoot it or not.

"Papi? They can't *all* be dress extras!" I choked on my okayed lemonade – my mother had to whack me on my uncrushable back. She loved to make me laugh with our own brand of "inside" humor. At times like these, my father and Tami were the outsiders. I tried to explain it to Tami, who felt left out of a happy moment.

"Tamilein, when we need people to fill a scene, you know, like in a bus or on a street, we get 'extras.' But if the director needs men and women in evening dress, real elegant, like here, central casting hires people from a special list that says they have their own evening attire of good quality and can look like real ladies and gentlemen. They report to the set, all groomed, brilliantined, and marcelled, and dress the set. That's why they are called 'dress extras.' They also know how to dance politely. The slow fox trot, waltz, and sometimes tango, but not for musical numbers – just background dance-floor dancing. They are usually older actors who haven't made it, and they are very, very careful with their clothes."

"They sound like sad people, Katerlein."

I always liked the way Tami made my tomcat name sound soft and small.

"It must be terrible to get work only because you own an evening dress. What if something happens to it?"

Tami was the most compassionate human being I ever knew. She felt protective toward everyone except herself. If her destiny had not decreed that she be the sacrificial lamb of my mother and father, what a wife and mother she might have been.

But we had talked enough. One did not indulge in private conversation at my mother's table. She led the conversation, she did not join in, unless she was in her disciple role, the one automatically assumed when in the presence of "great" minds. With von Sternberg it had been okay. In later years, though, she overplayed it terribly, literally at their feet in blatant adoration. Noël Coward thought it false and in bad taste; Cocteau just adored it – naturally; Orson Welles, who knew her, smiled and went right on eating; Hemingway told her to get up; Patton snorted with pleasure and slapped his crop; Edward R. Murrow, Adlai Stevenson, Sir

Alexander Fleming actually blushed, and de Gaulle thought it only proper – didn't everyone worship him? Tami and I certainly never belonged to that charmed circle, so we sat up straight, turned our heads away from each other, and paid respectful attention to my father giving an inspired dissertation on the merits of black cherry sauce over the recommended Seville orange one for that evening's roast duck.

So, it looked like I was having duck. At least, a change from my liver. Let's see – that meant: lots of fancy fluted artichoke hearts done like little pale green baskets, filled with a mousse of spring peas, glazed pearl onions cascading over individual bundles of braised Belgian endive tied with plaited ropes of chives. But before that, we had to survive the appetizer, soup, and fish courses. At least I had my digestive lemonade to flush it all down, but the grown-ups went through five different wines, besides the dry champagne served while my father was planning dinner and the sweet one, served with the dessert. If you are counting, you might ask, "Why *five* wines when there were only four courses left unaccounted for?" Wrong – the cheese! That just had to have its own special bottle too, something called after some banker Rothschild or something! I had lost track of all those labels. Besides, my wine training didn't start seriously until I was thirteen. I just wondered how they could drink all that stuff. The evening went on and on. My back felt permanently fused. My jaws hurt from chewing all day. My mother looked as though she had just had twelve hours' sleep. My father's clever nap kept him going. Tami wouldn't dare wilt, even if her life depended on it. If I fell asleep on top of the Camembert, I'd never be forgiven! I pinched my leg as hard as I could, that always startled me awake – for a while anyway.

Someone came to our table to greet Dietrich. He looked as elegant as my father, spoke French, and must have been important, for my mother stood as he kissed her hand. My father had risen, of course Tami and I jumped up. The waiters must have thought we were leaving before the crepes Suzette! Dietrich always rose for elderly ladies and those she designated as deserving of this sign of her respect. With my orders to stand up whenever she did, it could look very strange at times. As famous people went to famous places, there to see other famous people, someone was always approaching our table to kiss the hand of "Marlene." Usually, up she stood, with us like fishing floats bobbing to the surface to join her as expected. Sometimes we must have looked as though we were all waiting for a bus! My father was discussing the right technique of chafing-dish flaming, when I finally asked to be allowed to walk Teddy, and, "Please, could Tami come too?" We got a:

"Yes! But don't be long, your lemon soufflé tarts will be served soon."

Once outside, the fresh air felt wonderful. We put our arms around each other's waists and Teddy walked us.

"Tamilein, do you think it is possible that Maxim's lemon tart could be made with yesterday's squeezed lemons?"

The picture of us, frozen stiff from exhaustion, waiting for Papi to straighten out Maxim's and their faulty lemons, struck us so funny, we got the giggles and couldn't stop. We were so punchy we were hugging each other, crying with laughter. Teddy stopped, to allow us to lean against a lamppost and get hold of ourselves! When he considered we had, he gave us a "tut-tut" look of censure and conducted us back to Maxim's.

Of course, the hundreds of daily telephone calls never ceased during this time. My mother phoned Berlin often, sometimes spoke to her mother and sister. No conversations really, just telling them her news. She rarely ever asked anyone what they were doing anyway, so these calls were my mother giving information, while those in Berlin listened attentively.

"Mutti, this work is ridiculous, no one knows their business! The songs are stupid. I have to change all the words. All they can write is songs like for *The Blue Angel*. You know how I hated *The Blue Angel* – all that terrible vulgarity! Rudi made this contract, so I *have* to do it, make all these records – he says I need the money! I make all that money in Hollywood – how can I already need money? But he insists. This hotel he found is beautiful and very expensive. But you know him, he only gets the best for me and The Child. The hotel and all the reservations in Austria are made for you and Liesel. We will arrive from Paris before you get there. Rudi has sent you your tickets. You will not believe how The Child has grown – even more than on the pictures. Did the coat I sent fit Liesel? I took an extra-large size. She can wear that on the train and look nice. Let me know what else you want from Paris. Don't worry, Rudi has got time to go shopping. Here is The Child – she wants to say something."

"How are you behaving yourself?" Without waiting for my answer, my grandmother went right on in that headmistress manner of hers. "Do not be in your mother's way. Remember, always be helpful wherever you can, but know your place, Maria."

When my mother spoke to her sister, her tone was softer, as though very patient with a slightly backward child, her German not so sharp around the verbal edges.

"Lieselchen, did you get the wool stockings? Aren't they wonderful? Just perfect? I know you always like to be warm on your legs. Yesterday I sent you those laces for your shoes. Rudi found them – he finds everything! . . . Bring me books when you come, German books are the only intelligent ones. . . . Mutti said you liked the brown coat and that it was not too big. Do you have a hat that you can wear with it for the train? . . . Do you need a new handbag too? . . . What? You want something from here? What can I get for you, Liebling? . . . Anything! The works of Molière? . . . In French? I will tell Rudi, he will get it for you. But won't that be a lot of books? . . . No, no – of course it isn't too expensive. You can have anything you want! . . . I just thought you would like to have something nice to *wear*. Don't worry, you will have your books *and* a dress, to go with the coat! Here is The Child . . . ," she handed me the receiver. "Sweetheart, say something nice! . . . to Liesel."

"Hello Tante Liesel . . ."

"Oh, Heidede," she still called me that. She got so easily confused by change that I never told her that now I was known again as Kater. My Tante Liesel always reminded me a little of Tami. They were both so petrified of displeasing their superiors that they made constant mistakes just from trying too hard.

"Sweet Heidede – I can't wait to see you again, sweet child! When we see each other, you must tell me all about America and Hollywood and your big house with the swimming pool and your mother, who works so hard and is so very, very beautiful. She was always so beautiful! Did you know that?" She was happily rattling on, as she always did when excited. My grandmother must have reprimanded her, as she often did, on her lack of self-control, for Liesel suddenly caught her breath and whispered, "I kiss you, child, and see all the wonders of Paris," and quickly hung up the phone.

While we worked, fitted, and ate, von Sternberg was writing *The Scarlet Empress* and fighting with Paramount. My mother didn't discuss her next film, she was really not interested. When everything had been created, settled, and approved to her "leader's" satisfaction, he would let her know and only then would we return to Hollywood and report for work to embellish his concept. Von Sternberg was the only man who ever received this utter professional trust from Dietrich. After they parted for good, she kept looking for his protective genius in every director. Only when her desperate search ended in constant disappointment did she release her own genius where Dietrich was concerned, and leave his far behind. She did have the intelligence to know that every tool she used so skillfully in building her own shrine came from him – originally. For many years, Dietrich's extravagant public acknowledgment of von Sternberg's greatness, in relationship to herself of course, embarrassed – even angered him at times. He should have been revered for more than just the discovery of one unique woman. He may have suspected, early on in his association with my mother, that he wouldn't be.

My mother received an official cable from the almighty "front office." First she frowned while she read it, then she laughed.

"Papi, listen to this . . ." and she read the cable out loud: " 'Mr. von Sternberg has informed us that he has been in telephone conference with you and has outlined to you the trend of the story. Stop. Will you please wire your acceptance of this subject so that we can officially advise Mr. von Sternberg to proceed. Stop. I hope that you are in good health and having a pleasant rest. Stop. With all good wishes, Emanuel Cohen, Vice-president in Charge of Production.' Isn't that too funny? Jo has been telling them that we have 'telephone conferences' together! They are so stupid, they believe him. What do we need conferences for? He will tell me what to do and I will do it. Very simple! And *they* are going to 'officially' advise *Mr.* von Sternberg? They should kiss his feet, instead of De Mille's behind. Those Russian Jews were little furriers, and now they think they are God!"

With that, she licked the end of her stubby pencil and cabled her answer to von Sternberg – not to Paramount:

JOSEF VON STERNBERG
PARAMOUNT STUDIOS
HOLLYWOOD CALIF=

TAKE FOR YOURSELF FROM MY IMMENSE LOVING AS MUCH AS YOU NEED STOP NOT SO MUCH THAT IT WOULD DISTURB YOU AND NOT TOO LITTLE EITHER THAT IT WOULD GIVE YOU TROUBLE ETERNALLY YOUR GREATEST FAN SHOULDER TO SHOULDER STOP A KISS FROM PAPI UNSIGNED

WHEN IT WAS TIME TO CUT THE RECORDS, my mother did not take me with her to the recordings. My father conducted me to the Cathedral of Notre-Dame instead. It was so beautiful! Just like in *The Hunchback of Notre Dame*, but much bigger and with many more gargoyles than I remembered. Once inside, I stood transfixed beneath an enormous window. It was round, like a giant jewel – aglow with color! That's something you missed in movies – the color of things! Like this unbelievable blue, translucent yet even deeper than my mother's sapphire ring or my famous Christmas tree. And the reds! As if all the rubies in the whole world had been mixed up together. My father was telling me that it was called a rose window, that it was thirty feet across and had not shifted over more than six hundred years! That it was used as an example of perfection for all master builders. Clear glass, still soft, was "flashed" – dipped into molten ground colored glass, where it received a thin film of color. Metallic oxides (whatever those were) were mixed into the glass when it was made, copper for green, cobalt for blue, manganese for purple. He didn't say what made the beautiful red, so maybe it was ground rubies after all! I tried to pay attention to my lesson, but the heavenly petaled window made me feel so dreamy I missed a lot of what my father was trying to teach me.

"Now, come over here, Kater," and I learned what exactly made an arch Gothic. The next time I saw one of our papier-mâché ones in the Prop Department, I would show off with all this new architectural knowledge. I took a furtive peek into the shadows of a nave. . . . Mr. Chaney and his poor hump might still be lurking, somewhere. My father taught me not to turn my back on an altar with its crucifix, and that one had to curtsey before kneeling down to pray. I knew from seeing De Mille films, but I had never done it myself. It was all cool and peaceful inside that great vaulted church. My father said I could pray if I wanted to. I remember being embarrassed, I didn't know how one did that correctly inside a church. It seemed sort of phony to do it like in the movies, but I really felt like saying something "good," so I decided to thank God for a special day. I hoped it would pass as an acceptable church prayer. We lit a tall candle before a little altar. My father paid for it by putting coins into a slot above a metal box. They made a terrible clanking noise as they slid down the chute, but no one minded. When we came out, the sunshine was bright in our eyes, as though the reflectors had been set up for a scene. I remember being strangely happy that day. My father had made a convert to all churches, if not exactly to Catholicism.

We had room service that evening. My mother didn't want to change. She told me of the day's work and how much she had missed me sitting in front of her while she sang. I was glad that she didn't ask what I had done that day. I felt instinctively that she wouldn't like enthusiasm about a church. Notre-Dame as a history lesson would have been all right, but as an emotional experience, that would be disapproved of for sure. My father was not so perceptive.

"Mutti, I took Kater to Notre-Dame today, and she prayed!"

My mother swiveled in her chair toward me, smiling. "You prayed? You are just a child, you cannot know how to pray – seriously!"

She turned back to my father.

"One of the violinists today was terrible, a real amateur! I showed him how, but it was useless. We had to change him and lost valuable time. That would never have happened if you had allowed us to record in *Berlin*!"

My father's mouth set, a muscle twitched along his jaw. He rang for the waiters to clear the table.

Religion was a taboo subject, to be avoided with my mother. That is, if one believed in anything! Dietrich did not like God. He could make things happen over which she had no control. This frightened her and made Him the enemy. She believed that if one needed a deity, it was a sign of personal weakness.

"That unknown thing that is supposed to float around up there – with angels? What do they all do up there? Get in each other's way? Ridiculous! Of course, the Bible is the best script ever written, but you can't really believe it!" She was proud of her logic and consequent disdain toward all religions. But she picked them up when it suited her. In later years, whenever my mother flew, at take-off time out came a little chamois bag from which emerged a gold chain, hung with:

> one cross
> one miraculous medal
> one St. Christopher medal
> one capricorn insignia
> the Star of David
> – and a rabbit's foot

My mother wasn't taking any chances. Maybe something was up there, after all! When the plane landed, she removed the chain from around her neck and put it back into its little bag, never to be used again – until the next flight among the clouds. On earth, Dietrich felt no need for the added protection of her good-luck charms.

I had a new dress for the opera! It just appeared on my bed out of nowhere, like Cinderella's! Forget-me-not blue silk, with scalloped lace collar and matching bolero jacket. The obligatory white gloves were of real kid leather, as were my Mary Janes. For this special occasion, even my ankle socks were of silk. My father was again resplendent in his tails, this time with black pearl studs and carrying his marvelous top hat. It had emerged from its special box as flat as a pancake and sprung up into its proper shape when slapped against his bent knee. Just like a black silk jack-in-the-box. I had waited to be allowed to slap it open for him. Sometimes he let me when I had my gloves on. I was very good at snapping top hats, my mother had dozens of them and this was one of my jobs, but my father didn't trust me with clothes the way my mother did. This evening, she was a vision in white chiffon, the fine material sculpted to her body like a second skin, a Greek statue. I had helped her tape her breasts with wide strips of adhesive tape, the way we did at the Studio, to make the breasts appear naked and perfect, not needing the support of a brassière. She had diffused the sculptured effect by multiple layers of white fox stitched to yards of chiffon cut on the bias. She looked as though she had wrapped herself in a cumulus cloud. Why did Dietrich always appear so tall, when she really wasn't? The height of the heels was not the reason. She never wore shoes with the four-inch variety. Those she called "whore shoes." That word – she used it so often and I never did know really what it meant, only that it was okay to look like one for a film but *never* in life.

We drove in all our splendor to the Place de l'Opéra and its opera house, all lit up like a giant birthday cake for a crew party. Tami did not come. Maybe our good fairy had not fitted her out for this evening. We swept up one grand staircase, flanked by golden winged statues, and up another equally imposing set of stairs covered in royal red carpeting that cast a pink glow onto the white marble banisters. We had our own box. As we approached, it was unlocked for us by a liveried footman who bowed as we entered. Swags of ruby velvet, clutched aside by gilded cherubs, crystals bouncing light from huge chandeliers. Again, the thousands of colors made the scene fantastic. Mr. Chaney was here, too – right there, under that vast stage, hiding his horrible face, waiting for the lights to dim. And talk about dress extras!! For my end-of-picture gift, Brian had given me a delicate pair of opera glasses – all gold and mother-of-pearl. I had never been able to use them in Hollywood, but now I made up for lost time! I brought into focus stunning women in repose, bored men, most of them old and older, dowagers all done up in fresh beauty-parlor curls and silver lace, gentlemen with elegant watch chains looped across prosperous stomachs. A lot of fussing with programs, opera gloves, and long strings of pearls. From the "ritzy" section, I shifted my glasses up and there I saw excitement, anticipation – young people who seemed so happy to be there. Wherever I looked, there were opera glasses looking right back at me, or more correctly, at our box and its special attraction. I can't remember what we saw that memorable evening, I was too excited by all the trappings. I do know that the lady who sang so beautifully was very fat and that her makeup needed Mr. Westmore badly, and although the baritone matched his loved one's bulk, his voice didn't, and my mother and I agreed: He should have been "synched." During the intermission, we strolled elegantly along marbled halls. Everyone drank champagne and tried to get closer to my mother, who behaved as usual as though she was alone on a desert island calmly smoking her cigarette, while ladies and gentlemen stared, pretending that they weren't. Little chimes, like those on a ship, summoned us back to our red velvet nest and another exhibition of "what could never sell a single ticket at the Roxy" began.

"*That* should have been much better!" my mother said as she rose to leave. After hours of sitting, there was not a single wrinkle on her — anywhere. How did she do that? I quickly tried to smooth the marks from my silk behind. Dietrich never understood the problems we mere mortals faced when trying to keep up with her. That extraordinary staircase was just as wonderful going down as it had been going up. Outside, as we stood waiting for our chariot, a young man with a rather ugly face approached and reverently kissed my mother's hand. She was definitely flattered by his gesture. I wondered who he could be. They spoke in French, as though they knew each other. After a few minutes, he lifted a slender white hand in farewell and disappeared down the marble stairs. A bevy of pretty young men fluttered after him, their white satin-lined evening capes fanning out behind them, like elegant little bats.

We met Jean Cocteau often over the years. My father thought he was an over-lauded mediocrity. I think Gabin did too. Remarque once said to me that he wished Cocteau would stop trying to be a poet who thought he was also Picasso. My mother kept all of his little notes to her. She too commented on his habit of drawing faces amidst the text.

"Why can't Cocteau just write a simple letter one can read! Instead of creating little treasures for posterity! I suppose it makes them more valuable. You can sell them and get a fortune, some day!"

It was so late, we went to a nightclub for dinner. That turned out to be a better show than the opera! A giant Cossack, complete with sheep's hat and carbine strapped to his ample back, opened our car door. This gave you a pretty good idea of what you were in for inside. Sure enough, Czarist Russia lay before us — aglow from the light of a thousand candles and bits of burning meat stuck on thin rapiers. Balalaikas moaned and my mother swooned. All her life, Dietrich embraced the drama of White Russians, as they were referred to, fleeing their homeland and the terror of the Russian Revolution. Despite having Tami's flight as proof to the contrary, my mother visualized it all as if it were a reworked Tolstoy script directed by Eisenstein. She romanticized Russia. She always wanted to play Anna Karenina, and hated Garbo for doing the film and refused to see it. She identified with characters who "died for love." Whether in reality my mother could ever have loved anyone sufficiently to actually be driven to throw herself in front of a moving train, I doubt. But that she could visualize herself doing so, in sable-edged velvet and violets, of that I am certain. Long before *The Scarlet Empress*, Russia meant Cossacks on wild horses, weeping balalaikas, lacquered red sleds with lovers nestled amongst wolf skins careening over Siberian wastelands, while healthy peasants in high-collared tunics sang their sad Slavic songs, waving them on. Neither Karl Marx nor Stalin ever changed Dietrich's lyrical version of Mother Russia. The siege of Stalingrad in the forties was right up her dramatic alley, and when we were all jubilant over our then ally's heroic stand against Hitler's armies, Dietrich felt her long fidelity to all things Russian vindicated. Her triumphal tour of the Soviet Union in 1964 only solidified her devotion. Thereafter one learned to keep one's opinions on Communism to oneself – unless one enjoyed being subjected, for the umpteenth time, to one of Dietrich's favorite doctrines:

"The Russians – only they know how to treat artists! They respect us! They are all intelligent! They feel with their souls! Americans should learn from them. But they are so brainwashed, they are so afraid of Russia, they shiver in their beds and play baby!"

"Rasputin" bowed low – waiting to take our order for dinner. Russian restaurant ordering was a little easier. Out went the wine discussions, in came the vodka and all the appetizers were replaced by caviar. The vodka carafe had to be frosted with cold, the caviar fresh beluga in five-pound lots with bone or mother-of-pearl spoons to eat it with; but, as these necessities were automatically met by any self-respecting Russian establishment, my father never had to get as fussy – as fast. Shashlik always took the place of my liver. I liked the drama of meat on fire.

"Mamutschka," my father could also be very theatrical when the setting demanded it, "the cold borscht for the chicken Kiev, but if you insist on the stroganoff . . ."

I ladled another mountain of caviar onto my plate; it was midnight and I was starving. As my mother had very strong views on Russian cooking, having learned it all from Tami, she didn't give in as easily, it might be a while before they agreed! I watched the way everyone was drinking their vodka. Thumb and third finger around shot glass filled to the brim, a deft lift to the lower lip, head slightly back, tip entire contents straight down the throat, lower glass with sharp downward gesture. Choke, eat – repeat procedure. I filled my shot glass with water and gave a brilliant performance. My choke was worthy of Sarah Bernhardt.

"Look! Papi! What The Child just did! Sweetheart – how did you learn to do that so perfectly?"

My mother made me do my whole routine over again. She loved it!

"Did you see that? Marlene Dietrich's little girl is drinking – *vodka*!"

A shocked voice stage-whispered at the next table. My mother suddenly noticed that she and her child were being observed and censured.

"Sweetheart," she whispered. "Do it again! They really think I am letting you drink real vodka. 'What Movie Stars allow their children to do!' I can see the headlines: 'Dietrich lets daughter drink in Paris nightclub!' How stupid people are, the same all over the world. Now, let's do it together and really shock them!" and in perfect unison, we slung back our liquor and went back to our caviar. From then on, whenever we were in a Russian restaurant, I had to do my act. It always played to a packed house of outraged spectators and my mother enjoyed every performance.

The first cuts of the new records arrived. With great ceremony, we all had to sit and listen, while my mother watched our expressions and controlled the gramophone. Listening to my mother's records was always a solemn occasion, full of pitfalls if you didn't know the rules. Unconditional congratulations were expected, except from respected professionals and me. After the first three times, the "civilian" listeners were excused. The favored few had to remain for another four or five run-throughs before she was satisfied that we had absorbed and savored all to the fullest. Only then would she accept our comments and possible criticism. Once she respected your opinion, she took constructive criticism marvelously. She even improved on your suggestions – if you were clever enough to present them in such a way that it left her room to find her own improvements.

Everyone was sent the new records. She had ordered her usual dozens. Packing them all was a big production. The 78s were thick and broke like glass. They also weighed a ton, but that didn't matter, everything had to be mailed by ship or rail in those days anyway. The first two packages were addressed to von Sternberg and de Acosta.

Brian was coming! I shined my best shoes and brushed my navy blue dress, spitting on my clothes brush as my mother had taught me, to catch the tiniest speck of lint. Maybe I could take him to Notre-Dame. I wouldn't have to mention Lon Chaney to him, Brian would be looking in the shadows all by himself! But there was no time to ask him, he arrived late, just had time to give me a fast kiss and was whisked off to dinner. Tami, Teddy, and I had room service and listened to the music that drifted up from our rehearsal hall that had been given back its proper identity of ballroom.

The atmosphere was very strange the next morning. If I had not been trained not to ask questions, I would have. No sign of Brian. Not even a phone call. I was very worried about him. Two days later my mother walked into our sitting room, her usual coffee cup in one hand, a letter in the other.

"Papilein, a letter from Brian – finally!" she announced. He had gone back to London? He just got here. And I didn't even get to tell him about not using the word *alas* when he wrote to her! Why did he leave? What had happened?

12 June 1933

My darling love,

Have I made you very unhappy? I have certainly made myself most bitterly miserable. I never hope to spend a worse twenty-four hours, but oh! I don't want you to be unhappy.

It is all Rudi's fault. I have not been so impressed by a man for years. His integrity, his honesty and his dignity, and above all his simple goodness, were more than I could bear. If he had been hostile or awkward with me I would have understood and would not have minded: as it was I was deeply touched by the proud and loving way in which he spoke to me of "my wife" and the way in which he held your hand and looked at you, and by your own stories of his devotion. Each thing you told me made me feel cheaper and cheaper – though heaven knows there is nothing cheap in my feeling for you – until as we were sitting at dinner I suddenly felt that the situation was more than strange. It was impossible. I watched you leaning on his shoulder and I knew that I loved you very deeply and wished I did not. I wanted to crush you in my arms and not let you go at all, but beyond you I could see Rudi and then I wanted to burst into tears instead. Life is so incredibly complicated and confused and there seems so little we can do about it. I watched you drive off and then I turned and went up to my room and sat down in my coat, all flushed with champagne and emotion. I was so tired I could not think clearly any more. I got blindly to the Gare du Nord and sat dumbly staring out of the window thinking of you all the way to Calais. Your happiness means more to me than Rudi's, or than my own amour propre.

Do you understand all this and will you write and tell me what you think? There is one fact that stands out above all else. It is very mysterious but absolutely real – I love you. There is just no discussing our thinking further about that.

I will come instantly by aeroplane if you think it would help to talk, but there are only two things that matter – I must not make you unhappy and I must be square with Rudi. How can these things be reconciled?

She finished reading Brian's letter. She handed it to my father and went into her bedroom, leaving the door open. In her annoyed voice, she placed a person-to-person call to London. She sat on the edge of her bed, smoking, drinking the rest of her coffee, waiting for the hotel operator to call her back. French phones didn't ring like normal ones, they gargled. She lifted the ivory-and-gold receiver off its tall gilt prongs, saying:

"Brian? I just received your ridiculous letter! I don't know what is the matter with you! Sweetheart – you must be joking! All this soul searching about poor Rudi. He is my husband! What has that to do with it? You can't be *that* bourgeois. . . ."

"Kater! Go to your room," my father said in that tone that made me scurry.

Brian did come back. Tami even got to go out to dinner with them, completing a foursome, but Teddy and I had room service. I didn't mind too much, at least Brian was okay and back. Besides, it was difficult being friends with someone in public when my mother was holding court. I put myself to bed quite happily, with the present Brian had brought me. A beautiful book, with strange pictures. By the time Alice fell down the rabbit hole, I was fast asleep.

It was time for our scheduled meeting with my mother's family. Out came the rolls of tissue paper, suitcases, hatboxes, and trunks. Some would accompany us to our first Austrian rendezvous, the rest would travel on to Vienna with Tami and Teddy. I don't remember where we met up with my grandmother and Tante Liesel. It must have been chosen very carefully, for it was hidden and no reporters found us there. A Heidi-type village, complete with gabled Madonna shrines on hilly footpaths and mountain flowers embroidered on everything. The hotel looked like a cuckoo clock and had mountainous eiderdowns covered in red-and-white checkered linen.

I was made a fuss over by my aunt and calmly observed by my mother's mother. I did not really remember them, as people – just the feeling one had when with them. That hadn't changed. My grandmother still made me think that I was about to be judged by the highest court in the land – for my own good. Not an "unfair" feeling, just a little uncomfortable. Liesel was still like an escaped canary, who flew to your shoulder hoping you would keep it safe until it could find its cage again. I met her son. He looked sort of Wagnerian and wore dark brown shirts. We disliked each other immediately.

The hotel sitting room was cool. The afternoon sun cast shadows on the hand-carved wooden frieze of squirrels and acorn leaves; the geraniums, lipstick red outside the six-paned windows made a pretty picture. We had tea and little cakes on blue Dresden china, on white linen draped over a pedestal table. My father was not with us. The eldest lady present poured. My mother sat very straight, her hands folded in her lap. Her mother did not ask her what she preferred in her tea. She poured in cream, sugared it, and handed her daughter the cup across the table.

"Thank you, Mutti. Please, The Child will have no cream." My mother hated cream in her tea, but I loved it. Did she want me to switch cups with her? I didn't see how I could manage to do that, with her mother right there watching, she who never missed a . . . I nearly dropped my fragile cup. Suddenly, like in the funny papers when a light bulb appeared above Dagwood's head to indicate he'd had a bright idea, I sat stunned in my carved chair realizing that my mother, who ruled us all with just a lift of her eyebrows, was scared of the lady serving us tea. Like finding out that your boss can get fired too. It was a heady thought. My grandmother spoke in her governess voice:

"Lena, this is a charming hotel. But it was not necessary to have two bathrooms. One would have been quite enough for us. The extravagance of a separate room for Liesel's boy also not necessary."

"Mutti, please. It is bad enough that you have to come here, that Rudi won't allow me into Germany – "

Her mother interrupted her: "Your husband has his reasons. They may even be justified. The political climate is to be observed carefully, not taken lightly as many do. Germany has need of a leader who will restore its national pride. A messiah? No, that borders on fanaticism, an explosive danger within a scarred nation."

I hung on her every word. What a fascinating lady she actually was. Liesel touched her mother's arm with a trembling hand.

"Please, Muttilein, please – lower your voice. Be careful – please!"

The waitress entered with a fresh pot of hot water. My aunt quickly put a finger against her lips, pleading for silence. My mother took her sister's other hand, unclenched it, patting it comfortingly.

"Lieselchen, you must not be frightened. We are in Austria!" but my aunt kept her finger pressed against her lips, beseeching.

The waitress closed the door behind her. My aunt turned toward my mother, words tumbling out of her mouth like pebbles rolling down a steep hill:

"Oh, Pussy Cat! You don't know. You don't know! Children march and listen – secretly! They are *told* to listen! And report what people say! And they do, they do! They are proud of it! At night, they roam the streets and sometimes people get hurt! And no one does anything to stop them. No one! Why? Pussy Cat, why? Our beautiful Berlin, that we loved so! What is happening?"

I wanted to hold her, but didn't dare. My grandmother was very annoyed at this outburst of her elder daughter. My mother seemed more concerned by her sister's fear than by what she had actually meant to convey. My cousin looked sullen and very ill at ease. I wondered why. We did not stay long in that gingerbread hotel.

My mother cried like a little girl lost the day she kissed her mother good-bye, who told her,

"That is sufficient! Lena, you really must learn to control your emotions!"

Liesel and I hugged each other, we were the two who liked to touch people and lived with those who never did. She whispered in my ear:

"Heidede, take care of your mother and kiss her for me and tell her that I thank her so much for . . . *everything!*" and stepped back quickly, before her mother caught her talking out of turn again. I curtsied, shook hands correctly, and said good-bye to my mother's mother. She looked down at me from her imposing height.

"You have turned out to be a good girl. A credit to your mother's upbringing."

Rare praise indeed. My mother was very pleased! I just had time to glare at my cousin, who glared back at me, before my father herded his three charges to the waiting car and then on to the railroad station for their return to Berlin. My mother and I waited at the hotel for him to return and repeat his specialized train-taking service with us. My mother seemed sad. She had not been able to persuade her mother to leave Germany and come live with us in America. I watched her as she stood by the geranium window. Perhaps she felt that her mother didn't want to live with her, no matter where it was? I was sure I would not be able to please both of them all the time, if we lived together.

Our next hotel suite looked like Viennese pastry done in sculpted plaster. Curlicues, cupids, bunches of grapes, urns, and turtledoves; the walls hung with gilt-framed mirrors, reflecting flowered satins in saltwater taffy colors. It could have passed for a very royal nursery, except for our usual florist shop display. The spotted elephants really disturbed all this fragile beauty, and for once I didn't mind my mother's mania for unpacking everything immediately upon arrival anywhere.

She had changed into a lounging pajama of black velvet with white silk braid that would have looked perfect on the back of a Lipizzaner being put through his paces.

"Sweetheart, at last – *Vienna!*" She flung open the French windows, stepped onto our rococo "Juliet" balcony, lifted her arms as though to embrace the city. "The city of music and poets, laughter and dreams! Sweetheart, come and see it!"

Her German had acquired a charming Austrian lilt. I joined her and together we breathed "the air of Mozart." She ordered her long dreamed of "real Viennese coffee with *schlag.*" I learned that this constant, ever-present *schlag* was actually only very thick, very rich whipped cream, and that the Viennese could not live without it. Even my mother had to admit that they put it on practically everything.

"Papilein, the Viennese probably *do* it with *schlag!*" she would say, and everyone would laugh. The "it" escaped me, but the words sounded funny, so I laughed right along.

I began my job of collecting the flower cards. Brian had sent masses of white and yellow tulips. Good, she liked them, especially if the colors were mixed. I would have to find some American pennies to put in their vase. For some reason, copper kept the tulips from drooping, and my mother insisted that her tulips stood at attention. Von Sternberg sent white roses, thank God not yellow ones. Those signified "the end of an affair," whatever that meant. My mother had some strange sayings about flowers. Now, red roses were only for the "beginning of an affair." She hated that color in roses anyway, especially when they were the long-stemmed kind that didn't fit into any vase and were too tall to put on tables. Even their names she couldn't stand, like "American Beauty." De Acosta had goofed. Her card nestled among a group of orchids, the big purple ones at that. They would certainly be given to the chambermaid immediately on being spotted; Mae West would have loved them. Paramount's arrangement of lilies, white irises, and snapdragons would follow close behind. There were even "those awful gardenias that shop girls wear at dances" from someone I did not know. The chambermaids were going to have a lovely haul.

Very few people really knew how to please my mother in the way of flowers. If you wanted to make Dietrich happy, you sent her a geranium pot! She also loved lilies-of-the-valley, cornflowers, white lilac, mixed European field flowers, and, in the thirties, tuberoses. But a bright red geranium was her very favorite, and just a single plant in a common flowerpot, not a fancy bowlful. Chevalier's offering was the best that day. His was a huge bouquet of white lilacs with an accompanying vase of cornflowers – for my father. I was proud of our Frenchman. My mother had noticed the cornflowers immediately – now she snapped off a blue flower and slipped it into my father's lapel:

"Papilein, isn't he sweet. He remembered how you love to wear a cornflower in your buttonhole and how we searched all over Beverly Hills that time, trying to find some for you. I drove him crazy! We looked everywhere, we even went as far as Hollywood Boulevard. I think Maurice loves you as much as he loves me." My father smiled.

The next day, reporters and adoring Austrians followed us to the House of Knize, the famous tailors, where we ordered tails, tuxedos, evening chesterfields, double-breasted suits, single-breasted suits, overcoats, dressing gowns, shirts in all categories, for both my father and my mother. That was the first day at Knize. The second day, we spent just choosing the cloth. Now my mother really enjoyed herself. These clothes she wanted to wear, looked forward to wearing. Besides, she always maintained that men's tailors knew what they were doing, that they were the real craftsmen, even those outside Hollywood, and Knize tailors – the very best in the world. She never changed her mind about Knize, and she was absolutely right. Years later, when having escaped to America before World War II, Knize opened his shop next to the St. Regis Hotel in Manhattan, she was the first jubilant customer, later allowing them to make all of her tails and accessories for the masculine portion of her stage performances. She even permitted them to make a special shirtfront, which was then sewn onto her secret foundation – to facilitate her famous fast change. No greater trust had Dietrich than to allow her foundation to be seen, let alone touched by strangers.

While waiting for the first fittings, we sat in sidewalk cafés, went to concerts, and ate. Either Mozart made you sick or the *schlag* did – you had a choice. I wished, just once, one of those constant strolling violinists, who insisted on sawing soulfully in your ear at every opportunity, would break into the opening bars of "California, Here I Come," but trills and frills is all they ever came up with.

They had adjoining fitting rooms. I couldn't make up my mind who looked better in their new tuxedos, my mother or my father. Each day Teddy and I wandered from one to the other, inspecting and approving. No need to do my mirror trick at Knize. They ripped out sleeves even before the Dietrich-Sieber contingent could find any imperfections.

We were in the middle of breakfast when my father gasped, gripped the sides of his back, jerked up, his chair falling backwards, his face pasty, glistening with sudden sweat. He was obviously in terrible pain! Frightened, my mother jumped up, demanding what was wrong with him. Tami, her arms wrapped around him, was trying to make him lie down on the settee. While my father was trying to handle the waves of pain, my mother placed emergency calls to Hollywood, London, Paris, and New York, looking for the world's greatest specialists for "very bad pains in the back." In the meantime, my father recovered sufficiently to phone the hotel manager, requesting a doctor to be sent up.

My mother was furious!

"You want some little hotel doctor? What will *he* know? He needs a hotel to give him patients! I am getting you the greatest specialist! He will know what it is! Not some little Yiddishe doctor!"

She was pacing, smoking, waiting for her calls to come through, when there was a discreet knock on our palace door. Tami hurried to open it, and there stood a little man, straight from central casting. Striped morning trousers, cutaway, celluloid collar and cuffs, pearl stickpin,

spats, and a pince-nez perched on an imposing nose. He was perfect!
Paul Muni could have played him. He walked over to the gentleman he
assumed was Herr Sieber, the one gritting his teeth on the settee, opened
his little black satchel, extracted the tools of his trade – all, without even
a fleeting glance in the direction of our "famous movie star." I liked him
immediately. I gravitated toward those not automatically impressed. My
mother withdrew to await her important calls in the privacy of her room,
our Viennese professor calmly went about his business of examining his
patient.

"Herr Sieber, you have just had the misfortune to experience a kidney
attack! Very painful – Yes – Very painful. A stone, or possibly several
of those offending particles have formed in your kidney and are presently
proceeding to depart this organ toward your receptive bladder. Hence the
pain of passage. You are most fortunate, most fortunate indeed, this has
occurred spontaneously. Otherwise, it might have been your misfortune
to be forced to contemplate the necessity of surgical removal of those
offending granules."

He wrote out a prescription, clipped the fountain pen back onto his
breast pocket, packed his bag, shined his lenses, replaced them on his
nose, shook my father's hand, nodded politely to Tami, and, with a last
admonition to his patient to drink at least three liters of mineral water a
day, left our premises. I felt like applauding. My mother, having heard
the diagnosis, called room service and ordered cases of Vitel to be sent
up and took command.

"Papilein, go to bed! Tami, find the housekeeper and get extra pillows.
Also hot water bottles for Papi's back. I am going downstairs to make beef
tea. This hoity-toity hotel must have filet mignon in their kitchen – but
probably *no* glass jars to boil it in! I will find some. Kater, you take the
prescription downstairs to the concierge. Have him send a bellboy right
away, although it probably won't help Papi at all . . . and put that dog
in Tami's bathroom – out of the way!"

The phone rang.

"My Hollywood call – Finally! – Jo, sweetheart! Rudi is in pain! He
has kidney stones! Oh – some little Jewish hotel doctor, looked like he
wandered in from another set. Can't be any good, but you know Papi
. . . has to have *his* way. But now, *you* find out who is the best doctor
out there for kidney stones. Didn't Pickford have some trouble once? So?
It's the middle of the night in California. So what? Call Pickford, that
husband of hers is probably still up, practicing his fencing. He certainly
can't be doing anything else around there at night!"

My mother hung up. The phone rang.

"Mercedes? Sweetheart! Rudi has kidney stones – I have to find a great doctor. Didn't Garbo have some trouble with peeing – or was that Stroheim when she made that awful picture with him, where she looked like a bleached chicken?"

My father passed many stones over the years. He collected them, kept them in a green leather stud-box from Florence, telling me that he planned to make a necklace with them one day, for me to wear. As they looked like little balls of pumice stone, I didn't think they would make up into a very pretty piece of jewelry and hoped he would be cured before he had enough to string them up together and make me wear them with my "uncrushable" blue velvet! For years, whenever we were "en famille," everyone would stop and listen for the distinctive *ping* as my father emptied his bladder. If we heard it, we cheered!

As my father was still "the patient," I was recruited to escort my mother to the various operas, ballets, concerts, and plays that the Vienna season was justly famous for. For my new job, I received two organdy dresses, a white with sky blue piping, a pale yellow with an embroidered hem of daisies, and my favorite, a long-sleeved navy blue linen that hid some of the extra rolls the *schlag* had created around my middle. As I was really the only unattractive object within my mother's aura, I felt if I couldn't even compete with the furnishings, I should at least attempt to fade into the woodwork. As the white and gold architecture made this a bit hard to do, I opted for shadowed places to disappear in – navy blue was great for that.

I was told to wear my yellow daisies the day I escorted my mother to see Vienna's matinee idol, Hans Jaray, in his latest triumph. It must have made quite an impression on me. I can't remember whether it was an operetta, a straight play, comedy or drama, or even its title. But my mother's performance, that was memorable. We sat in our box in one of those rococo theaters that reminded me of a Hollywood ice cream parlor that served sixty-nine flavors, when onto the stage strode a man in what I remember as being something very "Hapsburg-Hussar." Shapely legs encased in wrinkle-free white tights, a voice that Valentino should have had for the talkies, a face so dreamily romantic it could take your breath away, if you were so inclined, which my mother was! She leaned forward in her chair.

"Sweetheart! He is – Beautiful! Those eyes – look – Look at those eyes!" she breathed in a stage whisper that could have been heard in Yugoslavia by the deaf. Heads turned toward us and "shushed." Even the favored gentleman pecked with one so-"beautiful" eye in the direction of this adoring exclamation. Whenever my mother's emotions "pounced" in public like this, I cringed. Dietrich had a way of "falling in love" that was kamikazelike. Hans Jaray became her Viennese interlude and I wondered

ABOVE, LEFT: Looking very beautiful with well-behaved child.
LEFT: Teddy, Tami, Dietrich, and child, all dressed up as cute Austrians—except the dog. He refused.
BELOW: In her favorite Tyrolean mayoress outfit and decorative cow.

LEFT: In Salzburg, Marlene
and Rudi look even more like
brother and sister than usual.
BELOW: I posed continually.
My mother's trusty Brownie
was always pointing my way.

how von Sternberg, the White Prince, Chevalier, Fred Perry, my father, and Brian would react to this newcomer in tights. Most of all, I worried about Brian – the others, I was sure, knew how to protect themselves, but Brian might not.

We swept backstage. People backed aside to let us pass. Mr. Jaray bent over her extended hand, brushing his full lips across her alabaster skin. He raised his eyes and looked deep into her soul! I had to admit he was *something*! If there was such a thing as a "whipped-cream look," he had it! If it wasn't for that awful accent, he might have a chance in Hollywood. They were always looking for a Ramon Navarro type.

"The Child adored you," my mother trilled. Their eyes hadn't unlocked since the hand-kissing bit.

"She says she must have a photograph of you for her room." When Dietrich spoke for you, it was wiser to go along with her proclamations. As she was convinced that her opinions were the ultimate truth, it did not leave room for dissension. The fact that I thought Mr. Jaray was a pretty man who had nothing more going for him than a mushy look and my mother's present interest, had nothing to do with my expected attitude toward him. So I behaved in character – curtsied and was *very* grateful for the four lovely eight-by-tens he autographed to "Sweet Little Heidede" and, secretly, wished they were of Clark Gable. My mother received an even dozen.

She swept into my father's room, clutching the photographs to her body. She was a vision of "young girl aglow with love." If she had been wearing a big straw hat, it would have trailed blue satin ribbons!

"Papilein! He is beautiful! The way he moves! And the clothes – perfect! His eyes – you know how I hate dark eyes in a man, but – His? Are Perfect! He gave me all his pictures. Look. You can see what I mean!" and she spread Mr. Jaray across my father's bed. My father's brown eyes surveyed the images laid before him, smiled indulgently at his wife.

"I told you, Muttilein, he would interest you, that you *had* to see him. You see, I was right."

"Oh, Papilein. Yes, yes, you were so right! But then, you always are! You always *know*!" She swooped the glossy images back into her arms and floated out.

Tami, fussing with the pillows behind my father's head, asked me how I had enjoyed the performance, but I saw my father giving her one of his "shut up – be quiet" looks, so I asked only if he was feeling better and left the subject of my mother's latest pastime alone.

Strauss waltzes surged throughout our suite, setting every teardrop crystal a-jingle! Lilting, lyrical, lithe Vienna! Romance in dappled sunlight! My mother donned flowered chiffon and drifted about. I cranked the gramophone and turned the records. We kept ordering replacements for the "Blue Danube." "Hans" this and "Hans" that became her favorite topic of conversation. We listened attentively to: how wonderful he was, how sensitive, how sweet, how tender, and how he must have new shirts worthy of his beauty and accompanied her to Knize, where she ordered a dozen silk ones to hug his "perfect shoulders." Dressing gowns and pajamas came next.

Great bunches of lilacs filled every room, not sent by Chevalier. Every morning we did the mail, the cables, and the calls. Long letters from von Sternberg arrived. His loneliness seemed to be annoying her.

> Beloved,
>
> You told me this morning on the phone that you did not send me any news because you did not hear anything from me. During the first weeks when I got news from you every day and heard you missed me a little, it went well, but there was a big silence and suddenly my poor mind was disconnected. Then all of a sudden I heard you were doing wonderfully, which made me very happy and only afraid I could spoil your happiness with my complaints. I am so low anyway since my film at MGM didn't work out. But it was not possible to make the film and I was glad to come out of the matter as quickly as that because deeply I knew that *without you all was* meaningless. Now, here I am alone, tucked away in a little corner, smelling of moth powder. I just can't describe how much *I miss you*. It goes through my heart and soul like a stifling never-ending fog which throws a veil on the day and the night. And it carries a lot of suffering with it. I would have liked so much to come to Europe to see you for *an hour only* but I understand how crazy this would be to come without you being enthusiastic about it.
>
> Today I am better since I talked with you. Everywhere I go people feel sorry for me.
>
> Your answer, I know it already: "*You deserted me. You left me.*" I know and as you told me on the phone from Vienna, you find it good that we are apart for a while and that I miss you so desperately. I am sure that all that brings me suffering is good for me.
>
> *Everyone* disapproves and criticizes me and I am sure I must deserve it. People just love to tear me to pieces. I hope that you stand up for me sometimes, not because it is your duty but because you love me a *little* and understand me better.
>
> Now I have talked enough about myself. Your stay in Vienna is surely pleasant. I hope to get more details in a letter from you but I can imagine you don't have the time. I also want to know why you stayed so long in Paris. Is *Forst* making a new film there?

My mother called to my father in the next room:
"Papilein – Willi Forst again! Jo is back on Willi Forst – he is even

jealous of the people I knew *before* I met him! Really – such melodrama!"
and went back to reading her letter:

What do you do and how do you live and where do you go and *what do
your new clothes look like* and who are your new friends? IT'S TERRIBLE
NOT TO KNOW!

You probably heard enough already about your film. The cutting was
boring and the film ended badly, it was saved only through your part in it.
I believe you will be loved by all, although the film will not be appreciated
by everybody. In some parts of the film you are wonderful and I decided
– because I got sort of jealous – to bring these parts into my next film
to full bloom. Aherne has been pulled to pieces by critics, which in my
opinion is unfair since he is very good, as much as the part allows him
to be. Where the part fails, from the wedding on, he becomes silly and
dull but that is the failure of the script and of the direction – it becomes
so apparent that one must really be very stupid to make the Englishman
responsible for it.

Mamoulian makes the Garbo film and I think that Nils Asther will get
the male lead. Otherwise I hear little about it (sorry, I am also not very
interested).

Nothing new at the studio. At present we are going through a very dull
time. A propos, I wanted to tell you as well that Gable got sick (corns or
something like that) and I was lucky not to have made the MGM film,
since the film wouldn't have been worth it without him, there was nobody
else for the part of the prize-fighter, the others are just plain pansies.

Cooper and Chevalier hang around here . . .

"Papi," she yelled. "Now Jo is on the Cooper thing again. He will never
believe me. He still thinks I had a 'thing' with him. Ridiculous! All Cooper
can do is say 'Yup' and 'Huh?' Lupe Velez had to do it *to* him."

She continued reading:

. . . and greet me in a friendly way with a crazy look in their eyes.

I think my small talk is ending. Let's talk about important things! The
new film. The milieu and the part are fantastically interesting. I want
to develop a flirtation between the Empress and the Archduke's "Bed
mate." It is outrageously amusing to have the Empress fall in love
with the young man whose duty it is to sleep with the Archduke.
The miniature whorehouse where the young girl is growing before
she becomes Empress is great to work on. And then the 50-year-old
monarch courting her, believing she is a virgin, her cleverness and
being in love in spite of the consequences, the political enemies which
she develops because of her favors and her heart, the attitude toward the
former Empress and toward her rivals, her courage and way of living in
an epoch well known for its pestilence, revolts and sudden deaths, the

manners and fashions of that era, eating without a fork and knife, with their fingers, continuous hand-washing, the furtive looks of those who are constantly watched, the dangers which are threatening the Empress, the endless series of beheadings, poisonings, witches, the old jealous archduke stalking around, masquerading politicians – only the end is not quite clear yet – whether we have her get away or should she be beheaded for political reasons, as they say, or should she be gladly beheaded because she refuses to deny her love for the young man and, as she historically said, prefers to die as his woman than to live as Empress of Russia.

"Papi," my mother shouted, "you – ."

"Mutti," my father shouted back. "If you want to *talk* to me, come in *here!*"

We switched sets and sat on the foot of my father's bed – my mother continued her sentence.

"You have to read this – Jo is doing a whole script in his letter. If I play all the things he says here, the picture will run for five hours! *That* he has to forget!"

We were all quiet as she read on:

I have never started with so much material available and I have never started with such a wonderful character. For now I will keep the character flexible so that you may influence your part as you wish in the last stages before we begin the film and when you are here.

The costumes are also very sweet and fun, although the Holbein paintings are usually stiff and lacking in charm.

The preparatory work for the film is very difficult and it is nice that we have so much time later on to work it all together. It's a shame I can't tell you about this during hours and hours. Of course, I would be incredibly happy if you could bring enthusiasm for the idea together with confidence in my decisions. There will be again a series of historic films and I would like to be up front.

You can study the possibilities, the charm and grace and humanity of the Empress and the corresponding life before becoming an Empress. If you did so you would help me a lot. As soon as you feel the slightest enthusiasm for the character please cable me and make me happy since I know you will be happy with the film when it's finished and it would be great if the whole work and the planning could count on your invisible enthusiasm. Forgive me my intensity as director – I realize it's not always pleasant for you.

My mother finished von Sternberg's letter; shaking her head, she handed it over to my father, saying:

"Jo is getting much too involved in this film. He sounds like he is

planning to make an epic! Why not just shoot a beautiful picture of a
tragic Russian empress and leave the big 'to-do' to Eisenstein? Read it,
Papi, and then tell me what to say to him tomorrow when I call him.
I have to wash and set my hair."

I followed her out, to help with the hairpins.

Each day, looking divine, my mother left for lunch somewhere, to
return in time to change and leave for the theater – always to Jaray's play
and always alone. This routine was never discussed – it just happened
without comment, accepted by her retinue without question. Like making
a film – one followed the script. The constant waltzes were getting a bit
much and the huge silver frame enshrining Hans Jaray's face, installed by
my bed by my mother, I could have done without, but apart from that,
it was rather nice having her so occupied with someone else instead of
me. My father drank water and brought his ledgers up to date. Tami
embroidered napkins with wonderful Russian designs and taught me
how to play solitaire. In the evenings, we all had room service without
too much fuss and read our books until bedtime, like a real family I had
seen in a movie.

One morning my mother arrived back in time for breakfast, and
announced: "I need underwear!"

My father looked up from his paper. "'One never knows, said the
widow as she pulled on her black lace panties'?" he asked, smiling.

My mother laughed. It was one of those often quoted tag lines that I
grew up with, never knowing the joke it belonged to. Actually, Dietrich
never wore lace panties "in life."

"Lace rolls between the legs and gets wet – makes a sausage and sits
there. When you walk, it looks like you have worms under the clothes"
was one of her favorite doctrines, and "Lace panties are for *cinque-à-sept*
and starlets who wear those white whore shoes."

Dietrich had very definite opinions on underwear in general. Slips she
never wore, those were sewn directly into all of her clothes, becoming an
integral part of every garment, both private and professional. "Slips are
for women who buy cheap clothes and have to try them on in stores."

Men's undershirts she hated too, never went to bed with a man who
wore one. If for some reason a new lover revealed himself in such a
"working-class" undergarment at the first "unveiling," he was in trouble
even before he got into bed. She once told me of an up-and-coming
actor, who is now such a talented old codger he deserves to remain
anonymous.

"Can you believe it? He wears undershirts! Like a man who digs holes in the street! Now, really! And in Sunny California! How low-class can you get? I laughed so hard I had to pee – so I had to run to the bathroom. Very romantic! When I came out, there he is in bed, looking at me with cow eyes, all adoring, and now . . . he has *hair on his chest*! You know how ugly *that* is! Thank God, he was impotent, so it was nice and cozy!"

I often wondered if the poor man was afflicted before the discovery of his undershirt or right after it. Dietrich's ridicule could have reduced Casanova into nonperformance.

Now my mother phoned Paris and ordered a selection of lingerie to be delivered to her in Vienna immediately. No one thought it excessive in the thirties for a store to send one of their staff by overnight train with a selection of their merchandise to please a valued customer.

Two days later, an angular lady, in brown serge travel ensemble and prim felt cloche, presented herself at our door, complete with black cardboard sample case.

"Madame, I have arrived this moment from Paris with the selections so requested through the telephone," she announced through thin lips in a tired face. Unbuckling the two leather straps, she displayed her wares just like the Fuller Brush man who came to our kitchen door in Hollywood. Only these were no vegetable brushes! These were dreams in satin, crepe de chine, and gossamer silks – peach and pearl, fern and palest lavender, cream and white meringue. Everything whispered and slithered about. Unimpressed, my mother selected what she wanted – no need to try anything on, everything had been selected and made to her specific measurements. She also chose a few less ornate nightgowns for Tami and then dismissed Mlle. "Brown Serge."

"Sweetheart, call the concierge to order a cab. When does your train leave back to Paris?" she turned to ask the lady packing her treasures.

"Madame, in three hours' time."

"Sweetheart. Tell the desk that the lady who came from Paris for Madame Dietrich will have her lunch in the dining room and to charge it to me and that one hour later, a bellboy is to take her to the train station in a taxi."

Mademoiselle was overwhelmed by such largesse, and with many breathless "*merci*'s," departed to eat her fill in the hotel's luxurious dining room. My mother scooped up her new finery and went to show it to my father. Having done my telephoning chore, I entered my father's room as she was asking his advice as to which of the new nightgowns he thought she should wear for Hans that night.

"Oh, Mutti," I exclaimed, "wear the beige crepe de chine, with the inlaid lace – that's the best!"

My mother hesitated a second, then chuckled:

"The Child is right, Papi! What an eye she has – amazing. She knows everything about clothes for me. If you ever doubted that she is your child . . ." and, letting that sentence hang in midair, she left the room.

"Kater. Go check your room. See if the maids have done it properly. If not, report back to me!" my father said.

Not an unusual order. My father always kept a tight rein on hotel staffs and received meticulous service in return. They even respected him for it, in a way. Did my father really doubt that I was his child? Maybe, I wasn't his . . . then whose was I? Only my mother's? Probably. She was always telling me I was hers alone. I went back to report that my room was "perfection."

Fully recovered, my father decided to evacuate me. Leaving Tami with Teddy to hold the Viennese fort and assist my mother with her exits and entrances, he took me to Aussig on the Elbe to visit his parents. We drove up to the little farmhouse and there they stood! My grandmother, Rosa, all small and round, a cozy bundle of starched blue linen, with the sweetest smile in the whole world, and my Grandfather, Anton, tall and scraggly, an Austrian Lincoln, who had a silent way of looking at her that made you realize what the word marriage could *really* mean.

My grandmother held me close, words were never necessary. If she loved you, you knew it without emotional embroidery. It was real, just like her bread rising warm and sure in her big black oven. My grandfather placed his big heavy hand on my head and looked down at me with pleasure, as I looked up at him with joy. My father shook hands with his parents, then busied himself with our luggage, discussing our drive down in his new Packard with his father. I was shown to my room – my grandmother wondering if I hadn't grown too tall for my carved wooden bed with the painted bluebells.

My mother cabled she missed me and so we had to leave sooner than planned. My grandmother gave me a jar of her very best jam for my mother's breakfast and hugged me tight. I clung and cried. My grandfather gave me a perfect little fox he had whittled just for me, so I cried some more. My father told me to stop being so dramatic and to get into the car, made his formal good-byes to his parents, and we drove off. I didn't care if it was theatrical – I waved all the way down the hill. Four days only, but they had been wonderful!

"My angel! How I missed you! My life was empty without you! I did not sleep – the whole time you were not here! Tami doesn't know how to do anything right. She got all the flower cards wrong. Suddenly the service in this hotel is terrible. The reporters are outside, just waiting for me, I have to use the kitchen exit to escape them – in Europe! As bad as Chicago! Papi, why didn't you take Teddy to Aussig? Every time I needed Tami, she was out 'walking the dog.' By the time she finally got back, I had done everything myself!" She was kissing my eyelids.

"Your beautiful face. How I missed seeing your beautiful face!" She stood back, checking me over.

"Your hair – when did you last wash your hair?"

"I am sorry, Mutti. Look what Grandfather made for me," and I displayed the perfect fox in the palm of my hand.

"Sweetheart, go and change your shoes and wash your hands. Papi, you must read this cable and tell me what to answer," she said as she moved toward her desk.

In my room, I wrapped the fox in my cleanest handkerchief and put him way in the back of the drawer of my night table. I should have known better. She hated my liking presents from other people, I was supposed to love only hers. Maybe it would be better not to even mention Grandmother's lovely jam. Safer not to talk about my happy visit at all! Tami gave me a furtive kiss of welcome – she looked drawn, completely exhausted.

During our absence, Mr. Jaray must have done something wrong, or the press were getting too close, for suddenly, tissue paper wafted throughout every room and Vienna disappeared in a cloud of dust behind the Packard as we drove to Salzburg, the best ad for Austria that ever was; a floral mountain village, complete with Sleeping Beauty Castle, ornate Mozart-festooned fountains, oozing with culture from every crack amongst the cobblestones. Such an "operetta" setting of course demanded instant costuming, and off we marched to the world's best Tyrolean outfitters, Lanz of Salzburg. Dirndls, capes, hats, shooting jackets, skirts, frilly peasant blouses, buttons of silver coins or stag bone, and embroidered mountain flora and fauna on *everything*. You could have outfitted ten road companies of *The Student Prince* and never made a dent in their inventory. It took only a few minutes for my mother to transform herself. In a dark green loden skirt, black tailored jacket with its distinctive bottle-green scalloped lapels and silver coin buttons, the bottle-green repeated in a jaunty velour hat sporting a magnificent boar's brush, she looked like a very chic Austrian mayoress. Tami and I didn't fare as well.

"Muttilein, please! I can't wear all these beautiful things. Everything is much too expensive!" Tami kept whispering as my mother flung laden hangers into her cubicle.

"Tami – don't be ridiculous. You can't walk around Salzburg dressed like a Viennese grande dame or some tourist. Put on the blue dirndl with

the puffed sleeves and the red striped apron – and come out here so I can
see you!" my mother ordered, then concentrated on my problem.

"Sweetheart! Another size larger? Can't be possible. Come out here –
let me see you!"

A fascinated circle of customers had formed behind my mother,
appreciating her dedicated skills in clothing her difficult dependents. I
presented myself for inspection. An overstuffed tea cozy – a milkmaid
gone wrong! I was sure I heard the audience snigger.

"Yes – the vest is much too tight. Stand up straight! Slouching over
doesn't help to hide anything, just makes it worse. Maybe I can find
something in a dark color! Take that off and wait!" and off she
went, determined to achieve the impossible. My father joined the
metamorphoses, refusing only the lederhosen with edelweiss-festooned
suspenders. We finally appeared on the street, looking like the Trapp
family on tour. This set the tone for all future visits we made to Salzburg.
A new trunk was added to our luggage lists, marked "Austria – Salzburg
Special." Every year, until Hitler conquered Austria without any effort
whatsoever, we went there to play Milkmaids among the Buttercups.

"PAPILEIN – ," my mother's mouth was full of wieners and hot potato
salad – we were very consistent, menus usually matched the costumes.

"I want an Austrian peasant house – old and beautiful, with dark green
shutters, little windows and white lace curtains, the front all carved and a
poem written over the door, and flower boxes – full of red geraniums in
front of every window." She helped herself to more cucumber salad and
black bread.

"Hans could wear his beautiful loden jackets and Brian could walk, The
Child could make garlands of field flowers, Tami could feed the chickens,
I would cook all the vegetables from the garden, and you could sit on a
dark green bench in the sun and read your newspapers. We could even
have a *real* cow!" My father had his Hermès notebook out, listing my
mother's requirements for "rural happiness." None of us doubted his
ability to find a house precisely as ordered.

"Mutti, now it is much too late. You do not have enough time left, but
after the next film, yes. Now Hans is waiting for you, Jo is getting worried
about your starting the costumes – and you know we are scheduled to
leave here – "

"Yes, Papilein!" she interrupted him, "I know. First I have to make the money! The only good thing, Jo has me as a princess this time. With all those big period skirts, they are not going to see – the Legs!" she chuckled. "How Paramount will hate that! 'No legs in a Dietrich film?' . . . That's worth doing the whole picture for!" She motioned the waiter to fish out some more sausages from the steam pot next to our table. She was in a very good mood that day.

"Papi – wasn't Catherine the Great a lesbian? Must have been. She couldn't have ruled Russia like that if she was *normal*. At least, the costumes will be interesting to make. Travis Banton is probably doing 'research' like mad – and will have everything sketched very 'authentic historical' and all wrong for the camera! He is getting a reputation dressing Dietrich, and I do all the work. He knows nothing about 'line.' Why are the pansies all so fussy? They all overdress everything, but in this, we will use lots of Russian sable – That will cost a fortune! Let them scream, Jo will handle the Studio bosses. We could maybe let them sew on the skins – like they used to!"

The image of the Paramount hierarchy sitting cross-legged on top of their mahogany desks, plying their old furrier's needles, pleased her so, she roared with glee and attacked her wurst with added gusto. She actually seemed to look forward to the next film, which was very unusual for my mother. Our first "history" picture! It sounded like fun!

My father was going through the itinerary of cultural activities he had chosen for our education, when I heard we were scheduled to attend a concert of another string quartet, naturally playing Mozart. Mozart – Mozart – Mozart. Not again! I tried so very hard to like him! Everyone was so enraptured with his music I knew there must be something very wrong with me that it put me to sleep. As everyone seemed to be in such a jolly mood, I dared to ask permission to remain at the hotel that evening and go right to bed.

"What?" my mother turned to me. "Go to bed? Are you sick? Have you got a fever? Papi, the child – She doesn't look well! Sweetheart, what's the matter – Your stomach? Those greasy sausages and that heavy potato salad? Papi, you should not have ordered that!"

She took my hand and marched us into the hotel elevator and up to our suite. I was told to undress quickly, while she went for the thermometer. I unbuttoned the new embroidered vest, took off the frilly white apron, and tried to think of what to do next. To pretend I was sick seemed the safest way to handle this delicate situation. I prayed for a fever! A real high one! Please! Right away!

My mother returned, put the big flat thermometer under my armpit and waited. I squeezed my arm as hard as I could against my side, hoping the pressure might increase whatever body heat lurked there to make the mercury rise. No such luck.

"Angel, you are normal!" she sighed, relieved. I was told to stay in bed anyway, and she left to finish her coffee on the terrace. I never knew who or what made her realize the truth. I suspect it was my father, for an hour later I was given a message by one of the maids assigned to our suite, that Madame had instructed her to convey the following verbatim message to her child. The maid was very nervous, trying to get it all in the correct order:

"Fräulein Heidede, you are to get up, wash, dress for the evening in your pale blue silk, take your dinner alone downstairs in the dining room. It has been ordered for six o'clock, then to accompany Fräulein Tamara to the Mozart recital, which begins precisely at eight."

She bobbed a relieved curtsey and withdrew. When angry, my mother was never violent, never physically abusive. To show displeasure in such a way she considered low-class. Her favorite example to support this theory was Joan Crawford:

"That terrible, vulgar woman with the pop eyes beats her children. They are black and blue with wounds, and she always says that 'they just fell off their bicycles'! Terrible! Everyone knows what really goes on in that house, but what can you expect from that class – a cheap tap dancer! But all those children – why she ever got two of them is also crazy – they were all adopted and you never know, there may *be* something wrong with them."

My mother's methods of punishment were much more subtle, calculated to shame, and, thereby, reinstate obedience. My father learned her technique and also used it extremely well. The offender simply ceased to exist. Abracadabra! I was erased from her universe. She neither spoke nor looked at me; when I arrived at the breakfast table, she rose and left it. She did the flower cards, opened her own mail, put her cuff links into the shirt cuffs, shined her shoes, poured her coffee, and even ignored the pin I held out to her – using others from the box to set her hair. My father also shunned me. I hadn't realized he too was such a Mozart fan. It was lonely being so "invisible." I didn't mind Tami's timid withdrawal, I knew she wouldn't dare to be nice to me when I was declared *persona non grata*. Even Teddy couldn't comfort me; when he tried he received a sharp "No!" and got locked in the bathroom. I sat on my bed and thought about my Big Trouble. As even Hans Jaray seemed unable to distract her, this situation could last for weeks!

I was still being punished when I found out that Brian had made a "terrible mistake" too. He had written a personal letter to one of "the boys," confiding in them. Always a most dangerous thing to do. He should have known these types of people one never, ever, could trust. Of course, Brian's letter had been immediately sent on to Dietrich – with a lot of mental lip-smacking, I was sure. Poor Brian. Why did he have to be so innocent, and with Hans Jaray still in favor. He didn't even *know* about him! My mother received a cable from a still happy and unsuspecting Brian:

MARLENE DIETRICH
   HOTEL EUROPA SALZBURG
WILL BE LOCATION ON THE NEXT ALP STOP THE ROLE IS NOT INTERESTING
BUT THE WEEKENDS ARE PROMISING. I ADORE YOU CRAZY DIETRICH.
                                          BRIAN
HOTEL ALPENHOF, PERTISAU

She immediately cabled back, telling Brian not to plan on coming, that we were leaving Salzburg immediately to meet her mother in Switzerland. Next morning, we left for Paris, where Hans Jaray had been told to await her.

I was being talked to again, but wished I wasn't. I wished I could telephone and talk to Brian, help him with what to do, but although I worked out all the possibilities of placing a telephone call from Paris to Austria without anyone finding out, none of them were foolproof enough for me to dare to attempt.

The Plaza Athénée was very elegant and very proper. They served fancy afternoon tea in a hall full of little marquetry tables surrounded by embroidered chairs, tucked away in individual niches. Suddenly, it was permissible for my mother to reside within the city of Paris – not surprising, all things came right for Dietrich eventually! Brian, having read of her and Jaray's arrival in Paris, knew that she had lied to him.

BRIAN AHERNE

Dietrich,
   This will be short. You have hurt me more than I have ever been hurt by any person in my life. After all we have been to each other and all you have said to me it is unbelievable that you should have dealt me such cruel and terrible blows. If you wanted to get rid of me you had only to say one word to me. I am no Chevalier or de Acosta and I have too much pride to reproach you or plead with you, but if it is any satisfaction to you to

know it I have suffered damnably in the last few weeks and I can find no relief in anything or anybody. I have hurt people in my life, though never I think willingly, and it is awful to think it may have been as bad for them as this.

There are many Dietrichs I know and the one that has done these things to me is, thank Heaven, a stranger to me. I don't know her and I don't like her and I shall not write to her for if I did I should say bitter and ironic things.

I write instead to the Dietrich to whom I gave my heart and who gave me in return great happiness and content. She gave me tenderness and passion and comfort and a thousand memories which I shall always treasure. And if she has since taken it away again, what of that? It is a different woman with the same name – I am grateful to her and I love her now as I did then, and I shall always love her.

If you should come across that Dietrich again in some strange moment, if some scene or word should bring her to life for an instant at any time, would you please tell her that she still carries my poor heart in her hand and that my love for her is deep and real, though I know she is gone.

To you, who are all the Dietrichs, I wish bon voyage and happiness and success in Hollywood. I hope you found your heart's desire in Salzburg and Vienna as I hope you may always find it.

I shall watch your career with close interest for I have a belief in your talent, quite apart from my admiration for your beauty.

I shall meet you before long in the studio of course, but that need not embarrass you.

Will you please give my love to the dream child, who is very dear to me.

Aherne

My mother handed this letter over, as usual, for my father's opinion, and while he read it, skimmed through the latest billet-doux from de Acosta:

MERCEDES DE ACOSTA

Aug. 10th

Golden Beautiful One,

Today your letter arrived and I was so happy to get it because it seemed to me months since I had word directly from you.

I know you had a great success in Vienna and I read about you in the French papers.

I also read that you are buying many feminine clothes. I hope not too feminine! And I hope you will not give up your trousers when you return because then people can say (as they already do) that it was only a publicity stunt.

I see the "other person" all the time who is completely changed toward me – beautiful and sweet – and completely unlike last year. She had been having terrific difficulties in getting a leading man and finally had to decide on John Gilbert. I think a bad choice and I think she does too.

I will be happy to see your beautiful little face again.

Your White Prince

I was nervous and got "in the way." Everyone was very tense – maybe we were all just tired. Not my mother, of course. She was back in the city she loved most in the world, with a swain she loved most at the moment, letters to send, calls to make, luncheons to dress for and devour, romantic dinners to be beautiful at. As always with Dietrich, the more she had to accomplish, the more energy she produced.

The time dragged on. Every day I hoped to see the coffins lined up for packing, but they remained, ignored, in the hotel luggage rooms. My mother was also busy writing one of her own scenarios:

J VON STERNBERG
PARAMOUNT STUDIOS HOLLYWOODCALIF

SWEETHEART MISSED TODAYS SAILING AND MISSED NEXT WEEKS SAILING AND THE WEEK AFTER THAT STOP ETERNALLY GRATEFUL IF YOU WILL POSTPONE STOP WILL REPAY FAVOR WITH PRESS CONFERENCE ARRIVAL NEW YORK STOP KISSES

It was the first time I had seen her make a deal. I knew how much she hated press conferences – I also knew we hadn't missed a single boat!

HOLLYWOODCALIF 20 VIII 33
    NLT MARLENE SIEBER
    HOTEL PLAZA ATHENEE PARIS

DARLING OF MINE I AM DESPERATE SINCE I KNOW YOU WANT TO REMAIN LONGER IN EUROPE BECAUSE I HAVE EXPLAINED TO YOU HOW MUCH I WAIT WITH EVERYTHING AND HOW MUCH I NEED YOU STOP THE POSTPONEMENT OF FILM BEGINNING IS DANGEROUS FOR EXAMPLE BECAUSE OF COMPETITORS SINCE I WANTED TO BE THE FIRST WITH COSTUME FILM AND BECAUSE KORDA ALSO MAKES SUBJECT STOP IN SPITE OF THIS I OF COURSE AGREE WITH ANY DELAY WHICH WOULD MAKE YOU HAPPY AND ONLY WISH TO DO WHATEVER PLEASES YOU STOP YOU ALONE DECIDE UPON WHAT YOU DO WITH YOUR TIME STOP DO NOT THINK THAT BY WRITING THIS I REPROACH ANYTHING I ONLY WANT TO BE COMPLETELY HONEST WITH YOU AND ONLY CONFIRM THAT YOU AND ONLY YOU AS I ALWAYS TOLD YOU DISPOSE FREELY OF YOUR TIME BECAUSE I AM INCREDIBLY HAPPY

THAT I HAVE THE PRIVILEGE AT ALL TO WORK WITH YOU ONCE AGAIN STOP
KISSES KISSES KISSES

Her answer was immediate, but bought time by sending it as a letter:

> You send me a six-page cable to make me feel guilty if I stay on. Kindly
> cable explicit answer. What are "all the consequences" you are threatening
> me with? It is not necessary to manipulate me. I respond best to directness
> and honesty. You should be ashamed of yourself.

NLT MARLENE SIEBER 31 aug 33
    HOTEL PLAZA ATHENEE PARIS

WHY DO YOU WANT ME TO BE ASHAMED STOP I AM ALL ALONE WITH A
THOUSAND WORRIES STOP BELOVED THOUGH YOU WOULD ASK ME AGAIN I
WOULD ONLY TELL YOU ONCE MORE ALTHOUGH YOU WILL BE CROSS WITH
ME THAT DEPARTURE ON THE TENTH IS ABSOLUTELY NECESSARY STOP YOU ARE
SUCH A WONDERFUL BEING THAT I KNOW I CAN COUNT ON YOU TO DO YOUR
DUTY ALSO WHEN ITS HARD STOP DONT BE ANGRY AT YOUR POOR DIRECTOR

Finally, my father had enough and took charge. He booked us onto
the SS *Paris*, which was leaving in two weeks, and moved himself, Tami,
and Teddy out of the hotel and back into his Paris apartment.

Our Austrian returned to his City of Schlag; the time had come to
leave Europe. I kissed Tami good-bye, holding her close. I whispered
in her ear not to be so frightened of my father, to remember what I
had taught her, and to please take care of herself more. Then I hugged
Teddy till he squeaked. My father conducted us to Le Havre, handled the
reporters, permitting them just so many questions and no more, installed
us and the cabin cases in our staterooms, made sure that the trunks were
aboard and in the proper section of the hold of the ship, tipped the various
stewards responsible for our comfort with a lavish hand, delivered cable
forms, magazines, European newspapers, together with his packing lists,
luggage book, and catalogued keys into my mother's hands. Kissing her
cheek, he told her to now forget everything but the work awaiting her.
Not to worry, he would take care of Hans, her mother, her sister, her
refugees, and any shopping she might have to have sent from Paris. She
was to give his regards to Nellie, Dot, Edington, and de Acosta. Say hello
to Bridges the chauffeur, and "the boys," and send his love to Chevalier
and von Sternberg. I was told, sternly:

"Kater, look after Mutti and do not give her any more trouble, like
you did on this trip. Understand? And remember, the book I gave you
to read must be finished by the time the ship arrives in New York."

He kissed me quickly and disappeared down the ship's corridor. My mother smoked, looking forlorn. I poured her a glass of champagne, that always helped, then dared to ask her permission to go topside, just for a second! I ran so fast, I got there in time to see my father's jaunty Tyrolean hat appear on the gangplank. I waved and shouted, but he didn't hear me over the "Marseillaise." I watched until he vanished in the crowd.

The SS *Paris* was a little old, but like so many French ladies, very well preserved, still beautiful. This particular September of '33, the Atlantic Ocean decided to show all seafaring mortals, in their silly vessels, who was boss. Huge waves lifted our Gallic lady, then slid her back down – again and again. While the *Paris* tangoed frenetically across the rolling sea, I threw up – but I didn't care. *I was going home!* Nothing else mattered!

HOLLYWOOD – THE MAGIC YEARS

NO TIME TO LINGER at the Ambassador. We were in a hurry. "Mother Russia" was waiting among the orange groves. My mother scrubbed her face, hibernated, and wrote cables to Vienna – the telegram runs recommenced. I told my porter friends about the Eiffel Tower and how the inside of Austrian churches looked like circus calliopes. They, in turn, had news for me, of babies born, how Mr. Roosevelt had saved America, and what I had missed in the funny papers.

We were nearly there. In the dark, I crept down the ladder from my bunk, praying I wouldn't wake my mother underneath, carefully unlocked the door, slipped out into the corridor – still holding my breath – closed it, then ran along the Pullman cars until I reached my little outside balcony, just as the train entered the desert states. In my "for the train only" pajamas, I sat in one of the wicker chairs, hugging my knees, waiting for the dawn. The wheels clacked their rhythm, not really disturbing the stillness. The air was soft and perfumed with that unique smell of night-cold sand and tumbleweed. Magenta shadows formed, rimmed with just a glow of gold. Notre-Dame cathedral had been wonderful to see, but I was very sure that God lived in America.

"Back in this terrible country," my mother murmured, as she stepped off the train in Pasadena. Von Sternberg, Nellie, Bridges, the Cadillac, my bodyguards, Paramount's hand-picked reporters, and the luggage truck waited while Dietrich bent down to kiss her director's cheek. Cameras clicked.

I had already ducked into the car, out of sight. Since the kidnapping threat, I was not allowed to be photographed. It had something to do with being identifiable or something. All I knew was that in America, whenever I saw a camera, I had to hide. So, I followed orders and vanished.

We drove; my mother held court. "Paris is the only civilized city in the world! Papi made us eat all the time! I am fat – everything is too tight. In Vienna, there was nothing interesting except Knize – I bought you a dressing gown. I said, 'For Mr. von Sternberg,' and they had your measurements. But you should have seen Rudi that morning when he got sick." My mother launched into "Rudi's Vienna kidney attack." I leaned forward in my jump seat, thinking my own thoughts as I watched Pasadena go by. Why was my mother never interested in what other people had done during our absence? I have never heard her say, "How are you?" to a living soul I mused, not realizing that fifty-five years later, this would still be true.

It was a long drive. My mother smoked and talked. I waited to see where we were going to live this time.

The Bel Air community sits on gentle hills, between Santa Monica and Beverly Hills, protected by various imposing wrought-iron gates reminiscent of Buckingham Palace, complete with guardhouses. The very rich and famous hide there from each other amongst the thickest foliage known to man. They check themselves out of this lush compound to make more money or spend it – then check themselves back in, in those days safe from all exterior evils. Before television, youth, and lawyers changed the caste system of Hollywood, to live in Bel Air was the ultimate address achievement for a motion-picture star. The "Beverly Hills" actors, they had their mansions identified on tourist maps that faded New York actresses sold from beach chairs perched on street corners to the curious for a nickel. Bel Air shuddered at such crass notoriety. Nothing was allowed through its "palace" gates. If the Guard of the Day didn't have your name on his list, as either coming or going, you waited until the house you said you belonged to corroborated your statement. I don't know how they manage this strict security today, now that people jog and run about, but in those days, no one jogged – they didn't even walk. Only Japanese gardeners were ever seen on sidewalks, and actors from England, and they were usually stopped by the police and asked "Why?"

Our three-tone horn sounded our syncopated arrival. The uniformed guard, St. Peter at the Gate, with revolver on hip, peered deep into our car, recognized his new charge, but checked to make sure he had the name Dietrich on his clipboard, then saluted and waved us on. We rolled up the hill, around, then up again, and finally, into the driveway of the Colleen Moore house. And what a house! Real 1930 Movie Star Splendor! It must have had an address, but it was always known only as "the Colleen Moore house in Bel Air."

I thought we had crossed the border into Mexico! Terra-cotta shingles, cool tiles, urns, wrought-iron and bougainvillea trailing down every-where. The living room was enormous, dark blood-red à la Goya, with six-foot candelabra lining the walls. The whole place looked ready for Pancho Villa. Colleen Moore, a silent-movie queen as well as a real-estate aficionada, must have had a passion for ornate grandfather clocks, for they were all over the place – very *un*-Spanish, they chimed, tinkled, and boomed the minutes, the half-hours, the hours, and anything else worth making noise about. My mother had them disemboweled immediately, and they remained silent and forlorn during the Dietrich Occupation of their domain. "New Spain" might hold sway inside the house, but "Hollywood" took over the back. A covered veranda ran along the entire length of the house, crowded with Great Gatsby–type armchairs and couches done in chintz, "very Newport porch." To one side, among tall banana trees, stood a fully equipped miniature movie theater. That first morning in our new hacienda, I had immediate visions of selling tickets to my bodyguards, and oh, the whole household would come and I would show them to the blue velour seats with a special flashlight. Maybe we could even make popcorn in the huge kitchen before the start of "The Marx Brothers in their Latest Triumph!" But that never happened, so my "private" movie house collected cobwebs and smelled of desertion instead of melted butter. Talk about rolling lawns – ours swooped, past a Renaissance rose garden, continuing its descent until it was finally stopped by the biggest swimming pool I had ever seen. The pool house, a family of four could have lived in comfortably. The fact that my mother hated swimming, hated the sun, and existed entirely "inside," that von Sternberg never relaxed, that I had no friends, that Dietrich during this time never gave a party, this Hollywood splendor was enjoyed by one not-yet nine-year-old child only.

While my mother disinfected the toilet seats, then unpacked, reassured syphilis had once again been routed by her stringent efforts, I was allowed to try out my new swimming hole. Von Sternberg, installed on the porch in what would become known as Jo's chair, was given pens, pencils, paper, and told that if he insisted on working on the script, he could at least take the time to watch that The Child did not drown. He would have had to have binoculars glued to his eyes to have noticed me drowning at the bottom of that golf-course lawn. Von Sternberg worked and never looked up. He knew that I would tell my mother how Mr. von Sternberg had been aware of my *every* move, just as I knew he, in turn, would comment on my obedience whenever he had called out a warning of caution in my direction.

A new maid, all starched apron, white cuffs on black taffeta, hiked to poolside and, in a thick German accent, intoned that Frau Dietrich expected me "for to eat." I always felt like asking a new servant's name and introducing myself, but my mother had caught me doing that once and gave me such a lecture on maintaining the proper distance between a master and his servants, that I never dared – until I knew the "help" better and decided if they were the type to inform on my lamentable democratic attitude or not.

One of the oriental genies had turned on the sprinklers, hidden in the emerald grass. As I walked up toward the house, jets of water arched, cascading about – a little Versailles of a million misty rainbows. The roses caught this manmade dew and cradled it on soft pink petals. Tiny hummingbirds, all metallic blue and poison green, hovered like slow-motion jewels, and I fell in love with my very own magical back lot. Of course I got into trouble for being wet and making grown-ups wait while The Child changed her sundress, but, I decided, as soon as I could get away I would take my rainbow walk back down again.

"Beloved, I plan to cast an unknown in the part of Count Alexei."

"Who?" my mother asked, as she sliced the boiled ham.

"Count Alexei – the emissary sent from the Imperial Russian Court – to escort the Princess Sophia Frederica – that is you, as you may remember?"

"Oh, you mean the man she falls in love with," my mother interrupted. "And why the sarcasm right away? I came all the way back here because you want me to do this Russian picture! I would have stayed in Europe!" She served von Sternberg more cucumber salad. Indicating a row of tiny roast chickens, she turned to me:

"Angel – eat! These are for you. Jo, where are Travis's sketches? I expected them here when we arrived! And Nellie has not seen a single wig sketch either. What is everyone doing at Paramount? Hiding W. C. Fields's gin bottles? All you do is beg me to 'hurry back,' and then, when I rush, leave poor Papi to do everything, you are still writing the script!" She bit into a big slice of rye bread thick with liverwurst. "The costumes for this film will take *months* to make, and you are concerned about some unknown actor?"

Von Sternberg put down his knife and fork. Slowly wiped his lips, leaned back in his chair.

"Mutti, do you at least like this *house* – that I found for you?" he asked.

"Yes – very, very grand, very 'old-time' movie star! The kitchen is good – not 'American' at all, and finally, there are enough bedrooms for the trunks." She started to clear the dishes. Von Sternberg said he had an appointment at the Studio and left, and I walked back down among my rainbows.

AS WE DROVE THROUGH the Paramount gate, Mac saluted:

"Good morning, Miss Dietrich. Hi, Miss Heidede! Welcome back!"

I was home. Studios never change. Oh, they expand, get modernized, acquire black-glass office towers, but the feel of them, that is constant: The winding streets between the soundstages cluttered with cables, booms, generators, tripods, trucks, lights, leftover odds and ends, a junkyard array of valuable equipment parked on the outside for lack of room on a working set; there a dusty cowboy talking to a Comanche; over there Salome drinks her coffee from a paper cup in the shade of a prairie schooner. Sets are being built everywhere, the hum of saws, the smell of freshly-cut timber – of all the perfumes in the world, that was my favorite. While my mother was busy being "annoyed" with Travis, I strolled through my Studio and caught up on its news. Mae West had finished *I'm No Angel*, and her leading man was our shirt salesman from *Blonde Venus*. I liked Cary Grant and was glad that he was getting ahead. To work with Mae West was to take the best crash course in comedy timing in the world! Besides, she liked him and would do her best for him.

I checked out the Hair-Dressing Department. They had acquired a new coffee urn, Make-Up still smelled of greasepaint and cold cream. The Commissary had a new green Jell-O salad on the menu, but otherwise, nothing had changed – my world was steady and secure.

The Bekins van had arrived. Today we were unpacking the storage boxes marked Dressing Room-Studio. The towels and bath mats, the dishes, the ashtrays and cigarette boxes, the mirrors, makeup, hairpins, pens, pencils, sharpeners, paper blocks, rubber bands, photo mailers, gramophone, records, vases, phone books, special hangers and thermoses . . . I hurried. I had my job to do. My mother was already waiting for me. Quickly, I looked for the box that I had helped pack after *Song of Songs*, the one marked Cleaning. As everything was written in German, it always fell to me or my mother to identify the cartons. While Paramount's leading female star did battle with her favorite germs, I looked for the one carton never identified by content – only No. 1. My mother was frightened that a box bearing the words Dietrich – Dolls, even if in German, would be stolen. She was probably right. After all, they were not only her mascots but famous stars in their own right. They had sat on Lola's dressing table in *The Blue Angel*, Amy Jolly's in *Morocco*, and Helen Faraday's in *Blonde Venus*. Smuggled into every Dietrich film, they would now find a special place waiting for them, even in imperialist Russia.

We were still on the fringe of preproduction, when I was given a pair of whippets, probably to populate some of that rolling lawn. They looked like high-gloss porcelain replicas of themselves, carried the regal monikers of Lightning and Streak. Someone really goofed there, but their pedigrees were a mile long and my mother was swayed by their air of fragility. She was right, as usual. They died of double pneumonia the next day. The whippets were replaced by four white rabbits, that multiplied at an alarming rate – hippity-hopped about as they ate bald spots into the luscious lawn.

The sun shone bright, hot and clear, eight a.m., and breakfast on the veranda; my mother was reading our daily bible, *The Hollywood Reporter*. It was consumed each morning with the orange juice by everyone connected with the movie business. My mother never drank orange juice. "Only Americans would hit an empty stomach with acid – and then even put ice in it!" She read her *Reporter*, with coffee and a cigarette. This morning, "the boys" had reported for Marlene's "divine scrambled eggs." Now having finished their rhapsodic appreciation of my mother's version of instant cholesterol death, they were busy devouring the rest of the table, when my mother announced:

"The *Reporter* says that Mayer is thinking of Jeanette MacDonald for *The Merry Widow* – ridiculous!" My mother had never liked Jeanette MacDonald.

"Now you tell me how all that affected sweetness can sell tickets? Those awful rosebuds on everything, the trills through ever so slightly parted lips – the 'flutter,' the 'little steps' in satin slippers – ever so dainty! People can't believe all that! *She* . . . is *big* box office? Chevalier says he can't stand her. He told me she smells of cheap talcum powder, and I said 'In what place did you smell it?' So, of course, he was stuck – and couldn't answer!"

Whenever my mother had a fawning audience, she played into it with rapierlike glee. I sat and waited, hoping she would finish with the *Reporter* so I could read it. But that morning, there wasn't time – we had to leave for the Studio to design the opening dress of *The Scarlet Empress*.

"Young! Young! She must be YOUNG, Travis! Young on Dietrich is not like young on somebody else! No one will believe virginal innocence. With Dietrich, you have to overdo the look!"

I didn't quite understand *virginal*, but what she was getting at, that made sense. Von Sternberg had told me she had a long way to go in this film, from young girl all the way to an Empress. As usual, Dietrich would create this through visual transition, then let the acting ride along on that impact.

Travis's face was even more flushed than usual. He was very sensitive to criticism, particularly from his greatest asset. Perhaps he knew instinctively that Dietrich was as brilliant a designer as he and threatened his talent, as it built his reputation.

While they squabbled, my mother would call it "discussing," I lifted the heavy stack of costume sketches off the desk and arranged them in sequence on the floor. My mother liked to look at sketches this way – from above.

I didn't want to be rude to Travis, but as he had let me do this before, I figured he wouldn't mind and it might break up the "discussion." She turned and we studied the artistic splendor spread at our feet. There it was, the offensive "young girl" dress – all lace and bows and crinoline, the swatches of baby blue taffeta for the bows, the shell pink lace for the bodice, pinned to the cardboard mat that framed the delicate sketch. The breathtaking Wedding Dress had its swatches of pearls and diamonds embroidered onto antique silver lace; the Review costume, which would become the most famous of the film, to be made in blue velvet and ermine; the Ball Gown, off the shoulder, with enormous hoopskirts, appliquéd with a thickly embroidered swirled design, to be executed in black velvet – white seed pearl and silk cord embroidery, high tiara; and pearls, pearls, pearls everywhere. As von Sternberg had not finished writing the film, many costumes were still to be designed, but what had been done was magnificent.

"Travis, this is beautiful!" My mother bent to pick up my favorite – the "reviewing the troops" sketch.

"Why don't we make this in bottle-green velvet, instead of blue, and do the fur in mink. The way you have it, the white of the ermine will make the trim too distracting against the dark material . . . and such a high hat is better for the face when it is dark. The face is important, not the hat. . . . Give the jacket a slight puff on the shoulders, to make the sleeves appear more narrow, and how about continuing the jacket *over* the hoops, like in a riding costume, and end it in two points in front, with a wide band of mink to cut the hoop line. The braid fastening you have is good, but go all the way down with it and don't do it high on the collar – just up to the throat. With that hat, the neck will disappear if we cover it too much. You want high boots for this? And a short crop – maybe? We already have perfect gloves. . . . I got them in Paris. Sweetheart, we bring the box marked Dark Green – Short tomorrow to show Travis. I want to see now what Jo is doing with the palace. With these huge skirts, the doors will have to be wide," and we left to corner von Sternberg in the Art Department.

The doors were wide enough to park a ten-ton truck sideways. My mother immediately increased the span of her hoopskirts to exaggerated size and nearly upstaged von Sternberg's Russian icon doors. How he loved his doors. As tall as a lighthouse, their ornate brass handles six feet off the floor, all done in individually designed panels of enamel and gold bas-relief of religious images of the seventeenth century. Not one alike, not one scene repeated on seven doors. No need for an actor to fake their weight when having to open one in a scene, they were exactly what they seemed – huge, massive, incredibly heavy works of art. And the sculptures! Gaunt, brooding men, El Greco faces, and gnarled, spidery hands. They clutched wood from behind in an agonized embrace, making themselves into the backs of thronelike banquet chairs. Everywhere, these haunted, haunting specters. They held flickering tapers in macabre processional groups, framed oval boudoir mirrors, with their bent spines became tortured newel posts and sorrowing banisters. Like Frankenstein, their suffering was palpable, making them more pitiable than frightening. They were von Sternberg's ghosts, his creation, but then, *The Scarlet Empress* is all Sternberg – everything was conceived by him or through his glorious artist's eye. It was the only film my mother ever made where the sets vied with her for stardom, and she knew it. But von Sternberg was a generous genius and gave her his lighting, so she left him his sculptured excesses and kept her critical observations to a minimum.

"All those depressing faces – all over the place! Every time I come around a corner, there is another corpse looking at me. Russia wasn't *that* bad! I know Jo wants 'decadence,' but isn't he overdoing it? But he probably wants contrast. Like when he put all those fat, ugly women behind me on the stage in *The Blue Angel*."

As Dietrich never discussed her work as actors usually do amongst themselves, her observations were sort of flung out, toward anyone who found themselves within her immediate radius – in fitting rooms, dressing rooms, kitchen, or in her bathroom at night, when I would sit on the edge of her bathtub, watching her scrub her face with Castile soap and water – just keeping her company.

Now, she scrubbed her face dry, brushed her teeth with precise vengeance, rinsed them with her French mouthwash that turned the water red and tasted of dried rose leaves, and between spits, continued:

"We fit the white wigs tomorrow. They must have a high shine – not look like cotton. The hair the Studio gets from all those nuns in Italian convents has to have all the color bleached out and that makes it look dull. Those long corkscrew curls on the sketches look like everybody's. Straight out of the books. Who wore a wig like that? *And looked stupid?*"

She put on her pajama jacket, turned off the bathroom lights as I followed her out, saying, "You mean Toby Wing, Mutti?"

"Yes, that one who is always in Bing Crosby's dressing room and then gets parts in little pictures."

She got into Colleen Moore's ornate bed, as usual using only the edge of the mattress, as though she were sleeping on a soldier's camp bed. I wound the clocks, set the alarms, kissed her good night, and turned off the lights. She was asleep before I closed the door.

In the dressing room the next morning, von Sternberg asked, "Mutti, have you read the diaries of Catherine the Great that I left for you?"

"Oh, Jo – why? I am sure Bergner will have to – especially with Korda. You tell me what to do and it will all look beautiful! Do you know, Travis wants the mink hat to flop over, like the French Revolution! Doesn't want it to look like Garbo's hat for *Queen Christina*. I told him: 'Hers will look like a fur fruit basket!' Everything looks 'put on' on her – like a hanger. But Travis is petrified they will say he copied Adrian's designs. I told him: 'Ridiculous! No one ever remembers what Garbo wears!' Sweetheart, your beef tea is in the green thermos." She turned to me, "Angel, come," and we left for the Costume Department.

Actually, Dietrich enjoyed making *The Scarlet Empress*. Playing her first monarch appealed to her, she felt comfortable being her aristocratic self. The fact that her one-time idol and girlfriend, Elisabeth Bergner, was filming the same story in England didn't bother her in the least. Any brilliant performance Bergner came up with couldn't compete with Dietrich in a tall fur hat, reviewing her private guards. She was right again – ask any movie buff, "Who played Catherine the Great?" and without a moment's hesitation, they will answer, "Marlene Dietrich."

WE WERE ENGULFED in bolts of cloth. While my mother and Travis searched, found, rejected, and examined, they chatted. I sat waiting for my mother to find what she decided was what they were looking for, sipped my malted, and listened.

"Travis – I know we have a blacker black than this velvet. The nap is too short on this to look rich on the screen, and where is the georgette we didn't use in *Blonde Venus*? Did you use it for Lombard? That old satin you draped her with for those publicity stills – really! – off the shoulder?

À la 'vamp'? Lombard? She looked silly . . ." My mother crawled under a pyramid of stacked bolts, searching. Her voice sounded as though it was coming from a padded cave.

"Talk about silly, where *did* you get that sailor outfit they put on her? Really, Travis, you can't do that! Lombard can be very funny. If she gets the right pictures, she can become a big star. You have to watch what Lombard wears. She loves to look like me; why not make her a 'Dietrich' suit out of that white flannel we found – but she will need a shorter jacket than I wear. She has an American body. Also a behind, so watch the skirt line."

My mother surfaced from her cloth cave.

"Travis, where *is* that black? We had it. It can't all be on Miriam Hopkins's back!" She attacked a stack of bolts by the door.

"Did you see what they did to Dolores Del Rio over at Warner Brothers? All she needs is castanets! That wonderful face – they are ruining it! And what is Adrian doing over at MGM? I saw pictures of Jean Harlow in *Dinner at Eight*; he put layers of ruffles on her arms! Like lampshades! And *then*, she wears a dressing gown where the sleeves are *wrinkled feathers* – they look like those things they wave about at American football games! Has he got something with sleeves? But he is good with Marion Davies – probably scared of Hearst!" She held up a bolt of gossamer white chiffon.

"*This*, we have to use someday! Hide it, Travis. 'You never know, said the widow . . .'"

Travis finished our "black panty" saying for her. He was one of the inner circle and was allowed such liberties.

Weeks passed with endless exhausting fittings. Sometimes even Dietrich balked:

"What is the use of designing shoes, nobody will see them under all these hoops. Besides, Jo uses long shots only to carpet the cutting-room floor!"

But still, she spent hours fitting shoes and boots, just in case. On our lunch break, she wrote letters in her dressing room.

PARAMOUNT PICTURES

14 October 1933

Dearest Papi,

Enclosed drawing is of same design as the Hermès desk set, that was very successful. Of course also of leather and square this time instead of round – something new. The sample of the monogram R.C. style is on the other side. If they don't work, then choose other very modern letters. I am very depressed. The suspicion has become a reality that Jo has or always had – or has taken up again or started one during my absence, an affair with his secretary, the magnitude of this shock for me probably only you can fully appreciate. You have gone through all the troubles – that in the light of this becomes even more terrible and completely incomprehensible. His exotic trips – I never complained about but to think that like some little bourgeois he slept with his secretary, that he even brought her to help me, that I trusted, I can only laugh at my own gullibility. I thought he was true, so honest in his love for me – I believed in him and to think I even reproached myself that *I* was making him so unhappy. My thoughtfulness of not allowing anyone who belongs to me from coming here. It is all a comic tragedy. Everything has changed – I can't find any direction.

I'm sure by now you are pale with shock. It *is* terrible news. I should be sensible now and behave as if I knew nothing until I have collected enough proof to throw at his head.

Yesterday I saw her car in front of his house until quarter to 12 and this morning, when I asked him what he did last night, he said he went to bed early. This of course is the real proof, because if he didn't have to hide her being with him, he wouldn't need to. I am too weak for a long investigation – don't know what to do. The thing I do know is that he is lying.

I'll cable you the moment I have more news. By now, I'm sure you are saying, "Good, now she can do as she wants." That's true, but the shock remains, not because of sleeping with a woman but the betrayal without reason all through the years.

I kiss you a thousand times – you are the only friend – I love you.

Your Mutti

Von Sternberg was refused entrance to the dressing room, and his goulash was no longer bubbling on our stove. I was worried. What could our little man have done that would get him into so much trouble? My mother was stony faced. Called Vienna, told Hans how much she missed him, how divine his love letters were.

Suddenly, the usual mood of exhilaration, when creation was in high gear, changed. "What do you mean, we can't fit tomorrow? The Studio is closed for Thanksgiving?" We were in our dressing room, my mother was talking on the phone to Travis across the street.

"You can't be serious. . . . A whole studio stops functioning to eat *turkey*?" . . . Every two minutes, there is another 'holiday' in this country – but this one is really ridiculous! All this 'family schmaltz' . . . and the eating! If they are really so 'thankful,' then go to work and earn money for the family, instead of spending it on too much food!"

Thanksgiving has always been my favorite holiday. The day before, the Commissary served a full turkey dinner – for lunch! I somehow managed each year to escape my mother's condemning eye and had my private celebration at the Studio, with all the "fixings." With Dietrich, all holidays, human or celestial, were taboo. Anything that closed shops, stopped people from being on call to satisfy her demands, enraged her.

Dearest Papi,
Here it is Thanksgiving, so we are not working. Mamoulian is supposed to have made a very bad film with Garbo. Saw secret sketches – so it can't be the clothes. Tomorrow they start to shoot retakes and a new end.
Try to find something on the Bergner film. Here the English can't call their film "Catherine the Great" because our title was registered first, but for over there, we can't do anything. We are making very few stills because we don't want to give away too much of the decor before release.

Kisses

Christmas and New Year passed without memory. We had a film to make – all our energies were geared to eighteenth-century imperialist Russia. The redesigned Young Girl dress was perfection, with its layers of fluttery chiffon ruffles and perky bows – it resembled a Victorian christening dress, done in spun sugar. My mother gave it her ultimate approval – she kissed Travis's cheek, tucked the sketch under her arm and marched off to design a wig worthy of it. Little bangs, soft, soft yellow curls – a confection of blond lights all held together with a baby blue taffeta ribbon.

The "young-young-young" must have gotten stuck in her mind, for when she finally did her first scene in *The Scarlet Empress*, she played it so "wide-eyed innocence," with so many shy curtseys and bobbings, that she looked like the village idiot dressed in a bassinet. But then, acting "pure" was never Dietrich's forte, either professionally or in life – although she believed the opposite, as did a lot of her lovers.

MY MOTHER was shooting costume tests of the completed black banquet dress. Holding the fort in the dressing room, I was busy signing my mother's name to a stack of fan pictures. It was one of my "jobs," that took concentration and skill. Dietrich's signature duplicated on a brass stamp had to be inked evenly, then banged down onto the surface of the picture with force and precision, otherwise the edges would blur and give away the trick that she had not signed it personally. I was allowed to ruin three or four of the pictures, but no more. It was one of the jobs I hated. I was always scared of not getting it right; besides, after a hundred pictures, the constant banging got to me and my arm tingled.

ABOVE: The future empress of all the Russias being taken to the set of *The Scarlet Empress* in our special farm wagon, so her costume wouldn't be crushed in a car.

BELOW: In this film, "Maria, daughter of Marlene Dietrich," became a one-day movie star, playing her mother as a child, and got Dietrich as her hairdresser.

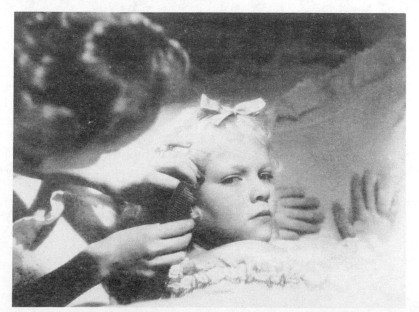

OPPOSITE: Von Sternberg, on his boom, loved shooting the "arrival in St. Petersburg" scene for its contrasts of the white of the fake snow and the ebony black of the coach and horses.

ABOVE: I thought the silver wedding dress fabulous, but my mother didn't. She thought it "too out of the costume books," not visually arresting enough to match the others in this film.

The most famous of all the famous looks in *The Scarlet Empress*, the review costume—my mother's favorite and mine. Dietrich helped design its perfection. It became the most remembered costume in this film.

The screen door squeaked, Dietrich entered; Dot, Nellie, and a bevy of Wardrobe girls at her heels:

"Angel! You are going to be me!" she announced. I stopped a *bang* in midflight and stared at her.

"Mr. von Sternberg is looking everywhere for a beautiful child who can play me as a princess. But I have the most beautiful child in the world – Right Here! So, you are going to play Catherine the Great – as a child!"

Everyone was beaming at me. I was stunned. I couldn't play my mother. I wasn't pretty enough. Besides, my ankles were too thick for a princess. My mother was always saying how real aristocrats had thin bones – like racehorses – that was why her bones were so thin. A plow horse suited my bone size! And what about all those orders never to allow myself to be photographed? What happened to that all of a sudden? Being seen on a giant movie screen all over the world – that was okay suddenly?

"Stand up! Wardrobe has to take your measurements. Nellie, The Child will have to have an exact duplicate of the wig I wear in the first scene."

Von Sternberg, followed by his harried assistants, appeared with Travis in tow.

"Marlene, I have written a new scene for the child – more interesting. It will convey a mood, be superimposed onto your first shot, which I plan now to do with you on a swing, before you are summoned by the archduke, your father." Von Sternberg had a way of talking, like setting up a scene, that annoyed my mother. When she had to listen to him, as now, you could see her wanting to interrupt him with a "Get to the point!" but, of course, didn't in front of people. She knew her place of "pupil" to revered "master." Von Sternberg never asked or expected this of her, it was Dietrich's choice to accord him her deferential homage – in public.

I was standing engulfed in tape measures, still speechless. Von Sternberg looked me over with professional eyes, for the first time since taking those famous portraits of me and my mother two years before.

"Everyone! Leave Miss Dietrich's dressing room! Wait outside – until I call you."

"Everyone" knew to obey immediately whenever von Sternberg cleared a place, be it soundstage or dressing room. In a flash, we were alone, just the three of us. Von Sternberg looked at my exasperated mother and asked, "Marlene. How old is Kater now – nine?"

"Oh, Jo! You know how they are always trying to make her older. She is only seven and a half!"

Funny, I had been sure I was "just nine." But mothers had to know the correct age of their child, so I must have gotten it wrong again.

"Well, whatever age she is, she will look too old for the scene – too tall. I have set it in the schoolroom of the castle, but I can put her in bed – she has a cold. Close up, many pillows, dolls – her size won't be seen, only her face, and that is always very young."

He gave me another of his scrutinizing looks, seemed satisfied, turned to my mother, saying:

"Call them in. Tell Travis to design a nightgown. All we will see is the top – lace at the throat and on the wrists. I want to shoot her baby hands. Keep the idea of copying your wig." Calling to his assistants, he left, marching down the dressing-room street, dictating his orders: He wanted an eighteenth-century princess's bedroom, built, decorated, ready to shoot in two days.

While Wardrobe resumed its fussing over me, my mother told Travis what she and Jo wanted; Nellie called Hair Design to alert them we were coming over to measure my head. All I could think of was, thank God, they are going to cover my peasant wrists!

The day I reported on the set for work, my entourage boasted Marlene Dietrich, dressed in a white uniform, sporting a hand mirror and comb. She looked just like me – in Big – and I looked just like her, about to be in bed – Small! Von Sternberg led me over to my chair, a special gift from the crew – MISS SIEBER – newly stenciled on its canvas back. He told me, "Sit and don't move." The wig was hot and itched where the spirit gum glued its outline lace to my forehead and temples. The long nightgown was strangely heavy, but felt silky and nice against my bare legs, its ruffles prickled through. My eyes felt funny, the mascara kept sticking my lashes together. My face was stiff with greasepaint and face powder. My lips tasted of Vaseline. My neck ached from trying not to dislodge the preplaced curls. I had been up since five a.m., worked and fussed over for hours, I was hungry. I sat in my chair as "lightweight" as I possibly could, knowing I mustn't wrinkle my costume. I was *very* uncomfortable! I was a real movie star!

My "princess room" had only three walls, and those were braced in the back, but what there was of it was very pretty. I wished I could have a fluffy, feminine bedroom someday, instead of my serviceable room with the extra-stiff mattress and flat horsehair pillow. My mother's mother always said, "Sleep flat! Makes a strong back!" My mother, of course, agreed, adding her special touch to the homily. "Soft pillows are for women who have nothing to do and stay in bed all day, eating chocolates from bonbon boxes."

My mother knelt to take off my slippers. Six people helped me climb into bed. More hands arranged lace-edged sheets, damask cover, satin pillows. Von Sternberg put my shoulders, neck, and chin into position, told me when, how, and what to say.

"Angel – wet your lips," my mother coached from the dark.

"LIGHTS!"

I knew I must not allow the glare of the lights to get into the center of my eyes – my eyes would tear and make the mascara run. Take a breath, but don't move! What had von Sternberg told me to say? And when? WHEN do I have to say it? She will be furious if I do it wrong! She will be ashamed of me! I am supposed to know all about making movies – I'M GOING TO SNEEZE! I KNOW IT! Or throw up . . .

"ROLL 'EM."

"SCARLET EMPRESS – SCENE ONE, TAKE ONE!"

The slap of the clap-board was like thunder! PANIC! I DON'T WANT TO BE IN MOVIES!

"ACTION!"

I DIDN'T SNEEZE OR THROW UP OR DISGRACE MY MOTHER!

"CUT! PRINT THAT!"

"Good, very good, Maria – I want you this time to take a pause. . . ."

I was being given DIRECTION by JOSEF VON STERNBERG and had graduated to an un-angry "MARIA" ALL IN ONE MORNING!

"Let's try it again," said the director.

"QUIET ON THE SET!" the assistant director shouted.

"Jo," my mother hissed from behind the camera, "the pillow on the right has a crease by her cheek line, it's making a shadow," and into the shooting set, or "hot set," as it is referred to, my "handmaiden" stepped, smoothed out the pillow, blotted a spot of sheen on my nose with a powder puff, ducked back between the light stands, saying, "OKAY – SHOOT IT!"

How the crew allowed my mother such unheard-of license was astounding. She fussed, corrected, and generally got in the way the entire day, and no one said a word or tried to stop her interfering. It embarrassed me. But if von Sternberg didn't mind, that's all that mattered. I was a real veteran by the time we broke to set up for my close-up. It would be a long wait while lights and camera were repositioned. Maybe I could have a Coca-Cola? Perhaps even a peanut butter and jelly sandwich? The makeup would have to be retouched anyway. My mother, on hearing my wishes, rushed off to fulfill them. Boy! There were real compensations in being a "star."

I was alone when a lady pulled up a chair next to mine, smiled, and asked if my name was Maria Sieber. I said yes, and she shook my hand.

"Now you will have your lesson, little Maria," and she produced a schoolbook, copybook, pencils, and erasers from her copious handbag. Placing a cardboard chart of the alphabet on my lap, she pointed to the letter *A* and, still smiling, sweetly asked, "Do you know what that is?"

I thought she was so nice, I better answer her and play along, so I said: "AH," pronouncing it in the only way I knew, in the German way.

"No, no, dear. That is incorrect. Try again – Now." Still smiling, her finger tapped against the big black letter.

"AH," I repeated, obligingly, beginning to wonder what this was all about.

Her smile had slipped a little.

"No, child, that is not an aaaaaahh. You must know what a simple *A* is!"

I saw she was getting a little upset. So I tried to distract her by continuing the alphabet, to show her I wasn't dumb. I pointed: "That is a BAY and that is a CZAY and that is a DAY and THEN only comes the AYE."

The smile vanished as I pointed to the letter *E*, pronouncing it in German, which happens to be the same sound as the letter *A* in English.

"What are you doing with my child? How DARE you! JO! There is a woman with The Child! There is a STRANGER on the set!"

My mother was shouting. Like a pack of hound dogs, von Sternberg and half the set converged on the once-smiling lady, now scared out of her wits!

"And who are you?" In the voice of a hanging judge, von Sternberg led the interrogation while my mother clutched me to her rib cage. I could have reached her bosom but I was so intent on "being small," I still had my knees bent.

"But . . . but . . . Sir! She is a working nine-year-old child! She is supposed to have proper schooling. I am the Studio School Teacher. It is the law!" the lady wailed in righteous indignation.

Von Sternberg was about to say something calming to get her off the set, when my mother whirled!

"What *law*? Who *dares* to say that my child has to go to school? My child is brilliant! She doesn't need to go to school. She can speak *two* languages. Can you? Tell your bosses, what my child learns – I *decide*. Not some *stupid* law!" My mother was on a "high indignation" role. She spelled it out to the quivering schoolmarm.

"We are making a *moving picture* here. That costs a great deal of

MONEY – more than you will ever see – and you are interfering with our work with your stupidity! So leave and take your *little* alphabet with you! My child has a CLOSE-UP to do!"

The result of my being in the movies was a taste of fleeting stardom, my own Hollywood chair, and a teacher who came to our house each day and taught me that an *E* was pronounced as *EE* – not *AYE*. It was the law! Even Dietrich could not afford the publicity of having a truant daughter. I also found out, as I first suspected, that I was, after all, nine years old.

I loved, finally, having real lessons in the language of *my* country. My schooling was not consistent, it got juggled around – according to what scenes I just had to be at the Studio for and which ones my mother felt could be shot without my holy presence. No one from the board of education ever came to check on what was really going on. I do not know if Paramount had a hand in making sure their star was left alone, but as long as someone taught her pride and joy, it seemed to satisfy the law.

Once my teacher saw she had a pupil who "ate" books like peanuts, her educator's spirit soared. It crash-landed when she attempted to impart the black art of arithmetic. She finally decided on a course that was to be followed voluntarily by every tutor I ever had. If the child loves reading so much and is hopeless in every other required subject, why complicate both our lives by beating a dead horse? So I wallowed happily in what I liked best, while my teachers relaxed, got paid, and enjoyed the novel experience of having a contented pupil. Through the years, some of them did touch briefly on such subjects as Egyptian, Greek, and Roman history. Then I would tell them stories of Cecil B. De Mille, smuggle home a Wardrobe book, and teach them a thing or two!

I was careful to keep my English reading pleasure to myself. My mother was already annoyed by what she referred to as my "two hundred percent Americanism." I did my best to always remember to speak German whenever my mother was around, and when I was told to "find a book to read," to either choose Schiller, Goethe, or Heine from her bookshelf. My German lessons continued. As neither tutor cared to inform themselves of what that "foreigner" was teaching their charge, it could get very confusing. It's not easy being in the reeds with Moses' basket in German, fighting the Spartan wars in English, and making a film with Dietrich about Czarist Russia – all at the same time!

On seeing the rushes of my scene, everyone was *ecstatic*! " 'The Child' was *magnificent*!" The Academy Award loomed on my limitless horizon. The Publicity Department jumped for joy and went to town on "the beautiful little girl, the talented daughter of . . ." My mother did not annihilate them, she didn't even try to stop them. She ordered fifty dozen fan pictures to be printed of my close-up stills and I was allowed to sign them, personally, in *purple ink*!

Von Sternberg set up a screening for me to see myself up there, on that big, big screen. The ultimate visual exposure, the acid test of that profession that is so merciless! Well? I looked five years old but, except for this dubious accomplishment, the scene was too contrived, sullen, and monotone, and boy! was my face FAT! Right then I decided that, as with Ruby Keeler and the tap dancing, now Shirley Temple had nothing to fear from me either. My "stardom" fizzled out quickly, and I was able to get back to signing my mother's fan pictures, instead of "Maria – Daughter of . . ."

There was a time in my childhood when I actually believed that was my name. I remember writing a thank-you note for some gift I had received and signing it "Sincerely Yours, Maria Daughter of Marlene Dietrich." My mother, on checking it over, declared my note "perfect," and sent it off. That memory still embarrasses me.

MY LESSONS WERE SUSPENDED. We were about to shoot "the arrival in St. Petersburg," and education just couldn't compete. The set smelled of horses and fake snow and overflowed with cowboys, all dressed like the doorman of the Scheherazade in Paris. Big black mustaches glued to their faces made them look like real "fierce Russians," hiding their California grins. Fake manes and sweeping tails, courtesy of Hair-Dressing, disguised the fact that their small wild Siberian horses were really polo ponies rented from the Riviera Country Club's chukka team.

But Dietrich's furs were real. A voluminous floor-length cape with rounded hood: Russian sable, silver-tipped and female! A king's ransom, she had insisted was absolutely necessary to give the film that look of authenticity. Secretly, I think she enjoyed watching the producer Adolph Zukor tear his hair! Her eyes held a wicked gleam, as she said to me:

"For once, Paramount doesn't have to be convinced *why* something costs a fortune. They remember what good fur costs! But, do you think they *ever* sewed on *real sable*?"

Dietrich's stand-in, her cape made of brown squirrel, stood on my mother's marks, while lights were being focused around her. It was believed that the job of stand-ins required a real facial resemblance to the star. Not really – the height, build, and coloring was all that was required, plus strong legs, endurance, and infinite patience. Although some stars adopted their stand-ins, giving them employment within their private entourage, using them as gofers, even confidants, often taking them along when changing studios, Dietrich never did.

The stand-in had been told to move to the door of the royal coach. It stood in the center of the winter set, all ebony and glass, with huge spoked wheels, silver lanterns, and tasseled pillion seats. Its perfectly matched black eight-horse team waited quietly, rippling their hides now and then beneath the unaccustomed weight of the ornate harness. They were veterans, stagecoach trained, and probably thinking, Tom Mix movies were a lot easier – there you galloped full out, worked up a proper white foam, got rubbed, fed, and sent home! This standing around all day, in this sticky white stuff that gets up your nose and smells awful, is no fun! When horses were working, the crew boasted an extra member – the Sweeper. It was his job to scurry between stomping hooves, ever ready to swoop on whatever "plopped," his shovel poised. The more horses, the more conscientious little men. Elephants were their recurrent nightmare! And goats drove them crazy – those little black balls had a way of bouncing about and getting lost. They preferred shit to lie there, peaceably, waiting for them.

Von Sternberg was astride his favorite toy, the boom camera. He rode it like a witch on her broomstick, sometimes, it seemed, devising shots for the sole purpose of enjoying the ride!

"We are ready for you, Miss Dietrich, whenever you are." The assistant director just missed bowing. My mother put on her sable cape and secured its hood to frame her face, Nellie fluffed the baby bangs with a deft twist of her comb, Dot redewed the lips with a brush dipped in glycerine, the stand-in relinquished her position as Dietrich claimed her rights. She looked all soft and cuddly, like a silky caramel teddy bear that had decided not to hibernate in order to gaze, in wide-eyed wonder, at Russia in the depth of winter! Dietrich was still convinced of the need for "innocent wonder" and held onto it tenaciously until much later in the film, when a scene occurred that was always referred to only as "the final dissolutionment." I thought it a very silly scene: A handsome palace guard pursued her into the bushes, then, suddenly, fade-out? It made no sense to me, but after that my mother dropped her "little girl" act. Von Sternberg was actually heard to utter a sigh of relief the day his star stopped flitting about, lowered those famous eyelids, and gave him back a face to light!

Dearest Papi,

I finally have the time to write to you. Have the first day off and that is only because I worked at night for the last week. Looks like the film will be good. Pictures on the way to you. You should have some already. Jo is very nice – Happy I have been so interested up to now. That I am even concerned with everything, including him. I look very sweet in the film, very young – as I said, in the film. In life, I have wrinkles on the cheeks as you already discovered. I'm just getting old. The mask from Arden that Tami got for me is very good. I still don't have a good night cream though.

Here it is warm. Had a cable today from Vienna, where it is snowing. He writes sweet letters but who does that help? Monday I sign the life insurance $100,000 death payable to you, $200,000 if death by accident. (Sure I won't die in bed.)

For the next film, you have to come here and work on it with us. Please think about it – you can really help us. Now we are, for the first time, involved in the earnings of the film. You could really help if you took a job in the company.

I love you,

Mutti

My father answered:

. . . about your and Jo's idea that I come to work for you on the next film – sounds fine – but what will you find as a proper position for "Mr. Dietrich"?

During the filming of *The Scarlet Empress*, I hardly ever saw my teachers. My bored bodyguard had a fight with our head gardener – the lawn mower had shaved off the tip of his brand-new saddle shoes while he was resting in the grass. The maid with the thick German accent was discovered trying on my mother's garter belts. Our sexy chauffeur was supposed to have done something "shocking" to either the laundress or the butcher boy. The rose garden was being devoured by voracious aphids, and the latest dog, I think it was the chow chow, had eaten one of the, now sixty, rabbits for breakfast! Sometimes, one didn't know what to choose, home or the Studio – both were so interesting!

Sunday mornings, my mother drank a tall glass of warm water mixed with epsom salts, trying to lose weight on her only day off. Between running to the bathroom, we answered the private mail and did the telephone calls. First to my father:

"Papi, if I suddenly have to go, talk to Kater." He knew the epsom-salt routine and needed no further explanations. "Jo is being very difficult again! I can't be blamed if Cooper keeps trying to get into my dressing room –" She laughed. "I said *dressing room*! Really, Papi! . . . And Maurice keeps calling. I cook Jo's dinner every night and every day make his beef tea for the Studio. I call Hans only when he can't hear me – and still, he gets angry! He doesn't understand that I am here *only* for him. . . . Quick, talk to Papi. . . ." She sprinted to the bathroom while I kept the line open to Paris.

"Hello, Papi. How are your kidney stones?"

My father was only halfway through his lecture on the urological state of his body when my mother returned and continued their conversation.

"Why don't you call Jo, Papi! . . . Tell him I only love him. That's why I am *here*, making this difficult picture. Do I have to *do* it with him all the time before he believes me?" She handed me the black-and-gold receiver, whispering:

"Sweetheart, tell Papi – you miss him."

"Papi, it's me again. I miss you."

He didn't answer, so I continued.

"How is Tami? Did she get my letter about my new dog eating one of the rabbits? May I say hello to her for a minute, please?"

My mother had left the room . . . I had to talk fast.

"Tamilein? . . . Oh, I miss you so! Yes, the film is going great. Everything is very Russian – you would love it. But there isn't one *real* Russian – anywhere! I wish you were here! We have hummingbirds and their wings really hum when they fly. I wish you could see them. Please write me a letter, I will write one to you right away, I promise. I love you. Kiss Teddy." I hung up – just as my mother returned.

Next, she called Berlin:

"Muttilein – did you get the photographs? Yes, they are very beautiful. Of course, the big portraits will only be done after the film is finished. Yes, very hard work, but I need the money. If you need anything, Rudi is in Paris – just call or cable him. Yes, put Liesel on. . . . Sweetheart? Yes, I am working. It is a very important film and Mr. von Sternberg is making me very beautiful. No – *he* does it! *He* makes me beautiful. I told Mutti to call Rudi if she needs anything or wants to leave suddenly. What? Liesel, they are not listening on this telephone line – they haven't gone that far yet! All right, but you must realize I am speaking from America. *Here* it is safe! Here is The Child . . ." she beckoned to me.

"Talk to Liesel . . . she always gets so dramatic!"

I took over:

"Tante Liesel, you would like our new house. It looks Spanish. Our garden has real banana trees and a rose garden, with the roses growing on little trees, not on bushes!" She had not said a word, so I asked, "Tante Liesel – are you all right?"

"Katerlein – tell Pussy Cat not to send those American newspapers. . . . Mail gets opened, and if they come to search the house . . . Tell her she must be careful of what she writes!"

"Yes, Tante Liesel, I will. Don't worry, please. I send you a kiss." I handed the receiver back to my mother.

She spoke a few soothing words to her sister, then hung up, saying, "Really, Liesel seems terrified! 'They' this and 'they' that! Always – Hitler. Why doesn't some Jew kill him and get it over with? Angel, now we call Hans in Vienna," and again I went through the intricate maneuvers required in 1934 to telephone Europe. When the operator finally rang back with Jaray on the line, my mother took the call in her bedroom and stayed for hours. We did not call Brian. Still no word from him. De Acosta was "tragically sulking," suspecting she was on the wane. "The boys," though, were deliriously happy. My mother had managed to get one of them into the film in the part of a courtier. He got to wear satin knee breeches, embroidered coat with a little peplum that fell just over his tidy behind, much lace at neck and wrists, and . . . high-heeled satin pumps! Divine! They absolutely adored it, and, of course, their Marlene – for making it all possible!

My teachers waited – the birth scene was ready to shoot.

She lay against the mound of silken pillows. Her white hair glinting like moonlight on still water, her softly tired eyes survey a large diamond pendant that sways, rotates on its delicate diamond chain that hangs suspended from one perfect finger of her alabaster hand. The jewel catches light, refracts it as the tips of her fingers make it twirl. The fine gauze netting that envelops the bed and her, like a white fog, first appears in microscopic focus, then begins to blur, becoming vaporous, as jewel and hand sharpen. Now they, too, recede, giving way to the ultimate perspective – a face, so breathtaking you do not realize that your eyes have just been led through three dimensions.

My mother always said, "We did not know we were making masterpieces! We did our job! Now, they write books about films, and professors discuss 'the meaning' behind every shot. Why this was done, what was meant, and how . . . big to-do! We had a film to make and we made it! That's *all*!"

Maybe. But that day on *The Scarlet Empress* set, members of the crew stood in small groups in the shadows, whispered, and watched. The huge soundstage was dark – except for that hot, white circle of light, where a little man with a droopy mustache practiced his consummate skill on the face and profession he loved – and everyone felt the magic and knew they were privileged to be a part of it.

THOSE EVENINGS when my mother did not need my company in her bathroom, I was told to stay in my room, not to come out, and go to bed early. Usually, though, I sat on my bathtub perch, listened, and watched her get ready for bed. I had stayed home that day studying something, so she was telling me of what I had missed: the first day's shooting of the Banquet scene. She spat into the pink marble basin,

"You should have been there today – it was terrible. First, Jo has built a table – as long as the street in front of the dressing rooms. That's already impossible! Then, everybody has to sit in those enormous chairs, with those corpses hanging over you! You can't imagine what shadows they throw on the face. More corpses all holding candles, everywhere – on the table, by the chairs, against the walls – between the hot wax and the lights, the *heat*!"

She peered in the mirror, worked on a pimple she had discovered on the side of her nose.

"That awful little man Jaffe keeps complaining about his wig that it 'looks crazy.' He is *supposed* to be insane. So? What does he want? To look like Barrymore? Probably! You know, he hates Jo. His behavior on the set is unheard of. All the time, says he is from the '*theater*'! He should go back to New York and stay there. Such a ham!"

She sat on the toilet, pulled off a corn pad, and massaged her reddened toe.

"Those beautiful black shoes we made? For nothing! Under that table, no one will ever see them. Even when I stand up, in that terrible costume, who can see anything? You can't see anything but *pearls*. Travis has gone crazy with the pearls! I don't know why I allowed it. I look like Mae West with a tiara à la royalty! Sweetheart, give me a new corn thing. My Paris shoes never do this – can't they learn to make shoes in America?"

She turned off the lights. We left the bathroom and she crawled into bed, but instead of lying down, she fluffed the pillows behind her back and sat up. That meant she wanted to talk. I was not allowed to sit on my mother's bed when she was in it, so I brought a chair over to the side and sat down to listen.

"That set dresser – what's his name? . . . Not important. He also has gone crazy – must be a friend of Travis's – with the fake food. This you have to see! Enough for two hundred people and what are we, at that never-ending table . . . fifty? You can't imagine it! Boars' heads painted so they shine! Stretched-out pigs . . . and pheasants decorated with so many feathers, it looks like orange and brown bushes growing out of their behinds. The platters of painted food never end! The *scene* never ends! It goes on and on. . . . Sweetheart, get me my nail file."

I returned from the bathroom and handed her the file she preferred, the one she had used in *Morocco*.

"Why don't my nails grow? Like Crawford's. She has talons – like a hawk!" She laughed.

"That pretty son of Fairbanks probably likes it that way. I am telling you now – this banquet scene is going to be a big bore, no matter what Jo does to it when he cuts the film. He was furious with me today. He cleared the set and said, 'Miss Dietrich will now *cry*!' But I didn't cry – you know how I get when he yells at me, just sick to my stomach. He can be so low-class sometimes, even with all that genius. Everyone hates him and wants to walk off the picture, so I have to show them they can't do that. But wait till you see that table! And the glued food melting in that heat . . . and the bracelet! You haven't seen that bracelet! Travis put it on my arm to try to hide how fat my arm looks – it goes from my wrist all the way to my elbow! In *pearls*! *Not* to be believed! And now it's been in the establishing shot, so I can't change it, I'm stuck with it. I tell you, this whole scene will be a disaster! Sweetheart, set the alarm for four-thirty. I want to be ready and catch Jo before he goes to the set in the morning."

She curled down on her side. I kissed her good night, turned off the lights – but I don't think she was asleep when I closed the door.

The next evening, I was waiting for her in the hall, impatient for another installment of the banquet saga. She didn't disappoint me; the moment she walked in the front door, she announced:

"Jo yelled at everyone today! If we *ever* finish this picture, it will be a miracle! Lubitsch came on the set and talked to Jo, trying to calm him down! I think somebody must have called him. You should have seen it . . . Lubitsch playing the role of 'head of a big American studio.' Jo says he will be – nebbish! He should do his funny pictures and stop trying to be so 'grand' and leave Jo alone. I got them to put real grapes on one of the platters – and picked up a bunch and started to eat the grapes, one at a time. *Slowly*. Jo is going to do a close-up of it! He approved – I just did it to give her *something* to do, instead of just sitting there in all those terrible pearls."

She removed her cuff links, handed them to me, and, rolling up the sleeves of her striped shirt, marched off to the kitchen to cook dinner for her director and her child. I went upstairs to put the cuff links in their box, hung up her polo coat before reporting to the kitchen to wash the salad.

The next day, my teachers had a nice long lunch on the sunlit veranda while Bridges brought me to the Studio – just to see that table. It was exactly as my mother had described it! But those banquet chairs . . .

they were truly fabulous! Shadow throwing or no shadow throwing. The atmosphere on the set matched the "corpses." No one was speaking to anyone, unless they absolutely had to, and if looks could kill, von Sternberg was a goner – from every direction. My mother, looking splendid despite the junk jewelry weighing her down, plucked her grapes and calmly viewed the brewing carnage. During the lunch break, von Sternberg came to the dressing room for his beef tea. My mother was redoing her makeup. She looked at him in the mirror.

"That girl, who plays the whore – very pretty. Can't take her black eyes off you – might be interesting – Jo?"

"Mutti – are you procuring or checking on her availability?"

My mother chuckled and turned back to the mirror. Somehow, von Sternberg seemed to have had the last word. He put down his glass, was at the door when my mother called over her shoulder, "Want to share?"

The screen door banged. I kept on sorting the makeup towels. These two did have the strangest conversations at times. Gary Cooper scratched on the screen door, said, "Hi, Beautiful!" but went on. Oh dear – von Sternberg must have passed him on the sidewalk. It just didn't seem to be Jo's day!

Dietrich was ready to review her palace guard. The costumes had become so elaborate, the hoops and crinolines so exaggerated, my mother could not fit herself into the car to get her to and from the set, so Bridges was told to park himself and our useless hearse away in the Studio parking lot, and a truck took its place in front of our dressing room. With its slatted sides and high chassis, it looked like an old farm wagon. It was fun! I felt like we were potatoes being carried to market! The carpenter's shop built us a set of lean-to steps: we would climb up, hold on to the sides, and rumble along the Studio streets, while my mother's huge skirts swayed, danced a jig all by themselves.

The day she wore her bottle-green velvet and mink masterpiece, its hoops were so wide she couldn't even see our special steps. It took Nellie, Dot, me, and a blushing truckdriver to finally hoist her onto the truck. Quite a feat, considering that we dared not touch the costume in any place where our fingers might mark the velvet. Once up there, my mother tried to hold herself and found she couldn't! She was wearing a pair of her famous "frozen" gloves, and her fingers wouldn't bend! We finally figured out a way to keep the Empress of Russia from falling off the truck. She wrapped her arms around my waist, I braced my legs and held on for both of us. We rumbled to work, laughing all the way.

When the crew saw Dietrich in her Review costume, their whistles bounced off the soundstage walls. Motion-picture crews are a blasé lot. They see, have seen, and know they will see about everything that can be fantastic, sublime, superb, or just plain marvelous, somewhere, sometime. It lies within the possibilities of their profession. So, if they even notice you, it's a rare treat. If they *show* you their appreciation and approval by whistling, that's a wonderful sound! To receive the ultimate accolade, their applause – that, I think, most actors would die for.

Tall men, in a row, all even, all handsome, stand at attention. Von Sternberg calls, "Action!"

She materializes. Stands there, looking as no one has ever looked – or ever will again. Not just beautiful, not just "Dietrich" – much more! A Ming vase, a Monet painting, Michelangelo's David. A rareness – a one of a kind, a true work of unsurpassable art. She tilts her head, slightly, looking down her row of lovers slowly – very slowly – up and down, lingers a downward glance for a split second below their waists, sucks on a thin piece of straw held rakishly between her teeth – and makes motion-picture history.

This image of Dietrich inspecting her personal guard, in tall mink Cossack hat, became the visual identity of *The Scarlet Empress*, just as the garter belt and white satin top hat is *The Blue Angel*'s. Only when I was much older did I realize that, once again, she had superimposed her special brand of bisexual eroticism onto this scene. With her hair slicked back, hidden under that famous hat, she had the face of a beautiful young boy. The downward gaze then becomes an even greater accomplishment of silent acting. The fact that my mother was not aware of what she was doing has always astounded me. For many years, I couldn't believe it. She had to have known *what* she was doing, just had to! That innocent boy's face looking down for those expected erections – that didn't just happen, she *must* have planned it! But No! When, many years later, I finally had to ask her, my mother answered me:

"You must be joking! What do you mean? I was playing Catherine the Great. What has a boy's face got to do with that? You can't wear a fur hat like that on top of female curls – it would look ridiculous on the screen, so I got rid of the hair, that's all. . . . And it looked wonderful. You've seen the pictures Jo took of my face with that hat – they are beautiful! Anyway, all hats look stupid with hair hanging down."

Dietrich achieved the look of hybrid sexuality long before it became acceptable. As always, she didn't even know she had done it! With Dietrich, wondrous results just happened.

TENSIONS INCREASED, von Sternberg verbally abusive, while Dietrich, refusing to sink to the level of "fishwife," as she called it, flayed him with written accusations instead of public ones. As she wore only wigs in the film, and therefore, did not need to wash her hair during her lunch hour, she used this time to tell him what was wrong with him, his picture, his ideas, and his background, punching out her fury on her portable typewriter. Dietrich never reread what she had written in anger, never doubted her absolute right to say anything she wanted to anyone, any time.

It was my job, or Nellie's when I wasn't at the Studio, to be the courier, delivering my mother's letters to von Sternberg's office across the way. Dietrich always kept carbon copies of what she wrote. She liked to refuel her anger and justification by referring to her letters to her victim, if necessary, at a later date. Von Sternberg sometimes answered her by letter. He wrote in German, perhaps trying to reach her more fully, plead his case.

After reading his letters, she stuffed them into envelopes and sent them to my father, without comment.

MY TEACHERS RESIGNED THEMSELVES to never seeing me again. Catherine seizing the throne of Russia was about to be recorded on film. Von Sternberg wanted an Eisenstein montage of Cossacks charging up the palace portico. The stunt riders were ready. The horses, sensing the tension, pawed the sawdust on the perimeter of the set. The specially reinforced palace stairs loomed before them, the horses rubber-shod to help cushion the expected shock. A slim young man dressed in my mother's all-white hussar's uniform, splendid in tall ermine shako and long regimental sword, looked exactly as he should – a slight, amazing woman in military garb at the head of her loyal cavalry. He checked his snaffle rein and, once more, the angle of the charge. They all knew what was expected of them, what had to be done – what the director demanded. It was difficult, dangerous, and utterly insane. Quite the normal state of affairs for stuntmen. Still, they were apprehensive. There was not enough room for so many horses rushing up that flight of stairs at full gallop – someone would have to get hurt in such a crowded frenzy.

"QUIET ON THE SET!"

Horses snorted, some whinnied, humans held their breath and prayed.

"LIGHTS – SOUND – ROLL 'EM!"

Strong hands tightened their grips on reins, leg muscles increased
their hold.

"ACTION!"

And – *they charged*! Fast – Wild – They surged – Uncaring. Man and
beast threw themselves against those stairs – attacking them – Up and up
they ran, the crash of hooves tremendous. . . . A high frenzied scream
wails above the deafening sound.

"Cut! Cut!" yelled the assistant directors through their megaphones. A
horse lay writhing on the steps. Loving hands gentled him, stroked down
those beautiful legs, and found the break. This was my mother's favorite
scene in *The Scarlet Empress*, although she was not actually in it.

"Listen to those hooves . . . listen to that sound! That's what makes
the scene great! The Sound!"

I wished I'd stayed home that day.

I was coming back from a courier run, when I saw Nellie standing guard.
Whenever my mother had a "special" visitor, the dressing-room door was
closed, locked, and Nellie put outside on "sentry duty." Well, it couldn't
be Jo this time – I had just delivered one of my mother's mean letters to
him on the set. So, who could it be? Who was on the lot today, but not
busy shooting? Certainly not our so-called leading man! Although he was
tall, dark, and sort of handsome, for some reason my mother had not been
interested.

"That John Lodge – where did Jo find him? Boston? No wonder – what
a bore! Jo does that so I won't be . . . Ever since *Morocco* and Cooper . . .
he gives me either pansies or bores. Jealous! Ridiculous!"

Maybe Chevalier was scheduled for a wardrobe fitting? or perhaps
Cooper had finally decided to stop scratching on the screen door and go
inside instead? My mother had not had company like this for a long time.
During *Song of Songs*, the dressing room had been locked often, but not
during *The Scarlet Empress*. I walked over to Nellie, who looked worried
– her usual expression when guarding my mother's privacy. I did like her
so, this birdlike woman. Nellie was miscast; with her bony body, thin,
pointed nose, and bleached curls, she looked more like a dim-witted Billie
Burke than the skilled Hollywood hairstylist that she was. Nellie and I
had become good friends over the years. We supported each other, did
yeoman service in the employment of our star. My mother is supposed to
have given her a one-hundred-acre orange ranch, cars, houses, fortunes in
clothes, and hard cash. If so, none of it was necessary. Nellie did not have
to be bribed, as so many others needed to be. Unconditional faithfulness
was her middle name.

I asked her the usual necessary question: "How long do I have to stay away?"

She twittered, "Your mom was so exhausted! She just had to have a little rest! So, be back in one hour, hon, but not before. Okay?"

I had on my new wristwatch that our producer had given me for being in the film; it had a red patent-leather strap and numbers that glowed in the dark. I checked the time.

"And, hon – your mom left orders at the Commissary that you can sign for anything you want!" she added. I knew that. Whenever the dressing room was locked, I was allowed to go and eat everything – for free! All I had to do was print my name carefully on the little piece of paper that the waitress handed me.

A whole hour! I had a whole hour! I could have a . . . melted cheese and bacon on white . . . a large root beer . . . even a piece of lemon meringue pie . . . and still have enough time to sneak onto the De Mille set and watch Claudette Colbert being Cleopatra!

I kissed Nellie's cheek and was on my way. Why did Nellie always say that, about my mother – "having to rest"? She knew that my mother never rested, was never tired, like normal people. As I passed, I noticed that Bing Crosby's dressing-room door was closed too, his Studio driver on "guard duty." I got to the corner and ran!

Between shooting the cavalry charge and Dietrich's last scene in the film, I ate myself through ten varieties of pie, deciding that Paramount's coconut cream was the best in the world! I had a waitress friend who would cut me extra-big slices, but only charged the regular twenty-five cents on the bill. I wished I could give Maggie something for herself! But I wasn't allowed to sign for a tip, and real money? That I never had. I decided I should try and find some, so I could give it to my nice friend. I knew it was no use looking through my mother's pants pockets – she never had *real* money either. Von Sternberg's office paid all our bills – the rent, the salaries, the stores; everyone had expense accounts that they turned in at the end of each week. Bridges bought gasoline, all the newspapers and magazines. My bodyguards, any incidentals I might need. I thought of raiding my mother's "extras" supply cupboard, maybe taking one of the large bottles of perfume from Paris, which were stored there by the dozen. But I felt funny about giving Maggie such expensive perfume when she had to work so hard to earn her money. It was my first realization that cash, as such, did not exist in our life. By its very absence, it became intriguing and very precious to me. I just had to find a way to get some – but how? CHEWING GUM – THAT'S IT! I can ask for money to buy chewing gum!, then keep what they give me, until I have at least – a dollar? I could move my jaws now and then, so they wouldn't get suspicious! Before leaving for the Studio the next morning, I asked my nighttime bodyguard, who was still on duty, for money to buy some chewing gum. Smiling, he graciously handed me his fresh pack of Juicy Fruit. So I tried Bridges – who gave me Wrigley's spearmint. Mac at the Studio gate gave up his Black Jack to please me. Everyone was so generous with their gum! What could I pretend to want that required actual money to buy? Maybe I could make a deal with Travis? He always asked me what I wanted from him for my birthday and for Christmas. Although it was only February, I cornered him on the way to the beading rooms:

"Travis, instead of giving me a birthday present this year, can I have real money instead, please? And can I have it *real* early – *now*?" I pleaded, · scared stiff. Of course, he thought I was joking and repeated how amusing I was to my mother!

"Maria! Come here! Travis just told me you asked him for – money? You have dogs, a swimming pool, a doll's house that cost a fortune, a garden to play in – you are allowed to be here in the Studio with me! You have everything – all for you. You can even *sign* at the Commissary! Everything you want you get, for *nothing*! . . . I work for you only! Bridges has the car outside – he will drive you back to the house . . . you even have a *chauffeur*!" and she turned her back on me and walked away toward her dressing table.

I was thoroughly expelled for the day. On the way back to Bel Air, I kept thinking about what she had said. I mulled over the word *work*. Those funny kids, in the *Our Gang* movies – what did they always do? THAT'S IT! LEMONADE! The moment I got back to the house, I raided the icebox, took all the lemons, stole a bag of sugar, found a huge Baccarat pitcher with matching tumblers, lugged a crate from the garage to the entrance of our imposing drive, and set up my lemonade stand. My bodyguard brought out his beach chair and installed himself in the shade by the road, first helping me with my sign. It turned out really nice – dark yellow and orange crayon lettering on white drawing-block paper:

STOP! FRESH LEMONADE!!
3¢ A BIG GLASS!!

I waited all afternoon. My Limoges saucer, ready to receive all that loot – remained empty! Thirsty people didn't seem to exist around Bel Air. My bodyguard helped me hide my stand in the gardener's shed before my mother returned that evening. After she left the next morning, still not talking to me, my "business partner" drove down the hill and bought more lemons, then dozed in the shade while I, with a fresh supply and renewed confidence in my ability to make a fortune, waited. The cut crystal sparkled pretty colors in the sun, I sat next to my crate and read forbidden comic books – and the lemonade boiled! My bodyguard got so thirsty, he offered to buy some of my hot lemonade. But I couldn't charge him – he had been so nice to help me hide my stand and everything! At six, we gave up and went into the house to get ready for my mother's return. If Brian were still with us, I wouldn't have all this trouble. He would have given me . . . oh! . . . at least a whole dollar bill and would never even have asked me what I needed it for, although I could have told him. For just a second, I thought of asking von Sternberg – but quickly rejected it. Poor Jo! That locked dressing-room door must be getting him down – it always did.

They came home together and must have had "discussions" in the car, because my mother's lips were tight, eyes blazed, and nostrils flared. She served dinner with cold resentment and the air could have been sliced with a cleaver. Jo and I were both in the "Dietrich Doghouse," so we kept silent, stuffed our mouths, and hoped to get out of the dining room as soon as possible.

The day Catherine the Great's final triumphant close-up was scheduled to shoot was the worst. Dietrich and von Sternberg arrived on the set angry, and continued to verbally stoke their antagonism until they had a mighty blaze going. He – was a Tyrant, a Jewish Hitler, a Mean Little American, a Vicious Monster! – was her version. She – was "incapable of doing anything correctly," the "most simple acting was beyond her," "cried the instant something did not suit her" – his version.

Von Sternberg cleared the set at least three times that day. Each time, I had to go outside. I was afraid these two might kill each other! Although they were violent only with words, wounded each other with their sharp minds and vitriolic tongues, there always was the possibility of them one day reaching a saturation point and resorting to physical violence. I would stand outside in the bright sunshine, feeling cold, hating them both for being so angry and scaring me.

She had to ring the great cathedral bell, proclaiming her victory and herself Empress of all the Russias. To simulate the ringing of the huge bell, the thick pullrope had been rigged on counterlevered pulleys and weighted with sandbags. A massive mahogany crucifix, rimmed in steel, was attached to the end of the rope to keep it hanging taut. As she pulled on the rope, stretching her entire body up high, then bringing it down, all the way to her knees, the crucifix slammed against the inside of her thighs, and down her calves. Over and over she repeated this action, until she had executed the required eight strokes. She must have been pulling twenty pounds of dead weight with each motion. This, in fully resplendent uniform complete with cavalry shako and dangling regimental sword.

"Cut! . . . Miss Dietrich, what do you think you are doing? Ringing for the butler at an elegant dinner party in Vienna? . . . These are the bells of the Kremlin! Let us *try* for some *reality* in *that*, at least!"

On the twelfth take, "Miss Dietrich – could you manage some expression of exaltation on that pretty face of yours? You are *not an Austrian milkmaid calling in her cows*! You are seizing a throne!"

On the twelfth take, she was biting her lips so hard, Dot had to rush onto the set and redo her mouth.

On the twenty-fifth take, she, who never perspired, had beads of sweat on her face that had to be blotted and repowdered.

On the thirtieth take, her hands trembled on the rope. The crew watched, shocked. No break – no rest – and still no sound of protest out of her!

On the fortieth take, her legs began to buckle.

On the fiftieth take, her face of joyous victory had become a silent, agonized scream – and *that* was the shot that von Sternberg chose!

"Cut! Print that! Thank you, ladies and gentlemen," and he walked off the set.

So ended *The Scarlet Empress*. When we pulled the skin-tight white pants off my mother's legs, the blood had just begun to soak through the cloth. The sharp metal edges of the crucifix had shredded the inside of her thighs. Nellie was crying:

"Oh, Miss D.! You have to have the Studio doctor look at your legs right away!"

"No!" my mother barked out a command. "No one must know about this. Do you hear me? No one! Get me washcloths, the big bowl, and the alcohol. Kater! Lock the door. Don't let anyone in!"

She took the big brown glass bottle, put her foot in the wide bowl, and just poured the surgical-strength alcohol onto her lacerated legs. I felt the searing pain, all the way over by the dressing-room door. She didn't even flinch! We bandaged her legs, using her linen hand-towels, securing them with the extra-large safety pins from Wardrobe. We drove home in complete silence. That evening, she cooked her special Hungarian goulash with broad egg noodles, just the way von Sternberg liked it. When he had not appeared by seven-thirty, she called him:

"Jo – sweetheart! Where *are* you? I have your dinner ready! . . . Don't be ridiculous. Why wouldn't I want to see you? . . . You don't have to hurry if you still have work to do. I made your special goulash – it can wait!"

We sat at opposite ends of the long Spanish dining table. I glaring at him, he subdued and strangely hesitant. My mother served us – limping. No one spoke, my mother hovered.

"Jo, sweetheart, is it good? Do you want more sauce?"

As usual, she did not sit down. I asked to be excused and left the room. I didn't care how mad anybody got at me – I hated that mean little man. My mother did not call me back.

The next morning, von Sternberg's car was still parked in our driveway. We all had breakfast together on our sunny veranda, and I was made to apologize to him for my inexcusable behavior in leaving the dinner table. My mother limped a little less, but moaned softly when she tried to cross her legs. Von Sternberg kept looking at her, with cocker-spaniel eyes.

"Jo, sweetheart. It is not bad . . . really," she kept reassuring him. "You were right – I did not know how to give you that moment, the look you wanted. But now you have it, so you have something to cut to. Now you can fix it! I should not have given you so much trouble!"

I asked to be excused to do my German homework.

I was too young to know what my mother was really doing within the security of those locked dressing-room sessions. Even if I had, I would not have understood it, nor the ramifications – the emotional consequences – of her behavior. Still, I wish now that I had not been so fast to judge that pitiable man. Von Sternberg's Packard moved in, next to our Cadillac. My mother did her special brand of penance, the expedient way, using the emotional need of others to purify a tricky situation and punishing the perpetrator – all in one coup!

WE WERE BUSY in the dressing room doing the end-of-film gifts. I was labeling, Nellie was checking the lists. My mother had gone over to Wardrobe to see what she could salvage. After each picture, fur, jewels, beading, anything ornamental that could possibly be removed and reused was meticulously stripped from costumes and carefully stored for future productions. I sometimes think my mother's mania for saving every scrap of fur, no matter how ratty, stems from this frugal Hollywood custom. Travis always let her dig through the fur edgings, letting her keep whatever she found she wanted. My mother had not asked to buy her marvelous sable cape from the Studio, a usual procedure by stars that saved them a lot of money and pleased the Studio accountants. True to form, Dietrich expected Paramount to present her with her Russian sables as a gift. But such an extravagant gesture was not their style. She never forgave "the front office" for their "lack of manners."

That day, when she was scrounging through The Scarlet Empress scraps, if she had known about not being given her cape, I am sure she would have managed to steal it. But she was still innocent of her loss, and returned from her Wardrobe foray with only the trim from her Boudoir dress and the tall mink hat, hidden under her polo coat. I thought I would try, while she was in a good mood:

"Mutti, I finished the sound-crew gold lighters and the alligator wallets. The Cartier watches arrived and the engravings are all correct. Don't you think it would be nice to give something to the waitress, too? You know, the one who always takes care of us when we need something sent over from the Commissary?"

My mother agreed, took up the lists, and wrote at the bottom of one of the sheets.

"Waitress – Commissary. Autographed picture," and left to visit von Sternberg in the cutting shed. I thought at least I had managed a crisp new five-dollar bill for my friend! I appropriated one of the many wristwatches that had been allocated for "secretaries, script girl, assistants, Wardrobe, Make-Up and Hair," and, taking a signed picture from the ever-ready stack by the door, slipped away to give Maggie her end-of-picture gift. She couldn't believe it! Marlene Dietrich had remembered her? She kept going around, showing the other waitresses – exclaiming: "Look – what I just got from Miss Dietrich! Can you believe it! Isn't she something? Gee – a picture with a *real* autograph! That's the best present of all!"

The wrap party was held on the banquet set. The fake boars' heads were replaced by the usual giant platters of egg salad sandwiches, sliced hams, and, naturally, huge bowls of "Russian" salad. That concoction of old water-logged vegetables, glued together with mayonnaise, appeared at every shindig the way chicken à la king does at fund-raising luncheons. Although everyone was happy the film was over, no one was having a good time. After the bar table had been visited a few times, the atmosphere became more cheerful. I helped carry in the big grocery-store boxes, filled with my mother's extravagant gifts. She handed out each one individually, being shyly thanked or kissed as the position of the recipient warranted. No one spoke to von Sternberg. He stood alone, watching her. When she approached him, carrying his special gift, he tried to withdraw further into the shadows, but Dietrich pulled him into the crowd, announced so that all could hear:

"For my master! The only man who knows how to make me beautiful, how to light me, the *genius* who guides me, makes me do what he wants because he alone knows what is right! I SALUTE YOU!" She bent and kissed his hand in homage.

Everyone applauded her gallant gesture. We left soon after that. Jo did not come with us.

Almost immediately, we went into the portrait sittings. To duplicate the "Review" face, my mother called von Sternberg over to the portrait gallery to recreate his lighting, which he did, with just a small alteration. He improved it. No one attempted the "birth" look. Not even its creator. The star of this session was the face with the tall fur hat. Everything else paled in comparison, except some "Dietrich in private" poses taken at this time. In one, she wore one of her white Knize suits, her favorite white felt slouch, and, to soften the masculine effect, added von Sternberg's navy and white polka-dot silk scarf, Chevalier's emerald, and her new wedding ring from Jaray. I hoped Jo, on seeing the proofs, would think she was wearing his.

My mother had a lovely collection of wedding rings. They were kept in a Hermès sewing case amongst the threads and odd trinkets sent to her by fans. Over the years, the needles and spools disappeared, and the ring count increased. I used to love to take them out and line them up in assorted stacks. Gold bands in all widths, from the very understated thin circle to the exaggerated thick and wide ones from those few who really believed they could claim possession. The diamond array was my favorite. They, too, came in thin, medium, and wide. Some had dates engraved, others a private phrase or, simply, a nickname. It seems that every man and woman presented Dietrich with a wedding ring somewhere along in their relationship. They all dreamed of possessing the unpossessable. Sometimes she wore it, when they were around, but mostly she would enter her bedroom, take off their symbol of undying devotion, and add it to the growing trophies in the sewing case. I would keep the count and inventory up to date. I never found her real wedding ring. That one she must have mislaid long before we started shopping at Hermès.

Although von Sternberg had been editing during the making of the film, he now began cutting in earnest. As he had done with every one of his pictures, he put on those special white cotton gloves that protected his hands from being cut by the sharp edges of the celluloid and its surface from human fingerprints, locked himself and the "official" cutter into the editing room with their Moviola, and neither was seen again for weeks. My mother started her special nighttime soup-kitchen deliveries.

A studio at night is an eerie place. Everything is suddenly so very dark, so quiet, lifeless and suspended. The night watchman knew our car and waved us in, busy fiddling with the knobs of his big wooden radio, looking for a clear station to keep him company. We would drive slowly through the back lot, headlights picking out a kaleidoscope of impressions – unrelated, yet familiar – a New York lamppost, a Little Italy tenement front with its well-worn stoop, cobblestones of old San Francisco made our car jiggle, New Orleans's filigree wrought-iron balconies, a pyramid appears and disappears as quickly. Silence! Everywhere!

We turn the corner and – blazing light! People, cameras, pumping generators! Everything in frantic motion, making noise. Steam rises from the mobile Commissary truck; it is a night shoot and the ten-gallon coffee urns are kept busy. While small worlds stand dead around them, this one of nineteenth-century London is vibrantly alive. We pass, drive on until we arrive at our destination. An old clapboard three-story building, cracks of light shine along the edges of the black roller-blinds that cover the second-floor windows, behind which two genies cut and splice the work of many talents into one worthy example of their craft. We deliver the thermoses of soup, broth, and coffee, the chicken, ham, and salami sandwiches, the dishes, cups, and damask napkins. My mother is shown the results that they are most proud of. She has a profound respect for the art of editing, an uncanny talent for recognizing what will work. I sit quietly and listen. After a few hours, we leave them; the night watchman waves as we drive out the gate. It is three o'clock in the morning and the streets are still deserted. We make good time; Bridges gets us home by four.

We saw the rough cut before our scheduled departure. The projection room was packed. My mother sat next to von Sternberg and kept up a running commentary in her usual "whisper" that everyone could hear.

"That's where you took forty takes – and *that's* the one you picked?"

"There you made me do it over and over – not worth it!"

"Where is the scene we made that beautiful velvet dressing gown for? You *cut* that?"

"See, I was right! I said no shoes would be seen in this picture!"

And, at the final bell-ringing scene, "Jo – you should have made me do it *another* fifty times. You were right – I am terrible. You shouldn't have stopped. I could have gone on until I did it *right* for you."

I hoped I would get to see the finished film someday – with silence.

I had packed the mascots, the dressing room was stripped. The coffins and larger confetti elephants were on their way to some New York pier. The herd of smaller elephants awaited our departure. I said good-byes to the maids and our overly sensitive gardener – dog and rabbits had already been gotten rid of – and followed my mother and von Sternberg out of the door. The Colleen Moore house had been rented for another year – it would be there when we returned. I liked the novelty of knowing where we would live the next time! On the train, I took two fifty-cent pieces out of the tip saucer, tied them in my handkerchief, and so entered the Waldorf-Astoria with *real money* in my pocket. It felt *grand*!

Brian was in New York. I did not get to see him, but my mother talked to him on the telephone for a very long time and when she came out of her bedroom, looked soft, and ordered Earl Grey tea with thin cucumber sandwiches from room service. That was good enough for me! Brian was back and accepted again! I was so happy – I nearly didn't mind having to go back to Europe.

My father picked us up at the boat train. Tami and Teddy were waiting in our suite at the Plaza Athénée. We were back in my mother's Paris. I wondered if the young girls were still skipping about, picking those wild strawberries. She placed her calls to von Sternberg, Brian, Chevalier, Jaray, and others. My father saw to the distribution of the luggage, tipping according to his foolproof system that never failed to bring instantaneous fawning results. It went something like this: When entering a hotel, *tip everyone twice* the amount normally expected – this establishes your credit, ensures service by anticipation for future generous donations. Do not tip again until you leave. If you plan to ever return to the establishment, tip again – lavishly. If *not*, ignore everyone, give *nothing*. You had the attentive service out of your original investment. It's their loss in believing there was more to come.

I had been prepared for imminent departure for *schlag*-filled Vienna, but we stayed. *The Scarlet Empress* had whetted my mother's appetite for furs, so we went fur shopping!

Africa, Alaska, and most of Siberia lay at my mother's feet. She stood in the center of a sunburst of pelts: leopard, tiger, cheetah, all the foxes – red, silver, gray, and white – beaver, nutria, seal, ermine, broadtail, chinchilla, zebra, snow leopard, mink, and our famous silver-tipped sable. A conservationist's nightmare, but in those days, no one cared. She pointed to the bundles of skins, indicating what should be made from them: a floor-length mink cape, to go with the stolen Review hat. Red-blond fox got a nod for a three-quarter-length cape. Two silver foxes, complete with dangling legs and shiny black noses – their snouts to be joined – for flinging casually across black-suited shoulders. Smoky foxes to do the same, on gray flannel suits. Baby seal trenchcoat, for wearing with white flannel trousers. A nutria polo coat for those cold, going-to-the-Studio mornings. Ever since my father's criticisms on her departure ensemble that day in Berlin, my mother had decided not to like leopard or tiger. All patterned fur she now considered fussy, detracting the eye from the wearer. Ermine was only for "royalty," for those "who wear silver lace and old tiaras." If their little black-tipped tails were left intact, she would shudder and exclaim: "Now *that's* really for old queens and costume pictures." Chinchilla was her pet hate, only suited "old dowagers – with blue hair and those big, sagging bosoms." Its only redeeming feature was its wonderful weightlessness, which my mother resented in such an "ugly fur."

In 1980, the talented screenwriter and old friend of my mother's Walter Reisch told me, "Your mother called me one day and said that she had just received her new record and wanted to play it for me. At that time, she was renting one of those apartments of Mitchell Leisen, you know, the ones above Sunset Boulevard. She didn't have anyone to drive her, so I said I would come to pick her up around one o'clock. She insisted on waiting for me on the sidewalk – and there she stood, in the hot sun, carrying her gramophone, dressed in a long chinchilla cape – looking as always, *magnificent*! When we got home, she played us her new record – twenty minutes of nothing but applause, cut out of her London album. That was the same day Lubitsch died."

Dietrich wearing an evening fur in the daytime? In the hot sun *and* in the loathed chinchilla? This nice old man went on:

"Do you know, when von Sternberg died, your mother did not come to his funeral? But, when his second wife came home, there was Marlene, waiting for her. She had flown all the way from New York – just to be with her. She said she hadn't gone to the funeral because 'she didn't want to take the attention away from Jo.'"

This was told to me in a tone full of reverence and respect. With all he knew about my mother, he was still a fan. He continued, conjuring up his *important* memories, "There she sat, in front of Jo's wife, looking so sad and so beautiful – all in black, wrapped in a long chinchilla cape." That cape my mother never owned sure got around! I did not correct this sincere old man, he might just have a fixation about chinchilla.

"There she stood, dripping . . . diamonds," would have done just as well, although Dietrich never owned enough diamonds to "drip" in. Just as people have said, "There she stood in the doorway, in her marabou negligee" – an old, terry-cloth bathrobe stolen from some posh hotel, more likely! Or, "Marlene was walking down the street in Las Vegas in that shimmering dress of hers" – only she NEVER walked, and on a Vegas street? Never! And the "shimmering dress" was only for the stage, and once sheathed in it, movement became restricted to a geisha trot! This superimposing of illusion on reality, without conscious thought of plausibility, happened all the time. Her aura, and that of other manmade legends, is so powerful it confuses even those who should know the difference. Fantasy becomes reality and, by sheer repetition, accepted fact. Thanks to Walter Reisch, I have a name for this phenomenon: The Chinchilla Syndrome.

I also got a new fur coat, to replace my outgrown white rabbit. It had a matching beret and was made of softest mouse-gray squirrel. I would rather have had wool and fed my coat nuts instead.

Strange, my mother seemed in no hurry to go to Jaray. She spoke to him in the mornings and late at night, but when I put the "Blue Danube" on the gramophone, I was told to play one of the Bing Crosby records instead. She might be critical of his dressing-room activities, but she adored his singing. Actually, I think Jo would have been pleased to see how very "Russian" we still were. We saw Stravinsky conduct his own *Firebird*. Serge Lifar, Nijinsky's heir, was rapturously exclaimed over as he sprang and pirouetted in the air, all muscles, both front and back, rippling under white tights. In our darkened opera box, my mother turned to my father and whispered:

"Has he got Kotex stuffed in there or is that all him?" I had never gotten around to asking Nellie what Kotex was. I knew American toast was supposed to taste like it, and now it could be used as some sort of stuffing as well? I looked through my precious opera glasses to see what my mother was so interested in.

We also "ate Russian" every day. We should have had Korniloff's cater the banquet scene. We stuffed ourselves, and, except for having to do my "little girls' room" sentry duty, I loved eating there – until the night of The Black Bread Disaster!

I don't remember if Paderewski was in our party that evening or not, but we made our usual awe-inspiring entrance. Dietrich, resplendent in black evening dress, diamonds, and new floor-length cape of mink, tuxedoed handsome husband, uncrushable velvet child, attractive child's governess, also in full evening dress, and assorted famous guests. The press had recently decided to give Tami a set "identity" within the Dietrich household, and I got her. I never dared to ask why me and not where she belonged: my father. The day I heard my mother ask the hotel doorman if he had seen "Miss Tamara, the governess of her child," I decided to leave it alone and not question it. If no one else wanted to claim her, I loved having her. So, there we were, being fussed over. The reigning queen of Paris glides toward her usual table. Her minions follow in splendid procession. All heads lift and stare. By a wave of my father's manicured hand, we are placed correctly and sit. I fold my hands in my lap, lock my spine, and wait for the discussions and ordering to commence. German, French, Polish, Czech, and Russian bounce around the table. My father spoke most languages well enough to discuss and order food in. He was very charming that evening and extremely patient with his charges. Everyone wanted something different, no one followed anyone else's lead. "No . . . no . . . no, fresh caviar?" – *pressed* was the only way to begin this type of meal. My mother immediately led a debate on the virtues of fresh beluga versus pressed beluga. I thought we might get to the main course around midnight! Finally, the sturgeon eggs controversy was settled – and my father had everyone organized. The exhausted headwaiter was dispatched to execute his commands. I was so hungry, I could have eaten Teddy's piroshkies that he was daintily picking at under my chair. At the soup course, it happened! Like all great natural disasters, without warning! My father checked his borscht. It looked perfect, the glop of glistening sour cream like an iceberg floating in a purple-red sea. His eyes searched the table – a small frown appeared. I looked around to see what could be wrong. . . . It couldn't be my lemonade – he had pronounced it freshly squeezed and given his permission to swallow it. . . . My father lifted his tuxedoed arm. The headwaiter shot to his side.

"Where is the black bread?" my father asked in that soft undulating voice that boded no good.

"Oh! Monsieur Sieber! A million pardons! Just this very morning, our baker – the one who was the bread-maker to the czar – his wife, a beautiful young girl from Minsk, died while presenting him with a child! Such a tragedy . . . we all cried! The child will be named Natasha for – "

"You have served borscht *without* black bread?" my father interrupted this interesting novella.

"Oh, Monsieur! Such a tragedy! She was so young – "

"Are you telling me that you do not *have* black bread?"

"*Oui*, Monsieur, *da, da*!"

The poor man was shaking. Slowly, my father removed the large linen napkin from his lap, placed it by the side of his red soup, and rose. The entire table followed suit, and like zombies, we filed out in regal splendor, following our hypnotic leader. Dietrich never let her husband forget *that* memorable dinner party. It prompted her to create the first "clutch" evening bag. The fashion world thought it a smart new Dietrich innovation. We knew she designed it to hold the slices of pumpernickel she carried from then on, whenever we went to a restaurant that served borscht.

"Sweetheart! Don't forget Papi's black bread – we are going to have borscht tonight!" she would shout to me, packing one of her new bags for the evening, and before we ordered, always announced in that voice that carried to every corner of the restaurant: "We can have borscht tonight! I brought Papi's black bread."

No matter how embarrassing that famous evening was, I think my father got paid back for it – in spades! My mother never gave up her game of carrying bread for him to restaurants.

Looking ravishing in her new red-fox cape, my mother finally left for Vienna, accompanied by forty suitcases and my father. I didn't have to go! No *schlag*. No Mozart. No drooling over Hans Jaray. How wonderful! I stayed with Tami and Teddy in my father's apartment. I wasn't allowed into his private rooms, but as usual I snuck in anyway. He had recreated his Berlin monastery. Walking into his bedroom, you expected to be met by a monk! I hadn't noticed last time how somber everything was. The smell of beeswax and incense was overpowering. How could Tami stand to sleep in that sepulchral bed? Like being laid out. Jo should give my father one of the banquet chairs – he would love it, a "corpse" would look perfect at the base of that bed!

The "kids" left behind had a wonderful time. We did everything. We walked in the Luxembourg Gardens, made paper and twig sailboats, and floated them among the classy store-bought ones in the big fountain. We strolled the Champs-Elysées, *un*noticed, *un*adored, *un*followed. Everywhere we went, we were just like real people: nobody! When we stopped to eat, we ordered all by ourselves and exactly what we wanted, and so fast, sometimes the waiter couldn't get it written down. When that happened, we giggled at our private joke. This feeling of being free was bliss. We wished it could last forever.

My father phoned, ordered the flowers to fill the hotel suite and for me to move back amongst them. "Mr. and Mrs. Rudolph Sieber," better known as Marlene Dietrich and her husband, were returning sooner than scheduled.

The atmosphere was ominous. Something must have gone wrong in Vienna. But then, why should Tami look as though she had been crying? Jaray had nothing to do with her. She had been so happy, looked so well, even seemed, finally, to have gained some weight – it didn't make sense. My mother was very angry about something. Spoke for hours on the telephone, shutting the door so I couldn't hear. My father stalked about, looking sullen, and Tami became more drawn each day. Hans Jaray could not accomplish *that* much misery. He wasn't that important in our lives. Perhaps Hitler had done something terrible that no one could tell me about? I just worried about Tami . . . why was she suddenly so fragile, so lost?

One afternoon, I was about to enter my mother's room when I heard, "Jo? I called. Where were you? I have been waiting here for you to call me back! It's Tami. Do you know what *that woman* has done? . . ." she slammed her bedroom door, so I couldn't listen. "That woman?" For Tami? That was like me being called Maria! It meant *big* trouble. What could she, of all people, have done that was that bad?

Amidst strain and silence, we packed, said our individual good-byes, and left.

The SS *Ile de France* sparkled like a bottle of French perfume. She was the pride of the French Line. Still another year before the great *Normandie* would take that title away from her and from every other luxury liner that ever was or would be. But while the future queen still reclined in her shipyard berth, the *Ile de France* played coquette and held court. In the spring of 1934, her beige marble staircase suited Dietrich's entrances, and her opulent first-class dining room was the perfect background for a "famous" encounter.

The first meeting between Ernest Hemingway and Marlene Dietrich took place one evening at the bottom of that grand staircase of the *Ile de France*. The famous story goes something like this: Dietrich, wearing a backless white satin evening gown with a plunging neckline, dripping in diamonds, descends the staircase. Her long satin train, edged with chinchilla, spread out behind her, she approaches her host's dinner table. Seeing that she will be the thirteenth guest, she recoils in superstitious dismay. Unknown young man, in ill-fitting borrowed tuxedo, who has crashed first class from steerage, steps up to beautiful, distraught Star and says:

"Don't worry, Miss Dietrich. I'll be the fourteenth."

As *A Farewell to Arms* had already been published and acclaimed, sold to Hollywood, a film made of it starring Cooper and Helen Hayes, and as Hemingway was on board returning to America from his first safari, it might be assumed that he owned a tuxedo by this time, could afford to travel first class and probably did, that he was an invited guest to the same dinner party that Dietrich had agreed to attend for the sole purpose of meeting this man whose work she knew and admired. For this she wore a black velvet evening dress, closed back, high necked, long sleeved, with just *one* diamond brooch. After all, she was dressed for a private dinner party, not doing an imitation of Josephine Baker at the Folies-Bergère. But isn't that first version better? More suited to these two soon-to-be "living legends"? When you get a fable *and* a chinchilla syndrome to overlap, you really have something. Combined, they will defy all logic and last forever.

That Dietrich and Hemingway were real pals, that is true. That she called him Papa and he referred to her as The Kraut or Daughter, as he often called those adoring ladies of his inner charmed circle, is also true. That they were ever physical lovers, that is not true. That he liked the world to think the opposite and that she wasn't angry at him for doing so – *that's* true. She even helped, by continuously denying, ever so "vehemently," any allegations that they had been or ever were lovers. For my mother, Hemingway was the dashing War Correspondent in the turned-up-collar raincoat; the Hunter, shotgun cocked, standing strong in the path of a charging rhino; the Lonely Philosopher of the bleeding hands clutching his fishing line. Whoever he visualized himself being, she accepted and believed in. She, the infatuated fan to all his fantasies, adored him and was convinced that she was the best friend he ever had. He adored her for being intelligent as well as beautiful, basked in her effusive adulation with shy pride. When, in 1961, this sad and gentle man splattered his beautiful brain against a wall, my mother went into mourning, repeatedly asking me:

"Why would he do such a stupid thing? Must have been that wife of his. She drove him to it! *That* must be the reason. . . . What else was there? Or do you think maybe . . . he had cancer?"

If their destinies had been reversed, *his* ability for friendship would have known and understood all *her* reasons. She should have understood his. His letters to her are full of his private dreads. I have them all. I wish his widow had allowed me to include some of them in this book. They are as the man – quite wonderful! But my mother saw only what was easy to see on the surface of people.

I NEVER KNEW why the New York Harbor customs shed was called a shed. It ran the length of the pier, the size of a football stadium, and except for a vaulted-glass roof, just as open. The icy winds blew off the water, freezing our feet while we stood waiting to be inspected under a large sign bearing the first letter of our legal last name. As usual, the twelve coffins surrounded us – a Stonehenge on the Hudson! Sixty-odd pieces of additional luggage, piled high, we waited under the big red letter *S*, for Sieber. For the world, we belonged under *D*, but for the U.S. Customs, we knew our place. As the alphabet began at the entrance to the shed nearest to the gangplank, from the *G*'s on, people wrapped themselves in lap robes especially left out of the luggage for this purpose, buttoned their fur coats, smoked, and resigned themselves to a known ordeal. The cement floor was so cold, most of the women climbed onto their trunks and got comfortable. Silver flasks were handed around, people met and talked for the first time after having crossed together on the same ship for days. There was a sudden camaraderie – all those people suddenly finding each other, sharing an initial. I wished we too could sit on our trunks and have a party. But ours were too tall to climb up on and my mother did not approve of being gay while awaiting a "serious occurrence." In a way, she was right. Smugglers *should* be serious. This time we not only had the usual fortunes in gowns, dresses, suits, handbags, shoes, hats, and feathers, but all those new furs as well! My mother never accepted the existence of customs inspectors. Her entire life, they were the "enemy." She hated them, the system that allowed them authority, the look in their "beady little eyes," their opening line of: "Miss Dietrich, have you anything to declare?" while they had my father's prepared and doctored five-page declaration folder tucked under their arm. Most of all, their ominous request, usually issued in the most dulcet tones – a type of soft death knell: "Would you open them, please? All of them!" I never knew what was worse, doing customs or knowing that when they were through with you, the reporters, lying in wait outside the shed, got you! No matter what happened, we usually managed to leave long before even the *K*'s were done. Paramount sent conscientious young men to help with "the Dietrich arrival." They were usually on a rotation system, probably to cut down on nervous collapses. Also, in those days, all the great hotels sent their representatives to assist important incoming guests. The Waldorf-Astoria man was a veteran organizer. He awaited us with his own staff of trained helpers and a moving van, his hotel uniform pockets stuffed with five- and ten-dollar bills. The tip charge on my mother's hotel bill could run to three hundred dollars just to get us off the pier – and that was during the Depression!

I liked the Waldorf Towers, that inner sanctum of the Waldorf-Astoria Hotel, with its private elevators and played-down side entrance. We were staying a while. I did my flower cards, made friends with the chambermaids and the waiters assigned to our apartment in the sky, and snuck out, with my bodyguard in hot pursuit, to take a fast look at the new Empire State Building. I stood on the sidewalk, rocked back on my heels trying to see all the way to the top, and got dizzy. Most mornings, I unpacked the latest daily deliveries from the bookstore, removed the stack of Goethe from my mother's night table, replacing them with Hemingway, Faulkner, Fitzgerald, and Sinclair Lewis. I was relieved my mother was finally being extricated from her German "gods." It took that nice friendly American Hemingway to do it! She was having a great time. I rarely saw her except when she came back to the hotel to change her outfit between literary luncheons, small dinner parties dedicated to "intelligent" conversations, the theater and serious nightclubbing. It was so rare for Dietrich to be part of a group. Now, as later during her "Gabin–French patriots" period, she was involved with many instead of only one. Even our language changed. We spoke English, and probably because of all this American influence, my mother had a gaiety completely foreign to her. It was great! Sometimes she took me along to lunch. I would sit quietly, eating my smoked salmon, watch and listen. Now that Prohibition was over, everyone seemed to be making up for lost time, drinking innumerable cocktails from tall, lily-shaped glasses instead of old, thick coffee cups. Dorothy Parker was being cleverly brittle. A tense lady with a funny name slurred sharp retorts back at her husband, Scott Fitzgerald. I liked him, there was something special about him, a little-boy sweetness, except when he chastised his wife for her heavy daytime drinking while consuming a bottle of scotch all by himself. Most of them were on their way to or had already worked in Hollywood. How they enjoyed dissecting it! Their verbal brilliance, so lethal, so precise, while luxuriating in the money it paid them.

New York was so alive. After Europe, you felt the full impact of its American energy shaking you awake until your back teeth rattled. Toscanini was at Carnegie Hall, Martha Graham was being "gray cloth in fluid motion" on naked feet, George M. Cohan tried O'Neill's *Ah, Wilderness!*; Melvyn Douglas, drawing room comedy in *No More Ladies*; Helen Hayes, a youthful Mary of Scotland; Fanny Brice *was* the Ziegfeld Follies; Jerome Kern gave Broadway *Roberta*; Rockefeller Center was nearing completion. You would never have guessed that soup kitchens existed, that desperate men sold apples on street corners for a nickel apiece! When my bodyguard and I took my walks, I used my whole stolen dollar buying apples and felt guilty I didn't have more. He lent me money, noting it on his expense account as "fruit – for The Child."

I made friends with one of the Waldorf doormen. I would go down in the evenings to the main entrance to watch the limousines arrive, disgorge their human finery, then pull away from the curb to make room for the next imposing chariot. My new friend, resplendent in his long frock coat adorned with many brass buttons and plaited chevrons, could whip open a door with such flourish you had to marvel at his skill. From him, I finally found out what a flophouse was, in between his helping people out of their Rolls-Royces.

I was having a real problem understanding all these paradoxes. I asked my mother one day what the Great Depression really was.

"The American Depression? Oh! That happened when I first came to do *Morocco*! All the millionaires on Wall Street jumped out of skyscrapers, just because they lost some of their precious money. All they had to do was stop being so dramatic and get a job! Tonight, I need the beige satin handbag that goes with these shoes – and I am wearing the mink cape."

I was not present when my mother bought her emeralds, but this time, when we boarded the 20th Century Limited en route to Chicago, their custom-made jewel case joined our "special hand baggage" count. They were "mysterious" jewels. Their acquired origin unknown, their final end had so many versions, all enacted with such dramatic conviction by my mother, that the actual truth has gotten lost amidst too much invention. But while they were part of our life, they reigned sublime. They became like my younger sisters – I had charge of them. Their safety and well-being were my responsibility. They lived in a brown leather case, the size of my mother's gramophone and about as heavy. Each piece was perfection. No emerald smaller than a large marble, the smallest diamond no less than four carats. Three bracelets in various widths, two large clips, one large pin, and one unbelievable ring. The main diamond bracelet was as wide as a man's shirt cuff and housed the largest emerald. A perfect cabochon, the size of a Grade A egg, set horizontally, it spanned the entire width of my mother's wrist. Because of its size, this was the only emerald permanently anchored into its diamond setting. All the others were interchangeable! This unique feat of engineering made my mother's collection justly famous. It was my job to assemble whatever combination my mother had decided to wear.

"Sweetheart – today I need one clip, the ring, and one medium bracelet," and with one deft twist, I would click the giant marble-shaped emerald into the ring setting, repeating the maneuver with the other emeralds until the required pieces were assembled, ready to be worn by their mistress. Miniature green lakes embedded in white fire! I was very proud of my "siblings". All the way across America, I clutched the jewel case close to my body, never letting it out of my sight; I didn't even sit on my little balcony, I was too scared the last car might swerve sideways suddenly and whip the case from my grasp! If I could have, I would have locked myself in the drawing room and never come out until we pulled into Pasadena.

AS USUAL, everyone was ready and waiting to greet us. In the car, my mother showed von Sternberg her magnificent present to herself:

"Jo! Aren't these wonderful? The big bracelet is too 'Mae West,' but it will be good for photographs – very – 'important-looking,' what Dietrich would wear! Sweetheart, show Mr. von Sternberg how they work."

Our car rode so smoothly, I showed off my clicking skill without a jiggle.

Jo seemed subdued. I wondered if he thought his lovely sapphires from now on would take second place. . . . Like Teddy, I poked my face out of the car window and breathed the orange-blossom air. I was home! I had a restolen dollar tied up in my handkerchief. I even knew where we were going to live – so why did I feel sort of sad? I didn't know.

We unpacked, disinfected toilet seats, de Acosta and "the boys" phoned, flowers awaited from Brian, Maurice, Cooper, Jaray, Lubitsch, and Mamoulian. Telegrams from Hemingway, Dorothy Parker, Scott Fitzgerald, Cocteau, Paderewski, Lifar, and Colette. Paramount delivered my new dog, and Jo stayed for lunch. Everything was back to "normal."

We had been home about a week when my father called. Shopping talk, orders for him to buy and send the numerous items that my mother always seemed to desperately need from Europe, no matter if we had just been there or not. Then she handed me the receiver, with the usual "Say hello to Papi."

"Papi. How is Tami?"

I had no time to be diplomatic, to work my way around to asking about her. After the way she was when we left, I wanted to know.

"Kater. You are being rude. One does not speak that abruptly. One says hello first. You have been in America only a week and already you are forgetting your manners."

For the first time in my life, I defied him.

"May I please speak to Tami?" I said.

"No! Let me speak to Mutti!"

I handed the phone back to my mother and went to my room. I knew I was going to be sent to it – might as well get a head start! My mother appeared in the doorway.

"Your father says you may not go into the pool today. You must stay in your room and read. So I have to now go to the Studio – alone!" She closed the door and left, annoyed at this inconvenience I had caused her.

I was really worried about Tami. I just had to figure out a way to get to talk to her. I would know right away how she was if I could only hear her voice. No use sneaking out of my room and placing a call to Paris, my father always answered the phone himself – then I would be in *real* trouble. Okay, tomorrow I will do it their way and get to talk to Tami for sure!

"Mutti, I am very sorry that I was so rude to Papi on the telephone yesterday. I didn't mean it. Are you going to call him again today? If you do, may I say I am sorry?"

"Hello, Papilein? Kater is so sorry about making you angry. She is right here and wants to apologize to you."

"Papi? Please forgive me for yesterday – I didn't mean it. You are right. It was not nice."

My father was pleased with me. I was careful to take my time, make conversation, answer his questions. The minutes were dragging on . . . soon he would say, "This has cost enough money," and hang up!

It was now or never: "Papi, how is Teddy? Is he eating all his vegetables and behaving himself?"

I was told all about how exemplary his dog was, how well trained, and, therefore, obedient.

"Papi, and how is Tami? Is she less nervous? Not such a problem to you anymore?"

"She is much better, Kater. Yes, it is difficult for me, sometimes – her behavior is so uncontrolled."

"Yes, Papi, I know, but you are always *so* patient! I have watched you – it cannot be easy sometimes."

"Kater, Tami is right here – do you want to say hello?"

"Yes, please, Papilein."

Finally, Tami's sweet, tender voice . . .

"Katerlein . . . I miss you and send you a kiss."

"Oh, Tamilein, me too, me too!"

I heard her tone, I knew she was better. That's all I needed to know. I handed the receiver back to my listening mother and went to swim in my pool.

My mother checked the baby grand, ordered it tuned immediately, and gave Bridges a long list of records to be picked up at the music store. Chopin piano concertos crescendoed through the house, ricocheting off the Spanish tiles in pre–hi-fi resonance. I wondered who it could be. Whoever it was, his background music was certainly more exciting than Jaray's Strauss! I tried to form an image to suit the tones. Tall, muscular, all angular bone with burning passionate eyes, a little wild – "unharnessed" – a Paderewski type? My mother resurrected the fringed, embroidered piano shawls that had been draped over everything when we first took over our "hacienda." She had stuffed them immediately into storage boxes, keeping them only because they were itemized on the inventory lists. The evening our new beau was expected to eat his first Marlene-cooked dinner, we redraped the Spanish shawls over everything, just as they had been before. All the candles were lit. Dark red roses vied for their color with the Goya walls; the piano, tone perfect, had its lid raised to concert height. Toledo sherry reposed waiting on a silver tray. I had a feeling . . . he was Spanish *and* played the piano. He was, and he did, but that was all I got right! José Iturbi was short, squat, chunky, and kind of "cute." He looked like a conscientious accountant, but give him a piano, and his chubby baby hands could fill the air with passion and glory. That he thought my mother was all his dreams come true was immediately obvious. That she thought him a musical genius was apparent in the way she reverently kissed his hands, sat leaning against his little knees in adoration. From then on, I was given a lot of free time to read, swim, pick oranges off our trees, and get acquainted with Lord Hamlet of Elsinore, my new Great Dane, who looked like a fawn-colored pony and ate like a horse.

Von Sternberg was very sarcastic about our piano player, but then, Jo was really miserable about everything. Whenever he came to the house, he had to remove a Spanish shawl off his chair. To get a piece of paper from the desk, he had to wade through Jaray's love notes that favored such Valentine-card phrases as, "Your mouth is so far away and yet close because it is in my heart!" or "When do I feel again your beloved head on my chest?" Of course, if my mother left her private mail open all over the place, Jo would read it – I had! Just because it didn't bother me didn't mean it wouldn't hurt Jo. I started to police the house, hiding love letters whenever I knew von Sternberg was expected. I began to suspect my mother didn't really love him after all. She took everything that he had to give her and then just put up with him as though she was doing *him* a favor.

ON EVERY STREET CORNER across America, newsboys shouted:

EXTRA! EXTRA! READ ALL ABOUT IT!
WOMAN GIVES BIRTH TO FIVE!

and we all went crazy! My mother sat by the radio all day, listening to the news bulletins that kept us informed on the condition of each tiny girl. Then she called von Sternberg at the Studio:

"Jo! Have you heard? A woman had *five* all at once. What do they *do* up there in Canada? . . . And did you see the pictures in the papers? She's ugly and he is a 'mennuble'!" Another of my mother's favorite Yiddish words, it meant small, clumsy, nondescript, colorless, ineffectual, and a born loser. "And now – they are going to have *five ugly* daughters! – But five at once? How is that possible? . . . And the *work*! I could go there and help. They could use me! Find out from the radio station how to get there. If there is a train that goes there – call me back."

I hoped she wasn't going to take me with her to make lists!

Dietrich never got the chance to organize the Dionne quintuplets. We went into preproduction for *Caprice Espagnol* instead. Our new film had an array of titles. It began with the title of the book, *The Woman and the Puppet*. After Rimsky-Korsakov's music was chosen for the score, it became *Caprice Espagnol* – until Lubitsch decided that no one would pay to see a picture with a title they couldn't understand and chose the more provocative *The Devil Is a Woman*. That one stuck. But it didn't help. The public had already decided it did not want to see Dietrich in another costume picture, but we didn't know that then.

We began our visits to Travis at the Studio.

"Marlene! You look marvelous! A cape – in red fox! The color of your hair – simply *perfect*! That suit . . . If only they would let us do a modern film. . . . Those shoes! We would *have* to use those shoes!"

"Travis, we're going to need lace for this picture. Not French frilly, but heavy – the Spanish kind. What do the books say? Is it still going to be in the same period as *Carmen*? Or has somebody changed that too by now?" She stood by the desk, leafing through the big research books.

"You lingered in New York, dear. . . . Was it as exciting as always?"

"Some of the things were very good – some were terrible. I saw Ziegfeld's *Follies*. Those girls of his are very pretty! But much too tall for women – *must* be men. And those things they have to carry, strapped to their heads! I was frightened they were going to fall down all those stairs! Don't you think that whole to-do is a bit exaggerated? For the screen, I can understand, but on a stage? It looks like 'circus' . . . and that ugly woman. Fanny Brice! What is *she* doing with those beautiful Ziegfeld show girls? No one can be that ugly! The Nose! Have you seen *that* nose? How Jewish can you get? No one can allow themselves to go around with a nose like that and then sing! Travis, do you know where that accent of hers comes from? There is no country in the *world* that has an accent like that. What *is* that?"

Travis was laughing:

"I think it comes from a part of New York called the Bronx."

"I don't believe it! And she keeps it?"

Thirty-three years later, I was with my mother when she saw Barbra

Streisand play Fanny Brice in *Funny Girl*. In the dark movie house, Dietrich's voice rose, clear and distinct above the film's sound track.

"Well, she has the *nose* for it!"

IT WAS ONLY TWO A.M. My mother had returned early from the party she had gone to, at William Randolph Hearst's home. I was waiting for her in the hall.

"That drive is ridiculous! It takes longer than going to the Studio from Santa Monica!"

We started up the stairs.

"Who does that man think he is? Louis XV? You should see that place! It is like a museum – a bad one!"

We entered her bedroom.

"Nouveau riche is not even good enough! That Marion Davies doesn't know any better, but you would think *he* could pay somebody to teach him – to tell him he can't have a Pompeii floor, red marble columns, and shepherdesses standing about, holding stags, all in one room, and expect people to *eat* there! The solid gold cutlery – that *must* be Davies – and the plates! She must have bought those from a desperate Hungarian prince, or Asprey's told her that the Queen of England didn't want them anymore. Who would?"

I started to unhook her gold evening dress.

"I counted the row of forks and thought, they must be joking! Ten courses? There wasn't anyone there intelligent enough to make conversation to last through the soup!" She stepped out of the dress. "That dress has to go to the Studio. The left sleeve rides up. Travis has to fix that. . . . Don't forget the bra has to go with it."

Walking to the bathroom, she unhooked her gossamer stockings from the beige satin garter belt. I held her bathrobe ready, she removed her brassière, slipped her arms into the sleeves, sat on the toilet taking off her stockings while I went to pin the brassière to its gold dress. I had to wait before I could put the evening shoes away in their chamois drawstring bags. They had to cool off first. So I sat on the edge of the bathtub, holding the shoe trees, waiting.

"Sweetheart, when is the manicure girl coming in the morning?"

"At nine o'clock, Mutti, and the girl to dye your lashes comes at ten-thirty."

She examined her face in the mirror.

"They need it. Why the Americans don't allow dyeing of eyelashes is ridiculous! Did you get the French dye out of the 'extra makeup' bag?"

She rubbed her washed face with witch hazel, inspecting the cotton pad for signs of leftover dirt. "Gable was there tonight. Shows you what one successful film can do. . . . And Harlow! That also shows you the level of intelligence there tonight." She poured shampoo into the basin, swooshed it around, and began washing her stockings and panties.

"*You* would have liked it. There was Coca-Cola and apple pie. Apple pie! On those terrible plates! The whole awful mess was just unbelievable. Hearst can afford a good cook after all. But *he* is not so bad, just rich and vulgar. Of course, 'Dietrich' was the one on his right. Later, when I said I had to leave because my child was sick and needed me, you should have seen the fuss! I had a difficult time getting out of there. To get to the front door took me an hour! I kept running into footmen! Only an American millionaire would have footmen in knee breeches running about! I told you he thinks he is Louis XV and Marion Davies thinks she is Madame de Pompadour! But she has pretty thighs; that doesn't show on the screen. That terrible dinner. I didn't eat anything except some fish in pink jelly . . . even that was too much!" She bent over the toilet, stuck her finger down her throat, and threw up. I gave her a wet washcloth. She flushed the toilet, started to rebrush her teeth. "Don't forget, if anyone calls tomorrow from the Hearsts, you are supposed to be sick." She threw back her head to gargle.

I put away the cooled shoes, unpacked her beaded evening bag, then wrapped it in black tissue paper, labeled it, and put it with the others. My mother climbed into bed. I wound the clocks, did the lights, kissed her good night, and was at the door, when she sat up, turned on her lamp, and said:

"Sweetheart, you know what I want? Two slices of rye bread with liverwurst. *Now* I am hungry!"

I hurried downstairs to the kitchen. When I returned, my mother was out of bed, examining her gold gown.

"That pull is here . . . on the inside seam, under the armhole. The sleeve has to be taken out and reset."

I put the lacquered tray down on the bed and went to get her cuticle scissors, the ones my mother liked for opening seams. I knew she wasn't going to wait for Travis and Wardrobe to do it. So, there we were, at three a.m., resetting the sleeve in her thousand-dollar dress, munching liverwurst sandwiches. She sewed while I threaded the thin, thin needles that Mme. Grès had given us in Paris.

When von Sternberg wasn't pouring out his heart in letters to my mother, he was writing the film. At least, he was trying to get it written, badgering

John Dos Passos, who lay weak and wan in some Hollywood hotel. Jo
kept saying:

"That poor, sick Dos Passos. The Studio ships him out here. Nineteen
hours on an airplane, and now, all he can do is sweat and faint. In between
attacks, I try to teach him how one writes dialogue for a motion picture.
It will never work this way. I will write it myself and let Lubitsch think
his special 'Spanish' poet did it all!"

On hearing "sick," my mother rushed to the kitchen, Bridges was sent
to Beverly Hills to buy thermos bottles, and "poet at death's door" soup
deliveries began. Sometime later, Mr. Dos Passos must have recovered
sufficiently to return to New York, because we stopped making chicken
soup and resumed filling thermoses with Jo's beef tea instead.

My mother stopped eating. The serious costume discussions, designing, and fittings loomed. The less script there was, the more my mother
concentrated on the costumes. She felt instinctively that this would be
primarily a visual film. Her clairvoyance did not tell her that *The Devil Is a
Woman* would be the zenith of the Dietrich image, von Sternberg's parting
gift to the legend he helped to create – and what a glorious gift it was!

The first test stills, those were terrible, but on purpose.

An outraged Travis greeted us: "Marlene, the Head Office wants test
stills! They are mad! Nothing is even designed! You and I haven't even
talked. And they want to see? What, for heaven's sake? Never, in all the
years . . ." Travis's nose looked like a stop sign.

My mother took charge, a battle glint in her eyes.

"Travis, where is that terrible lamé abortion you always insist on using
for publicity? The one you draped Lombard in, two years ago?"

"Marlene! You can't wear that! It is ghastly!" Travis gasped.

"Yes, I know. Also get me that cheap veiling – the wide one, with all
the swirls. Sweetheart, send Bridges back to the house and tell him to
bring one of the piano shawls – the big one back of the couch."

While Travis looked sick and the Wardrobe girls stared in horror, my
mother draped herself in the sleazy material, leaving many folds and loops
across her chest, made long gloves out of the veiling, telling the girls to cut
and hem them just above her elbows – "messily." She plopped the ugliest
section of the patterned veiling on her head, draped more yards of the stuff
around her shoulders, finishing the whole hideous effect with our piano
shawl. Left hand on hip, naked elbow protruding from sloppy glove,
other arm positioned on raised right hip, displaying drooping fringe,
she posed, cocked her head, tucked in her chin, lowered her lashes, and
giving Travis a real Mae West bedroom look, intoned in a Lupe Velez
Tijuana slur: "*Sí, sí, señor!* Eet took a lot of *caballeros* to change my name
to Concha!"

Travis was rolling on the floor, the girls shrieked, and we all applauded.

"Now, everybody, we go! And give them their stills! The only terrible thing is they are so dumb, they will probably think we are serious with this outfit and like it! But, it will shut them up so we can work without being bothered by their stupidity."

We traipsed over to the Still Department, shouting "*Olé!*" She was right on all counts! The Head Office approved of the costume and let Banton and Dietrich be. They never really understood what those two supreme artists finally conceived for that film. But then, very few did; not even Walter Plunkett's designs for *Gone with the Wind* can top them. Although he reigns supreme in historical-context design, the costumes for *The Devil Is a Woman* are not hampered by any accepted guidelines; except for a rather oblique aura of "old Spain," all is pure imagination, poured onto living perfection. With Sternberg's sublime camera work, Dietrich never looked as beautiful before or since. It was her favorite recorded image of Dietrich, the only film she wanted to own a print of, and did. My mother was always able to recognize unique perfection of inanimate objects. Dietrich, forever the instinctive connoisseur, able to sense sublimity.

Lace – I didn't know so much different lace existed. It was everywhere. Real, antique, and just wonderful, and *heavy* – nothing fluttered. If lace could be considered "dramatic," the room oozed drama. Like a merchant in an Arabian bazaar, my mother moved about inspecting the wares, gossiping with Travis as they liked to do:

"I had to go to that dinner at the Hearsts. Absolutely awful! The Child will tell you. She laughed so when I told her all about it. Only one interesting man – one of Garbo's lovers. I don't understand how she gets them. He was drunk, the whole evening, but if you have to go to bed with Garbo, you *have* to drink. We have to use this . . ." She flicked over a bolt, unrolling some gorgeous handmade white lace. "This is very good. Do a dress for it and maybe make a large type of hat. If Jo puts light behind it, it will show the pattern."

"Wonderful, absolutely wonderful!" Sitting on the corner of his desk, balancing his big pad on his lap, Travis sketched – elegant sweeping lines, that would one day become a masterpiece in white silk crepe and antique lace.

"Did you see Clifton Webb in that play of his in New York?"

"Marlene – when do I ever get a chance to leave here!? I haven't had a vacation in years! . . . I like Clifton. You know, he never goes anywhere without his mother, Maybelle. That's why he has never married."

"Oh? I thought he wouldn't do that anyway."

Travis laughed. "Dear Clifton – does liven up a party. Wonderful sense of humor. We must have combs . . . all sorts of Spanish combs. Some very tall, others smaller – with rounded edges. We'll have some made in tortoise shell and some in ivory." Travis continued working on his sketch.

"Travis, don't go crazy with the mantillas. Don't give me too many of those curtains hanging down my back. Everybody does that when they want to look 'Spaneesh'! Talking of curtains, did you see what Orry-Kelly did to Dolores Del Rio in that costume picture at Warner Brothers? She looks like a window of a French château. He is going to have real trouble dressing that one with the pop eyes and the frizzy hair – what's her name? Jo says she is a wonderful actress. She just did that film from the Maugham book."

"You mean Bette Davis?"

"Yes, that's the one. But why must they be so *ugly*? You don't have to be ugly to act! . . . Stockings – we have to do something about stockings. A woman like that wouldn't wear stockings. And bare legs are no good with heels. Why don't we run embroidered lace up the front . . . right on the stockings, then, when we show the legs, they will look like part of the costume. Hasn't been done. Call Willys – have him come over!"

"Wonderful idea, Marlene! Wonderful! Willys won't sleep for a week! He will love it!" Travis picked up the phone and called Willys – The Hosiery Specialist to the Stars.

MY FATHER AND TAMI were coming to America! There was even a rumor that they would stay for a while – that von Sternberg had put Dietrich's husband on *The Devil Is a Woman* payroll. How Tami would love the hummingbirds in the rose garden.

"Of course, the Nazis killed him." My mother sounded very anxious. She was on the phone to my father discussing the assassination of the chancellor of Austria. "I want you to come now, right away. Don't wait. Bring Mutti and Liesel. Leave the dog – really, Papi! You must have some friends in Paris that will take your precious dog! If Mutti makes any problems, tell her I will get her a house. She doesn't have to live with a movie star."

Was that the reason that her mother didn't want to live with us? I had never thought of that. My mother continued:

"If that son of Liesel is in the Hitler Jugend – that's the father. Tell her I told her long ago he is no good! She can't sit there trembling in her shoes . . . praying he will change. He is a Nazi! Always was – even before there *were* Nazis, and when you come, you can help me with Jo and this picture. It's getting more stupid every day. Jo writes, that famous author of Lubitsch's writes – probably half the writers' building is secretly typing out dialogues – that Jo will throw away anyway and then do another close-up instead."

When my father finally arrived, only Tami accompanied him. That was fine with me, but my mother was furious with him for not being able to convince her mother to leave Germany. Tami settled into her room, down the hall from my father's, and I showed her the tiny hummingbird nests hidden among the rose thorns. I hugged her hard and asked, "Are they still angry at you?"

She shook her head, cried a little, held me, and said she was fine.

When my father was "in residence," my life always changed. The absence of any formal schooling infuriated him. So teachers of many sizes and shapes filtered through our Spanish living room where my father had the perfect decor for his inquisitor tactics when interviewing potential employees. Always economical, he finally engaged a bilingual tutor. In the mornings, she was to follow a German curriculum. In the afternoons, an English one. How was I ever going to keep up with the costume designing, the hair meetings, the fittings, do the flower cards, unpack the dressing room? My father really had a way of putting a damper on everything that was important! All the personal maid chores were shifted onto Tami, so I got more sleep, but we had a film to make! How could he be so naive and book me up with such unimportant things. For two weeks, I struggled against my new schedule. Then help came from an unexpected direction.

One morning, my father entered my schoolroom, interrupting Goethe. I swung around in my chair with joyous relief.

"I beg your pardon, Fräulein Steiner, but Maria must go to speak on the telephone – it is urgent!" my father intoned through set teeth. I ran into my mother's bedroom and picked up the receiver.

"Hello?"

"Maria?"

It was Nellie, and she sounded harried.

"Nellie, what's the matter?"

"Listen, hon – Bridges is coming to get you. Your mother wants all the carnations she got that time in Paris. She says you know where they are and that you are to bring 'em."

"Okay, but what am I supposed to do about my lesson?"

"I don't know. All your mother said was, 'Get Maria to bring the carnations . . . she knows.'"

My father was furious, my teacher utterly confused, but I couldn't help that. Quickly I assembled the carnation boxes and was ready, waiting, when Bridges drove into our driveway.

"Finally!" My mother strode toward me as I entered the dressing room, and grabbed the boxes out of my arms. She sat at her dressing table, "Now look! If we put the comb in back, over on the right side, and then place the flowers across, in a curve, on an angle to arrive just on the forehead – good?" She held them to her head, looking at me in the mirror. "Sweetheart?"

"Mutti, that line may photograph too dark against your hair. Why not do a red one – then pink – then a lighter red?"

"You see!" my mother turned to the assembled hairstylists, designers, wigmakers, Travis, and Nellie.

"The Child walks in – and right away knows! Sweetheart, now we have this hole – how about some bangs? Nellie, get me some bangs – very thin – wisps, like baby hair."

We worked all day on that famous carnation hairdo of *The Devil Is a Woman*, while my teacher sat and my father fumed.

For two weeks I was hauled out of my lessons and delivered to Paramount, until every one of the hair designs was completed. The only indication I got that my mother was having some difficulties with my father was when she said to me, "Sweetheart, if you finish all your work at *night*, then no one can say you can't come to the Studio."

From then on, every morning at eight sharp, my copybooks lay open and ready for inspection. Grammar, arithmetic, and assigned compositions done – not well, but done, and I was off! My new teacher became friends with my bodyguards, swam in the pool, and stopped feeling guilty. My father decided my dog needed training and concentrated on fashioning Lord Hamlet into an example of canine obedience; Tami was housekeeper and superb cook – Dietrich's retinue functioned satisfactorily.

I GOT INTO TROUBLE. We were designing the hair for the white fringe dress; an enormous Spanish comb had been especially made to perch at the back of my mother's head. For this, she had pulled her hair back – finishing the line with a large figure-eight knot hairpiece at the nape of her neck. But the effect was too elegant – too clean – so she placed an exaggerated inverted question mark curl in the center of her forehead. It looked outrageous – wicked – and utterly fantastic. So wonderful, in

LEFT: The "pom-pom" look in *The Devil Is a Woman*, the face that von Sternberg shot his gun at.

BELOW: At the time of their final parting they pretended to them-selves, as well as to the press, that they were still together.

The carnation hairdo from *The Devil Is a Woman* that Dietrich designed.
The inverted-question-mark curl was added later in the film, although the
much-worried-over eyebrows are already in place.

fact, that she kept it for most of the film. The first time I saw it, I loved it, so without thinking, I launched into:

> There was a little girl
> Who had a little curl
> Right in the middle
> Of her forehead.
> When she was good,
> She was very very good –
> When she was bad,
> She was horrid.

The moment those last words left my mouth, I realized what I had done – but it was too late! There was nothing I could do to cover them up. Bridges was not sent to pick me up for a whole week, and so I missed the creation of the famous white lace picture hat.

When we didn't work on Sundays, we did "outings." Jo, my father, Tami, my mother, and I would pile into our car and be driven to the Riviera Country Club to watch polo matches. Everyone was allowed to dress in correct "Sunday spectator attire" – except me. I was always told to wear my organdies, newly ordered and delivered from Bullock's, complete with matching wide-brimmed hats. One in particular I hated, white stiff organza, appliquéd with bright red strawberries everywhere, scalloped hem, and itsy-bitsy puffed sleeves. The reason for these ridiculous outfits must have been to make me appear younger. I have photographs of us in our box – I look like an angry strawberry sundae.

FBI agents killed America's Public Enemy No. 1, and *The Scarlet Empress* opened to disastrous reviews. Neither of these events caused much of a stir in our lives. My mother had no respect for movie critics, considered their views beneath contempt, and as 1934 was long before her "I love gangsters" period, she had not met Dillinger. Besides, we were in a deep makeup crisis.

"Something is wrong. The face is wrong – no mystery – no exotic bird. This face does not go with the clothes," my mother had been muttering for days. Like a chant – you could hear her on the toilet in the mornings, while standing at the stove, and on the long drives to the Studio. It became like an incantation! Dot and Westmore tried everything. The entire Make-Up Department became involved in the quest to find Dietrich the face she sought. The dressing-room floor was covered with stills and portraits. Every face, every look Dietrich had ever achieved was scrutinized, analyzed, and then rejected. Nothing fit the stylized exaggeration of the costumes she had helped create. When

Jo asked, "Can I help?" he was told that this was not his worry but her responsibility. He had more important problems to solve and should go and solve them. As every fitting became more wonderful, more superb, her dissatisfaction with her face increased. Everyone thought she looked ravishing. I knew that didn't mean a thing. Dietrich had to look ravishing to Dietrich – no one else counted. One day, she was chopping onions, sniffing up the tears that trickled out of her nose.

"The eyebrows!" she shouted, waving her eight-inch cleaver in the air. I dropped a bowl of peas I was shelling and we raced upstairs to her bathroom. While she plucked out all her eyebrows, I watched – holding my breath in anticipation, not apprehension. Like her, I knew she was right, had found the solution! We both couldn't wait to see the whole effect. The cooking was forgotten, Bridges was summoned, and we left for the Studio. There my mother put on a full-screen makeup – everything as it had been planned. Nellie came to do the carnation hairdo, Dot, Travis – everyone watched and waited. When everything was done, my mother sharpened one of her black wax eyebrow pencils with her paring knife, and with a steady hand, drew two soaring arches above her lids and – every exotic bird that ever was swooped into that room and grinned. She had the look! The magic that had eluded her!

There are people who know something is missing even in apparent perfection, and then there are those who realize it only after they are shown what it was. My mother was one of the former – most performers belong to the latter. It may be one of the subtle differences between Legend and Star.

ON ONE OF OUR SUNDAYS, we all went to visit Jo's new house. He had built it in a remote region of heat, dust, and orange groves known as the San Fernando Valley. A deserted place, lonely and dry, where, forty years later, my father would live on a half-acre corner lot and think himself lucky to have found so much land in such a crowded area that was still as dry and dusty as when I first saw it in 1934. It took us hours to get there. My mother kept complaining about the rough country roads.

"Another one of your madnesses. *Why* do you have to live way out in an oven? Only *you* would consider Beverly Hills not good enough. . . . Even Malibu is not as bad as this! How can you live way out here and get to the studio in the mornings? . . . And if this *is* only for Sundays, why build a house? Rent a shack if you have to play the hermit."

Jo was driving his car, my mother grumbling in the backseat. I tried not to be carsick, Tami worried I would be. Up front, my father fiddled with Jo's car radio, hoping to distract my mother with something musically soothing. We were too far out in the country, all he got was crackle. And I got carsick. Suddenly, a clump of trees, dense and wonderfully green – Jo swung the car around them, and there it loomed! A Jules Verne illusion. A fortress of shining steel, a futuristic castle. No turrets, no windows, but a real moat, its still, clear water reflecting the sheen of steel, aglow with sunlight! I caught my breath – all woozy stomach forgotten. I blurted:

"Oh! Jo! It's wonderful! The light – you have captured the sun!"

He smiled, one of those rare gentle ones that reached his eyes.

"Behave yourself! First *Mr.* von Sternberg has to stop the car because you can't control yourself. Now suddenly, you're all happy," and my mother stepped out of the car.

I followed, keeping my enthusiasm in check. But it was hard to do. What a house! All the Knights of the Round Table could have held their meetings in the main hall. The stairs, leading to the open second level, were perfect "medieval castle," and Jo's bedroom – a private planetarium. One huge dome of circular glass, purple mountains and sky like rear-projection, until the clouds moved across it and you realized it was real. At night, it must have felt like sleeping with the stars! I had to clench my teeth to keep from babbling. My mother had gone to inspect the bathroom.

"Jo, what is this?"

He followed her.

"Where are the curtains? Haven't they been delivered yet? – Like in the bedroom?"

"No, Beloved – there will be no curtains. There are no other houses for miles. No one around to see or be seen. I don't need to shut out the sky."

"You are going to sit on a toilet in a glass bathroom?"

"Yes, I am even going to shit with the sky watching me!"

"Don't use words like that – The Child is here! I don't understand you. If you have to live in a *set*, why here? . . . And you can't be serious and expect me to douche in a glass bathroom! What have you done to the kitchen? Is that also an aquarium? You better have gas – if the stove is 'mohderrn,' as Fanny Brice says, you will not get your favorite goulash!" and we all followed her back down the Lady Macbeth staircase to a marvelous kitchen.

"Again metal! What is this thing you have about steel? Are there at least wooden spoons, or are they, too, too old-fashioned for you? Such affectation! Trying to be ever so avant-garde! No matter what you say,

Jo, sometimes you are very bourgeois. And who will be able to keep all
this metal cleaned? How are you going to get servants to come way out
here? . . . Or are you planning to train the Indians?"

As we passed through the living hall on our way out of the house, I
spied two of *The Scarlet Empress*'s banquet chairs placed on either side of
a lovely chess table. The brooding specters looked so right, leaning over
the backs of those chairs, as though contemplating their timeless move.
But I didn't say a word about them. That's all my mother had to see!
Poor Jo would have been told off about his chairs as well.

We drove back to our beshawled hacienda. My mother smoked, telling
my father to finally find something on that stupid radio or stop fiddling
with the knobs. Tami worried who would be left for dinner. Jo drove
silently, both hands gripping the steering wheel. I concentrated on my
stomach and felt so sorry for his spoiled surprise. Von Sternberg never
did get curtains, and Dietrich never did live there with him, although
the one had nothing to do with the other; I can still see that glorious
burnished shield of a house and feel his pride and disappointment. We
arrived back to find José Iturbi in residence, limbering up with a Bach
fugue. My mother swept into the house to greet him. My father and
I made ourselves scarce, Tami went to serve the sherry, and Jo drove
down the hill and out of the Bel Air gates – too fast.

My friend and lemonade partner was fired. I was sad and wondered if it
had something to do with helping me. Just because he was nice to me
was no reason for him to lose his job. But, one day, he was gone and
a new revolvered gentleman had taken his place, so I never found out
the real reason. Perhaps I had said too often that I liked him? I knew my
mother did not approve of my making friends. She often told me, "You
say right away people are your 'friends' – like an American. You don't
even know them! Or, even if they want to *be* your friends – like a dog,
you wag your tail when anyone just smiles at you. It is not done!"

That must be it! I let my liking for my kind bodyguard show and lost
him his job. That was awful! I must be more careful in the future – and
with Tami too. I had noticed that if we baked a cake together, it suddenly
had "too many raisins," was "too sweet," "too fat," "didn't rise enough,"
whereas the same recipe baked by Tami alone was accepted and consumed
without criticism. "Open friends" were out! Like my train-porter ones,
better keep everyone I liked a secret. I wondered if it could be made to
work on purpose? I decided to test that possibility. Thanks to my father,
poor Lord Hamlet had become a very unlikable dog, a statue of a Great
Dane that breathed. I knew this wasn't the dog's fault, but just the same,

I began to wish he would get exchanged. For the next few days, I told my mother how much I liked him – what a really good friend this dog had become. When she called me to find something for her, I was "busy with the Dane". . . . My new dog was a Highland terrier, with stumpy legs and a cocky attitude. I loved him on sight and never, ever let it show! I felt guilty, though, having used poor Hamlet for my experiment. I asked Bridges if he knew where he had gone. When he told me he thought Lord Hamlet had been sent to Joan Crawford, I was relieved. I knew Miss Crawford approved of anything trained and instantly obedient.

Some evenings, we had "intimate dinners." My mother cooked all day. Tami and I peeled, stirred, and washed up. My father drove to Los Angeles to search for the proper wine in "this wasteland of culture." Everyone oohed and aahed over every dish, then shifted to the living room for coffee, rhapsodizing over the quality of my father's selection of brandies, before settling themselves into the blood-red couches and Spanish mission chairs for the evening's recital. While Iturbi played his Chopin, my father warmed his snifter between pale hands, de Acosta burned with Spanish patriotic ardor, "the boys" looked appropriately appreciative, I was politely quiet, my mother, enraptured, leaned against the vibrating piano, and Tami tried not to worry about the mounds of dirty dishes waiting for us in the kitchen. Jo just sat, looking tired, and left early. Even when our dinners were "German," when my mother made liver dumplings, stuffed cabbage, and beer soup for the "Berlin colony," Jo never stayed long. I always had the feeling he only showed up to prove to the others that he still "belonged," not because he really wanted to be there.

Those foreign groups of Hollywood were interesting. Like a species, they bonded. Forming their pseudo-security within a strange land, based on national characteristics. The British colony, because it shared a common language with the natives, was the largest group and boasted the most Stars. They reinforced their identity by importing English breakfast teas and ignoring ice cubes, walked with tightly rolled black umbrellas on perpetually rainless streets, sported tweeds, trilby hats, old school ties and regimental ones – rarely acquired through actual affiliation with these illustrious establishments (who in America would know the difference?) – spoke the king's English, even if born in Manchester (again, who could tell?), and played lots and lots of serious golf in plus-fours.

The French colony knew where to find drinkable wine, soft cheeses, wore berets, worked on "charming," and watched for Charles Boyer to tell them what to do next.

The German colony was the most structured group. Unlike the British, they did not allow class digression simply because of American innocence.

The aristocrats, or those who could pass themselves off as such, read Goethe, wore pigskin gloves, and came into their own playing Nazis during the forties. The immigrants, comprised of burlesque comics, gag writers, composers of popular music, and agents, adopted American clothes and searched for bagels. The intelligentsia – writers, lyricists, and directors – carried fruitwood sword canes or short crops, depending on their degree of insecurity. As always, Hungarians, Austrians, Czechs, Poles, Bulgarians, Rumanians, and Yugoslavs were lumped under this same Middle European banner – together they kept it flying by their consumption of marinated herrings, sauerkraut, and liverwurst; adored or loathed the Nibelungen; searched longingly for accordion players, real coffee, and lager beer; and shared their German newspapers and English-language teachers. As their English improved and the flood of refugees swelled their ranks, they became the most influentially creative group in the industry. Deservedly so – a Billy Wilder is not to be taken lightly. Most of them recognized and embraced their good fortune and applied for American citizenship, gave up the Fatherland for obvious reasons, but treasured their memories nonetheless.

Our José was replaced by Leo Robin, only at the keyboard though, and only for a very short while. Rehearsing the songs for the picture had begun. Upstairs, recopying my composition entitled "Autumn Is Here!" I listened. What I had found to write about, living in a seasonless place, intrigues me, but never mind, that's not important. I was laboring over my schoolwork when I heard a man's voice raised in song in that intense bellow indigenous to all songwriters when selling their latest gem:

> Three sweethearts have I,
> One is a son of a . . .

long pause – then again,

> One is a son of a . . .
> *baker!*

This continued without shame, until most of the professions had been accounted for, ending in a mighty crescendo. Utter silence ensued, then . . . the front door slammed! Unable to stand the suspense, I abandoned my "falling leaves from palm trees" and ran downstairs. My mother did not disappoint me:

"Did you hear that? That's a song? They must be joking! . . . And the other one is even worse – something about Pain and Love! What has happened? He wasn't so bad with the songs for *Morocco*! But already in *Blonde Venus*, he started being strange, and now, with that other idiot that we had who wrote songs – these two have gotten together! *Blonde Venus* was bad enough, but at least there we *had* to be cheap. But can you see me, all glamorous in those beautiful costumes, trying to sing about a *baker*? . . . We all should decide this film is a comedy and make Lubitsch happy!"

Dietrich sang those songs in *The Devil Is a Woman* and broke up each time. Even when hearing the playback, she couldn't keep a straight face. Why these songs remained, were not changed, rewritten, or cut, is a complete mystery.

"Sweetheart, try to find out what is wrong with Tami. Make up some story about how you want to have her take you to the beach – and you think maybe she is getting a cold and, if she has a cold, you can't go to the beach and that's why you want to know. Papi says it is just 'nerves.' What's she got to be nervous about? Everything is paid for, she doesn't have to work – she is a lady of leisure! So how can she have 'nerves'? I told Papi, 'Kater will find out.' "

My mother left the room to phone Jaray. I was concerned by Tami's behavior. She seemed depressed. Not like Jo, who got sad; she seemed lethargic, like a deep tiredness inside. It would be difficult to reach her with a stupid lie about the beach. I didn't want to question her, so I just told my mother about what I thought was the most important symptom – that Tami seemed very tired, knowing that a dissertation on "some people's lack of stamina" would surely follow. It did. Then she picked up the phone and called one of "the boys":

"Sweetheart? What is the name of that strange doctor you two found in Pasadena? The one who gives injections that are supposed to make everyone feel terrific? Well, call him and tell him you have a friend who is always tired and that she will be at his office tomorrow morning for his 'shot.' You pay him and tell me how much it costs and I will tell Jo's secretary." She hung up and left to inform Tami where she was going the next morning. What kind of a shot? What kind of medicine was there that could make you feel good right away, like that? And how would "the boys" know a decent doctor anyway? The next evening, Tami chatted away about everything and anything. Her eyes sparkled, her hands expressive, she was clever and amusing. Triumphantly, my mother turned to my father:

"You see, Papi. All she needed was a shot! From now on she must go to that doctor at least two or three times a week. I will tell 'the boys' to make the appointments. You can drive her there to make sure she goes!"

Tami was so happy she had made everyone laugh, that my father approved of her scintillating behavior at the dinner table. That night, she couldn't sleep. The whole night she tried, but it was impossible. Probably that nice, too exciting evening was the reason. In the morning, she mentioned her wakefulness to my mother.

"What? You couldn't sleep? First you were tired – then you are all awake and now, suddenly, you can't sleep? All you have to do is take a pill. I will call the drugstore to send them over."

"Oh, thank you, Mutti. I am sorry to be all this trouble. You have to do so much with the film. Rudi told me about going to the doctor, how you have arranged it all for me. Thank you so very much. I really think those injections will help me. You are right. I felt so good yesterday evening – I even made you all laugh. Remember in Berlin, you used to say I could always make you laugh?"

That night, Tami gratefully took her new little pills and slept. The next morning, after two cups of strong black coffee, she was ready just in time for her drive to Pasadena and that lovely injection that made her feel so wide awake and attractive.

"JOEL MCCREA is going to be in the film."

We were unpacking the dressing room, Jo had stopped by with this important casting news.

"He is a good actor, has just had a big success, and is available. He will make an interesting Antonio."

My mother looked up over the rim of a storage carton.

"Is that the one who did the film with Dolores Del Rio?"

"Yes." Jo turned to go. My mother's voice stopped him.

"He is beautiful! And tall! Nellie and Dot will swoon! And Kater will ask for his autograph. And he even has light eyes!"

Von Sternberg shot a test of Joel McCrea. After the fiftieth take, Mr. McCrea walked off the set, the Paramount lot, and the film. I never did get him to sign my autograph book. Cesar Romero, an actor my mother always referred to as "that gigolo dance teacher," replaced him and joined the ranks of Dietrich's forgotten leading men.

My mother was mumbling again. In the evening, in her bathroom, she just stood staring at herself in the mirror. All the hairdos and hairpieces were right – the combs, carnations, shawls, mantillas, hats, costumes, parasols, gloves, stockings, shoes, fans . . . even bird cages had passed inspection and been okayed. The eyebrows looked as though they could take off any moment and fly south for the winter. So what was left to mumble about? The day after she saw the test of the white lace hat, her muttering increased. I didn't know exactly what we were shooting that day, I think it was a test for the silver lamé costume. I had escaped my father's schoolmaster eye and been spirited off to the Studio. I had not visited the Commissary since our return and ran over to say hello to Maggie and gobble a cheeseburger before reporting to the set. The red warning light was off. That meant they were not in the process of filming – so I opened the big padded door and slipped inside. I waited for my eyes to adjust to the inner gloom after the intense brightness of the sun outside, then picked my way across the floor cables, ducked under the standing lamps, and reached my mother's mirror – just as she walked *into* it! I caught her just in time, or she would have walked *through* it! She peered intently into my face and said:

"Oh! It's you! What was that thing I hit just now?"

"Mutti, what's the matter? You walked right into your big mirror!"

"Oh, that's why it looked so shiny! . . . Where's the set?" She turned on her heels and walked toward the light and – crash! – down went a lamp. She went right on walking, calling:

"Jo? Are you there? Can you hear me? What do you want to see next? The 'Carmen' costume? It's ready . . ." and, still talking, walked out of the padded door into the street. Nellie and I raced outside. There she stood, in that incredible silver outfit, sparkling in the sun, looking at us – with huge, myopic eyes.

"How did I get out here? Those drops are crazy!"

"What drops? Mutti – what are you talking about?"

"Miss D, I told you – you shouldn't," Nellie chirped.

"Sweetheart, it's a *secret*! Don't say anything to Jo. I want to have dark eyes! In this picture, only dark eyes will look right. Beautiful! Give a mysterious look. So, I got drops from an eye doctor – they open the eyes, dilate something, make them big, so they will photograph dark! But don't say anything. Open the door, Nellie, and show me where the camera is – I want to surprise Jo when he sees the rushes and suddenly, I have *black eyes*!"

We got her to the edge of the set, gave her a little directional shove, and, blind as a bat, nonchalantly she sauntered into Cesar Romero. That did it! Jo grabbed her by the shoulder:

"This has gone far enough! What have you done to yourself? Tell me the truth."

"Jo, take a look in the camera. I have Spanish eyes! . . . But it's not going to work! I won't be able to see anything throughout the whole picture. I can't hit my marks if I am blind!"

Jo had such a sweet expression on his face, as he listened to her disappointment.

"Beloved, why didn't you tell me you wanted dark eyes? I can give you dark eyes!" He walked over to her key light, shifted it slightly, tore a piece of paper off his large memo pad, taped it along the top edge of the little lamp, and said, "You must always tell me what you want – that I can give you."

The next day, my mother was ecstatic. In the projection room, she screamed when she saw herself in the day's rushes, with dark, Spanish eyes.

"Yes! Yes! You have done it! Genius! You are a genius!"

"It was a wonderful idea, Beloved. As usual, you knew exactly what was missing. Although, with light eyes, she would have been perfect too."

"No. *Now* she looks right!"

JO WAS SHOOTING his BB gun in the garden. Ever since the kidnapping scare, my mother was frightened of guns, wouldn't have them anywhere near her except in my bodyguard's holster. This morning, Jo had stayed on for breakfast and then insisted on doing target practice against my movie-theater wall. My mother was angry, but he paid no attention to her. He had taken a handful of balloons out of his jacket pocket and asked me to help him blow them up. He was very good. Each time I pinned a new balloon in the center of the chalk circle he had drawn, he popped it with a pellet. My mother was shouting at us:

"Jo! Stop that noise! Kater – move back! Out of the way, you are too close! Get back!"

When all the balloons were gone, Jo came back to the breakfast table.

"Beloved, is it really so bad for you? I have an idea – the opening scene: a wonderful effect to introduce the face of Concha – the first close-up."

"All that stupid banging was for that? What is it – what 'idea'?"

Whenever von Sternberg spoke of a special camera shot, he sounded like a man describing the woman he loved:

"You are standing in an open carriage. It is trying to make its way through a milling carnival crowd. Your face is completely hidden behind a mass of toy balloons. A man is watching. He pulls a slingshot from his back pocket, we cut to the balloons. Suddenly, they explode, and – there, revealed for the first time, is her face. No quiver, not a single flicker of her eyes – no reaction whatsoever to that miniature explosion. Nothing can faze her, she is fearless, unreal, perfection, untouchable – *woman*!"

"You are planning to explode balloons in my face and want no reaction to show on a tight close-up?"

"Yes . . ."

"For that, we will need a special look – maybe now we can use a mantilla to get a feeling of height after the balloons collapse. Who is going to shoot?"

"I am – no one else I could trust to take such a chance."

"If *you* shoot, then the timing will be right. Anyway, it is the beginning of the film. So, if you shoot me in the eye, we can stop the film to rewrite and design eye patches!"

Jo actually laughed. The next day we had an "important meeting" with Travis.

"Travis, for the Carnival dress, we have to design a special look – also change the top of the dress. Jo is going to hide me behind balloons. So, we need to see just an outline at first, above them. Here we can maybe use one of those exaggerated too-high combs you love so."

"Jo is planning to cover your face with balloons? What for? Why?"

"He knows what he is doing. We do what he says. Now – all those balloons will certainly be in light colors, so she should be in dark. What have we got in black that we can hang over that comb?"

"What about that gorgeous scalloped lace we haven't used yet?"

We went to scrounge through the material storeroom. We found the blue lace that was eventually used for the famous hospital costume but nothing suitable for our balloon one. Where she finally found it, I'll never know, probably ordered it made. Not lace this time, the effect needed to be as airy as the swaying balloons, so thin millinery veiling was chosen, on which were sewn hundreds of small black pom-poms, repeating the rounded shape of the balloons in miniature. Her shoulders, upper arms, and neck were left unadorned – naked, their pearl sheen a wonderful contrast. The flame-red mouth, the only color, highly glossed, open in a smile to end all smiles, a fragile wisp of a lacy mask covering just the tip of her nose, somehow accentuated the seduction of the white-rimmed, dark eyes more than it defused them. The wicked curl just barely visible, then a seven-pronged Spanish comb took over. It is my mother's favorite face of all the awe-inspiring ones in this film. Although I don't believe anything can ever top Dietrich's cock-feather costume in *The Shanghai Express*, there are some in *The Devil Is a Woman* that come very close. There is a saying: "The camera is in love with the face." Of course, it helps if the cameraman is in love with it, the director is, the writer, and the entire crew. But it is true, there are some faces that can do no wrong. Special faces that look marvelous recorded by anything that prints an image. Some say it is the bone structure; maybe, but pictures of skeletons aren't particularly gorgeous – so it can't be only the bones. Some think it's skin! As this magical love affair with a lens encompasses men's faces as well, luminous, fragile skin cannot be the answer either. Inner beauty? The beauty of the soul? Now that should be close. But I know from personal experience that this is really the least necessary ingredient. It shouldn't be, but then, nothing is fair that concerns looks. So what is it? I don't know. In her prime, one could not take a bad shot of Dietrich, even if one had wanted to. When the motion picture camera saw her, it sighed, melted, worshiped, and adored! Film ran along its ratchets, documenting its loved one's perfection. Von Sternberg took photographic credit on *The Devil Is a Woman*. For the first time, he was both director and cameraman officially – and about time!

"Roll 'em! Start the carriage! Marlene – hold the balloons higher . . . ACTION!"
  Bang!
  And there it was – revealed: a face to launch a trillion ships.
  "Cut! Wonderful! Print that!"
  "No, Jo! I felt my left eye flicker – let's do it again!"
  Balloons were inflated and replaced, horses and carriage backed up onto their starting marks.
  "ROLL 'EM!"
  Jo took aim . . .
  "ACTION!"
  Bang!
  "Jo, forgive me. My lower lip quivered – "
  This went on until we ran low on helium and I worried that Jo's aim might begin to waver. Then, once again . . .
  Bang!
  Von Sternberg would write, years later:
  "Not a quiver of an eyelash, nor the slightest twitch of the wide

gleaming smile, was recorded by the camera at a time when anyone
other than this extraordinary woman would have trembled with fear."

It really is an incredible moment. One remembers it in color, but then,
the entire film as shot by von Sternberg has such interplay of light and
shade that the eye forgets it is seeing black-and-white images and registers
them in color onto one's visual memory.

Books have been written, lectures given, on the inner meaning,
the proof of von Sternberg's obsession with Dietrich as he perceives
her in this film. How he really depicts himself in the role of the
older lover, used, degraded, deceived by the heartless whore. Some
sages have even gone so far as to point to Lionel Atwill's wearing
a mustache in the part as being proof positive that he is, therefore,
portraying the mustachioed von Sternberg. All of these deep studies
only prove one thing, to me at least: that the material must be very
rich to warrant so much study, support so many different, profound
interpretations, all of which could be correct, yet no one can ever
be really certain they are. Years later, my mother would get furious at the appearance of yet another dissertation on the Dietrich-von
Sternberg simile in *The Devil Is a Woman*. Reading them, she would
exclaim:

"What? That ugly man who played the policeman is supposed to be
Jo? What are these people talking about?" She would read on, shaking
her head. "Sweetheart! Now this is *too* much! Listen to this: 'When
Atwill declares his love for her, despite all this, Dietrich's retort is
like a dagger which von Sternberg, the director, has turned against
himself! "You have always mistaken vanity for love."' *Now* they have
gone too far! A line from a script they think is real? Can I sue these
people? How can they be allowed to write about things they don't
know anything about? Do they think they are God? Outrageous! . . .
These *little* people, who know nothing, get paid and think they are
professors, as Hemingway called them. Oh! Listen to this! Here they
say I wore black in the hospital scene because it is the color of death!
Big deal! We made the costume in dark because the wall in back of
me was white – and because we had that beautiful lace we wanted
to use! Such affectation to invent deep meanings for a costume! And
you know what? It wasn't *black*. It photographed black, but it was blue
taffeta!" She chortled, "Of course, I *had* to stay with the policeman. She
can't stay with that actor who looked like a dance teacher . . . What was
his name – Cesar . . . Romero? Yes, that was his name. If Paramount
had let us keep the handsome one with the light eyes, now what was *his*
name?"

"Joel McCrea?" I said.

"Yes, that's the one. Now *he* was good-looking. If we had had *him*, she could have ended up with him in the end and the picture wouldn't have been a flop!"

When I heard that Brian was going to play *Romeo and Juliet* on the New York stage, I asked my teacher for a copy of the play. She didn't laugh at me in ridicule, but she laughed: I was too young; "Why, we haven't even studied the Ancient Greeks yet!" – and similar reasons were given in that vein. What did the Greeks and my age have to do with reading a simple stage play? Couldn't be harder than a movie script. On my best light blue stationery, with the slim *M.S.* in raised white, I wrote Brian a letter. I asked him for a script of *Romeo and Juliet* and wished him luck playing the male lead.

"Brian sent you a present. Only an English actor would send a young child Shakespeare!" my mother said, as she handed me an elegant-looking book.

"Also, he has written you a letter. He really treats you as though you were grown up. But then, he doesn't know, he has no children."

I hugged my book, waiting for the right moment to disappear. When good old Travis called from the Studio, "to speak to Miss Dietrich," I sprinted down to the pool house. It had become my sort of "out of the way from underfoot" place. The hike down there took so long not everyone bothered to walk the distance when looking for me. Oh, boy! This was no movie script! No wonder theater actors felt so superior to us. If they had to learn all those difficult words and act them all in one go, with no time off between takes, that must be very hard to do. But then again, they never had to worry how they looked in a tight close-up, shoot out of context, do a love scene or die at nine a.m., after being in makeup since six! They probably could sleep all day, work a couple of hours at night, and be through. Still, it couldn't be too easy with plays like this one.

Brian's letter was full of news. He was not playing the lead, Basil Rathbone was Romeo. He was someone called Mercutio, a part he had taken away from a talented young actor called Orson Welles. Another young actor, not as talented but prettier, Tyrone Power, had the part of his friend. Somebody called Katharine Cornell was Juliet, Edith Evans was a nurse, and that Orson Welles now had the part of Tybalt. He told me to read slowly, not to be frightened or put off by all the words that I would not understand, and included a synopsis of the plot. He also suggested I keep a dictionary handy to look up words, since they were already spelled out they would be easy to find. The next day, I waited for my mother and Jo to leave for the Studio and my father and Iturbi to go shopping for sherry. As it was Saturday, my teacher wasn't coming, so I was free to sit in my hiding place and try to figure out why a simple Boy meets Girl, Boy loses Girl, Boy gets Girl should need so many words, make such a fuss, then end up with them dying by mistake! For weeks I snuck off to my retreat and struggled through my "romance." Juliet on the balcony reminded me a bit of my mother in Vienna. Brian would have been perfect for Romeo. All he would have had to do was behave the way he usually did when he was around my mother. The nurse reminded me a little of Nellie, and Mercutio, under all that cleverness, sounded so sad, Jo might have been like him if he talked that much. I loved Shakespeare! Everybody was so *real*, with words that at first seemed so *un*-real. As no one asked me about my new book, I didn't volunteer any information. I did ask my teacher what else Shakespeare had written. I remember writing Brian how much I loved my wonderful present, how much I loved him for sending it to me, and would he please send *Hamlet* someday, that I wanted to read that one next as I once had a dog with that name. I slipped my letter amongst the stack on Jo's secretary's desk. Letters were picked up six times a day by the boys from the mail room. At our house, my father counted every letter, weighed them on his delicate brass scale, then recorded their weight and value of stamps in his ledger marked "postal costs." He would have found mine and either opened it or asked me what it said, depending on the mood he was in. Paramount sent my letters flying, without questions.

RICHARD BARTHELMESS seemed a nice man. Sort of young, though, to have been such a famous Silent Screen Star. I don't know how he joined our little family. One day, his car was parked in the garage and he was there. Iturbi did not like him at all. Jo tried to pretend he didn't exist, while my father told him where to find the best dessert wines and looked forward to going to his house for Sunday brunch. Barthelmess owned one of those marvelous estates that could be bought in the twenties for practically nothing, when Beverly Hills *had* hills and the arid acres stretched for miles, just waiting to be bought. Being an "old" property, his trees were huge bewhiskered eucalyptus; they lined the long winding drive to the top of a hill on which reposed a Movie Star Mansion. Red brick, begabled, ten-chimneyed royal Hollywood Tudor. Being an American, he joked and was easy to know. He had a family and I loved it when we went to visit. Tami was not allowed to come. Usually, she had to tell Iturbi or Jo whatever scenario my mother had invented for that day's absence. We all hated the intricate, sometimes stupid lies my mother concocted for us to tell whenever she thought a situation warranted them. When Dietrich expected a performance from one of her minions, there was really no escape. Doing what my mother commanded was perhaps the coward's way out, but for those of us who had no other place to go, a state of acquiescence became a permanent character fault. It also warped those who were paid a salary and needed to hold onto their job.

Travis designed some very smart "brunch" clothes – lots of pleated skirts and natty blazers, worn with laced oxfords and knotted foulards. Barthelmess had an agile mind, could carry conversations as well as instigate them and on a wide range of subjects. I noticed he avoided those relating to home life, marriage, bringing up children, and pianists. He was an intelligent man.

I WAS TEN when I found out, at last, what Kotex was really for. It frightened me when I bled into the water while taking my bath. I thought something inside me had torn apart! Someone called my mother, who appeared, "white of face and quivering lips." I was told it was nothing, to get out of the bath and dry myself. My mother rolled up a washcloth, told me to put it between my legs, that from now on I would have this happen to me once a month, that it was Nature, and to never *ever* allow a *man* to come near me – and left the bathroom. It was very difficult to keep that washcloth clamped between my thighs. I hopped over to my chest of drawers, took out one of my all-in-one camisoles, and put it on. At least it helped me to hold my mother's roll in place. I got into bed and thought seriously about "nature." Maybe I could ask Brian to explain its mysteries to me. On that comforting thought, I fell asleep. The next morning, I was told by a maid not to leave my room until Bridges had returned from the drugstore with "my things." I waited, wondering about "things." Finally, Tami appeared to instruct me in the intricacies of my new pink satin sanitary belt. She told me that God had given me a little room inside me, where one day my baby would sleep, waiting to be born. That once a month my "room" was cleaned, all nice and tidy to keep it ready and fresh for its eventual tenant. I listened with bated breath. I had never even questioned from where babies were born. Living exclusively with adults who knew and, therefore, were no longer curious, I had never been either. Tami hugged me, cried a little, and told me I should be very proud to be a woman. I walked downstairs to breakfast, feeling very special! I was a Woman with a Room! My mother, dressed all in black, looking attractively wan, greeted me with a tremulous sigh. I wondered if someone had died. I drank my tea, she sipped her coffee in silence, Jo read the *Reporter*. When they left for the Studio, I went back upstairs for my lessons.

I was scheduled to appear in Travis's office in the afternoon. First I delivered the beef tea to Jo's office, then I stopped by the Hair-Dressing Department to say hello to Nellie. She greeted me by throwing her arms around me and asking how I felt. I replied, "Fine. Why?"

Some of the hairdressers, busy as usually, curling and gluing, stopped to give me "understanding looks." Everywhere I went, people stopped what they were doing and smiled kindly. Travis greeted me with:

"Hi, little *lady*! Feeling okay?"

My mother must have given out a press release! It seemed as though all of Paramount Studio knew! It was an uncomfortable feeling. Later, I was returning from a courier run when I heard my mother on the telephone. I stopped outside the dressing-room door and listened:

"You will not believe this! The Child started her period today! At nine years old? Must be the California weather! In the heat, all girls mature faster. Look at the Italians – and the Mexicans are even worse. I should have kept her in Berlin, where it's cold. Isn't it terrible? I couldn't sleep all night. How my mother brought up two girls all alone, I will never know. I don't know how she did it. They are so difficult!" and she hung up. Why had she said that about . . . difficult? I didn't think I was so difficult! I went to bed when I was told, stayed up late when I was needed, ate everything on my plate the way she liked, studied, ran errands, helped with hairdos, and never, ever talked back, in two languages. Also, I wished my mother would get my age right, just once! For a long while after the "momentous occurrence with The Child," tiny puffed sleeves came back with a vengeance. Even my books were examined, some confiscated, replaced with beautifully illustrated editions of Grimms' fairy tales. Romeo and Juliet escaped the purge. They lay in the pool house, hidden under the carpet behind the heavy couch.

MY FATHER DROPPED TAMI OFF after taking her to Pasadena and continued on to Beverly Hills, searching for "edible" foie gras. She changed her clothes, then walked into the garden and cut all the roses off the pretty trees. I ran down to her. She stood, horrified, staring down at what she had done, and began to sob. I took her in my arms.

"Katerlein, what did I do? Oh, Kater! Why? Dear Jesus! Why?"

"Easy, easy – it's not so bad. Easy," I crooned, rocking her in my arms. I felt so helpless.

"What will Papi say? And . . . Mutti?"

Now *there* I could help. That fear I could handle. I picked up the flowers, took Tami's hand, and walked us back up the rolling lawn. We arranged the roses, placed them around the house – and I told my father the gardener had brought them to the back door. Tami was still so upset by her inexplicable behavior, she broke one of the measuring cups while preparing dinner. We had guests that evening. I think Iturbi and Rachmaninoff were there. Tami served. My father, pouring the wine, turned to my mother.

"Mutti, I think we will have to fire the gardener. He cut the roses off the trees. Tamichka! Don't you want to say something to Mutti?"

Tami had stopped dead still on hearing the "rose" line. Now she looked at my father, pleading.

"Remember? Didn't you break something of Mutti's today?" he coached her.

"Oh, yes, Mutti. I am so very sorry. I broke one of the glass measuring cups from the hardware store. As always, I was not being careful enough."

She resumed serving the potato soufflé from the left. My father's voice followed her, mercilessly:

"Of course, Tami will pay for it. I have deducted the fifty cents from the allowance she gets from me."

I rose from my chair.

"Let me help you serve that, Tami!"

"Kater! SIT! We have guests!"

"Yes, sweetheart," my mother chimed in. "You are being rude. Eat your dinner. Tami!" stopping her escape to the kitchen, "when you come back, we need more bread! Then you sit down too."

In the night, I snuck down to the pantry to make sure MacDougal was all right; I thought I had forgotten to fill his water bowl. Passing my father's door, I heard him lecturing Tami about something. Why couldn't he leave that poor woman alone! I got back into bed and stayed awake, listening for the usual opening and closing of doors that meant that Tami was safely back in her room. Lying in the dark, waiting, I decided that my father had a natural cruelty that I did not like at all! The next time he played a mean game like that, I would do something to stop it. I didn't know what, but I just had to find a way.

As *The Devil Is a Woman* progressed, Dietrich's and von Sternberg's lives began slowly to separate. Destiny had decreed that this would be their last film, yet only Jo felt the needle of his inner compass change direction. My mother sensed no such warning. Each day, Jo gave yet another gift to that phantom up on the screen. Emptied himself with daily gestures of farewell. He may not even have known he was saying good-bye – his way. It could have been that his desperate need to go created the volition. All I knew was that every day Jo seemed to leave us, pulled away a little more. The heated messages still flew across the Studio street. My mother left them casually thrown open amongst fan photos and full ashtrays for all to read.

> My dear Marlene,
> You get worked up unnecessarily. At first, you get angry at me – then everything is all right – so many arguments all the time! Stop being angry with me all the time, you know I cannot change everything.

Even his notes had begun to sound distant, as though he felt too empty to care.

I was stamping pictures when Jo entered the dressing room. I saw his face and stopped.

"I have just informed Lubitsch, I will make no more films with Dietrich. Naturally, he was overjoyed."

"Oh? Once again you are throwing me to the wolves?" My mother stood facing him, deathly still – just looking at him.

"Yes, if that is what you believe. I am tired, beloved. No more, please."

"What a luxury! To drop me whenever you decide!"

"I would not call it a luxury as much as a sad necessity."

"What have I done that is so terrible? Everything you wanted, I have given you. Every look you needed, you had!"

"Yes. You were always a sublime inspiration. I have never said you weren't that."

"So? Then why are you deserting me?"

"Oh, if you don't know the answer to that yourself – no use my trying to explain it to you."

"Jo, that is a woman's line."

"Is it? Yes, I suppose you are right. Interesting – perhaps our roles have become reversed."

"Don't be clever – for the sake of appearing superior! You made me come to this country and now you abandon me to people like Lubitsch?"

"No, you deserve a box-office success. With him, you are assured of one."

"But I will look like I did in *Song of Songs* – like a potato!"

"You are nearly as skilled with a camera as I am. You will once again enjoy showing them how it should be done." Jo turned to go.

"Are you leaving me?"

"Yes, my love," and he walked out the door. My mother lit a cigarette.

"Leaving like that, in the middle of an important discussion! What could be so important that he had to go – now!" she asked me, not expecting an answer.

Had she really not understood Jo's exit line? Or did she not want to? I felt my mother had just lost the best friend she ever had, maybe would ever have, and didn't even know it.

Work continued on the film. Nothing further was said. My mother cooked Hungarian goulash, baked Viennese cakes, and, if you looked for her, she could most often be found sitting on the floor at Jo's feet. All suitors were told a crisis was in progress, that Miss Dietrich was unavailable, for the time being. Jo's office was flooded with dark red carnations, silk dressing gowns, and extra beef tea. Now I carried love notes across the street, and in the evenings, was told to stay in my room. My father took Tami and went to visit members of the Berlin colony, making sure they would return only when our young lovers had gone upstairs. I had seen my mother being "young girl romantic" often enough to recognize the symptoms. I wondered if Jo would forget he wanted to leave. This sudden overdone devotion seemed so phony to me, maybe it wouldn't to him. He had taken so much, maybe he would decide, after all, to take some more.

I have a special memory that came from this twilight courtship. One Saturday, when Jo went to his usual football game, my mother, for the first time, was willing to accompany him, and allowed me to go along. Smart British lap robes had been delivered from Bullock's, sterling silver flasks filled, hot coffee in thermoses. Our weather was the ever-constant "southern California hot," but these were the props for going to a football game. It must have been UCLA against USC that day. Our hometown teams were always battling it out. Jo had a special box. It was great! I could see everything. The stadium was so vast and full of people! He bought me a hot dog, oozing with that light yellow mustard my father disliked so. I sat on the edge of my seat, so excited I was afraid it would show too much and annoy my mother. What an afternoon! I got everything! Touchdowns, soaring passes, even one of the players carried off the field on a stretcher! Jo tried to explain some of the rules to us, but when my mother said:

"Why don't they just give each player a ball? Then they can stop fighting over it and everybody can go home," he gave up.

I whispered to him, "Will you give me a book on football, please?"

He answered me, hardly moving his lips, which were partially hidden behind his droopy mustache. It was amazing how he could speak secretly like that.

"Yes, and next time you can come with me – alone."

When we arrived home, I kissed Jo on the cheek. I didn't have to stand on tiptoes to do that anymore and thanked him for a wonderful time.

My mother was ignoring me. I was told by a maid to stay at home. I did what was expected of me and tried to think what I had done or said that could have angered her. Usually, I was able to identify my mistake almost immediately, but this time I drew a blank. So I stayed in Bel Air, was particularly careful, and hoped my mother's displeasure would wear itself out. I did not know yet that she could be jealous of a child.

An interesting friendship with Dorothy di Frasso stirred on the horizon, the great John Gilbert, rumored no longer involved with Garbo, though still drunk, was about to enter our lives. Fritz Lang, director of such masterpieces as *M* and *Metropolis*, joined the German colony as revered refugee and became a steady admirer of my mother's goulash. Ronald Colman hosted intimate afternoons on his yacht, Brian signed a contract with MGM and would be returning to us, and von Sternberg made his final move.

The morning papers said it all:

SVENGALI & DIETRICH
in Final Split

Interviewed on the soundstage at Paramount Studio, director Josef von Sternberg stated that "The Devil Is a Woman," the film he is now shooting, starring Marlene Dietrich, would be his seventh and last picture with the great German beauty.

"Miss Dietrich and I have progressed as far as possible together."

Asked if there was a personal motive to his decision, von Sternberg replied, "Everything I have to say about Miss Dietrich I have said with the camera."

My mother was stunned. She called everyone, reading them Jo's press release, saying how Jo had never even *hinted* at anything so cruel. Why couldn't he have said something? He could have told her, to at least shield her from the terrible shock of having to see his decision in cold print! He knew how much she loved him! Would not work without him! She even phoned Lubitsch's office and, for the first time, spoke to him directly. This enemy of von Sternberg agreed wholeheartedly. Jo had certainly done a most dastardly deed and to the one person he owed all of his fame to.

"No, no, Ernst! Jo was a genius! Everything! He taught me *everything*! He was the master. It must be my fault that he has now left me like this!"

Lubitsch invited her to have lunch with him, just the two of them, in his private dining room. If not now, whenever she felt lonely and in need of a sympathetic friend. Lubitsch wrote scenes for himself that were almost as slick as the ones he invented for Herbert Marshall. My mother promised she would remember that he was "there," whenever she needed him, and hung up, saying:

"Sweetheart, you know – Lubitsch is not so very bad. Jo always behaved as though he was *so* terrible. But now we know that Jo has been going crazy for a long time!" The use of the past tense in reference to von Sternberg disturbed me. The lunch break was over. It was time to report back to the set.

The messenger from the German consul in Los Angeles delivered into my mother's hands a copy of an editorial that had appeared in the leading German newspapers at the personal suggestion of the minister of propaganda of the Third Reich, Dr. Joseph Goebbels:

> Applause for Marlene Dietrich, who has finally dismissed the Jewish director Josef Sternberg who has always cast her as a prostitute or other fallen woman but never in a role which would bring dignity to the great citizen and representative of the Third Reich.
>
> Now Marlene should come home to the Fatherland, assume her historic role as a leader of the German film industry and end allowing herself to be the tool of Hollywood's Jews!

My mother's face was ashen. Quickly, she hid the paper behind her back.

"No! No! You must never read this!" her voice had a hollow sound. "Go! Sweetheart! Run to the set and get Jo! – and find Papi!"

I knew this was very serious and ran! I only hoped that after all that was going on, Jo wouldn't refuse to come with me. The light was out, thank God! I dashed onto the set. He listened to my fast explanation, turned to his assistant, told him to kill the lights, and left. I brushed off the questions being thrown at me and ran out along the streets, asking everyone if they had seen Miss Dietrich's husband. It was as though he had suddenly disappeared. Maybe he had decided to go home? Someone thought they had seen him go into Mae West's dressing room. Here I was running all over the lot and my father had been next door all the time? I rushed back, knocked urgently on the closed dressing-room door. Mae West's outraged voice boomed:

"Where's the fire!"

But, when I answered: "Please, is my father there? Miss Dietrich must see him right away!" she opened the door herself, tying the sash of her dressing gown.

"He's here, alive and kickin'! Don't fret, honey." She called to him over her satin-clad shoulder: "Rudi – your German lady wants you! Tell her I *l-l-l-like* her taste!"

For hours, production was halted on the film while Dietrich, her husband, her agent, and von Sternberg discussed and planned her next move. Finally, the head of Publicity was summoned and told that Miss Dietrich had made her choice: She would apply for American citizenship and sever her ties with Germany forever. I noticed my mother's eyes were swollen. She kept turning her head away. She must have been crying.

A momentous decision, made under pressure and within hours, as usual, worked for her as though it had been strategically planned. If Dietrich had filed her application for citizenship just a few months later, she would still have been a German citizen at the outbreak of the Second World War. As it was, five years later, she would receive her first American passport – only four months before that fateful September of 1939.

Did this mean I would finally be an American too? I read all the press releases, but none of them said anything about me becoming a citizen some day. No one told me anything, and with all the different moods running rampant at the house and the Studio, I didn't dare ask. Jo's secretary knew practically everything – so I went to her and got my "how to become an American citizen" information. The next morning, I looked my teacher right in the eye, and in my best Rudolph Sieber manner, informed her that from now on we would be having lessons in American history and government! That it was imperative for her to impart to me, her pupil, the Constitution of the United States and anything else that made my future country tick. I didn't know if I was going to get to be an American, but I was certain that when my mother finally took the Oath of Allegiance, she would not have studied any of the things required, so one of us better learn something! Deep down, I held the faint hope that if I could answer all the questions correctly, they might let me in too.

The final weeks of *The Devil Is a Woman* were slick, professional, and expedient. My mother was glacial. Jo wrote one last time:

I am tired, beloved. I can no longer fight with you, with Lubitsch, who despises me almost as much as I detest him. And I can add nothing to you.

I'm only plagiarizing myself. My parting gift to you will be the greatest "Dietrich film" yet. In it, I give you all my talent. You will see the ultimate Dietrich and it will be your favorite of our seven films.

After reading Jo's note, my mother handed it to my father – without comment. She did the same with the one delivered by messenger to her dressing room the day *The Devil Is a Woman* came to an end. Sometimes the German language becomes very touching. Trying to translate feeling is always hard to do. When von Sternberg wrote:

Danke, es war himmlisch, auf wiedersehen,

he meant:

I thank you, it was heavenly. Till we meet again, good-bye.

My father kept this sad little note – my mother never missed it.

We did the portrait and the publicity pictures. I was told to bring my green charges to the Studio, and for the first time, Dietrich was photographed wearing her emeralds. Another "first" were the new eyebrows. She kept those soaring arches until *The Garden of Allah*. Even after that, using them in "life" whenever she wanted to look particularly "Dietrich." Whenever Jo's lighting was desperately needed, he was called, arrived promptly at the portrait gallery, did his magic act, and left. The faces that emerged from this sitting are some of the most superb ever taken of Dietrich. They sparkle, glow, enchant – nothing behind her eyes distracts from the perfection. But that is the awesome discipline of this profession and what attracted my mother to it the most. Personal problems were off limits. Nothing, absolutely nothing was allowed to infiltrate and harm the product. No excuses made for emotional sloppiness. Let a personal grief show, just once, and the camera will zero in on it, record the actor's secret vulnerability, and become his enemy. Only very great actors sometimes are able to use their private misery to enhance a performance. What my mother lacked in talent, she more than made up for with her discipline.

Jo called. The edited print of *The Devil Is a Woman* was ready for her to see. She went alone, returned home, and said:

"What work! One face more beautiful than the next! The film is not good, but we all knew that at the beginning. But that isn't important. This picture should be studied by all people who think they know how to shoot film. I held Jo's hand all the way through. I even cried. What he has done! Unbelievable! I told him so and kissed his wonderful hands. I said he was a god and he smiled at me and said, 'If you like it, then I am satisfied.'"

Von Sternberg left the next day on one of his journeys to strange and distant places. Unreachable, alone, and, I suppose, convinced they would prove curative. Unfortunately, no place was ever far enough to exorcise his personal Lorelei. In one last effort to save himself, he had torn the lifeline that tethered his genius. Scattered sparks of his brilliance would glow again over the remaining years, but they were the afterglow of what had once been celestial fire.

Soon, it was as though Jo had never existed except that preparing for a film was never again as exciting nor the results as visually wonderful. From then on, Dietrich no longer recreated her image – simply perpetuated it – still requiring very hard work, just less inspiration.

MY MOTHER was going to a party! This was so rare that it created quite a stir in our lives.

"It says here, 'Wear old clothes!'" My mother was reading Carole Lombard's invitation to her party in the fun house on the Venice pier.

"What does she mean, 'old clothes'? Just like her, trying to be ever-so-different and cutesy! Get me Travis at the Studio."

I dialed and handed her the receiver:

"Travis? Have you heard about Lombard's big party? Well, what does she mean with 'old clothes'? Old clothes 'history' or old clothes 'no good anymore'? . . . Oh! Is a fun house really *that* dirty? Then why give a party there? Do you know what she is going to wear? Knowing her, she will have alerted Publicity and there will be photographers. . . . Really? Now everyone thinks they can wear trousers – so, what do *I* wear? I am coming in! Think! We will have to make something 'OLD CLOTHES'!"

She went to the fun house party wearing shorts, her legs bare, little-boy shoes and socks, a jaunty kerchief tied around her neck; the photographers went wild, and my mother arrived home a bloody mess! I was waiting for her in the hall.

"Sweetheart, help me upstairs! Don't look at my legs! I don't want you to get worried! What an idea for a party! We had to sit on potato sacks and slide down enormous slides! I thought we were going straight through the wall into the ocean! . . . And barrels that rolled! We had to run through them trying not to fall! It was awful! Everyone was crashing on top of each other and they were *laughing*. They thought it was fun! You know those horrible mirrors that make you look like a midget or a giant or fat? She had those too. Who wants to see themselves fat? I can have *that* right here in my bathroom and not look like I have been in a war! Remember our shirt salesman? He got in all the pictures next to Lombard. He must have spent the whole evening watching where the photographers were going, and managed to get there before them. 'Ready and handsome,' in position! My god! Look at my knees! They didn't look this bad in the car!"

They were really bad. She looked as though she had fallen off a bicycle at high speed on a gravel road. She had worn a shirt made of the same thick raw silk as the shorts, so her arms had gotten some protection, but even that was torn at the elbows and the skin peeking through the holes was scraped and oozing. We cleaned the caked blood off her knees and shins, then she soaked in a hot bath loaded with epsom salts. While she winced, she let off more steam:

"All this for a party? The worst thing of all was something called 'the whip.' An enormous bowl, with a little platform in the center. First we had to sit on this itsy-bitsy shelf. Then suddenly the thing started to spin, so we all flew off, down into the bottom of the bowl! But that wasn't the end, because whoever was on the platform when the thing stopped, was the winner! So, there we are – terrified! – on our hands and knees, trying to crawl back up, while this monster machine whips us around and throws us back down again. I *know* somebody threw up! I must have done these knees on that thing. Of course, I had to join the mood. Everyone was watching. But such children! Typically American! Fun, fun, fun! Barthelmess is old enough to know better. But he just loved that whizzing thing! . . ."

I helped her out of the bath and into bed.

"Of course, Lombard's trousers protected her legs. Her legs *should* be covered!" and she went to sleep. The next morning, she was blue, overlaid with a lovely shade of puce, and stiff as a board. As it was Sunday and everyone was home, she kept calling people on the phone. Her opening line:

"I went to a *marvelous* party that Carole Lombard gave in a fun house! Well, let me tell you all about it! . . ."

As the day progressed, every call became more and more outrageous. When Barthelmess arrived for dinner, limping, we all got hysterical! My mother said he deserved it for trying to act "young." He was only forty at the time but wasn't annoyed. He laughed right along with her, he was really nice about it. He was also madly in love with her, which helped.

MY FATHER'S TRUNKS APPEARED. He and Tami were booked on the
Ile de France to return to Paris.

"Tamilein, how am I going to know anything about how you are?"

We were alone by the pool, having our last talk.

"Kater, I am all right again! You see, I haven't done anything stupid
for a whole week! You must stop being worried about me so. You are
too young – just enjoy the sunshine and be happy."

"I'm not too young! I know how Papi is mean to you – "

She gasped; her hand shot out, covering my mouth.

"Kater! You must never say that about Papi! He is kind and patient.
A wonderful man. You must always be proud that he is your father.
And Mutti too! There is no one in the whole world more generous.
Always giving, doing everything for everyone – and you are her whole
life. She loves you more than anyone else. You must love her always and
Papi too."

"Be sure to write me, Tamilein."

"I will . . . but it is difficult. Papi doesn't like me being silly in letters
– sometimes I do Russian spelling, so I have to show them to him before
he sends them off."

"Listen, Tamilein. You can write me a private letter in the park, when
you take Teddy for his walk. Then you can go to the Plaza Athénée,
buy a stamp with your household money, and give it to the concierge
to mail for you." I wasn't the daughter of the best private scriptwriter
for nothing! At moments like these, my mother's training came in very
handy.

"Oh, I don't think I should do anything like that. Besides, how would
you get it?"

I had maneuvered her letter out of Paris, but into my hands instead of
my mother's. That was a real stumbling block. I sat in the pink wicker
chair shaped like a curled sea shell, thinking frantically. Paramount? The
mail room? No – they would tell. So would Make-Up and Wardrobe.
Nellie? No. Not meaning to, she would chirp, "Miss D. . . . here is
a letter for Maria. It was sent to me!" My new bodyguard? He was
too new – I did not know him yet and people tended to be on the
side of those who paid their salaries. . . . My teacher and the maids
were out, for the same reason. . . . Bridges? Never, he flattered my
mother only because she liked it. But I knew he didn't really mean it
– I didn't trust him at all. Even Brian was out. With his proper sense of
things, he would never condone receiving mail "behind one's mother's
back." Who? Who was there? Just somebody . . . ? I suddenly felt all
cold inside. There seemed to be no one. Not a single person I could trust
to do something very important just for me, without my omnipotent

mother being informed of it. I remember feeling utterly alone and being frightened by that reality. As these unrelated moments in childhood have a way of doing, it marked me.

They left, my father laden with his new polo-watching clothes, American gadgets, and my mother's shopping lists; Tami, with my mother's suits she had been given and a year's supply of glass vials and colored pills. She would not have to miss a single exhilarating injection nor a moment of deep, deep sleep.

The patient swains resurfaced from out of their individual holding tanks. New ones hovered on the perimeter. Everyone dedicated themselves to helping "Marlene" get over the shocking desertion of her creator and the departure of her husband. A tidal wave of flowers, phone calls, and invitations swept into our life. Parties, parties, and more parties – in the thirties, the only casual relaxation available to Hollywood stars. These people, who worked each day in make-believe, came together seeking company inside their manufactured reality. They had no other place to go. Except for a small handful of passable restaurants, like the one in the shape of a derby, painted brown, and known by the ingenious name of The Brown Derby on Hollywood Boulevard and Vine, stars had no choice but to create their own entertainments inside their homes. Maintaining mystery and protecting it was also an extremely important reason. Movie Stars, and all that label represented, did not mingle with the masses. Today, this attitude would be condemned as snobbism, but not then. The public would have felt cheated had these "celestial beings" shown the slightest inclination toward normalcy. They expected, and got, their idols always beautiful, always glamorous, always handsome, unreal, perfect, and divine.

In the "glamorous" Hollywood time, this envied minority entertained each other within the privacy of their compounds, believing everyone would then feel free to relax. They could have thrown their parties open to the public, for they never did let down their visual guard, even amongst themselves. Their houses were built with party needs in mind. Sunken living rooms had the seating capacity of hotel lobbies, private movie theaters, billiard rooms, dens that sometimes dwarfed the "lobbies," bars in all sizes and decorative motifs. Swimming pools that were impossible to crowd, pool houses boasting six bathrooms done in various shades of Italian marble, lawns for "garden games," and "come to a real small-town picnic" gatherings. In the forties, barbecues, to rival any Texas ranch's, joined the requirements necessary to be socially self-sustaining.

Newcomers were very rare to this elite group. The same glittering people saw the same glittering people over and over again. "Theme" parties became very important for this reason, disguises helped to make the too familiar appear "unknown" – if only for just a moment. This extended to homes. Interior designers were often given houses to redo between parties, just so one could have that refreshing sensation of thinking one had, somehow, come to the wrong address. Clothes were a guarded secret – continually new and exciting. Studio designers and their workrooms were kept busy, making sure their stars outshone those of the rival studios, even in private.

When I was allowed to accompany my mother, it was "magic time." Jean Harlow in silver, sipping a Pink Lady, laughing slightly up at William Powell. Wallace Beery ever so solicitous to a shy chorine named Ginger Rogers. The "drinking buddies," John Gilbert and John Barrymore, helping each other find the bar – each a romantic dream on its way to a nightmare. Joan Crawford in clinging red, determined that Franchot Tone will look her way while she hangs on Douglas Fairbanks, the "Junior's," arm. Mary Pickford, in baby-blue taffeta, nibbling petit fours while Douglas Fairbanks – the real one – concentrates on holding in his stomach and looking younger than his son. Jeanette MacDonald in tulle is looking for Chevalier, who is having a charming tête-à-tête with Claudette Colbert in a Travis Banton matte satin. Charles Boyer wishes he could hear what they are saying, as he is certain they *must* be discussing him. Lionel Barrymore and his sister Ethel are looking for their brother, John. George Raft, Clark Gable, and Cary Grant are in the billiard room being instructed in the finer points of snooker by Carole Lombard, while Gary Cooper leans against the oak paneling, just watching. The Frederic Marches arrive with the Rathbones. Ronald Colman wanders dreamily into the garden. Gloria Swanson, in jet black and diamonds, throws back her head and laughs at the joke Edward G. Robinson just told her, and Marlene Dietrich, in her tuxedo, smiles softly up into the boyish face of a very young Henry Fonda. Add the great supporting players, like Eugene Pallette and Edward Everett Horton, the composers, Gershwin, Porter, Berlin, the directors, writers, favored agents, studio heads, and some producers, and you have a "once upon a time" Hollywood party. Usually, my mother skimmed over the invitations, then threw them in the wastepaper basket. This one she reread, the "theme" intrigued her.

"Sweetheart, get me Travis on the phone. . . . Travis, have you heard the Rathbones are giving another party? I don't believe Rathbone's wife thought up this idea. I think she got it from the Countess di Frasso. Interesting woman. But why do these rich American women always insist on marrying poor European aristocrats? Just for the title? I suppose to an American being a 'countess' is important. Apart from that and being

Gable's mistress, she is quite intelligent. It says people have to come as The
Person You Most Admire. Are you going, Travis? Why don't you get out
the cock-feather dress from *Shanghai Express* and go as Dietrich! I don't
know who else they have invited. Gable will come as Louis B. Mayer –
he doesn't know anyone else to admire – and you know Crawford will
come as Crawford! They will probably *all* want to come as themselves!
I am going to be Leda . . ." There was a long pause.

"Travis? Don't make me change my mind about you! I always say you
are an educated man. You must know the fable of Leda and the Swan! A
magnificent white swan seduces a beautiful virgin, she falls in love with
him, and they stay entwined, forever. . . . Yes, that is the correct story!
. . . Well, that is how *I* learned it!"

I sat listening, trying to visualize my mother as a virgin. I wasn't too
clear about what that was, but it sounded sort of delicate.

"We will have to make a swan. Otherwise, no one will get who I am.
She has to look 'enfolded' inside him. We have a whole week to make
the costume. Order the swan feathers. We need the long ones that come
from the wings and, don't forget, we will also need very short ones to
make the neck. . . . What? Of *course* jeweled eyes. Travis? Is something
wrong with you today? You can't give a swan blue eyes. Swan eyes
are always green! . . . Don't forget, we will have to work at night
so no one knows what I am going to be! If Louella Parsons finds out
about the feathers, she will have it in her column that I am going as a
sea gull!"

No film costume was ever worked on and perfected more than the
one for Leda and her swan. When Dietrich was finally sewn into that
costume, what an incredible sight! Clustered short "greek statue" curls
framed her face, leaving her neck bare for her swan to curl his neck
gently around it and pillow his head on one swelling breast. Her body
sheathed in sculpted white chiffon, she stood within his all-enveloping
passionate embrace. They were truly "one." There might have been
some who did not know the story of Leda and her swan, but no one
could misunderstand the emotion my mother represented. Her escort
for that evening was "Marlene Dietrich." Elizabeth Allan had become
a friend and went as her idol, my mother. She was a pretty actress,
with a porcelain shepherdess face. She had appeared one day for tea
and stayed through dinner. I think she was brought to the house by
Ruth Chatterton, a skilled stage actress and a fellow Paramount star,
although not in my mother's exalted category. Chatterton flew her
own planes and had a direct manner. In later years, she played the
parts that weren't important enough to be given to Mary Astor. My
mother was enchanted by Elizabeth Allan's "English tea rose" delicacy.

She had Travis cut down one of her precious sets of tails and we all helped to dress her. Nellie did her hair, I put the pearl studs into the stiff shirt-front, my mother helped her into the pants, smoothing them with her hands down the legs, making sure they were not too long for the patent pumps. Then she positioned one of her best top hats, showed the overwhelmed girl how to put her hands in her trouser pockets and stand "à la Dietrich," and laughed in appreciation of her perfect imitation. There were so many feathers, it took us twenty minutes to settle our Leda and her amorous swan inside the car. Fortunately, our new Dietrich was such a wisp of a thing, she took up very little space. They drove off together to be the sensation of the party! Travis and his covey of seamstresses went home. Dot and Nellie helped me clean up; my mother never liked maids touching her personal things.

My mother was having a marvelous time. Sometimes she didn't even come home – just phoned to tell me she loved only me. Sometimes Nellie would come in her lunch hour or after work, to see how I was and pick up things my mother needed, wherever *she* was. As Brian had sent me the requested *Hamlet*, I spent most of my time in the pool house, deciphering Shakespeare. I decided I liked *Hamlet* much better than *Romeo and Juliet*.

Brian came back from wherever he had been and sometimes picked me up in his car and we drove to the beach. He always let me sit in the rumble seat. That little, hidden bench that folded down into the back of the car, just above the trunk, was a little like my train balcony – a special place. The wind would swoosh into your ears as palm trees whizzed by. Sitting in a rumble seat on the way to the beach, one was always the first person in a car to smell the sea. We would park, take off our shoes and socks, walk along the sand, I with my bucket, Brian with our shoes tied together over his shoulder. I was a little too old for a metal bucket and matching blue spade, but I loved to dig up the sand crabs, then watch them rebury themselves. We didn't talk much. When he brought me back, I hoped he would stay for tea. Most often, finding my mother still absent, he kissed the top of my head, told me to give her his love when she returned, tell her she should call him, and left.

THE WOODEN CRATES filled with squirming blue-black creatures, all entangled in dripping seaweed, were delivered to the kitchen door. We were scheduled for a crawfish dinner, my mother's true claim to culinary fame. It was my job to pick up each crustacean, scrub his belly with one of Mr. Fuller's vegetables brushes. These miniature lobsters were feisty, they hated being tickled while being prepared for death. I couldn't really blame them, being plunged alive into my mother's bubbling cauldron couldn't be considered an easy demise! Dietrich's crawfish dinners were justly famous – as long as Louisiana could deliver the required twenty dozen, we feasted.

Ronald Colman looked at the huge platter, heaped with reddened bodies, and turned ashen. My mother, busy ladling out the succulent champagne broth in which they had drowned, did not notice. I, in my special presenting attire, sat primly watching an interesting drama in the making.

"Ronnie, sweetheart – eat! Eat, don't wait! I never sit!" my mother trilled. Since falling in love with her latest, she trilled often.

"Marlen*ah*, my dear*ah*!" Mr. Colman had a way of putting an *ah* on everything: "You must join us – please! My dear*ah*!" Through the whole meal, between choking down what he obviously abhorred, the "my dear*ahs*" floated about like punctuation without much else in between. My mother didn't mind a bit. She fussed, and served, showed him how one dismembered the tiny bodies, pulled their meat from out of their pink armor without breaking their flesh, paid absolutely no attention to his valiantly disguised shudders as empty claws, legs, heads, and bodies were flung into the big bowl in the center of our table. When finally all had been consumed, all gloriously praised, she took "Ronnie" by the hand, he rose, looked at her longingly, she looked back at him tenderly; their arms entwined, they moved as one, out our front door, drove into the starlit night in his green convertible. This romance with Colman was a "floater." It came and went at the oddest times, without ever enough substance for upheaval. As they rendezvoused mostly on his beautiful sailing yacht, very "British Buccaneer," I didn't get to play along.

Dearest Papi,
Have forgotten how to type so forgive my mistakes. Pictures are on the way from the last sitting that I lit myself and a publicity picture of me and the car. Now to the work – by the time you get this everything will probably have changed again. I can't get a finished script out of Lubitsch – although he and 3 writers have been working on it for months. After many letters and threats, yesterday – I got the first 2 pages. Very banal and the worst of all – is they introduce me – my very first scene – the first time one sees me in this "so different" type of role – the moment everyone is waiting for – (Lubitsch after all has proclaimed, "We are going to remake

Dietrich!") – so the first close-up of this "New Woman" – Are you ready
for this? – Are you on the edge of your seat? – The first shot is . . . MY
LEGS . . . IN THE CAR, CROSSED. A whole written description of
how one leg slides down – then the other lifts and crosses over again . . .
You're awed – right? From this "brilliant" beginning – you can imagine
what little hope there is for the remaining script. I am still waiting for
an answer from Lubitsch – when I will get it, a full script, and when I
start. Locke is taking my costumes and a cameraman to Spain to shoot
exteriors, so stupid. But Lubitsch *loves* exteriors, so I have stopped any
costume work so he can't go and am demanding a FULL script. If it is
no good – I won't do the film. *Hotel Imperial* is ready and as told to me –
charming. I still hope I can do *Hotel Imperial* first. My clothes for *Necklace*
are nothing special – as it all plays in the car and we need nothing but
"driving" costumes.

Yesterday Jo started working on *Raskolnikov*. He called and was so
desperate – said the whole day his heart was heavy and how wonderful
it was with me. I understand that so well. Of course, you're now saying
to yourself: When they were together – all they did was fight. *I* decided
not to say that to him – I just comforted him – what is the use of all the
fighting in comparison to the feelings of love and trust.

Saw *Morocco* again – please see it. It is again proof of the idiocy of
people who all say that in the early days I was so natural and in the last
films so stiff – they all should see *Morocco*. I hardly move, speak once
an hour with calculated inflection – yes – and am half as pretty as now –
am inhibited and even the legs are better now than then. Look at it – one
forgets.

I now play tennis – mostly with Gable, Frank Lawton ("David
Copperfield" grown up), Jack Gilbert, and Elizabeth Allan (a sweet
woman without "chi-chi") mostly up in Gilbert's house or at the Bel-Air
Club. Gilbert has emerged out of his "trunk" and enjoys life again like
a child. Everything was really easy until he fell in love with me – then
it got difficult, because he has a force that one always secretly yearns for
and when one finds it – one gets frightened. He is out of his mind that I
don't want to and I don't really know why I don't – because he would
really be worth it and it would make him so happy, but I am not so
sure it would be so easy to get out of it again – the passion is too hot.
So one says better to live alone if one can't find the one right person to
belong to whose whole happiness is you – then when one can have it
– one doesn't want it. I am sure it also has a lot to do with that I was
very close to Ronnie (Colman) and still hang on that. Although he really
disappointed me. He is so cool – despite that face and that voice. . . . Not
cool because he doesn't want to but because he can't – went through a
terrible time with his wife who for 14 years refused him a divorce until
he was completely virginal and inhibited. I tried to bring him to "glow"
and he loved me – I am sure – but I didn't like the nonchalant "How
about next Thursday" and so I walked away a little because I felt I was

losing something. So I don't live tragically as I used to, only sad, which is already a big improvement.

Buy yourself Stravinsky's *Sacre du printemps* – the most exciting music that ever was.

Well, my angel, I must stop – my fingers hurt – Iturbi is coming to dinner – crawfish soup – stroganoff – pancake crepes with cheese filling. Ruth Chatterton and Lang (he goes through everything with me – helped a lot with Colman – gave me advice – and as he loves me too – his efforts are even sweeter). Aherne couldn't come, making a test with that Shearer. By the way – his new flame is Merle Oberon, a real common piece. He suddenly got real masterful – tried to start again with me, and when I got furious – he rushed off and threw himself at her. It looks as though he has already had enough because all ashamed he again came back to me. That's all the gossip there is.

A thousand kisses, my love – Kiss Tami – I envy you both – the "searching" is so unpleasant.

Mutti

I WOKE UP TO *Rhapsody in Blue*, and like the macabre prayer that little children are taught to mouth, I thought I had "died before I awake" and gone to heaven! Gershwin? . . . Gershwin before breakfast? I washed and dressed like lightning and ran downstairs. My mother, in tennis attire, a white ribbon holding back her hair, greeted me with: "Good morning, sweetheart! Let's have breakfast."

I must have died. I just didn't know it yet. My mother, who considered all salutations a waste of breath, had actually said one – to me, of all people! And in English! John Gilbert came into our life, and from then on, my mother spoke to me in English, reverting to German only for tragic announcements, big secrets, special sarcasm, and while under the influence of anesthesia and alcohol. Her tennis shoes gave her a bouncy walk; we proceeded outside, where she surveyed the breakfast table and said,

"And where is the orange juice?"

I sat down, hard, on the nearest chair. Wonders kept right on happening! She summoned the maid and ordered toast and a whole plate of crisp bacon, then went back inside and changed the record. Benny Goodman? At eight o'clock in the morning? She brought her tennis racket with her, tightening the screws of the wooden press.

"Sweetheart. What that man is playing – is that what they still call jazz?"

"Yes, Mutti," I croaked. Shock had dried up my saliva. She sounded as though she were doing her homework.

"And is that what is called a 'hot' piano?"

I just nodded.

"Sweetheart, Mister John Gilbert is coming. You will meet him. He is beautiful . . . his eyes are like coals – burning! Look at his eyes when he comes. You will see what I mean."

I was going to meet the great John Gilbert? What a morning!! I did not have much relationship with the silent-screen actors. My mother never admitted, even to herself, ever having been one of them. But John Gilbert, like Valentino and Chaplin, he *was* Hollywood. I just had time to run upstairs and get my autograph book before the front door chimes announced his arrival. Talk about "burning coals"! You could get scorched being looked at by him! He had also a sweet, half-sad smile that could break your heart. He took my hand. I made my best curtsey, looked up, and got the full treatment – coals, tender smile, the lot!

"My darling . . . she has your eyes." That voice could melt steel! He turned back to me. "I have a daughter just about your age. I call her Tinker." He gave me another one of those devastating smiles and they left.

I closed the front door, my legs all woozy. I felt a little disloyal to Brian, but I hoped Mr. Gilbert would stay with us for a long time. He did, but not long enough.

While their relationship lasted, my mother must have seemed the glorious reality of all his dreams long dreamt. How she mothered him! She smothered him with it and he loved it. She enjoyed her new cause tremendously.

Where Garbo had failed, Dietrich would succeed! She alone would save this man from the "demon drink." After all, "alcoholism was nothing but a degrading weakness, suited more to low-class men who spend their time in rank bars, disgracing themselves." Chicken soup bubbled on our stove. The special beef required for my mother's elixir was delivered to Gilbert's home. She set up her beef-tea laboratory in his kitchen. When telling me of this time, she said:

"I used to hide his bottles. I got his Filipino houseman to help me. For a while, it was nice. But he always wanted me to do it! You know me . . . all I wanted to do was cook for him and be 'cozy,' not all that to-do in the bed. But he thought that I didn't love him if I didn't. So I did. He wasn't very good . . . those that 'look' it so much never are."

I used to love finding his notes, stuffed into empty thermoses, in pockets of her tennis cardigans, or tucked inside her box of tennis balls:

> I swear you have drugged and intoxicated my brain. Thinking of you and longing for you makes me dizzy.
>   I love you.

> Just because you are so sweet and generous and fine. How nice a world if all people were like you.

> Pie Face,
>   Wouldn't you be in a hell of a fix if I should actually stop drinking and smoking and staying awake nights – and our sex life were satisfactorily active and I didn't remain too positive in my opinion? You wouldn't have anything to squawk about. The difference between us is – I love you – just as you are. Of course – I know – don't tell me – naturally I love you just as you are – because you are perfect. You see – I guessed it. But you once thought, for ten fleeting seconds, that I was perfect too. Oh, bitter loss!
>   I love you.

How can one not be enchanted by a man who addresses a goddess as Pie Face? The first time I heard him call her that, I held my breath, then noticed the twinkle in those glowing coals and admired his audacity. He was so American! He kidded, something no European ever learns to do properly. Americans can make fun of each other in the most outrageous ways and remain lovers and friends. Europeans never quite know what not to take seriously. They often confuse American humor with ridicule and react accordingly.

"Gilbert called me 'Pie Face'!" she would say. "Why? My face was never round! Joan Bennett, she had a moon face, but I never did. I never understood Jack when he got 'cute.' He also called me 'Love Face' – but *that* I could understand."

Bullock's delivered new bathing suits, sundresses, even a navy blue pool robe; I was given a smart sun hat to complete my new wardrobe and sent to the desert with Nellie. A manmade oasis, of one street, four Indian souvenir shops, a riding stable, an exclusive tennis club, and one luxury hotel. El Mirador looked like a mission, had the obligatory swimming pool, lawn, and lots of tall date palms all around. The little town was called Palm Springs and became my favorite place in all the world. Instead of just seeing the desert from the train, I was actually in it, and everything was as wondrous as I had imagined it must be. Little lizards dozed on bleached rocks, never ran off when I came near; people were so new, they assumed the place still belonged to them and felt safe.

The heat penetrated deep inside our bones. It felt glorious! Joshua trees and yucca stood tall, like conscientious sentries guarding their infinite territory. The sand was the shade of my mother's favorite color, soft beige. It had a way of absorbing sound, so that one became aware of hearing silence. The snap of a dry twig, the screech of a golden eagle, a horse's muffled hooves – all emerged as isolated sounds within their own intensity, individualized. Where man had brought water, everything sparkled, erupted into lush, vibrant color. Where he had not encroached as yet lay hot and silent, all dusty pastels. The San Jacinto mountains soared above, seemed to stretch forever. They were just as I had seen them first from my train balcony: magenta shadowed with tips of snow white. I ate cactus candy, all sweet and sticky, drank the juice of freshly pressed passion fruit, feasted my eyes on the wondrous array of turquoise jewelry at the little Indian training post, made friends with the staff who came from the Agua Caliente reservation, saw my first real prairie dog sitting up by his burrow, like a little, fat, golden squirrel without its tail, discovered the gossamer, sloughed-off skin of a rattlesnake, asked my Indian friends to help me make a snake stick. When they told me I must not wander in the desert without boots, I begged Nellie to buy me cowboy ones. She did, a real pair! With slanted heels and inset butterflies of white leather, and every day and every night I was quite simply in paradise! Bridges drove my mother down. I think she brought someone unsavory, probably "the boys." We moved from the main hotel into one of their private bungalows, nestled amongst the hibiscus trees.

"Sweetheart, you are so brown! Like an Indian. This terrible heat. Why do people have this passion for roasting themselves in the sun?"

The first morning, wearing sporty lounging pajamas with kimono sleeves and a wide-brimmed linen hat, my mother typed letters out on our shaded porch. Of course, she had immediately discovered my snake stick and forbidden me to ever again venture beyond the hotel grounds, chastising Nellie and my bodyguard for permitting me so much dangerous freedom. So I stayed in the pool and had a nice day anyway. My precious cowboy boots were safely hidden, just in case.

The radio announced Will Rogers had been killed when his airplane crashed; my mother immediately phoned Brian. She was furious:

"You see what happens when someone is crazy enough to fly? You, who want to be an aviator – you see what happens? Anyway, it's just one of your affectations – buying a plane! Will Rogers was just somebody who told stories, but someday, someone really important will be killed, and then, suddenly, everybody will understand what I have been saying!"

That evening, while katydids sang and the mock orange perfumed the warm air, my mother held court. We listened, while she complained about Lubitsch and the film he was writing for her.

"He is so stupid, he thinks I will do whatever he says just because he is the big comedy director and now the head of Paramount – and Jo is gone. He keeps trying to put his hand up my crotch. He sticks that wet cigar in my face, trying to look passionate. He is such an ugly little Jew! I told him my child was sick in Palm Springs, to get away from him. Gilbert says to ignore him, that my contract calls for Lubitsch to direct the film, and as long as his name is on the credits, he will make sure that it is a success. Papi agrees, but says I have to do the film to get paid. Edington says I must not be off the screen too long after the box-office flop of *Devil Is a Woman*. Lang wants to do the film for me – Barthelmess doesn't say anything, just sulks, he is jealous of Gilbert. Jo always took care of everything. Now, suddenly, I have to do it all myself!"

Waiters arrived from the main hotel with after-dinner coffee. My mother had brought sugared-vanilla crescents from the Viennese bakery that had opened in Beverly Hills. While delicate little moths clung to our screens, basking in the moonlight, we munched, while my mother read us the letter she had written to John Gilbert:

Jack!
    I am sorry to have hurt you – I didn't do it intentionally – as you know – I made a joke – but you were hurt by it.
    Since you started drinking the last time I have been in constant fear and every sign of weakness made me more afraid.
    You have done some things to me – intentionally! – that hurt me terribly – you did them nevertheless because you felt like it. I hurt you without knowing that as a result of it you would ask me to leave your house. You have said to me that in spite of all the pains I had through your weakness you could not understand that I wanted to throw away something so beautiful as the happiness we've had together – and you said that if I could make an end because I was hurt – it would prove that all the happiness didn't mean much to me.
    I say the same words to you! You probably are relieved that you can have all the drinks you want and will probably ruin what I tried to build upon – maybe my method wasn't always right – but be assured that it sometimes was a task and only the most beautiful and unselfish thoughts were behind everything I did.

She had made her usual carbon copy and I went over to the hotel to mail it to my father. One of "the boys" drove Gilbert's letter to his home. He called at the crack of dawn. I heard my mother croon and laugh softly. Then she ordered the car to report to the bungalow and left. She was smiling and seemed happy as they drove off. I made another snake stick and was too. I was glad my mother was returning to stay with Mr. Gilbert – I liked him. People living together had no unusual connotations for me. In our life, Tami lived with my father, von Sternberg lived with us, sometimes so had many others. My mother had not slept every night in our hotel in Vienna, nor in the one in Paris. So why should she not sleep at Mr. Gilbert's house? Adults have a way of assuming that their awareness of sexual connotations are universal. Children first have to know what sex is, before they can make a judgment on its basis. The natural naiveté of children, although a dangerous purity at times, is also a formidable armor against the darker realities of those who have the right to govern their existence.

Clark Gable had discovered the electric charms of Carole Lombard, Gary Cooper was becoming boring so the Countess di Frasso decided to return to Europe and rented her house, her English butler, her cook, her ladies' maids, her housemaids, and her dog to her girlfriend Marlene. I was brought back to Beverly Hills instead of Bel Air and, thereby, found out that we had been moved. From "Spanish somber" to "Hollywood glitter" was some jump! What a house! If a wall didn't have mirrors glued to it, it was covered with tropical birds looking exotic, perched amongst silver-leafed branches. Tables were mirrored, so were lamps and every single door frame. Versailles was prettier, but in reflective glass, we just might have been able to give it considerable competition. The carpeting throughout the house was 1930s "hairy white." The downstairs looked like the floor of a New Zealand shearing shed. Where the floor *could* be seen, it was lacquered black. This edifice boasted a "game room." Here, stalking panthers replaced the ornate birds, jungle foliage "à la Gauguin" the silvered branches, and scattered zebra hides the hairy sheep. Four individual bemirrored backgammon tables stood forever ready, their playing pieces cut from golden agate and milky jade. The dining room seated twenty, at a mirrored table on mirrored chairs. The plumed Audubon display gazed down from yet another dark blue and silver jungle. When that mile-long table was laden with its mirrored candelabra, massive silver, stretched floral centerpiece, and never-ending food, those weird birds staring down at you with their mean red eyes could make you feel very apprehensive. Naturally, our staircase "curved," perfect for Gloria Swanson-type entrances. The upstairs was a bit more subdued. The ornithology exhibits and Hollywood "lush" were confined to where they would impress – downstairs. The whole place oozed decoration, exaggeration, and "money is no object." Outside, gardenia bushes continuously in full bloom, the horticultural triumph of four manic

Japanese gardeners, bordered a meandering garden path that ended at the aquamarine swimming pool and its mandatory pool house. Sheltered by a wall of thick conifers lay the tennis court, in red clay and white-chalked splendor. The lawn had been designed for croquet matches, its perimeter for the serving of English high tea. Circular wrought-iron tables, shaded by that symbol of success, the large, scalloped-edged, cotton-fringed garden umbrella, stood waiting, always ready. Our two-hundred-page inventory listed so many tea services and "covered crumpet dishes," we could have lent some to the Queen of England for her annual Garden Party and never missed them.

My mother once described her friend and landlady as: "One of those rich women who always wanted to be a movie star but is too ugly. So, she sleeps with them and entertains them instead," adding, "but she is nicer and more intelligent than those types of people usually are."

As a child, I thought Dorothy di Frasso a fun-loving lady, who could and did anything she desired. Years later, a lonely one, who wore too much makeup; unlike the other Dorothy, she seemed to have lost her magic shoes along the way. But, while we inhabited her Beverly Hills Oz, it worked its charms. This was the first house where Dietrich gave real parties. Guest lists, engraved invitations, place cards, even finger bowls. Because of its "fan fantasy" interiors, she also permitted the first "at home" photo sessions for the fan magazines, who all believed it was her own decor. That house was probably "overdone ghastly," but my mother and I thought it very glamorous. The croquet gatherings brought in people like C. Aubrey Smith, Ronald Colman, and Clifton Webb, who thought he was Oscar Wilde and worked very hard at being outrageously witty. He became one of my mother's "buddies," too gentlemanly to be one of "the boys," although at times he forgot himself and behaved like them.

The British colony appeared often, more for di Frasso's cook's famous English crumpets and thick raspberry jam than to knock wooden balls through little wickets. Chaplin liked his crumpets dripping with warm butter and honey, smacked his lips, licked each finger, then departed. Our Ronnie preferred jam. George Arliss balanced his delicate teacup and kept score.

One evening, someone brought Clara Bow. Now a "has-been," she still looked pretty in her bright green pajamas, jumped on top of the piano, drank lots of champagne cocktails up there, then spent the rest of the evening throwing up, while her Great Dane, Duke, guarded the powder-room door. That didn't create any problem though, as we had three more powder rooms ready for business. The Barrymores

had a way of arriving singly, then leaving as siblings. Dolores Del
Rio came with her husband, Cedric Gibbons, to play backgammon.
My mother was a Dolores Del Rio fan, she thought her the most
beautiful woman in Hollywood. I had my chance to study her. Not
that beautiful; the mouth – yes! – that was worthy of adulation. When
she was still, she projected such an aura of infinite mystery, it was
hypnotic, but when she "came to life," you smelled tortillas curling
on heated stones, chilies drying in the sun, sweet babies clinging to
her skirts, one suckling at her breast. She would laugh, rattle the
dice, throw, slap the stones into position, then challenge her husband
with her dark eyes. They made an interesting couple. He, the most
respected Art Director in the business, one of the brilliant jewels in
MGM's opulent crown, and she, the Mexican Madonna – draped in
skin-tight satin.

John Gilbert walked among the guests being genuinely charming. He
must have been responsible for most of them being there, they were
not my mother's usual types. I got so many autographs, my book
was nearly full. During this time, I began my "portraits of the great
stars" collection. My mother's guests were really very kind about my
request for an autographed picture. "Please, and could I have a big
one?" Most of them didn't forget to tell their secretaries to choose
a nice pose for them to sign and send to Marlene Dietrich's little
girl. When they arrived in those distinctive photo mailers, I would
get out my magnifying glass and first make sure it had been signed
by hand, not stamped, before I made a frame of passe-partout and
window glass.

Everything during our stay in the di Frasso house was sort of
special. My mother even posed for the very first "leg shots," wearing her little tennis shorts, and allowed di Frasso's Afghan hound
to pose with her, which he did, superbly! The Paramount Publicity
Department was ecstatic, explaining Dietrich's metamorphosis as being
the result of von Sternberg's yoke having been finally lifted from
their star. No one suspected that it was John Gilbert and Countess
di Frasso's decor that made Dietrich suddenly so un-European and
accessible.

Lubitsch must have finally gotten something down on paper, because we
went to the Studio and started "our talks" with Travis.

"Well, you wanted a modern picture, Travis . . . now you have one!
You will see how difficult it is going to be to design fashion that won't
be out of style by the time the film is released!"

"Marlene, my dear, this is not the first time – "

She interrupted him: "But not with Dietrich. Nobody cares what your other stars wear, not even with Lombard. You have put her in that 'nightgown cut' for years and nobody even notices. This will be the most difficult and boring film we have ever done. Without von Sternberg, we will have no mystery. Nothing that will be remembered. Oh, amusing perhaps, with some glamorous moments from you and me, but nothing else. I will bet you a hundred dollars I will have a round face and look like a very beautiful dressed-up doll!"

Travis poured my mother's coffee.

"There is a rumor that Coop will do the film."

"Travis, do you know what he said to Lubitsch? He said that now that Jo was gone, he is 'willing' to work with me again! Have you ever *heard* such egotism? A cowboy? Making judgments? He should go look at *Morocco* and learn some humility! But he never was very bright. We have to design some very good hats for the opening scenes, otherwise it will be nothing but crossing and uncrossing of the legs. And if Lubitsch makes up his mind if the man *can* be in the bedroom or *can't* be in the bedroom with her, we will know what kind of nightgown we will have to make. De Mille can get away with bazooms hanging out all over the screen and his ugly orgies – just because it's 'history' . . . and we have to watch out so a bed doesn't show in the back of me when I talk to a man, fully dressed, at the door! I like Mae, but it is all her fault that we have the Hays Office and this childish censorship. So American – to see sex everywhere and then try to hide it. Travis, have them bring you *Vogue* and *Vanity Fair* and any of the other ones – study them so we won't do anything they have done."

They kissed and we left.

"Papi, I am going to get Gilbert a part in the film, that is now called *Desire*. Don't ask me why – you know how Lubitsch loves 'naughty' titles, like with *Devil*."

It was Sunday, and we were making our calls to Europe. "No, I am at home. Ronnie's boat has a leak and Jack was drunk. I let him sleep and came home to do the calls. Of course, Lubitsch is jealous already. But Jack can play the part of the head of the jewel thieves. It won't matter how old he looks for that – so I will have Lubitsch give him a test. If you need me, call Nellie, she knows where I am. Here's The Child."

I spoke briefly to my father, being careful not to ask about Tami until he had mentioned her first. When he told me that she was out walking

Teddy, I made my polite good-byes and hung up. It felt strange, suddenly speaking German again.

Someone called Huey Long was shot, and the great John Gilbert was made to test for a minor role in a fluff of a film. Senator Long's assassination was the more merciful of the two. My mother was triumphant. She called Paris:

"Papi, Lubitsch okayed the test. I did it with him. Jack didn't want me to – he kept telling me that I, a 'big star,' should not appear in a little test like that. But of course I said I would not let him do it *alone*. Travis and I designed a very good costume, with a big pattern, black and white polka dots, and a perfect hat, so the eye would be on me, distract from Jack's face. I set the lights myself, washed out all his lines. Then we all looked through the camera and told him how young he looked. The hat and the polka dots looked so good, I insisted on stills. We can use them later for publicity – when I have retouched them. I will send them to you, then you can see what I mean – with my lights Jack looks ten years younger."

Paramount cast John Gilbert in the part of Carlos Margoli in *Desire*, and, for my birthday, he gave me a new autograph book. It was garnet red Moroccan leather, with real gold corners, and I treasured it.

My mother kept calling her Pasadena doctor, telling him to go to Gilbert's house and give him some shots, that he was sick again. One day he arrived to pick her up in his car. I had not seen him for a while and the change in him scared me. Now, those glowing coals burned in violet sockets and his smile had become forlorn. I thought my mother was taking care of him. All that beef tea wasn't doing a thing! I wondered if Mr. Gilbert knew a doctor of his own that *didn't* live in Pasadena.

I was glad I had made him an extra-special Christmas present. That year, it was felt bookmarks for everybody, embroidered in motifs suited to the recipient.

My mother decided that Gilbert's little girl should be given a special Christmas by her father, and so we went shopping. I am sure there must have been times when my mother wished she actually had a "little princess," the daughter of frills and bows, the spun-sugar little girl that the fan magazines wrote about. Dietrich often "adopted" such little girls in need of a fairy godmother. She would shower them with feminine gifts – princess dolls, tiny heart-shaped pendants, delicate charm bracelets that jingled, and basked in their wide-eyed gratitude. Eventually, their adoration would begin to pall, and, like

ABOVE: In 1935, Dietrich, now on her own, unhampered by her discoverer, goes public. At lunch with her girlfriend the American Countess Dorothy di Frasso and a very interested Clark Gable.

BELOW: A rare picture. It isn't every day that a woman can be photographed with three lovers at once. Ronald Colman, looking very nonchalant; Richard Barthelmess, the silent-screen idol, smiling bravely; and Brian Aherne, my favorite ersatz father, who had the grace to look embarrassed.

ABOVE: In the rented opulence of the Countess di Frasso's Beverly Hills house, Dietrich poses for fan magazines as if it were hers. BELOW: And by its pool, she permits the first *ever* At Home cheesecake shots of her legs.

ABOVE: John Gilbert, one of the great loves of my mother's life, leaning over her shoulder. Her friends Cedric Gibbons and his wife, Dolores Del Rio— whom my mother thought the most beautiful woman in Hollywood— approved.

BELOW, LEFT: Dietrich and Gilbert, in love, chaperoned by Mary Astor.

BELOW, RIGHT: Loretta Young was one of my mother's pet hates. I wonder why this snapshot was in her private collection, marked "Only for Maria's book."

ABOVE: Party time in Hollywood. Carole Lombard threw a bash at the Fun House on Ocean Pier, where my mother, wearing cute shorts, banged up her knees. She said that Cary Grant came running whenever he saw photographers. Richard Barthelmess was her escort.

LEFT: The theme of the Rathbone costume party was "Come as the one you most admire," so she molded herself into swan feathers and came as the legend of "Leda and the Swan." Her friend Elizabeth Allen came as "Dietrich." They were a sensation.

Mary Poppins when the wind changed, Dietrich was no more. Still, the little girls never forgot her, remembered her always, their childhood innocence intact. John Gilbert's daughter became one of my mother's "little girls."

We bought out Bullock's. We took over the dining room and used the mile-long table to wrap on. Another first for this time: The Wrapping of the Christmas Gifts. The German custom was to allot each family member a surface on which their unwrapped presents were displayed, a sort of tidy church-bazaar effect. No wrapping expenses, no wasted time, no cozy paper mess around the tree – no anticipation, no magic! Very sensible – very Prussian. Now, for the first time, as would be Dietrich's custom for many years to come, she was "wrapping" presents, and they were coded. Silver paper and silver pine cones meant me; gold paper and gold beribboned fragile roses were for Gilbert's daughter, Tinker. My mother never wrote tags, she would tell you your "motif," and automatically you would know which of the thousands of packages were yours. Weeks before Christmas, you would be informed:

"This year, you are 'porcelain bells.' Tell Brian he is 'brown velvet bows.' Clifton has 'gold tassels,' his mother is those birds we found at the stationery store. Ronnie is 'silver leaves.' 'The boys' get silk rope this year, and Nellie is 'baby blue knots.'"

This meant that there were no more porcelain bells available in the whole state of California, nor any of the other mentioned decors. In New York, in the fifties, my mother once placed sculpted Florentine angels, costing fifty dollars apiece, on a hundred and twenty packages, and made Bloomingdale's even richer. Soon after that memorable Christmas wrapping feat, this store remodeled its main floor. On entering, my mother would pause beneath the giant new crystal chandelier, look up, and say:

"That's the one I paid for!"

This first wrapping time, in 1935, we got organized. Scissors tied around our necks, glue pots ready, paper rolls stuck in tall wastepaper baskets, one per color. Two big stacks of presents, Tinker's and mine. Like conscientious elves, we worked for days, immersed in glitter and golden flowers. There were so many boxes, I sometimes got confused whether one was a "pine cone" or a "rose."

"Mutti, I'm sorry – is this one for her or for me?"

"Is it a bracelet with the little hearts or the dogs?"

I peeked into the slender velvet box.

"The ruby hearts."

"That's for her."

When everything was done, Bridges loaded the huge cardboard boxes, brimming with our splendid work, into the car and took my mother and her bounty to Gilbert's house. She arranged his child's gifts that he had never seen under his tree, warned him once more that they were all supposed to be from him, *not* her, and left – so he could enjoy his child's Christmas joy. In the meantime, I wrapped the presents I had made, using the paper I had secretly added to the silver and gold buying spree. I thought it was divine! Little snowmen, in a pretty snowstorm, wearing Dietrich's top hat. Never having seen a real one, I was partial to snowmen. Brian brought his gifts, they were the only ones I didn't know the contents of. He admired our sumptuous wrappings – they did look splendid under the tree the butler had set up by the piano. Although, no music, no surprises – I was now too old for all that anyway – still, we had a nice Christmas that year. My mother cried a little when we talked to her mother and Liesel in Berlin. I got weepy wishing Tami Merry Christmas, but otherwise, we had two pleasant days . . . and *The Merchant of Venice* from Brian was my favorite present.

John Gilbert could not be in *Desire* after all. Before New Year, he suffered a heart attack and the Studio refused to take an insurance risk on such an easily replaceable actor. My mother spent her days preparing clothes at Paramount and being Florence Nightingale up on Tower Road.

"Travis, that wonderful white chiffon we hid . . . now we can use it. Must she wear a 'negligee' in that scene? They are so boring! Everyone wears them, even that ugly Miriam Hopkins."

"Whatever we do, Marlene, it has to be seductive . . . she is trying to get something out of him, or has *that* been changed also?"

"Who knows? If they would let Cooper take his vacation in Mexico instead of Spain, the whole picture could be taken out of Europe and Lombard could play my part. She would be very good in it. Why don't we make a bias cut – in chiffon? Then it will fall against the body . . ."

"We can do a bias cape, maybe border it in fur – to weight it?"

"That's very good."

Travis beamed. She continued.

"But we need a long line underneath. How about putting in some gathering over one knee, so it can break, and continue the line down from the thigh?"

"Dear, what about using some really gorgeous white fox?"

"But double width, otherwise it will photograph 'poor.' We must taper down so the skirt is tight. At least, I am *really* thin for this picture. I told Jack that the one good thing that came out of his heart attack – I don't have to worry about being too fat for the clothes."

"Can we have a long train, dear? Not necessary, but it would give it a pedestal look in the long shots and on the stills."

If you ever have a chance to see *Desire*, take a good look at the white chiffon creation those two consummate artists concocted! Seduction and sublimity make a heady potion. Dietrich leaning against that French door, swathed in fox and chiffon, is quite intoxicating.

We were in Wardrobe, working on the later scenes. My mother had just come over from the Music Department.

"Travis, wait till you hear the song! *Not* to be believed! What has happened to Hollander? – too much Hollywood living? The songs he wrote for *The Blue Angel* were not *great*, but at least they had *something*! And I could sing them – but this! Just listen to this! 'You're here, and I'm here,/With your lips and my lips . . . *awake*!'

"I have to scream the end of that line – he goes up a whole octave! Don't think that is all . . . it goes on, 'In a dream so divine . . .' and something awful like that . . . then the big finale!: full of innuendoes . . . 'Can it be that tonight is *the night*?'

"Can you believe it? . . . There I am, at the piano, in those wonderful black egret-feather sleeves we made, singing this abortion. . . ."

For days, she went around the Studio singing: "Your *ear* and my *ear*, With your lips and my lips . . ."

No one noticed she had substituted "ear" for "here." They thought she was just rehearsing. Travis and I got hysterical. Later, when we filmed that scene, Travis made a special trip over to the set. When she saw we were there, watching, waiting for *the* moment, she actually spoiled a take on purpose, singing loud and clear:

"Your *ear* and my *ear* . . ."

When Borzage, who was the director by that time, yelled, "Cut!" Miss Dietrich was heard to say:

"Oh, did I say ear? I seem to do that all the time. I am so sorry. Shall we try it again? Such a *moving* lyric . . . Oh! Just a moment! What is it again? 'Here' – you're *sure*? Not ear?"

Travis and I were stuffing handkerchiefs into our mouths, and Nellie had sprinted to the portable toilet. She had to go when she laughed too hard . . . just like my mother.

That scene came later, now we were still in preproduction. While *Desire* took shape, I started on Ancient Greece and struggled through long division. We designed and fitted until late at night.

"Travis, she can't wear trousers, but – a man's blazer? . . . Double-breasted, maybe in a blue linen, not too dark, with a straight white skirt.

For that, I have shoes! You won't believe this, but I wore them in Berlin in a play – and they are still modern today! Like the ones you liked so, but in white, with lizard. At least in this film we will see *shoes*!"

"Wonderful, Marlene. We can use mother-of-pearl buttons on the jacket to accentuate the cut. Maybe even a carnation in the buttonhole?"

"If we can get away with it – yes! That whole scene is so stupid, at least this way there will be *something* interesting to look at."

Lubitsch decided to only produce *Desire*, handing the directorial chores over to Frank Borzage, a rotund little man who wore vested business suits, signet rings, and floppy white tongues on scalloped shoes. Travis took one look and immediately ordered a pair for his collection. My mother dubbed Borzage a "mennuble" and threatened to walk off the picture. Edington did some of his fast talking, assured her that, of course, Lubitsch would always be there watching his every move, ready and willing to solve any problems that might arise. My mother calmed down and treated her director through the whole film as though he were Lubitsch's office boy. Fortunately, Borzage was not an egotistical man. He quietly sucked his habitual pipe, listened attentively to everyone, then went about his business of bringing his film in on time and on budget.

Chevalier was off somewhere with Grace Moore. "Another one of his warblers," as my mother put it.

Desire, costarring Dietrich and Cooper, began principal photography.

Gilbert seemed fully recovered. His notes recommenced, some giving her gentle advice. He probably was a more gifted director than he was an actor. I wish she had not been quite so involved in her role as "savior to the afflicted," had listened, and, perhaps, learned. He had much to teach her. She saved only a few of his sweet notes. I wish she had treasured them all:

> Oh, Love Face!
>   I am so happy today, and it's such a nice feeling.
> Remember
> Keep Alive!
> No Placidity in scenes!
> No white mystery!
> No ghost!
> No matter what happens to us – please
> remain an alive animal.
>   I love you

There are so many versions of my mother's role in the death of John Gilbert that it is a hopeless task to attempt to unravel the maze of lies and suppositions. I believe my scenario to be the only one that matches Dietrich's pattern of behavior. Nothing, no matter who says they know for sure, has ever been discovered to change my mind. On the contrary, my mother admitted to me being in his house that night.

Sometime, during the predawn hours of January 9, 1936, John Gilbert began to die. As the first convulsion of the massive coronary hit his chest, he screamed, awakening my mother. She knew immediately what was happening. Lifting the receiver of the house phone, she summoned the Filipino valet, cautioning him not to wake the other servants and that this was an emergency, to enter through the connecting bathroom.

Next, she dialed one of her string of unsavory doctors, who could be counted on to keep their mouths shut. Gilbert's breathing was rapid and shallow. His face had grayed. A film of sweat appeared. Quickly, she dressed and began erasing any evidence that Dietrich had ever inhabited his room. Despite her many indiscretions, scandal had never touched her. Now it was staring her in the face! This was the thirties, a world star, married, the proclaimed epitome of pure motherhood could not be discovered in a lover's bed! Be he alive or . . . dead. The all-powerful Studio, usually so ready to cover up all improprieties of their human property, could decide to invoke the Morality Clause contained in every contract and, thereby, ruin Dietrich professionally. She rushed into the bathroom, collected her things, returned with a wet washcloth, handed it to the distraught servant, ordering him back downstairs to admit the doctor. Gilbert's skin pulled tight against his cheekbones, his eyes glazed.

She dialed Nellie, ordered her to come at once, park at the bottom of Gilbert's driveway, extinguish her lights, and wait. If she managed to escape before the police and press arrived, Nellie's unimportant car might be overlooked. Hers was too famous to go unnoticed. A rapid knock. She ran to unlock the bedroom door. Gilbert's back arched high in agony. The doctor injected a powerful stimulant, not directly into the laboring heart. He was neither skilled enough nor equipped for such an emergency. My mother had stuffed her clothes, toilet articles, cigarettes, lighter, telephone book, alarm clock, my picture into one of the pillow cases – she now grabbed it and ran. Nellie was there, waiting. She jumped into the car, they sped off to Beverly Hills and safety.

I heard the news on the radio. They said John Gilbert died alone. I wondered why. I went to look for my mother. I found her in her bedroom, dressed in a monk's robe of black velvet, arranging dozens of tuberoses into vases placed on every available surface. The room lay in deep shadow. The heavy drapes were drawn and secured with safety pins. Small flames flickered in red-glass votive candles; they stood before

John Gilbert's picture, throwing a soft blush onto that gentle face. In a voice of woe and abject misery, my mother sent me from her room.

"Now I am alone. First Jo, now Jack!"

I was ordered not to disturb her until summoned, and she locked the door behind me. For days, she remained entombed. I can still smell the heavy cloying scent of those tuberoses. It and my mother's gramophone playing Rachmaninoff permeated the house. When she finally emerged, her face was as thin and white as the man's suit she wore. We left for the Studio and work.

This was the first time I witnessed my mother mourning as a widow. In the years to come, she did this so often that by the time her real husband died, her grieving widowhood had become a déjà vu.

Months later, I asked permission to visit John Gilbert's grave. I didn't understand why that made my mother so angry with me. I was forbidden to come to the Studio for a whole week. She wouldn't even talk to me. My favorite bodyguard understood. He drove me all the way to Forest Lawn, where all the stars were buried, and I laid some of our special gardenias on John Gilbert's grave and said my own good-bye. We got back before anyone had missed us.

My mother launched herself into "bereaved-child mothering" and "lost will searching" and her recuperation was complete. My father was kept informed by telephone.

"Papi, the last wife of Gilbert's, that gold-digger Virginia Bruce, she has stolen his last will! . . . Yes! She *has*! She gave them the will he made *before* the heart attack, the one where he leaves *her* everything. Of course, he made a new will! I told him he could not leave everything to that awful woman, that he had to give every-thing to his child! But now, nobody can find that will. So I said 'I *saw* him write it' – so now, of course, everybody is searching and that Bruce woman is shaking in her shoes! I got his Filipino servant a job at the Studio – you know who I mean – in the Art Department. He deserves something. He is so loyal and doesn't *talk*. I also gave him money. Gilbert's child is here. We are taking her to see a movie. Kater is looking in the newspapers for a film good for a child. Papilein, you know, without Jo, Cooper is so much nicer! Tomorrow I am making my chickens for him. Do you know what he wants for dessert? Ice cream! Can you believe that? A grown man? Only Americans eat like children! Now, I have to send Bridges to the Beverly Wilshire Drugstore every day to get ice cream for the dressing-room lunch."

My father must have said something funny, for she chuckled appre-ciatively, then replied:

"Papilein, of course he has enough time to . . . *eat* it. But you know, he is jealous of Lubitsch? . . . Order him some heavy silk pajamas, like yours, from Knize . . . but in white, with dark green piping. Those legs of his are so long, he can't find any here that fit. Travis has his measurements – I will send them to Vienna. Talking of Vienna, did you call Jaray? Did he get the pictures? Did you call Mutti? Did she get the box with the books? I put money in the pages. You never know when she will need *real* dollars – fast! Yesterday I sent off some more of Tami's pills and those injections, so she has enough now for a while to be normal. Here is The Child . . ."

Wills were suddenly so important, my mother decided that *she* needed one. As she typed, I read over her shoulder. She had so few tangible assets, it became a one-page document. To my father, she bequeathed her car, Tami, her clothes, Nellie, her furs, and me, her jewels.

"Oh! Goody! I get to keep the emeralds!" I blurted. My mother whirled, furious – then laughed and phoned "the boys":

"I am writing my will! Of course I have to! You never know – they still haven't found the last will that Gilbert made before he died – that *I saw*. So, now I have to make sure that everyone knows what they are getting. Of course, everything is for Maria. You know what she said? – 'Goody-Goody! I am getting all the jewels!' Can you believe it? A child? She already *knows* how much they are worth? . . . *You* are getting my cuff links, the good ones from Cartier. No, you both can use them. You can get elegant parts with them. Rudi has enough cuff links already."

I listened and felt ashamed. I hadn't meant to sound greedy! I had only been happy to have been granted permanent custody of my green charges. I never did inherit them – they too disappeared, long before the final end.

Now that Jo was no longer with us, everyone seemed to be courting Dietrich. Their daily floral offerings choked the dressing room. We were forced to stack the larger baskets outside, on our stoop, where Mae West "stole" them. She called it "pinching," saying that Dietrich wouldn't miss them anyway.

"Sweetheart – look outside. Has Mae West stolen the flowers again?"

"I think so . . . Mutti, but it isn't *real* stealing. She just thinks if you put them out that you don't want them."

"Well, they still belong to *me*. From now on, we put only the ugly ones outside!"

It became a game they played. My mother got rid of the hated gladiolas, delphiniums, and roses, and Mae had fun decorating her dressing room with her floral loot. I never told my mother that long-stemmed red roses

were our neighbor's favorite flower. That became a private joke between
Mae West and me. They had other games as well: One morning, my
mother, half-hidden behind the screen door, kept peering down the street.
Travis had told her of a new negligee, an elaborate extravaganza of silver
lamé and lace, bordered in black fox, that would be delivered to West's
dressing room. The Wardrobe girl was just rounding the corner when
my mother spotted her. She sprinted along the sidewalk, intercepting the
startled girl, snatched the heavy garment bag from her arms, saying:

"Miss West asked me to accept this for her. She hasn't arrived yet!"
and sprinted back inside our dressing room, calling to me:

"Quick! Stand outside and watch! Tell me the second Mae West
drives up!"

"Mutti," I whispered urgently, through the screen door, "her car is
just pulling up."

Dietrich, resplendent, trailing lamé and fox, positioned herself before
Mae West, who screeched: "That's *mine*! That's my brand-new hostess
gown!"

"Oh, no, angel! It can't be! Travis made this just for *me*! Do you like it?
Not *too* vulgar?" She turned slowly in front of the irate little woman.

"Now just hold it! You mean to tell me that Travis Banton dared to
copy one of my designs for you?" Suddenly, her sharp eyes noticed my
mother clutching all that extra material over her not-so-ample chest, and
her voice resettled into its famous creamy register:

"W-e-e-l-l-l, sweet thing, it does look mighty swanky on that pretty
body of yours. Let's you and me go inside and discuss li'l ol' Travis's
treachery!"

In perfect syncopation, they turned, wiggled their tidy bottoms, and
sashayed into Mae's dressing room, closing the door firmly behind them.
The appreciative minions left behind on the sidewalk applauded.

My mother disappeared often into Mae West's dressing room during
this time. Sometimes George Raft or Cooper joined their pranks, but
mostly they enjoyed amusing each other. I had a lot of time to stuff
myself at the Commissary and investigate who was working on my
home lot.

Fred MacMurray was always around. He seemed to be in every film
Paramount turned out that year. Harold Lloyd was filming. W. C. Fields,
Lombard, Margaret Sullavan, the brunette Bennett, Burns and Allen of
radio fame, Zasu Pitts, and a funny woman who had arrived from the
New York stage called Ethel Merman. She had refused to allow the Studio
to change her name, kept muttering how ugly she looked on the screen,
and how much she hated Hollywood. I watched her work and thought
she was great. She was just frightened and had no von Sternberg to protect

her. I had a lot of favorites, usually those my mother disliked. I was a Loretta Young fan, especially when she was being "lyrically devout." I saw De Mille's *The Crusades* four times. For some unknown reason, she was one of Dietrich's all-time hates. For nearly sixty years, one could not drive into Beverly Hills without being subjected to Dietrich's special venom regarding this lady:

"See that big, ugly church on the corner over there? Loretta Young built that. Every time she 'sins,' she builds a church. That is why there are so many Catholic churches in Hollywood!"

I didn't care. I got a lovely autographed picture from her, but I did not tell my mother. Building churches was a beautiful thing to do, I thought, no matter what the reason.

Desire was such an easy film, I was called to the Studio so rarely, I got through all of Ancient Greece. Occasionally I escaped my studies of the Olympian gods to mingle among the real ones. The day my mother shot the "driving scene," I was on the set to witness the fun. No one suspected she didn't know how to drive. Coolly serene, she sat behind the wheel of a slick little roadster, minus its wheels. It had been jacked up before the rear-projection screen. The moving road behind her, the crew members jiggling the chassis off-camera, the wind machine fluttering the chiffon swag on her peaked hat, would give the required effect on the screen that Dietrich was driving happily along the country roads of Spain. The film began to roll behind her, the wind blew, the car bounced, the road curved to the left – Dietrich swung the steering wheel to the right! The road made a sharp right, she turned . . . left! She swung the wheel as though she were steering a schooner around Cape Horn during a typhoon.

Borzage yelled, "CUT!"; the road stopped running, the wind died, the grips straightened, resting their backs. Borzage strolled to her side.

"Miss Dietrich, there seems to be a problem with the synchronization between you and our rear projection. It is necessary to turn in the same directions as the image behind you. It is also necessary to slow down at certain moments and shift gears. Could you move your head slightly, to appear more relaxed?"

"You are joking! If I move my head the wind will blow my hat off . . . and the lamp over there by the boom will throw a shadow across my left shoulder!" Never taking her eyes off her mirror next to the camera, she spotted a curl slightly out of alignment. "Nellie!"

Nellie ran into the shot, black comb poised. Borzage faded back into his safe shadows. All morning, like a slapstick routine, Dietrich and her road missed each other. We broke for lunch. Borzage was seen heading toward Lubitsch's office. My mother grabbed my arm and whispered:

"Sweetheart, get Hank! Tell him to come to the dressing room!"

ABOVE: My mother arranged to have Paramount test the great John Gilbert for a small part in her film *Desire*. She designed a costume to distract the eye from what she called "his aging face." You would never have known she was supposed to be in love with him at the time.

BELOW: Dietrich and her only Studio pal, Mae West. They were friends for years but never saw each other off the Paramount lot.

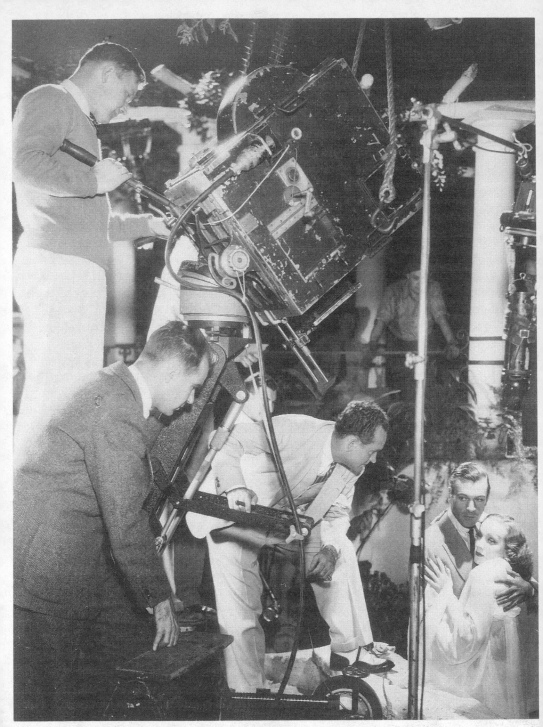

OPPOSITE, TOP: With Gary Cooper during the filming of *Desire*, 1936.
OPPOSITE, BOTTOM: One of my favorite Dietrich faces. She is in the Paramount Commissary, wearing her celebrated emerald collection, reading her script.
ABOVE: Shooting a tender, intimate love scene in Hollywood.

In costume for *Desire*, signing autographs for VIP visitors to the set. She wore some of her own jewels in this movie about jewel thieves; special Pinkerton guards sometimes outnumbered the crew.

I ran. Hank was one of her favorite grips but had been assigned to the Crosby picture instead of ours. I brought him back with me.

"Hank. I have one hour to learn how to drive a car. Have you got one off the lot?"

"Sure, Miss Dietrich. I got it parked around the corner on Melrose. But why don't you use your own car? It's parked in front!"

"And have everyone see? Come. . . . We go," and we scurried into our black hearse to be driven outside the Paramount gates, where a burly man in overalls taught Dietrich to shift and I kept track of the time. When we reported back on the set, she had it down pat. Borzage did not ask questions, he was just relieved. Hank had been sworn to silence, given a generous check, a long kiss, and drifted back to Crosby in a golden haze. That evening, a scarf tied around her head, my mother sat up front, next to Bridges, and watched him drive us home. Before falling asleep, she said:

"How can anyone want to drive a car for a living? But you know, it is interesting that something that is so dangerous can be so *boring*!"

On the last day of *Desire*, my mother strode into Travis's office, came to a dead stop in front of his desk, her hand outstretched. He too had seen the daily rushes and was ready for her. Extracting a crisp one-hundred-dollar-bill from his elegant billfold, he placed it on her palm. As her fingers snapped shut around it, she laughed. Dietrich loved collecting on sure bets. *Desire* was the first film of my mother's I enjoyed as a spectator. It was fun, a real cute movie, not an awe-inspiring experience. In my opinion, she had made the transition from "art" to "entertainment" rather well. It would take four years before she did it again.

Paramount, expecting *Desire* to be a Dietrich success, gave her a week off, then rushed her into the next film.

"Have you heard the title? No one will buy a ticket to see Dietrich in something called *Hotel Imperial*, and me – another peasant! How many 'braid hairdos' can we invent?"

We were in the dressing room at night, working quietly with Nellie. My mother sipped her strong coffee.

"I thought – finally after *Desire*, things would be better. Why – why must I be forced to do an old Pola Negri script? Edington says that only Lubitsch can produce my films. My contract says so."

Nellie interrupted her.

"The latest rumor is that he is leaving Paramount."

"Good! Then I don't have to make this stupid picture!"

For the first time in days, she looked happy.

"But it is not a bad idea that this Henry Hathaway has. When it was first called, even worse, *I Loved a Soldier*, he told me about it. Not bad his idea to let love transform her in front of the camera. It will not save the film, but it is a good idea. Making the transition, that's easy. First we do no false lashes, use only a light brown mascara on my own, do a thin mouth, powdered down. Leave off the nose line but shadow the sides. Set the key light lower – make a baby face. Also, no inside white line in the eyes, so they will be very round. Then we slowly add . . . first the mouth fuller, then the nose thinner, then *very* slowly, we bring the mystery into the eyes, move the key light higher for each take until we have – Dietrich. All that is *easy*. They think it is a *big idea*, but that alone will not save the script."

She was right. Fortunately, Lubitsch did leave Paramount, Dietrich invoked her contractual right and walked off the film. I would have loved to have seen her do that transformation though.

To avoid irate Paramount executives and Louella Parsons's insistent telephone calls, we escaped to a small mountain village of log cabins, Ward Bond types in checked flannel shirts, Marjorie Main beginghamed ladies, and tall dark pines encircling a glacial lake. I loved Lake Arrowhead. My mother thought it overdone "rural America." The first time Bridges drove us to the general store, she took one look at the cracker barrel by the potbellied stove and asked:

"What film are you shooting today? Is Rin Tin Tin in it?"

While my mother ordered thick sweaters to be delivered "immediately" from Bullock's and cooked gallons of lentil soup to keep me warm, I collected symmetrical pine cones, fed glossy squirrels, lay on pungent pine needles looking at postcard skies. If I stayed very still for a long, long time, blue jays and crested cardinals came to rest a while on the pine branches above me. Sometimes a trout would break the still surface of the lake, then, in an explosion of color, off the birds flew to decorate another tree.

During this time, our address was changed. I never did know why we were moved from "fan fantasy" to "stucco yuk." Again, my mother must not have seen the house prior to our arrival, for when we pulled up to the painted door with its horseshoe knocker, she rolled down the glass partition separating us from the chauffeur and asked:

"This is it? This is the new house they found? Are you sure you have the correct address?"

Inside, all was "studied gloom." Lots of faded pea-soup green velveteen, shellacked mahogany, and floral throw rugs. The backyard was exactly that – a yard. If there had ever been a lawn, which was doubtful, nothing remained except scattered patches of graying crabgrass. A clump of azaleas withered decoratively against a peeling fence. The only concession to the Beverly Hills address was a concrete tennis court by the compost heap. We didn't stay in this house for long and never missed it after we left. Its importance stems from the two memories it invokes – my first party and the making of our first color film, *The Garden of Allah*.

Unexpectedly, my father arrived, had long meetings with Edington, approved of the new contract with David Selznick, stood over my mother as she signed for her first picture away from her "home studio" since becoming a star, did her taxes, persuaded her to accept the lucrative offer from Alexander Korda for a film to be made in England, checked my schoolbooks, replenished our wine cellar, discovered a superior source of ice cream for Cooper, found that the butcher was charging too much for our weekly supply of soup bones, and left.

Tami had not accompanied him. She was being given a luxurious "rest cure" in an exclusive spa. My mother said that it was very expensive to send her there, but worth it . . . if she learned, finally, to control herself. It was the beginning of many such "cures" that Tami would be made to endure over the next ten years. After a while, this polite wordage was dropped and "treatment" or "sanitarium" took its place. Finally, those too were replaced with an even more suitable phrase – "mental institution."

To break a human being is a slow process. To injure a mind beyond its border of recovery takes concentrated dedication. The people I called "parents" were thorough – they took their time.

IT FELT STRANGE arriving at Selznick's Monticello, instead of our old Paramount gate. When we exited our new studio after the first conference with the costume designer, Dietrich breathed fire. She waited, mouth tightly set, until we were safely in the car, then she issued her order:

"Bridges! Drive straight to Paramount!"

Nothing further was said until she swept into Wardrobe:

"Travis! Tell your secretary not to allow anyone in and lock the door. We have trouble!" She lit a cigarette and paced. I sat out of the way.

"Now listen! That so-called 'designer' that Selznick hired for the film is a complete idiot! I tried to get one of the sketches to take out with me to show you, but he is tricky. He said 'they have to stay on the lot – boss's orders!' That's how he speaks, a vulgar man. We will have to make the clothes here, in secret; then smuggle them over to Selznick. We can make up a story that they are my private dresses and that because they are the right color, I am going to wear them in the picture – "

Travis tried to stop her: "Marlene, we can't – "

"Don't tell me *you* are suddenly going to go with the rules! No one will know what we are doing. You will be making private dresses for me, like always. No one will think they are for another studio. . . . I will tell that idiot and Selznick *I* have the perfect things to wear for the film. They are so dumb, they will believe it. Now . . . we must order that film in color that everyone is talking about and see what they did *wrong*."

When my mother screened *Becky Sharp*, she was so intent on the new three-color Technicolor process, she hardly noticed that one of her pet hates, Miriam Hopkins, was its star.

"Everybody is so excited to have suddenly *color*! So, of course, they use too much of it!" she observed.

The true artist in Travis Banton had caught fire and left his scruples far behind.

"Marlene, your film plays in the Sahara desert. Use light chiffon in the same color as the sand! If they can print pastels, it will be the first time it has ever been done on film!"

Triumphantly, she turned to me: "You see! Now you know why I rushed back here to him! That is how a true artist thinks! They will wet their pants when they hear I am going to wear beige! They will say it *can't* be done – because they don't know how to shoot it. But you know who does – JO! He will know!"

Somewhere, somehow, my mother found where von Sternberg was, called and told him what she needed. Again we returned to Paramount.

"Travis, now listen! Jo says: 'To shoot color there should be a third camera to shoot in black and white. Lighting for color, you must first see it as light and shade. Until new cameras are invented and the technique is perfected,' he says, 'all photography is based on the balance between light and dark'! Isn't he wonderful? On a telephone! Miles away! He knows – what here, they are all still learning! I am going to tell Edington to tell Selznick that I insist on having a black-and-white cameraman also. Selznick is already looking at me with cow eyes."

The Garden of Allah was doomed from the beginning. A ludicrous story, with a Polish director trained by Stanislavsky in Russia, who believed he was Rasputin dressed up as Stroheim, leading a cast of European hams. A tower of Babel, each one with a different accent as thick as old cheese. Joseph Schildkraut, a master of the art of overacting, convinced he was upholding his famous theatrical name, was given a betasseled fez and left to his own thespian devices. To watch Schildkraut being "beguiling," a flower tucked behind one ear, playing a sort of effeminate Moroccan Fagin, is an experience to be avoided. A beturbaned Basil Rathbone, ever so long-nosed British Empire, petrified astride a wild Arabian stallion, and Dietrich, meticulously coiffed, looking like a dress dummy from a Berlin department store, are no better. On the other hand, Charles Boyer, playing a morose, defrocked, uncelibate monk as though he were a French headwaiter, his toupee marcelled like a gangster's moll, that might be worth the price of admission just to see how that could be possible! If one sees *The Garden of Allah* in the context of high camp, it can be very amusing. Those of us involved in the making of this film were in deadly earnest, except for my mother, who vacillated between anger and ridicule. The latter often helped her to endure the filming of assured flops. She was making a terrible picture that had absolutely nothing to redeem it, and she knew it. As she would in the many mediocre films to come, she compensated by overemphasizing the one category she could control – the way she looked. She tried everything and anything – burnooses of silver lamé, heavy shimmering satin, capes, and turbans, achieving nothing but an unrelated look of draped confusion. The clandestine sessions with Travis were too difficult to be completely successful. To keep her secret, she was forced to accept some of the designs executed by Dryden. If you ever see *The Garden of Allah*, take a look at Dietrich in that jodhpur outfit. You really can't miss it. It is nearly the ugliest costume in the film, a perfect example of the credit costume designer's mediocrity. His floor-length satin number is no better. Then, take a look at the way the desert breeze sculpts palest silk chiffon against Dietrich's body, transforming her into a "Winged Victory" amongst the sand dunes. It is easy to spot the genius of Banton and Dietrich. Together, they were unique.

I was also in this gem. For some reason, my mother allowed me to be one of a group of girls who filled the background of the convent scene. All I remember is the weight of the false braid Nellie plaited into my hair, the snottiness of the professional child actors, the "convent" uniform bloomers that itched, and the seventy-five dollars I was paid for my day's work. I spent it all on a huge bottle of perfume for my mother, which she gave to the maid.

When I was not at our new studio, watching everybody being ridiculous, I was panting and sweating. My new tennis teacher had been given strict orders to slim me down or else! He would whiz balls into alternate corners, making me run as fast as my chubby legs would carry me. At the age of "nearly" twelve, I had hit puberty with a bang! I had heard my mother so often describe "fat" people as being "ugly," that I was certain she was ashamed of the way I looked. So I ran as hard as I possibly could, weighed myself at least ten times a day, never lost an ounce, and was so miserable at my hopeless failure that I just had to make myself a peanut butter and jelly sandwich!

"You are going to a party for 'children,' " my mother announced. "Bridges will deliver you there at seven o'clock and pick you up at ten." *Children?* What children? I didn't know any! What would they expect? What was one expected to do? I was scared and ran to ask Nellie what children did at "children's" parties.

"Well, honey . . . you play pin the tail on the donkey."

"How does one do that?"

Nellie was a bit out of her element. She had no children, but tried her best:

"Well . . . they tack up a big picture of a cute donkey on the wall . . . then everybody gets a tail with a pin. Then they blindfold you, turn you around a couple of times so you get good and dizzy, then they point you in the right direction and you have to try to pin your tail where it belongs."

I stared at her.

"Why?"

That shook her a bit.

"So you can win a nice prize! Oh! They do all sorts of great things at kids' parties. Like . . . um . . . musical chairs. I'm sure you will play musical chairs!"

"Can you teach me how to play that, please?"

"Oh, honey! It's easy. . . . All you have to do is run around some chairs while the music plays. But when it stops, you have to sit down quick! Or you're out!"

"Nellie – are you sure? Just – run and sit? What do I do with my tail?"

"Oh, no, no! The donkey game has nothing to do with musical chairs . . . and you don't really have to run, just skip. It's fun! Really!"

I was so sure that Nellie must have gotten it all wrong, I went to ask Travis.

"What fun! Your first party! What are you going to wear? Does your mother want me to make a nice party dress for you? I'll give her a ring. You will love drop the handkerchief. Only don't get caught! Or you will be IT!"

I was used to professional discussions, thinning eyelashes – maybe a little excitement when kidnappers lurked, but this sounded like some junior Olympics!

The big day came. My mother washed my hair, using her own shampoo. Nellie put in a finger wave and secured a large butterfly bow on top of my head. At seven precisely, I was delivered to a small house somewhere in Hollywood. My teacher shoved me into the gaily lanterned garden and disappeared to gossip in the kitchen. The place was full of non–grown-ups who seemed to know each other. They laughed and chatted, making up comfortable groups. They sounded so American, I was sure my accent would show. I drew back into the shadows of the porch.

"Were you invited?" a slippery voice said from somewhere. I turned in its direction and answered it:

"I don't know. My mother just told me I was going."

"Who's your mother?" the voice was curious.

"Miss Marlene Dietrich."

"Oh, boy! She's great! She's really famous! Do you like being the daughter of a famous movie star?"

I hesitated. No one had ever asked me that before. I had nearly answered "no" without knowing why I would want to say that. It surprised me. The voice slipped about the shadows of the old-fashioned porch:

"Do you hate being fat? Do you hate your stupid dress?"

"Yes! And how! But how do you know that? And where are you?"

A chuckle gurgled, the porch swing creaked.

"Over here. Come on, sit here. What's your name?"

"My real name is Maria. But nobody calls me that except when they are angry at me. Most of the time I am 'Sweetheart.'"

"Gee – who calls you that?"

"My mother."

"You like that?"

"I don't know. My mother calls a lot of people 'sweetheart.' It doesn't really mean anything. Sometimes she calls me Angel, and sometimes I am The Child. She calls me what she wants to."

It was nice and cool on the porch. The children were having a good time in the garden.

"Who brought you? Your father?"

"Oh, no. Our chauffeur, my teacher, and my bodyguard."

"What do you need a bodyguard for?"

"I was going to be kidnapped, once. You know? Like the Lindbergh baby? We got real ransom notes and the FBI came with guns! But nobody ever came to get me. My mother thinks they still will someday, but she is only afraid in America."

"You're making it up! I don't see any bodyguard!"

"No! It is true! Really! He is hiding behind the trees. He does that all the time."

We sat, dangling our legs, side by side, the swing creaked as we swayed slowly back and forth.

"It's my party." The voice had lost its pretty lilt.

"It is? Then why are you sitting here all alone? Don't you like your own party?"

"I'm tired. I worked today. I'm in the *movies*."

"You are? How wonderful! What's your Studio?"

"MGM."

"I'm Paramount. But yours is my favorite. They make the best pictures. What do you do?"

"I sing. I act too – and tap. I'm being 'groomed for Stardom'!"

I turned and took a good look at my companion. She wasn't "Shirley Temple sugarplum-pretty" at all! Big brown eyes in a little white face. Her front teeth jutted forward, giving her mouth a sweet pucker. She looked . . . cute, vulnerable, and very, very real.

"Do you like being 'groomed'?"

"No! It's horrible! They pinch me and measure me and weigh me and won't let me eat. Everybody fusses, everybody touches me – DO THIS, DO THAT, DO IT RIGHT, DO IT AGAIN, BE GOOD OR THEY WILL DROP YOU. When I sing, they stop. They leave me alone. Then it's great! But I get scared. Maybe the boss will decide not to make me a *star*."

"You will be a star! I know it! A really big one, just like my mother. Even bigger, because she can't sing very well at all. You can even tap! Do you have a key light?"

"They tried it but it made me look fatter."

"They just put it too low. You have to check that yourself. When you sing, don't let them light you for a tight close-up – your facial expression will have to be too constricted and you will feel uncomfortable and that will show on the screen."

The smell of cooking frankfurters wafted our way.

"I wish I could have a hot dog! But I am not allowed to," sighed the voice longingly.

"Listen. Would it be all right with your mother if I asked for two?"

"You're an 'important guest.' She'll give you anything you want!"

"Okay, then. What do you like on your hot dog?"

"How do you like yours?" the voice tingled with excitement.

"You'll *love* it. First, I put mustard, then ketchup, then the onions and the relish, then another squirt of mustard. Okay?"

"Swell! And Coca-Cola, lots of potato chips, and don't forget the cole slaw! And make sure no one follows you back here!"

I found a cardboard box by the barbecue pit and took everything I could get my hands on, even corn-on-the-cob, dripping in butter, made a careful detour by way of the garage, to lose any unexpected "tail," and arrived back at our swing, laden and in the clear. We feasted. We giggled. We told each other secret truths. We became important to each other, we became friends. We rarely met. Sometimes it was years, but when we did, instantly, without hesitation, we again became two little fat girls sitting on a back-porch swing.

"Well? Did you like Judy Garland's party?" my mother asked as I walked in the door. I chose my words carefully. This was not a new dog – this was my first very own friend. I wanted to keep her. I said what I knew my mother was waiting to hear:

"Yes, it was very nice. Thank you for letting me go, Mutti. But I like our parties better. They are much more interesting."

My mother was very pleased. She even mentioned that I might be allowed to go to another "party for just children" someday. I didn't sleep for a long time that night. I had so much to think about. Also, I wondered if I should tell Nellie that donkey tails was passé and something weird called spin the bottle was in.

AN ADVENTURE! A real live adventure! We were going on "location." Nowadays, we would be shipped to Africa. In those days, we went to the "Sahara" in the state of Arizona. The stars were to be housed in an air-conditioned hotel in Yuma, the company in a tent city being erected amongst the sand dunes of the Arizona desert . . . miles out of town.

My mother prepared for our exodus as though we would never return. With the intensity of a field marshal, she assembled her troops for battle. The dressing room became our headquarters, Paramount studio – our supply depot. Bullock's delivered cavernous trunks that we filled with enough "maybe needed" makeup and hair preparations to supply fifty remakes of *War and Peace*. So convinced was she that the savage Indians of Arizona were ignorant of the existence of toilet paper that she bought six cases, marking the cartons: "Garden of Allah – Marlene Dietrich – Bathroom, Private."

It was a very long drive to the little whistle-stop town of Yuma. While my mother sterilized toilets and reorganized our hotel, I was sent ahead into the desert with my charges: "Dressing Room Trunks" – Nos. 1, 2, 3, and 4.

Canvas flapped in the hot wind. Like something out of Kipling, tents stretched among the sand dunes as far as my eye could see. Except for the maze of wooden walkways, the trucks, generators, reflectors, arc lamps, sound booms resting lopsided in the fine sand, I expected Gunga Din to materialize. Filming "on location" is always a little like being on military maneuvers. Our locale gave it added drama.

Nellie, stolen from Paramount by what devious tactics I never knew, arrived, comb poised, and we went to work. My mother became so busy leading the actors in daily mutiny against the dialogue that I was granted my plea to be allowed to move out of the hotel and join the crew. She also seemed involved with a gentleman sent out to us by the Studio. His official title was rather vague, but he was slim and "understated New England." I knew that would appeal to her. If his presence made it possible for me to remain out in the desert and not be forced to return to the hotel, I was on his side one hundred percent, whoever he was.

Bugles didn't blow reveille, truck engines did. When I heard those mighty motors cough up their nightly ration of sand, I knew my time had come! The Pre-Dawn Patrol was moving out! In my precious cowboy boots and resurrected snake stick, I reported to the Snake and Scorpion Detail. It was our duty to secure whatever dune had been designated for that day's shoot. It was our job to clear the area of all that scurried, crawled, and slithered. The really lethal, those that walked erect, were not included in our "search and find" orders. Bundled up against the fierce desert night, hands protected by tough leather gloves, our flashlights playing polka dots, we would search in the sand, probing for those vulnerable creatures, who, unable to adjust their body temperature, lay sluggish from the cold, waiting for the sun to warm them back to life. We did not kill our catch, we kept them caged and had quite a lovely little zoo by the time we were recalled.

After us came the carpenters, with their platforms and walkways to support the cameras, sound booms, generators, star dressing rooms, portable toilets, tents, people, and the precious director chairs. As *The Garden of Allah* was one of the first exterior pictures to be filmed in color, we depended on natural light. It decreed when we could film. To catch the translucency of the shell-pink desert dawns, the blood-orange reds of the sunsets, we worked at any time and as long as possible. Whenever the "light was right," everyone had to be instantly ready and in position. Nature had a way of escaping. She also took no notice of union rules. The intense heat also governed our lives. The 130 degrees in the shade made working between eleven and three impossible. Even if the director had wanted to, he couldn't: The film would melt! Many things were learned the hard way. As was the custom under normal conditions, the site of the next day's filming was chosen at the end of the previous day's work.

"That sand dune – over there – the big one on the left. We'll set up there for tomorrow."

Next day, at the crack of dawn, men and equipment were ready to roll, but . . . where to? Where was that dune? The desert had a way of moving her mountains right from under your nose. We played hide-and-seek with sand dunes for eight weeks. An assistant to an assistant director of an assistant director was given the new title of "Dune Watcher." He was such a conscientious young man, when everyone went to eat, he wouldn't leave, kept right on watching his desert until one of us came to relieve him. It felt sort of silly, sitting there waiting to catch a sand dune moving. After I did it a few times, I rather liked it; it was a very relaxing occupation, sort of Zenlike. And sandstorms! For two weeks, every day at precisely two p.m., they hit us. They roared through our canvas town, determined to destroy it. The howl of those winds had an angry sound! Suddenly . . . they stopped . . . dead! Utter silence, very eerie, like after an earthquake. Then came the blowing of many noses, the coughing, spitting, cursing, and the clang of shovels as an entire motion-picture company began its daily task of digging itself out. Then . . . the gasps! Each time, it took you by surprise! Each time it shook you. You looked . . . and the world had changed! The desert had moved toward a new horizon.

At first, water was trucked out to us once a day, then twice, and, finally, three times. Although an entire laboratory had been set up, the film was found to be too sensitive to be developed under those conditions and had to be driven back to Hollywood for processing. The infirmary was kept busy behind the lines. Our specialties were sunstroke, blistered skin, diarrhea, infected eyes, and lacerated shoulders. For some reason, the camels hated the Arabian horses. To emphasize their loathing, they spat at them whenever they came near. Those high-strung aristocrats retaliated by rearing into the air, hoping to slice those ships-of-the-desert in half with their razor-sharp hooves. The handlers, usually caught in the middle of these grudge fights, ended up having their eyes washed and their shoulders sewn. The cowboys, looking very Valentino-ish in their Arab disguises, could handle those crazed horses, but the mounted actors trembled whenever a camel was led into a scene. Everyone continually searched for an unoccupied patch of man-made shade and sweated profusely. My mother, dry as melba toast, fussed with her already too perfect hair and concentrated on her campaign to force Selznick to allow the dialogue to be rewritten – her way. Considering that one of her lines, repeated twelve times in the script, was "Only God and I know what is in my heart," she had a point. My mother just went about it the wrong way. But then, Dietrich never believed in using honey to catch her flies; vinegar it was for her douches and vinegar it was for her flies. Boyer only worried about his toupee. It refused to stay put, perspiration made it come unstuck until my mother carried it back to Yuma one day and cleaned its hair-lace with gasoline. The next morning, shampooed and marcelled, she glued it to his head using half a bottle of spirit gum. She did such a good job, it stuck through the whole morning. Boyer was thrilled – until the close-ups of one of their inane embraces, when the toupee suddenly popped loose, dumping a torrent of accumulated perspiration into Dietrich's upturned face! We broke for two hours and lost the light while she redid an entire Technicolor makeup. From then on, whenever she knew Boyer had to bend over her, she first patted his head, making sure there was no little Niagara Falls lying in wait for her.

Our shooting script called for a "a crystal pool, encircled by waving palms" . . . an "oasis in the vast Sahara." My mother phoned Travis:

"Now . . . you *must* come. You will not believe this! It is getting funn-e-ee! . . . They are building an oasis! . . . Yes! Of course there isn't a real one in Arizona. There isn't one like this in the real Sahara either! If Jo could only see this. . . . Remember in *Morocco*? How wonderful he made the desert with nothing? . . . Of course, that Selznick goes by his precious script and says, 'Build an oasis!' They are digging a hole big enough for ten swimming pools! And they keep falling into it with sunstroke. Boleslawski keeps throwing up. . . . They think he drank poisoned water, but I say it is the script! You cannot imagine what it is like. He is a bad director when he is *well* . . . now . . . I just laugh. When you come, bring me one of those new 'home movie' cameras that Kodak has invented. Bring a lot of film for it . . . I have to record this abortion on film! Also, bring me sauerkraut and some black bread. All they have here is American Kotex."

Travis never came to visit us, but he sent a studio car with the things she had ordered. My mother loved her little movie camera. It became a new item on our dressing-room list. For a few years, she was never without it.

When our "pool" was ready, the palm trees arrived. They came, bouncing happily along in convoy, transported to us courtesy of the California desert. When they were planted around our "crystal pool" they looked a little un-Moroccan, but they waved attractively in the slight breeze, and by then, who cared about authenticity! Some of those scraggly mastodons had arrived still clutching their dates to scaly bosoms; the nurserymen gave me a whole handful. The bigwigs didn't get any – we, of the crew, munched them all in secret.

My mother always believed that horses belonged only on racetracks, preferably running very fast, while looking *very* beautiful. To ride one, as a "civilian," for pleasure, she considered a complete waste of time and, therefore, anathema. So, the stuntwoman, dressed in a duplicate of Dietrich's costume of thick wool jodhpurs, twelve-inch cummerbund, and inverted-chamber-pot turban, galloped into the oasis and stopped on her marks.

"Cut!"

Our Dune Watcher approached.

"Miss Dietrich, we are ready for you now," he breathed in awe.

My mother walked up to the horse. The scene would now continue with her dismounting. A slight problem . . . first, she had to get up onto the horse's back. I, who had been taught to ride by the stuntmen and, through their kindness and infinite patience, had progressed all the way to bull-dogging, watched. I had taught her the graceful slide from the English saddle, but she had refused to learn how to mount, saying that as it was not in the scene, it was not necessary. The grip placed a box at her feet, ready to help her.

The box began to sink into the sand, the horse shied, the handler stepped to the horse's head, Dietrich gave him one of her "Prussian officer" looks, he came to attention, tightening his hold on the bridle. The box was repositioned, began sinking, the horse jumped. Dietrich switched her look and nailed that skittish little mare right to the ground. The searing hot sand might have burned her trim ankles, but that mare stood ramrod still and never moved again – that horse knew a Dietrich Look when she felt one! The cameras rolled, our star slid expertly down onto the ground into the waiting arms of her costar, and one of the most boring scenes in motion-picture history was enacted to the ecstatic satisfaction of our director, Boleslawski, who died soon after the film was completed. My mother, on hearing the news of his death, intoned:

"We all should have died after *The Garden of Allah*. But *he* should have died *before* the film!"

That "oasis" day, after the seventh take, she looked up at the sky, checked the light, knew we were losing it, and decided to end the day's fiasco. She breathed, "A-a-a-ah" and fainted. Dietrich never fainted! Anything so lacking in control didn't suit her. In later years, she passed out a lot, but that had nothing to do with fainting. Actually, Selznick's

Publicity Department gave her the idea. She had been furious at the press releases:

PICTUREGOER Weekly

Marlene Dietrich felt slightly faint as she stood up and stepped out of the meagre shelter of the sun-umbrella. . . . The short walk was an effort for her, but she struggled on, trying to smile, trying to let no one know how she felt. Everyone else probably felt the same way, in this blazing heat. . . .

She reached the wide doorway of the large tent, resisted the temptation to grasp the canvas for support. . . . Her old friend, Charles Boyer, with whom she was to make the scene, warned her, with a smile, that this "take" would be an endurance contest. She tried to smile in return, as she took her place before the camera. She had a flash of pity for Charles, in his heavy suit.

There were black dots gyrating before her eyes. . . . Director Richard Boleslawski, quick in his perceptions, asked: "Do you feel all right, Marlainah?"

She nodded – and then, suddenly, limply, she dropped. Marlene, for all her will power, had fainted.

She had called Selznick to complain: "I am *not* some delicate female who droops. That 'old lady,' Boyer, does that enough for everybody. He puts ice bags on his wrists! Even the camels are dying of the heat, while I sit under the hair-dryer! I resent you releasing stories without my approval that make me look like one of those wilting flowers that think they are professionals and are only amateurs."

Selznick had calmed her down, promising more heroic press releases in the future.

Now, Nellie, seeing my mother prone on the sand, shrieked. I grabbed her and whispered:

"It's a fake. Don't worry. But we better play along." I rushed to my mother's side, who fluttered her eyelids in a fine imitation of Janet Gaynor at her most wan, and sighed.

"Oh, Mutti, Mutti!" I exclaimed. "Speak to me!" I must have overplayed it, for she opened one eye and glared! I suddenly felt she had expected me to be fooled as well.

One of the Studio doctors, who ensured their four-car-garage lifestyle by adjusting their diagnoses to suit a picture's shooting schedule, took Dietrich's normal pulse, proclaimed it rapid, and advised an immediate rest in a cool place. The ailing director saw his chance. We broke for the rest of the day and returned to Yuma and air-conditioning. My mother was in high spirits:

"Well, they keep writing about my fainting, so I decided to try it! To do that scene seven times was ridiculous. That idiot director thinks if he keeps doing it, it will get better. The only thing to do is to cut it out of the film. You watch – they will keep that terrible scene in the picture just because they built that whole oasis and are in love with it." She looked at me.

"Angel, how did you know that I did not really faint?" She sounded annoyed. So I had been right! She didn't like my not being really worried about her. I tried to say the right words:

"Oh, Mutti, I just thought that you would never faint!"

She turned to Nellie.

"You see how the child knows? She knows how I was brought up to endure, never complain. My mother always told me: 'A soldier's daughter never cries!' It is all how one is brought up. Speaking of that, you have been with those low-class people out there long enough. Nellie, tell our studio driver to bring Maria's things back to the hotel!" She attacked her platter of corned beef hash with gusto.

There were lies I was made a part of, there were lies in which I was given the role of spectator, and there were lies that pertained to me. It took more growing up before I could recognize which were which.

"Sweetheart, order some more beer and we need butter." She pushed the empty platter to one side and started on the only sandwich ever given the Dietrich sanction, the mighty "club." "I have a new name for that awful horse: Mrs. Once-a-Mayer-Daughter-Selznick!"

Mr. Selznick was busy writing his famous memos:

April 28, 1936

Dear Boley [Boleslawski]:

I am getting to the end of the rope of patience with criticism based on assumption that actors know more about scripts than I do, and am disturbed, worried, and upset by telephone calls that are now pouring in. . . . actors are getting together and ganging up about scenes, would appreciate your having a frank heart-to-heart talk with Marlene and with Boyer, either separately or jointly, telling them the problems that both you and I are up against. . . . Marlene's pictures have been notorious for their ghastly writing, Charles is yet to have an outstanding American picture, and neither of them has ever had a single picture comparable with any one of fifteen that I have made in the last years. Tell them very brutally that this comes from me. It is high time for a showdown, and I am perfectly prepared for it because I am not going to face, or have you face, six or seven weeks of this nonsense. I wish you would lose your temper with

ABOVE, LEFT: The very bored stars of *The Garden of Allah*. Charles Boyer was never one of Dietrich's loves. The only film they ever made together was always referred to as "that disaster in the desert with 110 degrees in the shade when Boyer's toupee never stayed glued down!"

ABOVE, RIGHT: David Selznick tried everything, visited the set often, but even he could not save this picture.

BELOW: The tent city that Selznick erected to house the crew for this early Technicolor epic of a noncelibate monk and his passion for a beautiful, soul-searching woman.

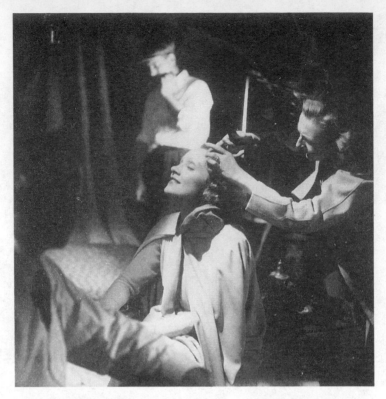

ABOVE: Nellie, Dietrich's one and only film hairdresser, whom she stole from Paramount, tried to do her work in the tent dressing room. My mother's smile is there only because this is a shot for the Selznick Studio Publicity Department.
BELOW: A poignant farewell against the sand dunes of the Arizona desert that doubled for the Sahara.

them, and I will have a lot more respect for you if you turn into a von Sternberg who tolerates no interference. . . . This is actually the very first time in my career as a producer that I have had to put up with this fantastic stuff that I have heard about for years but never had to personally experience, and I shall need your cooperation and toughness to do it. . . . Make clear to the actors that if they choose to sulk through scenes and give bad performances I am perfectly prepared for this too and am not going to add hundreds of thousands more to a fabulous cost to satisfy their temperament, but will release the picture with those performances. . . . If they will only do their job and give a performance, that will be enough. That is all that they are being overpaid for.

I always thought that the reason Selznick and Dietrich disliked each other so was their basic similarity. Both fanatical perfectionists, devoid of self-doubt, brilliant when their fanaticism worked for them – complete disasters when it didn't. Selznick had an amazing innocence for such a powerful man. He generated a constant flow of enthusiastic energy that seemed to stem from his being absolutely convinced that he alone could make a silk purse out of a sow's ear.

Finally, he had no choice but to recall the company, with special instructions not to forget to bring some Arizona sand. It seemed that the sand of the California desert was a different shade of beige from the one we had been filming. So we came home to the Studio dragging our sand trucks behind us. From then on, we duplicated our pink dawns, swayed howdahs as though they were strapped onto camel backs instead of scaffolding, sprayed glycerine sweat onto air-conditioned brows, landscaped dunes, and continued making the same bad film – this time in comfort. Selznick memos were now hand-delivered to the set:

To: Mr. Richard Boleslawski   June 17, 1936
Dear Boley:
     Would you *please* speak to Marlene about the fact that her hair is getting so much attention, and is being coiffed to such a degree that all reality is lost. Her hair is so well placed that at all times – when the wind is blowing, for instance . . . it remains perfectly smooth and unruffled; in fact, is so well placed that it could be nothing but a wig.
     The extreme in ridiculousness is the scene in bed. No woman in the world has ever had her hair appear as Marlene's does in this scene, and the entire scene becomes practically unusable. . . .
     Even today, on the set, having the hairdresser rush in between takes to put each last strand of hair in place looked so nonsensical, when you could see the palms blowing in the background.
     Surely a *little* reality can't do a great beauty any harm.
     I wish you would go over the contents of this note with Marlene, who, I

am sure, will realize that what I say makes sense; and if you will remind me, I will go into it with you and Marlene again when I am next on the set.

DOS

That was Selznick! He never gave up. This unfaltering tenaciousness made his great *Gone with the Wind* possible – but it couldn't save our opus.

We didn't skip town exactly, but six days after the completion of *The Garden of Allah*, we left America. By the time Dietrich appeared in her next disaster, the one before was quite forgotten.

Nellie was again purloined from the Paramount Hair-Dressing Department, and so we were three. Accompanied by twenty-one steamer trunks, thirty-five large suitcases, eighteen medium ones, nine small, fifteen round hat boxes, and one magnificent Cadillac complete with handsome, liveried chauffeur, we embarked. England was in for a rare treat!

Other stars worked frantically to attract the publicity that fueled and maintained their fame. Dietrich never bothered. She had no need to work at being a Star. She was one; it was her natural state. The world press, sensing this phenomenon, accorded her their constant interest. From *The Blue Angel* on, Dietrich never needed to solicit publicity – it came to her voluntarily.

If I hadn't been going to Brian's country, I would have been really sad. I did not like the idea of having to stay in Europe for all the time it would take to prepare and make a whole film. My mother was so pressed for time, we could have taken the *Hindenburg*, but she refused. Zeppelins floated in the air, making them immediately "suspect," and this one was not only Nazi-built, but Nazi-run. Although she insisted that her Uncle Dietrich had once commanded the *Hindenburg* – which I found very confusing.

We left by sea, to the ennobling strains of the "Marseillaise." Is it possible to fall in love with a ship? I believe it is. The SS *Normandie* was not really a ship. Oh, she had tonnage, ballast, captain, and crew, but they were merely camouflage, assumed by an incredible goddess to enable her to transport her temple and its worshipers across the seas. All of us privileged to know her loved her.

She was the greatest ocean liner of them all! Nothing could top her. Nothing ever did. A gluttony of the senses that the French seem to be such masters at creating. From the first moment you saw her, lounging elegantly in her berth, you caught your breath in wonderment and never breathed normally again! For me, as a child, she was a magic kingdom. My own 1930s Art Deco Disneyland! The *Normandie* was built to represent the supreme artistic achievements of a nation. She did her country proud. She was so representative of what France stood for then, the epitome of style, taste, quality, and artistic perfection. For all her opulence, her grandeur, her majesty, she had a loving nature, a caring serenity, strength, and dependability. The *Normandie was* France.

We had the Deauville suite, one of four *"appartements de grand luxe,"* individually designed by the leading decorators of their day. Ours boasted an oval salon, two double bed chambers, marble bathrooms, circular dining room, ceiling-to-floor French windows opening onto our private sun deck, white baby grand, walls draped in Aubusson tapestries, everything in a shade referred to in the history books as rosé-beige. A Napoleonic bonbon box that can only be described by one word: rich. It became "our" suite. As from then on, we only traveled on the *Normandie*, it became more "home" than many of the houses we lived in.

My mother had been sent so many bottles of champagne, one wall of our rosé dining room was lined with coolers resting on their silver tripods. I twirled the various bottles, selected the Veuve Clicquot, 1928, looked at the card, saw it came from our New Englander. Well, he learned fast.

I was trying to think of a good reason to be given permission to leave, when my mother said:

"Sweetheart. Go downstairs and ask the purser what evening they are showing *Desire*."

I handed her the glass of champagne, closed our rosé door politely, and . . . ran! I hadn't dreamt of getting free so fast! We were so high in our exclusive crow's nest, I got lost three times trying to get down to the main lobby. On the way I discovered the Grill Room: Tall mirrored columns reflected the dance floor, all was black calf, gleaming steel, and refracted glass. The Countess di Frasso must have gone crazy the first time she saw it. Although the *Normandie* had the most astoundingly beautiful First Class dining hall, which seated seven hundred people in an area the size of a football field, festooned with rows of soaring columns of light in the shape of upside-down wedding cakes of Lalique, aglitter with Christofle silver, Limoges and De Haviland porcelain, and shimmering Baccarat, the *Normandie* also offered her passengers the added luxury of an exclusive grill room. While the very rich ate their pâté de foie gras in the main dining room, the *very* rich *and* famous nibbled theirs above in the Grill. Before the Second World War, such snobbish exclusivity was accepted, condoned without question.

I found the main lobby and stood transfixed, surrounded by four massive, free-standing elevators, their cages sculptured black iron filigree encrusted with golden scallop shells. Even the Waldorf had nothing like this! No palm court – no spinsters sawing on their strings. Here Irving Berlin and Cole Porter syncopated notes slid, jumped, and swung! If Fred

Astaire and Ginger Rogers had spun by, cheek to cheek, I wouldn't have been surprised. The whole ship was a Busby Berkeley production . . . with *class*!

The Goddess shuddered. Whistles blew, horns blared, the band played louder. I caught a sea-shell elevator going up, ran the rest of the way to the top sun deck, and in the shade of one of the *Normandie*'s unique, slanted funnels, watched as she slipped silkily into the Hudson River.

I knew my mother would be getting angry. I hadn't done the flower cards or anything – but I had to stay and wait for the Lady. If I saw her on the way out and made my wish, I knew it would come true. I always made the same one – "Please, please let me get back home."

As protocol decreed that one did not "dress" the first night out, my mother saw no reason to make an "appearance." She went to bed early and was asleep in her rosé-beige cream-puff bed before I closed the door. I dashed into my own bandbox splendor, throwing my lace-ups in one corner and my navy linen into another, emerging cautiously ten minutes later in uncrushable sapphire velvet and lily-white Mary Janes. I was ready – to "do" First Class!

What wonderful treasures I discovered! Rooms for the art of letter writing, where gold-leaf tigers gazed down as they silently lapped from golden ponds. Rooms for the art of smoking, raisin-suede chairs amidst murals depicting the life of ancient Egypt that would have made Tutankhamen envious. Playrooms for happy children, with little fat elephants in bright green tailcoats, sporting golden crowns, cavorting on the walls, the whole place geared to fun. Even delicately decorated rocking horses, their sweeping white tails tied back with bows of chartreuse taffeta. The Winter Garden, an orchestrated jungle of cascading orchids and rare ferns, scrolled wicker chairs nestled among the lush greenery, facing a curved wall of glass that reflected the night sky. I curled up inside one of those curled chairs and watched the dark ocean play catch with the moonlight. Around me the air was warm, smelled of damp moss and wood violets. A worried steward shook me awake. I ran. First thing in the morning, I would have to find the chapel with its stained-glass windows, and all the different theaters. I decided that four days would not be enough time to discover all the wonders of the *Normandie*.

The evening *Desire* was shown was designated as a "gala." I helped tape my mother's breasts, poured her into a masterpiece of pleated crepe de chine, and assembled the emeralds. Buttoned myself into a scalloped silk, especially made to complement my mother's dress, and following politely behind, accompanied her as she swept into the Grand Salon.

A small Versailles, done in Aubusson and Lalique fountains, filled with Dress Extras. The men, in white tie and tails, all looked like Cary Grant and William Powell at their best. The ladies, willowy visions in Lucien Lelong and Patou. As they strolled, they manipulated their long trains, ever on guard against the danger of some clumsy foot. My mother surveyed this sumptuous scene, smoothed her evening gloves, and observed:

"All the women look like Kay Francis!"

With the ladies and gentlemen of the Grand Salon following in regal procession, we made our way to the *Normandie*'s full-size movie theater. The lights dimmed and Dietrich saw *Desire* for the first time. Sitting next to her, I was, as always, the appreciative recipient of her professional comments.

"So – they did keep that shot in! I told Travis they would never cut a close-up of Dietrich wearing that hat with those feathers.

"Look at that! Now that is a long shot to remember! Gorgeous! Look how that chiffon falls. Wonderful! She looks breathtaking!

"That awful song! I said it was stupid, but look how the light catches the tips of those feather sleeves.

"Of course, as usual, they didn't know what to do for an ending. But the shoes were good. . . . All through this picture, the shoes were right!"

The lights came up, the audience rose, applauding the star in their midst. My mother smiled politely, took my hand, and we exited quickly, the applause fading out behind us. She spent the rest of the evening dancing and being adored, while I watched, enjoying the glamour and the tiny spun-sugar petits fours.

When we docked in Southampton, my father and the usual horde of reporters, press photographers, Studio personnel, primed Customs officials, and selected baggage handlers awaited us on the quay. My mother's new boss, Alexander Korda, must have had a lot of pull, for we were whisked through the formalities to board the special train to London. My mother shoved the presentation spray of red roses into my arms, removed her movie-star hat, and, crossing those justly famous legs, leaned back against the ruby velvet seat.

"A real Victorian carriage! Look, sweetheart – it has little lamps with pleated silk shades! And cabbage roses in the carpet! Only the English know how to do trains! Papilein, we saw *Desire* on the way over. You know, it is not a bad picture after all. I was not bored the way I usually am when I have to see a film."

My father removed his vicuña overcoat. Although it was summer, it seemed to have passed this new country by.

"Papi, that is a very good cut on that suit. Is that one of those I bought for you at Knize?"

He said it was, handed my mother *The Times* of London, me, *The History of the Tudor Kings* in German, and settled down to study the luggage lists I had handed him on arrival.

LONDON AND BEYOND

FROM FRENCH SUPER OPULENT to one of the hallmarks of British understatement was quite a contrast. The famous Claridge's hotel was so correct, so regal, so properly toned down, one felt compelled to sit very straight, hands primly folded, conversing in hushed Oxonian tones. My mother, her arms again laden with roses, marched straight to the master bedroom, exclaiming:

"Why can't they learn to cut the thorns off roses before they make up these funeral sprays? . . . But if they were not stupid, they wouldn't be working in a florist shop!" and threw the flowers into the bathtub, calling to me:

"Sweetheart, ring for the maid to clean the bathroom." It became one of my duties to cut thorns, as well as to see to the general care and maintenance of flowers. Although the great hotels employed "flower girls" to cut, trim, water, arrange, and oversee the floral displays of their hotel and its guests, my mother preferred her own staff to do it. It eliminated one more "outsider" having access to her suite. Except years later, when she stayed at the Savoy. That monarch of all London hotels employed very young ladies, of the debutante type, delicate as the flowers they were paid to cosset. Dietrich was always very cavalier when admitting them and their watering cans. She would pat their soft hands, smiling at their blush of confusion. When we remained at the Savoy for any extended time, I noticed that the flower girls assigned to our suite were rotated. The managers of the Savoy were very genteel diplomats as well as prudent ones.

As my father had already organized Claridge's, that left my mother only the toilets. While Tami and Nellie unpacked, I got rid of the fruit. Why did hotels always insist on filling our suites with baskets of fruit? Most arriving "goddesses" probably liked such juicy offerings – ours would have preferred pickled herring! Dietrich considered anything other than apples a waste of time.

I think the British press mentioned my height, and by their tone, questioned my supposed age of "just ten," for I was excluded from many Studio meetings and given orders to do "something constructive with Tami" instead. Once again, Tami became my official "governess," a solution to a ticklish situation I always profited from. Obediently, we rushed off to the British Museum and rediscovered each other as we discovered the Elgin Marbles. She seemed better than when I had seen her last in the Bel Air house. Thinner perhaps, her beautiful Slavic bone structure a bit more angular, too sharp in places, but her laugh was free of the faint note of hysteria I remembered, and she no longer picked at the skin of her fingers. Maybe the "cure" that my mother had said was so expensive had really done some good after all. We explored London together and I was reassured by Tami's new air of health. The slight tremor of her hands, the hesitancy before being able to swallow, that did not hit me until a few months later in Paris.

We usually met for breakfast in my mother's suite. My father made his appearance from the direction of his adjoining sitting room, Nellie from her room on a different floor, and Tami from her usual single down the hall. As was her lifelong custom, my mother carried her coffee cup while she walked and talked at us. Dietrich rarely talked with anyone. That would have required a certain interest in another's opinion. As my mother believed only her opinions worthwhile, she saw no reason for wasting time listening to those of others.

"Papilein, did you know that Robert Donat is married? On the screen, he doesn't look like that at all! . . . He is so beautiful! In this film, they won't know who to look at first – him or me. But when you talk to him, right away you know he *has* to be married. What a waste! A bourgeois mind with such a face! A little like Colman – you think something must be there – but it isn't. . . . And his voice – like music! Can you imagine a voice like that talking about . . . hollyhocks? He told me all about how he has won prizes because of the special fertilizer he uses in his garden! It is not going to be easy in this film, making with the Grand Passion with a gardener!"

Poor Mr. Donat. He didn't have a chance of becoming a member of our exclusive "beef-tea club." I hoped my mother would find someone, though, she was easier when she was busy being "romantic" with someone. I needn't have worried. Soon, she donned superbly cut dresses that screamed, ever so understatedly, "woman." On entering a room, she flung her furs nonchalantly onto furniture, and left her trousers hanging in the closets. Browning replaced Goethe, paper-thin watercress sandwiches and Earl Grey tea, liverwurst and lager beer. She referred often to having played Hippolyta in *A Midsummer Night's Dream*. I wished it could all be for Brian's benefit but knew it wasn't.

Her voice took on the cadence of the BBC. She became a very, very "British" lady to the manner born. I expected at least a duke to make an appearance, but no crested invitations to Blenheim Palace arrived. No one surfaced until one day as we were once again crossing the English Channel on our way to Paris. We were making this trip frequently, to see the collections, fit, shop, and eat. This day, a dashing gentleman, complete with dark red carnation boutonniere, joined us, as though by merest chance. His eyes never left my mother's face. His hands touched, his immaculately tailored body bent toward her, at the slightest sway of the boat. Her girlish laugh trilled with "young love." They were definitely not strangers! I had recognized him immediately, his face was known – his name even more so. From then on, wherever Dietrich went, her swain was sure to go. She thought him "divine"! Alternated between being a Gainsborough maiden, an effervescent flirt, an irresistible siren, and a glamorous movie star. This did not stop her from making fun of him when discussing him with her husband:

"Papilein! He is really so funny – a real child! He wants to be knighted! Isn't that sweet? Being an American he thinks that having a title makes you a real gentleman . . . but isn't his father a Jew? You can't have a father who swings on ropes . . . and expect to become an aristocrat! But he is trying, and you know . . . he really *looks* the part. He may make it. If he does, he will have to stop using that stupid name. *That* really won't go with a Sir! He says he wants to 'present' me to Marina, the Duchess of Kent. He thinks I need him to do that. Isn't that sweet? But, of course, I let him think he is the only one who can do it . . . that *he* will be the one to give Royalty: DIETRICH! What is that American expression, Papi – means something like 'showing off'?"

My father, engrossed in the "London expenses" ledger, looked blank. Impatiently, my mother turned to me.

"You always know all those American things . . . what is it? It means being cocky."

"A feather in his cap?" I ventured.

"Yes, yes, that is it! 'A feather in his cap.' I am the shining feather in his nouveau-riche cap!" She laughed so hard she had to run and just made it to the bathroom. Her mood was "young bride" gay. Feeling desired by a handsome man always put her in an excellent mood, as it does most women. We all benefited from her joie de vivre and looked upon this new member of our family benignly. I never liked him as a person, but that had nothing to do with appreciating his effect on my mother's disposition.

Everything was such dedicated "hearts and flowers," such heavy breathing, such visions of walking hand in hand into the sunset, even to the exchanging of wedding rings, that Tami took hope.

For the first time, I too considered the possibility of my mother divorcing my father. I wouldn't mind a new father . . . if he was an American and the head of the house, then maybe I could go to school, have that lunch box, even be allowed to ride a bicycle, have child friends, have a birthday cake with real candles and sugar roses, have a family to celebrate Thanksgiving with, maybe even become a real American! I knew these wonderful things existed: I had seen them in the movies. But to have such a dream come true, it needed someone nice and settled . . . like a doctor or a lawyer. Even a businessman would do, but not a so-so actor trying to be a la-di-da titled Englishman and fooling no one but himself.

As Brian, Gilbert, Jo, and others had done before him, he too complained at times, expressing his hurts on paper, safer than confronting her face to face. True to her pattern, after reading his letters, my mother left them open for all to see. I read them before my father filed them for "posterity":

Darling,
   . . . I thought your hugging Mrs. Edington and later your definite and outspoken flirtation with Gloria Vanderbilt was, to my banal, sophomoric *taste*, too much!
   I do not reproach you for your feelings in any way, sweetest – I can only wish I knew them earlier. . . .
   With all my love and God Bless you, my Dushka,

I could never decide if the "Dushka" was a suggestive reference to her trusty douche bag or the influence of the Russian theme of the picture she was making when they fell in love. Probably a bit of both. Everything he gave her had "Dushka" all over it. He gave her a gold cigarette case with it written across the lid. Years later, when he and the memory of this time were no longer important, she looked at it and said:

"You know – he wasn't bad. He knew how to dress and had very good manners. But he had no taste in presents. Look at this cigarette case! Stuck full of little charms that probably had special meanings to us then, and, of course, he *had* to write Dushka all over it – so now I can't even give it to someone for a present!"

My father played his roles of "husband when needed," "manager to famous movie-star wife," and confidant, while Dietrich filmed *Knight Without Armour* at the Denham Studios outside London, was in love, and enjoyed the heady novelty of being a big Hollywood star in a foreign land. Tami, Nellie, and I did our assigned duties efficiently and disappeared at the proper times.

An old friend from the di Frasso house days wrote and made my mother laugh. It didn't matter that Clifton Webb knew he was amusing, because he actually was. My mother often read his letters aloud, pointing out where she thought him especially clever or outrageous. Knowing how she hated *The Garden of Allah*, he addressed her by her name in the film:

The Lombardy
One Eleven East Fifty-Sixth Street
New York

August 25th, 1936

Dear sweet Miss Enfilden,

I was more than happy to get your postcard if for no other reason than to know that in all of that dizzy whirl you still remembered little me. . . . I arrived, en suite, last week, and the shrieks of "Le (or perhaps I should say "La") Webb" could have been heard in Laurel Canyon, the ex-abode of that vibrating raper Brian Aherne, or maybe I shouldn't have brought that up. On the train coming back was Granny Boyer, which practically made the trip perfect and filled with excitement as you can well imagine. . . .

Madame Dracula de Acosta came over to the house to go to dinner with us on the day of your departure. She was thrilled to the bone because you had sent her "eight dozen lilies" which she said was "The Old Sign," whatever that means. Well dear, I happened to be in the florist you had sent your flowers from and in a very nonchalant manner . . . inquired if you had sent eight dozen lilies to anyone. When the florist fainted dead away, I knew then and there that Mme. Dracula de A. had been lying just a teeny weeny bit. . . .

. . . N.Y. is grand, and I must say it is a relief to get back to people who do talk of something else but "my public, my long shots, my close-ups." . . . All one has to do is to get away from that self-etherized group to realize how little they mean outside of that glorious sunlit terrain.

My mother looked up:

"You see why I like him? He is one of the intelligent ones, like Noël Coward!" and went back to reading her letter aloud to us:

I shall probably be crying for it this winter when I am up to my "whatsis" in snow and slush. . . .

My days of "whoopie poo" are at an end. I go into rehearsal next week. Am doing a play with the Theatre Guild, about the grandest part one could wish for. I almost did *On Your Toes* in London. I had visions of being crowned along with dear David at the Coronation.

"Papi! I was right! Now we know! If Clifton Webb calls the King 'dear David,' he *must* be a *pansy*! I like them, but they can't be *kings*!" She lit another cigarette and continued:

> I also had visions of all the crowned heads of Europe at my feet – and spots North – and I must say I was greatly excited for a very short time at the outlook. . . .
> If you see Noël, just casually ask him what went on in Garbo's flat in Stockholm. My dear girl – I SAY NOTHING! . . .
> By now you are probably palpitating over some illegitimate son of a frowsy old Earl. On the other hand, perhaps not. If I remember rightly, the English haven't got enough of that "zum, zip and zowie" for you, my puss.

My mother chuckled, and took a sip of her coffee. I noticed my father was in his "smoldering" mood and wondered why.

> Do, if you have a chance, and even if you have not a chance, drop me a line and let me know a little bit what goes on. . . . I love you so very much, and even though you are the toy of London, being whoopsed off your feet (in more ways than one I HOPE!), shall be delighted to get any news. As you know, I am MAHD for you. Love to Maria and Rudi if he is with you. Bless you,
>
> Your, little mother
CLIFTON
(Public gentleman number 1)

Occasionally, my mother was back in time to join us at breakfast, then the conversation reverted to her special brand of noninterruptive monologues:

"They say that Edward will definitely marry that frightful Wallis Simpson, no matter what the old Queen says. I said, 'Then he has to abdicate!' . . . You can't have an American commoner on the throne of England! Impossible! But you know, Papi, that woman must be very clever to get a king so crazy about her. Or she is very good at 'doing' what he likes. You know what everyone says he is, and that kind always love their mothers! So, maybe he will listen to Queen Mary. We had dinner again last night with the Duke and Duchess of Kent. Now, that's a beautiful woman. Wasn't she a Greek princess once? Everyone made very polite conversations. No one dared to mention The Scandal, but of course, were dying to find out what the Kents knew! I think one of the things that attracted the King to this Simpson is that she is so flat. She looks like his favorite – young boys. But *why* does he want to *marry* her? He must be *very* stupid!"

To read newspapers was a waste of time when you had Dietrich as your very own town crier! I hoped she would give us further bulletins on the "scandal of the century." She did! A few weeks later, she strode into our suite and announced:

"I am going to see the King! I told the Duke of Kent last night: 'Send me! I can do it better than Wallis Simpson – and with *me*, you can be *sure* I won't try to be the Queen of England!'"

She was on her way to the Studio. Nellie and I collected the thermoses and usual paraphernalia. I opened the door and stood aside for my mother to precede me. Pulling on her gloves, she called back over her shoulder:

"Papi! When the Prime Minister calls, take the secret phone number of the King and call me immediately at the Studio."

The night that Dietrich's distinctive, one-of-a-kind Cadillac was discovered parked in the shadows by a side entrance of Buckingham Palace, the press went wild. My mother declared herself to be "thoroughly shocked at the stupid behavior of her chauffeur – for it undoubtedly was he who had taken her car, without her permission, in order to see the sights of London." It was amazing how quickly that rumor died and the press dropped the story.

It was one of my mother's favorite secrets, one of a few of her manufactured intrigues that, when mentioned, produced an immediate Mona Lisa smile, accompanied by a very wicked twinkle in the eyes. If Edward VIII had not given up his throne for the woman he loved, I am certain we would have heard much more of Dietrich's contribution to the preservation of the British Empire.

Knight Without Armour was filmed without my usual necessary presence. My father evacuated me for a time to Paris, where I lived with him and Tami. While Dietrich was busy, fleeing rapacious Bolsheviks, draped in diaphanous gowns copied from *The Garden of Allah*, protected by a too-too courageous Robert Donat in cossack disguise, I sat in my father's apartment reading *Mein Kampf* and trying to understand it. As I felt my mother would soon tire of allowing my father jurisdiction over me, I tried to make the most of this free time with my friends, Tami and Teddy. I hadn't realized how much I had missed my four-footed pal until he greeted me at my father's front door. His welcomes were not like other dogs'. No tail wagging, wriggling, standing on hind legs with excitement. If Teddy thought you were special, you rated "the look": Front paws planted firmly, hindquarters in respectful sitting position, head slightly cocked, ears perked – he would survey you. His eyes, doubtful, spoke volumes: "Are you really here? Finally? If you knew I missed you, would you care? If you hug me now, then I'll know!" and you would fling your arms around his strong little body and hold him tight. Then, only then, when he was sure of no rejection, would he give you a kiss and wag his stumpy tail. Teddy was a very special being.

So was my Tami. She tried so hard to please and nothing was ever good enough. My father, in his own domain, was terribly strict. He expected things to be done only according to his rules. If he suspected the slightest hesitancy in obeying an order, he shouted. His fury was usually out of context to the supposed misdeed. His rages frightened me, they galvanized Tami into frenzied panic.

"Tami – what is this? . . . I was speaking to you! Look at me! What do you call this? . . . Answer me! You call this a *steak*? . . . How much did you allow them to charge you for this? . . . Show me the bill! . . . Well, give it to me! . . . You can't, can you? 'Lost it' again? Like you do everything else? Can't remember anything? Careless and stupid? . . . YOU *never* do anything right. We know that, don't we? . . . You think you are now so much better? No, you are just the same – hopeless! You will now take this disgraceful piece of meat you bought back to the butcher, get my money back, then come back here and give it to me!" He slapped the meat into her shaking hands.

Her face was white, her eyes those of a hunted animal at bay.

"Rudilein, please, please, it's already COOKED . . . I can't . . ."

"Oh, now the excuses? You make mistakes – You have to pay for them! I said GO! . . . And don't try to come back here with any excuses!"

"I beg you . . . Rudi, please don't make me – "

"What do I have to do – DRAG YOU THERE MYSELF?"

Sobbing, Tami ran into the hall, clutching the offensive piece of meat. I rose from the table, feeling sick –

"Sit! This is none of your business! Next *you* will be in trouble. Finish your lunch!" My father poured himself another glass of his excellent Bordeaux, leaned back in his special chair at the head of the table, sipped – watching me.

I tried to help. I went marketing with her, making sure that Tami

While shooting *Knight Without Armour* in England, my mother expected Robert Donat to be as romantic as he looked and was very disappointed when only his asthma attacks generated any kind of emotional upheaval. Halfway through the film, she decided she was making a flop.

ABOVE: We used to cross the English Channel to shop and eat in Paris. Although I always obeyed the order to step out of frame whenever a photographer materialized, this time I hadn't stepped back far enough.

BELOW: A rare picture of Dietrich's daughter, husband, and dog together at lunch in Paris.

OPPOSITE: Young romance in London, 1937. Dietrich and her Knight looked so handsome together I sometimes thought that they kept up their relationship long after the emotion was gone because of that.

ABOVE: Our Knight joins his Lady's family and is costumed for a sojourn in Salzburg.

BELOW: On one of her many transatlantic crossings, Dietrich finally got to meet someone whose work she admired and whom she, therefore, adored. Ernest Hemingway became a lifelong friend. They danced well together but preferred listening to each other being "brilliant."

got all the sales slips and that the centime count tallied. Checked the buttons on his shirts . . . if he found one missing, he might decide to kill her! Polished his shoes for her, brushed his clothes, filled his cigarette lighters, dusted his books, sharpened his pencils, filled his pens, ironed his handkerchiefs. I took over some of the cooking when Tami cut her hand. We both prayed we would get through each day without getting into trouble. At night, Tami took some of the new pills they had given her at the Spa and welcomed oblivion, while I read a madman's manifesto and wondered what made some people so ugly.

One of the things my mother learned during her time amongst the British aristocracy was their penchant for getting rid of their children as fast as possible. Starched and dedicated nannies received heirs wrapped in gossamer shawls and carried them off to the nursery wings, from where their charges later emerged, properly behaved and groomed, for special occasions only. As soon as Beatrix Potter and her cute rabbit palled, nanny was pensioned off, her young ones fitted for knee pants or pleated skirts, blazer and cap, handed a lacrosse stick, and sent off to illustrious, ivy-covered establishments dedicated to "building character." These, in turn, were later exchanged for denser ivy at even more "Hallowed Halls," until the young were fully grown and properly "finished": girls to advantageous marriages and their own nursery wings, boys to inherited grandeur and heroic conduct on some battlefield.

Although I was too old for the nursery, I was not for the scholastic residency. My mother decided that, as a German aristocrat, her child too needed "finishing." Knowing the rather orthodox attitude the English have toward the process of education, my father must have convinced her that I would never be able to pass their entrance exams. So, saying that her decision was based solely on her wish that I learn French, she instructed him to find "the best boarding school in Europe where girls learn to speak beautiful French." My father, the consummate procurer, found it in Switzerland, convinced them to save Marlene Dietrich's daughter from the purgatory of utter ignorance, and I was inscribed as a paid-up pupil entering in September of 1936. Age: 11. Name: Maria Elizabeth Sieber, Hollywood.

I came to love Brillantmont. If I had known then that they had put me down in their record books as being "Origin: Hollywood," I would have loved that school even more.

As Brillantmont required its pupils to supply their own linens, my mother arrived in Paris and bought me a trousseau; dozens of pure Irish linen sheets, heavy and slippery in their perfection, enormous napkins, of the same luxurious cloth. It was linen woven to last through generations of hopeful new brides. It was the only trousseau my mother ever bought me. She ordered my name to be hand-embroidered onto every article – none of those vulgar name tapes for a descendant of the Dietrichs! I was thrilled with my sumptuous hope chest and couldn't wait to make my first perfect bed at boarding school. I did not know that to be accepted by one's peers, it was better to conform to their standards, that to be different made one stand out and be judged, often unfairly. Never having lived in a real world, I had no guidelines to go by. I acquired those later, along with French. But I treasured my linens even after I learned to apologize for their ostentation.

My father delivered me to school; I thought perhaps my mother couldn't face the wrench of parting or was too busy with more important emotions. I was much too excited and scared to worry about why she wasn't there; to face things without the blinding glare of her presence was easier anyway. My father, very precise and informative, charmed the reserved headmistresses: this school was so elite, it had two of them – then told me, for what I hoped would be the last time:

"You are being given this opportunity to finally learn something. You will be watched. Here you will not be allowed to get away with anything. Remember, it is because of ME, not your mother, that you were accepted to this school. Here it will not be your usual Hollywood circus, where you can get away with everything because you have a famous mother. Only girls from the best families come to this school. I have given them my word that you will obey and behave yourself at all times. Your mother cannot protect you. Here a movie star's daughter does not count. Have you understood? . . . Then repeat it back to me. I want it word for word, so I know you have got it through your head!"

As this lecture was administered in front of my assigned roommates, I was dying of embarrassment. I hoped they couldn't understand German! He left me standing on a neat gravel path, bordered by decorative stone urns filled with matching flowers, below a Daphne du Maurier–type château that overlooked Lake Leman.

There were girls who cried and were miserable with loneliness, those came from "happy families," where people really loved them. Then there were those who, having grown up in boarding schools, were accustomed to the depersonalization, the uniformity of communal living. And there were us, the ones on vacation from being either hated or loved too much. We enjoyed boarding school, secretly envying those who had something to cry for.

At first, it was very difficult. We were allowed to speak only French, a language foreign to us all. This drastic method worked. It forced us to learn quickly in order to be able to communicate. For me, who had never learned how to be a real pupil, let alone most of the subjects required, the language barrier added to my panic of inadequacy. I didn't even know what "geography" was, suddenly I was expected to name the rivers of the world – in French! It didn't take Brillantmont long to find out that I couldn't spell in any language. That shook them a bit. I don't think they really knew what to do with me. I think they just gave up. But they were kind and let me stay, hoping that by some miracle I might catch up someday. If all else failed, at least I would be proficient in French and play an acceptable game of lacrosse.

My mother moved to 20 Grosvenor Square, the same address as her London lover. The girls at school talked a lot about "lovers." They too had mothers who had them. They even had fathers who kept something called a "mistress" – who wore "vulgar" clothes, "shocking" black lace underwear, "took" money, cars, jewelry, furs, even houses from a father, in exchange for their "favors." I hated to show my ignorance by asking what that meant exactly, but as none of those requirements for "a mistress" fitted Tami, I rejected that category for her instantly. The girls were so vehemently convinced that those women of their fathers were evil, avaricious, and dirty, that I decided my tender, gentle Tami, who had never been anything but a loving wife to my father, was not a "mistress type" at all! My mother didn't fit the image of "mother with lover" either. She didn't "hide," go to "out-of-the-way-hotels-in-seaside-resorts out of season," make up lies to "fool" her husband. I had a mother who took a lover whenever she felt like it and it suited her – then told her husband all about him. I was a real misfit! Even my parents didn't conform to the accepted behavior of adultery. I stopped joining the secret "tell all" night sessions under the bed covers and missed a lot of valuable sex education that might have helped me a few years later.

My mother telephoned me constantly. Harried ladies would trot from the headmistress's office, knock hesitantly on classroom doors, requesting the urgent release of Mlle Sieber . . . to take an important phone call from Mme Dietrich, her mother. Even tests were interrupted. It seemed that the unimpressionable Swiss were not movie star-proof after all. I would curtsey, excuse myself, embarrassed by the unsolicited attention, hurry to the *bureau*, apologize to whatever spinster happened to be in the seat of power, lift the waiting receiver to hear, not for the first time nor the last time that day, how miserable my mother was without me, how she missed me, nothing worked without me, the director was worse than our sick one on the last picture, that no one in England knew how to make films, that all the Kordas were "Hungarian Jews" – so what could one expect from "gypsies" – that Nellie had another cold and was useless with a nose that constantly dripped on the wigs, and, "Where did we pack the extra lashes?"

I listened and waited for her to hang up, without saying "good-bye," which was her custom. Then, curtseying, I did my apologizing act in reverse until I was once more behind my wooden flip-top desk – under the disapproving eye of the teacher. There was no escaping those calls. They hauled me in from hockey matches, even calisthenics! I tried hiding in the toilets – but those determined Swiss ladies would stand outside and wait, whispering urgently through the keyhole for me to hurry, to remember it was long-distance! If a scurrying lady dared to request that my mother call back, as her daughter was in the midst of attempting to conjugate Latin verbs, they were given such a tongue-lashing on the rights of motherhood and its priorities, that they flew, tore the chalk out of my hand, begging me with eyes gone pink and lips atremble to *please* get my *mère* off their backs. For more than sixty years, I tried to escape my mother's phone calls and never made it! She could find me anywhere! If Dietrich wanted you, you were doomed. Her private "homosexual fan Mafia," an adoring organization that circles the globe, were immediately alerted to "seek and find." As they also functioned as informants, lying to Dietrich as to one's whereabouts, in order to escape her, was useless. One year, my husband rented us an apartment in Madrid that had no phone. Ah! Bliss! Then cables began arriving every hour on the hour, until my mother remembered a fan in Barcelona and called him. He knew of a lovely antique dealer in Toledo who had just returned from a "divine" weekend in a gorgeous villa in Hammamet that belonged . . . the next day, we got a telephone! My mother was triumphant. In Spain in those days, people had to wait, sometimes for years, to get a phone. They didn't have Dietrich for a mother!

At school, I became the star of mail call. Other girls received letters, postcards, even small gifts. I got autographed pictures from my mother, but, best of all, the *Los Angeles Examiner* funny papers, rolled around a jar of peanut butter, from my favorite bodyguard. He never forgot, never missed a Sunday. The whole American contingent of Brillantmont was able to keep up with the adventures of Flash Gordon.

Although the school counted princesses, heiresses, and many prominent "blue bloods" among its pupils, I found, just like everyone else, they too regarded an autographed picture of a movie star a coveted trophy. One could even use it as barter: Two Dietrichs got you a Hershey bar, three, a lovely bottle of lavender toilet water, four, your neighbor's portion of roast beef on Sunday. It cost me three Dietrichs, the toilet water, Hershey bar, and two Sundays of my roast beef for a small autographed picture of Clark Gable! My mother would not have appreciated the rate of exchange.

I also found that I had the only parent whose profession was known to all. It fascinated them. The outside world wanted to know everything that concerned mine. I found that very interesting and a little heady. The bankers' daughters were never questioned on how their parent made his money. No one asked the Indian princess about her family. When my mother called, I asked for more autographs, but did not tell her about my wonderful American care packages from my bodyguard. She would have been jealous and spoiled it by saying something sarcastic about "funny papers" and the stupidity of Americans for reading them.

For my birthday, my mother sent me the contents of all the florist shops in Lausanne. A lot of the girls were jealous and made fun of me, and the headmistresses were shocked by such senseless extravagance. I apologized for being the cause of a "disturbance," donated the flowers to the infirmary, and hid in my room for the rest of the day.

At the beginning of Christmas vacation, I waited in the hall, next to my suitcase, for someone to pick me up. I hoped it wouldn't be my father. At the age of "just" twelve, I had taken my very first exams ever and done badly in everything but English Literature, and Religion. I prayed the latter would somehow placate my father's wrath but doubted that it would. My father strode through the big glass door, acknowledged my punctuality, and passed along the hall toward the inner sanctum of the headmistresses. I sat back down on the bench, wishing I could have spent Christmas at school. Looking as angry as I had feared, my father reappeared and signaled me to follow him out to the waiting taxi.

I think the sleeper we boarded was the Orient Express, but I was too frightened to notice if the marquetry was in patterns of overflowing fruit baskets or the plain geometric-chips-of-wood variety. I did get up the courage to ask where Tami was, was told she was visiting her brother and would not be with us for the holidays. Brother? I didn't even know she had a brother. I folded my hands and hoped my father's disposition would be improved by the usually impeccable lunch served before our arrival in Paris.

This time we were staying at the Hotel George V, in 1936, not quite as elite as the Plaza Athénée but a bit more famous. As I entered my mother's regency suite, she gasped:

"Oh! No! What has happened to you? What have they done to you in that place! . . . Papi! Didn't you notice? Look at her hair! . . . Call downstairs and tell them we want someone up here to cut Kater's hair. We also have to buy her clothes that fit! What do they give you to eat in that school? . . . Bread and potatoes?" She hustled me off to the bathroom to be weighed and washed.

From then on, whenever I reappeared from having been "away, together with a lot of strangers," I was disinfected along with the toilets. While my mother scrubbed, I ventured to ask her about Tami. She answered too fast, her voice high, a sure sign that she was lying without preparation:

"Oh, poor Tami! She had to have a little vacation. You know how hard she works to take care of Papi, so I told her: 'Go to Cannes and rest. I will pay the hotel – don't worry.'" She attacked my ears. I felt we were doing the washing scene from *Blonde Venus*! Could Tami's brother be living in Cannes? I doubted it – certainly not at a luxury hotel. Usually, my father and mother got their stories straight, very seldom did they not tally. Or, had I been just too young to notice? No, I decided, I had never been *that* young! They were both lying. Something was very wrong. I would have to be careful and find out the truth.

Although my mother had sent me away expressly to learn French, she was never actually convinced that I knew the language, and continued using it while discussing anything "that The Child mustn't know." She also considered that, as French was the recognized diplomatic language of aristocrats and monarchs, it must be beyond the capabilities of the mere masses. I could never figure out how she justified the population of France speaking it, but then, Dietrich had a way of ignoring realities whenever they didn't suit her that was phenomenal. She would say to me:

"Sweetheart. Call Hermès and tell them to send over scarves for me to choose from. You can speak to them in English – shop girls can't speak real French. Like maids and delivery boys, they all come from villages and are dumb. Most of them don't even know how to read."

I tried to tell her of my linguistic progress, but she looked dubious:

"Sweetheart. You – think – you – speak – French? No . . . no . . . it will take a long time before you are able to speak that beautiful language correctly. I learned my perfect French from my French governess. Girls from good families always learn to speak languages from their governesses."

I decided it was best to keep my knowledge of French to myself, and heard some interesting things that way.

Thinking that I was expected to talk about my life at school, I mentioned our lacrosse matches.

"You? Play that barbaric game? With those little nets on a stick? . . . You don't mean you run around in that Swiss cold, waving a pole!?"

Well, that hadn't worked, so I tried again:

"Mutti, I have a wonderful roommate. She is Norwegian and her family sends her big brown cheeses that – "

"Papi! Did you hear that? She has a roommate with cheese! No wonder she is so fat!"

I quickly tried to change the subject:

"Oh, Mutti. I told some of the girls about having a room – you know, that gets cleaned out every month for a baby someday? They thought it so nice – "

"What? What did you tell them? What room? What baby? Papi! – *that's* a famous school for girls from fine families? They talk about *babies*! What *is* this place you put the child into? How old are those girls Kater is living with? Those homes they come from can't be so very *fine* if they talk about private things like having . . . periods. She is there to learn *French* – not vulgarities!"

This went on for days. When her outrage was finally over without dire consequences, I was so relieved. I had feared she might decide to remove me from my school. I never said another word about my new world, reverted to being completely engrossed in hers, and assured once again of my exclusive devotion, my mother stopped feeling threatened and was content.

One afternoon, she took me along to visit a lady for tea. Actually, there were two. One thin and ugly, the other roly-poly with sharp little eyes and a long thin mouth. They were as honored by my mother's presence as she seemed to be by their invitation. That intrigued me. Dietrich was rarely impressed by women, and unattractive ones even less. The apartment needed only velvet ropes used in museums to mark off exhibits. Many years later, this is exactly what was done to it. A fabulous collection of glass paperweights covered every surface, paintings adorned the walls, framed photographs and delicate bric-a-brac arranged on a large black marble mantelpiece. One could feel that the pudgy lady was the boss, that she gave the orders. She made my mother's eyes sparkle with her conversation, while the other carried in the tray, poured the tea, then stood by the large armchair . . . ready to be of further service. There was definitely something extra-special about our hostess. I couldn't understand her rapid French, but it sounded so eloquent, so fluid, one felt she was being brilliant without having to know what she said. She patted my mother's hand as punctuation and laughed with delight at some of my mother's rebuttals. Miss "Thin and Prim" remained silent and attentive. I caught her looking me over and I sat straighter, trying not to rattle my delicate blue cup. The thin-lipped lady's mouth had softened, her bushy red hair seemed to flame in the late afternoon sun. She rose from her deep chair and my mother followed her out of the room. The angular one remained watching me, her eyes strangely attentive, her body poised as though anticipating a summons. We waited for quite a long while. I didn't know where to place my empty cup.

It was dark when we returned to our hotel. As we entered our suite, my mother, full of enthusiasm, a spring in her decisive step, announced:

"Papilein, Colette was wonderful!"

The next lady to open her door to us looked like one of von Sternberg's specters from *The Scarlet Empress*. My mother brushed past this shadowed skeleton to greet an apparition in an austere sitting room. I had a feeling she might be a female but couldn't be quite sure. She was built like a truck – square, heavy, solid – above her man's shirt and tie emerged the head of a bulldog. I was shown to an antique piano stool and told to sit. My mother curled herself against the armchair containing the "Truck" and looked up reverently into the beaming face of the mastiff. The "Angel of Death" poured. She looked so ominous doing that, I decided not to drink the tea. The Venus flytrap next to my seat could have it! Again, the atmosphere seemed full of unleashed power, like an electric charge, it tingled. Very similar to the one that sparked whenever Marlene Dietrich materialized. Here, instead of visual beauty, it was generated by mental energy. I had felt this in the presence of Fitzgerald and the vibrant red-haired lady, and now, this one. She sounded American and very sure of her brilliance. I was so preoccupied trying to pour my tea into the flowerpot without getting caught, that I didn't concentrate on what she was saying. I wish I had – it was the only time I ever met Gertrude Stein. As with our other tea visit, my mother withdrew with our hostess, while I sat waiting politely, being observed by a strange woman gripping the back of an empty chair.

CHRISTMAS MUST HAVE BEEN MEMORABLE that year! I can't remember a thing about it, except that my mother didn't really like the scarf I made for her in knitting class. Crossing the English Channel the day after that I remember. That body of water is terrible at any time of the year and in December, it was worse. Even my mother felt queasy, but endured gallantly, saying to my father – in French:

"He wants me in London with him on my birthday. He says we will celebrate tomorrow all day in bed. Then go dancing all night at the Savoy. You must admit, Papi, he is much more romantic than Jaray was."

Well, if my mother was going to celebrate her birthday in bed with our Knight to Be, maybe I could dare ask permission to go to the Natural History Museum and see the dinosaurs.

Grosvenor Square was always posh, even before the American embassy dominated one side of it. My mother's apartment at Number 20 was nothing special, just convenient for getting back and forth from her swain's penthouse above us. The next morning, she appeared briefly, shrugged off birthday wishes, changed her clothes, approved of my father taking The Child to see all those "old bones," and vanished for the next few days.

My father was never mean in museums. Like churches, they brought out the best in him. It was a little like being in class, but he was an enthusiastic teacher, interested in his subject and, therefore, never boring – no matter how detailed his lectures got. I was sure my mother could not be having half as much fun staying in bed all day with her "knight" as I was, learning about the life cycle of the dung beetle.

NINETEEN THIRTY SIX WAS NEARLY OVER. England had buried an old king, crowned his son – who deserted his country for "The Woman I Love," and replaced him with a much better one, his brother Bertie, George VI. Three kings – in one year. That must have been some historical record! Dietrich had made three films during the same time period that made no history whatsoever, lost the genius of von Sternberg, let John Gilbert die alone, picked up a few mediocre diversions along the way, and earned a great deal of money. *Gone with the Wind* was published, Monopoly was invented, MGM's genius Irving Thalberg died at the age of thirty-seven, Roosevelt was returned in a landslide election, our Fred Perry won his third Wimbledon title. Adolf Hitler took the Rhineland without being stopped by anyone, his friend Franco seized Spain, Mussolini slaughtered Ethiopians, Stalin his own countrymen. Fred Astaire and Ginger Rogers became the world's top box-office draws, and I welcomed 1937 by getting influenza!

When neither the charmed beef tea nor the "special" chicken soup cured her child, my mother panicked and called the Duchess of Kent for the private telephone number of the King's physician, saying to me:

"Rulers always have the best doctors. They have to be kept alive to rule. Look at that Queen Victoria . . . she went on forever! Even Roosevelt, with his Infantile Paralysis, runs America only because his doctors are brilliant!"

Sir Something-or-Other, very tall, long-fingered, immaculate in Savile Row gray pinstripe and stick pin, appeared as though sent over from central casting, shot me full of horse serum, and left (in those days, before penicillin and antibiotics, the only thing available). Everything would have been fine except that I was allergic. By the evening, I had swollen to twice my size, my lips looked like two eiderdowns sewn together, my eyes had turned "Chinese," my hands matched my lips. My mother, magnificent in black velvet and broadtail, stopped by my room to say good night, took one look, screamed, and ran to the phone.

Our eminent physician was tracked down attending a royal banquet at Clarence House. Bridges was dispatched, with orders to haul him over to Grosvenor Square. As he came through the door, resplendent in orders and tails, my mother pounced, beating her fists against his starched shirtfront, yelling:

"What have you done to my child? What kind of a doctor are you? How dare you go to banquets while your patients are dying!" Her pummeling dislodged his pearl studs, they now popped out onto the floor. His heavily starched dickey snapped and, like a roller blind, ricocheted up under his chin. She kept right on punching his bared chest.

"Madam! . . . Please! . . . Do make an effort to contain yourself!" the royal physician murmured, backing off while trying to unroll his shirtfront. I lay there like a beached whale, enjoying the performance through my slits.

I recovered, although too slowly to suit my mother's medical timetable. What was missing? What was still necessary? Of course . . . sea air! So, I was bundled up in shetland and cashmere and shipped off to Bournemouth. In February, that was a real "seaside resort – out of season." Now I understood what the girls at school had meant when they spoke of mothers with lovers going to one. Deserted boardwalks drenched by pounding waves, barren cliffs, and empty tea shops damp and fogged from kettles kept constantly "on the boil" in case some lost mariner should wander in through the salty mist. Whenever I see Hitchcock's *Rebecca*, I remember the sea breaking against those cliffs, and when Trevor Howard meets Celia Johnson in that little "caff" in *Brief Encounter*, instantly I am back in Bournemouth, warming my hands around a steaming cup of milky tea, my fingers sticky from Banbury tarts.

The nurse who had taken me to the sea brought me back cured, and my mother was once again vindicated on the healing powers of salt air.

"You see, how much better the air is on this side? 'The air of the North Sea.' That's what my mother always said: 'That is the one that cures!' not that hot pond we have in California. What is it called, Papi? You know I never know such things . . ."

"The Pacific Ocean, Mutti."

"Why is *that* one called an ocean? What is the difference?"

I was very pleased to learn that my mother didn't know geography either.

I got an extra dose of curative air as we crossed the English Channel back to France, and Paris, where my mother discovered Schiaparelli. She had never paid any attention to this avant-garde designer, calling some of her outrageous designs "just cheap publicity getters." I do not know what decided her to visit this couturiere, perhaps it was the influence of her romance, the pretentiousness of her companion – whatever reason, we went to Schiaparelli, and my mother flipped. As my father's mouth got tighter and tighter, and I shuddered inwardly, she rhapsodized and *bought*. When my mother goofed, she did so on a royal scale! Astrological symbols in silver sequins on night-blue velvet. Brocade ropes that looked like writhing snakes appliquéd onto garish pink figured damask, tight-waisted feminine suits with black fox overvests and matching powder-puff hats. Lots of odd fake jewelry, ornate buttons, decorations, bits and pieces – overdone, overstated, overworked. Everything startling, highly visible, and none of it Dietrich. Schiaparelli became a girlfriend-buddy. They traded secrets and gossip. My mother rarely wore any of her clothes more than once but kept on buying them nonetheless, the complete opposite to her relationship, years later, with Coco Chanel.

I returned to Brillantmont late, because of having been ill, to find that roommates had been changed around, as was the school's policy. It kept the pupils from learning each other's language instead of French. While I unpacked and stored my belongings according to the rules, a thin, dark-haired girl, with strange light-gray eyes, observed me. After a while, she asked, in very precise English:

"Did you inherit the legs of your mother?"

I was as startled by her courage to speak in English as by her question; I nearly dropped my sponge bag. That was the first time I was asked what would become a much too familiar question over the years. I always wondered why people would think it so vital that they abandoned all manners to ask it. If I had inherited Dietrich's legs, I might have been less embarrassed by the question, but as I didn't, I was. It took years before I stopped feeling guilty for having to disappoint them with a negative answer. I have even had people lift my skirt while inquiring about my legs. It is amazing how they are either pleased or disillusioned when they finally see them. I decided to keep out of the Gray-Eyed's way, which seemed to suit us both. The third girl in our room that term was an Indian princess, as delicate as a newborn butterfly and just as pretty. She smiled a lot, flitted about on silent feet, but did not mingle.

My mother's calls kept me abreast of her news:

Selznick had offered our Knight a starring part in a big swashbuckler. My mother had to convince him to take it – apparently he was a bit sensitive about playing anyone who flourished a sword. After he accepted the film, she began coaching him on "anti-Selznick" tactics, which included "how to handle that terrible man, who does nothing but write memos long enough to be books."

Lubitsch was preparing a new film for her that this time he would also direct. It had no title as yet but was "something about a wife of a titled Englishman who falls in love with a man in a Paris brothel, pretends to be someone else until they all meet and find out who is who." It was supposed to be very sophisticated comedy, she said, adding:

"It can be a real 'Lubitsch touch' film *if* he doesn't get too cute or vulgar."

As the Countess di Frasso was still in Italy, our favorite house would be available and wasn't it "a funny coincidence" – our Knight had rented one just down the street from us?

My mother managed to extricate me from school early, and I arrived in Paris in time to help pack the trunks. Tami was back, I hugged her with relief – then saw she had been crying. My mother was stuffing tissue paper into hats, holding court. She was in a good mood. My father made the lists and labeled the keys. Tami folded scarves, I bagged shoes, my mother packed and talked:

"Papilein, remember I told you how I liked Colette? Did you see what she wrote about *The Garden of Allah*? . . . all about my too-red lips – terrible! Why would a great writer like that consent to do a film review? Graham Greene wrote one too. He said our desert looked like craters of Swiss cheese! But he isn't as good a writer as Colette – and probably needed the money."

We broke for lunch at my father's apartment. Tami had not had time to remove the butter from the refrigerator, so it was still too cold for easy spreading. My father gave her a biting lecture on her lack of memory, organization, and efficiency. She sat very still, head bent, submissive, letting the sarcasm wash over her, then broke and ran from the room. I followed. In the corridor, she shook her head, motioning me to return, not to get into trouble because of her. I was about to reenter the dining room when I heard my mother say:

"Papilein. You must not be so harsh with her. You must understand that Tamilein is only trying."

My mother defending Tami? How wonderful! I stood by the door, listening.

"But, Mutti. You can see that she is just impossible!"

"Papilein, why do you let her get that way? Haven't the pills helped? What did they say at that place we sent her to? Don't they know *anything*? They must know *something* about what makes a woman get pregnant all the time. I don't, because I get up and do something about it. Is she just too lazy to douche afterwards? There must be a reason? It isn't just the money for the abortions – you know I don't mind paying for them all the time, that is not the problem. But how she lets herself get that way, *that* we have to find a way to control. Can you imagine if that happened to *me* every time? Someday, someone is going to find out – no matter where we hide her. Can't you *talk* to her? Can't you force her to get up and go to the bathroom after? A little discipline, *that* she *has* to learn – Sh-sh . . . here is the child!"

I returned to my place at the table. They switched to French. I could not quite follow their rapid discussion, but I had already heard enough in German.

That afternoon, I looked up the word I had not understood. I knew very few grown-up words in any language. Now I learned what "abortion" meant. I sat, locked in the toilet, the dictionary open on my lap, wondering how a baby was first made, how one killed it, and why. I was absolutely certain that Tami could never do such a thing on her own. My mother and father – that was different. They were capable of anything.

WE SIPPED PERFECT BOUILLON while reclining in our reserved deck chairs, cozy under cashmere lap robes, walked the Promenade Deck, bet on the wooden horse races in the Solarium during afternoon tea, watched the skeet-shooting competitions. My mother, looking divine, danced every night in the Grill Room. I explored my beautiful *Normandie* and, except for having to leave Tami with my father, was happy.

In the opulent movie theater, I saw Norma Shearer in *Romeo and Juliet* and thought that Brian would have made a much better Romeo than Leslie Howard. When a lady's voice whispered urgently somewhere behind me in the dark, "Oh! I hope they are going to get together in the end," I turned and whispered back to her, "No . . . they don't, because it's Shakespeare!"

We steamed past Ambrose Light and – there she was! Constant and true. I waved and thanked her. I was back home!

BOX OFFICE POISON

WE TOOK OUR SUBTERRANEAN ESCAPE through the Waldorf kitchens while the press lay in wait for Dietrich above. My mother sniffed the pungent aroma of garlic and thyme, calling to me over her shoulder:
"They have Lamb Provençal today. We have to order that! Smells *good*!" and disappeared into the service elevator.

She removed her arrival costume and did her toilets, while I organized the waiting mail. A short cable from our Knight, who was about to follow us, she would like first, and a poetic effort from von Sternberg.

"Sweetheart, put a call in to 'the boys,' then ring for room service." She lit a cigarette, I handed her the two cables:

DIETRICH WALDORF ASTORIA NEWYORK
GETTING TERRIBLY EXCITED SHALL I PACK VINEGAR OR DO THEY SELL IT
THERE STOP BLESS YOU FOR RESTING AND FOR BEING MINE

We had ordered our lamb by the time her Hollywood call came through:

"Sweethearts, did you get my list? Did you see Bridges when he arrived? And the car? Make sure he knows what time we get to Pasadena and tell him we'll go directly to Paramount, and to bring the thermoses. Order the crawfish to be delivered for Friday and don't forget to get the dill. I saw Colette in Paris. . . . Who? Colette. The great French writer! Being in Hollywood is no excuse for stupidity. Besides, you haven't been there that long! Even there, you can read good books! Call Travis – tell him I am bringing clothes from Paris that we can use in the film and not to tell anyone. . . . Are the bodyguards ordered for The Child? . . . I saw Jo in London. . . . Oh, yes – still making with the cow eyes . . . I just received a cable from him, listen: 'My heart is without rest I follow the clouds and the sunsets from which the color of your eyes and your hair drop from the sky stop if it were possible to forget or to sleep some place until one could wake to a new life and being called back from the forgetting sleep of death even then I would feel you stop you who are of my blood stop what is there when the rainbows lose themselves in eternity.' He could have said all that on the telephone! Probably not, looks better written out! . . . Don't forget to order the champagne and tell Nellie to make sure the water-cooler man puts in a fresh bottle in the dressing room."

My mother kept me so busy while we crossed America, I hardly had any time to visit with my porter friends. But when I was sure she was really asleep, I escaped to my magic balcony and breathed the rich air, marveling as always at the vastness and majesty of this country I loved.

Travis was waiting for us with open arms. I settled myself into the leather armchair by his desk, ready for a long session. I had a feeling they had missed each other.

"Travis! Wait till I tell you about the Korda film!"

"Well, I heard all about that bath scene! The papers here were full of it. Did you really do it, Marlene? You? Naked? With nothing but bubbles?"

"Of course not! You know me . . . but don't tell anyone! They think that scene will save the film at the box office – but I doubt it! It is all so booorring. But, what can you expect from an industry that stops shooting every afternoon at four so people can drink tea. I was told that they did that in England, but I didn't believe it until I saw it! Even their grips 'sip.' Can you see one of ours drinking – tea? . . . I saw Jo in London. He is going to do Robert Graves's *I, Claudius* with Charles Laughton and that Merle Oberon. Can you imagine . . . that Singapore streetwalker à la Roman poisoner? I am sure poor Jo *has* to take her because of Korda. He never used to do things like that, but *now* – he allows it. I don't know what has happened to him. Jo is much too good for them. They don't understand his genius. Laughton is a ham. You can imagine what is going to go on with *both* of them trying to be 'great' directors at the same time. Laughton should just listen and learn, but you know actors . . . they never know when to shut up!"

The coffee arrived. Travis poured, my mother lit another cigarette.

"I saw Cole Porter in Paris. He looks more and more like a hungry jockey. They say he can't live without cocaine. . . . I must say, his nose looks *very* peculiar. Strange little man. I don't like his music, but his words – they are brilliant! Is it true that he is madly in love with Cary Grant? What does Mae say about *that*? I went to his apartment – all black gloss and white pigskin, full of zebra skins scattered about. *Very* masculine, and *ever* so 'hired interior decorator chic.' Such bad taste! I thought he came from a good family? . . . I saw a picture of Lombard in something you did for her – in that black monkey fur . . . you want to give her a banana! Really, Travis! But in that film . . ." She turned to me. "What's the name of that film, where we saw the photographs and I said, 'Finally, Lombard looks beautiful!'?"

"*The Princess Comes Across*," I answered.

"Yes – a bad title – in that film, you finally did something for her. She looks just like Dietrich. I hear she calls you 'Teasie' – how very 'cutesy-poo'!" She had been riffling through some of the test stills on Travis's desk; now she held up one of Irene Dunne in a period ball gown, an exaggerated confection, its surface strewn with thousands of tiny sequins and enormous tulle bows.

"Travis . . . have you any tulle *left* in stock after making this dress? I know she must be 'the bow kind,' but haven't you exaggerated it just a *little* bit?"

Travis giggled.

"Oh, Marlene! How I have missed you! You are so right! Each bow we put on, I thought how *you* would hate it!"

"You were right! As long as you *know* that this sort of thing is terrible you are still all right. But when you start doing clothes like Orry-Kelly – *then* I start to worry. Did you see what Adrian poured on Crawford? I saw the pictures. The whole thing nothing but bugle beads – like a second skin! *What work!* Beautiful! But on her, with those hips, it just looks vulgar! But then, everything looks cheap on Crawford. Has Lubitsch told *you* what we have to make for this film . . . or is this going to be another one of those talked about but never written down pictures of his?"

"Marlene – didn't you get the script? It was supposed to be waiting for you when you arrived in New York."

"I gave it to Clifton Webb to read. I knew by the time we arrived here, Lubitsch would have rewritten it, no matter whose name appears as the official writer. I know she is supposed to be the wife of an English lord. So, we do white chiffon blouse with ruffles along the neck and wrists, with a very simple black velvet suit and beautiful thin-heeled shoes . . . white kid gloves, very little jewelry, and a calm face. That's easy. I have all that. We don't even have to design it. What about the 'other man'? Who is he? Who's playing him?"

"Melvyn Douglas. He is a talented light comedian, but for my taste, not a romantic lead. He has no glamour – no sex appeal. Very unexciting to look at."

"Between Herbert Marshall and this Douglas, Dietrich is supposed to be elegantly sexy? Charming! At least the last time I was Marshall's wife I had Cary Grant to leave him for. Now I get a cold fish?"

She rose. I guessed she had decided it was time to read the script of her next film, *Angel*.

The exotic birds still perched on their silver branches, the mirrors sparkled, the panthers prowled, the gardenias bloomed, the di Frasso house was exactly as we had left it. Even the Afghan hound still posed in the shade of the magnolias, as though he hadn't moved in a year. Except for the change of lovers, we picked up where we had left off. Our Knight, ever the chameleon, now took on the trappings that proclaimed: attractive Anglophile returned to his origins of southern California. Flashed his famous inherited smile, bronzed his body, and looked handsome by and in our pool. We made beef tea for Herbert Marshall and George Raft, goulash for Lubitsch, Anna May Wong got her green tea piping hot at four, and John Barrymore his whisky, smuggled to him in the thermoses on the set by ten every morning. We designed hairpieces with Nellie and set up the dressing room.

It had been redecorated as a "welcome back" gesture from the Paramount bosses. Massive Art Deco chairs and matching chaise longue covered in a white fuzzy material that rested on geranium red carpets. My mother loved it, calling the furniture her "white teddy bears," never gave them up, took them with her when she finally left Paramount for good, and kept them in storage where they hibernated for the next fifty years! Mae West never liked our "fuzzy bears," saying that they made her behind itch, but I think that was just jealousy. She continued to snitch the flowers from our stoop: Life was back to normal.

My mother, appalled at the pretentiousness of Lubitsch's script, stopped going to see him for weekends at his beach house, called Edington, gave him hell, told him it was time he did something to save this latest disaster because she was through being "nice" to an "ugly little man with a big nose and cigar"! When Clifton Webb wrote her that he liked the script, she got angry at him too.

410 PARK AVENUE

Sunday, March 28, 1937

My Pretty,

I read of your going to the Rathbone party in your tails and dancing with all the girls. Evidently spring is having a decided effect on your glands. I wish I could have seen it.

I have read your script *Angel*. It should be great for you and you should be divine in it. I feel however that you should have a good toss in the hay in Paris with the other man. That sitting-in-the-park scene might have been all right for Jeanette MacDonald. But not for you, Toots. Not if I know my Miss von Losch . . .

Suddenly, our pool was minus one tanned "knight" and my mother's bedroom remained unlocked.

Darling,
 . . . I feel that you have taken our relationship and my stormy intense devotion to you too much for granted.
 If one shares one's life to the extent of setting up, within certain necessary limits, a household and practices domesticity to the same degree that we have – then there are certain obligations. . . .
 I believe that if you found it necessary to change your "one man woman" viewpoint then the proper thing to do would be to sit down and say to me that it was something you wished to do, and at least make a thoughtful attempt to make me understand. . . . I don't think it exactly respectful either to yourself, to me or to our relationship to treat me as though I were a gigolo – anxiously awaiting "milady's whim," i.e., if you feel like having me with you – then over I trot – if you have other plans then I'm expected to adjust myself accordingly and stay home until called for again. . . .
 Between two people who are in love there must be concessions, respect and a coordination of heart and mind and soul. These cannot be demanded or asked for – it must come out of mutual or necessary desire. . . .
 I'll not say anything more except . . . God bless you, dearest Dushka.

Their romance vacillated a great deal. When it was back "on," they kissed, held hands, dressed up, went to parties, did the night spots. The perfect couple – both beautiful and handsome at the same time. When "off," he prepared for his film, felt sorry for himself, blamed her for his unhappiness, and suffered. While she prepared her film, handed me his wedding ring to put away amongst the others, and managed, quite easily, to forget him without any emotional churning whatsoever. Although he did crop up in telephone conversations with my father and "the boys."

"Papilein. Tell me, why did I think he was so wonderful? Was it all *only* . . . London? The way he is there? Or could it have been because he was not working? Because now, here in Hollywood, he is behaving – suddenly – just like an actor! 'I–I–I, Me–Me–Me.' No wonder that father never sees him. I am even beginning to understand that terrible ex-wife of his. Do you think I maybe fell in love with him because he looked so wonderful in tails?"

The day the *Hindenburg* burst into flames while trying to dock in New Jersey, we heard it over the radio in the dressing room. The announcer broke down trying to describe the disaster. He was sobbing. My mother was jubilant:

"You see? Remember how I wouldn't let us take it? Even when Papi said we should? It must have been sabotage! Very good! Now the Nazis have to spend money to build another Zeppelin that nobody will go on because they will be too frightened after this!''

Somewhere along the preparation for *Angel*, my mother lost interest. For the first time since *The Blue Angel*, she allowed herself to get sloppy, and in the one category in which she had always been the most brilliant, the way she looked. Travis Banton, by now so confident to let Dietrich lead them, went right along, and together they made one error after another. It culminated in the only film they ever worked on that lacked their unique sense of style. Especially sad, as it was to be their last one together. The famous "jewel" dress from this film, an encrusted sheath of fake rubies and emeralds designed so she could wear her real ones, owed its notoriety more to its weight of fifty pounds and cost of four thousand dollars than to its photogenic perfection.

The whole film is slightly "off" – nothing works. Maybe my mother sensed this long before anyone else did, acknowledged the hopelessness of the situation, and just gave up. Of all the thousands of stills and portraits Dietrich kept of herself from every one of her films, she only saved a few from *Angel*, and those are mostly of her wearing her own "Tante Valli" velvet suit with the white ruffled blouse. By the time *Angel* was nearing completion, we no longer kept a supply of Lubitsch's favorite cigars in our dressing room; they were no longer on speaking terms.

ON THE 30TH OF MAY, 1937, the Independent Theater Owners of America took out an ad in all the motion-picture-industry trade papers:

The following stars are
BOX OFFICE *POISON*
Joan Crawford
Bette Davis
Marlene Dietrich
Greta Garbo
Katharine Hepburn

Suddenly these ladies supposedly had lost the ability to draw the paying public into the movie houses on the power of their name alone. Under pressure, Paramount canceled plans for Dietrich's next picture and put her out to pasture. Columbia, which had been after her to play George Sand, dropped the project.

ABOVE: In 1937, filming *Angel,* a script she disliked, Dietrich hoped that with Ernst Lubitsch directing, the picture could be saved.

LEFT: Travis Banton and Dietrich—the magic pair. Between them, they designed some of the greatest clothes for a film star ever seen. *Angel* would be their last film together.

BELOW: Dietrich, looking for a possible flaw in the reflection of the big mirror that was always stationed next to the camera. She knew she was in another flop, but that was no excuse for imperfections.

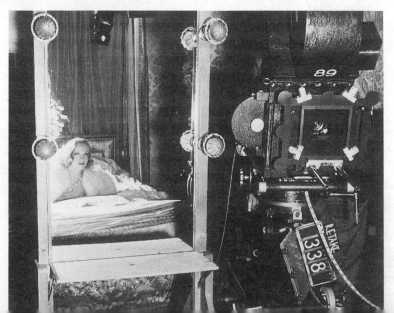

ABOVE: In *Angel.* Playing a "lady" always meant a black velvet suit with ruffled silk blouse.

LEFT: In 1937, branded "Box Office Poison," a star bids adieu to Hollywood, and leaves on the SS *Normandie* with just enough luggage to see her across the ocean until she can shop in Paris.

For the first time since coming to America, my mother was un-
employed. She called my father:

"Papi, we are leaving America. They say they can't sell Dietrich films
anymore. Those idiots, *all idiots*, of course, they can't sell them . . . because
they are *bad* – nothing to do with Dietrich. Even Garbo is on that list. The
pop-eyed one, that is possible, who wants to pay money to look at her –
but Hepburn? Yes, she is named too. Not to be believed! So now, who
have they got left? Irene Dunne maybe? *That's a star?* A real madness."

We packed up the dressing room, stripped it of everything that wasn't
nailed down. Storage vans drove it out through the Paramount gates and
that was that. No tearful good-byes, no "walks down memory lane." The
battle won and somehow lost, our soldier left the field – unbowed. Next,
we packed our things. We had always been gypsies anyway. Canceled the
house, paid off the bodyguards, servants, and tennis teacher, stored the
Cadillac, handed Bridges glowing references, and boarded the train, now
called the Super Chief because it had acquired air-conditioning. I waved
to Nellie long after the train had pulled out of Union Station. An era had
come to an end.

I don't remember anything about that trip east, except for a feeling of
loss, a hurting deep inside me. Even my little balcony was gone, replaced
by streamlined chrome. Fast and cool, travel had become expedient – no
longer an experience.

Once in New York, my mother enjoyed herself enormously. Being
"box office poison" might damage her fame in the "nickel-and-dime"
people category, but could not influence the rarefied circles she preferred
to move in.

Someone must have alarmed my mother about my safety, even in
Europe, for my head bodyguard was rehired and told to get east in
time to accompany us to France, and why not go the whole hog, make
it a really comfortable summer: my mother persuaded Paramount to give
Nellie a leave of absence so she too could join us. Just before we were
scheduled to leave, my mother called my father:

"Papi. Call Mutti. Tell her to call the doctor who cured The Child's
legs – tell him she is growing too fast. Something must be wrong inside
– she will be a giant. Every week nothing fits! Not only her fatness, but
the bones are growing. He has to tell me what I should do – maybe he
knows what is wrong. He can come to Paris to examine her."

Oh dear! I hadn't slouched enough! I hoped I wouldn't be locked away
in one of those "spas" like Tami.

The day we all boarded the *Normandie*, I was in such despair, even that
wonderful ship couldn't give me the usual euphoric lift of anticipation. I
stood in the very back of the ship. I wanted to see the Lady as long as

possible; the way my mother was behaving, it might be for the very last time. I made my wish but didn't really believe it had a chance of coming true. My grandmother cabled to the ship:

RADIO TELEGRAM
BERLIN
MARLENE DIETRICH
S.S. NORMANDIE
DOCTOR NOT ALARMED SAYS CHILD COMPLETELY NORMAL.
GROWING AS NATURE COMMANDS. ABSOLUTELY WITHOUT DANGER

MUTTI

I knew my mother wasn't completely convinced – she still kept looking at me speculatively, though not as often. I hoped once we got to her precious Europe, she would stop worrying about my bones.

My father, ready at his post, met us in Le Havre, accepted the mighty luggage lists, and herded our expanded group onto the train for Paris.

What the *Normandie* was to ocean liners, the Hotel Lancaster was to hotels. Discreetly hidden down a side street off the Champs-Elysées, it functioned as one's own private château in Paris. Baccarat chandeliers, brocaded chairs, priceless antiques, beveled mirrors, Aubussons, ornate friezes, Versailles doors, swagged satin-taffeta-organdied French windows, flowers, flowers, flowers everywhere, dewy fresh in hues of perpetual spring, their perfume never allowed to intrude, only delight. In those days, there were other great hotels that could also boast such visual perfections. What the Lancaster achieved over and above its superb luxury was absolute privacy. For nearly three years, we lived there. It became our base, our European headquarters, and never, in all that time, did I meet or ever see another guest! How did they do that? How was it possible to run a hotel where every chambermaid, valet, porter, and waiter became one's personal servant? Where rooms were cleaned and beds changed without one ever being disturbed or made to conform to anyone's timetable but one's own. How is it possible to run a hotel without a lobby? Without bells or bustle or elevators that never come. How can you maintain one without the sound of one vacuum cleaner at least being heard one time down some corridor? The Hotel Lancaster did! They didn't even expect you to register. After all, why should one be required to sign in on arriving at one's own château? Here we never entered by way of the kitchen. Although the French press and the adoring fans crowded the narrow side street, they parted like the Red Sea to let us pass. Once inside, nothing and no one could follow. Bribery of the Lancaster staff was unknown, unheard of, impossible – I am sure, if ever attempted, punishable by the guillotine.

My father had discovered this jewel but came to regret it, passionately. Fans and reporters kept their devoted vigil: night and day, rain or shine, the Rue de Berri was choked with people. Into this bottleneck, my father's big green Packard was expected to make its way whenever Madame Dietrich needed to be conveyed somewhere. This disturbed my father tremendously. After months of poring over paint samples, corresponding with Packard officials, he had repainted his precious car. Like a smitten youth, he was so enamored of his new, dark green patina, he glanced adoringly and fondled his fenders whenever near. He was also ferociously protective of his expensive paint job. We would emerge from our "château," the crowd surged forward:

"MARLÈNE! MARLÈNE!" excited voices shrieked. Flustered gendarmes, looking chic in little capes and spotless gloves, lifted their matching white truncheons in mild protest. Of course, *amour* triumphed over law and order! The crowd pushed forward to glimpse their idol, but my father's pride and joy blocked their way, so they pushed against it. Strange hands touched his glowing green metal and my father went berserk!

He bellowed: "My God! My sheen! My sheen! . . . Don't touch my *sheen*!" and Dietrich, this time, *didn't* make it to the toilet. She was laughing, peeing, crying. We had to cancel the fittings at Schiaparelli. From then on, the borscht and black bread story took second place to "Papi's paint."

"You should have seen it! People, hundreds of people, rushing toward me, and Papi? He wasn't worried about me – all he worried about was the paint on his precious car!"

In order to avoid Germany, we took the train via Switzerland to Austria and reached Salzburg in time for us all to be "costumed" for dinner. Nellie looked pretty in her patterned blue dirndl, with its dusty rose apron. She even got a jaunty straw hat with a bushy white feather that bobbed when she skipped. I was in cornflower blue that year, with a big, dark, dark blue apron that hid everything my mother had decided needed hiding. At first, my bodyguard, positioned outside the shop, refused to enter and be transformed, but when he saw my mother's disappointment, he relented and accepted a loden shooting hat sporting a big silver pin of a stag at bay. Tami and Teddy were spared as they were still being driven across borders by my father in Packard splendor.

My mother spent the evening talking to Jaray in Vienna and our lonely Knight in Beverly Hills. Nellie wrote postcards, my bodyguard oiled his revolver, I locked myself in the bathroom with its swan-shaped spigots and read *Gone with the Wind*, which I had "borrowed" from the Wardrobe Department. Its size made it terribly hard to hide. I kept my precious book in my knitting satchel from school, hoping no one would offer to carry it and feel how heavy it had become! Nellie knew, but she was my friend and wouldn't tell. *Gone with the Wind* became a sort of lodestone for me. Far from home, I read about a time in my country's history and felt less isolated.

My mother, looking like the most gorgeous milkmaid that ever was, my father, in leather shorts and Tyrolean knee socks, Tami and I in varying examples of flower-embroidered finery, got into the Packard, whose color matched our loden capes, and we were off. Nellie, bodyguard, and luggage followed by hired taxis. The road show of *Heidi* was about to begin!

Of course, he had found it! Exactly as his wife had ordered it. There it stood! Green shutters with cut-out hearts, gingham curtains swagged on six-pane windows, green bench sitting in the sun, bright red geraniums everywhere. A water pump, a wooden trough, red-and-white checkered tablecloths, feathered beds, working cuckoo clocks, even a pungent barn – courtesy of our very own living cow. Like a master set dresser, he had done it all! My mother stood before her ordered dream of an Austrian farmhouse and said:

"Papilein, are there enough closets for the clothes?" and without waiting for an answer, went to investigate for herself. But she couldn't fault him; she tried, but she couldn't. We stayed there for quite a while; that is, Teddy, I, and the cow stayed. My father was kept busy, chauffeuring and escorting my mother back and forth to nearby Salzburg and its famous festival attractions. Tami filled her usual role of "cover companion" to whoever was actually my mother's boyfriend for the evening. Those mornings when my mother was in residence, she rose early to keep an eye on the caretaker farmer as he milked her cow, warning him that should he hurt her in any way – he'd be *very* sorry. We would sit around the beautiful old farmhouse table, coffee and fresh bread keeping warm on a porcelain stove, while our group, resplendent in Knize silk, satin, and marabou, forgot our rules as "quaint peasants" and played sophisticates, reading the morning papers in Noël Coward style instead. Tami and I never read, we listened. We were always ready for the "breakfast" show.

"Papi! They finally are married! Now that awful Simpson woman is the Duchess of Windsor! The King has decreed that his brother can be addressed as 'Your Royal Highness,' but not she or any of their children. Well, they are never going to have any – *that* we know! But good, at least she can't call herself a 'Royal Highness'. 'Duchess' is already too good for a woman who is, after all, only an American divorcée!"

A few days later, we heard that the wonderful Jean Harlow had died at the age of twenty-six of uremic poisoning. My mother was livid:

"That mother of hers! That terrible Christian Science mother! She killed her! She wouldn't allow a doctor in the house. William Powell finally took Harlow to the hospital himself . . . but it was too late. They couldn't save her. Somebody should kill that *mother*. Maybe Powell will do it, but he is probably too heartbroken. Louis B. Mayer might. She was a real star. Wonderful body, wonderful hair. I never liked her when she opened her mouth, too low-class American, but . . . *silent*, she was beautiful."

One of our side trips that summer of 1937 was to visit my father's parents in Aussig, on the Czechoslovakian border. This time my mother came along. Tami and the livestock were left back on the farm. I tried not to run into my grandmother's waiting arms. I knew this might hurt her, but too much overt enthusiasm shown by me toward my grandparents would only result in my mother being jealous and becoming sarcastic with everyone. Dietrich stepped from the Packard to greet her mother-in-law, who wiped her hands quickly down her blue apron before timidly shaking the gloved hand extended toward her. When my mother turned to bow to her father-in-law, I grabbed my sweet grandmother and gave her a fast squeeze. The visit turned out to be even more complex than I had anticipated. It was so difficult to keep my grandmother from hugging me, stroking my head as she talked, showing her affection as loving warm people did sometimes in "real life," I couldn't even try to explain to her that my mother had to believe I loved only her and no one else – for ever and ever, amen! It would have been incomprehensible to this simple, uncomplicated woman. My grandfather's way of dealing with "the star come to call" was interesting. He flirted with her and she fell for it! I had not realized what an intelligent man he was until then.

My father was pleased with his parents' proper deferential attitude toward his famous wife. Nevertheless, he remained constantly on guard in case they forgot themselves and spoke before being spoken to first.

We only stayed two days. I bent down to kiss her soft cheek and whispered:

"I love you, Grandmother. Next time, we will bake together and then you can teach me how to make your special chocolate cake. I promise! Please tell Grandfather I am sorry, but I just couldn't play checkers with him this time. Tell him I love him and that I still have my fox."

With my father watching my every move, I got into the car. Farewells were formal and very correct, and we drove away. I didn't even try to look back and wave. I would have cried and been told to control my emotions. I would be a grown woman before I saw them again, they – too old and war-worn to recognize me.

Back on the farm, our cow was giving birth and having a hard time of it. Immediately, my mother became the midwife, shouting instructions to the worried farmer trying his best to pull the calf from its resting place.

"Pull! Pull! Can't you see it's stuck in there?"

"Moo!" bellowed our frightened bovine.

"Listen to her! You are hurting her! Stop it! Stop!" shrieked the visiting movie star. Dripping with sweat, face red, the farmer wrapped burlap sacks around the two protruding hooves and pulled anew. Nothing budged except the laboring cow.

"It's stuck! We need oil!" Lifting her peach-satin dressing gown above her waist, Dietrich sprinted through the steaming manure toward the house and her supply cupboard, returning seconds later with the first lubricant at hand, a big bottle of Elizabeth Arden's Blue Grass Facial Oil, which she proceeded to pour into the heaving cow's behind. My mother took hold of one leg, handed the other to the farmer, and as though she were crewing a sculling race, counted:

"One – two – three. Pull!"

"One – two – three. Pull!" and out plopped the best-smelling calf ever born in the Austrian Tyrol. For weeks, the barn smelled of Arden's signature scent, while the poor cow tried to lick the stench off her newborn. My mother ordered a case of her oil to be sent from New York, so the farmer would have it handy for all his future "birthings."

Our breakfasts, as always, continued to be informative.

"Everybody says that *Othello* is a big success. Brian is in it. Can you imagine him playing Iago? Probably slinking around the scenery, looking ever so handsome. Ridiculous! First, he isn't a good enough actor to play that part, and second, he is too English to be a convincing Italian villain. . . . Noël Coward has another success – he just goes on and on! He is really brilliant! Remember when he cabled and asked me to come to his dress rehearsal to watch him? And how he said in that slightly affected English of his, 'Marlenah! I must not appear effeminate in any way. Do be a dear – watch for anything that could be considered less than "butch," if you see me being at all "queer," tell me immediately.'

Now with him, I would do a play. Look what he has done for Gertrude Lawrence. A little, low-class soubrette. Now she is considered 'elegant' . . . all because of Coward. . . . Hitler has officially thrown Elisabeth Bergner out of Germany because she is Jewish. . . . Soon they won't have any talent left for their big 'cultural Reich' – except of course, that terrible Riefenstahl and Emil Jannings. *They* will stay, and those two 'well-poisoners' – the Nazis deserve!"

When I wrote to Brian, congratulating him on his success as Iago, I told him all about our new perfumed calf in our barn filled with the aura of Arden, and would he please send me a copy of *Othello*, so I could know what he was being so good in.

My mother was often away that summer. Besides the daily visits to Salzburg, she traveled to London, Paris, Venice, Cannes. On one of these "side trips" to England, she met George Bernard Shaw for the first time. She often told me *her* version of their meeting:

"There he was, that wonderful man . . . looking old even then, with that beard and parchment skin. Eating only vegetables always gives people a funny color. I sank down on my knees in front of him, and those light eyes of his just looked at me. He loved women at his feet. We talked all day . . . it was dark when I left. He said he would write a play for me, but he never did! You know he liked Hitler? Strange, how brilliant men can sometimes be so very stupid, but about the Russians, there Shaw was right! He loved them as much as I do. We recited our favorite poems to each other. He couldn't believe how many I knew by heart. You know, Shaw didn't look like a writer at all! More like an actor. He behaved like one too . . . very egotistical and full of himself!"

My father's version of this coming together of these two "living legends" was somewhat different:

"During the time we had the farmhouse in Austria, Mutti found someone to take her to meet George Bernard Shaw. When she came back from spending the day at his house, she told me that when she sank down on her knees in front of him he unbuttoned his fly, took out his 'thing,' so she told me, 'Of course I had to do *it* before we could talk!' She never went back, but she always said that he was a brilliant man."

It was not unusual to be told varied versions of the same thing. As an adult, I was often used as a sounding board for the different scenarios constructed by my mother, her husband, lovers, friends, enemies, and "also-rans." After a while, one became quite expert at recognizing the lies from the truth. It became a sort of distasteful parlor game my family and I played with skill and a certain voyeurism. Dietrich "fell on her knees" a lot in front of famous men. Ever willing and proud to prove her absolute homage. She must have been very convincing. Once, after visiting the great sculptor Giacometti in his studio, she emerged a few hours later, her arms cradling one of his plaster statues, her knees only slightly red.

MY MOTHER STOOD in the doorway of our farm kitchen, pulling on her gloves:

"Papilein – if California calls, I am in Vienna for fittings. If Vienna calls, I am in Paris for fittings. If London calls, the same. And you don't know what hotel."

It seemed that our Knight, Hans Jaray, and someone in London were out of favor.

"Mutti, as your husband, I would be expected to know where my wife is staying!"

"Don't be ridiculous. Just tell them you don't know!" and she left for her supposed fitting in Salzburg.

My father's lips thinned. He never objected to lying to my mother's lovers – only being made to look a fool in their eyes. He was very vain as to their good opinion of him.

I never met the "Salzburg" boyfriend. He was, after all, only a summer replacement and didn't last long. But, while he did, Dietrich rhapsodized about *Faust*, good and evil, retold her "young girl's dream" of someday playing the devout Margarete, and did the famous prayer as an encore at breakfast.

My father was busy with his accounts and making sure that the hired couple didn't cheat Dietrich on the price of potatoes. My bodyguard was staking out the village, Nellie wrote postcards, Teddy quivered watching butterflies alight, Tami embroidered linen tablecloths with beautiful borders of Slavic design, and I read my "official" books sitting on the green bench. It was peaceful and sunny and calm. I was glad my mother had, once again, found someone to occupy her.

The peace didn't last long. My mother's mother arrived, accompanied by her elder daughter in dark brown wool. Neither one of them had changed, except to intensify their basic characteristics. My grandmother, cool, composed – commanding; my aunt, hesitant, fearful, and cowed. Tami and I were given the job of baby-sitters to this trembling dumpling of a woman, which the three of us thoroughly enjoyed, but were careful not to let show, except to each other. Discussions and arguments filled the house. My mother became more and more vehement:

"Mutti! You have no choice! You *have* to leave Berlin and come to America with us. If the Nazis now think they can bomb places as far away as Spain, there will *have* to be a war. The Americans are not going to do anything. As usual, they won't even know what is going on in the rest of the world. The English can't make up their minds – but the French won't allow such behavior and *will* go to war. My friend Hemingway, the great writer, told me so!"

"Lena, you do not understand. Franco is trying to liberate Spain from the oppression of the Loyalists! He is a good friend to Germany. All this talk of our new Luftwaffe being involved in a bombing of a small Basque village is nothing but anti-German propaganda. It never happened! Otto Dietrich is now the Party's press secretary, and I believe him!"

My aunt's hands clenched in her lap. All through this visit she had been trying so hard to stay out of discussions. Now she failed, could no longer remain silent – and plunged:

"No! It's not anti-German propaganda! It happened! Everything is true! Terrible, terrible things – and no one stops the evil . . . no one." Her hand flew to cover her mouth as the words left it, shocked at her own audacity.

"Liesel! *That* will suffice! You are only a woman neither intelligent enough, nor sufficiently informed, to consider yourself equipped to make moralistic judgments. Behave yourself, before you become an embarrassment to this house."

"Tante Liesel – let's go and pick some field flowers for your room," I chimed in, and led her quickly from the room. Tami followed in hurried pursuit.

We sat in the poppy field, making little bouquets, and listened to my aunt as she told us about a place called Guernica, as ever afraid to speak above a frightened whisper; even the flowers might be listening for the Gestapo.

When the time came for my mother's family to return to Berlin, I held my aunt close, wishing she could remain safely with us. My grandmother shook my hand, looked me in the eye and said:

"Maria – the world is about to change, for better or worse, only time will have the answer. But loyalty and duty, those will remain constant and never ending. It is *they* that set intelligent men apart from the rabble. Remember that!" She kissed my forehead, patted my shoulder, and stepped into the waiting car.

I never saw her again. She lived in her house in Berlin throughout the Second World War, dying shortly after the fall of Nazi Germany – whether in celebration or defeat, I was never sure. My mother stood watching the car wend its way down into the valley of St.

Galgen, stepped back, and slammed the door. This time she did not cry.

I HAD PROBLEMS that summer. The "happy farmhouse" mood generated lots of cooking at the big iron stove, with me sitting at the kitchen table, being told to taste the copious results.

"Papi! I don't know why the child is getting so fat! She is beginning to look – ugly!" my mother would exclaim periodically, as she marched off to the kitchen to make me a four-egg omelette, followed by those special, just-baked-by-Tami vanilla cream puffs. When I hesitated to stuff myself, I was told:

"What is wrong? Are you sick? No? Then – *eat*! Eat. It is good for you – I made it just for you, sweetheart!"

So, I ballooned, split the cute bodices of my peasant finery, while my mother shook her head in consternation, and ordered ever-larger sizes to be sent out from Salzburg as she slapped a pound of butter into the pan for my daily ration of fried potatoes.

When they found my *Gone with the Wind*, that was the worst. All my English books, even my precious Shakespeare, were confiscated. I thought for a moment they were going to burn them in the village square! No one spoke to me for a week. Austria was never a lucky country for me.

Even the cow got into trouble. The summer evenings were so mild, the farmer had decided to house her in a slotted lean-to above the makeshift garage. She liked it there, relieved herself copiously, chewed her cud, while her highly acid urine seeped through the slats, splattered my father's precious Packard. The hot sun did the rest. The car acquired an interesting pattern of chartreuse polka dots burned into its dark green sheen. Our poor cow was presented to the local butcher without a chance of reprieve! The Austrian farmhouse had had it! We hung up our checkered aprons, changed into silk and gabardine, and left for Paris in the pockmarked Packard. It was the last time we were in Austria. By the next spring, Hitler had added it to his collection of shotless victories.

Maybe Hans Jaray had been told to follow her to Paris, maybe it was the Salzburg swain, or perhaps she had decided on a repeat performance with Chevalier or Colette – whoever or whatever was responsible, Dietrich went off on her supposed own and, as my father was immersed in negotiations for a new paint job, Tami and I were free to explore the great Exposition of 1937. The whole world had come to Paris that year to show off. Every country was represented by its own pavilion housing the finest examples of that country's achievements in every category imaginable. The architecture was very nationalistic. The Germans, ever faithful to Hitler's favorite Greco-Roman style, erected a skyscraper-type temple, on which they perched a twenty-foot eagle clutching a massive swastika in his vicious claws. Facing it was the U.S.S.R. pavilion. Looking like an Art Deco, off-center layer cake, it was topped by a twenty-foot statue of a charging comrade brandishing his lethal scythe. France electrified its Eiffel Tower for the occasion, built a lot of plush restaurants, displayed priceless art – even dedicated a building to the glories of my love, the SS *Normandie*. Siam represented itself in the shape of a golden temple bell, filled with jade Buddhas and delicate water lilies. Italy, a hodgepodge of da Vincis, Michelangelos, handmade fettucini drying on wooden trestles, interspersed by photographic proof of the glorious progress achieved by Mussolini's Fascism. Spain, still free, displayed its Cordoban leather, Valencian lace, toreador suits under glass, fountains in patio settings, and, in a special room off the main entrance, an enormous mural painted by someone called Pablo Ruiz Picasso. It was so ugly, it shocked. Gaping mouths, stretched in soundless screams, eyes that bulged, forever blinded by the horror they had seen, man and beast thrashing in the agony of violent death, crying their terror into hopeless silence. You felt it in color, yet it was done in black and white. Like death – colorless! I read the plaque: "Guernica, 1937," and I knew what my Aunt Liesel had been trying to tell us, understood what had happened in that Spanish town, what the Nazis had done.

Back at the Lancaster, I tried to tell my mother about what I had seen and felt that day. She wasn't interested:

"I don't like that Picasso. He paints only ugly faces. Crazy man. Hemingway thinks he is a great artist and a patriot. But then, anything to do with those people who keep fighting their civil war in the Spanish hills is *sacred* to Hemingway. . . . Tonight we are going to the Danish pavilion to eat their fish in dill sauce . . . then Papi wants to go over to the Turkish one to taste their baklava. I told Cocteau he and his friend can come and take me to the Yugoslavian pavilion to eat the little wild blueberries with sour cream instead. Sweetheart, you and Tami can go and have your favorite red pudding in Bulgaria – and we all meet in Java for coffee at eleven."

Tired and full of a thousand impressions, I sat, ate my flamed bananas à la Javanese, and listened to Cocteau gossiping. Elsa Maxwell and her party joined our table. A very elegant group. The ladies, their hair cropped close to their heads, evening dresses clinging against startlingly thin bodies, gloves to elbows, evening bags suspended from real diamond chains; their gentlemen, tuxedoed, exuding that aura of wealth, not necessarily worked for, but acquired with flair. When I heard Gertrude Stein mentioned, I paid extra attention. Finally, they were discussing someone I had met.

"Oh – *that* bull dyke? She gives me a pain in the ass!" lisped Cocteau's friend, a fair-haired Dane with milk-white hands that fluttered. That expression confused me. Not the part about the "ass." I heard that one often – it was my father's favorite expression, but a "bull"? A bull was a bull and a dyke was a type of water barrier the Dutch were partial to. What had the coupling of these two words to do with describing a woman?

"Oh, look – quick! Over there!" Excitedly, my mother pointed to a beautiful woman drifting by in layers of lavender chiffon and Parma violets, trailing Guerlain's Shalimar.

"See her? The one done up like Irene Dunne? That's a *he*! Gorgeous!" My mother turned to Cocteau. "Do you know him? Introduce us!"

By the time the lovely lavender "lady," who wasn't a lady at all but a twenty-five-year-old apprentice to a pastry chef in Toulouse, had satisfied my mother's curiosity, been given tips on how to thin out his false eyelashes, and solicited numerous autographs for his many friends who filled éclairs back in the provinces, I was falling asleep in my carved teak chair.

It had been a long summer.

"PAPILEIN, *MUST* THE CHILD GO BACK to that school with all those strange girls? She has nothing more to learn there . . . she knows everything already. She spoke French to the overseas operator yesterday and they understood her."

Fortunately, my mother's pleas did not sway my father, and I arrived back at school for the 1937–38 winter term. It was nice to be back in solid Swiss reality. I hoped that this time I would be allowed to stay for the full semester.

No such luck! Two months later, Tami was sent to Switzerland with orders to haul me out of school. My mother *had* to see me in Paris. Those final exams? Not important – they could wait. Glad to escape having to translate Homer, I flung some clothes into my suitcase – they would all be considered too tight, old, or whatever, and be replaced anyway – curtsied to the disapproving headmistresses, wished them a breathless "Joyeux Noël." and jumped into the waiting taxi. We had a train to catch!

Tami seemed gay – nearly too much so. She spoke in rapid bursts, as though in a hurry to get the words out before others crowded her mind; her gestures were animated, unrelated to what she was saying; she fumbled with her wallet, paid the taxi too little, apologized profusely, then overpaid, searched frantically for our train tickets, found them, handed them over to the porter, dropped his tip, scrambled to retrieve it, took my hand, and hurried us after him and onto our waiting train.

"Water – didn't buy water? And newspapers? Passports? We have passports? Katerlein, you want chocolate? Yes! Yes! I will run and get some – is there time? When does the train leave? Do I have Swiss money? How much will it be? Will they take French francs? They don't, do they? . . . Maybe not enough time? Why didn't I think of the water – how stupid of me! Maybe they will have some on the train? Will they take French francs?" She hesitated by the door, at a loss, unable to decide what to do, where to hurry to.

I put my arms around her, turned her gently, sat her down, tried to assure her: We did not need papers; we each had a book; the train not only had a dining car, but vendors; water was easily accessible. All alone she had managed to travel from Paris to Lausanne, pick me up, then get back on the right train all by herself without a single mistake – all was well. She had done it. She could relax now – we would certainly make it back to Paris without any big trouble.

Like an exhausted child, she put her head on my shoulder and quietly fell asleep. My God, what was happening to her! I held this fragile, tormented soul and wondered what her demons looked like.

We were pulling into the Gare de Lyon. She tidied her hair, put on her hat, smiled shyly at me through the mirror. "Katerlein, you won't tell Mutti and Papi – anything about my being so silly? They are so good to me, have so much patience."

"Of course I am. I am going to walk into the Lancaster and say, 'What a trip! Nothing but her usual stupidities! Really, can't *that* woman learn a *little* discipline!'" I said in my very best Dietrich imitation, which made Tami laugh.

When our taxi pulled up to the hotel, my father was waiting on the curb. On ushering us into my mother's presence, he remarked:

"Mutti – they have arrived! And all in one piece! Amazing! The blind leading the blind!"

My mother was busy kissing my eyes.

MY MOTHER WAS ESPECIALLY BEAUTIFUL that winter. After I was disinfected, had my hair cut, been reclothed and reshod, she cried, kissed me good-bye, and left for America, stopping in New York to shop for hats and fall in love with a lady called Beth, before continuing on to Hollywood. *Knight Without Armour* had opened and flopped. *Angel*, opened the first week in November, also laid a rotten egg.

My billet was moved to a small, threadbare hotel just off the classy Place Vendôme, where from my window I could watch the comings and goings at the mighty Ritz; that is, when my new English governess permitted such "common" curiosity.

My mother, installed at the Beverly Wilshire Hotel, wrote my father her news:

> The Beverly Wilshire
> Beverly Hills, California
> November 30, 1937
>
> Dearest,
>   I will try to write you a letter full of facts, because when I start to complain, it is hard for you to take.
>   First, the film that Paramount owes me won't start before February and may not be made at all because if they have to pay salaries while everyone waits, it will be too expensive. Maybe I will try to work someplace else and do the film for Paramount only in the New Year.
>   The trip was very bad. In the train suddenly Tauber stood in front of my door, singing his heart out. Then for days he poured his heart out to me. He is so unhappy. He sang here yesterday – so beautifully – better than ever. We all cried during *The Grenadiers* by Schumann. Reinhardt had such tears rolling down his face, that I wasn't embarrassed that I was crying. It was a marvelous success for him here and he was happy – for a few hours. In the train we sang together – all the old songs and Berlin was suddenly with us again – so near, so strong, that we were lost and forlorn when we arrived in Pasadena. Lang is looking after me. D. I have not seen. He wrote me this morning that he has found himself – and that his life is "calm" and purposeful! I am glad that everything has been solved so calmly. I wrote to Beth a farewell letter, because in New York I didn't have the courage to tell her that everything was finished between us. Edington is loyal and good, with him and Lang, I hope to get through this difficult time. I am so lost without The Child. In this country, that remains so foreign to me, as it always was, that only through her joy I could feel close to, became a home because of her – now makes me miss her even more.
>   Adieu, my heart. I am lying here in bed – and no door opens – from anywhere – and that is frightening.
>   Always yours,
>
> Mutti

For Christmas, Tami was sent to "pull herself together" in a mountain sanitarium. My father's plans were so obviously veiled, they had to be clandestine, and I was delivered to an English country estate, with turrets, pomp, and circumstance, straight out of a Sir Walter Scott novel. My room boasted a canopied bed, all white ruffles and Elizabethan drapes, curved window seat beneath Tudor windows, an Adam fireplace whose ever-ready logs were lit by a uniformed lass each snowy morning before she awakened me with: "Miss, Miss, the fire's lit, your bath's run. Do hurry, the breakfast gong will be sounded shortly." My hostess was the model British lady, gracious, genteel, to the "manor" born. Her husband, a younger version of C. Aubrey Smith with a lot of Michael Redgrave thrown in, sat in a majestic, high-backed chair, knitting argyle socks in rapid five-needle perfection. He had become proficient in this awesome skill while recovering from war injuries to his hands. The picture he made, so elegantly nonchalant in that so-British chair, clicking away, his eyes never concerned with his sock in progress, is a treasured memory. Their daughter was very nice to me, it was not her doing that I felt alien in a world I wished I belonged to.

We took horse-drawn sleds to neighbors' stately homes for festive balls, were given real dance cards that kind Sirs, Lords, and Viscounts down from Eton and Harrow were kind enough to write their illustrious names in. On Christmas morning, the real one, I woke to discover a pillowcase at the foot of my pretty bed stuffed full of gaily colored gifts, and one incredible evening, guests in full-dress kilts, all black velvet, reds, greens, blues, and silver-buckled shoes, sat at our own banquet, given in our own ballroom, as pipers in tartan regalia marched around the laden table, piping their thrilling tunes welcoming in the New Year!

Never *ever* has one homeless child been handed such a perfect Christmas. It became my yardstick of what this holiday should and could be. Whenever I hear bagpipes, I see that lovely house, feel the warmth and security, and thank those kind strangers for giving a make-believe child her first taste of tradition.

Once back at school, my mother's calls continued their interruptive pattern. She had been forced to go to a big gala opening and just had to tell me all about it! She didn't even give me a chance to thank her for letting me go to England for the holidays.

"Sweetheart! Listen! Listen! You won't believe this! I had to go to an opening. Klieg lights, fans, red carpet, everyone dressed to the teeth à la real glamour, radio interviews – everything. Like a real big movie première. I had to do the whole movie-star to-do! Hair, furs – even all the emeralds! The beautiful white chiffon didn't fit because you weren't here to tape the breasts. Anyway, all this glamour *to-do* – and you know for what? *Hopping rabbits!* Even you would have been too old for that! But you should have been there, just to hear the screaming when we stepped out of the car – box office poison or no box office poison, the people went wild – they pushed so hard against the barricades that some of them fainted from all the excitement and got stepped on!

"Afterwards in the car, I said: 'Now, tell me one thing! *Who* is going to go to see that? A full-length picture of nothing but "cutsey-poo"? . . . Except for the wonderful stepmother . . . it is for two year olds! And all those ugly little men, like midgets, and that Prince – looks queer. . . . You can't allow somebody who does Mickey Mouse to become a movie producer!' Sweetheart, you have to see it! [I couldn't wait!] They have a 'cleaning scene' . . . I nearly peed in my pants! Little 'birdies' and fluffy squirrels, all helping the village idiot! And terrible music. All sugary doodle-do. . . . They can't allow such things and then even have premières for them. And for this abortion I had to dress up? . . . Sweetheart, I tell you one thing – it will never make money!"

The power of Disney's first full-length cartoon was such that when I finally did get to see *Snow White and the Seven Dwarfs*, even my mother hadn't been able to spoil it for me. I loved it – "birdies," "queer prince," and all!

Dietrich's old contract had until the end of February to run. Paramount, still owing her a picture, was now willing to pay her off. She wrote my father.

I have already used up too much time and money hoping that the Studio would come up with something that could erase the "Box Office Poison" but they have nothing to offer. I have been advised, discreetly, that they are willing to pay and forget it, but that for appearances I must have a lawyer write to them, etc.

The $250,000 will keep us going for a while. Something will come up eventually, and then things will be all right again. I have to believe that Hemingway was right when he said that it did not happen only by Jo's hand, that much came from inside me.

Here it's very expensive but you know the mentality around the studios. I don't dare have the smell of "has been" or even "out of work star." So, I'm spending what I have in order to appear very glamorous, when really I am lonely and bored and – to you I can admit it – frightened.

Hitler marched into a welcoming Austria. My mother moved out of the expensive hotel into a little house in Beverly Hills.

My father delivered me into my mother's arms for spring vacation. I hadn't been in school long enough to deserve one, but the other pupils had, and so, I got one too. Tami, I was told, was once again "visiting her brother." I worried where she had been hidden away this time and if she had been forced, once again, to kill a baby.

My mother was beautiful that spring. Vibrant, talkative, and in command of her handsome Knight. He too seemed at his very best. They laughed and played the "lovers" to perfection. But there must have been someone else, for once or twice, I was told to say she was busy discussing scripts, when I knew she wasn't – and when he called early one morning, I had to pretend she was still in bed when, actually, it hadn't been slept in.

We went to have tea with one of her old girlfriends. I wondered if now Dorothy di Frasso and my mother had something more in common than just having rented her house. Our countess was about to rush off to Italy – to kill Mussolini. She had a foolproof plan. Sticking a fresh cigarette into her long ivory holder, she told us all about it: It seemed that tiger's whiskers, once ground and mixed into food, would perforate human intestines like a thousand fine needles, bring on agonizing death through peritonitis.

"Marlene – one's insides turn into a sieve, shit pours into the stomach – and *basta*! Stinking death!"

Once back in Rome, she was planning to throw a party, invite all of her titled Italian friends, hand each one tweezers, send them out on a scavenger hunt with orders to return with the whiskers of tigers.

"But, darling, once they're ground, how are you going to get them into Mussolini's food?" my mother asked, fascinated.

Our elegant assassin chuckled: "Silly girl – that's the *easy* part."

My mother threw back her head and roared.

We stayed the whole afternoon, going over the details, planning Mussolini's demise. It was agreed that as there were only two mangy tigers left in the Rome Zoo, di Frasso had to take airplanes to get there in time before they died and got carted away, so we would bring her Afghan hound over by ship when we came. Like two courageous legionnaires about to venture into dangers unknown, they kissed each other in gallant "farewell."

On entering our car, my mother exclaimed: "Oh! How I would love to be there! Watch her fuck and feed him to death!"; then realizing what she had said in front of me, tried to cover it up by quickly talking about our taking the dog to Europe, while I was desperately trying not to laugh.

With no other film offer on the horizon, her Paramount affiliation now severed, my mother became restless. Having put in her time on American soil required by law for those awaiting U.S. citizenship, she was ready to leave, anxious to get back to Europe. We joined my father, who had preferred to amuse himself in New York. He had a pretty redhead in tow and seemed very busy being shown the sights of the city. While my mother, with her friend who answered to "Beth" and clung, my father, and his Palm Beach debutante did the town, I got a chance to talk to Brian – told him all about his England being so special for Christmases, my worries about Tami, my constant incomplete marks at school because I was never really there, my mother being disturbed by my fat ugliness and growing bones. He listened. He was always ready to listen to my childhood woes, then tried to help – really couldn't, but just being able to talk to him was comfort enough.

I watched Rockefeller Center still being built, bought a secret copy of a new book, called *Rebecca*, with money I stole from the "tips," listened to the radio, learned all the words to "Flat Foot Floogie with the Floy Floy" so I would be the only one at school who could sing it, and wished, for the umpteenth time, I didn't have to leave.

Our rosé-beige apartment awaited us, the *Normandie* ever ready to enfold us in beauty, carry us to the opposite shore. The band played – horns blew. At "just thirteen," again, I was leaving "home." This time I had returned, but I doubted that I would ever be so lucky again! I prayed extra hard, hoping the Lady wouldn't mind if I thought of myself as one of those "homeless, tempest-tost" she was so willing to protect and love.

I tried to drown my sorrows in the *Normandie*'s ornate swimming pool, but my pining California spirit missed the sunlight. "Forgetting" at the movies was easier. Even my mother joined me. We saw *Marie Antoinette*. The *Normandie* was very partial to Norma Shearer films.

"She looks much better now than when that husband of hers, Thalberg, was alive," my mother's voice boomed out of the dark. The audience "ssshed" in unison the voice that had disturbed. Dietrich took no heed.

As she considered films were shown for her benefit only, she believed movie houses the world over to be her private projection rooms.

"Sweetheart . . . look at that work! Best designs Adrian has ever done. Of course, they have nothing to do with the real Marie Antoinette, but nobody cares about that anyway – and Mayer wouldn't know the difference." Her comments came hot and heavy. The "shushing" increased. "The wigs! Look at those wigs! The work! That Sydney Guilleroff! Did he design all of them? . . . A bit overdone but . . ."

"*Mais, alors!*" muttered an exasperated gentleman behind us. My mother turned. He recognized her, apologized profusely for having disturbed her. She continued:

"Between the ostrich plumes, the cascading curls, the velvet bows, the jewelry . . . she looks ridiculous! Like a circus horse . . . but beautiful. You know, if Marie Antoinette had looked *that* good, they would never have cut off her head."

My father was occupied playing shuffleboard with a cute brunette. I often wondered if all those "cuties" really were interested in him or just wanted to sample what belonged to Dietrich. This holds true all the way down the genetic scale: If you can't get the queen, try the consort, or her princess. Fame and its aura are so desired, even grandchildren become coveted bed partners for no other reason than their illustrious genes. It is a real struggle of survival to exist within that spectrum. If the creator of this magical attraction is a Mme Curie or an Einstein, it is no less wearing, but at least a little easier to understand. If this sick obsession is generated by nothing more than physical beauty, it becomes, at times, unbearable.

"Sweetheart, I'm wearing the Alix with the satin flounce. Barbara Hutton is giving a party up in the Grill. Who do you think is her latest boyfriend? Our shirt salesman . . . from *Blonde Venus*! Amazing how these American heiresses go for pansies! . . . Cole Porter is probably furious and wishes he hadn't written 'Night and Day' for him!"

I was returned to boarding school just in time to prepare for exams before the summer break. I didn't even know what had been taught. My new roommate was a girl whose father had once spent a weekend at the Hotel Ambassador with my mother, so we were practically related! Sometime during that very short term, my official family came to visit me. My mother, my father, a resurrected Tami, and Teddy stopped off in Switzerland from Somewhere to Somewhere, signed me out for a sumptuous lunch in Lausanne, then delivered me back to school, where my mother signed autograph books, patted youthful cheeks, was gracious, regal, impressed everyone with her perfection, and cried as she bade me a Chekhovian farewell. Despite the moving scenes of a "mother's farewell," she seemed in a dewy haze, utterly in the throes of some new "perfect" love. It was very "Anna Karenina." I waved good-bye, had time to feel sorry for our Knight and Beth before reporting to "French Lit – Room B," where we were deep into Proust. The interruptive telephone calls came hot and heavy, but this didn't get me into trouble anymore. Brillantmont had given up trying to fight my mother. I didn't blame them, I knew the feeling!

Her voice soft, she spoke in lyrical German, her best "à la Heine": "Jo is here. They are showing his films in this festival. He is very famous here – being feted, so is never around. Sweetheart! Venice must be seen only at twilight or dawn – in the light of Tintoretto. We drink Dom Pérignon as the golden light paints the sky, silhouetting the domes of a thousand churches! We walk over little curved bridges and listen to the gondoliers sing – they all sound like Caruso!"

I wondered who the other half of the "we" was . . . he knew his painters.

"Oh, sweetheart! If you could see it! We are in a small fishing village – little boats on a blue-blue sea, white sails billowing, fishermen repairing their nets in the golden evening sun, beautiful barefoot women carrying their water jugs on one hip to the village well. We eat little fish roasted over coals with fresh thyme from the Provence and breathe in the perfume of pine trees that grow right down to the sea. At night, we listen to their beautiful Italian songs of love and the sea makes little wave sounds onto the soft sand."

I was dying to meet the other half of that "we."

"Sweetheart – the grapes! Everywhere you look, little sturdy vines. Today, we are driving to drink white Burgundy in a little country inn . . ."

She sounded more and more fairy-tale happy, with overtones of "German breathless"! I decided her new lover must be German, a wine connoisseur, an artist, a true romantic worthy of her, certainly someone very special.

I NEVER KNEW why my mother ordered me back to Paris, for when I arrived at the Hotel Lancaster, she wasn't there. But the lilacs were!

ABOVE: Meeting and loving von Sternberg in Venice.
BELOW: A rare candid picture of my mother having a good time in the golden sun of Italy.

Someone must have bought out France in white lilac. You couldn't see the furniture for the flowers, and breathing was definitely difficult. Suddenly, my father materialized from behind the vases, said hello, and introduced me to my new governess, who inspected me without enthusiasm. I curtsied, removed my train gloves, we shook hands, I was told to put my gloves back on as we were leaving, I was being moved to another hotel, where I would henceforth reside with "Mademoiselle" as guardian and chaperone. This was the beginning of sometimes being billeted apart from my mother when she had a new lover in residence. Suddenly, at the age of "just thirteen" in my mother's mind, I had attained the age of perception.

The Hotel Windsor was brown. Furniture, walls, carpeting – even the dried flower arrangements looked like baked mud. Our "special wing" boasted a pretty bay window, otherwise it was just as somber as the rest of the establishment. Except for my memories of the time spent in a perfect little park nearby, the Hotel Windsor had nothing to recommend it. In the square, Rodin's huge statue of a depressed Balzac brooding on top of a massive pedestal set the tone of the area.

My father, having installed his charges, left. While my governess unpacked us, I observed her. She was not easy to cast. She was not a Zasu Pitts, certainly not a spinster version of Claudette Colbert – if there ever was such a thing as a Colbert with overtones of spinsterhood. What made this woman interesting was that her lack of personality – such a necessary requirement in a proper governess – was there, but in her case seemed purposely acquired. Her costume was right: prim navy serge suit, immaculate white blouse, cameo at throat, sensible black leather shoes, very proper, unattractive, out-of-fashion hair in serviceable bun at nape of neck – all correct, and yet, completely false. She looked the colorless spinster lady, but wasn't – her walk was wrong; it undulated, enticed – she wouldn't have gotten past my friend Mae West with her camouflage! She might have fooled a casting director. Certainly my usually sharp father must have been taken in, but I wondered . . . had he seen that walk? Noticed the way her shoulders followed the lift of each hip, how she glanced furtively at herself whenever she passed a reflective surface? Perhaps he hadn't been hoodwinked at all – had been so intrigued by her too-carefully hidden attributes and decided to engage her for future inspection? I had noticed that whenever Tami was put away somewhere, he had a certain type of woman ready at hand. I hoped this one wouldn't be one of them. Being the girlfriend of the boss might give her airs. This one had enough of those already. Trusting someone who played a lie so cleverly could be dangerous. She must really need this thankless job to have gone to such lengths to get it. I decided to find out why.

My new life became rather structured. In the morning, waiting for my mother's summons to report to her at her hotel, I did my homework while my governess caught up on her "hidden beauty" sleep. Promptly before lunch, refreshed and accurately prim, she delivered me into my mother's waiting arms and disappeared. I did the mail, helped my mother dress for whatever luncheon rendezvous was scheduled, listened to her, saw her off, tidied her bathroom and makeup, put away and filed her evening clothes from the night before, did the flowers and cards, was told by my father not to dawdle, gave Teddy a fast hug, tried constantly to find out where Tami had been hidden this time, then helped my mother change for dinner, tidied and refiled her day wear before "Mademoiselle" reappeared to collect her charge, conduct us back to our somber abode and our usual room-service dinner of Poached Sole Jardinière. I was left to finish my fruit and cheese course by myself as Mademoiselle needed time to prepare for our nightly "outing." Her long hair looked so pretty, all combed out, curling down to her shoulders; I thought the lipstick she wore was a bit too crimson, but the lip gloss was effective; the floral silk clung, molding her body, very high heels accentuated the walk that had first given her away. Swiftly, we made our way through the empty lobby and to an already waiting taxi. We would sit silently in our respective corners, the lady of the evening and her young charge, until the lights of Montmartre and the dome of the Basilica of the Sacré-Coeur heralded our arrival at her destination. She would pay the taxi fare from her little purse that swung jauntily from its silken cords, push me ahead of her through a small hidden door, sit me down in the remotest corner of the candle-lit bar, vanish up a flight of creaking stairs, trailing a scent of cheap musk. I learned to like the taste of cherry brandy that June of '38! A sullen woman with dirty hair kept replenishing my glass with the sticky elixir. As the hours passed, I, the child of censored movies, whose only concept of human relationships was lyrical, adoring romance, or cruelty, sat obediently, waiting for my governess to return from wherever she was and take me home. If someone had told me then I was sipping brandy in a brothel, I wouldn't have known what they meant, and as my school friends' descriptions did not really fit my governess, the label "prostitute" never entered my mind. I had been told by my father's appointed authority to *sit* and *wait*, and like Teddy, I did; behaved myself until Mademoiselle, all smiles and tangled hair, reappeared and took me home. As she was especially lenient and permissive after these clandestine soirées, I quickly learned to keep silent and reaped the benefits of her approval of my cooperation of her "little secret."

In the daytime, I continued shuttling between the airy white-and-gold beauty of the Hotel Lancaster, returning to the brown gloom of the

Windsor whenever my mother and her new lover resided in Paris. It never occurred to me that the year of "The Child might discover" had begun. My mother's behavior did not change, just where I was housed, and even this was so erratic that I never could figure out when I could be "viewable" and when not. Finally, I gave up trying to understand the elaborate attempts at subterfuge and continued to play dumb as far as my mother's romances were concerned. It had always worked in the past, it surely would keep everyone reassured in the present. I had my father's slick example: Befriend and charm all who enter here, wait them out until they and their accompanying rules were replaced by others.

The white lilacs kept arriving in unparalleled abundance, accompanied by cases of Dom Pérignon and some of the sweetest love letters I had ever seen. I had yet to meet the man responsible for them and the retraining of Dietrich's palate for champagne. Whoever he was, his influence over her was complete. Goethe had been replaced by Rainer Maria Rilke, all the Hemingway books by one entitled *All Quiet on the Western Front* in multiple languages by someone called Erich Maria Remarque. I never could understand this strange German penchant for calling boys by my name.

My mother swept through the lilacs, pulling a reluctant man behind her:

"Sweetheart! Come here. I want you to meet the most brilliant writer of our time – the man who wrote *All Quiet on the Western Front* – Mr. Remarque!"

I curtsied and looked up into the face of an intriguing man. The eyes veiled, giving nothing away, mouth as vulnerable as a woman's, a face to be sculpted.

"Kater? Is that what you like to be called? I am known as Boni to friends. How do you do?" he said in a soft, aristocratic German, as though reading good poetry.

"No, no – my heart! The Child must only address you as *Mister* Remarque," my mother cooed, melting herself into his side. She locked her arm in his and strolled him out of the lilac bower. I went back to unpacking *Mr.* Remarque's books, thinking – this one might really be worth mooning over!

Remarque and I became close friends. I always thought that he had the look of a debonair fox, like an illustration out of the *Fables* of La Fontaine, even the tops of his ears pointed slightly. He had an innate theatricality – an actor in a heroic production standing perpetually in the wings, waiting for the right cue; in the interim, he wrote books in which all the male roles represented the powers within him; in life never placed together to form one whole character, just the most intriguing parts of himself, doomed never to meld into one complete man. Not because he didn't know how to, but because he felt himself undeserving of such exemplary completion.

My mother used to describe her first meeting with this charming, complex depressive. The scene went like this:

She was having lunch with von Sternberg on the Lido in Venice, when a man approached their table.

"Herr von Sternberg? Madame?"

Although my mother resented strangers approaching her, his deep voice, with its cultured tone, intrigued her. She looked up into the finely chiseled face, the sensitive mouth; his falcon eyes softened as he bent toward her.

"May I introduce myself? I am Erich Maria Remarque."

My mother held out her hand, he raised it to his lips in homage. Von Sternberg motioned to the waiter for another chair, saying: "Won't you join us?"

"Thank you. May I, Madame?"

My mother, enchanted by his impeccable manners, smiled faintly, inclined her head, giving him permission to sit.

"You look much too young to have written one of the greatest books of our time." Her eyes had not left his face.

"I may have written it solely to hear your enchanting voice tell me so." He flicked his gold lighter, extending it to light her cigarette, she cupped her pale hands around his bronzed ones, inhaled, the tip of her tongue dislodged a speck of tobacco from her lower lip. Von Sternberg, the consummate cameraman, left quietly. He knew a great two-shot when he saw one.

"Remarque and I talked until dawn! It was wonderful! Then he looked at me and said, 'I must tell you – I am impotent!' and I looked up at him and said: 'Oh, how wonderful!' With such relief! You know how I hate to do 'it' – I was so happy! It meant we could just talk and sleep, love each other, all nice and cozy!"

I always imagined Remarque's reaction to her enthusiasm at his supplicant confession and wished I could have seen his face when he heard her utter it.

They looked very strange, all that blackness against the white and gold of our Lancaster anteroom. I had arrived to help my mother dress for lunch and been told she was busy, to wait until summoned. So I sat, watching the two men guarding our living-room door, behaving as though they belonged there. Both were young, thick-necked, square-jawed, steely-eyed, and very blond. They could have been twins. Even without all those silver eagles and swastikas all over their uniforms, they would have looked menacing. They scared me. I sat very still, hoping the "Siegfrieds" wouldn't deign to notice a mere "Aryan" child. I wondered who they were there to guard and why my mother would consent to a meeting with a Nazi! The door opened, expert clicking of heels, lips brushed elegantly across my mother's extended hand, a clipped "Heil Hitler," and a tall German strode out of our suite, followed by his henchmen.

"Papi – have you ever seen such a thing? How can such a well-educated man like Ribbentrop believe in Hitler! He is an intelligent man, from one of the best families in Germany, so you can't tell me that he doesn't *know* any better. I had to hide Remarque in the bathroom! After they burned all his books, I was afraid if those 'well poisoners' saw him – a ridiculous situation! *I* have to be careful – just because Mutti and Liesel refuse to leave Germany? Next time you talk to them, just tell Mutti they *have* to leave – so I don't have to go through things like this. But . . . did you *see* that uniform? How those shoulders fit? That's where all the Jewish tailors have disappeared to! They have taken them to make their costumes! Sweetheart, get Mr. Remarque – he can come out of the bathroom now."

Remarque didn't like being locked away, even if it was for his own safety; he stormed into the living room:

"Marlene – never, never dare to lock me away again! Do you hear me? I am not an errant child nor an irresponsible idiot bent on defying reality for the sake of irrational bravura!"

"Oh, my only love! I was only frightened for you! You know how they hate you because you, a non-Jew, left Germany. They might have been sent here just to find *you*! All that story about Hitler wanting me to be the "Great Star" of his German Reich . . . that is all not true! The only reason he keeps sending his 'so important' officers to get me to come back is because he saw me in *The Blue Angel* garter belt and wants to get into those lace panties!"

Remarque threw back his head and roared. He, who so rarely found life amusing, laughed with complete abandon on those rare occasions when he did.

My flighty governess was given excellent references from my father. Her services were no longer required. Tami had returned, restored once again to surface health, clutching a handful of new prescriptions guaranteed to keep her happy, at least through the summer. My mother, on seeing her, had commented:

"Well – all the money was finally worth it. You look human!" and we left to vacation in the south of France, *en famille*.

The Hôtel du Cap d'Antibes, perched white opulence overlooking the Mediterranean, in 1938 still sapphire blue and crystal clear, its water so clean one swallowed it without fear while swimming in its cool beauty. As one of the most famous hotels along the Côte d'Azur, the so-called "beautiful people" of the thirties gathered there to observe each other and exchange their privileged gossip. They were different from those of today. Maybe it was the silks and linens they wore, the Patous, Lanvins, Molineuxs, Schiaparellis – the absence of jeans, sneakers, and unisex – that gave them such an aura of real chic. Just as the movie stars of the silver screen were visually unique, they too had special individuality seldom seen today, even on the most luxurious yachts anchored in Monte Carlo's harbor. The men, whose business acumen or inherited wealth made all this effervescent luxury possible, they haven't changed as much, although their 1930s prototypes had a bit more style, looked classier, were better mannered.

Our summer palace was, and still is, a truly great hotel, one of those rare few in the world that have defied change of any kind. The Dietrich entourage had connecting suites, Remarque, my mother, my father, and the luggage. Tami down the hall, I, up the hall. Teddy divided his loyalties like the diplomat he was.

There is a special summer light along this part of the French coast. Stark, intense, hot, and white, making all color come into its own. That first summer in Antibes, Dietrich forsook her beiges and blacks, wore flowing beach robes in Schiaparelli's invention, "shocking pink," and looked divine.

A nondescript woman and her secret machine became the latest discovery in the never-ending quest of the rich and famous for "eternal youth." This clever ex-postmistress from Manchester had built a contraption that was rumored to possess the powers of immortality. A black box, the size of my mother's portable gramophone, it was festooned with Frankenstein-like filament tubes, lots of serious-looking knobs and dials, above which stretched a wide band of milky rubber – the type used in surgical gloves.

"Now, Miss Dietrich, give me your finger. Just a little prick of this pin, a tiny squeeze – and observe, we have a lovely sample of your bright red blood. That did not hurt at all, now did it? . . . Now, onto the magnetic surface it will go," and she would grasp the bleeding finger, rubbing it and its blood onto the rubber surface. This done, the "patient" was asked which one of her organs was giving her the most discomfort. My mother, who was always sick to her stomach because of her enormous consumption of Epsom salts, said in dead earnest:

"My liver – I am sure it is the liver why I feel carsick all the time."

"Aha! I thought so! The moment I came in through the door, I felt it! I said to myself, 'There is a peakish liver!' I shall now set my machine to the frequency generated by this organ, and through this drop of your living blood, treat your sluggish liver magnetically back to health!" and fiddling with the dials, making her radio tubes glow, she rubbed, spreading my mother's blood back and forth along the strip until the rubber squeaked. My mother, fascinated, watched, felt the surge of electricity course through her afflicted organ, and announced:

"Wonderful! I feel better – let's go eat!"

Over the years, that clever lady was paid enormous sums. As she claimed her machine could cure "in absentia," drops of blood were continually drawn, soaked into pieces of white blotting paper, then sent on to her by mail. While she rubbed her rubber and cashed checks, my mother was convinced she felt ever so much better. Of course, Tami was the first of us who was made to try it. When the woman asked Tami which organ needed magnetic attention, my mother answered for her: "Her head!"

Because of her "liver" cure and no scheduled film, my mother, for the first time, embraced the process of acquiring a tan. Of course, all this new exposure was possible by another, much more extraordinary invention: the "built-in bra." We had found a jewel, a French seamstress who made brassieres cut on the bias, darted underneath. The first really perfect support for Dietrich's breasts. When this genius suggested incorporating her idea into bathing suits, the first ever exposure of Dietrich's body to summer was born, and the admiring glances were legion!

First thing every morning, it was my job to mix and distribute the sun oil, guaranteed to bronze and hold, a mixture of the finest olive oil and iodine, with just a hint of red wine vinegar. This was funneled into glass bottles, corked, and handed out to those ready to brave the herculean task of acquiring an even tan. That summer, everyone smelled like a salad! Laden down with books, bottles, makeup cases, sun hats, and beach robes, we commenced our descent to the rocks below, on which perched our candy-stripe cabanas, like something left over from the Charge of the Light Brigade. We also had stick huts, little houses like those in *The Three Little Pigs*. I think I once counted a hundred and fifty steps from the hotel to the beginning of its sloping, formal, mile-long esplanade that finally brought one down to our boulders along the sea and – collapse!

We had to descend those never-ending stairs before the sun could heat them to "frying an egg" temperature. God forbid if anyone forgot something. It took an hour to get back up to our rooms and then back down again, if you survived sunstroke! The hotel, aware that no one would ever make it up to lunch in their beautiful dining room, compensated for those distances by building a superb restaurant that overlooked both the sapphire-blue pool as well as the equally blue sea, and called it the Eden Roc Pavilion.

Remarque had his own table, at which his newly acquired family ate and enjoyed his superb choice of champagnes and wines; where my father, for the first time displaced as table authority, took out his frustration on the only things still under his jurisdiction: Tami, Teddy, and my lemonade. At the age of "just thirteen," I had arrived at an astounding conclusion: All those years of shaking in my "sensible" shoes over the possible unfreshness of my lemonade could so easily have been avoided had I only had the sense to order mineral water instead! I was amazed at myself. How could I have been so stupid not to do that long ago? With this newfound intelligence, I decided to switch beverages, and at one momentous luncheon, announced that henceforth I would prefer Vittel with my meals, "Please," to which my father replied:

"What? Expensive mineral water for a child? Certainly not! You are having fresh lemonade, Maria!" and so ended my teenage rebellion.

I remember most vividly the sparkle of those lunches. Everything in shimmering Technicolor – the tall fluted goblets, the ornate silver, the elaborate ice sculptures, changed every day, of leaping dolphins, Neptune rising from foaming seas, reclining mermaids, majestic swans – amidst flame red lobsters, pink shrimp, orange salmon, purple sea urchins, midnight blue mussels, silvery fishes, primrose langoustines, and pearly gray oysters. Luncheons lasted the required three hours, followed by rest periods in louvered, darkened suites to ensure the energy necessary for the nightly balls, galas, and intimate dinners of fifty in nearby Cannes and its summer mansions sprawled along the Mediterranean coast, or public "slumming" in Juan-les-Pins, a nearby village where the artists' colony camped out.

Remarque began working on *The Arch of Triumph* that summer. He wrote in German, on lined yellow pads. His script small, neat, precise, the sharp tips of his pencils never breaking under exaggerated pressure. The large tub of meticulously sharpened pencils he kept forever ready wherever he was, ever hoping for inspiration, was one of the most revealing things about him. Of course, he modeled his heroine, Joan Madou, after my mother. His "hero," Ravic – on himself. He even used that name in some of the many letters he kept writing to my mother, whether they were together or not. He also invented a little boy, who would talk for him when even my mother withdrew herself from their relationship. Little "Alfred" was such a touching child – I grew very fond of him. He called my mother Aunt Lena, always wrote in German, and was highly articulate for an eight-year-old! Sometimes, when I read one of his many letters that kept being pushed under her door, I wished he were real – I would have liked to talk to him.

While our "famous author" labored in his shadowed room high above the sea, his lady, sexy in fitted white bathing suit, befriended the sexy Irish politician on the cliffs below. The American Ambassador to the Court of St. James was kind of rakish. For a man with such a patient little wife, who had borne him so many children, I thought he flirted a bit too much, but outside of that, Mr. Kennedy was a very nice man, and I thought his nine children were – wonderful! And I would have gladly given up my right arm, the left, and any remaining limb, to be one of them. They looked, and were, so American. All had smiles that never ended, with such perfect teeth each of them could have advertised toothpaste.

Big Joe, the heir, broad and chunky, a handsome football player with an Irish grin and kind eyes. Kathleen, a lovely girl who assumed the role of the official eldest daughter, although she wasn't and seemed to have matured too soon because of it. Eunice, opinionated, not to be crossed, the sharp mind of an intellectual achiever – her constant identity. John, affectionately known as Jack, the glamour boy, the charmer of the wicked grin and the "come hither" look – every maiden's dream, my secret hero. Pat, nearest my age, but not gawky, nor fat, with not a pimple in sight, a vivacious girl already on her way to womanhood. Bobby, the "fixer," the one who knew everything and never minded being asked to share his information. Jean, a quiet, gentle girl who picked up forgotten tennis rackets and wet towels – a concerned mother in the making, and then came Teddy, on his chubby little legs, always running, always eager to show you love, trying to keep up with his long-legged siblings. Rosemary, the eldest daughter, the damaged child amidst these effervescent and quick-witted children, was my friend. Perhaps being two misfits, we felt comfortable in each other's company. We would sit in the shade, watching the calm sea, holding hands.

Mrs. Kennedy was always nice to me. She even invited me to lunch at their private villa adjacent to our hotel. Tami told me not to be nervous, nevertheless, I changed my sundress four times before I was satisfied that I didn't look dressed too "aristocratic European," could pass for just a normal child coming to lunch. Their table was so long! We, the younger children, listened while the older ones discussed topics and issues proposed by their father, while Mrs. Kennedy supervised the serving of lunch by her staff and the table manners of her youngests. Never once was a critical comment made without corroborating evaluation. No sarcasms. No one "starred" and yet, all had a starlike quality. After Ambassador Kennedy became a regular visitor to our beach cabana, I stopped going. I didn't want any one of his family to feel uncomfortable. Although I had heard a spindly lady in nautical linen say, in one of my mother's type of whispers: "That's the American Ambassador over there . . . the one with all those children, who is Gloria Swanson's lover!" So maybe they were as used to their father disappearing as I was my mother.

My father was very angry about something. With Tami and Teddy in the back seat, he drove his Packard out of the hotel gates and left for somewhere. Remarque stayed, continued to write his book by day and drank by night. My mother told everyone how she searched for him in every bar between Monte Carlo and Cannes – afraid he would be arrested and news of his disgraceful conduct hit the world headlines.

"Everyone already knows that Fitzgerald is a drunkard, and Hemingway drinks only because he is a Real man, but Boni – he is a *sensitive* writer. Sensitive writers are poets, so they are delicate, they can't lie in gutters and get sick!"

That summer, I was reassigned my dresser duties. I would wait in my mother's suite for her return from the many parties, help her undress, file away the clothes, then leave. I was putting away the cooled shoes when he strolled in. Remarque was in favor, so was permitted entrance to the suite unannounced.

"Boni, why is Somerset Maugham so dirty? I mean dirty vulgar, not dirty unwashed. Does he do that just to be clever and shock, or is that him really?" my mother called from the bathroom.

"Like most gifted homosexuals, he mistrusts normalcy to such an extent, he has to embarrass those that practice it." My mother laughed. "Like women who see a rival in every woman they meet and must discredit them, so Maugham plays the vindictive bitch. Thank God, when he writes this leaves him – most of the time."

"He is a *wonderful* writer!" my mother retorted, annoyed by what she

considered Remarque's criticism of Maugham. "*The Letter* – what a script
that is. Now *that* woman, I could play – and right!" She squirted paste onto
her toothbrush. Remarque removed his cigarette case from his dressing
gown, extracted a cigarette, lit it, leaned back in the armchair, crossed
his pajamaed leg, and said:

"My beautiful Puma, most roles of deceiving women you could play
magnificently."

My mother gave him one of her "looks," spat into the decorated sink,
noticed I was still in the room, told me that was all – to go to bed. I kissed
her, Remarque, and left them to their heated discussion that I knew was
brewing.

At lunch the next day, my mother repeated Remarque's assessment of
Somerset Maugham to their guests as though it were her own, adding:

"It is only those young boys he keeps surrounding himself with that
gets too much. Where does he pick them up? On Moroccan beaches?
Noël does that too, but at least he does it politely, sotto voce. That's
what is such a relief when you are with Hemingway, finally a *real* man
– who writes!"

I quickly looked at Remarque and caught the slightest wince before he
covered it up by telling my father that he had ordered the wrong year
for the white Burgundy to complement the poached turbot.

I was delivering something forgotten back down to the Rocks when a
dowager, in orange toweling turban and matching robe, stopped my
descent.

"Do you know where Marlene Dietrich's little girl could be?"

"Why? Are you looking for her?"

"Oh, I've got to see her. I've read so much about her. Do you know
she is her mother's whole life – her only reason for living? She makes all
those films, is a star, only for that little girl of hers?" gushed the plump
lady, flashing diamond rings too tight for her pudgy fingers.

I had the feeling that if I said "Here I am – it's me!" she would be
terribly disappointed. No angelic smallness, no porcelain delicacy – no
miniature replica of the star she obviously admired – so I pointed down
the walk and said helpfully:

"Madame, I think I just saw her skipping down toward the cliffs."

The orange lady went in search of me.

My father and his "family" had returned for Elsa Maxwell's summer ball,
being paid for, as usual, by someone else. Elsa Maxwell was shrewd,

coarse, an opportunist – and ruthless. But, once your friend, she never stabbed you in the back, never tried to hurt and had a sense of pity for the "Followers" of this world of which she was one. She recognized my position and often was very kind. I was taken to a lot of her parties. She always made sure I sat next to "nice" people, who rarely asked me to tell them all about my mother, even made sure my assigned table was far removed from my famous parent. Being ugly herself, she recognized the insecurities of those who knew they were unattractive in the midst of the beautiful and never forced me into the limelight. As I remember every single person who was ever kind to me, I remember that often maligned woman very well.

Everyone had been sent an invitation on gold-edged cards, printed in thick raised letters by Cartier and, because the teenage Kennedys were going, I was allowed to go too. My mother even bought me my very own first ever evening dress, stiffened white net with a wide, inset cummerbund encrusted with chips of multicolored glass. I looked like a mosquito tent with sparkle. I wanted to hide in a very dark closet, preferably die! Newly tanned, my mother in floating white chiffon, looking like silky butterscotch poured into whipped cream, slapped some calamine lotion onto my peeling nose, pinned a net bow on my head, and pushed me into the waiting car. The huge ballroom looked like Aladdin's cave à la humans – the whole place a travel poster perfection. Miss Maxwell had assigned me a seat at a table amidst the potted ferns, with people who were kind, who didn't pay any attention to me. She placed my mother, my father, Tami, and Remarque miles away across the room. It turned out to be a very special evening, for Jack hiked all the way across the ballroom and asked me to dance the latest rage, the Lambeth Walk! A breathtaking dream who, at the age of just twenty-one, has the kindness to ask a net tent to dance, you must admit is truly wonderful!

I don't remember who started the rumor that Mars was scheduled to collide with the Earth that summer of 1938. True, every evening, the red glow from that ominous planet seemed to be getting closer and closer! Beatrice Lillie kept eyeing it, shaking her head, murmuring, "Doomed, my dears – doomed!" while the Sitwells prayed; the historian Will Durant, very disturbed, packed, ordered his car, and drove off at top speed – my mother always maintained – in the direction of Maugham's villa. The more curious gentlemen ordered powerful binoculars, telescopes, and books on astronomy to be sent down from Paris by car and train, then busied themselves calculating when Armageddon was certain to occur, while their ladies made beauty appointments and wondered

ABOVE: The moment Erich Maria Remarque lit her cigarette, my mother knew she was in love with him.

BELOW: The Mediterranean, the pool, the cliffs below the Hôtel du Cap d'Antibes—the summer of 1938 was luxury in high gear.

ABOVE: Dietrich on a schooner, posing in a real bathing suit—and tanned. Very unusual. But then, the summer of 1939 was special for many reasons. BELOW: A gala evening with Dietrich's "family" in attendance. Remarque, who never did get used to the constant snapping of pictures, tried to shield his face, as though the whole world didn't know he was one of Dietrich's lovers.

ABOVE: Our cabanas above the sea. My friends the Kennedy children had theirs next to ours. Jack, Pat, Bobby, Eunice—I thought them all wonderful and yearned to be part of such a joyous family.

BELOW: My father took this picture. He wanted to prove to my mother that the outfit she had donned for her rendezvous with Ambassador Kennedy was a little overdone, even for Antibes. She retorted that her latest, the Pirate, loved it.

which of their many evening gowns would be most suitable to enter eternity in. Lying on rocks roasting, observing the calm waters of the Mediterranean, wondering if it was time yet for lunch, or time to begin dressing for dinner, had begun to pall a little, and so, the movements of the flaming planet became an exciting and appreciated diversion. Evelyn Walsh McLean, who owned the infamous Hope diamond, rumored to strike dead anyone who dared touch it, decided to throw caution to the wind, removed her lethal gem from the hotel vault, and let people fondle it if they dared. We all agreed that it was a most appropriate jewel to wear for the first party to be given to celebrate the annihilation of the world.

On the designated fatal night, everyone threw each other a gala. The gentlemen, resplendent in white mess jackets or full dress tails, their ladies trailing satin, chiffon, lace, organza, and piqué, everyone was truly breathtaking. Huge crystal bowls of caviar nestled amongst mountains of shaved ice on ornate silver platters, Dom Pérignon, Taittinger, Veuve Clicquot in their tulip-shaped Baccarat, bubbled pale gold in the moonlight. Some preferred Black Velvets, considering Guinness mixed with "bubbly" more suitable for the last toast; others chose Pink Ladies or Stinger cocktails in delicately frosted Lalique. It was a gorgeous farewell party! It lasted until the pink dawn shimmered across the surface of the silvery sea, when everyone suddenly realized that their world had not come to an end after all – and went to bed, just a little disappointed. The next summer, not Mars, but a little man in Berlin changed the course of human history.

I WAS RETURNED to my brown Paris exile, where a new governess awaited me. Gray of hair and vestments, she smelled of lavender sachets and spinster purity. Cherry brandy was replaced by English tea, brewed correctly in a pot, clandestine junkets by bedtime at eight and Milton's *Paradise Lost*. I wondered why I wasn't being sent back to school.

"That stupid man, Chamberlain, thinks he can persuade Hitler?" My mother paced, the morning newspapers in one hand, her coffee cup in the other. Her family listened while buttering their croissants.

"What does he think? That the Prime Minister of England going to Berchtesgaden, *that* will impress the "Führer"? Always the British behave as though they are an empire!"

"That may be the attitude that will save them in the end," Remarque said in his soft voice.

My mother whirled:

"Boni! You of all people! You, the great authority on the suffering of war, how can you think this stupid trip of Chamberlain's to Hitler is going to do any good?"

"Marlene, I did not make a judgment on a political maneuver but an observation of a national characteristic."

"Papi," my mother turned her attention from my latest father to my primary one:

"What do *you* think? When Boni uses that 'professor' tone of his . . . Kater, sit up straight. Finish your egg. Tami – don't fidget, and watch The Child. Papi? Well? Boni and I agree if war is inevitable . . . The Child must be evacuated! She must be saved. . . . Boni, you too. . . . I am safe, they won't dare touch a Dietrich! Anyway, Hitler, with this thing for garter belts . . . do you know he kept a print of *The Blue Angel* for himself when they burned all the films? . . . Kater, get ready – *you are leaving*! Papi will tell us where you have to go to be safe from danger!"

Remarque placed his napkin by his plate, rose, and said:

"I would recommend Holland. They have ports. Ships will be able to leave from there for the safety of America and the Dutch will not capitulate."

"You see," my mother was triumphant. "Only a man who knows real war thinks correctly when one is about to happen. Papi: Holland! Tonight! The Child goes to Holland tonight! Tami can take her!" and she left for her fitting at Schiaparelli. My father called Thomas Cook.

I wondered what one packed to flee a war. My mother returned in time, said refugees must be unhampered by baggage, and gave me one of her special overnight cases. Handmade especially for her by Hermès, it was of such delicate pigskin, it boasted its own canvas slipcover to protect it. The interior of cream suede was fitted with cut-crystal bottles, jars and tubes for creams, face powders, soap, and toothbrushes. The lids to all this glass splendor were of inlaid enamel of geometric design, in shades of petal pink and lapis lazuli. Empty, this small overnight case weighed a ton – which is why my mother never used it. With the added weight of pajamas, shoes, skirt, blouse, sweater, and book – if I had had to flee across borders, I wouldn't have made it. My mother removed our hats, tied woolen scarves around our heads, with big safety pins pinned dollar bills into our underpants, saying, "You never know, said the widow," cried, kissed us good-bye, handed her refugees over to her "train-taking" husband, and, cradled in the arms of her lover, sobbed:

"To safety – to safety – go! Quickly!"

Tami was shaking like a leaf. With nothing but her very dubious Nansen passport, a true museum piece of glued-together permits that looked like a hastily constructed tail of a child's kite to cross Slavic frontiers, I with my German eagle-festooned one, we boarded a sleeper in the dead of night – to The Hague. I don't know who was more scared. Probably Tami, who was not only reliving her original flight from Russia, but was being separated from the man who had, for some inexplicable reason, become her whole life. She looked so forlorn, huddled in the corner of the faded plush seat, I took her into my arms, held her as the train sped through the night. At the border, we got the works. The inspectors took one look at the swastika on my passport and my mother's elegant case was torn apart: every jar opened, her face powder left over from when she had once used the cases, dumped, sifted through with the tip of a pencil, hems were squeezed; heels were tapped for possible hollow sounds. They were calm, cool, silent, and extremely thorough. I felt completely guilty, just for being the focal point of their precise attention. Funny feeling, being afraid – though innocent. Later, one remembers the sense of utter helplessness, more than the fear.

Neville Chamberlain returned from signing the Munich Agreement, proclaimed to the world that he had achieved "Peace in our time," and my mother's "refugees" were recalled from Holland. I didn't want a terrible war, but I had so looked forward to going home to America, I returned to Paris a little disappointed. In anticipation of war, my governess had been let go, so I was housed with my father. The tongue-lashings of Tami recommenced, so did my efforts to shield her from their cruelty. My mother, who had returned to Hollywood, called me to tell me about what had happened for Halloween:

"Sweetheart! The whole country has gone crazy! A radio show did it! Unbelievable? Yes, yes, all over America – panic! Real panic! Something to do with little green men from Mars landing in spaceships in – New Jersey? And they believed it! Just a man's voice doing all this through the radio! *Him* – I've got to meet!"

Orson Welles became a true buddy of hers. They fed each other's fame, recognized and respected their manufactured flamboyance, and never, ever, tattled on each other.

Finally, I was allowed to return to school, had my fourteenth birthday amongst my mother's floral extravagance, labored over exams that I had no hope in hell of passing, watched as happy girls left for Christmas at home with families. Reported to my father's penitentiary in Paris, smuggled an exhausted Teddy into my bed, listened to him snore contentedly, while waiting for the lectures and subsequent sobs to die down in my father's bedroom.

After the Christmas holidays, instead of being returned to school, I was moved back to the Hotel Vendôme. Maybe I had been expelled? For never being there on time and doing badly? I wanted to ask but didn't – I was too scared to hear the answer. My new, very British governess was strict and noncommittal, considered it a comedown looking after a mere movie star's offspring, while informing everyone in the park she was employed by the famous "Miss Marlene Dietrich."

I wondered when I would be called to report and where and why I had been put back into a hotel, when my father had an apartment in the same town. On January 30, 1939, my mother cabled him what I have always considered to be one of the prize examples of a true Dietrich cable.

HOW ARE YOU DOING STOP WHEN IS WAR STOP CABLED TAMI FOR DAY AND CLEANSING CREME ETTINGER CHEEK ROUGE OLD COLOR CYCLAMEN ARDEN POLISH RECEIVED NOTHING KISSES LOVE

In February, ready to leave America, my mother cabled that she was not allowed to leave the country because her English earnings were being investigated by American tax authorities, that she now would only receive her first American passport on the 6th of June. That the sum in question was one hundred eighty thousand dollars, to kiss me, then quoted a favorite line: "It was not meant to be because it was too wonderful."

In March, Hitler took Czechoslovakia, and I worried so – my sweet grandparents, what would happen to them? Why hadn't my father brought them to Paris long ago? So many questions can sit in the heart of a child that are never answered, even if asked.

Suddenly, I was taken back to school. I didn't know whether to be grateful or repentant, so concentrated on being invisible, cause no one any trouble.

In June, I was sent into my school's summer "holding tank." A mountain chalet amidst Swiss buttercups. I stored my things at Brillantmont, curtsied, said my good-byes – not knowing it would be thirty-four years before I would see that lovely school again.

ON A SWELTERING JUNE DAY in 1939, the world press ran the picture of Dietrich becoming a U.S. citizen. Eyes downcast, looking bored, she is leaning nonchalantly on the desk of the magistrate administering the Oath of Allegiance. He in vest and shirtsleeves, she in a winter suit complete with felt hat and gloves. A very strange pose for such a momentous

ABOVE: While Nazi Germany gnashed its teeth, Marlene Dietrich became a U.S. citizen in 1939.
BELOW: Accompanied by the Countess di Frasso's Afghan hound, she returned to Europe on the SS *Normandie* and was met by Tami.

ABOVE: Looking every inch Marlene Dietrich, she exits her hat designer's atelier in Paris, waiting for her chauffeur.

BELOW: Tami, who was also ordered to always step out of frame whenever the press pounced, was next to me but not seen in this candid photo of "Dietrich and her husband and child."

occasion. In Berlin, *Der Stürmer*, Dr. Goebbels's preferred newspaper, ran the photograph with the caption:

> The German film actress Marlene Dietrich spent so many years amongst Hollywood's film Jews that she has now become an American citizen. Here we have a picture in which she is receiving her papers in Los Angeles. What a Jewish judge thinks of the occasion can be seen from his attitude as he stands in his shirtsleeves. He is taking from Dietrich the oath with which she betrays her Fatherland.

My father called me in Switzerland, told me that I also had been made a citizen of the United States – not to let it go to my head – asked about my algebra, and hearing the answer, hung up.

Was I really? It seemed too good to be true. Was I finally – actually – a *real American?* No more vicious eagles, no more German? I ran to my room, from under the bed pulled out my shoe box of hidden treasures, found the little American flag I kept to celebrate the Fourth of July, set it on my marble-topped night table, saluted it – and cried my heart out!

My father must have gone to America to try and help with the tax situation, for he was supposedly there to star in yet another famous Dietrich script that played on the day the *Normandie* was scheduled to sail from New York to France. As I have absolutely no memory of this supposed drama, except through my mother, her often performed scenario will have to do; be it altered truth or pure fiction, it has enough Dietrich flavor to warrant repeating. It is entitled "The Day the Tax Gangsters Seized Papi!"

Certain that no one would ever see the cable she had sent back in February proving she knew this was all going on long before boarding the ship, her story goes like this: Dietrich arrived at Pier 88, boarded the SS *Normandie*, entered her Deauville suite, and found it empty. Her eight steamer trunks, thirty pieces of assorted luggage, and one husband had been seized – were now back on the pier being guarded by agents of the Treasury Department.

She rushed off the ship, clasped her husband to her beautifully tailored bosom, and in tones that could have curdled milk in Jersey, demanded:

"What are you doing with my husband?" and was told she owed the United States government three hundred thousand dollars in back taxes for monies earned for the film *Knight Without Armour*.

"Why do I have to declare in America what I earned in England?" was her dumbfounded retort. My mother always told this next part in a voice filled with rage, became speechless for just a second, then continued: "I had to leave poor Papi there between those American gangsters and ran

back up the gangplank to plead with the captain of the *Normandie* to hold
the ship until I could call Roosevelt. Of course, he held the ship, but
said something about 'the tide.' Anyway, I got through to Washington
– the President was out, but Joe Kennedy's friend, the Secretary of the
Treasury, Henry Morgenthau, I got, and he said he was shocked that I
should be treated like this right after becoming an American citizen and
maybe the tax people had received an anonymous tip that I was leaving
America forever, taking all my money with me. I said, 'What money?'
'Well, maybe,' he said, 'the tip came from the American Nazis as revenge?'
That would have been just like them! But *he* was no help – So you know
what I did? I hung up, rushed back down the gangplank, handed the tax
gangsters all my beautiful emeralds, and they gave me back Papi and the
trunks, and the *Normandie* could sail!"

At other times, my mother claimed that as a distraught supplicant,
she had gone to Washington clutching her jewel case, handed her
emeralds personally over to Secretary Morgenthau – sometimes President
Roosevelt, depending on who was listening. In 1945, she told everyone
that she was forced to sell her precious emeralds to have money to live
on, because she had sacrificed her earnings to serve in the war!

When she arrived in Paris, I was called back, this time to live with her at
the Lancaster. Remarque was at his home in Porto Ronco, overseeing the
packing of his many treasures for shipment through Holland to America.
I did my usual chores, wondered why there was no one new on my
mother's romantic horizon, and was happy that Boni had managed to
last out the year.

Jack Kennedy called, said he would be coming through Paris and asked
me out to tea. I was in seventh heaven! I had three days to work at getting
thin and disguise my pimples. My mother was not pleased. She considered
it bad manners for a "schoolboy" to invite a "child" to tea. She called
Remarque, who saw nothing sinister in such an invitation, and suggested
she buy me a pretty dress for the occasion. She relented, took me to a fancy
children's store where they did not go up to my size, stormed out, took me
to another where I tried on whatever she flung at me; finally bought me a
dark green crinkly silk with huge white and red daisies printed all over it;
a green cummerbund encircled my thick waist, puffed sleeves completed
this vision. Even with the blended camomile lotion all over my face, I
thought I looked better than usual, almost okay.

"Your governess will accompany you," my mother announced, and
my bubble burst.

"Oh, Mutti! Please, no. He will think I am a baby!" I gasped.

"You will be chaperoned or you will not be allowed to go." My mother
was adamant.

I secretly called Jack: "I have to tell you something – I have to come with a chaperone, so if you want to cancel, I'll understand, really!"

"Don't worry – we'll stuff her so full of éclairs, she won't have the time to be nosy!" Jack always made everything seem easy.

We met upstairs in the glass-enclosed tea room of the Café de Triomphe on the Champs-Elysées. First, Jack kissed my cheek, which made my knees wobble, seated my governess at one of the small marble-topped tables, ordered her a tray of French pastries, then guided me to a table of our own. He answered all my eager questions, told me all the latest goings and comings of his big family. We had a wonderful afternoon.

Our summer exodus to the Cap d'Antibes began. Remarque called from Switzerland to say he would drive his Lancia down to the south of France and meet us later in Antibes. Our suites were waiting, the hotel as serene and opulent as always. Nothing had changed. I always loved it when places stayed the same. It felt so comfortable being sure of something.

Even the Kennedys were back, vacationing from all their official posts and important schools. For the first time in my life I had friends to greet. Quickly, I put on my bathing suit and robe and, before anyone could call me to perform some service, I escaped down the esplanade toward the cliffs.

None of my friends had changed, except to enhance their special individualities. All, except Teddy, he was even cuddlier. Some rare children can do that, retain their cherubic sweetness, unaffected by having to grow up. Bobby caught my arm:

"Rosemary has to take her nap – come, we are going to dive for octopus. Joe has a terrific new gun – it shoots under water, like a harpoon. He wants to try it out. The President gave it to him!"

The Kennedys always had the most fascinating new inventions that they wanted to test. If no one had ever seen it, if it couldn't be bought yet, if something was hot off the drawing board, they already had it.

"Octopus? They'll grab our ankles and pull us down! I'll watch you from the rocks!"

"Ah, come on! These are Mediterranean, they are small! They don't attack! They hide between the rocks. All you have to do is dive, pry them loose, and bring them up. When they squirt their ink at you, just close your eyes and surface. They wrap themselves around your arm – so it's easy!"

"Bobby, is everybody diving for octopus, even Jack?" I asked, hoping he would say no.

"Sure, come on. Nothing to be scared of. We do it all the time. If we catch enough, we can have them for supper."

It worked just as he said. Following Bobby's instructions usually did.

Remarque's Lancia, just as he described it in *Three Comrades*, purred to a halt. He had called ahead from Cannes and my mother was waiting for him. He took her face between his slender hands, cradling it, just looking down at her. Without heels, my mother always appeared so small, although she really wasn't. They kissed; then, taking her hand, he introduced her to his best friend, his car. He was anxious that his "gray puma" would understand his love for the golden puma and not be raked by jealousy. My mother loved the imagery of being presented as a rival to a car. Remarque took them both for a drive along the coast to get acquainted.

That evening he arrived in my mother's suite, especially handsome in his white dinner jacket, carrying a German schoolbag, just like the one I always wanted when I was little. He removed some yellowed papers. While waiting for the carpenters to crate his paintings, he had found stories he had worked on in 1920 but never finished.

"They were good then and they'd be good today, but I couldn't finish them now. I no longer have that wonderful bold immaturity." As he leafed through the pages, his golden eyes dulled. "Twenty years ago, when there was a war and I wrote this, I thought only of saving the world. In Porto Ronco a few weeks ago, I saw that another war looms, and I thought only of saving my collections."

My mother moved over to kiss him, saying: "My love – how ridiculous. You are a *great* writer – what else do you need? Look at Hemingway. *He* never worries about how *he* feels or what *he* felt long ago. It just comes flowing out of him, all that beauty!"

I was wakened by: "Papi, Papi – are you awake?" My mother's voice was shrill as she shouted at my father over the house phone. I looked at my travel clock: four a.m. Something was wrong! I put on my dressing gown and crossed the hall to my mother's suite.

"Papi! Wake up! And listen to me. Boni and I had a fight. You remember how strangely he behaved at dinner. Well, later he accused me of sleeping with Hemingway. Of course, he wouldn't believe me when I said I didn't. He said terrible things to me, then stormed out. Probably he went to gamble at the casino and get drunk. Get dressed – take the car and find him! Maybe he is lying somewhere and strangers will find him! Call me the moment you know something!" She hung up, noticed me, told me to order coffee from room service, and began pacing the floor.

Two hours passed, then the phone rang. My father had found Remarque in a bar in Juan-les-Pins, drunk, desperate, but unharmed.

That summer, our blood and rubber lady was absent, but we had another medical sensation that my mother had discovered. This one came in a tiny tube, all the way from Russia, and was guaranteed to cure the common cold. My mother was explaining the application procedure to Beatrice Lillie when I happened on the scene.

"Bea, sweetheart! It is absolutely amazing! Never has been seen before – give me your arm. No, no, turn it, this stuff has to be rubbed inside of your arm, where the pulsing vein is." The cap clamped between her teeth, she squeezed a big glob of yellow grease onto the skin, screwed the top back on, began rubbing the ointment savagely into Bea's arm. The spot reddened, a slight swelling appeared where the "pulse pulsed."

"Marlene, did I say I had a cold?"

"Of course you did – you said you were 'stopped up.'"

"Oh, is this good for constipation as well?"

By now, the spot is nice and red, and Bea Lillie is trying to get her arm back from my mother.

"Marlene – what is this goo made from?"

"Snake venom. It inflames the tissues, then dries them up, and suddenly, you can *breathe* again!"

I never saw anyone get down our walk that fast! My mother stood watching Bea Lillie sprint toward the pool, a confused look on her face:

"What is the matter with that woman? Noël always said she was so funny – but I thought funny 'ha-ha,' not funny 'strange.'"

One day, everyone was "a-twitter." They congregated along the rocks like hungry sea gulls, searching the surface of the sea. A strange ship had been sighted making for our private cove. A magnificent three-masted schooner, its black hull skimming through the glassy water, its teak decks gleaming in the morning sun, at the helm, a beautiful boy. Bronzed and sleek – even from a distance, one sensed the power of the rippling muscles of his tight chest and haunches. He waved at his appreciative audience, flashed a rakish white-toothed smile, and gave the command to drop anchor among the white yachts. If he had run up the Jolly Roger, no one would have been surprised. The first thought on seeing him had been Pirate – followed by Pillage and Plunder.

My mother touched Remarque's arm: "Boni – isn't he beautiful? He must be coming here for lunch. Who is he?" She watched him being rowed ashore. Dressed in skin-tight ducks and striped sailor's jersey, he climbed the steps leading up to the Eden Roc and turned from a sexy boy into a sexy, flat-chested woman. At a time when "madcap" heiresses were a dime a dozen, this one was a dedicated adventurer and explorer – owned ships, developed and governed her own islands, was known as "Jo" to her intimates, became my mother's summer of '39 interlude, and was the only one who ever called Dietrich "Babe" and got away with it. Her majordomo was a two-ton truck. Although she wore her tailored suits with a skirt and painted the nails of her sausage fingers deep red, this made absolutely no difference to the general effect of – ugly male. With close-set eyes, bulk that overshadowed her pylon legs and very small feet, her resemblance to a rhinoceros was startling. I expected any second her ears to wiggle and a pilot bird to pick insects off her hide.

While Remarque labored in his shuttered rooms over his yellow pads, and drank himself senseless at night, my father checked hotel expenses and improved his already perfect tan, and Tami swallowed any new pill guaranteed to bring on instant happiness given to her by solicitous dilettantes, I swam, watched the Kennedys being a happy family, and helped to dress my mother for her daily rendezvous on her "Pirate's" ship, hoping she would return before Boni emerged from his day's entombment to be with her.

We were having breakfast in my mother's suite, when my father answered the telephone and announced that a call from Hollywood was coming through. My mother frowned.

"At this hour? You take it, Papi – must be something stupid."

My father handed her the receiver.

"It is person-to-person from Joseph Pasternak."

My mother was definitely annoyed.

"Who?"

"Remember? He used to be around Ufa during *The Blue Angel*. He is an important producer now at Universal. You better talk to him."

My mother gave my father a dirty look and took the receiver.

"This is Marlene Dietrich. Why are you calling me in the south of France?"

I remember my mother's eyebrows as they arched even higher in utter surprise and her glacial good-bye before she slammed the receiver and said:

"Now *that* is a real Hungarian idiot! Do you know what he said? He wants me to be in a Western! Starring Jimmy Stewart! Ridiculous. They get more stupid every day out there in Hollywood!" and with that, dismissed the topic for the rest of the morning until she told it as a joke to Kennedy over lunch.

"Papa Joe . . ."

We had so many "Joes," she had begun to refer to Ambassador Kennedy as "Papa Joe" to avoid confusion between his oldest son, von Sternberg, and the Pirate.

"Papa Joe, you must admit – it's too funny. Dietrich and that mumbling baby-faced beanpole? And trying to be ever so 'real American'?"

"How much are they offering you?"

"I didn't even ask. You think it's not such a crazy idea?"

"Marlene, if you want me to, I'll talk to Universal. Pasternak may just have hit on a brilliant combination."

My mother turned to my father: "Papi. Put a call in to Jo. Tell *him* about Pasternak. Ask him what he thinks and to call me back before seven o'clock tonight, our time, then book a call to Pasternak for eight." She turned to Kennedy: "Are you free then?" She rose. "I want to ask Boni about this," and left the table. By seven p.m., everyone had been consulted. Von Sternberg had said that in his opinion Stewart was like another Cooper, only with more acting ability, and that playing a Western "dance-hall floozie" was simply taking "Lola" out of Berlin and plunking her down in Virginia City, and that she was insane if she turned it down. Kennedy told her the money offered was too good to refuse and gave her the name of Charles Feldman, who became my mother's most trusted and beloved agent of her professional life.

The Pirate loved the idea so much, she promised to rent a mansion in Beverly Hills – to be near her "Babe." She was already planning to give my mother her island in the Caribbean, population included! Even Remarque liked the idea of Dietrich going "Western."

Still, she hesitated: "Papa Joe – what will happen if there is a war? Do I have to take everyone with me to America, or can I leave them here? You are the Ambassador to England, you must know that that gaga Chamberlain with his pretty boy Eden, they are not going to be able to stop Hitler. So what will happen? I can't be away making a stupid film if anything happens!"

Kennedy assured her that if and when he felt the danger of war was imminent, he would evacuate his family back to England and safety and that her family would be given the same protection as his.

My father ordered up the trunks, made the travel arrangements; my mother, Tami, and I packed. Before being driven to Paris, my mother took my hand and laid it into Remarque's:

"My only love – I give you my child. Protect her, keep her safe – for me!" Calling over her shoulder to my father: "Don't forget to call Paramount. They have to release Nellie to do my hair at Universal." She stepped into the limousine.

Between costume meetings, flirting with Pasternak, and song-writing sessions with her *Blue Angel* composer, Frederick Hollander, and a "sweet" man she called "a fresh, but talented lyricist," Frank Loesser, my mother kept in constant touch by phone.

Vera West wasn't Travis, but it didn't matter. She was designing the clothes herself anyway, making a dance-hall dress in the "nightgown cut" that Travis always loved so, but with her built-in bra so she could move in it, and in short, that would be the "look" of the film. Stockings made of a new invention called nylon were amazing; they lasted through a whole day without laddering! Her name was "Frenchy," to justify her far-from-Western American accent. She and Nellie were working on a "honky-tonk saloon tart" hairdo, all fake curls, like big corkscrews – "like Shirley Temple, only sexy," is how she described it; and the director, George Marshall, was sweet; Pasternak was tricky, like all Hungarians, just as she had expected, but sweet; her dressing room was a house – "Yes, a real little house, not like our cupboard rooms at Paramount"; and Jimmy Stewart was not at all "cowboy boring" but "very sweet." She was practically bubbling, and with everyone so "sweet," I figured she was having a ball and wondered which sugared individual would win out.

Hitler and Stalin signed a nonaggression pact, and the Kennedys left sooner than anyone had expected. The moment had come that everyone had been waiting for, praying that somehow it wouldn't happen. The message ran through the hotel like a flash fire:

"Go, get out. Leave France – fast!"

From across the world, my mother pulled her mighty strings and secured passage on the *Queen Mary*, scheduled to sail from Cherbourg on September 2, 1939. We left Antibes in convoy. Remarque and I, in his splendid Lancia leading the way, my father, our luggage, Tami, and Teddy in his Packard, trying to keep up, following behind. Nobody had said, "The Germans are an hour away," but that's how we evacuated Antibes. We stopped only to refuel, but we were slowed by long columns of mules and horses that were being mobilized.

"Kater, remember this," Remarque urged, "memorize it so you will always have it! The feeling of despair, the anger of these French farmers, their hopeless faces, the shadowed colors as they herd their black mules off to war in twilight. Mules and horses – against the Wehrmacht and the Luftwaffe."

As we passed through the French countryside, there was a sense of defeat before the war had even begun. No patriotic fervor to join up, no heads held high singing the "Marseillaise." Those farmers were not marching to war with their animals, they were trudging as though to defeat, stopping on the way to sit dejected by the wayside.

"Boni? They already know they're going to lose?"

"Yes. They are old enough to remember the last war. Look at the faces, Kater. Remember – war has no glory – only the sound of mothers weeping."

I was a young girl witnessing a new war in the making, with a man who had known, had lived through the old one, captured its horror for the whole world to read, to bear witness. I felt very privileged being with such a man as another war was about to begin.

The Lancia began to overheat. We stopped at a garage. It was abandoned. Boni let the radiator cool, there was no time to fix it. We had to get to Paris in time to take the boat train to Cherbourg. He folded the hood up on his side for ventilation. It blocked his view, so he drove holding his door ajar, leaning out the side in order to see the road. He cursed his beloved car for deserting him, berated his Puma for being a coward in the face of danger. His fury had nothing to do with his car. I wished I could share in his sense of loss. I had never felt I belonged to Europe, but knew that for Boni this time was immense, that he was about to confront a profound leave-taking, convinced he could never return – for he believed that Hitler had the power of evil, would win the war and become the master of all Europe.

Paris was dark, we drove slowly. I looked for the Eiffel Tower, which had just been illuminated the year before, and saw only its somber outline against the night sky.

"Paris – the City of Lights!" Remarque whispered. "Beautiful Paris, suffering her first blackout. Never in modern history has she been forced to extinguish her brilliance. We must toast her and wish her well. Come, while Papi says good-bye to his furniture, you and I will go to Fouquet's, sit on the Champs-Elysées one more summer evening, and say good-bye to Paris."

We drove to his garage. He gave his keys to the owner, instructing him to guard his friend from the Boche, adding:

"But, if you must flee the city with your family, take my car. Pumas are good at escaping." One last look, then he took my hand and we walked away in the direction of Fouquet's.

The great Burgundies, the 1911 cognacs, the special champagne,

Fouquet's famous cellar was emptied that night. The citizens of Paris crowded the Champs-Elysées, everyone drank – no one was drunk.

"Monsieur," Remarque's favorite sommelier bent low, offering a dusty bottle cradled lovingly in his arms, "we don't want the Boche to find this – do we?"

Remarque agreed. He filled a small glass for me.

"Kater, this you will never forget – neither the taste of this wine, nor the occasion for it being uncorked." He was right on both counts.

That night, Boni and I became friends, not a girl and a man, a child and an adult, the daughter of the woman he loved, nothing to do with that. We were comrades, experiencing something tragic together.

In New York, under the cover of darkness, the *Bremen*, her lights dimmed, with only her German crew aboard, slipped stealthily into the Hudson on the night tide. She had been ordered to get back home to the Fatherland with all speed and at all cost.

Hitler bombed Warsaw and invaded Poland.

My father, Tami, and, thank God, Teddy, met us in Cherbourg. I was so happy to see that sturdy little fellow in his black-and-white fur. I don't know why, but I had been afraid my father would leave him behind to be captured by the Nazis.

The *Queen Mary*, so regal "empire" elegant, felt like a disappointed hostess whose party has somehow gone awry. No band, no gay abandon, hundreds of people scurrying about with tense faces and worried looks. My father told me that the swimming pool might have to be drained to accommodate cots, sections of the main dining room had beds in it. Some people had suggested that the billiard tables could be slept on. This was destined to be the last crossing of the *Queen Mary* as a luxury liner until after the war. Immediately on arrival in America, she would be painted gray and converted into a troop ship.

One day out at sea, the ship's loudspeakers announced that Great Britain and France were now at war with Germany. The *Queen Mary* was committed to making the dash across the Atlantic. There was fear that German submarines might now take action against our English ship. We watched the sea for telltale periscopes; at night we imagined U-boats stalking in the depths.

Daily lifeboat drills were ordered. I asked our steward if he would help me sew extra-long ties onto my life vest, so if we were torpedoed, I could hold Teddy inside. He was so nice he did, even helped when I practiced. At first, Teddy was very uncooperative. He didn't like being clutched, but after a few tries, he understood I wasn't being "dramatic," just "prepared," and curled against me real small.

Gentlemen expounded their theories on how to win a war around crowded card tables enveloped in rich cigar smoke. Jewish families huddled in groups, prayed, wept for those left behind, unable to escape in time. There were those who, never having lost freedom, considered it their permanent right and behaved as though this were a normal crossing. The children played, dowagers wore their life vests to dinner and carted their jewel cases wherever they went.

Our captain announced radio silence for the remainder of the crossing. We sailed alone, out of touch with the rest of the world. There were rumors that we were changing course, that the *Queen Mary* had received orders to avoid an American port and would make her way to a Canadian one instead. When my mother was informed by the British consul in Los Angeles that the ship might be rerouted, she sent Studio representatives and lawyers to Canada to await our arrival there, but told those waiting in New York to stay put until further notice. Between issuing orders to Immigration lawyers and shipping agents, my mother began filming *Destry Rides Again*.

The top decks were crowded; we rounded Ambrose Light and – there She was! Such a cheer welled up, I'm sure it could be heard all the way in New York City. We had made it – We were safe – We were home! Of course, I cried, but this time I had so much company, I didn't feel silly at all.

We were such a motley group the Immigration officials had a hard time sorting us out. Remarque, with his special refugee passport from Panama, my father with his German one, Tami with her Nansen, which, of course, was a never-seen-before curiosity. Finally, thanks to the lawyers my mother had sent, after a long day of discussions and waiting, we passed through Immigration. I, as a minor, offspring of a legal American citizen, Teddy as an accompanying disease-free canine, the others as "pink card" aliens. At times like these, the power of fame becomes very acceptable.

WARTIME

WE CHECKED INTO Remarque's favorite American hotel, the Sherry Netherland on Fifth Avenue, and my mother's refugees called her on the set at Universal. We took turns talking to her; she insisted on hearing each voice to be certain we were all there. Of course, I was delirious with joy. Secretly, I couldn't help thinking that with a war raging in Europe, my mother would be stuck in America and I would be spared having to go back there all the time. So, when my turn came to speak to her, she got no regrets from me having been forced to leave the Old World behind:

"Mutti, it's wonderful! Everything is wonderful! Do you know they have a World's Fair here, right here in New York City? May we stay and see it – please?"

"Angel – you can *all* stay. Nobody has to rush. The film is difficult. This little studio is not Paramount. The director, George Marshall, is sweet, so that is all right. Some of the songs are good, and Stewart has something, I don't know exactly what it is, but there is something so sweet about him."

She paused, then continued, softly:

"Don't tell Boni, you know how he gets jealous about everything, like Jo. Put Papi on the phone. I want to tell him where to get money so you all can stay there."

Tami and I spent days at the fair. Like the Paris one the year before, it had absolutely everything – this time, with added American razzmatazz. I even got Boni to come with us. He was so sad, for so many legitimate reasons, I kept coming up with all sorts of excursions, hoping to distract him a little. My father was just as depressed. Of course, Tami believed she must be the cause of his unhappiness and shook.

When we finally arrived at the Beverly Hills Hotel, my mother had our assigned quarters ready for us. She had her private bungalow, Remarque had his next door across the way, my father had a suite in the main hotel, Tami a single down the hall from him, I a single next to her.

There was a hand-delivered letter waiting for me from Brian, telling me he had married a lovely woman who was sure to make him eternally happy, that he was so sorry I couldn't be there for the wedding, that he loved me, welcomed me home, would try to see me soon. I looked at the letter again for her name . . . oh! Joan Fontaine. She *must* be nice because her sister was playing Melanie in *Gone with the Wind*.

Dietrich was news again. *Destry* was rumored to be a Box Office Smash in the making. The chemistry between its costars was described as "sizzling," and "See What the Boys in the Back Room Will Have," a song written for the film, was certain to be a hit. The Studio Publicity Department was ecstatic. Pasternak, the genius innovator at Universal, had done it again! This renewed glare of the limelight bothered my mother. She had become used to the Europeans' nonchalant attitude toward "unconventional" households, but America was different. Trying to keep secrets from the diligent American press was always dangerous – especially ones that had anything to do with moral behavior.

"Those terrible Puritans," my mother used to say. "America is full of them. Is that because of those awful people who came over on those ships? The ones who started that Thanksgiving thing you love so?"

As she now had a few too many "husbands" about, she tried to convince Remarque that New York was the place for "brilliant authors," not this cultural wasteland known as Hollywood, and got nowhere. So, she concentrated on the one she could order around and sent my father with his dog and Tami back east to live. I was allowed to stay. I was happy I had escaped the purge.

I and my new bodyguard took them to Union Station. My father had given me his lecture on behavior, loyalty, and filial duty in the car, so there was little left to say. He kissed my cheek, patted my shoulder, told Teddy to precede him, and boarded the train in deep discussion with the porters. Tami and I hugged each other good-bye.

"Please, please – be more careful with yourself, Tamilein! If he ever hurts you, if you need help, promise you will call me right away. Promise!" I whispered, foolishly believing she would ever do so or that I could really help if she did. I waved long after the train had left, hoping Tami and Teddy could still see me. It would be four years and an emotional lifetime before I saw them again.

That took care of one problem. Next, my mother called her Pirate, acquired the services of her Rhinoceros, then housed this "woman" and her "beloved Child," just the two of us alone, in the back of the hotel in one of the apartments above the garages in the alley. Now began a

time when I saw my mother by appointment only. My days were spent
finishing whatever grade I was supposedly in. My tutor was a lady who
arrived at ten, chatted, drank her coffee, opened a few books on the
subjects I liked best and excelled in, then departed, having had a nice
visit – with pay.

Remarque remained, by day a virtual recluse, forcing himself to write,
only to tear up each day's work before my mother returned home from
the Studio in the evening. He lived for the sound of her car pulling up in
front of her bungalow, the ring of the telephone telling him that she was
alone and he was now permitted to steal across the path, and take her in
his arms. Sometimes, when she was very late coming home, especially
Saturday nights, when she usually didn't appear until the evening of the
next day, I sat with him, keeping him company during his sad vigil. Of
all the people I knew during my youth, Remarque was the only one
who ever understood that where my mother was concerned, I was not
a child, probably had stopped being one at the age of six. My mother's
current passion, one could not really fault her for. Half the women in
America would have given their eyeteeth to be where Dietrich was on
those Saturday nights. Remarque not only suffered from utter rejection,
but like Jo, from self-hate, because he loved her too much to leave her.
He needed to be close to her, just see her, hear her voice, even listen to
her telling him about her new love, which she did, asking his advice on
how she could make the moments spent in her new lover's arms even
more wonderful than they already were.

"She expects me to write her 'love scenes,' phrases to enchant.
Sometimes I do, then she bestows on me her wonderfully romantic
smile and goes to make me dinner. Kater, it is such heaven to please
her," he would say, looking out the window, watching for his Puma's
return. This lovely man had become a pathetic voyeur, a Beverly Hills
Cyrano.

The Studio released a rumor that Dietrich, having found out that
Stewart was a fan of the comic-strip hero Flash Gordon, had ordered a
life-size doll to be made for him. She giggled when she heard it and didn't
get angry. She had changed. She was still the dedicated perfectionist, the
professional tyrant, but in *Destry*, when she had achieved acceptability
in those categories she believed her duty, she allowed herself to relax,
have fun. Of course, it helped that Jimmy Stewart was the designated
box-office star. If the film failed to pull in the money, he would be the
one blamed – not she. This had not happened to her since *The Blue Angel*
and Jannings. Now she found it wonderfully relaxing, once again having
another carry the burden of stardom. This letting go of responsibility
resulted in Dietrich giving a very good performance.

She tried to persuade the director, George Marshall, to let her do her own stunt work for the saloon fight. He said no! The stuntwomen had been hired, rehearsed, and would deliver on film a wild and rowdy brawl with their usual expertise. Dietrich and Una Merkel, properly bloodied and disheveled, would then take their places for the medium shots and close-ups. She might have gotten Pasternak to agree to her scheme, but the possibility of both˙performers being injured was just too great a risk. The fight had been choreographed for professionals. But the prospect of the enormous publicity that would be generated from Marlene Dietrich brawling in a saloon finally outweighed any objections the worried Studio could come up with. To my knowledge, Miss Una Merkel, the other contestant in this grudge match, was never given a chance to withdraw.

I had never seen so much press crowding a movie set. *Life, Look*, all the wire services and fan magazines, photographers everywhere. Dietrich doing a Western had sparked excitement in the first place, now she was fanning the flames, playing it raucous and rowdy all the way – no holds barred.

A first-aid station had been set up outside the soundstage, just in case. The stuntwomen, ready to take over, watched from the sideline. Una Merkel and Dietrich took their places, the cameras rolled, my mother whispered, "Una, don't hold back – kick me, hit me, tear my hair. You can punch me too – because I am going to punch you!" and with a snarl, jumped on Merkel's back, knocking her to the floor. They kicked each other, screamed, grabbed handfuls of hair and yanked, slapped, scratched, rolled on the dirty floor – were oblivious to everything except trying to kill each other, until Stewart stepped into the fray and dumped a bucket of water over them.

Marshall yelled "Cut!" and the set exploded in applause. The press called it the best "slug-fest since Tunney and Dempsey." My mother was stronger than Una, that nice lady suffered a lot of ugly bruises, but that fight and the fantastic press coverage it received resulted in turning *Destry Rides Again* into a Dietrich film at the box office.

I had just helped her dress for a date with her romantic "beanpole" when Remarque wandered in, unannounced. He stood looking at her in wonder, her body molded in black silk jersey that pedestaled into a thick flounce of absinthe green satin, her black turban repeating this color in a crown of minute, closely laid bird feathers – a Juno balanced on green fire.

"Well, why did you come over?" she asked impatiently. I handed her the evening bag with the emerald clasp, packed with her diamond compact from Gilbert and the Knight's cigarette case.

"Did you know when Sigmund Freud died in London, it was of cancer?"

"Good! All he did was talk about sex and got people all mixed up," she threw over her shoulder as she ran out of the door. Her "date" had honked his horn.

Dietrich had utter disdain for all forms of psychiatry and those who needed such "talking to on couches by strangers." Instinctively, she probably feared this science – it delved, discovered, invaded, exposed, all very dangerous words within my mother's private universe.

My special friend had become a star – a real, MGM star! I had told her she would. I was so proud of her. I was sorry, though, her breasts had to be tied flat, and hoped it hadn't hurt. It wasn't easy pretending to be twelve when you are sixteen. I identified with the Dorothy of *The Wizard of Oz*: Toto was like Teddy, the Bad Witch I knew, the Good Witch I would like to meet, a home I would also like to come back to, and Oz I lived in. Only the magic shoes I couldn't imagine ever escaping in.

Winston Churchill became First Lord of the Admiralty. The French waited, secure in their belief in the Maginot Line, winter rolled in over the Atlantic, nothing happened. American war correspondents had no war as such, dubbed it "the phony war," and Marlene Dietrich, the new citizen, voted, for the first time, on the set of *Destry*. She hadn't a clue who, what, or why, but she looked so glamorous contemplating her decision, the Publicity Department, which had set it up to remind the paying public that Dietrich was no longer a foreigner, milked it for all its worth. The Americanization of Lola was complete.

Destry opened in New York City in November 1939 and was a smash hit. Russia invaded Finland, everyone went to see Garbo actually laugh in *Ninotchka*, although some felt a grimace of painful embarrassment could hardly qualify for mirth.

On my mother's thirty-eighth birthday, she attended the West Coast gala opening of *Gone with the Wind*. It had already been acclaimed at its first première in Atlanta, and so everyone knew they were about to see a motion-picture masterpiece. I listened to it all on the radio, the screams as Gable and Lombard arrived, the oohs and aahs as gorgeous stars appeared in never-ending cavalcade – the Kings and Queens of America on parade! My mother's comments on this milestone of motion-picture history?

"Now I have seen everything! Leslie Howard, with orange hair!" She stepped out of her velvet evening dress. I began soaking the adhesive tape off her breasts. "That girl who plays the lead, the one who is so in love with Noël's old boyfriend who is so handsome and a good actor, *she* is very good, but the one who plays the saint? Not to be believed! *That's* Brian's sister-in-law? *That* – he doesn't deserve!"

Dietrich had many monologues on *Gone with the Wind*, but that was the first.

Rationing began in Britain. Hitler was about to overrun Norway and Denmark, Russia took Finland, and I dreamed of one day being allowed to have a black dress. Cautiously, I asked my mother, and got a "What? *Children* don't wear black!" I was very sad. A few days later, a big elegant box was delivered to the alley apartment, bearing my name. I cut the fancy string, lifted the deep lid, grabbed thick hunks of silky tissue paper and, there it was! A real, honest-to-goodness black dress! It was so grown up, Deanna Durbin could have worn it! And, when I tried it on, it fit! Not since my Indian suit had I felt so smart. For the first time in my whole life, I thought I looked terrific! I showed myself to the Rhinoceros, who said:

"I *am* pleased that you like it so much. I was a bit worried I wouldn't choose the exact style you wanted," and I realized it was she who had bought me the lovely dress.

Confused why she would give me such a big present, I thanked her very, very much, adding:

"How did you ever get my mother to allow it?"

She chuckled.

"If you want a black dress so much, why shouldn't you have one? And you look so nice in it. We just won't tell your mother you have it, shall we? It will be our special secret." Not since my lemonade stand had anyone employed by my mother hidden anything from her for me. A week later, I received my first pair of stockings – nylon ones! Then, a pair of shoes, in black – with two-inch wedges! Never had I dreamed of ever owning a pair of real "wedgies." After a while, I had so many "secret" treasures, all I needed now was a secret occasion to wear them. I was so terribly innocent – I didn't know I was being courted.

When I voiced a desire to become an actress, the gift-giving Rhinoceros, whose one aim it seemed was to grant me whatever my little heart desired, presented my wish diplomatically to my mother, who called one of "the boys" and arranged for him to give me acting lessons to keep her child "happy." Every afternoon I had to report to her empty bungalow to be coached by a know-nothing actor with a thick German accent in the "art of enunciating Shakespeare."

While he preened and I gnashed my teeth listening to him doing Juliet's soliloquies à la Weber and Fields, my mother began preparing her second film for Pasternak. She brought in her favorite designer, Irene, and both, thinking they were being truly inventive, had fun. The white tails from *Blonde Venus* were turned into a white naval officer's uniform; the striped, white-tipped-feathered negligée from *The Scarlet Empress*, into a concoction slightly more vulgar but still as effective.

The same team that had given her "See What the Boys in the Back Room Will Have" for *Destry* did not do so well for *Seven Sinners* – although "The Man's in the Navy" came close. She always wanted Noël Coward to sing it – which he never did, because he hadn't written it, but mostly because that tasteless a homosexual he was not!

She enjoyed her resurrected fame, was still "in love" with one "cowboy" while eyeing another, clowned on the set, was very American, calling the crew "Honey!," munched sticky doughnuts, drank coffee out of Commissary urns without making any sarcastic comments, palled around with Broderick Crawford, charmed the ever-so-pretty Anna Lee, flirted outrageously with her new leading man, brought him beef tea, tried to ply him with gifts – and got nowhere!

John Wayne and Dietrich made three films together over three years, and each time out came the beef-tea jars, gold watches, silk dressing gowns – and each time Dietrich struck out. Wayne became such a frustrating thorn in her side that she began concocting stories about him, told so often and to so many that they found their way into the Dietrich lore and were believed by all as gospel truths. One of her favorites: that John Wayne was such a complete unknown that, after she spied him entering the Studio Commissary, she had to persuade Universal to hire him for *Seven Sinners*. She embellished this by further stating that after the f irst day of shooting, it was so evident that Wayne was such an "ungifted amateur" that she had to call her agent, Charles Feldman, and instruct him to hire an acting coach for her new "so untalented" leading man. The fact that Wayne had been superb in John Ford's brilliant film *Stagecoach*, released in 1939, a year before *Seven Sinners*, seemed to vanish from everyone's memory when Dietrich was telling *her* version of things. Somewhere, sometime, John Wayne must have made Dietrich really mad about something to get her that riled.

Many years later, in London, Wayne and I had dinner together with mutual friends, and I finally got my chance to ask him what magic spell had so protected him against the siren's onslaught. He laughed with his eyes, took a slug, shifted his big frame on the too small chair, and grunted: "Never liked being part of a stable – never did!"

In *public*, Dietrich claimed to have no great love for "screen cowboys" in general.

"Those long drinks of water, like Cooper and Wayne, they are all alike. All they do is clink their spurs, mumble 'Howdy Ma'am,' and fuck their horses!" and people believed her – of course.

I had always wanted to go to Catalina, that little island off the coast, where big abalone shells, all iridescent shimmer, were sold as souvenirs. My mother refused. It was just a day trip there and back, but "No!"

The Rhinoceros spoke: "I do think that as Maria has worked so diligently, her behavior has been so exemplary, she deserves an outing – she has earned it, Miss Dietrich" – and lo and behold I got to go to Catalina. This strange woman really wanted to be my friend, even lied for me. Grown-ups didn't behave that way for children of "important people"! But this ugly woman was ready and somehow prepared to do battle for me, stand up to the all-powerful, omnipotent Marlene Dietrich, Star of the Silver Screen. I had never had a friend like *that* before. It felt sort of – nice. She even bought me a beautiful abalone – "To remember our day," as she put it.

Remarque finally had enough, moved out of his bungalow into a rented house in Brentwood. It was a temporary place, a nice one but not what Boni would have chosen for himself as a permanent frame. Only one of his paintings was hung, van Gogh's *Yellow Bridge*. The rest were stacked against the walls. To me, it was amazing that all these priceless treasures had safely crossed the ocean, the American continent, to finally arrive in that nondescript house in sunny California. He bought himself two dogs, proud Kerry blues, that kept him company. I visited him often. Even with his passionate "affliction," he was saner than anyone I knew.

Remarque owned Daumier's *Don Quixote*. It was my favorite. I loved the texture of its untreated canvas, its unconventional size to accommodate Quixote's long lance. Remarque enjoyed watching me; I could sit for hours feasting my eyes.

"One day it will be yours. I will leave it to you in my will, Miss Sancho Panza. But your taste is sometimes too emotional." He would shuffle through those hundreds of canvases, looking for what he thought I should learn to appreciate on any given day. He'd say, "Let's have a van Gogh day."

I was very courageous with Remarque. Sometimes, I'd say:
"No, I really don't feel like a van Gogh day."
"Then what kind of day do you feel like?"
"How about Cézanne?"
He'd smile, nod, flip through his paintings.
"Watercolor or oil Cézanne?"

Most of the time, I'd ask him for El Greco. His somber style suited my worries. I think Boni knew something was very wrong, but he was afraid to ask for fear he couldn't help me after he knew. It would have shattered him to be impotent in friendship as well.

I asked him why he didn't hang his paintings, he said that it was a foreign house, that it was not his friend. He hoped his home in Switzerland would wait for him. Remarque kept busy unpacking his museum crates, placing his Tang dynasty treasures around the empty rooms without joy, kept his priceless carpets rolled along the walls – his treasures were his only friends, his dogs his only companions, and writing to my mother his only release. As always, he wrote to her in German most often, referring to himself as Ravic:

> Look at Ravic, scratched all over, caressed, kissed and spat upon. . . . I, Ravic, have seen many wolves that know how to change their appearances, but I have only seen one Puma of this kind. A wonderful animal. It is capable of manifold transformations when the moonlight sweeps over the birches, I have seen it as a child kneeling over a pond, speaking with frogs, and while she spoke, the frogs grew golden crowns on their heads, and because she put such will into her eyes, they became little kings. I have seen her in a house wearing a white apron, scrambling eggs. . . . I have seen the Puma as a panting Tiger-Cat, even as the shrew Xanthippe, close to my face with fairly long nails. . . . I have seen the Puma go away and I wanted to shout out to it, to warn – but had to hold my tongue. . . . My friends, have you ever noticed how the Puma walks like a flame, dancing to and away from me? How's that? You say I'm not feeling well? That on my forehead there is an open wound and that I have lost a tuft of my hair? That's what happens when one lives with a Puma, my friends. They scratch sometimes when they mean to caress, and even when asleep, one is never certain when they might attack.

Each time he wrote to her, she called him, swore she loved *only* him, sometimes allowed him to love her, then in the early morning sent him packing again before going to the Studio. This turning on and off of emotion played havoc with his creativity. After a

while, the yellow pads remained empty; the ever-ready pencils waited
– unused.

THE FIRST THOUGHT that comes when disturbing a secret grave is –
Did I really have to bury it *that* deep to feel safe? Once opened and
exposed, milky sensations float to the surface like specters from some
Halloween greeting card. . . . The weight of her huge body, pushing
me down. A hand probing into places that had been mine alone. The
sudden revulsion, without understanding what was being done to me.
The cold – that terrible, terrible cold – that started the trembling, that
nearly stopped the heart beating, that choked the silent scream I thought
I heard aloud.

I did not know I was being raped – that word only took on meaning
long after the fact, when I learned that what had been done to me *had* a
name. Nighttime became a soundless crying and I thought I had learned
what sex was and shuddered at its approach. When she was through
with me, I pulled down my nightgown, curled up small, pretended she
didn't exist, and escaped into sleep, convinced I was being punished for
something unspeakable I had no knowledge of.

In some ways, I was trained for rape. Always obedient, always trying
to please those in charge of me, pliable, an owned object, conditioned to
usage. If you don't have an identity and someone helps themselves to
you, you respond more passively, you're so unaccustomed to the right
of question. Oh, I ran. In my own way I ran, but I had nowhere to go,
no one to listen and be kind – even if I could have found the right words.
So I went to the only place I knew, thought was safe, the inside of me.
Hid it – let it fester, become my private hell. Becoming damaged through
the instigated negligence of the one nature and society recognize as your
"loving" parent begets a special hell.

Why had my mother chosen that woman, then put me with her
– all alone? Did she want it to happen to me? What had I done to
deserve that? Mothers were supposed to love their children, protect
them from hurt. I had been a good girl. Why did she want me
punished? Why did she want me hurt? What had I done? Was I
that bad?

These searing questions stayed deep inside me, and despair was born
to lie beside the damage already done. I was convinced that my dream
of someday being allowed to have a real home with a husband who loved

me was lost forever, and that it must be my fault because I had allowed such a terrible thing to happen to me.

Yet, I must have still believed in miracles, for I asked for an audience with my mother. I don't know why I did. All my life, I have wondered what I thought I would get to comfort me – probably simply instinctive, to run to one's mother when hurt. Stupid, just the same. Desperate need often begets such stupidity.

I was told my mother was ill but that if I had to see her, I could come over to her bungalow if I made my visit very short and undisturbing.

The blinds were drawn, the room lay in cool shadows. Wan and strangely listless, she lay amongst the cushions of the deep couch, one slim hand clutching a soft woolen shawl to her chest.

"Sweetheart," she sighed, as though even this small expulsion of air cost her too much effort. I thought she might be dying. I knelt by her side, her hand fell gently onto my head, like a benediction. Nellie hovered close.

"Your mother needs a little sleep now, honey. Come back again tomorrow – okay? She'll call you, I promise."

With a last look at my mother's fluttering lids, I left. . . . Maybe she knew? Didn't want me around anymore? . . . No, just bad timing. Never turn to your mother for help when she has just had an abortion.

My mother played Camille for the next four days, and by that time, my desperation had turned onto itself. It was too late for miracles.

God was kind, and my time was safer. No angel dust, no ice, no crack, no street-corner pushers, no needle parks. The drug of my youth was alcohol, one that takes a little longer to achieve one's need for self-destruction. It deadens the done-to-hurt, to hurt oneself voluntarily: It beguiles you into thinking that for *this* degradation, *you* are in control. So you hurt yourself more than others can and feel safe – an insane self-delusion; and are truly lost.

I stayed within my self-punishment, kept my famous owner satisfied, kept my despicable owner at bay when I could – kept myself? Not at all. I wasn't worth that much effort. Booze nullified what was left. Life went on. It has a way of doing that, despite everything.

TO KEEP ME "HAPPY," I was enrolled in the Max Reinhardt Academy, now housed in a nondescript building next to a filling station on the corner of Fairfax and Wilshire Boulevard. Why Dr. Reinhardt, now one of the illustrious refugees, thought that his elite drama school had a chance always astounded me. No one, in those days anyway, came to Hollywood to "act." Handsome boys and pretty girls flocked to California to be seen, be discovered sipping ice cream sodas at Schwab's drugstore, their pointed breasts sticking way out in too-tight sweaters. Lana Turner had been – why not they? The boys, they stuck out all sorts of things on Santa Monica beaches, hoping for the same magic results of instant stardom. Who needed to act? And learning it in the laid-down rules of a strict Germanic curriculum? Who was kidding who? So pupils in the once-renowned academy were few, the Herr Doktor mostly absent, the teaching chores left in the hands of his wife, Helene Thimig – a fine actress, mostly out of work, except when Warner Brothers needed another Nazi landlady or Gestapo informant. She became my champion, taught me her craft with dedication, patience, and skill. Dietrich could now proclaim, "My daughter is a theater student at the Max Reinhardt Academy – just like I was as 'a very young girl,'" and everyone was impressed and "happy."

A gallant armada of little ships chugged bravely out onto the night sea, lifted off three hundred thousand trapped men, and brought them home to England. Dunkirk became the first symbol of what this "tight little island" and its courageous people were capable of. Glued to our radios, the still-free world listened and cheered.

Winston Churchill became Prime Minister, Roosevelt ran for an unprecedented third term, France fell, Hermann Göring vowed to bring England to its knees, and the Battle of Britain began. Many of the British colony left Hollywood to stand by their countrymen in their hour of need.

Smoking and pacing, my mother was arguing with Remarque when I entered her bungalow to deliver the mail.

"Sweetheart – I just got back from taking Noël to the station! Boni, it was so touching. He looked so proud going off to war to fight for his beloved England. We stood there together, like two old soldiers, not knowing how to say good-bye. He nearly missed the train, when the whistles blew he had to rush. I stood and waved until the train was gone – and cried!" Her voice conjured up two exhausted comrades intrepidly wending their desperate way to the last evacuation train. Remarque was smiling.

"You know, Aunt Lena, it's a touching scene, seeing a dear friend off to war, but it would play better if you had taken him to the troop ship in Canada. Saying good-bye in Pasadena . . . it misses something!"

She whirled: "You're the one who's 'missing something'!" Sympathy for a patriot who does his duty, puts on the uniform of his country, goes to face the enemy . . . like a real *man!* And, for Noël, that is something already!"

"Well, for bayonets in no-man's-land, I could empathize, but today it was still Pasadena and a chauffeured limousine – and he wore a pinstriped suit with a red carnation, he had two chorus boys with him, was armed with an alligator briefcase, and arrived safely in his drawing room on the Super Chief without a shot being fired. Also, there was no fog."

"I said nothing about fog!"

"You were thinking it."

Unable to compete with Boni in this type of repartee, my mother turned up the radio. She had developed the habit of keeping a radio on, to hear the latest news from Europe, complaining that there never was any, that the Americans, in their usual way, knew nothing of what was going on in any part of the world but their own.

"Just look at them. War is raging and the Americans, what do they do? Make pictures, play gin rummy, and stay neutral!"

Remarque answered her in English:

"Give them time. The future of the world rests on their shoulders. It is a burden that requires all the time they can get."

"Well, if you are suddenly so pro-American, you better do something about your German accent. You sound like a Berlin butcher trying to be a gentleman! After all, you are supposed to be a 'famous' refugee!" In the "European days," she would never have treated him with such disdain, but those days were over – he was no longer her "sublime love." White lilacs had lost their magic. Remarque sighed, started to leave.

"Puma, do you know what Robert Graves wrote when the Spanish Civil War forced him to abandon his home? 'Never be a refugee if you can possibly avoid it. Stay exactly where you are, kiss the rod, and, if very hungry, eat grass or bark off the trees . . . but never be a refugee.' Of course, he only had Franco to contend with, not Adolf Hitler."

Determined to break England's morale, Hitler ordered nightly bombing raids on its civilian population. How we waited by our radios for that wonderful voice, that deep, honest growl that announced: 'This is London,' that led us, made us see, feel the terrible struggle, the devastation, the astounding bravery of its besieged people. So vividly did Edward R. Murrow bring the London Blitz into the consciousness of the American people that they began feeling slightly guilty for being still neutral. As Murrow set the scene vocally, Hollywood began to do it visually.

We packed Bundles for Britain, loved everything that was English; Mrs. Miniver became our symbolic heroine, were proud when American flyers left to join the glorious RAF and formed their own Eagle Squadron, worked full-time, around the clock, to send England whatever she needed to hold Hitler at bay; unconsciously were being emotionally conditioned to be willing, once again, to fight a war far from home.

MY MOTHER WAS SO FROUFROU FRENCH in *The Flame of New Orleans* – like meringue, its sticky sweetness hurt your back teeth. Nothing could be that overdone "ooh-la-la" and be a success at the box office. It deserved to flop, which it did. This film screamed "give me Lubitsch," was directed by a famous French refugee, René Clair, who should have known better. Still, the only thing Dietrich hated about this film was her leading man. She called my father in New York.

"Papilein, I have another dance teacher!" Considering she meant Bruce Cabot, she had a legitimate beef. "Why would Pasternak give me a gigolo? With von Sternberg we know why. After Cooper, he only gave me leading men he was *sure* I wouldn't like – but Pasternak? He can't be jealous already – I haven't slept with him yet! I told him 'No! Not until after Hitler loses the war!'"

Charles de Gaulle escaped to England, and my mother fell madly in love with him, began wearing the Cross of Lorraine with Free French fervor. The Nazis goose-stepped down the Champs-Elysées and 20th Century Fox announced that they had signed France's reigning male star, Jean Gabin.

"Boni, that unbelievable actor from that magnificent film, *Grand Illusion* – They are bringing him over to be in cheap American films? He probably can't even speak English. They will ruin him! He is perfect the way he is – and there will be no one to protect him. Can one still call France? Isn't Michèle Morgan in love with him? I could call her and find out where to reach him?" my mother asked, not mentioning that as far back as 1938, she had cabled my father from Hollywood:

I HEAR GABIN MAY BE COMING HERE. FIND OUT. I SHOULD GET HIM
FIRST.

Using his American contract to get out of Occupied France, Jean Gabin
was on his way – Dietrich's arms were waiting, ready to enfold him. He
didn't know it yet, but his doom for the next few years was sealed.

Remarque decided to move to New York. I helped him pack.

"You really have to leave her?"

"The dock cannot leave the ship that sailed the night before."

"Must you, Boni?"

"Yes, Sadness. If I could turn you to happiness I would stay, but I am
short of my former powers."

"You call me 'Sadness.' Why?"

"I call you many tender things, a gasp for breath because your mother
breathes up all the oxygen around you."

"I don't love her, you know." It felt so good saying it!

"You must. She loves you as she perceives love. But her rpm's are a
thousand a minute, whereas ours are a normal hundred a minute. We
need an hour to love her, she loves us as well in six minutes and is on
to everything else she must do, while we are wondering why she isn't
loving us as we are loving her. We are mistaken, she already has."

His Studio installed Gabin in the bungalow Remarque had vacated. A
chauffeured Rolls-Royce and a yacht were at his disposal. Anything he
wanted, Zanuck was prepared to give his new star. He was the new king of
Hollywood. Poor Gabin! All he knew, was comfortable with, left behind,
his beloved country lost. He, who hated all pretense, assumed glitter and
ostentation, was now expected to behave like an Important Star within an
insular foreign community, in a language he hardly knew. Jean was such a
simple soul, a little boy in a gruff man's body, easy to love, easy to hurt.
Over the many years, we became distant friends, rarely were together,
never really talked – yet, somehow, felt a kinship. In Jean's concept of
things, a man did not involve his mistress's child in his adult passion. I
always thought Jean Gabin was the most instinctive gentleman of all my
mother's lovers.

His waiting "general" prepared the field for combat. All he had to do
was surrender himself into her loving hands – and lose the battle. Holding
on to her bungalow, but to escape prying hotel eyes, my mother rented a
little house up in the hills of Brentwood and transformed it into a bit of
France. Called Gabin at the hotel, said in her beautiful French:

"Jean, c'est Marlène!" and one of the great romances of the 1940s

New start, new Studio, new image, new love. Dietrich as Frenchy in *Destry Rides Again,* with Jimmy Stewart. They enjoyed each other.

ABOVE: On the set of *Seven Sinners*, with costar John Wayne, director Tay Garnett, and Broderick Crawford.
BELOW: In her favorite costume from that film, the naval officer's uniform, designed for the Hollander-Loesser song "The Man's in the Navy."

ABOVE: The froufrou French look of
The Flame of New Orleans, with René
Clair and Joseph Pasternak.
RIGHT: The wonderful hooker look of
Manpower.
BELOW: The French cowboy look of her
new consuming passion, Jean Gabin.

ABOVE: Lunching with two of her pals, Ann Warner, a confidante, and Noël Coward, a devoted friend who knew all, kept her secrets, and stood by with compassion.

BELOW: Gabin and his *Grande*. Still "happy times" in 1943.

was born. Their love affair was to be one of the most enduring, most passionate, and most painful of both their lives, and of course, Gabin suffered the most.

But now he ran into my mother's arms like a floundering ship finding its home port. She reveled in his dependence on her. For his homesickness for his country that he felt he was deserting in its time of need, she recreated France for him in sunny California. She wore striped jerseys, knotted a jaunty kerchief around her neck, and took to wearing berets over one eye. Chevalier would have been proud, had he not been busy entertaining the Nazi occupation forces in Paris.

This French cocoon my mother enveloped Gabin in was not constructive. He had to earn his living in America, work with American actors and crews; making no effort to meet them halfway did not help him. Jean Gabin, the man of the people, through Dietrich's influence became the aloof foreigner, and this affected his work and popularity.

One day before the anniversary of Napoleon's try in 1812, Hitler invaded Russia.

My mother was making *Manpower* at Warner Brothers with her old pal George Raft, and one she had no liking for: "Ugly little man – why is *he* a star?" Edward G. Robinson. She did her job, achieved one "look" in a raincoat and beret that was superb, hated the film as it was "just for money" and took her away from being with the "love of her life."

Manpower was such an easy film, there were many days Dietrich was not on call. She had time to devote herself to taking care of her "man." When he came home in the evenings, she greeted him at the door of "their" house, enveloped in her big apron, the pungent perfume of her cassoulet filling the air. On Sundays, she cooked crawfish and pot-au-feu for Hollywood's French refugees. The directors, René Clair, Jean Renoir, Duvivier, Gabin's friend from *Grand Illusion* Dalio, and many more. Feeling far from home, they reveled in this Gallic sanctuary. She allowed no foreign intrusion into the safety of their little French household. Only Jean's inner male clique were welcome. It was "bistro" time in Brentwood.

Gabin called her "*Ma grande*," one of those wonderfully romantic expressions that are so difficult to translate. Literally "My big one," it really means "My woman," "My pride," "My world." The way my mother looked at him when she said "Jean, *mon amour*" needed no translation. She loved everything about him – especially his hips: "The most beautiful hips I have seen on a man." The only part of him that she had the slightest reservation about was his intelligence. His background and education lacked the sophisticated polish that attracted her so to Remarque.

She set to work on Gabin's English pronunciation. His French accent did not have the lilt of Chevalier's, nor the sexy softness of Boyer. Gabin growled; in French his voice could give a dead fish goose pimples, but in English, he sounded like an angry headwaiter. She fought for him at his studio and made enemies for him in absentia. She even persuaded someone to assign her old lover, Fritz Lang, to direct Gabin's film. Fortunately, he was replaced in the first four days of shooting. As it was, the film turned out to be such a nonentity, it wouldn't have mattered who directed it! Still, Lang must have had enough time to have a man-to-man talk with Gabin, for he came home one day and accused her of having had an affair with Lang, to which she replied, utterly amazed:

"*That* ugly Jew? You must be joking, *mon amour*," and enclosed him in her embrace.

Throughout her life, Dietrich did that constantly – erased lovers from her memory as though they had never existed. Not just a convenient trick to get out of a sticky situation, but true mental erasure. She could do it with other things too, a frightening trait.

MY APPRENTICESHIP DONE, I graduated to being permitted to perform on stage, and chose a professional name for myself – "Maria Manton." I thought it sounded strong and un-European. I was given the leading role of Lavinia in *Mourning Becomes Electra*, a Greek tragedy set in New England, that our director had switched to the Deep South, revolving around the hatred between a daughter and a mother. Interesting choice! My mother came to the opening night with "the boys" and de Acosta, didn't understand what that "depressing" O'Neill was talking about, thought me superb except my hair was too curly, and the rented antebellum gown should have been made especially by Irene, and why didn't I tell her I had to wear "period"?

Her agent, now a producer, offered her a picture to be called *The Lady Is Willing*, at Columbia. She accepted without knowing the director, full script, or leading man. Charlie Feldman was pleased, though a bit surprised. I wasn't, she trusted him, and, for the first time in her life, was so in love – work had taken second place.

Once installed in her dressing room at Columbia, reality hit a little, but unfortunately, not strongly enough. The director, Mitchell Leisen, worshiped her, had been, was, and would be her fan forever, so she was in the driver's seat, and between them, they managed a production that can only be described as high camp. In the forties, this took real, concentrated effort to achieve, not as easy as it is today. Of course, everyone was convinced they were shooting a marvelous picture with the even more marvelous Marlene.

Poor Fred MacMurray. Ever the dependable workhorse of Hollywood's leading men, found himself in the midst of this gay extravaganza, and in his unflappable way, never said a word, did his job, took his paycheck, and like any normal breadwinner, went home to his little woman. No love was lost between the stars. Actually, the way everyone behaved, there was only one Star in this film – Dietrich.

A baby figured prominently in the story. One day, carrying it in her arms, she tripped, stumbled, and fell. As she couldn't very well toss the child like a forward pass, she twisted her body to avoid squashing it and broke her ankle. I was called, told to get to Columbia fast – my mother had been in a terrible accident! I found her looking gorgeous, reclining on a gurney waiting to be taken to the hospital.

"Sweetheart," her voice registered unconditional awe, "you know what that astrologer said about today? 'Beware of accidents'! Unbelievable! This morning I called him and he said I shouldn't go to the Studio until after lunch, but of course, I went – and see!"

From that moment, Carroll Righter became her all-seeing, all-knowing guru. That very skilled and very sweet man often regretted having warned her that day. He had to cast the horoscopes of all potential as well as accepted lovers, family members, coworkers, acquaintances, servants, decide travel dates and contract signings. Over the years, day or night, he was "on call" – interrogated, asked for advice and magic solutions. She rarely followed his counsel, but blamed him if things didn't work out to her satisfaction. Carroll Righter became my lifelong friend, one of the fathers I would have wished.

One of Dietrich's famous gams being injured while "saving the life of a little baby" knocked the war off the front pages.

She refused to hold up the film until the ankle was healed and the cast could be removed, insisted on a walking cast, very unusual in those days, and with all long shots eliminated from the shooting script, was back at work within days. Her only problem: appearing natural in medium shots without her upper body reflecting the restricted movements caused by the heavy cast and obvious limp.

"What did Marshall use to do? Remember – with his wooden leg? He had all those little tricks to look normal in scenes?"

We ordered a Herbert Marshall film and did our homework. She got his timing, his subtle distractions so down pat, few people on seeing *The Lady*

Is Willing can catch the point in the film where the break happened and the cast begins. This accident gave Dietrich "heroine" status, both privately and professionally, paid off at the box office, and allowed her to use a very elegant walking stick when wearing her male attire, without being criticized for this added, overly masculine accessory. Dietrich couldn't even break a simple ankle without profiting from it. After a while, this talent of hers to turn everything to her advantage took on the faintest diabolical overtones.

Finished at Columbia, she went immediately into another film with John Wayne at Universal, even finding a part in it for her old flame, Richard Barthelmess. Gabin, still uninitiated to my mother's emotional life-style, basked in the intense celestial fire of her all-encompassing love and was innocently happy. *Moontide*, his first American film, began shooting in November.

AT FIRST, when I heard it on the radio I thought it must be another one of those scary Orson Welles shows, but then, it sounded much too real to be just a script. I called my mother. Being Sunday, she was busy organizing a crawfish dinner, angry I had not arrived yet to scrub their bellies.

"What? They bombed ships? Finally! So, it took the *Japanese* to bring the Americans to their senses? Good! *Now* they will fight! Now it will all be over soon – like when they came into the war the last time, before I was born. I need more butter when you come. Oh . . . where *is* this Pearl Harbor?"

Overnight, every gardener disappeared. Flowers drooped, lawns withered in the hot sun. This marked the end of the era of manicured horticultural splendors of movie-star estates. For the landscapes of the Hollywood mighty of today, Mexican gentlemen labor diligently among the bougainvillea, but somehow, the sublime magic is gone – a little like the stars themselves.

A sign in a barber shop read:

Japs Shaved
Not Responsible for Accidents!

California, now so close to the enemy, panicked. A six p.m. curfew was ordered for all Japanese, their radios confiscated. All were potential spies, undoubtedly loyal to their Emperor Hirohito, whether American-born or not. All Oriental-theme pictures were shelved. The Studios geared up for "heroic propaganda" and "morale boosters," upgraded anti-Nazi scripts. Hollywood went to war its way and did a magnificent job.

Under the auspices of the Hollywood Victory Committee, stars volunteered their time and fame to help with the war effort. For once, my mother joined her peers. Mystery and aloofness were no longer prerequisites for glamour. This was 1942 and "realness" was in. Her early Berlin cabaret days now paid off. She went everywhere – did anything – cracked saucy jokes with Charlie McCarthy, joined impromptu chorus lines, broke into song whenever called on. As the wounded arrived from Pearl Harbor, she joined the hospital shows hastily organized, was a "good sport," a "regular guy," a "real trooper," and had a ball. She was in rehearsal for the biggest role of her life – "the gallant war entertainer" – but didn't know it yet.

Carole Lombard was killed when her plane crashed returning from a war bond drive. My mother's fear of flying was again vindicated.

"See? What do I always say? Never fly! Airplanes are dangerous. I never really liked her, but she could be beautiful when someone dressed her right. I wonder who Gable will find next?"

The *Normandie*, confined to her New York berth since 1939, being stripped of her finery to be converted into a troop ship, caught fire, rolled over on her side, and died. For us, who loved her, it was like a death in the family.

I now played leads, was mildly successful, began teaching, directing, and getting paid for it. I was coasting in the afternoons, drunk at night, hung-over in the mornings. Rot-gut bourbon had taken over from brandy; Stingers, Sidecars, and Alexanders I used as chasers.

The perfect lovers must have had a fight. Maybe over John Wayne, or Remarque's love letters were arriving too often . . . whatever, or whoever, when Gabin left to go on location, my mother was convinced that he was angry with her and would therefore have an immediate torrid affair with his costar, Ida Lupino. Poor Jean, he was being judged by Dietrich's rule of thumb, not his. She canceled a bond tour to devote herself to "pining" and recorded her yearning into a navy blue diary – as with all of her written outpourings, with an eye to posterity, later leaving it in a conspicuous place so Jean could find it, read of her magnificent love for him, "if" he returned. In later years, when Jean was no more, she would haul it out whenever she wanted to impress a famous author swain of her talent for lyrical French prose, inspired by her great love for "the one man who knew not what he gave up."

15th February. He has gone.

16th February. I am thinking in French. It's funny! 10 A.M. I am thinking about him – thinking about him I could sleep for years if only I could see him for one second.
He is with me like a blazing fire.
Jean, *je t'aime.*
All that I plan to give you is my love. If you don't want it my life is finished, forever. And I realize saying that does not prove anything – even saying "I will love you all my life long and afterwards too" – because even when I am dead, I will still love you. I love you – it feels good saying it without you having to answer: "I don't believe you." However, if you were here I could kiss you and lay my head on your shoulder and I believe that you love me. Because if you don't, all is finished for me – because if you don't want me anymore I intend to die.
I am in bed. My body is cold and I look at myself, don't find myself attractive, not attractive enough – I would like to be very beautiful for you. For you I would like to be the best woman in the world and I'm not. But I love you. You are all my heart, all my soul. I never knew what soul was. Now I do. Tomorrow I will sleep in your bed. It is going to hurt. But I will be nearer to you. I love you – I love you.

February 17th – I haven't slept. I took some pills at 3 A.M. but I was too cold to be able to sleep. I worked in the afternoon. I wait for you as though you were going to come back any time from the studio.
Please, my adored one, come back, please.

18th February – I slept so well in his bed. At first it hurt to be there without him – but I pretended he was there and went to sleep. Time passes so slowly! It is because I count the hours – even the minutes! I had lunch with George Raft and talked about him! Raft asked me how could he look at another woman?
I can't believe that only three days have passed since he went away. It seems an eternity to me, or a lost life. I am breathing, but that's all. I realize I am only thinking about myself. Maybe that is what one does when one really loves. I always thought that real love was not to think about oneself but it can't be true. I love him with every drop of my blood and I think only about one thing: Being next to him – to listen to his voice – feel his lips – his arms around me – and I think that I want to give myself to him for life.

Most nights I stayed in the theater, passed out on one of the prop couches stored in the loft above the stage. It was dark and cool up there, and much safer than where I was expected to be.

21st February – I still have the fever. My head is burning and so are my hands – this book I touch feels cold. I write slowly, my heart beats quickly. It's a good thing he doesn't know I'm sick.

Sunday, 22nd February – He called me. I am very ill. The doctor is coming at lunchtime. All those injections! What are they doing to the baby which I think is inside of me? But I can't have it if he is not free. And to have the child and say it is not from him, no, I don't want to think about that.

Sunday evening – If I only could touch his heart, however lightly, for him to see me as I am. If he said he loved me and wants me, that he needs me in his life just as much as he is necessary to mine – only this could end this misery which shrouds me like an eternal night.

Every day she wrote, page after page of her love and longing.

Thursday, 26th February. I sent him a telegram with the number of La Quinta. I'm going to wait for him there.

Like Garbo, my mother often went to La Quinta, then a hideaway oasis way out beyond Palm Springs. I sometimes felt this lush compound of discreet bungalows had been built for the sole purpose of movie stars' secret assignations. If someone was having a blazing affair with someone that was either illegal, scandalous, bad box office, or against their Studio's orders, off they flitted to the desert and "hidden" La Quinta.

Friday, 27th February, La Quinta – I woke up with the sound of his voice in my ears. He keeps me alive with his voice, to take the place of his arms and his shoulders. He gives it back to me with such a sweetness which touches me deeply. He knows he keeps me alive that way. Therefore he calls me and talks to me sweetly. There is no sunshine in this place which is usually so sunny. Maybe the sun is jealous of you. I think that prisoners must feel what I feel. They exist without really living. They wait for the day when they will get out of this misery to go on living again. I feel cold, my love. But if you were here, I would be clinging to your warm body and love the rain because it would be reason to go to bed. And you would ask: "Are you all right, my face?" Oh Jean, my love!

Saturday, 28th February – I didn't sleep at all. I kept thinking, thinking. Thinking . . . If I have his child, I am going to ask him to decide what we are going to do. I don't want to hide myself the last five months. If he wants, I'll have the child as though we were married. I don't give a damn what people think. I wouldn't be able to kill that child. But if he

wants to, I'll do it. I could get my divorce a lot sooner than he, but that
is not important. I hope that this time I am not pregnant because I am
afraid he would stay with me for that reason and not because he loves
me. In the future, when he is completely certain he wants to live with
me, then I will want a child – but only if he wants it – and not because
it happened without him wanting to. Oh, Jean, come – Come to cure all
my pain.

The Battle of the Java Sea was lost. The triumphant Japanese were
through to the Indian Ocean.

Sunday, 1st of March. I have a small tummy but no symptoms. Another
Sunday without him. My body feels warm because I was in the sun and
had a bath. I would like to go to bed but if I do, I'll be thinking too much
about him.

Thursday, 5th March. He comes tomorrow. Oh, Jean – I love you. This
is the last day I write in this little book which holds my deepest feelings
– my sufferings, my tears – my hopes.

Reunited, they stayed locked in each other's arms for weeks. They
came back to town dressed as sexy cowboys, both handsome, vibrant,
and tanned all over.

Only one flaw in this idyllic picture – she told my father on the
phone:

"And, Papi, after all the joy, Jean really loving me, something terrible
has happened. I'm not carrying his child after all. How is that? I didn't
douche on purpose. Funny, no?"

My mother decided the back-and-forth from Beverly Hills to Brentwood took too much time, let her hotel bungalow go, rented herself a
hacienda near her man, and moved me and my "constant" companion
from the alley to a house of our own down the hill in the next village
of Westwood.

"The Child – since she has that woman to look after her and is learning
to act – is so quiet. No problem at all. At least, I don't have to worry
about her all the time on top of work and cooking for Jean," my mother
told my father on one of her frequent calls to New York.

Singapore had fallen. After a desperate struggle, Bataan surrendered
in April.

Jean's film was going badly, and he knew it. Trying too hard to
be "Gabin," he became stilted, lost that enchanting actorless ease that

reminded one of how much he resembled Spencer Tracy. In later years, their style of just being wonderful without the least apparent effort was so similar, they even began to resemble each other physically, at times.

Jean had not only found my mother's planted love pourings, but also letters from Remarque, Pasternak, Beth, even ones from the Pirate to her Babe. Normal jealousy consumed him. He accused her of having an affair with Wayne.

"Between selling bonds, retakes that won't help another disaster, and cooking for your buddy-buddies, I haven't got time . . .", she snapped.

If he could be jealous, he must love her. She was once more sure of her hold over him and became abusive, accused him of being "bourgeois," "possessive," and "jealous beyond reason."

She would return to her house, summon me from mine, and let off steam:

"A peasant – and French! The worst kind, after Hungarians . . . but he can be so sweet. . . . What is the matter with him? I love only him. I die for him. He is my whole world! He does nothing but talk about 'poor France.' Only the war? Is that why he behaves so strangely?"

Between fights, they went dancing. Orchestra leaders seeing them arrive would break into the "Marseillaise" in Gabin's honor. He sat down quickly, embarrassed, while Dietrich stood at attention, singing fervently until the last note.

"I hate it when you do that French patriot act," Jean would growl.

"Have you noticed that you are the only one?" she retorted, saluting the band, bowing low to the leader, "and 'act'? What gives you that idea?"

Colonel Doolittle led sixteen B-25s off the deck of the mighty *Hornet* and bombed Tokyo! All ran out of fuel, crashed, some taken prisoner, three executed by the Japanese, but we had bombed Hirohito's hometown and morale was high.

I was in the midst of a "dramatic" speech in some play, my mother and her date George Raft were in the audience, so was the new rival to the mighty Louella Parsons, Hedda Hopper, when suddenly the air-raid sirens recently installed on the street corners went off! Everyone knew it couldn't be an actual raid, so sat listening to the play as best they could, waiting for the din to stop. Not my mother! She wriggled out of her row, sprinted outside, grabbed the filling-station attendant, made him haul his ladder to the lamppost, climbed up it, and stuffed her mink into the offending horn that had dared to interrupt her "brilliant" daughter's monologue. The show outside was so entertaining, the audience left us and traipsed outside to see it. Hedda Hopper was the only one who ever

ABOVE: My mother loved going out with Gabin, showing the world she belonged to him. He, missing France and worried about the war raging in Europe, went out only to please her.
BELOW: Her insistence on showing off her one-time skill on the violin in public places embarrassed Gabin, but he accepted it all with quiet charm.

LEFT: Whenever she was in New York, Remarque was there, ready to listen to and love her. My mother always had old loves ever waiting to embrace her.
BELOW: At Universal, on the set of *Pittsburgh*. Although John Wayne was Dietrich's leading man in three films, his refusal to become one of her many conquests absolutely infuriated her.

ABOVE: Dietrich joined the many stars who toured the States selling war bonds.

BELOW: Filming a scene in *The Lady Is Willing*, she tripped while carrying a baby. To avoid injuring it, she twisted her body and broke an ankle. The Columbia Studios Publicity Department rejoiced! They brought the baby to the hospital, photographed it with the "heroine star," and knocked the war off the front pages.

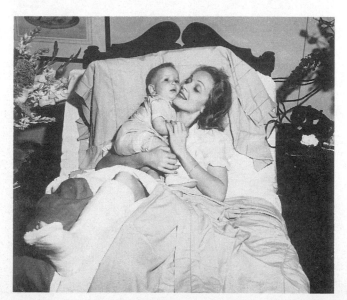

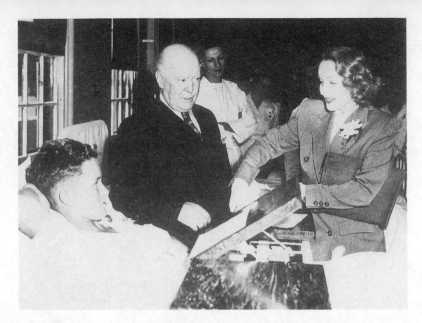

ABOVE: In 1943, organized military hospital visits by stars were a must. Guy Kibbee thought my mother's bedside manner was delightful. She loved cheering up "her boys," as she called them.
BELOW: Gabin in uniform, about to leave the United States to join the Free French Forces overseas, danced one last dance with the woman he loved. She swore to follow him to war, then kissed him farewell.

told this story with any sympathy for the rejected actors left stranded while Dietrich, her skirt hiked up to her hips, was performing *her* act in the parking lot. Everyone else took it as yet another proof of Dietrich's great devotion to her child. The siren silenced, she climbed down, lowered her tight skirt to the deep disappointment of the onlookers, herded them back into the theater, calling to us, rooted in our positions on stage:

"Go back to where he says, 'Darling – what is this all about?' so Maria can start her speech again." Turning to her adoring herd she instructed them: "Everyone – sit down! They are going to do it over again from the top. Okay! Dim the lights – you can start!"

Hedda became my champion. Whenever she wrote about anything involving my mother's "goodness," there was just a hint of tongue-in-cheek sarcasm, a flash of censure. The first columnist ever to buck the tide of "perfect motherhood." Over the years, she was very kind to me. Whether she really liked me or just disliked my mother wasn't really important. Anyone who questioned my mother's "sainthood" was okay by me.

AT A STRANGE COCKTAIL PARTY of dislikable people, a gentle, likable man took my arm, walked me out of there to his car, drove me to the beach – let the sharp sea air clean away the impressions of that unsavory gathering. He fell in love with me, this oh-so-good man with the lovely talent to make people laugh, and resurrected my spirit in the process – made life seem, once more, livable. Of course, I adored him, and not only because he wouldn't let "that woman" get near me from then on.

Very properly, we became engaged. I was walking on air. My mother was furious, hid it gallantly, and called my father to come "immediately" to California to help with the "craziness of The Child!" Their combined efforts of dissuasion hit a stone wall of British determination. My fiancé presented me with a beautiful amethyst ring, and complete with "smiling" golden-haired parents, we were photographed celebrating our official engagement.

The Rhino pawed the ground, breathed fire, and quit. My mother was so shocked at her sudden departure, she told my father to check for some ulterior motive. When he informed her some checks could – might – seemed likely to have been tampered with, she said:

"I knew it! I had a feeling she was stealing something – that's why she left so suddenly." Henceforth, always referred to her as "that woman – the one we had for The Child – the forger." Even after my father discovered

that others had embezzled huge sums of Dietrich's earnings, her moniker
was not reassessed.

Strange, I never really blamed that woman. She frightened me,
disgusted me, harmed me, but "blame"? Why? Lock an alcoholic into
a liquor store and he helps himself – who's to blame? The one who takes
what is made available or the one who put him there? Even an innocent
parent would not have put a young girl into an unsupervised, wholly
private environment with such a visually obvious lesbian. My mother
was certainly not an innocent.

All was suddenly such a real B-picture script, so "hearts and flowers"
perfect, I should have been more on my guard. But I was in such a daze of
"normal people" fairy tale, I was delirious; visions of wedding dress, veil,
and bridesmaids played tag with rice, honeymoon, and happy-ever-after.
I was once more an "untarnished" virgin, in the first throes of idyllic love.
That poor sweet man, loving me as he did, seeing this raw need gathering
momentum, rolling toward him out of control.

We walked along the sand, the early morning cool and still. Hesitantly,
he told me he was leaving, was returning to England to enlist, our
wedding would have to be postponed. He said he loved me, promised
he would come back, to wait for him. He meant it all. He could not know
the extent of my fears, that believing myself to be so rejectable made it
impossible for me to accept that anyone would ever want to return and
love me still.

I think I begged a little. That day has taken on the cataract haze that
seems to appear to envelop such hurts and subsequent foolish actions.
I saw him off – kissed him good-bye, convinced he had left for more
reasons than the love of his country and turned my back on his precious
gift of salvation.

My mother was very pleased.

"Good for him! He knew what he was doing. Don't be so la-di-da
romantic. He was twenty years older than you and a comic actor! No –
no! Good you are out of that – without any *big* problems!" and called my
father to tell him The Child was saved and back to normal. The Rhino
was also pleased and waited patiently, hoping.

My mother decided I needed further "curing." As undoubtedly it had
to be my misfunctioning glands that were at the root of my inexplicable
stupidity of falling in love, she put me into a hospital for metabolic
disorders in La Jolla. There I was given lettuce, gained weight, was
accused of bribing the staff to smuggle in candy bars, drank a bottle of
milk of magnesia the night before every Friday's weighing, made friends

with a nice lady who shared our adjoining bathroom, or she would have, had she been able to walk, which she couldn't because her legs were black from diabetic gangrene; and concluded that I had always known I would be put away into a "spa" like Tami someday. I was discharged at the same overweight I had entered with but wiser in the agony of gangrene, and resumed my quiet self-destruction.

The Reinhardt Academy failed – was taken over by a drama school run on expedient lines: "Got the money? Want to act? Be a star? Here you can – No waiting – No heavy classes – No classics – Only modern plays you can be seen in by talent scouts – An instant showcase – Learn while doing." A natural for Hollywood. I stayed on as one of the directors.

A breathless young student timidly interrupted one of my multiple rehearsals of *The Women*.

"Miss Manton? Please excuse me but," here she took a deep breath as though oxygen had become imperative, "there is a young officer in the front office asking for you." Her eyes shone, her slight bosom fluttered, "He is waiting for you in the lobby."

I was sure there must be a mistake, no one with that effect on women could be coming to see me!

There he stood, in that dingy lobby, looking like an ad for what joining the navy could do for a young man. His officer's whites immaculate, his cap set at an angle even my mother would envy, that rakish white-toothed grin – so handsome, so young, so alive, so American! Jack Kennedy said:

"Hi, Maria," and my knees went just as wobbly as they had so long ago.

At the drive-in next door, he bought me a cheeseburger, answered all my eager questions about his wonderful brothers and sisters, was kind, attentive, and a joy to be with. He never changed. When we said good-bye, he kissed my cheek, then walked away to his red convertible. As he drove off, we waved to each other, mouthing, "See you soon! Take care of yourself!" We never saw each other again. As to taking care of ourselves, we didn't do that very well either.

SUGAR AND COFFEE were rationed. The use of klieg lights that shone their long beams into the night sky were banned for the duration, and fancy movie premieres were no more. A hundred stars went to Washington, D.C., to launch the first billion-dollar war bond drive. Tyrone Power became a marine, Henry Fonda joined the navy, and

Bette Davis, with John Garfield as cofounder, had begged, borrowed, and finagled enough money to open the Hollywood Canteen. In the first six months, six hundred thousand men passed through its doors – seven nights a week, volunteers welcomed the boys far from home, showed them they cared. Where else would a young man waiting to be shipped out to the Pacific be served a cup of coffee by Ann Sheridan, get a ham sandwich from Alice Faye, a doughnut from Betty Grable, hold Lana Turner in his arms to the strains of Tommy Dorsey's orchestra, jitterbug with Ginger Rogers to Glenn Miller's band, twirl Rita Hayworth to the beat of Benny Goodman, while Woody Herman joined in on his "licorice stick"? Chew the fat with Bogart, Tracy, and Cagney, have an egg plucked from their nose by Orson Welles, finally find out that Veronica Lake DID have a second eye under that peekaboo bob?

The European contingent preferred the kitchen detail. Hedy Lamarr made hundreds of sandwiches, Dietrich scrubbed pots in clinging dress and attractive snood, up to her elbows in dirty dishwater – it drove Bette Davis crazy. I once heard that wonderful four-octave-range voice of hers declare: "If I find those dames back there one more time . . . I'll brain them! What is it with those hausfraus? Show them a kitchen and they're off! Like a horse to water! I need glamour out *here* for the boys – not in there with the pots! Oh, God! What I couldn't do with a dozen Grables!"

At the Canteen, those unreachable "gods" stepped down from the silver screen and turned into flesh-and-blood people, suddenly touchable. It had a profound effect on those young men, and, eventually, on the entire industry that supplied their entertainment. Once exposed, made human, stars lost their divinity and became "lovable"! When a Betty Grable film was shown in some tent behind the lines on some Jap-infested island, they knew her – they had actually held her a time-stop moment on a crowded dance floor. All the stars, both male and female, that made that bridge from make-believe to reality gained that special place – when an audience replaces awe with genuine affection. Garbo never appeared at the Canteen. A shame, it might have saved her from extinction. Again that incredible, completely intuitive weather vane of Dietrich's pointed her in the direction that would eventually prolong her visual fame by thirty years.

Gabin didn't resent my mother's giving her time to any cause that helped the war effort. It was my mother's all-consuming pleasure, the emotional high that her "war work," as she called it, gave her that made him feel even more the outsider, the ineffectual foreigner. When she came home brimming over with stories of how the GIs had held her very, very close, how she could feel their rising excitement, how sweet they were with those freshly washed faces, those innocent young boys about to be heroes, how she knew their last dance with "Marlene" would remain with them through the terrors of war, Gabin was jealous of her enthusiasm and emotional satisfaction that excluded him. She, never aware of such subtleties of another's sensitivity, was annoyed by what she called "his moods," accused him of being jealous of "her boys" because all he was doing for the war was "making a stupid picture."

My ever-devoted mother must have bribed someone, for I was given my final high school exams and *passed*. Amazing! For years I expected the California Department of Education would wake up one day and haul me off to jail. Now, after fifty years, I figure the statute of limitations is on my side.

Rumors of a massacre in a Warsaw ghetto were faint but there, still few believed them. The Allies landed in Sicily, bombings of Germany intensified.

I found someone who was willing to marry me and thought salvation was at hand. The day I packed my few belongings for this sad and foolish teenage marriage, my mother, her face frozen, stood watching me, walked out, returned, handed me my wedding present: a brand-new douche bag.

"At least, make sure he doesn't get you pregnant!" With that sage and loving counsel, I left my mother's house. I was married in a summer dress of gray, printed with purple violets – funeral colors, unplanned, but very appropriate. That poor boy, neither old enough nor trained to cope with the neurotic mess he acquired. Our "legal cohabitation" lasted just long enough to gain yet another gold star on my mother's "martyred mother" tally board. She searched and found a small apartment, a real feat in wartime, cleaned and furnished it. Created a little love nest of marital bliss for the ungrateful daughter that everyone knew had "deserted" her.

Of course, this desperate attempt at escape, this pathetic self-delusion of normalcy, was doomed from the start. The so-called "marriage" was finished before it ever began. I was left with three choices, besides an obvious fourth of working the corner of Hollywood and Vine, which in my drunken state I probably would have tried had I believed I could earn enough to survive on; the way I looked, I had my doubts. So, it was either returning to my mother or the ever-waiting Rhinoceros, or hitchhiking across America to my father's punitive asylum. I chose the lesser of those evils . . . my mother. I wasn't very bright. Maybe reading all that *Hamlet* at an impressionable age had gotten to me and so opted for the "ills" I knew. With her, at least, I knew all that awaited me, knew what to expect, including giving her the divine satisfaction of having "the love of her life" return, tail properly clamped between her legs.

And how she enjoyed it, for more than fifty years reminding everyone

– me included – how she took me in, welcomed the penitent home, the "ever-forgiving mother." She even added a touching scene of how in the dead of night, I crawled into her bed, whispered pitifully, "Mutti, I am back – please can I sleep here with you tonight?"

I returned at high noon, downed a slug of bourbon, and, gritting my teeth, went to do penance. But my mother wasn't home, she was still in Gabin's house. But her version is a much better script for a prodigal's return. And by this time, I didn't care what anyone did to me – worse, what I did to myself.

Gabin had had enough. His country defeated, his American film career going nowhere, he began pulling diplomatic strings to join up with the Free French Forces formed by de Gaulle out of England. Zanuck assured him he would not stand in his way. Not only did he sympathize with Gabin's loyalties, it would also relieve him of having to honor his contract – finding vehicles for an actor whose American box-office appeal was proving a dud. My mother wept, but was brave. Her man was doing what he *had* to do: "going off to war to do his duty." Somehow, she would find a way to follow him into the field. The impossibility of travel during wartime without official orders and her Universal contract kept her tied down in Hollywood for the time being. Still, she resolved to find a way. I was not present at their leave-taking, but it must have been a lulu! Probably fog and all!

Papilein,
   Jean went tonight to New York. You will see it in the papers when he arrives.
   My great love seems too much for him, and too sudden for him, after all that time when he thought that my love was not enough in comparison with his which included everything. I have promised him to eat and to take care of myself until he comes back.
   I will not work, have canceled the Camp Tour because in my misery I could not take all that.
   I only know one thing: that I have loved without being selfish, without any thoughts at the back of my mind, and I have always tried to give happiness even though I did not succeed always. After this, I will be more able to do it and I will try not to clutch myself to him, but I would like to have, finally, the chance to be a real woman and not to strive toward ideals that are in the moon and do not bring any happiness because one can keep them only for a while. Kisses and love,
                                                                            Mutti

Still, she couldn't let him go without a last lingering farewell and actually got into a plane and flew to New York, saw Gabin one more time, danced in his arms – she, ethereal in clinging black and feathered hat, he, wonderfully handsome in his French uniform.

"Sweetheart," she called on her return as she strode through the door, the chauffeur following lugging her cases, "flying is so easy! No different arrival clothes to pack, no endless cornfields, no lists, no tipping – not even that heat! Why did we always take trains? Next time, we must try it instead of boats!" Planes had arrived! Flying, given the Dietrich stamp of approval.

Now that I was once more housed with her, mail was again my duty. The flood of love letters from Gabin was never-ending. Wartime V-mail, opened first by French-speaking censors before being sent on microfilm, then printed in the States before reaching my mother's trembling hands, and she could sigh, cry, yearn while devouring the contents.

> 11th Febr. 1944
>
> . . . Ma grande, my love, my life! You are here before me, I look at you: La Quinta, you, me. I've nothing but that in my head. I'm alone, like a kid lost in a crowd. Is it possible to love this much? Do you think that one day we will be together again and will live together, the two of us, only the two of us! Will you wait for me . . . Will God want me to find you again, you, the greatest of all? . . . You are in my veins, in my blood, I hear you inside of me. For the first time, I tell you: I need you, I need you for all my life or I'm lost.
>
> J.

After a few months of this, Gabin's letters outnumbered hers. She was very busy adoring Orson Welles. They spent days together discussing his brilliance. As with anyone of higher intellect, she was his fan, and Orson, being Orson, saw no reason why he shouldn't agree with her assessment of his genius. As recompense, he taught her to perform as his assistant in his magic act. They did camp shows and appeared together in a big morale booster, *Follow the Boys*, that featured an array of stars. As I had worked for Orson on his Mercury Theatre of the Air, my mother was always a little jealous of my actor's association with him, became very possessive whenever discussing "*my* friend Orson Welles" with me. When Orson fell in love with Rita Hayworth, my mother had been shocked.

"An intelligent man like that? Falls for a Mexican hoofer? You, who think you know him, will you *tell* me why? Does he maybe like hair under arms?" She was very disappointed in him but forgave her pal, as she did all his future disastrous amours, by saying: "Orson needs it. Don't ask me why. He just needs to love somebody all the time – poor man!"

Leslie Howard, rumored to be a valuable British spy, was killed in a mysterious plane crash, and Hollywood was buzzing. The most believed story was that his plane had been purposely shot down by the British because they had discovered he was a double agent for the Nazis.

"See? What did I tell you. Such a terrible actor, he *had* to do something else. After that orange hair – anything was possible!"

I often wondered about my grandmother and Liesel. What had happened to them? My mother never mentioned them, never said a word, behaved as though they didn't exist. Ever so slowly, rumors of unbelievable horrors began filtering back, unknown names of places where Nazi cruelties and actions lost plausibility in the sheer magnitude of their evil. Still, no one had yet seen the visual proof of hell and, therefore, could not be expected to believe such things were possible. Over the next two years, my mother, ever so gently, let drop that her mother was safe in Berlin and that her sister was in Belsen. As horrific rumors became heinous reality, it was automatically assumed that Liesel was in *the* Belsen – the only Belsen in everyone's mind at the time. That concentration camps were simply given the name of the town they belonged to was not a concept that even seemed plausible. Just too normal, for geography to designate the placement of hell. I, too, had no reason to think otherwise, accepted my mother's tragic version, and worried about the fate of that tender little woman.

In New York, Teddy died. Strange to think of a world without him. Many years later, his spirit settled into a glossy black cat who appeared one day at my door, and stayed to be my friend. So like him to have no animosity toward felines.

My mother found out Gabin was in Algiers. How she got that information is one of those mysteries so often associated with Dietrich. This now galvanized her need to follow her man into battle. She began her campaigns at the top. Abe Lastfogel, of the mighty William Morris Agency, had been put in charge of camp shows for the USO – the civilian organization responsible for sending entertainers to lift the morale of America's fighting men wherever they might happen to be. Lastfogel and his power became my mother's primary target. The daily "Oh, Abe – sweetheart" phone calls came hot and heavy. He was impressed, promised to keep her in mind, do everything possible to grant her ardent request, adding his respect for her courage and patriotism. Jack Benny was already overseas, so were Danny Kaye, Paulette Goddard, and others. Ingrid Bergman was scheduled to spend New Year's with the troops stationed in Alaska. While waiting for her assignment, Dietrich signed to do a picture at MGM.

THE SKY WAS JUST TURNING PINK as we drove through the imposing gates of Metro-Goldwyn-Mayer. After fourteen years of envy, Dietrich had finally made it to Garbo's studio – three years after her leaving it. She smoothed her hands over her legs – it was the fifth time she had checked to make sure that the seams of her nylons were straight. She was nervous. She had much to be apprehensive about. She thought the script of *Kismet* was hackneyed and MGM an enemy lot, and her leading man, a former lover now married to a very sharp lady, might be difficult to handle.

"Sweetheart, remember how we all hated *Song of Songs* and that other stupid one I did for Korda in England? We thought those were awful, but at least they were made *before* the war! But this picture! Who will go to see Ronald Colman making cow eyes at Dietrich 'à la Baghdad'? You know him – he will be ever so British, no matter how many turbans they plunk on his head. Besides, why isn't he in England fighting? The only thing that will save this picture is, maybe, Dietrich looking unbelievably glamorous. Thank God Irene is here for the costumes and Guilleroff for the wigs."

Although Irene and she had been working on her secret foundation for years, using it for her private wardrobe as well as the costumes she wore in *The Lady Is Willing*, they now perfected its basic structure. In 1944, they still had to use thick silk. It was only after the war, when the great Italian fabric houses, like Birannccini, were able once more to manufacture their renowned materials, that my mother found the "soufflé." Aptly named, it *was* a "breath" of silk, delicate and weightless, a spider's web with the retaining strength of canvas, which she used from then on for her foundations for Las Vegas and throughout the rest of her career. The ritual of getting into her foundation never varied, always in secret, never taken lightly, always regarded as the most important duty, requiring her inner circle's absolute concentration.

First, she stepped into the garment, we fastened its thin inner belt around her waist, then she secured the triangular piece of elastic between her legs, adjusting its fit between the sides of her vulva to minimize the pain of the tension that would be necessary. Bending over until her breasts hung clear of her body, she slipped one arm into one capelet armhole, then the other. Next, she scooped up her drooping breasts and placed each one into the bias bralike structure, carefully positioning each nipple into its proper slot. Once they were placed to her satisfaction, she cupped her breasts from underneath, holding them and the foundation in place, quickly straightened up, and we zipped her in from the back. If a breast shifted, a nipple was just a hairline off, the whole procedure had to be repeated. If the specially made, incredibly delicate metal zipper snapped under the extreme tension, it was like a death in the family, although three dozen backup foundations hung, waiting, hidden under their silk covers, ever ready and willing to do their magic act of giving Dietrich the sublime body she craved all her life. Once she was in her gossamer harness, only two places could give her secret away to any probing eyes: the line that circled the base of her neck where the foundation stopped and the line of the zipper that extended from the back of her neck all the way down to the end of her spine. The neck she camouflaged with embroidery or necklaces, the other by managing to align the appliquéd zipper of the covering garment exactly with that of the foundation. Once placed, positioned, and zipped into her most treasured secret, my mother became a statue; breathing was a conscious effort, movement a calculated and limited luxury. For the film *Kismet*, she was placed amongst satin harem cushions and just froze herself into positions. Dietrich always admired soldiers who could endure long periods of "standing at attention," and so she welcomed such tests of physical discipline.

Irene's genius, the fabulous execution of Karinska, and tireless dedication to perfection resulted in some of the most flamboyant costumes Dietrich ever wore on film. Now they needed only equally inventive wigs to complete the exaggerated look. The genius of Sidney Guilleroff was up to the task. In the process of designing ornate wigs and hairpieces, he too discovered Dietrich's amazing ability and willingness to endure physical pain in order to achieve a look she felt impossible to capture otherwise. As Irene and she had pulled her body in to simulated perfection, so now she and Guilleroff pulled her face. The fact that she was tampering with a face that was already perfect did not seem to cross her mind. It was not a conscious decision. Dietrich simply did what she believed was necessary, never wasting time on the process of thought or evaluation. The instant that she had seen her face in *The Devil Is a Woman*, she had fallen madly in love with its perfection. From then on, no other image of herself ever satisfied her mind's eye completely. As von Sternberg was no longer there to create that face for her, she attempted to do it herself whenever she could and by any means at her command. Now, she and Guilleroff took minute strands of her wispy hair all along her hairline, braided them into tight little ropes, pushed straight hairpins, whose ends had been bent into miniature fishhooks, into them and twisted the little ropes of hair until the skin of her scalp could take no more. The pain was excruciating. The "instant face-lift": Now it is done often, then it was a very new process. During the lunch break, this procedure had to be repeated, as the tension of the little braids slackened, causing my mother's face to resume its normal beauty. She did a lot of crazy things in *Kismet*. She tried for any effect she thought was necessary. Perhaps it was her inner fury at shooting a preordained flop on Garbo's lot, or an impatience to

At the end of 1943,
finally having made
it to Garbo's studio,
MGM, Dietrich pre-
pares for her role
in *Kismet*.
RIGHT: Sydney
Guilleroff creating
a hair design.
BELOW: Dietrich's
idea of having her
legs painted gold is
the only thing any-
one remembers
from this Arabian
disaster!

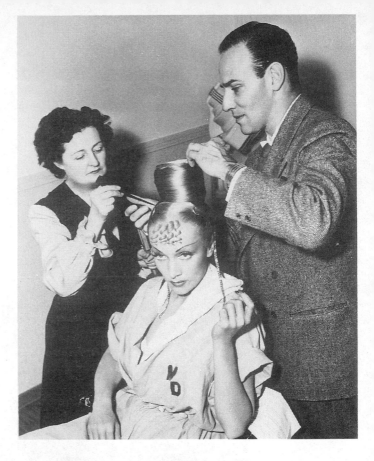

The golden legs looked great, but they weren't worth the possibility of lead poisoning.

get to war – probably a mixture of both. She kept trying to "save" the picture, at least make it into a "Dietrich" one. She and Irene designed trousers of tiny gold chains, looped like Victorian curtains that encircled her legs for the "harem dance" sequence in the film. My mother, who had never actually danced before on the screen, was very apprehensive. That day, she found herself in a hairdo that made her scalp bleed and her back teeth ache, breathing carefully for fear of cracking the zipper of her foundation, her body covered in barbarian embroidery of metallic thread that pricked her propped-up breasts like a thousand fine needles, her legs aching under twenty pounds of looped chains, expected to undulate her seductive form down the ornate staircase of the sultan's palace. I will say she tried – she looked like a desperate ostrich with a migraine trying to be a sexy snake, but she tried. The sound man finally saved her. Every time she moved her legs, the chains bounced, causing such a racket that it drowned out the musical playback. Everyone agreed that the chain idea had to go! She pretended to be upset at the loss of what everyone had thought was such a terrific idea, until we got back to the dressing room. There she opened a bottle of champagne, heaved a sigh of relief as we cut the chains off her legs, and smiled:

"Thank god, that's over! But what are we going to do now? That ridiculous dance – did you see me? 'Theda Bara à la Arabia'! Ridiculous! But now we have to think of something! They want that dance. But everything that moves makes a noise . . . so? What is exciting – that hasn't been seen before, that we can put on the legs – that doesn't move?"

Everyone had an idea that was rejected. Finally, Dietrich ordered brushes and cans of paint from the Art Department and painted her legs gold! The dressing room reeked of toxic fumes, the skin of her legs turned green under the thick coats of metal paint, her stomach heaved, she became dizzy for days, on the brink of lead poisoning, but: Dietrich's golden legs knocked the battle of Monte Cassino off the front pages! It is the only "look" remembered from that awful film.

My great treat during the preparation of this disaster was being on my friend's home lot at a time when she was working. Whenever I could, I escaped my mother's imperious eye and sneaked onto the set of *Meet Me in St. Louis*, a world of ruffled charm and sparkling talent. There is a feeling on the set of a hit picture in the making that cannot be explained. It's something in the air, like an energy field, that gives off an electrical current, that feeds, charges all talents to ever higher output. It is a rare phenomenon. It can happen within any artistic union, but when this force pervades an enormous soundstage, it is truly magical.

"Hi," said the Voice – now so famous, so instantly recognizable.

"Hi – god, you look fabulous! Can you breathe in that corset?"

"Enough," she took a breath to prove it. "But this wig is so heavy, my neck's breaking."

"It'll photograph wonderfully. And it *moves!* Just terrific. Guilleroff knows what he's doing. You should see what he and my mother have concocted for *our* picture! Real crazy! But that's how she wants it. We're doing a flop anyway."

The giggle still sounded like little pebbles rolling under water. One of her many attendants came to investigate who was monopolizing The Star.

"We are ready for you now, Miss Garland."

She got her "trooper" look. She always had that capacity to call up the discipline of her working childhood. Even when she was so sick, so finally broken, that tough vaudeville training kept her going. I wish it hadn't. It prolonged her suffering.

Halfway through our picture, MGM received security inquiries from the FBI for a Dietrich clearance as a loyal American. The Studio, happy to oblige, gave her the green light. She might be scheduled to leave before a second film could be put into production – they too had seen the rushes!

The day finally came when my mother received notice that her wish had been granted. She and a selected accompanying group were scheduled to go overseas to entertain the troops as soon as she had completed her present assignment at MGM. She took her first series of required inoculations the day before she had to shoot a love scene with our "Ronnie." Off the set they avoided each other so, it had become comical. No love was lost between them. She covered this up by telling everyone that Colman was so frightened of her, that was why he never dared to touch her, even avoided looking her way whenever possible.

"You know, he is frightened stiff of me! Probably his wife told him, before he started this picture, that if he went *near* me . . ."

She always allowed her listening audience to supply their own version of the dire punishment that Benita Hume might have threatened her husband with should he stray into Dietrich's clutches. The day my mother's upper arms were swollen, throbbing with the reaction to the tetanus-paratyphoid injections, Ronald Colman "forgot" himself, grabbed her violently in a fit of unleashed passion; she screamed, he recoiled!

Later, in the dressing room, we applied ice packs. She was laughing:

"Through this whole terrible film, he never dared to touch me! Then suddenly today, when my arms are inflamed from the shots, he gets 'dramatic'! Typically English! You can never tell with them – when suddenly they will decide to let themselves go and get passionate. Stupid man.''

I always felt our "Ronnie" knew exactly what he was doing, but kept that thought to myself.

Kismet ended as it had begun, a vacuum of nonexpectation. My mother was ready to follow her man to war. She did not go quite as far as the high-heeled shoes and silk dress from the last shot of *Morocco*, but the feeling was the same. Her orders were to report to USO headquarters in New York for rehearsals in preparation to being shipped overseas. She was triumphant.

> Papilein,
> My cholera-typhus shot is still swollen and red but does not hurt anymore. I have, I think, packed everything except the hand things I need for traveling. Please write to Jean and do not forget that mail is being opened so allude to me as "La Grande" or "Louise." Jean Gabin, French Liaison Office APO 512 c/o Postmaster New York City.

Spies were everywhere, all troop movements highly secret. Posters proclaimed, "Loose Lips Sink Ships." Fighting men never knew where they were being shipped to until after they had left U.S. shores. One even had to have FBI clearance to serve coffee at the Canteen! But Dietrich, the born German, knew she was being sent to the European theater of war and not the Pacific one. Amazing! Her letter continues:

> I am eating tonight with Gable – with the purest intentions. But the choice is difficult – because Sinatra hangs on the phone and he is small and shy. I'll send you his records, they are not for sale yet. Gable says he hasn't got lights or heat on his ranch, because of the storm, so it sounds as though it might get "difficult" – but I didn't want to cancel.
>
> I want to give this letter to the postman. It is almost ten o'clock. I hope to fly away on Tuesday but I will send you a telegram.
>
> Adieu my love,
> Mutti

All her belongings stored at a Bekins warehouse, my mother cried, put a check in my hand, and left to win the war.

I remained, teaching people who had the money to pursue their dream even if they had no talent, directed play after play, on the same level of mediocrity, drank, slept with anyone who said I was pretty or "loved" me, woke not knowing where I was or with whom, sought for ever deeper degrees of oblivion, ran, and ran – while standing still.

In a woodland shack in one of the canyons, I spent a weekend amongst the coterie of Henry Miller. One of his *Tropics* was then hot and shocking, and young girls flung themselves into his burly arms with rebel abandon. He considered such juicy offerings his due and took whatever he fancied, regardless of their, at times, very tender age. I did not sleep with him. Considering the fogged state I was usually in, quite an interesting achievement. Everyone *else* did. He liked multiple numbers and communal appreciation of his sexual prowess. Afterwards, instead of smoking a cigarette, he read from his banned book as though delivering the Sermon on the Mount.

GONE A' SOLDIERING

IN NEW YORK, my mother went into rehearsals. Her troupe consisted of an accordionist, a male vocalist, a comedienne – who would be her handmaiden and female companion, and a recently successful young comic, who would function as master of ceremonies, entertainer, and jack-of-all-trades. Lastfogel knew his business; Danny Thomas was the perfect choice for Dietrich. His humor clean, very American, he was also wise in the art of handling large, sometimes unruly, crowds. His youth and respectful attitude made him immediately acceptable to my mother. She listened to him, did what he told her, and learned invaluable lessons from a master. He taught her American comedy timing, not too far removed from her own Berlin humor, but more structured, less rapid, less sardonic. Routines were polished, an overall show constructed. Thanks to Danny's skill, the Dietrich troupe became a tight, highly effective unit.

Between rehearsals, she got her uniform. Irene and she had already made the gold sequin sheath that would become her real wartime uniform, and later, the basis for her stage costumes. Now, at Saks Fifth Avenue, she fitted her regulation one – not the army, air force, paratrooper ones that she was to be photographed in, only two months later and forever after visually associated with, but the civilian uniform of the USO, a sort of cross between World War I Red Cross and very early airline hostess. A little stodgy but quite adequate for riding in jeeps and doing one's job. Once overseas, my mother got rid of it quickly, acquired "proper" military attire, kept only her required USO arm patch, although she hated it, later even letting that somehow disappear, replacing it by the one of the 82nd Airborne, her favorite division. Everyone was so busy trying to win a war, no one had time to stop and reprimand a glamorous movie star for disregarding her civilian organization's dress code. Besides, Dietrich looked so very right in military garb that soon the Eisenhower jackets, complete with service ribbons and hash marks, tailored trousers, combat boots, and GI Joe helmet became her accepted, rightful costume of the day.

It was the best part she was ever given, the role she loved the most, the one that was to bring her the greatest success. She collected laurels for her heroic bravery, medals, citations, devotion, and respect. Worked her way through the enlisted ranks up to five-star generals, had a glorious time being a true "hero," and then got decorated for it. In her own words, "I never felt so happy as in the army." The Prussian was in her element; her German soul embraced the tragedy of war with all of its macabre sentimentality and – she had it both ways.

To hear Dietrich describe her tour of duty, one would believe that she was actually *in* the army, overseas for at least the full four years under constant fire, in imminent danger of death, or worse, capture by vengeful Nazis. Anyone listening to her became convinced of this, for she had convinced herself that this was so. Actually, on and off, she worked from April 1944 to July 1945, in between returning to New York City, Hollywood, and, later on, remaining either in Paris or at the headquarters of her favorite general in Berlin. Dietrich's laudable civilian contribution to the war effort is not to be downgraded by this, only put into its proper perspective. She was fearless, heroic, and dedicated. But so were many civilian women and many entertainers who were not given the Legion of Honor in three escalated grades or the Medal of Freedom. It is just that Dietrich was so much better at playing the valiant soldier and had the fame and beauty to be noticed doing so.

She spoke of her days "in the army" with reverence. Wrote her version of that time repeatedly. As with anything concerning her life, truth and fiction interlaced, in the end becoming accepted history even for those who had been there and should have known better. Legend and logic don't mix too well.

On the 14th of April, 1944, her USO troupe left in a hailstorm from La Guardia Airport, their destination "officially" unknown until after they were airborne, when they were told they were on their way to the African theater of war, and not the Pacific theater, as everyone had believed. Except my mother, of course. Her goal was Gabin, not Hirohito.

They stopped to refuel in Greenland and again in the Azores, finally landing in Casablanca, then went on to Algiers. Considering this was before jets and taking into account the different time zones, they could not have arrived there until at least the 17th of April. All this, while some biographers and, on occasion, Dietrich herself, have her searching through mounds of corpses, looking for her sister's at the concentration camp of Bergen-Belsen. As Belsen was liberated by the British on April 15th one year later, this does not seem likely, somehow.

The Dietrich troupe did their first show in Algiers. Danny Thomas opened the show, won the boys over with his special humor, then the comedienne did her act, she was followed by the male vocalist – then it was time for the main attraction. Danny announced:

"Fellahs! I've got bad news! We were expecting Marlene Dietrich – but she went out for dinner with a general and she hasn't shown up . . ."

This planned "tease" got the anticipated groans, the boos. Suddenly, from the back of the theater, the unmistakable voice called:

"No! No! I'm here! . . . I'm here!" in uniform, carrying a small suitcase, she appeared, running down the aisle toward the stage. By the time she reached the microphone, she had pulled off her tie, was beginning to unbutton her khaki shirt.

"I'm not with any general – I'm here! I've just got to change into . . ." She was down to the last button and the GIs howled. She "suddenly" remembered that she was not alone.

"Ooh! Sorry, boys, I'll just be a second," and disappeared into the wings.

Danny called after her: "That'll be a tough act for you to follow, Miss Dietrich. Let's save that for the end. I think they'll wait!"

That got the desired foot stomping and whistles. In a flash, Dietrich reappeared in her sequined sheath and *wow*! It really was Marlene, the screen goddess, who could be enjoying the luxuries of Hollywood but had come all the way to North Africa to entertain them, and the boys were on their feet cheering! She sang her famous songs. They loved her. She chose a boy from the audience to be the subject of Orson's mind-reading act. The boy stood there, gazing at her in the shimmering dress, she looked at him, then out at her audience:

"When a GI looks at me, it's not hard to read his mind!"

That was a sure laugh-getter. At the close of her act, she hiked up her dress, sat on a chair, put her musical saw between her legs, and played it! Pandemonium!

As was the custom between shows, she toured hospital wards, singing or just visiting. Raising morale was the primary goal of the USO entertainers. She loved to tell how the doctors would take her to dying German prisoners, would ask her to speak to them in German. How these suffering boys would look up at her and ask in their whispers, "Are you really, the real Marlene Dietrich?" How, "like to children," she would croon "Lili Marlene" in German, comfort them as much as she could, they had so "little time." My mother wrote scenes for herself that were worth believing.

There was a rumor that the front had been reinforced by an armored division of the Free French. She commandeered a Jeep and a driver from the motor pool, went searching for a tank division, and, before dark, found it. Tanks, spread out under trees, their hatches open, their crews resting on top.

"I ran from tank to tank – crying his name. Suddenly, I saw that wonderful salt-and-pepper hair! He had his back to me – 'Jean, Jean, *mon amour!*' He spun around, exclaimed, '*Merde!*,' jumped to the ground and took me in his arms."

They stood in their passionate embrace, oblivious to all those longing eyes, envying the gray-haired man holding a dream. The kiss went on – they doffed their corps berets, and cheered their approval, tinged with jealousy.

The sound of tanks starting up their engines finally broke them apart. He kissed her once more – "We go, *Ma grande, Ma grande, Ma vie* . . ." Held her to him for one timeless moment, then let go and leaped back onto his tank and down into its belly. Tanks began moving into formation. She stood in the clouds of dust they churned up, shielding her eyes, trying to catch one last glimpse of him, afraid she might never see him again.

I drifted – ketchup and hot water made a great soup and left money for the more important nourishment of bourbon. I remember a limbo time in San Francisco. How did I get there and why? I spent my time in bars and transvestite nightclubs. Earned booze money doing odd jobs. A trained-by-Dietrich dresser can function very nicely as handmaiden to a female impersonator of Sophie Tucker. His name was Walter, his fame quite legitimate and deserved. He kept his many sumptuous evening gowns, like museum pieces, in ventilated cedar-lined closets, his huge collection of accessories in catalogued archival boxes, let me bunk down in his boudoir, fed me, worried about me, protected me by his patronage, and very probably kept me from really being hurt. Why I have always remembered him – that bald, Rubenesque, outrageously flamboyant drag queen – who took the time to – care.

After playing North Africa, Dietrich's troupe was flown to Italy and assigned to travel with a Texas division. She sent snapshots: she in khaki, sleeves rolled up, washing in her upturned helmet; on the back was written: "To the sweetheart of the American Army. A swell G.I., Hqrts. 34th Inf. Div. Italy, 1944." She was laughing, the soldier's daughter had found "home." Other pictures followed: Holding her mess kit, she stood in chow lines, and whenever she was asked, "Can I have a picture taken with you, Marlene?" she put her arm around the boy's shoulder and smiled for his folks back home. Anything they wanted was theirs. If a boy was about to go into battle and she could make him happy one last time, why not? Dietrich considered the morale of all fighting men her sacred responsibility. To send a brave man into battle, his spirit renewed from having spent his last hours in the arms of a beautiful woman, had always been one of my mother's most romantic fantasies. Now she had the whole Fifth Army to inspire. There was one "tall drink of water" from Iowa who called her "Chicken" and was loved; another gangly kid from Missouri named her "Lammie Pie"; to a brash kid from Chicago, she was "Toots"; to another, "Princess," but whatever they called her, she was their dream come true amidst the hell of killing.

She had crabs often – looked upon them as part of being a real soldier and insisted one did not, absolutely *not*, get those from intimate physical contact. Years later, a member of one of my mother's troupes told me that it was their job to stand guard outside her billet, be it tent, bombed-out hotel, or Quonset hut, making sure the "traffic" ran smoothly. She wrote to her Brentwood neighbor and pal, Evie Wynne, secretly letting her know where she was by saying "Frankie's country is wonderful."

Still in Italy, my mother came down with pneumonia and was hospitalized in Bari. She always maintained that it was there her life was saved by the new miracle drug penicillin, and its discoverer, Alexander Fleming, became one of her medical heroes.

For me, life lost its color. Became a sameness. Meaningless hours – to meaningless days that ended in empty weeks that became meaningless hours on their way to infinity.

On the 6th of June, 1944, Dietrich announced the news of the Normandy invasion to an audience of nearly four thousand GIs. Soon after, her troupe was sent Stateside and disbanded. She came home dissatisfied. Being a restricted USO entertainer did not fulfill her need to go a' soldiering. A month later, on the 25th of August, my mother was still in New York when Paris was liberated. It galled her that she was not there to march at the head of the "victorious troops." Years later, she had her revenge when she did march in the anniversary parade commemorating this glorious day, was photographed and her war fame

ABOVE: She who had always feared flying now flew. Wartime made everything acceptable.
BELOW: Wherever she went, she played her musical saw and GIs cheered.

LEFT: No mere war could stop
Dietrich. She found Gabin in
Algiers just as she had planned.
BELOW: Strutting a routine with
Danny Thomas somewhere in
Italy, 1944.

ABOVE, LEFT: My mother in her element, feeding someone.

ABOVE, RIGHT: One of her favorites from her huge collection of wartime snapshots.

BELOW, LEFT: Anything and everything could become a stage when moving with the troops.

BELOW, RIGHT: She sent me this. On the back was written: "My tent is cosy."

Dietrich always looked so right in military garb.

was such that whenever this picture was printed, it was assumed it had been taken on the actual day of the Paris liberation in 1944. Somehow, no one noticed that in the photograph she is wearing her medals – only received after the war.

I began hoarding sleeping pills. Never ever waking had become nearly a necessity. Jumping from a high place – that scared me, so did the thought of pulling a trigger. Strange, how one can still be frightened when killing oneself.

In September, with a new troupe that again included her Texas handmaiden com-pal, Dietrich was on her way to France. Whatever official travel orders or carefully worked out and correlated military itineraries by the USO and the Special Services Division now vanished. Through her connections, she managed to be brought to the personal attention of one of her heroes, the flamboyant, pistol-packing Patton. It was one of Dietrich's most treasured stories, one she would haul out at the drop of a military hat:

"Oh! He was so wonderful! A real soldier! Tall, strong! Powerful! A leader! He looked at me and asked if I really had the courage to face the danger of going to the front: 'Could I take it? Was I brave enough?' Of course, I told him I was ready to do anything he wanted for his boys – only I was a little afraid of what the Nazis would do if they captured me. When I told him that, you know what he said to me? 'They wouldn't waste you. If you're captured, it is more likely that you would be utilized for propaganda, forced to make radio broadcasts like you did for us.' Then he took a small gun from the pocket of his windbreaker and said: 'Here. Shoot some of the bastards before you surrender.' Oh, he was wonderful!"

Dietrich now had the war she wanted. They were billeted in France in a town she referred to in her letters as "Sinatra's wife." From their *Nancy* headquarters, they drove to different installations near the front, did their shows with orders to return before nightfall.

From this point my mother's often-told "War Stories" take on the texture of film. The poignant drama of scenes augmented by her consummate skill as scenarist, director, and cameraman:

"That day, we did our show in an old barn – it was cold, bitter cold and dark – the noise of war was very close. In my gold sequin dress, they could see me with their flashlights – " and as she conjures up this moment, one is there – her memory's captive. . . .

Like a beacon, she stands. The sequins of her golden dress reflecting beams of flashlights trained on her body. The sounds of war mingle with the strains of a single guitar like an accompanying beat of hell.

Softly, she sings. The makeshift microphone cupped between caressing hands, she is to those war-weary men the half-forgotten dream of all women longed for. A shell bursts too near – old timbers groan – wood dust cascades, catching the faint light. The repetitive click of Zippos sounds like crickets who have lost their way from sun-filled places. She sings of "Boys in the Back Room" and young faces grin. "I Can't Give You Anything But Love" – Home may be Mom and Apple Pie – but here – now – is raw desire. "Move out!" A barked command, its heightened pitch betrays an edge of fear. Curses, as men return to their reality – prepare to leave her golden aura.

"See you, Marlene!" "You take real good care of yourself now, you hear?" "Hey, Babe – Adios!" "Bye, Sugar!" as they shuffle out to give death or receive it.

My mother's voice drops to a hollow sigh:

"I stood there, cold and forlorn – and watched them go. . . . Sometimes . . ." Her voice lifts in anticipation of a lighter memory. "We played far behind the lines – then the hills were full of men – wherever you looked, just a sea of young faces . . . hundreds . . . of them. I, on a little stage far below and their whistles floated down to me – like adolescent kisses and the war seemed far away."

And so it went, day in, day out – one scene better than the other.

Dietrich stayed attached to Patton's Third Army. He hinted that he had no intention of stopping for the Russians – that his job was to beat Germans, not play Roosevelt-Stalin politics. Of course, she loved this brash soldier, his bravado, his military arrogance, and supported anything he felt it his duty to do. He, in turn, basked in her utter devotion and kept her close to him as long as possible, until orders separated them in December of '44.

Dietrich says she was in the Ardennes, at Bastogne, when the Germans surrounded the American forces to which she was attached, among them the 101st Airborne Division with its commanding general, Anthony McAuliffe. She knew they were surrounded. Everyone did. She expected to be captured. She wondered what would happen to her. She waited. What she had done with her civilian troupe is a Dietrich legend no-no! She does not say, nor ever knew, that General Sepp Dietrich, probably a cousin, was one of the commanders of the Panzer armies surrounding her. Neither did she know that when General Luttwitz asked for the Americans to surrender, he got back the now-famous reply of McAuliffe's – "Nuts!" – an expression impossible to translate into German. As a matter of fact, it took the translators and interpreters two hours before they delivered McAuliffe's meaning to the Nazi general, who didn't really understand its implication even then. But the American troops had, and its effect on their morale was cataclysmic – it gave them renewed courage in the face of what they had only a short time before believed was a certain defeat.

My personal favorite Dietrich war story now takes center stage:

In the midst of what was to be known in the history books as the Battle of the Bulge, one concerned American general is supposed to have had the time to request, of another general, that Marlene Dietrich, being in danger, needed to be evacuated immediately. At once, a major jump was mounted. A whole planeload of the 82nd Airborne Division fell from the skies, so that their general could rescue one heroic movie star! It seems unlikely that a division of paratroopers would be ordered, in the midst of one of the fiercest battles of World War II, to risk their lives making such a jump. If the wives and mothers of those boys had heard that! But the legend actually brazenly upholds that the mass jump occurred and that the general was the first to find his quest. My mother loved to tell of how she sat on the ground, coughing, waiting in the snow-hushed stillness, when a mighty hum from above became the sound of an airplane, and looking up, she saw an American Flying Fortress, from whose hatch parachutes opened against the bleak gray sky, that the first paratrooper to land was the 82nd Airborne Division commander, General James M. Gavin himself, and the first thing he did – was find her. Isn't that lovely? "Jumping Jim Gavin" became my mother's favorite hero general, after Patton. Tall, handsome, young, and brave, he gained the devotion and respect of his heroic paratroopers by asking as much of himself as he did of his men.

Dietrich says that Gavin brought her safely back to Paris in his Jeep – not on a white horse – then left her. How this was done under USO regulations was never checked too carefully, but it's *so* romantic, who cares? She was billeted at the Ritz, which had been commandeered for the use of American officers, VIPs, and dashing war correspondents. I never did find out what happened to the accordionist, Texas comedienne, and comic – but I'm sure they were safe too.

I WAS A TWENTY-YEAR-OLD DRUNK living with a man who balanced on the hairline edge of true insanity. To prove that he was perfectly sane, he memorized the complete works of Freud and Jung, devoured the writings of any who deciphered the secrets of the human mind. His own schizophrenic brilliance was such that, when undergoing psychiatric examinations, he could answer whatever questions were asked him correctly within the accepted guidelines of normalcy and passed every test with flying colors. Some doctors sensed the virulent madness, but could not prove it by the rules laid down. Others were not skilled enough to even know they were being duped. One day, this "madman" handed me a book and ordered me to read it. Its title, *The Neurotic Personality of Our Time*, written for the first time in laymen's terms by a very (then) modern psychoanalyst, Karen Horney, and there I was – on every page! It was me – the Me of Me! She knew me. A startling revelation to find one's innermost wounds exposed, explained, known by a total stranger and without censure. That's the greatest discovery, that's what opens the door to salvation – that sudden realization that you are *not* alone. If your desperation can be written about, there must be others like you. Being one of many makes you feel so much less dislikable. One's self-hate becomes tempered by this sudden loss of uniqueness. I carried that book within me and its teachings saved me. Quite literally, saved me. Without it, I would have eliminated myself eventually – I am certain of it – and missed all the loving that was just waiting for me down the road. It took a long time before I could walk that road, but now I had a surface to balance on.

My mother continued fighting the war with songs, sequins, sex, and sympathy. Suddenly, she was ordered back to "Forward 10," the code name of the commanding general, Omar Bradley. She says she arrived at his trailer in the Heortgene Forest. He looked pale and tired.

"Tomorrow, we are going to enter Germany," she says he told her. "The outfit you are attached to is going in first. I've discussed this with General Eisenhower and we both agree that it is better for you to stay back. Playing hospitals and such."

She wanted to march with her soldiers into Berlin. She pleaded, but Bradley was adamant.

"We're afraid of you going into Germany. If the Germans were to get their hands on you, all hell might break loose. We could not stand the criticism if anything happened to you."

She wrote my father of this meeting:

He seemed distant, thoroughly uninterested in how much I cared to go in with the first troops. I must tell you one very important thing, all Generals are lonely. G.I.s go into the bushes with the local girls, but Generals can't do such things. They have guards around the clock, with machine guns strapped to their sides; they are surrounded wherever they go. They can never, never have a "kiss and tumble" in the hay or out of the hay. They are all desperately alone ever since the war began.

Dietrich never liked Eisenhower, like with John Wayne, always had stinging stories about him. I often wondered why. After the war, when Eisenhower's private wartime romance was exposed, then I knew. But General Bradley had no "lady driver" to stand between him and Dietrich, and so, lo-and-behold, she entered Germany, schlepping her troupe willy-nilly along with her on the way to Berlin. In Aachen, they took over the movie theater for a performance. With no fuel for heat, the building was like ice. The German caretaker brought his thermos, poured a cup of his precious coffee for Dietrich. The members of her troupe warned her not to drink it, it might be poisoned.

"No," she said, "they wouldn't do that to me," and she drank, thanking the man in German, asking him why he had wanted to share something so precious as coffee when, "You know I am on the other side."

"Yes, yes, but *The Blue Angel* – ah! I can forget what you are, but *The Blue Angel?* Never!"

There were no threats on her life, few insults. As they moved through the bombed towns, the German population paid her homage and genuine affection, so she maintained. Being such a good scriptwriter, all her scenes involving her one-time countrymen play well. Full of human pathos, adoration for her and respect, with none of the hatred that one would expect, considering all the ingredients of this human tragedy.

On the 19th of February, 1945, my mother was again in Paris. Why she was suddenly there and how she got there three whole months *before* the end of hostilities is another one of those "legendary no-nos." She sent my father the menu opposite.

It is headed by her observations: "You can imagine how the poor eat if *this* is what you get in a deluxe restaurant!" and "To have dinner you walk half an hour only to find this! My stomach is bad from the phenol in Army food and I have to eat 'fresh food.' This is it! 200 for the wine which is about the only good food you can find. Around 680 – together, which is $13.50. So, if you read that Paris is gay and there are terrific Black Market restaurants, don't believe it." The "luxury tax" gets a dig *[handwritten top]* I if this is what you get in' a' de luxe Resta...

[handwritten left of circle] Received 2/13/45

MENU

Café National; 5.-
Café Conn: 25.-

19 FÉVRIER 1945

HOTEL CLARIDGE – PARIS
GRILL-ROOM, RESTAURANT

Foie Gras à la Gelée
(70 Gr.)   200.-

Couvert: 10.-
Pain: 100 Gr.

DINER

Crème Solférino   10.-

Pommes Macaire (*mashed Potatoes*)   20.-

Soissons Bretonne (*beans*)   x.-

Choux Fleurs   Sauce Crème   20.-

-:-

Fromage   20.-

-:-

Pâtisserie   20.-

-:-

Taxe de Luxe: 38%
Service: 12%

[handwritten left block] To have dinner you walk half an hour only to find this!!! My stomac is bad from the phenol in this food and I have to eat "fresh food"! This is it! 200.- for the wine which is about the only good food you can find. Around 680- together which is $13.50. So, if you say that Paris is terrific Black Market Restaurants don't believe it.

[handwritten right margin, vertical] Jean has taken out on the banks all da same old...

too: "What luxury?" The margin is my favorite: "Jean has been out on the tanks all day, came all the way here to see me again and washes and eats his rations and hates it."

NEARLY FULL-TIME SOBER, I traveled to New York – hoping to find a job in the theater. Little money forced me to stay in my father's apartment. Between auditions, I took care of Tami. Her condition had deteriorated alarmingly. Shuttled from one psychiatrist to another by my "long-suffering" father, ordered and paid for by my equally "long-suffering" mother, she had been diagnosed as schizophrenic by some, a manic-depressive by others, a paranoid, an obsessive-compulsive, a hysteric, given other equally extreme labels for want of one correct diagnosis.

While she suffered her torments, my father, who had always believed that all she needed to come to her senses was stringently applied discipline, behaved according to his beliefs, thereby reducing this already damaged soul further, until she was a trapped animal that quivered in abject fear whenever he was near. My mother, who believed that psychiatry was only for the weak and unintelligent of this world, shook her head in disapproval of "Tami's stupid lack of self-control," paid the doctors' bills, and told everybody about her burden, "having to take care of Tami and her 'illness,' for poor Papi!"

I tried out at a big audition for a showcase part any young actress would kill for – and got it! I was now an employed actress and getting sober to boot. Life might be worth trying after all!

Foolish Notion, a Theatre Guild production starring Tallulah Bankhead, went on the usual weeks of tryouts on the road before opening on Broadway. It was exciting, and not only on stage. Our star, usually blind drunk and completely naked, liked chasing me down hotel corridors. Poor Tallulah, she hadn't managed to get "into Dietrich's pants" at Paramount, now figured she'd get into the daughter's in Columbus, Ohio, and points west. Trying to hold onto a job can get dicey under such circumstances, particularly if you don't let the star catch you. I did my job, kept my mouth shut, learned a great deal from good people, useful lessons from those skilled in self-projection, also understudied our star and disappointed her greatly with my agility for flight.

We finally arrived back in New York prior to the Broadway opening. After I put Tami to bed, I went to Forty-fifth Street and stood in front of the Martin Beck Theater. The theater was still dark, the lettering on the marquee still unfinished, but the giant blowups of Bankhead and her costar Donald Cook were framed and positioned on the columns outside the theater – and there, next to theirs, eight feet tall, was one of me, as though I, too, were a star. Neither my part nor my talent warranted such important exposure. It seemed that the fascination for the "daughter of" was just as intriguing to Broadway audiences in 1945 as it had been to movie fans in 1931. Seeing that huge poster, I had the disturbing thought that the first audition I had been so proud of getting might not have been on my ability as an actress after all! Changing my name to escape identification had achieved nothing. We opened. The reviewers referred kindly to "Maria Manton daughter of Marlene Dietrich" as showing "promise."

In April, President Roosevelt died at the beginning of his fourth term in office. In New York, we stood silent and shaken as Tallulah announced his death to the audience before our performance. To me, Roosevelt had been *the* President – the only one I had ever known, like a protective father, always there, and I mourned him as such. It felt so strange without him.

Hitler supposedly committed suicide in his bunker the end of that April, but no one really believed it until a week later, when we all went crazy celebrating VE Day. I couldn't help wishing Roosevelt had lived just a little longer to witness the end of the European war. Now the men, who had fought and survived one terrible conflict, waited to be shipped, not back home but to the other half of the war, still raging in the Pacific. When the play closed, I applied to the USO for a part in one of the many plays they were now sending overseas to entertain the occupation forces and those waiting to be shipped out. My mother wrote that she was back in Paris, I never did find out where her poor troupe was, nor did she elaborate – she was busy asking everyone who had travel orders to enter Berlin to deliver packages of food to her mother. Almost invariably the officers doing the errand of mercy were able to acquire extra items to augment her packages, their attitude being, "It's the least we can do for our gallant Marlene." Aware her accompanying, hand-carried letters would be read by censors, she wrote in English, using American wording:

28 June 1945

I hope the package reaches you all right.
I am doing all I can to come to see you or to have you come out if you want to.
I am worried about you and I am sending messages by everyone who goes there.
　Please keep well until I can come. I am in Paris now. Maria and Rudi are in New York, but Maria will come here soon to play for the troops and might also come to see you later.

I pray that I can see you soon. In the meantime I will send all my friends to see you, who go there where you are.

All my love.

God Bless you always.

Your daughter,

Marlene

On the 13th of July, 1945, Dietrich and her trusty and trusting troupe were shipped back Stateside. Her famous script starts with their lonely return on a rainy night when no one met them at La Guardia because "security" had not permitted their arrival to be announced. Hand weapons given her as souvenirs by adoring GIs as well as generals, she *says*, were confiscated by Customs. Outside the terminal, a surly taxi driver wouldn't open the door to his cab for them. It seems he was not impressed by their uniforms – he was too used to returning GIs who did not have American currency to pay for their ride. No one in the troupe had anything but French francs. Accustomed to army life, they had forgotten that civilians have to pay for transportation.

She asked the driver if he recognized her, and he did. She promised that if he took them to the St. Regis Hotel, he would get the biggest tip of his life. At the hotel, she cashed a blank check for a hundred dollars, paid the taxi lavishly, and split the rest of the money with the troupe so that they could get home. She said they stood in the lobby of the hotel with her, none of them wanting to make the transition back into this once familiar, "now so strange civilian society." My mother had them all go upstairs to her suite, where they took baths, ate, and talked. Apparently, no loved ones awaited them. Her story continues:

"I called Feldman in Hollywood, and you know what he said? 'Don't write any more checks – they'll bounce.' 'You must be crazy,' I said. 'No!' I was in the war too long not making pictures! So I was broke. So I said: 'Get me a picture!' That wasn't going to be so easy either, he said, because I had been off the screen for all those years."

This established once and for all her great sacrifice for the war and supported the "second" selling of the emeralds. After that, she called my father, said that she was going to move in with us in the morning, it was cheaper, that she had called Remarque and we were all going to the Stork Club to celebrate "a soldier's return."

In the heat of a New York July, my USO play, *The Front Page*, rehearsed in the dingy rooms of a dance studio on Forty-sixth Street. When everything was ready, we received our stage costumes, papers, uniform purchase orders, and inoculations. As I was playing the whore, my costume was easy – I just copied my one-time governess and looked very authentic. I got my heavy uniform, brogues, ties, shirts, waterproof overcoat, lined gloves, olive-drab wool hat, and wondered where in the hell we were being shipped to in August in long johns.

My mother had a confidential talk with me – to prepare me for war.

"Oh, those wonderful boys – they want to give you everything, Lugers, Mausers, Nazi daggers – you won't have enough room in your valpack to carry them all." She inspected my ready-and-waiting musette bag. "Soap, tooth things, shower cap, shampoo, makeup, towel . . . where is your douche bag?"

"I . . ."

"And your diaphragms?"

"I don't have one – I really don't think . . . I . . ."

She grabbed me, pushed me into the elevator, into a cab, into the gynecologist's office. An hour later, I was the owner of half a dozen little compacts containing what my mother called "the greatest invention since Pan-Cake makeup," adding, "How did you imagine you could go overseas to entertain soldiers without one? You never know . . . said the widow . . ."

She left for Hollywood before I was shipped out, wept, said we would meet again, didn't know where, didn't know when . . . but we would meet again. Sounded very familiar, like a lyric.

My company reported to Camp Patrick Henry in Maryland. We stayed at that big training camp for a while, waiting for our troop ship. I got very nervous around there. A lot of clenched-jawed men, with very blond hair and big POWs written across their backs, kept tidying up the manicured parade grounds. I had nightmares of one of them turning around one day and, on seeing me, yell: "Ach! If it isn't little Heidede, our Marlene's little girl!"

Our Victory Ship entered the Bay of Naples, trucks deposited *The Front Page* company in our billets in Caserta, where we were issued regulation summer uniforms in tall stacks, like jumbo loaves of sandwich bread, and I wondered how my mother, at the height of the war, had managed to have hers so beautifully tailored and all for the correct climate. Allen Jones and his operetta troupe were in Caserta on their way home. We exchanged news, got our PX cards, were lectured on the evils and precautions of VD, accompanied by colored slide shows and prophylactic demonstrations – and we were ready to move out.

For the next six months, we made our way through Italy, up and into Germany.

On the 6th of August, America unleashed the nuclear age and, in a flash, reduced eighty thousand living beings to powdered bonemeal. And those were the lucky ones. On the 8th, Russia declared war on Japan and invaded Manchuria. On the 9th, to make sure it would work a second time, we added another thirty-five thousand to the dust pile, in Nagasaki. America no longer needed the Russians to help conquer Japan, and the war was over.

In a quiet Italian town, we interrupted the performance, and I was given the honor of telling the boys the great news: Instead of being shipped out to the Pacific, they were now going – *home!* Their joy exploded, and those little milky balloons filled the summer air. This was not new, this had happened often. Whenever I made my first entrance in black-net stockings, four-inch ankle-strap shoes, and clinging dress, they usually floated in to greet me, a sign of yearning, intended vulgarity, anger, protest toward stupid actors who could come, make with the brave patriotic gesture, then be flown home, while they, having miraculously survived one war, sat waiting to be shipped out to fight the other half of it, this time surely to die. But this time was quite different. On this lovely summer evening, those little balloons looked like soft white blossoms swaying in the warm Italian air, were signs of gaiety, a naughty prank from men who suddenly knew they had the time to be the children they thought had been lost forever. Condoms afloat can be very pretty.

The Second World War was officially over. America had lost 300,000 of her youth, 600,000 wounded. This was a low count, for she was the only country whose civilian population did not need to be counted amongst the casualties. France lost a quarter of a million men, 30,000 of her civilians had been shot by firing squads. Britain counted her dead at 250,000, her wounded and missing at half a million, her civilian casualties at over hundreds of thousands. Russia lost 7 million men, another 14 million were wounded, her civilian deaths – a staggering 14 million. Germany counted three and a quarter million dead, 7 million wounded, and 3 million of her civilians killed. Japan lost $1^1/_2$ million, a million of her civilians dead, another 500,000 wounded.

Behind the lines, the Master Race had starved, frozen, mass murdered, gassed, incinerated, mutilated, exterminated 6 million human beings for being Jews. Seventy thousand "race-defilers," the sick, retarded, crippled, homosexuals, and gypsies, were also eliminated in these ways, for contaminating the purity of the Aryan bloodstream. For this, German generations to come would carry the mark of Cain, and should. But, in all probability, will not. As with all such man-made hells, they will be forgiven for creating it for some convenient reasons, then forgotten. Remembered only in books and through the pain of its survivors, who too will fade in time and their wails of outrage with them.

Gabin, now back in Paris, begged my mother to come, make a film with him, maybe even marry him? She answered by cable that she would do both. He cabled his delirious joy. She began working on getting the necessary postwar permission to get back to Europe. The USO needed entertainers to relieve the boredom of the thousands of men in the Army of Occupation, and Dietrich's request was welcomed with open arms. She also asked to be sent to Berlin. She had two reasons for wanting to go: her mother, and her handsome general now stationed there.

August 13, 1945

Angel –

You are completely crazy – and you drive me insane with your doubts. In *my* last letter, I spoke of *my* divorce of course. I think, after the film, will be the best time to do it. Rudi will try for a job in Paris. He naturally is completely in accord with the divorce – it is more the idea of it that shocks him – I have to admit me too. Just the idea of it, nothing more. We are both really such bourgeois, we have decided, if it is possible, not to be present but make the lawyers do it all. Please find out what are the most dignified reasons for getting a divorce in France.

The Claridge is fine if you move my things from the Ritz, because when I get there I must have warm clothes right away as I must go to my mother first. I hope you understand this – after that, I am all yours. If you are sweet to me, I will stay with you for the rest of my life – married or not married however you want it. But, if you want a child, then it is better if we marry.

I hope you got some of the things I sent from O'Hara. There are not too many planes now and one is not allowed to send things like clothes to France. Unbelievable but true. It is allowed to Holland though. I am bringing enough clothes for a regiment and boots for the winter. André, instead of bringing your make-up, mailed it direct. That was before I knew that one is allowed to send only food to France. So I told him to bring a new set here, so I can bring it. Jack Pierce from Universal brought me all the make-up I will need also I am bringing the oil for us to take off our make-up. Also I bring soap and for laundry, pens, razor blades and olive oil. I have been packing all day and if all these cost duty, I don't care. They are necessary for the film. Do you still love me, my angel? What is with your apartment? If you don't get it, maybe I don't need to bring all the sheets and linen. I am worried about my Visa – It said "Not for Work" on the form. If all goes well I leave on the 10th of September by *plane*. I'll cable before.

I kiss you as always my angel – I love you.

Your Grande

The news of her planned return to Europe preceded her. She received a cable that interested her very much indeed – from the man who was soon to be the supreme commander of Berlin's American Zone:

HAD A VERY PLEASANT VISIT WITH YOUR MOTHER. SHE IS FINE. THE 82ND IS
LOOKING FORWARD TO SEEING YOU SOON.

GENERAL GAVIN

By September, she was back in Paris, the romantic vision of marriage
and babies already dimmed. She wrote my father, who had been put in
charge of shipping Gabin's belongings, stored in Hollywood during the
war, to him in Paris.

Hotel Claridge
Avenue des Champs-Elysées
Paris

Sunday, Sept 16, 1945

Papi sweetheart,
I miss you terribly! Takes me so long to get used to the ways of Jean.
Why his nerves are in such a state I can't explain. The town is full of French
soldiers walking on crutches without legs – he came out of the war all in
one piece and is not happy about anything. I make all the effort I can but it
wears me out because I cannot pull him out of his depth. Finally, yesterday
he received his car. A Citroën 2-seat coupe, used, $4,000. I was told that
he sat in his room all day – only went out after dark – because he had a
car and is ashamed. He has the Presidential Citation and does not wear
it. I ask you if that's not definitely a complex! He hides out like Garbo.
Those two should have been married!
We have had a fight every night. About what, you ask? For instance: He
took one bedroom with salon for both of us. I said that it would be better
to have two adjoining bedrooms so we have two little girls' rooms, because
that is one thing that is uncomfortable and I tried to explain to him that
sometimes one wants "Privacy!" Whereupon he got up and dressed and
left. He took his shaving things and went back to his apartment to shave,
saying he did not want to disturb me. Instead of phoning downstairs and
taking two rooms with bathrooms. How can I live during the winter with
one bathroom making a film? Where one has to wait for the other in the
morning!! Is that insane? Last night we had another scene because a couple
we passed in the restaurant said "Bravo." He flew into a rage. I said that
wasn't so bad, as we had been the only couple on the dance floor, that it
was meant nicely and could happen anywhere. That ended the evening in
ice cold silence.
The enclosed letter came just now, Sunday evening. So you see, it is
always the same.

It was a sweet note of apology from Gabin, asking her to forgive his
behavior. He admitted being "unbearable," and he understood that she
must be very bored with him. He felt miserable because it was his fault that

she was in Paris and unhappy. He told her not to worry about anything except her mother and to forgive him.

She continued her letter to my father:

Monday morning
    His trunks arrived. Thank God!
    I am still waiting to go to Berlin. Promises, promises! It is impossible to telegraph Private Messages to Berlin from here! Easier from New York. Here the red tape is unbelievable.
    Please go to Bloomingdale's and pay for the next four months, each month one package to the same addresses: Coffee, olive oil (if possible), chocolate, good honey, rice, canned meat (if possible). Tell the saleslady to change the contents from month to month depending on what she gets in. The things needed are fats, meat, chocolate, rice, coffee, sardines. As it takes two months for the packages to arrive, tell them to send one every two weeks, so that they have the food during winter.
    Please send me books. I am starving for mental food. I will write more soon.

All my love
Mutti

As we had been overseas for several months, our company was given a few days off and I was able to get travel orders to France; and on a clear autumn day, I saw Paris again. Without the intense emotion of the last time with Remarque, or the effervescent elegance of when I had known it as a child – now a little shabby, a little worn, perhaps even a little self-conscious at being so very well preserved after such a devastating war.

I climbed the stairs to my mother's hotel room. She was waiting for me. She looked strained, a soldier without a "front," suddenly at loose ends. I took off my army overcoat.

"So why are you still wearing your skirt? How can you wear skirts when you have to ride around in Jeeps dodging shells?" she asked.

No use explaining that the bombings had stopped. My mother never did get used to the idea of Peace Time when there were still troops to entertain.

I had expected to see Jean and asked where he was.

"He's in the country, as usual fixing his house."

Perhaps, if I hadn't come, she could have gone to the country with him?

"No, sweetheart, I was waiting just for you!" She plugged in her hot plate to boil water for our coffee. There was a can of Nestlé's condensed milk and an open army ration of butter on the ledge outside her window.

I looked around the small room, remembering all those opulent suites we had lived in with extra bedrooms just for the trunks. Yet, somehow, this Spartan atmosphere suited her more.

"You know, Jean is still a rich man, but for some reason, he feels out of place in a place like the Lancaster, even if one could get a suite there, which is impossible. Jean likes living like the peasant he is. Now he is suddenly so guilty about everything – why?"

I wanted to answer but thought better of it. To try and explain Jean's sensitivity was hopeless, to defend him would only set her against him more – as a reaction to what she would see as my disloyalty to her.

"At least, here we have hot water on Saturday and Sunday, a real shower, and a real bed to sleep in – no rats running over your face with their ice-cold feet, like in the war. Last time I was here, I stayed at the Ritz. . . . Oh, it was wonderful, Papa was there. . . ." She stirred the coffee grounds. For a moment I thought, which Papa? Kennedy or Hemingway? Then knew it had to be the latter:

"He was there looking so beautiful in one of those war-correspondent trench coats. When he saw me, he roared, 'My Kraut!,' threw his big arms around me. He was so happy to see me . . . everyone just stared." She sounded wistful, as though wishing herself back to that day. "He has a new woman, a reporter called Mary something, who works for Luce, that awful man that that woman who wrote that awful play, *The Women* – remember, how Clifton hated it? – married. She was at the Ritz too, now a hoity-toity congresswoman. How can you write plays and then be in the government?" She got the can of milk from the window sill. "The Ritz gave me a double bed. It was wonderful, but I gave it to Papa and Mary – I was alone." Another sigh.

"One night they had a terrible fight. He was drunk, and of course, his cronies were too, and for some reason he shot her toilet! Don't ask me why. She got so angry, she screamed at him, called him terrible things, and he hit her – and, you know what she did? She hit him back! Can you believe it! And Papa was like a little boy – all upset! I sat on the bidet while he shaved and he told me he 'killed her toilet' and asked me to go and talk to her. 'Daughter, talk to Miss Mary. You know how,' he pleaded. A wonderful man like that, putty in that woman's hands. Amazing! He wants to marry her, and she has the chutzpah to tell him he has to learn to behave himself first! I told her: 'So – he shoots a toilet! So what? He is Hemingway!' But this woman insists on flushing it, and of course, the water gushes through the holes like an Italian fountain – and she stands there pointing and says, 'See?' I tell her: 'But he *loves* you! He is a *great* man! What more do you want?' That's what I mean about women – their brains are too small, they can't think straight. I went back to Papa's room and told him his 'Miss Mary' would forgive him. We drank a scotch together and just talked, about the war, what we did, what we saw, all the tragedy, the bravery . . . It was wonderful! Then he left, went upstairs to her where my bed was." Again, that wistfulness. She lit a cigarette, flicking her Zippo like a true soldier. "Did you know I saw Jean-Pierre Aumont? We met in a mine field. We had to get across because his Jeep was on the other side. You know what a 'perfect' gentleman he always *has* to be, so – he steps aside ever so politely and says, 'Marlène, you first.' Then suddenly remembers where we are and screams: 'No! No! No! Marlène – *I* go first!' and I say, 'No, No, No, Jean-Pierre, me!' By the time we got through 'No-no-ing,' we were across without stepping on a mine. But it was fun-n-n-eee!" She began slicing the butt end of a hard salami.

"I got some bread for you. Not like before the war, sour and just right, but bread anyway! The concierge had to stand in line for it. When he finally came back, he was so proud that he had been able to find some for me to give to my daughter who wanted some." She smiled. "Remember the night when Papi ordered his borscht and got so angry because they didn't have his black bread? . . . Another world! We worried about having the right bread to eat with what, and I designed evening bags so that we could carry it with us."

We drank our milky coffee, dunking our precious bread.

"Oh! I haven't shown you my lucky 'short-snorter'!" and jumped up to get it, held it out proudly for me to inspect. It was as thick as a roll of toilet paper. She unrolled it for me – all that paper money glued with Scotch tape, end to end, bearing the signatures, messages, names of boys she had known, played to, loved, sent out to fight. "See, that's Russian money. I got that when we met up with one of their units – wonderful peasant faces, angry and strong! . . . That's British, I have a lot of those. Sweet boys – always so polite . . . but the dollars the GIs gave me are the best. When I met Irving Berlin, I think it was somewhere in France, we compared our short-snorters. Of course, mine was much longer than his. He, the 'big army song writer,' didn't like that at all!"

I asked when she thought she would get permission to travel to Berlin to see her mother.

"General Gavin is doing everything! He is a *sweet* man, and then I can see him again. Naturally, Jean is jealous. He is sure I had an affair with him during the war. But I didn't – he didn't ask me. Of course, Jean doesn't believe me when I tell him I only have a fan-type crush on my general. Where are you being sent after this?"

"I have to report to Special Services in Frankfurt," I answered.

"Oh, what a terrible place *that* is! Like a giant PX! They have

everything! Because it is Eisenhower's 'supreme' headquarters! Very
hoity-toity! Even in the war, he always had all the comforts of home,
no matter where he was. Terrible man, the whole war he stayed so far
back, he never heard a shot!"

I left for Frankfurt, where I worked for the Armed Forces Radio with
a very talented GI Joe – freckle-faced grin, bouncy charm, loaded with
charisma, by the name of Mickey Rooney, then rejoined *The Front Page*
on our continued tour through Germany.

My mother, smart in her uniform, now all army, even to service ribbons,
no sign of a USO insignia anywhere, carrying the special patent-leather
case containing her musical saw, was met at Berlin's airport by an elegant
woman in a gray-tailored suit, tie, veiled hat, and silver fox – her mother.
They embraced. Her mother had serious news for her. My father's parents
had been thrown out of their house, interned in a refugee camp in the
Russian sector. They had sent a pitiable letter to her in Berlin, begging
for permission to come and stay with her. My mother immediately asked
General Gavin to issue her travel orders through restricted occupied zones
to find them. While waiting, she did her two shows a day and wrote to
my father, as always in German:

> Berlin – Chalottenburg
> Thursday, 27 Sept. '45

My Darling,
    Sometimes life is very hard – even for me. Was supposed to have travel
orders for Thuringen from the Russians early this morning – but didn't get
them. So I went home (How many "homes" have I had already? This one
is Klopstockstrasse – 15A in Zehlendorf West), and am now waiting if at 3
p.m. the orders come and can leave early tomorrow morning! Time against
human life! I should have been a nurse. They never have to explain why
they help people regardless of their nationality. Remember how I used to
say one day I'll cry my eyes out because I can't speak Russian? So now I
will stand there and try to put all my pleas into my eyes – but I'm afraid
that they have so often been prostituted by film – they will not be able to
communicate what my heart is saying. My mother answered your parents'
postcard of Aug. 23 immediately – where they told her they could come
to her – which is still allowed until the 30th. Since the 6th of August they
have been in the Refugee camp.
    Papilein, how sad this world is – our house at 54 still stands and although
it is full of shell holes, there are red geraniums on our balcony. No. 135 only
has walls left – is completely gutted – its balcony just hangs there and every
day my mother searched in the ruins, and on top of the rubble and ashes,
there lay that bronze mask of my face completely intact – for a long time

RIGHT: One of her favorite heroes, General George S. Patton, Jr. He liked her spunk. She loved his daring audacity. They got along like "jam on bread."

BELOW: General Omar Bradley was so scared of her, he usually granted anything she wanted, just to get her out of his headquarters.

ABOVE: Meeting up with General Gavin on some lonely country road. The look says it all.

BELOW: France, 1944. War or no war, whenever she appeared, crowds gathered.

ABOVE: In Berlin, in 1945, Dietrich, carrying her trusty musical saw, was met by her mother, who had survived the war.

RIGHT: Dancing with Gabin or Hemingway was delight-ful, but dancing with her very favorite general—the dashing James Gavin, commander of the 82nd Airborne Division—*that* was sublime.

BELOW: My mother cried when she saw the burnt-out shell of the church where she had been married.

In the winter of 1945, she entertained the occupation forces stationed in and around Berlin.

she sat there and cried! I take her everything to eat I can find. Since I've been here, I've only eaten bread. Look like an old soup-chicken – with a shriveled neck. All the people we knew are in Vienna. Henrich George (Big Nazi) shovels coal for the Russians! The Three-Penny Opera with Kate Kühl and Hupsi is playing. As I have two shows a day, I can't go. Femina Theatre on the Mollendorf Platz has *My Sister Eileen*. The Kaiser Wilhelm Memorial Church is bombed out, Bahnhof Zoo, Joachimthaler, Taumentzinnstrasse – all in ashes. Friedenau and here outside the city, everything still stands, nearly all. The Felsing store still stands. The Russians stole all the watches. For 5 days, they broke in and rifled the safe. Now Mutti repairs clocks and my old glass beads lie on a counter in the window. The big clock outside was stolen, too, and Mutti put up a wood one – that she painted! Claire Waldorf, who was not allowed to perform by the Nazis, is still in Reichenhall and doesn't have an apartment any more. All day long it thunders – like in the war. They are dynamiting to level the ruins – I haven't had the courage yet to go to my school in the Nürenbergerstrasse. One is already sad enough about one's lost youth when seeing old places again – without seeing this, this is just too terrible.

The Berliners love me, bring me everything from photos to their rations of herring. The language sounds familiar when I walk through the streets and the children play "Heaven and Hell" amongst the rubble. The Marmonhaus still stands and because it is in the English Sector, they are showing *Rembrandt* with Charles Laughton.

My Heart – I hope by the time you get this letter, you will already have good news from me by cable. I will stop at nothing – absolutely nothing (Don't tell Jean this!) – to get your parents out.

With all my love,
Your Mutti

Paris, October 9, 1945

Papilein,

Don't know where to start. You must have by now your parents' letter that I mailed from Berlin. When Mutti received the card from them in Martinroda, I immediately started to contact the Russians for permission to go there. That took three days. When I finally had the travel orders, which *nobody* else could get, I left at five in the morning, went to Leipzig, Jena, Weimar, Erfurt, and down to Martinroda. It took six hours as the autobahn stops all the time because of bomb craters. Had blankets, food, clothes in the car, jumped out, ran for barrack 3 and there was told they had left! You can imagine my despair. Went to Arisbadt, Amstrat, but as it was Saturday afternoon, all offices with the files where they might have gone were closed until Monday! I was told that they had been evacuated to families around the district. I went to the Russian Commander and arranged that Monday morning the information would be phoned to Berlin. That was all I could do as my travel pass was only for one day – and I had a show to do that night! I cannot describe to you the trip back, the disappointment, the helplessness, and the racing through rain against time.

We made it in time for the show. I stood as shaking and dirty on the stage as I will ever be. That night I had another car to take me home and the driver said that he thought your parents were at my mother's house, as he had brought my breakfast rations there as usual and had seen them. I nearly fell out of the car. I found them there! They had traveled all the way to Berlin just on that one postcard from Mutti. Now they were in another misery! They had gone to the police to register where they were told they could not get a ration card and would have to go to another refugee camp if they wanted to be fed in the winter. They were shaking with fright and said that now they would have to die. They told me how terrible the camp had been – bad enough for them to walk from Czechoslovakia all the way to Berlin without a penny, and they asked only that I explain to you that they have no other way out. I told them to sit tight and raced to do my two shows. Then I went to Gavin. It was he who had made that rule, because Berlin is so overcrowded and they have not enough food for the winter! By the next morning, I had heavy labor ration cards which give much more than the normal ones, and an apartment! I did not take the apartment as Mutti wants to take care of them, but later, if they want it, they can get it. At two p.m. that day, I left by plane. OK?

I was so exhausted mentally, seeing, hearing all those horrible things they had to tell – the nerves, afraid I would not succeed, no food for two weeks (I took everything from the table in a shower cap in my bag for them and Mutti before that), that I nearly collapsed. Besides, I had other emotional troubles about my private life.

OI YOI YOI is my life messed up! I wish I could stay with the Army – There everything is clear and easy.

Gavin could be Abelard, you know!

I love you
Mutti

Of course, my mother adored the legend of Heloise and her undying love for her Abelard.

On the 11th of October, General Gavin wrote to her from Berlin, signing his letter, "Your Jimmie". Some widows are very protective of their dear departed. Especially where love letters to others are concerned. So, the General's outgoings must be longingly imagined instead of read. Don't blame me – blame the laws of copyright.

During this time, my mother continued her life with Gabin, convincing him, when necessary, of her "true" love, half-heartedly prepared their French film she was really not interested in, while yearning for the organized life of the army and the commanding strength of compassionate generals.

> Papilein,
> . . . I wish you were here to tell me if I am doing right in thinking that I could not live like this forever. He has no friends except sports people and people who work for him. There is no mental food around anymore. If you were here I would not need anybody. . . . But when are you going to come?
>
> I am living in a tiny hotel, cramped in, without a maid, I do the washing, ironing, sewing because I don't make any money.
>
> Hollywood is decent compared to the business people here. The Jewish film producers are not back yet and the "goys" just don't understand how to make good pictures and treat artists.
>
> I am stuck on the Army I guess. Hemingway is expected here for the Nürnberg trials. Hope I can spend some time with him.
>
> What do you think I should do? Abelard flies in here today to see me. This has become quite serious. He is a wonderful man. Wrote me yesterday about having to go to England – to thank the villages where his men trained before Normandy. Sweet – no? Also worried about the 36,000 troops stationed in Berlin, said potential dynamite there and wants to stay – until British general can take over, that he would personally talk to the Commander of the 78th Division when they take over Berlin to take care of your parents. They are asking the War Department to give me the Legion of Merit.
>
> Thank God I can work for the Army, otherwise I would go nuts.
>
> I am still at the Claridge, hoping through the Embassy or the French to get a room somewhere else. That's why I feel a bit better now. Jean had wrecked my nerves for good when I returned from America. If one has a little hope around the corner, it is easier. He is coming to Paris Tuesday for one day. I called him Abelard in my last letter, you know who I mean, don't you? The 82nd? His name is very close to Jean's. Said he loves me too!

Gabin wrote her:

> . . . I know that you are in love,
> What you don't know is how much I suffer,
>
> J.

On the 6th of November, my mother's mother died in her sleep. Through military channels, my mother got a message through to me in Stuttgart. I immediately requested permission to leave the play in order to travel the three hundred miles to Berlin. I thought my mother might need me, that I should be by her side when she buried her mother.

As USO plays were produced under Equity rules, I was under union contract to perform, and my request to leave the play was denied. When the company manager gasped: "You can't leave! The show must go on!" I had the once-in-a-lifetime chance to reply "Why?" and left. I had no travel orders, no papers to move from one city to another – a very serious offense in occupied Germany in the winter of '45, but I was determined to make it to Berlin in time for my grandmother's funeral. I finally reached Berlin late at night, only to find that I had missed the funeral by a few hours. I asked General Gavin's aide-de-camp where I could find Miss Dietrich's billet and realized that he was choosing his words very carefully indeed. Suddenly, it dawned on me that my mother was already being comforted and that my overly dramatic dash to her side had not been necessary. So I inquired of the embarrassed colonel if he could possibly requisition a billet for me for the night. He did immediately, repeating all the while in a voice full of exaggerated sincerity that the only reason why he hadn't rushed me to my dear mother's side had been orders issued that "no one was allowed to disturb Miss Dietrich" that night! I assured him that I had no intention of demanding to see my mother, that I understood "the situation" perfectly, which relieved him enormously. He saluted and marched smartly into the night, his watchdog duty done. I went to bed, decided that as long as I had defied my union, my profession, and the laws of the army of occupation to get to Berlin, I could at least see my grandparents; I might even try to acquire a Jeep and driver to take me to my Aunt Liesel in Belsen. Why a former inmate would remain in such a place was beyond my comprehension.

My mother had not appeared by the time I walked through Berlin that cold winter morning. A shell of a town, ugly and scarred, filled with seemingly beaten people who shuffled amongst the ruins, their heads low to hide the hatred that burned behind their eyes. Everywhere women were clearing, piling brick upon brick, neatly organizing the rubble. I had seen this often through Italy. There it was done as haphazard clearing of roads, whereas in Germany, one had the distinct impression each brick was being saved for the future – to build another Reich.

My American uniform marked me; they mumbled in their Berlin slang that they had no way of knowing I understood. Some bowed to my uniform as they passed me, making sure their mask of deference was set in place. It was quite obvious that the Russian soldier with his ever-ready carbine was feared and therefore merited respect, while the

American soldier, handing out his ever-ready Hershey bars, was beneath contempt.

I broke the law, traded my army ration of American cigarettes for cuts of fresh meat on the black market by the Brandenburg Gate, my officer's liquor allowance for precious carrots, onions, and a whole loaf of real German bread. By the time I arrived at the apartment where my grandparents lived, I had the makings of a sumptuous stew stowed in my musette bag. Cautiously, my grandmother opened the door. How small she was! Seeing a uniform, she shrank back, eyes wide.

"It's me . . . Grandmother, Heidede – Really! It's me, Rudi's child," I said softly, not wanting to startle her. She just looked at me, clutching the doorknob. Her hair was all white.

"Grandmother, may I come in? I have fresh vegetables and meat." The door opened wider, I stepped into the dark hall. It smelled of furniture wax, just like I remembered, the special one my other grandmother had taught me how to properly polish with.

"Rosa? Who was that at the door?" my grandfather limped into view, no longer tall, no longer strong – a bent man whose age had become unfathomable.

"Who are you? What are you doing in this house?" he growled.

"She says she is Rudi's child," my grandmother whispered.

"I am, Grandfather. Really I am! See – I have brought you fresh food, all I could get . . ." I rattled on, not knowing what to say to make them accept me.

A little hand reached up, touched the insignia on my sleeve

"I have to wear a uniform because I act in a play for the soldiers . . ." I caught her hand. "It's me, Heidede. I love you, Grandmother – like I always did, remember?"

She reached up, pulled my face down to her, searched my eyes, and burst into tears. I held her smallness in my arms and cried for all the years of loving lost, the childhood that could have been, that never was. My grandfather moved beside us, I felt his big hand on my hand, and I was a little girl again in a sky-blue dirndl come to visit.

I told them about their son. Happy, good things, what they wanted to hear, making up what would please them, imbuing my father with a goodness I wished he had. They told me of their gratitude to my wonderful mother, of her goodness, and I shattered none of their necessary illusions. I could not stay long. My last memory is of them framed in that big oak door, a man and a woman grown old with a love as young as when I first knew them. They died the next winter within hours of each other. They never did like being separated for long.

In my best beguiling "daughter of" manner, I asked the general's aide for a Jeep and driver to take me to Belsen. It was cold, we drove fast. My driver, fully armed, didn't like being on a deserted Nazi autobahn amidst a dense pine forest. He only broke speed when bomb craters necessitated detours. I fully agreed with him – the metallic winter sky, the ominous silence, that dark forest, the memories so new of what this joyless place had been witness to and where we were headed, all made me shudder and want to have it over with.

Up a flight of stairs in a cozy apartment above a movie house, I found my aunt installed in a deep armchair. I bent down, held her close, and felt her healthy plumpness. Her eyes were fearful but they had been so since I could remember. Her attitude still timid and hesitant. She had not changed! This startling continuity of her so normal state shook me. This woman was intact. No concentration camp cadaver here, no still-breathing leftover skeleton. This had never been one of Jo's specters! What twisted script had my mother written now – to evade yet another truth from being known? This time, aided and abetted by the British as well as the American military? I gave my aunt the precious rations I had brought. No longer life-giving, now simply luxuries. Answered her usual fluttering questions about her beloved Pussy Cat in the context she wanted to hear them, shared her tea and cakes and loved her still. It was not her fault that I was angry. She was the victim she had always been, just not the one I had expected. I kissed her good-bye, my time was up and I had to leave.

We drove fast, it was cold. My fury burned deep inside me. I wanted to scream, bellow my rage, ask forgiveness of all those tortured souls whose misery still clung in that evil air, whose suffering had somehow been desecrated by an outrageous lie for personal convenience by one I was related to. You can't take the agony of a people and use it for your own aggrandizement and be allowed to get away with it I cried, knowing that Dietrich already had. My aunt lived in the town of Belsen until the day she died – it was her home.

My mother never changed her story. The power of "the legend" was such that whenever Dietrich dramatically announced that she had found her sister in Belsen, the listener had an instantaneous vision of gas ovens and cyanide showers – and she let them.

This time I had official travel orders to rejoin my company. My mother complained that as I had arrived too late for the funeral, I should at least be allowed to stay with her now, cried as she kissed me good-bye. Neither one of us mentioned her sister. I left, knowing she was very well looked after by her Abelard. A few weeks later, her letter caught up with me somewhere in Germany:

Paris, Thanksgiving 45

My Angel,

After you left I was so terribly miserable there that I couldn't get away fast enough. Three nice colonels from China-Burma drove me to Frankfurt. Then the train to Paris at six p.m. Without those three nice men I would not have been able to do it, but they took care of me like a baby.

Once back in my miserable room, the entire weight of all that had happened fell suddenly on me. I don't think that I was quite aware that my mother had died.

If you could only get out of the show and live with me. I need your advice for so many things.

Two days after I arrived, at five in the morning, Jean knocked at my door. He sat down and said, "Let me have it. I am prepared to hear everything." I couldn't tell him. Didn't have the courage, maybe.

Abelard arrived yesterday and was so sweet and tender and terribly kind and quite different from in Berlin, where he had to be so discreet and correct and impersonal in front of all his staff to whom his loving me would be misconstrued as a love affair.

And there I stood and was in love with him all over again. He is leaving middle December – and my wish came true. Their big parade on Fifth Avenue beginning in January. He was so happy about it – like a child. They'll all get new scarves and caps and they'll be "the best-looking soldiers of any army" when they march down Fifth Avenue. This all is still very confidential.

Then I thought of poor Jean while I was having dinner with Abelard at Korniloff's (remember?) and wished you were there to help me make order in my head and heart.

All my love. I love you terribly.

Mutti

She enclosed her note from Gabin:

My Grande –

I have just left you. I realize I have lost you forever. . . . I know that this letter is stupid and ridiculous in such a moment when you have such a deep grief. Please forgive me. I am deeply sad too. I don't know what to do next. I hurt, I hurt so much. I feel alone. I don't know what's going to happen. Doesn't matter! Adieu. I will never come back.

J.

She wrote my father:

Paris, December 1, '45

Papilein,

I have moved to the Elysées-Park. I sent this new address to you with a pilot who flew back to America three days ago.

Gavin goes home Christmas for the big parade. I have trouble here. Have no idea what to do. Where to live – and with whom. You never answered my September letters so I don't know what you think.

Love.

M.

Paris, December 5, '45

Beloved Papi,

Thank God your letter arrived. I was almost going crazy.

I have never been so alone and lost. Paris without you was from the beginning a strange town, but now it is worse than China. You can't even begin to realize how I live. True, I have lived in worse places during the war. But that was different. For one thing, everybody was young around you and one laughed about the misery of it all. And then one is not alone. But alone I have no more sense of humor.

It looks as if we fought the war for nothing. The people have changed so terribly, the great spirit that was there during the war has gone or maybe was never there in civilians. In Germany it is the same. Hitler has left his mark. Everyone still denounces his friends, only now to the other side, to get some good out of it. Nobody needs business and everyone is impolite. I mean the hotels in particular. Finally, through Adi Hollander who knows someone at the Préfecture, I have this two-room, unheated suite at the Elysées-Park. It is charming and cozy and I overlook the Champs-Elysées. I have, with a lot of tips, a wood fire burning in one room. The other one is ice cold. Most French people still have their apartments with black-market coal heat and their "pied à terre" and the swanky cars drive around.

Taxis are there only for deported and wounded although the people who ride in them don't look it. A carriage takes ages and costs: Fouquet's to Lanvin 200 Fr. 4$, which is coming and going too much. This is just to tell you how I live. I found no mention in your letter of Abelard. Maybe you are being careful, which I appreciate as Lin was not and wrote: "I was happy that Jim was with you," which is the letter Jean found, behind Kater's picture and he tore up everything in my miserable room as he had a suspicion about my staying in Berlin so long. And we have been parted ever since. And I was really behaving very well. Had no idea of anything else but, as you know, to live with him for good. But it was quite impossible. Scenes all the time. He had the new complex that I did not like France. You know how Jean sees only the black side. He now has a young pretty actress called Marie Mauban, he takes her out every night and thinks I am with my "Generals." He treated me so terribly, accusing me of sleeping with everybody I talked to, that I knew I could never live with him. Then, in Berlin, with all the emotional upset, I ran into the so suddenly open arms of "Abelard" like into a haven. And I did not sleep with him. Which does not make me any purer. Then he wrote me wonderful letters and wanted it to be the "great thing or nothing" and when it happened with Mutti he brought me there and was kind and did not push himself into the picture. He calls every night from Reims where the camp is and he will come here on the 18th and leaves for New York on the 21st. He will call you. Although he is very shy he promised to do it. Just say that you know of my admiration and devotion for him. So as to make it easier for him. He will get a divorce not because of me – his daughter is twelve. They live in Washington. He does not know what he will be assigned to. For your information he is the pioneer of the paratroopers, started with a handful of men in '41 against all odds. Went through the Sicily, Anzio Campaign, Normandy, Holland. Only Division which has four Combat Jumps. The red things on his shoulders are the Belgian and Dutch Fourageres. Maybe they will have the French by the time they get home. But for that they would need one more shoulder. He was born 1907, I am nine months older than he, see?

Actually she was six years older than her Abelard at the time, but then arithmetic always confused my mother.

I just made myself some tea, made a little sack of an old piece of panty, tastes awful, like soap. The food you sent was wonderful. Find out when one can send clothes officially, because civilians can't wear uniform things and no shop is allowed to dye them.

Got all the books. How do you like Remarque's new book [*The Arch of Triumph*]? Didn't you laugh that "Jean" kills me in the end? I wondered how Boni would solve the problem because he couldn't wait until I first played it out for him. It is badly translated and the love scenes are too "literattur" and boring, but it is a good film story with action once it gets started. He paints me worse than I am in order to make himself more interesting and he succeeds. But everything from Fouquet's to Scheherazade to Antibes, Chateau Madrid, Cherbourg, Lancaster Hotel, even "Jo" on the boat. Of course, he couldn't make it a woman and the actor he really makes ridiculous is in it. I am much more interesting than Joan Madou.

Jean has a wonderful story he is making for Gaumont. He wants me to play it, now that the other film is off. Two in a row together would not have been good. If I make that picture, I will stay here. First to be here as long as Kater is here, and then for that kind of a part it is worth it. Should it not work out and Gaumont wants a French woman, which might be an argument, then I will come back. No reason to sit alone in a hotel in

Paris. I will cable and write. Don't worry – my stars are wrong, that's all. Can't last forever. Carroll Righter has been right again. I told Jean to have the contract signed before September 12 and he did not. Righter said it was important because after that date there would be trouble. He was right. They have paid me only my expenses since Oct. 15. I hope I get the rest. I will let you know. Don't worry. I am tired, inside, not physically, emotionally.

All my love as forever,

Mutti

December 7 '45

Papilein,

I am going to Biarritz for a week. First to get away from here – am really too lonely, every evening, reading old Kaestner books and Rilke. That's fine if you are quiet inside. But I am too nervous after all the misery. I'll give lectures on films for the GIs at the University there and sing in the evening. Abelard called from London last night. They are moving there but he will come here on the 18th and leave on the 21st.

Was with Chevalier for a few hours yesterday. He stars at the ABC and then goes on to New York to sing for the Shuberts. He said that I was the climax of his life. He is so very much like Jean when he talks. He also said that he could understand Jean's jealousy. Must be typically French.

All love for now.

Mutti

For my twenty-first birthday, my mother wrote me a letter using one of her precious sheets of crested stationery. Whether the Dietrichs' or von Losches', I never did find out, and she never commented on it – just used it with aristocratic flourish when a "grand" occasion warranted it. As far as I know, it was the only memento she took for herself from her mother's house.

Still in Paris, being Jean's "*Ma grande*" while waiting for her Abelard, my mother went to a play, saw Gérard Philipe and swooned, told everyone how beautiful he was, what a brilliant actor he was, every night sat through his play – hugging her knees, on the edge of her seat – entranced. Went backstage, glowed, draped herself against his sinuous frame, looked up into his handsome face and – melted. He, very young, was flattered, enchanted, and returned the compliments.

ON A COLD WINTER NIGHT, we did our play in a deserted schoolhouse in Bad Hamburg. Icy rain beat against the fogged window panes. There was something ominous about all those regimented desks, still in place, where only a short time ago tow-headed youths had been indoctrinated. Their spirits hovered. I ran my hand along a scarred desk and felt the sharp outline of a swastika. Christmas Eve is not a time for such feelings.

In January, General Gavin wrote from Fort Bragg that he had called my father and had a visit with him in New York, adding: "A good man and I can understand your deep and understanding friendship."

Having done our six months, our show was sent home on a huge Victory ship jam-packed with jubilant GIs. My father was at the New York pier to greet me – without Teddy at his side, somehow incomplete.

A letter from my mother awaited me:

Paris, February 10, '46

Angel,

I am so blue it isn't even funny. I have lost all my last straggling ends of sense of humor. With you gone, nothing seems to matter. This Europe I loved so much has dwindled down to some vague form of memory. I still long for it, forget that I am here, and then realizing that it too has probably gone forever.

Only when I walk up the Champs-Elysées and see the Arc is it still the same place and just as beautiful. I am always looking for the Beautiful. That is probably what is wrong with me. During the war there was Beauty in the people but now all that seems to have gone. Everything is ugly. Everybody thinks of how he can outdo the other and schemes to get around the law and thinks nothing of it. Maybe all this is natural. I don't like it. And that's why there is no joy. Nobody is gay. They are too busy scheming to make money and keep it. Maybe that is natural too.

When you read this letter you will be in your "Holy Land" and probably you are hating the civilians just as I did.

Don't forget me. Here life with Jean is very difficult.

I love you more than life.

Mutti

Back in my father's penitentiary, Tami was my first concern. Her condition was deplorable. The many forced abortions endured over the years to ensure no scandal sullied the purity of my mother's marriage had finally taken their catastrophic toll. While my mother and father still believed that these "shocking" consequences of Tami's love for my father were entirely her fault, and scolded her for her irresponsible behavior, Tami, the conditioned victim, accepted the guilt and proceeded to punish herself for it. False pregnancies had begun to appear and disappear, first accompanied by euphoric joy, then black despair. As her emotional pendulum swung out of control, her desperate need for drugs had become imperative to escape from her worst nightmare, her own reality. To acquire them became the goal of her daily existence. When she ran along the streets of New York, from one drugstore to another, buying amphetamines, stuffing her handbag as she ran, her frenzy making her oblivious to her surroundings, as she searched for yet another and another source, I would follow, catch her, coax her into coming home with me, hoping we would make it back before my father returned and punished her for once again disobeying his strict order not to leave his apartment without his permission.

When she pummeled her bloated belly, trying to kill the child she believed was inside her, I grabbed her frail wrists, held her as she shivered from shock at her own bestiality. When she tried to ram a bread knife up inside her, I tore it from her hand, held her as she screamed – reentering reality, cradled her frail body as she wept her sorrows against my heart.

I tried to discuss her "treatment" with my father. I was highly critical of the doctors my mother had hired with instructions to "do something to make my friend, Miss Matul, behave – normally." But my father refused to discuss her, adding that if I insisted on questioning the expertise of respected medical authorities that my mother, out of "the goodness of her great heart," had found and was paying for, I could find myself another place to live. If I left, Tami would be utterly alone, completely at his mercy. I kept my mouth shut, cleaned her, fed her, guarded her, loved her, and stayed.

My mother's letters continued to arrive. Gabin, knowing how my mother loved Remarque's Cézanne watercolors, had given her two, throwing in a Degas for good measure.

. . . at first I did not want to accept them and then sometimes I think that I am very stupid always feeling like that. Jean has so much property here – is really a rich man.

A scrawny street urchin in a little black dress became the sensation of postwar Paris. With a big guttural sound, she sang of suffering, lost love, and impossible dreams. Hands on hips, legs braced against the onslaught of life, she epitomized the indomitable spirit of the French masses, and they adored her. Of course, my mother fell under Piaf's spell, and as always when enamored, mothered her, showered her with presents, advice, and whatever drugs her new love required. Gabin, always

Martin Roumagnac was filmed in France in 1946.
Its stars, Gabin and Dietrich, tried, but to no avail.
They had planned to marry after the film but, by
the time it was finished, my mother was in love
with another Jimmie and blamed Gabin.

One of my mother's prides: the day she marched, wearing her medals, in the military parade commemorating the liberation of Paris.

appreciative of raw talent, agreed that my mother had good reasons for her crush on Piaf the performer, but reserved the right to his opinion of Piaf the woman.

The script they had been working on finally became a reality, and they began shooting *Martin Roumagnac*. A film so full of self-conscious embarrassment, it is amazing they didn't stop after the first rushes and walk away from it. Gabin, his wonderful unself-conscious acting stilted even in his own language, hobbled by tricks and contrived characterization. Dietrich is just plain awful. Trying ever so hard to be "provincial, small-town French," she achieved a look and acting style that made you want to take scissors and, like a paper doll, cut her out around the edges. Jean must have seen it, for he tried, worked with her on the dialogue: "Don't speak so perfectly. Pull the syllables together, you are not playing a baroness." When she had a scene without him, he sat beneath the camera, coaching her. But even "Gabin and Dietrich" together could not lift this film out of its mire of mediocrity. They had been lovers too long for any vibrant sensuality to register on the screen and perhaps save the film.

When her old pal director from *The Lady Is Willing* called and offered her one hundred thousand dollars to play a gypsy, *and* at Paramount, she accepted without a moment's hesitation. Phoned Nellie to prepare a black wig "with long bangs to give the look of mystery, and lots of shine to give the look of hair – *greasy*. Gypsies always smear their hair with goat grease – that's why they stink so. If the hair shines, it will look 'real' gypsy!"

Of course, Gabin didn't want her to leave. They quarreled:

"But I need *money! American* money! *Real Money!*" Having made up her mind to leave him, yet always with an eye on "history" and to make certain that Gabin would be the one blamed, she wrote out all her reasons in one of her trusty notebooks:

> Paris, July 25, '46
>
> This is a story which I write down so I don't forget the facts of this strange end to my life with Jean.
>
> I also write it down so that I can prove to myself later that I did not dream it up or elaborate on it as time went by. . . .

Jean only sent a final letter, as always in French, delivered to her hotel. For "an uneducated peasant," as my mother so often referred to Gabin, rather beautifully expressed. My father thought so too – that's why he kept it safe after my mother sent it to him. A long true letter from a man who loved her – that ended with:

. . . Ma Grande, listen, there is a commonplace remark that has been said thousands of times, "You have been, you are, and will remain my one and only true love." I know, this has already been said to you but, believe me, it is said by a man who has a lot of experience. . . . I hope you will appreciate its real value. As I once told you: I would rather lose you alive than lose you dead and unfortunately, I feel I have lost you, although we did have such a good time together. I don't care about what will happen next, I don't mind what the future holds in store for me, I just remain with an immense sorrow, a deep pain within me and an infinite grief. There it is, that's all I wanted you to know.

J.

The only thing wrong with Gabin was his character and his love. Both were strong and unmalleable. Impossible attributes when in love with Dietrich, whose entire emotional structure was built on quicksand, that she shifted to suit herself – then blaming her victim for what she herself had manipulated.

Jean Gabin walked away from his damnation and I was proud of him.

SHOWTIME

A NEVADA divorce became possible, and I left my wounded Tami for my own selfish needs. As my mother was paying the legal costs and required a trained handmaiden, I was told to report to her in Hollywood after being granted my "freedom." We moved into a little house in Beverly Hills. All "bungalowy," a happy nest fit for contented mother and child. As the one bedroom contained an enormous bed, she absolutely refused to let me sleep on the equally huge couch in the white and petal-green living room, insisting we share the bed. I knew I wouldn't be there for long, a new romance was sure to come along soon and I'd get the couch.

"Good morning, Miss Dietrich. Good morning, Miss Hei – Oh! Excuse me, Miss Maria!"

We drove through the Paramount gate. The dawn pink, the air crisp. We had been assigned our old dressing room. Nellie, now the head of the Hair Dressing Department, stood waiting, wig block with greasy wig under her arm; Crosby crooned, saws hummed, the perfume of sawdust, that charged hush before a studio woke . . . I was home!

If ever *Golden Earrings* is remembered, it is for the look of Dietrich in that black wig and matching face. She out-gypsied every gypsy that ever was or ever will be. That hair dripped grease. The heavily black-rimmed eyes, with their inner line of stark white in a modeled nut-brown face so mysterious, could see into any future in any crystal ball. Barefoot, beragged, beshawled, bejeweled, bracelets, earrings, gold coins jangling, she smeared grime and dirt on herself, plucked fish heads from suspended black iron pots around smoky campfires, stank to high heaven, and had a wonderful time. She even had a costar to make fun of again.

"Now, really! *That* they pay! *That* is considered a star? Can't be! Probably Mitch has a crush on him and that's why he wants him in the picture!"

Through the whole film, Ray Milland very carefully kept out of Dietrich's way, appearing at her side only when a scene called for it, and then you could see the clammy sweat begin to form on his gypsy makeup. It drove his makeup man crazy, he kept having to run into shots to "blot." This moisture was not due to passionate desire held in agonizing check for his gypsy woman, but from trying desperately not to throw up in her face. The day of the campfire scene – that did it! My mother plunged her hand into the pot, stirred it around, extricated a big juicy fish head and sucked out its bulging eyes. Under his dark makeup, Milland turned dead white – and ran. I think she rather enjoyed turning her costar's stomach – it became a game to see what she could come up with to make him sprint to the bathroom.

In the evenings, going home in the car, she would be deep in thought, then murmur:

"You know, tomorrow, in the wagon scene – I could itch my crotch. All gypsies have lice. The petticoats pulled up, against the brown naked leg will look very good, then move the hand down the leg, pull off a hunk of bread, put it in his mouth . . . very gypsy! Shows she loves him that she gives him her food. I told Mitch when we do the disguising scene, I'm going to use my goose grease to smear him with . . . so it looks *real!*"

In later years, she always referred to Ray Milland as "That awful Englishman with the delicate stomach, who was finally taught to act by Billy Wilder and then never did anything again after that 'drunk' picture."

The hottest new find on the Paramount lot, an athletic young man fresh from his triumphant debut in a gangster film – *he* interested her in an entirely different way. Soon our weekends revolved around making him happy. As he was married at the time, he would arrive around ten in the morning and have to leave by five in the afternoon, so I never got to sleep on the couch. After seeing to it that his favorite foods were in the refrigerator, helping my mother put her special Irish linen sheets on "our" big bed, I made myself scarce, reappearing when I knew our young actor had gone. As handmaiden to the queen, my role had not changed, except that now I was considered old enough to listen to sexual tidbits of her romances, as well as changing the sheets.

She rhapsodized about her latest's physique. His amply muscled torso held special appeal. Between filming, I ordered gifts for him that my mother decided this "future star" required. The gold watch, the Cartier cuff links, the cigarette case, Hemingway to lift his mind from his "side show mentality," as she put it, up to her superior level, the cashmeres, the silk shirts, and opulent dressing gowns. One day, I was sorting the bills in the dressing room, when she turned away from painting on her gypsy eyes and said:

"Sweetheart. He wants a gramophone – No! What are they called now? Record players? – Yes, that's it. He is dying for one with all the 'very latest inventions built in.' That's what he told me. Can you get it for him? . . . The best they make and have it all ready on Saturday so that he can take it home with him in the car when he leaves. He can tell his wife the Studio gave it to him, so when you find it, buy it under the name of Mitchell Leisen – they can charge it to him – I already talked to Mitch about it."

Soon after the latest hi-fi presentation, our weekend visitor lost interest and faded out of our life. Over the years, my mother often referred to this "interlude" in her life as, "the time we made that terrible film with that English bore – What was his name? And that son of a bitch went to bed with me for a record player!"

He became one of the few lovers she never saw again, who did not remain a lifelong supplicant.

During the filming of *Golden Earrings*, we had a strike.

"A strike – for what? Who is allowed to strike in Hollywood? We make pictures – not cars," said our 1930s Movie Star and meant it. As a matter of fact, it had confused her for years that she now paid union dues and had something called an SAG card. "What is SAG?" she asked me, very puzzled.

"The Screen Actors' Guild, Mutti."

"Oh – I thought it was a union?"

"Well – it is."

"No, it is *not*! Says 'guild' – that's when actors get together, like that place in New York, where they all are so proud they belong to – You know – What's it called? Something . . . monk . . . something . . ."

"You mean the Friars Club?"

"Yes! That's the one! In Hollywood they call it 'guild.' In New York they call it 'club,' but it's the same thing. They get together to have drinks, sit in leather armchairs, and talk about themselves!" So, when her union, which was supposed to be only a 'social club,' informed all the actors working on the Paramount lot that they risked breaking a strike if they came to work, my mother was outraged and refused.

"Mutti, please listen. The strikers are lining the gates. There are rumors they are threatening to throw acid in the actors' faces if they insist on crossing the picket line." *That* got her attention.

"I am going to see Mitch about this stupidity," and she marched out of the dressing room.

The Studio was battened down for a siege. The companies of all pictures in production were ordered to stay on the lot, remain inside the Studio until the strike was settled. The Property Department heeded the call to arms – trucks hauled mattresses and cots out of their storage lofts and distributed them, pillows, blankets, and sheets were issued, canteens were set up for dinners and breakfasts and an entire Hollywood studio went camping.

In the Writers' Building, cots, pretty typists, and booze mingled in erudite abandon. The Make-Up and Hair Dressing Departments merged, set up their cots in one, then threw a party in the other. Dressing rooms became a fiercely contested possession; the stars having their own private ones reigned supreme. Everyone who had ever thought of sleeping with someone on the lot got their wish. They were "locked in – by order of the Studio," the excuse of all time – to live one night within one's fantasies *and* get away with it!

My mother's dressing-room door stayed securely locked, but Nellie didn't stand guard – she was busy somewhere else. I had my studio bicycle and rode around, listening to the radios blaring "Zip-a-dee-doo-dah," taking in the gay sights and squeals of delight!

The next morning, disheveled, bleary-eyed, and dazed, the Studio went back to cranking out its product, not quite sure they could take another night like the last one. My mother really did not blossom from one-night stands, especially when a very bad, very untalented actor had shared it, and so – was in a lousy mood. She was drawing the white line down her nose when I came back from dawn breakfast.

"Well – did Milland get you?" my mother asked, her gypsy eyes fixing me through the mirror. She had been making these innuendos through the whole film, irked that I wasn't having an affair with someone. Anyone would have done. Just as long as my behavior was worse than hers, it would make her feel more the "lady." I hated to disappoint her; besides, anyone who had spent a whole night with Murvyn Vye deserved something, so I gave her a present:

"Oh, he wasn't good at all," and seeing her satisfied smile, left to pick up her gypsy skirts from Wardrobe.

We had just come home from the Studio when the telephone rang. I answered it; that French growl I knew well, I passed her the phone. She said "Oui," her face quite calm.

Jean told her he was getting married. Her face whitened, she clutched the receiver, she began pleading with him. He was making a terrible mistake, no woman he had suddenly found "like that" could be good enough, could ever make him happy enough to warrant marrying her.

"*Mon amour*, sleep with her if you have to but MARRY? WHY? Is it all just to have a child, that you feel you have to be so bourgeois?"

But no matter what she said, how much she begged him, reminding him how he had loved her, how she still loved him completely, unconditionally, she couldn't sway him. Finally, he hung up on her. She put down the receiver. She looked drawn and completely lost.

"It's a mood," she whispered, "another one of Jean's moods. A trick, to make me come back to him. It wasn't necessary. All he had to do was call, tell me he loved me, and I would have rushed back to him – *after* we finished the film."

That evening we were scheduled to go to a big party at somebody's Bel Air mansion. I don't remember whose. Travis, now a disenchanted man running his own dress business, designing clothes for poolside cocktail parties and bored executive wives, had designed a special evening dress for the occasion, of palest blue chiffon, its trailing oversize stole bordered in blue fox. I, too, had a special dress, a spectacular black silk jersey made for me by Irene, so it must have been a very important affair. All I remember of that night are illuminated gardens that stretched for miles, playing marble fountains, the who's who of Hollywood dripping jewels and charm, and my mother floating about in a pale blue daze, getting blind drunk. It is my first memory of what was to become the tragic reality of the years ahead, of picking my mother up off the ground, hustling her quickly into a limousine, having her pass out in my arms, getting her safely inside her place of residence, to undress her limp form as she snarled invectives at me. Back then, in the fall of '46, I had been cold sober for twelve whole months and was determined to remain that way forever. In my so-new self-pride and crusader innocence, I believed that I could now help my mother to conquer her demons, but although I tried for more than forty years, I never managed to extricate her from the final dismal pit she dug for herself.

MY FATHER WROTE, saying that he had an offer of a job with a French film company and that he was eager to return to Europe. If, after a few months, he found that it worked out, he would give up his apartment in New York to live permanently in Paris. He planned to leave Tami in New York, send for her and their belongings if things went well.

"Good. Finally Papi has something to take him away from Tami's craziness"; and assuring him of her financial support, my mother involved herself in the arrangements.

She did wonderful gypsy portrait-sittings; we packed up the dressing room. The stench of goat grease clung to everything. I felt sorry for whatever star would be occupying it next! Apparently, Jean had not rushed into marriage after all, and so deep, intense astrological discussions began, until my mother was assured the stars were in the right position to return, persuade "the love of her life" that he truly was that and more, do away with all his foolishness, and be his – forever! Poor Jean, I wished him well.

As Carroll Righter advised against flying for all Sagittarians and Capricorns, we took the train to New York.

"Endless! This country never stops, and we used to do this all the time? Why? It takes forever – but then, we used to do a lot of crazy things in the early days – remember that heat, before this air-conditioning? Which is just as bad. Cook or freeze – always American exaggeration."

We still washed at the Blackstone, that hadn't changed.

My mother continued on to France by ship. I remained in New York to look for work in the theater and take care of Tami during my father's absence. A convenient solution for a tricky problem that gave everyone what they wanted: My father got his bachelor trip to Europe, my mother the safety of having someone take on the duties of nurse within the family, thereby eliminating the risk that was always present of possible exposure to the press of Tami's true position in the Dietrich household.

Alone, Tami and I were actually happy at times. Being together, without the powerful presence of our usual taskmasters, was a relief. I searched for the hidden pills, followed her on her daily foraging of unscrupulous pharmacies, fed her, washed her, helped her dress in my mother's cast-off finery, and tried to shield her from harm. I didn't succeed – I just tried.

My mother wrote from the new pride of the Cunard Line, the SS *Queen Elizabeth*:

> Angel,
>   These are notes as I think of things I need, not a letter.
> 1. Ask Dr. Peck if the depilatory he spoke about, the one that does not smell, is ready to send.
> 2. Also need Vitamin C, ascorbic acid, against my red hands.
> 3. Cream for Papi's hemorrhoids.
>   I have the same stewardess from the *Bremen* who asked me about "Little Heidede."
>   Saw *Darling Clementine* yesterday. How terrible – Ford, our greatest director, to make such a bad film! The title is so misleading, too. Gloomy tombstone in slow motion. Today we have *M. Beaucaire*, with that awful Bob Hope.
>   Unbelievable passengers. Unbelievable boat. I have made a motion to

give sunglasses with every passage ticket. The lights are hospital lights and so are the walls. The vibration up at the grill is so strong, your teeth chatter – and you are supposed to dance on a carpet! For that at the grill you pay extra.

Wally Simpson's husband, I mean Mr. Simpson, runs after me and I hide which is difficult with all these bright lights. People stare at me so openly, it is almost insulting. There are mostly rabbit coats and old fox coats worn over evening dresses and I leave my new coat in the cabin. Today we are going to the Cabin class dining room instead of the "Vibration" room.

Six days of complete boredom. "Next time, take the plane." Should you come over, ask Carroll and fly if possible. Although you might love the boat as you can sleep for days and days.

I think we have a good time when we live together. I love you.

Mutti

One of the string of quacks that my mother collected had convinced her that electric shock would certainly cure her friend and so, before leaving, she had issued orders for Tami to be taken for weekly treatments, signed a blank check, and hired a very strange-looking woman to make sure she went. When I promised that I would follow all orders laid down if only I might be permitted to take Tami myself, my mother fired the "Auschwitz warden" and said: "You'd better! I paid!" and stepped into the waiting limousine.

The doctor was near, I walked Tami to his office, then helped her as we slowly retraced our steps. Each time we went, she whispered: "Don't leave me." Each time we returned, I had ceased to exist.

In 1946, there were no tranquilizers as we know them today – three years yet before the first, Miltown, long before the mighty pacifier Valium. If any anxiety-reducing drugs did exist, the "doctor" hired to electrically unscramble Tami's brain did not believe in them. Two burly men, in white coats, lifted the trembling creature that I loved so, slammed her onto a metal slab, strapped her to its icy surface. The restraining cuffs around her ankles and wrists were thick leather, the straps securing her body of heavy canvas. A wired leather band was tightened around her head, electrodes placed against each temple, a wooden wedge jammed between her teeth, and the switch pushed forward. I remember noticing that the ceiling lights dimmed, just as they did in movies at an electrocution. As Tami's limbs jerked, a low scream escaped through her wedged mouth, like the howl of an animal at bay, a faint smell of singed flesh – then silence.

Some days it took hours before Tami emerged from that long black tunnel she had been slammed into, knew who she was. Other times only a few minutes, but with each "treatment," she lost a little of herself, her memory, her quick intelligence, her lovely humor, her giving tenderness. The essence of the woman that was Tamara Matul became diffused, bringing fear, confusion, and utter desolation into sharp focus. She had trusted me and I had stood by and let them torture her. Deep down in the depths of her madness, she never forgave me – neither did I.

Fordham University in New York was justly famous for its unique triple stage and innovative productions. Its theater department was headed by Albert McCleery, the one-time aide-de-camp of General Gavin who had been so diplomatic and protective of his general the night I arrived in Berlin. He called and asked if I would be free to assist him in directing his production of *Peer Gynt*. I agreed to come to a rehearsal and see what I could do.

When I walked into the darkened theater, I saw a lithe figure of a man focusing lights onto the huge barren stage. I turned to McCleery as he joined me, and said:

"Are those going to be the lights for the first scene? If so, aren't they too bright?"

The man on the stage turned, peering into the darkened auditorium.

"Who said that? Al? Is someone out there with you criticizing my lights?" He sounded very annoyed.

McCleery escorted me down to the apron of the stage and introduced me to William Riva, the university's teacher of scenic design. I, who had grown up in a profession that had practically invented "love at first sight," I, who had always ridiculed such unrealistic "Valentine's Day" behavior, who cringed when my mother swooned, fell madly in love, never regretted it, and never looked back. Although I came to realize almost immediately that the object of my sudden passion was a superb artist, a consummate teacher, and brilliant craftsman, it took him a while to get over his antagonism against "movie stars' daughters who thought they knew the theater and, worse, believed they had the talent to teach its craft." Besides knowing that I was hopelessly in love, I came to respect his judgment in things of true value. After forty-five years of loving him, I still do. I worked hard to gain his approval, but it wasn't easy. He watched me direct a scene and that seemed to impress him. I volunteered to work all night to finish building one of the intricate sets; that he liked. I joined the paint crew, found an old pair of pants, put them on, needed something to hold them up, couldn't find a belt, so tied an old curtain chain around my midriff – that got him!

I got a job touring as understudy in the Theatre Guild's first production of Eugene O'Neill's *A Moon for the Misbegotten*. Bill came to visit me whenever he could get away, and soon O'Neill, the great stage designer

Robert Edmond Jones, James Dunn, everyone smiled their approval of the romance traveling with our company through Columbus, Cleveland, Boston, and points west. When, in Kansas City, the police closed O'Neill's beautiful play because its language offended the decency laws of that fair city, I returned to New York, caught Bill on the eve of a dress rehearsal for another one of those complex, extravagant, exciting productions that the dear Jesuits of Fordham loved so. Three days without sleep, Bill was dead on his feet; I saw my chance, and asked him to marry me. He nodded his head – he was too tired to say no. Best thing I have ever done, as well as the most courageous.

I kept my mother carefully uninformed. This was never hard to do. Such mundane questions as "How are you?" "What are you doing?" "Tell me about yourself" were never part of her speech pattern, but I called Brian:

"Oh, Kater – my dearest girl. What wonderful news! God bless!" and went to visit Remarque, just to tell him of my love for Bill – not to stay long. We talked the night through, never noticing the time, until the electric lights became too bright with the morning light streaming in through the tall windows. Good friends can do that for each other – open old wounds, let accumulated poison flow, cleanse each other's spirit. He was so happy for me having found a home to set my love in. For him, the need for my mother remained unaltered.

The morning of my wedding day, I settled Tami in her favorite chair by the window, put a roll of tangled twine in her lap – she liked to pluck at the knots, a preoccupation that calmed her – kissed her and wished she were well enough to see me marry. On the 4th of July, 1947, I walked up the aisle of a beautiful church, feeling right in a very white dress, and married the man I loved – who loved me. No fuss, no extravaganza, no press, no photographers, no "world movie-star mother." But Albert McCleery, ever her fan, did manage to send our wedding picture via Reuters news service to her in Paris, and so, she managed to find someone in New York to break into our apartment and strew masses of fresh rose petals all over our white bed sheets. It was reported to me that she was furious, but made sure that everyone had the impression that she was only concerned about getting champagne and flowers to her wonderful daughter who was getting married – *without* her loving mother by her side.

She never got over my choosing to marry a man who had served overseas longer even than Eisenhower, sported seven hash marks on his uniform against her not too "official" three. In Dietrich's world, *she* was the designated hero soldier – certainly not some Italian-American with dark eyes and black hair. When later all my sons were born with their father's eyes, she shook her head in Aryan disapproval and was heard to mutter: "I knew it! The moment Maria married him, I knew her beautiful blue eyes would be lost forever! Those dark men – their genes always win!" For years, she waited for the moment she knew would certainly come, when I would return, my marriage another dismal failure, and gnashed her teeth as the years passed and I did not appear to whisper "Mutti – can I stay here with you tonight?"

JEAN MARRIED, and, completely distraught, my mother returned to New York and fell in love with the only man I ever thought the perfect husband for her. Elegant, handsome, intelligent, cosmopolitan, trilingual, and rich. Bill and I liked him enormously. The only thing that worried me was his gentleness, that and his genuine "niceness" might be a real handicap. This cavalier had so little armor to enter into an emotional siege with Dietrich.

Between being swept off her feet by her storybook Cavalier, she met my husband. He was polite, she was reserved but determined to make the best of what she considered was yet another emotional mistake of mine. She visited our third floor walk-up, commenting with girlish giggles how the linoleum on the stairs reminded her of the servants' quarters in her mother's house in Berlin, tasted my tuna casserole without comment, and shuddered at the roar of the Third Avenue El as it clattered past our bedroom window. Finally, a long sleek limousine drove her away – only to return an hour later, laden with boxes of expensive gifts: smoked salmon from the coldest rivers of Scotland, tins of perfect caviar, cheeses, breads, squabs, exotic fruits, bundles of white asparagus, cakes, and filigree cookies, and the inevitable bottles of Dom Pérignon.

My husband, who could not afford to lavish such gifts on me, was stunned. I was frightened, tried to laugh it off:

"Bill, love. Don't let my mother get to you. She is world famous for her overdone generosity and no one ever questions, nor understands her motives behind it. But I do. You know why she sent all this luxury? Because what she really wants to say to me is: 'You see, with him you have to eat tuna fish, with me, you would have caviar!' Let's have a party and get rid of all this junk!" A brave speech that I hoped would convince him that he was not letting me down by having only his love and canned tuna to offer the "daughter of a famous movie star." I knew he so wanted to give me the moon. He had yet to learn that what he had to give was much more precious to me, but the warning bell had sounded inside me. She knew this time someone might finally take me away from her, and desperate to repossess what she had always believed was hers alone, to keep forever, she would not stop at gifts of food.

Billy Wilder came to my rescue. He offered her the role of a nightclub singer trying to survive amidst the ruins of Berlin. She hated the character, the whole idea, but trusted Wilder and needed the money. She left for Hollywood in '47, quite sure that once she had designed the clothes, sung the Hollander songs, and made sure that "Billy won't insist that the woman was really a Nazi during the war," *A Foreign Affair* would become a Dietrich film. She duplicated the old sequin dress that she had worn during her GI time and looked fantastic. With an old German buddy as director, she had a wonderful time making the film. She phoned me constantly, sometimes didn't get me – which angered her – because, as I was teaching graduate classes at Fordham, I was not instantly available. Her leading man did not interest her. She referred to him as "that piece of petrified wood," and to her costar Jean Arthur as "that ugly, ugly woman with that terrible American twang." An attractive athlete she had met at one of Warner's many parties was paying her court. "Just like your Bill, '*ever* so Italian,' but not romantic-looking like yours, a little more low-class – like down more towards Naples. In the summer he hits a ball and then runs 'home' in that childish game the Americans are so crazy about – you know the one I mean. He is a little dumb – but sweet!"

So I knew my mother was well taken care of and hoped her Cavalier's corporate position would keep him safely in New York and out of the way until DiMaggio struck out.

With the recommendations of her admiring generals, the War Department announced that Marlene Dietrich had been selected to receive the highest honor the nation could bestow on a civilian, the Medal of Freedom.

She called me, sobbing, full of pride and elation:

"Sweetheart – I am having it framed for you. Nellie is going crazy sewing the little red-and-white ribbon I can now wear in the lapel of my suits. And I have a small medal to wear for state occasions – besides the official big one. Most children get medals from their father. You will inherit yours from your mother!"

I became pregnant, and my mother, ever the soldier's daughter who faces defeat with stoic resignation, returned to New York to oversee her daughter's "glorious" pregnancy, but not before asking me if I didn't really want to get rid of it.

"Once you have a child, you won't be able to get out of this marriage so easily. I know you keep harping on wanting children, but a child brings you nothing but trouble."

The look on my face must have frightened her, for she never dared to mention this subject again, allowing herself only to observe, in a tone laced with acid disapproval whenever I announced over the years that I was once more expecting yet another child:

"Again? Another one? Haven't you enough trouble already? What's wrong with Bill – won't he let you douche?"

In the spring of 1948, at the urging of her Cavalier, who knew the proper background his lady deserved, my mother rented the Lady Mendl suite in the Plaza Hotel. A four-room concoction of Vertès hand-painted murals of smirking nymphs scampering through watercolor woods of palest greens.

Bill was building a nursery out of a little storeroom we had, and as only oil paint was available in those days, we escaped the dangerous fumes engulfing our apartment by staying for a few days at the Plaza in my mother's suite. With her charming Cavalier in residence, everything was serene. Whenever he was not at his office or with his wife, he resided with us, showering his lady with superb gifts of impeccable taste. She lived up to his visual concept of her, wore beautifully simple suits, Valentino dresses, cut slim, unadorned, their line as elegant as a Ming vase. A figure-eight knot, first used in *Foreign Affair*, sculpted her hair against her neck; understated pearl earrings completed the look – Aunt Valli had come to stay, was living at the Plaza!

Russian broadtail and silver-tipped Russian sables were a must to complete this picture of ladyhood. Stoles were very fashionable in the late forties; my mother hated them. In her opinion, they had been invented by "fat old ladies who wanted to show that they were rich enough to own furs but couldn't afford the whole coat." It became a family problem what to have made in sable. My father, back in his apartment on the upper East Side, unencumbered by Tami, whom he had locked away in a sanitarium, preferred the full-cut Chesterfield-style coat. Remarque, still at the Sherry Netherland, a belted model with a flared skirt. I, horizontally worked skins. In Paris, Chevalier, when asked his advice over the phone, wanted cuffed sleeves. Noël's comment was a pertinent: "Whatever you do, Marlenah, make certain that you have yards and yards of the delightful stuff." Hemingway's laugh boomed over the Cuban phone lines – said it had to button. Piaf didn't like the whole idea:

"Why do you want to spend so much of your own money? Keep it. If he wants to buy you a sable coat, that's different – that's business!"

My husband was included in this summit meeting of pelts, by being asked to sketch the many suggestions. My mother smoked, paced the imitation Aubusson, and said:

"Have you seen that sable coat Tallulah wears? I don't know where she got it – but she looks like someone kept by a rich gangster!"

The Cavalier smiled his cosmopolitan smile, remarked:

"Whatever, you decide – Dietrich should be *wrapped* in Russian sable," and the idea for my mother's famous fur blanket was born.

She finally made a ten-foot runner of horizontally placed skins and, like a tall tube of Christmas paper, wrapped her body in sable instead of cellophane. She referred to it as her "Indian blanket." Years later, it became known as "the Thing" or "the Animal," and starred in one of Dietrich's renowned self-parodies:

"Do you see this 'Thing'?" pointing to the yards of sable taking up its own chair. "I looked wonderful wrapped in it when I arrived, right? No money – but covered in Russian sable! The story of my life! You know Rudi had it insured years ago for a fortune. I still have to pay every year for the insurance – waiting for it to get stolen, but you know, no one steals it! Everything else they steal – but not my Animal. So I think, why not lose it? One night, I just happened to leave it lying under my seat in the theater. No one noticed. So I call Rudi in the middle of the night to tell him the good news. The next morning, the manager of the theater appears at my door, beaming, and hands me my Indian blanket! Of course, I had to appear overjoyed and gaga grateful. He wouldn't accept a check, so I said, 'Tell me *how* I can thank you,' which, of course, was a dangerous thing to say – but all he wanted was autographed pictures for his whole family. I finally got rid of him. . . . I leave it in taxis – it comes back and costs me a fortune in tips. I let it sort of slide off as I walk through Bendel's or Bloomingdale's . . . and they find me wherever I am in the store and are *ever* so happy to bring it back to me. One time, I was on some ship crossing either to or from Europe, and we hit a storm. It was terrible. Everyone was sick – the ropes were up, wind blowing so hard no one was allowed on the upper decks. So, I put on my 'Animal' and took the elevator to the promenade deck, as though I wasn't feeling well and needed to walk, then I crept up the stairs to the top deck. The wind nearly blew me overboard – that would have been funn-eee!" She always laughed at the sudden thought of her going over the side together with her sable.

"So there I am, struggling to hold on to the rail – I loosen the 'Thing' so the wind can just take it and blow it away! In case some sailor might happen to see me, I couldn't just throw it into the sea – it had to look like a real accident. I was freezing, my hair, my evening dress completely ruined from the salt spray. It took me an hour to lose that thing! I got back to my cabin and immediately placed a call to Rudi to tell him the good news! Two hours later, the captain bows and hands me my Indian blanket! It had flown off the top deck and landed on a man's head in third class, four decks below! . . . I am jinxed with this thing. But the day I cancel the insurance – *that*'s the day someone will *finally* steal it!''

I had always dreamed of having one of those royal bassinets, all lace and ribbons and ruffled canopy for my firstborn. I looked all over New York City for one to live up to my exaggerated MGM-type concept, but as this was 1948, before Grace Kelly's Monaco princesses, there were none to be found.

"You want a Victorian bassinet, my darling? Easy. We'll make one," said my scenic designer husband and went in search of white organdy, eyelet for ruffles, and as I was determined to have a boy, wide blue satin ribbon. Ever the executive, the Cavalier had his secretary buy a sewing machine and ordered card tables to be installed in the Plaza suite.

My mother caught the bassinet fever, decided that Austrian field flowers were the only motif to complement the ruffles and ribbons, had the chauffeur drive her to the garment district in search of silk cornflowers and poppies. Santa's gnomes had nothing on us. Bill measured, cut, and pinned while the Cavalier sewed perfect ruffles as though born to the trade, my mother kibitzed, ordered coffee and sandwiches to keep us nourished and working. I, by now the size of a house, was allowed to sew the finished splendor to the wicker basket. I had to do so standing up, bending had become impossible. It was a happy time that I have remembered, because despite the rather theatrical circumstances, it felt so normal – like a real family.

In June, John Michael Riva was born and made Marlene Dietrich a grandmother. *Life* magazine ran a cover, proclaimed her "The Most Glamorous Grandmother," Walter Winchell called her "Gorgeous Grandmarlene," and *A Foreign Affair* opened to raves. The press kept pouring it on, until universally, she became known as "the World's Most Glamorous Grandmother," a title she secretly despised but officially embraced with seemingly passionate devotion; but never stopped blaming my husband for making me pregnant, thereby "complicating" her life. I, of course, was sublimely happy – my guard was completely down. A dangerous thing to let happen when Dietrich was near.

I even allowed her to play grandmother, or so I thought. Actually, she took on the role she preferred, the one of mother. Bill and I were young, in love, we wanted a few days together, and as I was not nursing, gave our baby to her to look after. It was late summer, friends had left the city, so she took over their house, draped off the downstairs in sterile sheets, scrubbed everything down with Lysol and Ajax, taped the windows against possible drafts, ordered nurse's uniforms, dressed in one, and moved our child from his sweet new nursery into Dietrich's Surgical Ward – and took over. Boiled bottles, made, remade, and remade again formula until she was certain no germs could possibly have survived, touched the baby only when absolutely necessary or to check if he was still alive. Fortunately, he was too young to be harmed by this exaggerated sterility. By the time we returned she had convinced herself that my son had sprung from her womb instead of mine. At the age of ninety she still accused me of taking him away from her:

"You left him with me and went off with Bill. He was mine! I got that house, moved all the furniture out, washed and sterilized everything, made that formula over and over – all that steam in that terrible New York heat. Never slept, listened every second to hear if it was still breathing and, when you came back, you *tore* him out of my arms and took him from me to your apartment!"

For years, I was confronted by outraged ladies, with: "Is it true you tore a baby out of your mother's arms and just marched out of the house after she nursed him for a whole year for you?" Sometimes, I actually caught myself explaining that I had only been gone five days, that I had actually borne him. Really, I could prove it!

Later, she loved to tell my son how I had deserted him, beat him when he was little, how she had been his only hope, tell him her "hidden secrets."

He was a young man, nearly grown, when he asked me:

"Mom. Is it true that you used to beat me when I was a baby?" He saw my face and quickly put his arms around me, held me close. "I'm so sorry, Mom. I knew it couldn't be true, but she used to tell me you did . . . all the time. I just had to ask you."

Charles Feldman called, offered her a film to be made in London for Alfred Hitchcock. She would have complete control over her choice of clothes and be allowed to pick any Paris designer she liked to execute them. She agreed to do the film. I called Charlie and thanked him. "You're welcome," he laughed. He was a good friend.

Before leaving America, the life insurance that von Sternberg had bought for her in 1931 matured, and my father and mother had one of their most vehement quarrels. It was my father's contention that as I had been the sole beneficiary of this policy, the matured amount was rightfully mine.

"But, I am still *alive!*" she screamed at him. "Anyway what would she do with sixty thousand dollars?" After a few weeks of this, my father found a lovely brownstone house on the upper East Side, convinced my mother to buy it with the proviso that she allow me and my family to live there until it could be legally gifted over to me.

"A house! Maria *has* to have a house? For what? All that work, rooms and stairs? The garden is good for the child, but who needs a whole house? You two are so alike – always talking about a 'home'! When she is with *me, then* she is home, and not in some house in New York with a strange man!"

My father persisted. Finally, she bought the house and lots of lovely rubies for herself with what was left over. My father knew that we had no means to furnish a house on our teachers' salaries. His plan had been to use the rest of the monies to make the house habitable and put a nest egg by for our son. But although he seethed inside, he knew when it was time to back off and be satisfied with what he had achieved. Years later, before he finally died, I was able to tell him of the house he found and fought for me to have, that became the Riva house, full of joy and love, children and grandchildren, youth and age – a real home, full of memories, and I thanked him for it. Over the years, my mother got so much good publicity out of this fabulously generous gift to her beloved daughter, I had no guilt about the house at all as far as she was concerned.

Clutching a dirty bib as a talisman of "her baby," my mother left for Paris and began making clothes at Dior. Remarque was in Paris and they saw each other constantly. He understood her longing for Gabin and the seething anger at his recent marriage. She encouraged Remarque's love and allowed him to share her suffering over Jean. Her Cavalier, still the innocent, followed her to Europe.

Paris, June 6 49

My Angel,
     The pain of having to leave you was all over me running like a fine toothache into my hand with the bib. Arrival at Orly, photographers, press. I played gay and almost felt like it. Had a date with Remarque at Fouquet's, we went to dinner at the Méditerranée and as we sat at our old table, I had the first funny dull thought in my head. The thought made no sense but it was there: Why isn't Jean here? The baby is expected in October. We joked that in France they now make babies in a much shorter time than it usually takes and said that it must have happened the first night he knew her.
     Anyway, that was the first evening. Remarque probably had a good time, knowing that Jean's expecting a child would close the door to any future between him and me, enjoying the dramatics of it all – and planning

to use it somewhere in his next book. He was sweet though, full of fatherly
pity and advice.

The next morning, after a night I passed somehow, I went to work. I
spent all day at Dior's while the sketches were made and materials picked
to be sent to London. Then I got sick like I cannot remember ever having
been, except when I was a child and had eaten unripe cherries. I had eaten
almost nothing since I arrived, but my stomach kept turning upside down
all night. I was so weak that I could not walk on the street. Chlorodine
helped but the weakness stayed for a week.

Like blood and rubber and snake venom, another one of those "great
discoveries": Chlorodine, came in tiny, very thin, cobalt blue glass
bottles with a tight cork stopper. Wrapped like Worcestershire sauce, its
parchment proclaimed this elixir could cure stomach cramps, diarrhea,
malaria, dysentery, influenza, typhus, cholera, and the bubonic plague.
Black, thick, and sticky, it looked like boiled-down opium – which it
probably was. My mother loved it, couldn't be without it, gave it to
anyone who had the slightest upset stomach, for years smuggled her
little blue bottles everywhere she went.

It's a holiday here, PenteCote, auf Deutsch Pfingsten. In Germany and
Austria they put young Birch trees or branches in front of their houses
and anyone can come in and drink young white wine. Here they go to
Deauville instead.

Dresses, shoes, stockings, gloves, handbags, coats, negligees, suits,
jewelry, foundations, scarves, hats – nearly all was ready, and so she
finally left Paris for London to make the wigs.

Her Cavalier awaited her with open arms at Claridge's. *Stage Fright*
began shooting in England on July first.

Michael Wilding had all the prerequisites to attract. He was handsome,
a storybook British gentleman, tender and shy, with a medical affliction
that marshaled all of her protective powers. They became lovers quickly
and remained so for quite a long time. In many ways, Michael reminded
me of Brian. Although he had a more pixie humor, he also had that
capacity to step back into the shadows whenever she became involved
with someone else, ready to emerge again with love whenever she
finished with his rival. Both men had the compassion of a saint and
the patience of Job.

During the Wilding time, my mother kept up her devotion to the
Cavalier, became involved with a famous American actress known
not only for her talent, pined for Gabin, received her baseball player
whenever he needed cosseting, loved Remarque, her charming general,

Piaf, a gorgeous Teutonic blonde who became her German pal, and worked full out at being indispensable to her immediate entourage.

After a romantic week with Wilding in the south of France, she returned to Paris in October, called, complained that it had rained the "whole time" in St. Tropez and that the fuss everyone made about the Côte d'Azur was ridiculous. "Before the war, *then* it was luxurious. Now *concierges* take their whole families there for vacations!"

Stage Fright finished, she booked passage for New York, called her astrologer, and then flew instead. Arrived back on November 5th, furious that American Customs had charged her one hundred and eighty dollars for the Dior clothes, worth thousands, that she had brought back with her. That night, she and her Cavalier had dinner at our house and she told her stories:

"You know how I worship penicillin, how it saved my life during the war, so I told Spoliansky, I saw them all the time while I was in London, I said: 'All I want while I am in England is to meet Alexander Fleming, the god who discovered penicillin. I want to tell him how he saved my life during the war!' The next day, the papers said I had gone over to Alec Guinness at a restaurant and said, 'You are the second most important man I want to meet,' to which he was supposed to have replied, 'Who is the first?' to which I answered: 'Sir Alexander Fleming!' Can you imagine my doing that? I was furious, but the Spolianskys swore they didn't tell anyone. But one evening, I go to dinner at their apartment and – who is there? Fleming! He just stood there and said: 'Hello.' I sank to my knees in front of him and kissed his hands. I must have been very boring at dinner. All I did was stare at him in awe – like a schoolgirl with a crush. Then we went dancing and the most terrible thing happened: When he held me, I felt him trembling! I couldn't believe it, so I said, 'Sir, are you all right?' – and you know what he said? 'Oh, Miss Dietrich, it is such an honor to meet you!' Can you believe it? A great man like that – the god who brought the world penicillin – turns out to be just another fan, like everyone else. Isn't that sad? I asked him for an autographed picture, and you know what he did? He sent me the very first penicillin culture under glass. I am going to frame it with his picture. Sweet man, but like all geniuses, only intelligent in the one thing they are interested in." She helped herself to more of the Camembert she had brought and cut a huge hunk of bread. As usual, she was starving.

"Let me tell you about Hitchcock! A strange little man. I don't like him. Why they all think he is *so* great, I don't know. The film is bad – maybe in the cutting he does all his famous 'suspense,' but he certainly didn't do it in the shooting. Richard Todd is nice but nothing there.

You know the kind of Englishman who has those thick white ankles? Also the hands? Todd's fingers are like little uncooked sausages and he's *engaged!* Jane Wyman, she is very sweet. Michael Wilding? Oh, a British version of Stewart. He mumbles, is ever so shy, and being English, gets through the film on charm. The best thing in the film is me doing 'la Vie en rose.' I called Piaf for permission. I didn't want her to think that I thought anyone but she had the right to sing it. Of course, she said yes and was flattered that I called her – and the *very* best is 'Laziest Gal in Town.' I did it with marabou feathers on a chaise longue, making fun of it. Cole will adore it – if he ever sees the film. The hair is very bad – the whole picture – too 'old lady little curls.' I always have said that the British can't make women's films – I should have listened to myself."

As she was between pictures, my mother now launched herself into the role of "fairy godmother" for the benefit of "her son." She had seen him looking at the pretty pictures in a book of fairy tales, and when next she appeared to take him to the park, she arrived in costume. Gone were the hospital-matron brogues, the surgical uniform, the antiseptic look of purity and dependability. She didn't walk into the house, she skipped – layers of starched petticoats awhirl about her beautiful legs. She hadn't been able to find glass slippers, but those she wore were see-through plastic and did the job. Golden curls bobbed on her shoulders, satin bows adorned her wrists, a blushing rose nestled in her cleavage.

My one-and-a-half-year-old was enchanted. "Puetty wady," he lisped, and they became inseparable – until he cried, then she quickly handed him over to me, worried that he might be dying and that she would not know what to do to save him: "With you, I was always frightened. Always! Never a day went by that I wasn't frightened about something happening to you. I drove Papi crazy in the early days with you in Berlin, then in America with the kidnapping – it only got worse." When she saw that my son was truly still alive, not threatened by some ominous unknown disease, she plucked him out of my arms, and they went back to happily cooing at each other.

My mother's new maid addressed her as "Missy Dietrich," and for some reason, my son liked the sound of "Missy," giving it his own pronunciation of "Massy," and that became the name my mother was referred to from then on by all of those within her intimate circle. A great relief to have found a name at a time when I was desperately looking for an acceptable substitute for "Granny."

Tauber died, and my mother went into her mourning routine, came out of it to voice her fury when the Kinsey report was published:

"Sex, sex, sex! What is it with people? Put it in, pull it out – *this* they have to *study?* And the money it costs! All that research – for what?"

Oh, how my mother objected to my second pregnancy.

"You have a perfect child. You need more?" she asked, genuinely confused by my obvious joy. When I answered that I hoped I would have many more children, she marched out of my front door in her best Nazi officer manner. All through that Christmas of '49, she suffered my obvious bulge with ill-disguised censure, throwing particularly juicy barbs when a dinner guest in my home:

"Look at her," she would point me out to my friends. "All her life she has hated being so fat – Now – Suddenly – She is as big as this house I bought for her and now she doesn't mind! She will find out someday the terrible trouble children are, then it will be too late!"

Convinced as she was that I could not give birth without her magical presence, she was once again in attendance in May 1950, when Peter was born. Although Bill was right there, it was again to Dietrich that the doctor came to announce that it was a boy. She played the role of husband so well, it was an automatic reflex for the doctor.

Hemingway sent her the galleys of *Across the River and into the Trees*. She brought them over to the house, plunked the long, thick stack onto my kitchen table.

"What has happened to him? Read this and tell me. Something is wrong, but I can't tell Papa until I know what it is!" She unpacked her schlepper, took out a tall jar of beef tea, put it in my refrigerator. "What have you got in here – Jell-O? You don't give *that* to the child? I'll make him fresh applesauce," and proceeded to do so.

"Pat took me to see a play, called *Death of a Salesman*. How depressing! And SO American. Little people with little problems, all done up like Big Drama! And you must see a thing called *South Pacific*. Not-to-Be-Believed! During a war – They SING! And big to-do because Mary Martin washes her hair on the stage with shampoo and real water? Now really!" The apples were boiling merrily. "She even does a cutesie-poo song, all about 'washing her man right out of her hair.' No! A bad Technicolor musical maybe, but not in the theater! And you can't even imagine the way the *man* looks – Old – Big – and Fat, like an opera singer. Which, of course, he is, but couldn't they at least have put him in a corset and dyed his hair?"

She was awarded the French Legion of Honor for her service to France.

LEFT: *Golden Earrings*
(1947), the gypsiest gypsy
that ever was.
BELOW: With Heming-
way. They met so often,
talked about each other
in such glowing terms,
the world believed they
must have been lovers.

LEFT: In June 1948, Dietrich became a grandmother. She thought the headlines proclaiming this momentous change in her status ridiculous hysteria. (Photograph by Arnold Newma BELOW: Photographers pounced when they caught Dietrich out with her daughter and son-in-law.

ABOVE: The fine talents that made *Foreign Affair* a success. My mother disliked everyone in this picture except the man in the hat, Billy Wilder. He was her German-speaking chum, and she trusted him and his talent. In such things, my mother was never stupid.

BELOW: *Stage Fright*, filmed in England, was another matter. Alfred Hitchcock was not to my mother's liking. They stayed as far away from each other as possible, and the film suffered. My mother didn't—she fell in love instead.

ABOVE: I liked Michael Wilding. He reminded me of another one of my mother's loves, Brian Aherne.

BELOW: An opening night somewhere. On seeing this picture, my mother said, "*I*, who can't stand jealousy in a man, went out with two of the most jealous men I ever knew in my whole life? Von Sternberg *and* Remarque *together*? Why would I do such a stupid thing? Must have been *quite* an evening!"

To be selected to become a member of such an exalted body was the high point of my mother's aristocratic life, topped only by being promoted from the rank of Chevalier to Officier a few years later by the then president of the French Republic, Pompidou, and finally, to the ultimate glory of Commander by Mitterrand. I certainly did not begrudge her this high honor, only wondered what she had done for France as a nation that was *that* important. Loving Gabin? Worshiping de Gaulle? Knowing the lyrics of the "Marseillaise"? And living in Paris just didn't seem enough, somehow.

"Jean should have been with me. He would have been proud. Why they never gave him one I'll never know. After all, he is still the greatest French actor they have. He even fought in the war. Strange, a German they honor, but a man of the people they don't. But then, I have always loved de Gaulle, a wonderful man and I always tell him so when we see each other."

The first rumors of war began in Korea. Proclaiming that if I insisted on having babies all the time, she had to earn more money for me, my mother signed to star in *No Highway in the Sky*, to be filmed in London. She had a tearful farewell with "her child," clasped him to her bosom, whispered, "Don't forget me, my angel," while my son tried to come up for air. My new baby didn't warrant a look. He didn't interest her. He had dark hair, like his father, was chubby, healthy, and unromantic-looking. And she left for Paris.

Dior was again given the singular honor of designing her costumes for the film. The clothes they conceived were so perfect, so utterly Dietrich, that throughout the film she looks as though she is doing a portrait sitting for *Vogue*. Although her costar was once again her old heartthrob from *Destry*, and even Elizabeth Allan had a part in this film, she never mentioned either of them. In her daily phone calls to me, she complained about the "lackluster script," the "half-asleep director," then spent the rest of the hour telling me how sweet Glynis Johns was on and off the set.

In December, she returned aboard the *Queen Elizabeth*, complained that the cabins creaked, that she really had enough of the British four-o'clock tea mania, but conceded that Elizabeth Firestone and Sharman Douglas had made the crossing bearable. She launched herself and her newly acquired salary into a frenzy of Christmas shopping. Her Cavalier was grateful to have her back. She had a new film, to be directed by an old lover, scheduled for the New Year in Hollywood, where Michael Wilding was waiting for her, and her favorite general was expected to pass through. My father was sorting and recording her European expenses, Tami was stashed safely away in a new asylum, my two-and-a-half-year-old had recognized her immediately when she walked into his nursery, and I, for once, was not pregnant – all was right in my mother's world.

LIVE TELEVISION, originating in New York City, had become the new marvel, the wonder that kept families at home together, clustered around their precious eight-inch screens. My mother had nothing but disdain for its amateurish growing pains and predicted television's rapid demise. Having handed down her obviously correct judgment, she ignored its existence until I called her in Hollywood and announced that I had auditioned and been given a starring role in an hour-long play on CBS Television. She was happily ensconced in Mitchell Leisen's apartment complex in the hills above the Sunset Strip. Michael Wilding, in better health than he had been when they were together last, was functioning as a most inventive lover, so her diary states at that time. Although she writes that she is "staining," she adds that hopefully it is Wilding's "steeple chasing" that is causing it and not something else. She goes on to say that she inserted a "firecracker," Dietrich's name for Tampax.

For the next fifteen years, not a day went by without her recording, in one way or another, her evaluation of her menstrual cycles, its erratic signals, its sudden absence or appearance, swelling, pressures; no symptom from that part of her anatomy was too minute to record. Her comments always underlaid with that silent panic that was to continue until 1965, when I finally forced her to face the possibility of cancer, and then hid the truth from her while she was being treated for it in Geneva.

So, when I called her that day in '51, she was happy with Wilding, worried about what "staining" might mean, in preproduction for the worst film she ever made, and knew it, and was in no mood to have me "prostitute myself for a few dollars, trying to act on that tiny, little stupid screen for little people."

Thanks to my husband's urging and encouragement, I summoned up the courage to try and was very successful. I loved television. I always have, working in it, or simply being a viewer. I always felt I belonged to it, that it was my friend.

A very special relationship emerges when an actor must wait to be invited into his audience's home. The welcome mat may be out the first time, but the performer must earn the privilege of being invited back. Once your host approves of you, you become a friend, a bonding not to be taken lightly. The live television camera has an uncanny perception. Its range of intimacy leaves no room for falsehoods. If by some clever maneuver they do get by, the viewer will eventually catch the insincerities and resent anyone trying to make a fool of him in his own home. As friends are supposed to be honest with each other, TV demands it.

My mother was afraid of this intimacy between a medium and its audience, and, therefore, hated it, had to discredit it whenever possible. For her very few TV appearances in later years, she drank herself into an anesthetized stupor. Her only TV special became a parody on herself, a personal tragedy.

EXCEPT FOR GIVING HER THE IDEA for a costume she was to embellish and perfect years later for *Around the World in 80 Days, Rancho Notorious*, the film she made in March of '51, had nothing to recommend it.

Since the day when Fritz Lang had "betrayed" her to Jean, he had ceased to exist as her one-time lover and friend. Now she erased him as a director as well. She showed her antagonism openly to anyone she chose, calling him "a Nazi."

"No wonder he did all those frightening pictures. A man who can do a film like *M* has got to be a sadist."

In April, her diary records the end of shooting with:

End of film – Another tough one –
No more Germans!!
Resolution!!

During this period, a "Jimmy" figures prominently in her diary as taking up her evenings "steeple chasing." Trying to decipher my mother's somewhat crowded sexual calendar could be confusing. There were so many Jimmys, Joes, Michaels, and Jeans, both the Anglo-Saxon and French versions, that one welcomed those lovers who sported such exotic names as Yul – it made them easier to identify.

Hitchcock was quoted as saying that Dietrich was "A professional cameraman, a professional makeup man . . ." and so on. My mother never noticed that he omitted "actress" from his long list, nor did it ever occur to her that he might, just might, have meant to be slightly sarcastic, enumerating her many accomplishments in every category but her own. But those of us who lived within her immediate control, we understood and sympathized. We knew that Dietrich thought of herself as an indisputable expert in anything that she decided was important enough to warrant her interest.

Medicine was one of her most dedicated specialties. She told doctors what diagnosis they should come up with, changed, replaced, and manipulated them without the slightest hesitation, bullied nurses, reorganized hospital routines, ignoring completely the wishes of the patient in her zeal to save his life as "only she could." All of us tried, whenever possible, to become ill only when she was safely out of town.

My father had major abdominal surgery while she was away working in Hollywood. She constantly phoned everyone, waking my husband in the middle of the night, screaming that the hospital would not put her call through to "her own husband" at two a.m., so that she could make sure he was still alive! When Bill told her, for the hundredth time, that I was in attendance twenty-four hours a day, she calmed down a bit, hung up, and turned her energies to instructing her lovers and friends to send telegrams to "Poor Papi – who is suffering without me in that terrible American hospital in New York, with only Maria there to make sure that they don't kill him. While I am stuck here making a film to get the money to pay all the doctor bills!"

"Poor Papi" was recovering rapidly when the telegrams started arriving. I was with him the day he opened his daily stack, while muttering angrily: "More! They only send them because she tells them to! Does she think that I am really so stupid that I believe they care what happens to me? She tells everybody, 'Send poor Papi a cable!' and so they do it for her! Not me! Never me!" With every word, his voice grew hoarser. I watched him. I knew that inner rage that burned inside him at his own weakness, his dependency both emotionally and financially on the woman it had become his habit to love. This impotent fury had already damaged his kidneys, destroyed three-quarters of his stomach, and I wondered what part of his body he would sacrifice to it next!

"Papi, please! Stop! Why don't you try to have a life of your own? Try just once to get away? Do something *you* want to do that she has nothing to do with, over which she will have no control. Take Tami and just go!" I pleaded. At least, if my father decided to escape, it would get Tami away from the dubious psychiatrists reorganized for her by my mother.

It took him quite a while, but finally, with borrowed money from his only true friend, my father bought a little ramshackle house in San Fernando Valley, California. With two rows of meshed cages and a few dozen scrawny chickens, he proclaimed his independence by going into the egg business. He was "his own man" once more; he was happy, he had hope, and Tami blossomed. My mother was furious. Immediately on hearing who had made his independence possible, my father's friend became her mortal enemy. Then she launched her campaign to make sure that her husband would return to his rightful place of pliant "family retainer," the position he had filled so well for nearly thirty years. From then on, my father's acre plot of dirt and dust, the rickety rows of lopsided cages and clucking hens became "My Husband's Ranch," giving it the intonation one might use when referring to L.B.J.'s four-hundred-acre spread in Texas. Later, when she had finally maneuvered the takeover of my father's debt, it became "Papi's ranch – that I bought for him." But by that time, my father knew he was beaten, was working on his second massive coronary, and just didn't care anymore. He had lost for the last time, and he knew it.

In the spring of '51, she returned to New York into the waiting arms of her Cavalier and, within days, was madly, insanely in love with someone else. As her love for Gabin had consumed her, so now did her infatuation for Yul Brynner. For four years, their secret affair blazed, flickered, smoldered, simmered, then flamed anew – only to repeat its erratic, agonizing pattern all over again. They kept up this emotional upheaval, giving it the name of "love" until, finally, her possessive romanticism began to choke him, and he walked away from what had been an impossible situation from the beginning. He always remembered her with tenderness and joy. She came to hate him with as much passion as she had once adored him. Thirty-four years after their blazing affair, she sent me a newspaper clipping of Yul in a wheelchair, looking pitiable, returning from yet another unsuccessful cancer treatment. Across his haggard face, she had written in her big silver marker: "Goody – goody – he has cancer! Serves him right!"

But in 1951, she thought Yul a "god," was wildly jealous of his wife, although relieved that she was supposed to have "mental problems," and spent her days sitting by her phone hoping he would call. He did. Every moment he could capture the privacy needed to dial Dietrich's number. He was the toast of Broadway, the catalyst force in a most demanding musical, ever perfecting his brilliant performance of the king in *The King and I*, which was to be his lifelong triumph. He would call the moment he arrived in his dressing room, during the overture, intermission, the second the curtain came down; escaped from friends, admirers, and dignitaries who expected him to join them for their after-theater celebrations, to rush into the trembling arms of his divine goddess. My mother rented a hideaway on Park Avenue, furnished it in Siam silk and gold to complement her lover's Broadway persona, stocked her kitchen with Russian caviar, superb champagne, and five-inch filet mignons, had my husband install strip lights under the base of her king-size bed, and – Dietrich was in business.

It was my mother who insisted on all the fanatical secrecy. She, who had slept with married men all her life as nonchalantly as lighting her cigarettes, now became the nun who sinned behind cloister walls – all to "protect" her lover's reputation. Soon her "King" appeared for breakfast, stayed through lunch, rushed to play his matinee, and, still in his dark body makeup, returned to take his passion to bed between performances. She, who adored romance, but usually complained bitterly about having to include the necessary sex in order to "keep the man happy," now gloried in Yul's seemingly inexhaustible virility. On matinee days, after he had left for the evening performance, she would call me to come over to see "the bed." As this was usually around six o'clock in the evening, when I was busy putting my three-year-old and my baby to bed, my husband would volunteer to go over to her apartment and play the appreciative audience. She so loved to show off her disheveled bed, particularly proud of her once-white sheets now smeared with Yul Brynner's body paint that he had been "too aroused" to take the time to wash off. Bill found all this very funny. It was easier for him, he was not related to her, he didn't need to feel the shame that I did at this tasteless vulgarity.

She enjoyed being raunchy with my husband. She constantly sought opportunities to be ever so "naughty" when in his company. Whenever she greeted him in public, she executed her specialty – a type of standing body-press. Arms around neck, feet firmly planted, her pelvis would slide into its forward motion until it connected with the recipient's pelvic region, then glue itself into position while the rest of her body followed into line. It was something to watch! It was a famous "Dietrich" maneuver. Later, she even used it on my grown sons, those she preferred, of course. Their embarrassment she never noticed, she was too busy pressing.

Yul, who had been a respected TV director before becoming Broadway's idol, counseled my mother not to ignore television's potential nor the role that he believed I would play in its development. As my mother never had any cause to be professionally threatened by me, she had always been renowned for her supportive attitude toward her daughter's acting career. Now, between waiting for Yul to telephone, appear, and love her, she embraced her new role of "mother to budding TV star" with her customary dedication. She crept into studios during dress rehearsals, so broadly intent on not attracting attention that all action stopped to pay homage to the important movie star who had kindly descended from her Hollywood Olympian heights to grace a lowly television studio with her presence. Quite naturally, the young pioneers of this fledgling profession were awed by her and the industry she represented and completely charmed by her whispered comments: "No, no. Don't let me disturb you. I am only here to see my wonderful daughter, Maria. . . . I don't want to be in the way." Out of the darkness of the control booth, the famous voice would ask: "Does that light really have to be so low on her face? It makes her nose too long. If you lift it just a little . . ." They listened, flattered by her interest.

Of the director, intent on his three cameras, viewing his shots on different monitors, making hurried notes for changes, giving commands, sponsors hovering, the incredible pressure of live television bearing down on him, she would ask: "Do you really want her to wear her hair like that in this scene?" or "Have you noticed that her hat is throwing a shadow?"

She drove them crazy, but after all, she just wanted to help her daughter, and who could fault a mother for that, especially such a famous one? I spent most of my first year in television being embarrassed by the undeserved spotlight my mother's presence gave me, apologizing for her interference and trying to convince my employers that I did not expect to be handed instant stardom just because of my relationship to it.

She asked my husband to find her a secluded beach house on Long Island, then rented it for the summer. Announcing she had made it possible "for the children to have a nice summer," she let us live there during the week, then expected us to vacate the place by Friday afternoon, so that she could arrive and prepare the house for Yul's late arrival Saturday night after the show. Sometimes Yul even managed to escape during the week, then we made ourselves as scarce as possible, hoping the children wouldn't make noise and disturb the young lovers. My mother was happy that August, and without telling Yul, tried to get pregnant. When she told me of her "secret plan," I listened, but refrained from reminding her that at the age of four months short of fifty, this might be a little difficult to accomplish. One, I knew she would never believe that she was older than thirty, and two, I had learned long ago that it was much easier to follow her delusions than try to oppose them. I also had learned that nothing seemed impossible for Dietrich to achieve once she had made her mind up. This time, though, I hoped the laws of nature would defeat her. Yul's little boy, Rocky, had enough trouble to face in his uncertain future, and my children certainly did not need a sudden "uncle" younger than they. Her diary reads:

August 21, 1951
Here till 3 am
Two thirty – Tried again

August 22
Northport

August 23
Heaven
Leave at 3:15 for New York
He bringing Rocky
I behaved well, but suffer

August 28
Terrible night
Knew that all my courage would be going once he left.
2 Dexadrine
Misery. Nothing helps.
He came at 4:30 – Better

On and on it went! Misery when Yul missed an hour, a day, when his sick wife needed him, when he tried to save his marriage or his child, or his work and all those responsibilities that went with being a star took up his energy. Euphoria, when he managed to stick to the strict schedule her life had become dependent upon. As she had done since 1941, she consulted her astrologer, driving him crazy with constant questions whenever she was uncertain, then ignoring his advice completely when she felt back in control. As with all her previous lovers, Carroll Righter had been sent Yul's date of birth the moment after she had met him, but not the actual hour that he was born, nor the place, which Righter, being the skilled astrologer that he was, usually insisted upon. As Yul was then still claiming to be a Russian gypsy by birth, and as gypsy wagons are supposed to roll through moonlit nights going nowhere, his place of birth needed to remain as vague and mysterious as the intriguing background that he had manufactured for himself. His looks and manner so suited this romantic fairy tale, no one wanted to spoil it by the truth. Mystery, after all, doesn't go with being born a Swiss.

September 12
Called at 5:30
Said would call tomorrow at 12:30
Fight with DiMaggio/Stork Club
Saw *him* there

September 23
12:30 called
Pictures of DiMaggio and I. God, I hoped *he* might worry.
Call Righter. Seven o'clock called. Called 11:45

September 14
Lunch, he ordered lamb chops. Small talk, I finally told him I could not

worry anymore about what he thought or felt. He then said that he loved me. Left at four. I on cloud. Called at seven. Sent him love letter. Will come after show.

Yul's dresser, Don, became their loyal confidant and go-between. As neither could use their distinctive first names in messages, to escape detection Yul invented monikers for them: He, of the shaved head, became Curly, my mother he christened Crowd, in my opinion, the most wonderfully appropriate name my mother was ever given by anyone.

As her evenings were structured by the running time and acts of *The King and I*, she was free between the hours of eight-thirty and eleven, so continued to see her Cavalier for dinners. Often her diary states that she waited for a call at one, spoke to Yul at four, and, as he had no time between shows, she went to her Cavalier's home, then rushed to be back at her apartment for Yul's eight-fifteen call. Later, Yul worked out a calling schedule that even included those moments during the play when he was not on stage. When Gertrude Lawrence was doing her big number, "Getting to Know You," the King, offstage in all his bespangled splendor, was probably once again dialing Dietrich's number.

Between yearning and glorying in Yul's appearances and calls, she managed to fit in Michael Wilding as he passed through New York. She so hated to disappoint lovers of days gone by and considered it only natural to allow them to partake of what, after all, had once been wholly theirs. I tried once to question the basic ethics of such generosity. She replied:

"But they are so sweet when they ask, and then, they are so happy afterwards. So . . . you do it!" adding coyly, "Don't you?"

All year, her diary continues to record the hours when Yul came, called, stayed, canceled, didn't call, or was with his wife, whom Dietrich always referred to as Her or She.

September 15
Left at 6 AM. Heaven. Called at 6:30
The world stood still. Called at 12:00.
Came here for breakfast.
Happiness!!!
Called afternoon.
Don called at midnight – message:
    "Don't forget I love my Crowd."
To Hell with "Her."

September 25
No word all day.

Misery
Flowers from him at 6:00
Call at 6:30. All is well.

My mother poured her heart out to those who "knew," which meant
my home became her daily forum. She either appeared between Yul's
visits or phoned me constantly: He called; he didn't call; had I heard
anything? What did I think? I was his friend – I should know. Had his
wife really left him? Was he lying? Was he perhaps still sleeping with
his wife? Was I sure that he loved only her? What did Bill, as a man,
think? Et cetera, et cetera, et cetera. When I was busy with my children
or in rehearsals, she either badgered my husband at work or left repeated
messages on the switchboard of CBS for "Maria Riva to call her mother
immediately."

Bob Hope left to bring Christmas cheer to the fighting men in Korea.
My mother was so in love, I don't think she even knew there was a war
going on. Certainly Dietrich never volunteered to entertain "the boys"
in this one. But then, this time her "only love" was safe on Broadway.

We were never allowed to celebrate my mother's birthday. The world,
yes. The famous of that world naturally, but those she considered her
family, never! That was punishable by her deep-freeze method of
ostracizing the offender from her hemisphere. A banishment to be
wished, but as it never lasted forever, the reentry was made so unpleasant
it didn't warrant the primary mistake. No cards, no flowers, no gifts, no
cake, no party. This did not mean that one was allowed to forget the date
of her birthday. She would call and say:

"You know who called me . . ." Usually there followed a list of
several presidents, political leaders, famous writers, musicians, physicians, and a sprinkling of privileged actors and directors – then came
the flowers line:

". . . and you should see the flowers! The baskets are so huge they
won't go through the door! The roses are too tall for all the vases! No one
can move! The apartment is like a greenhouse! I can't breathe and I don't
know where to put all the cases of champagne!" She paused for breath.

This was our cue to complain "pitifully":

"But, Massy, you told us not to send you anything – you don't want
us to – you gave strict orders not to do anything for your birthday!" so
that my mother could reply:

"Of course I don't want *you* to do anything – but I just wanted you to
know how everyone else makes such a fuss for my birthday!"

The fifties were full of fascinating men—Yul Brynner
(ABOVE), the King; Edward R. Murrow (BELOW),
the Crusader—to name but two who loved and were
loved in return.

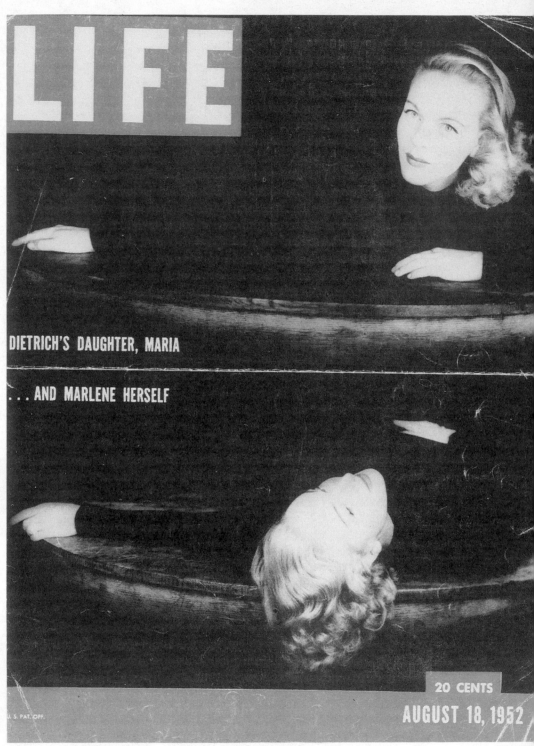

LIFE

DIETRICH'S DAUGHTER, MARIA

. . . AND MARLENE HERSELF

AUGUST 18, 1952

After only one year on live television, I made the cover of *Life*, with a "little" help from my famous parent.

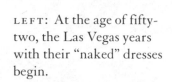

LEFT: At the age of fifty-two, the Las Vegas years with their "naked" dresses begin.

BELOW: Louis Armstrong, for the first time upstaged by a pair of gorgeous gams.

ABOVE: Each year she played Vegas we had to come up with new ideas for her big finale. This chorus line, à la Rockettes, caused a sensation. She used it later in her world tours.

BELOW: There was a reason her necklaces were placed so close to the neck—they hid the secret that was underneath.

It was a game we played for fifty years, until I heard from a trusted source that my mother had called, thanked an unknown fan for remembering her birthday, adding that his flowers and card had been especially welcome as "her daughter never remembered to send her anything." From then on, I cabled my mother or phoned her on the morning of her birthday, always beginning with the words: "I know it is against the rules, that you have forbidden it, but . . ." She still told everyone I had forgotten. But at least, now I knew she lied. My children were confused by all this game playing, and, when they were older, resented it terribly, as indeed they should. My husband simply refused to play. It did not endear him to her, but then, he had the strength not to care.

On December 27, 1951, Marlene Dietrich turned fifty. She had altered her birth year so often that very few people knew the truth, my mother least of all. She always had that amazing ability to believe unconditionally whatever lies she invented, so, as far as she was concerned, she was – maybe forty? And who was to say no? She looked no more than thirty and behaved, at least in her romantic life, like sixteen.

Noël sent champagne and an offering of Coward rhyme for the occasion:

> To celebrate your birthday most adorable Marlene
> I have been to an immense amount of trouble
> to get you this expensive little bottle of champagne.
> Please remember that my love's in every bubble.
> From Mr. Noël Coward with compliments to
>   Miss Dietrich and a smacking great kiss

She thought it extremely inferior. Not the champagne, that she drank, the rhyme she gave me to throw away. Yul gave her what she wanted. She wrote in her diary on that day:

> 12:00 – Evening
> Yes and Heaven!
> Wish my birthday was every day!!

As everyone had known, *Rancho Notorious* was a lackluster film. In the hopes of stirring up some interest, RKO announced it would present two of its stars, Dietrich and Mel Ferrer, "in person" the day the film opened in Chicago, in March of 1952. I never did know how anyone managed to get my mother to agree to do such a thing. Starlets were made to prance suddenly onto lit-up movie-house stages, to do their saccharine speeches into hastily placed microphones in front of ogling movie fans, but Dietrich?

I was scheduled to appear with Charlton Heston in a scene from *Jane Eyre* at a Westinghouse convention and promised to fly from there to Chicago in time to help my mother through the trauma this personal appearance was certain to be. I arrived on the 4th of March to utter bedlam. Once again, completely out of character, my mother had gone to Elizabeth Arden to find an evening dress to wear for the occasion. The style had to be exaggerated and flamboyant enough so that she could be seen down on the stage of that vast movie palace. Years later, she fully agreed with me that she must have been slightly deranged at the time to have gone to Arden in the first place, let alone choose a huge concoction of layers upon layers of ruffled, stiffened tulle in graded shades of hot pink! Dietrich, who had invented evening dresses with sleeves, now stood in this exaggerated lamp shade, the bodice of which left her shoulders and arms bare, her breasts flattened shapeless under pleated net. She looked like a huge boiled lobster in drag. As always in Dietrich's life, this ridiculous personal appearance, the awful dress, her desperate embarrassment and fury at finding herself in such a situation, having to show herself in the flesh for nothing more important than to promote a very bad film, caused her to come up with a solution that later contributed to her glorious success in Las Vegas. Still in her fit of madness, she had also agreed to warble the atrocious song from the film, plus a second one for good measure. I was stunned and decided her agent must have caught her between "heaven" visits from Yul, otherwise she would never have agreed to any of it.

She had designed a revealing dance-hall costume for the film that showed off her legs to perfection. After seeing herself in the lobster tulle, she knew that she had to get out of it as fast as possible, show the people how she really could look, and so, her later to be world-famous "fast change" was born. Fast changes, most under a minute, were a standard necessity in live television, and one of my specialties. I used to get jobs because I could do a sixty-second change from elegant evening dress to fleeing downtrodden refugee. It was "Iron Curtain" time, and I was escaping from the KGB constantly. I now taught my mother the trick and timing of underdressing. When she walked out onto the vast stage, under the voluminous skirts of her dress she already wore the black tights and high-laced shoes of her film costume. As she exited into the wings after her introduction, I ripped the dress off, she stepped into her foundation on which the entire costume, sleeves, swag, bustle, bolero, and jewels were sewn, zipped her up, and back onto the stage the "real" Dietrich stepped – from fat lobster to luscious dance-hall queen in sixty seconds! The crowd went wild, just like her GIs during the war. She had them, knew it, and basked in the feeling of power such moments always achieve. We did this magic act for the twelve, three, six, and nine-forty-five shows, and each time, it got the identical reaction of stunned surprise, followed by adulation that we had planned for.

When she returned to New York, she signed for her own weekly radio show, a concoction of espionage and mystery called *Café Istanbul*. Between agonizing, rhapsodizing over Yul, she rewrote radio scripts, recorded songs with Mitch Miller, kept up her close relationship with the Cavalier, took her favorite midnight planes that in 1952 still offered berths to Los Angeles, spent a secret weekend with her King in Palm Springs, and when he returned to New York, remained in Hollywood to guest-star on Bing Crosby's radio show, had dinners with Tyrone Power, indulged in a romantic interlude with a very handsome star who accompanied her openly to the homes of the James Masons and Van Johnsons. Her diary states that it was all "fun." A very unusual word for my mother to use in relationship to herself. I congratulate "Kirk" for accomplishing it.

Still in the "happy glow" of her new California romance, she returned to New York:

May 12, 1952
Arrived late 1 PM
Y here
Till 6 (He does love me)
Called at 6:45
Will come at 12:00
Am astonished but don't get too hopeful so not to be disappointed if it means nothing.
Y at 12:00 Midnight till 12:45
It means nothing

May 15
Decided I love him too much. Such longing is ridiculous after a whole year.
Lunch

May 17
Breakfast

Sunday May 18
All alone.
Remarque – dinner

May 20
All for nothing.
Make up my mind there is no love no nothing.

May 21
Y here breakfast tell him of decision.
Telephoned – All is well. Wilder dinner Stork.
Yul here

My mother always had the ability to create her own amnesia. She chose those realities that she feared or considered expendable and simply erased them from her conscious world. As she had done throughout her thirties, she recorded the first day of her menses in her diary with an X, not to be confused with the sign of the double X, which stood for sexual intercourse. My mother was in her fifty-first year, when she wrote on May 22, 1952:

X – Big Jump – Almost two months!

Stricken, she came over to my house and showed me her panties.

"You see? All this time you and I thought I was pregnant and now we know – nothing! But why did it stop for so long? Do you have that too? That it stops for no reason?"

I took her to my gynecologist, who put her on hormones and tried to explain what menopause was, but gave up when she turned to him and said:

"But, if you say these hormones are so great, why don't you give them to my daughter? I am sure she needs these shots too!"

One morning, she rushed into the house, the picture of outrage tinged with fury: "He says he cannot live without me and then – goes and fucks Taylor!"

For a second, the "he" confused me: "Who?"

"Michael Wilding! He married that English tart, Elizabeth Taylor!! Why? Can you tell me why? It must be those huge breasts of hers – he likes them to dangle in his face." And, a few months later:

"She got pregnant rather fast, don't you think?" and that finished poor Michael – that is, until they were divorced, when he returned, was chastised for his "insanity," and forgiven.

CBS Television had signed me to an exclusive contract and, as my face had become known to American audiences, Life magazine decided to do a "famous mother and daughter" layout. My mother and I had posed together once before for Vogue, but then I had only been "the daughter." Now I had a name of my own, an identity, so it meant something special to me. We reported to Milton Greene's studio in June; my mother always stated that it was her idea to have me pose looking down at her in the famous photograph, but it was Milton Greene who decided to print the composite photograph in reverse, so that I was the image and Dietrich the reflection. It was his version the editors decided was important enough to use for a *Life* cover. The article inside was mostly about Dietrich, but lo and behold, when it spoke of Maria Riva and there was no "daughter of" appendage, I knew I had made it – I finally had a name of my very own. My mother took to carrying *Life* around to people's homes along with her latest records.

"Isn't it beautiful? Of course, I told them – No, No. ME on the bottom – Maria must be on top. She is 'the star' and my hair looks better spread down. Of course, the article is on me, but they were nice. Good people at *Life*, they wrote about her big success too."

In August Yul was scheduled to go on a two-week vacation, after Gertrude Lawrence was due back after her two-week hiatus. Although my mother always maintained that "Gertie" was one of her best friends, never once do her diaries of this time refer to Miss Lawrence's failing health.

We packed training pants, spades, sandals, and teddy bears, bundled summer necessities into our Ford, and we were off to our little rented house on Long Island. My mother stayed, waiting for the phone to ring.

August 2nd
Breakfast 10:00 here till 1:00
Pretty vague laboring conversation about show. But then, why does he come here? Cannot be for that cup of coffee? Never saw anyone so preoccupied with himself. Flowers came while he was here and it suddenly occurred to me that he never sends me flowers or brings me something or makes the slightest effort to return all the things I do for him which should embarrass a man. Maybe he thinks he repays with the afternoons. What a horrible thought.

He is coming tonight. I asked him what he was doing tonight and he said – I could come to see you. I said you do love me if I have to ask.

He probably thought he was here yesterday and that takes care of his obligations. What horrible thoughts I have today.

I write all this to explain to myself why I swing back and forth and don't keep the resolutions I make – not to doubt his love.

Sunday, August 3rd
Sunday all alone. Time to think about my Sucker-ism.

August 6th
It is terrible now, he has not called or come. How inconsiderate, if he could not get out of appointments, he could call to say so.

This weekend with the maid on duty he could have even spent a good part of Sunday with me, including the evening. I'm his little whore, let's face it!

On the 6th of September, Gertrude Lawrence died of liver cancer, having suffered the agonies of this disease while continuing to perform in *The King and I*. She gets top billing in my mother's diary:

Sept. 7, 1952
Gertie died
Here for breakfast.

And, on the 9th, the day of her funeral:

Funeral, with Maria
Here 4–7:00
Y drunk
Ferrer dinner

Sometime during this period, my mother's Cavalier divorced his wife in the belief that she would marry him and attain the worry-free male-cosseted life my mother always claimed she so desired. During the years of emotional upheaval of her passionate affair with Yul Brynner, those years when she suffered, mooned over her "gypsy king," still managing to "keep happy," as she put it, Michael Wilding, Michael Rennie, Harry Cohn, Edward R. Murrow, Piaf, Adlai Stevenson, Sam Spiegel, Frank Sinatra, Harold Arlen, Kirk Douglas, and an impressive array of those ladies and gentlemen who must remain nameless for various reasons, yet never relinquishing her passion for Gabin, she often referred to the Cavalier's proposal of marriage with:

"Thank God I didn't marry him. Can you see me, the grande dame in Palm Beach, with nothing better to do than play canasta all day?"

JUDY BROUGHT BACK "two shows a day" at the Palace. We went to her opening *en famille* – well, not quite: My father was plucking chickens in California, so one of my mother's "pals" was her escort. That sweet voice, with its inner heartbreak, soared, filled that famous shrine of vaudeville, then left a bitter taste in my heart as it faded. The audience, on the edge of hysteria, screamed their adulation. My mother – who pretended to admire Garland but secretly couldn't stand her and never was able to understand her magical talent as it stemmed from inner creativity, not contrived, manufactured art, as it did in Dietrich's case – clapped as enthusiastically as the rest of the audience. Judy had become a homosexual fetish, and my mother, being another, knew she was being watched.

We went backstage to congratulate the star of the evening. I took her in my arms, it seemed the natural thing to do. I held her carefully, like those blown-glass souvenirs one buys at fairs – she seemed highly breakable. Our reunion was soundless and suspended. As the hordes of gushing admirers pushed into the dressing room, we let go of each other and the moment.

That evening, my mother insisted on holding court at the El Morocco, in her favorite, its exclusive inner sanctum, the Champagne Room. My mind was on other things than Dietrich being Dietrich, so much so that I did not hear Piaf say to my husband, in French, which he spoke very well:

"Well – how does it feel, living off your mother-in-law's money?" It shocked him so, he asked her to repeat it, to make sure she had actually said such a thing. She did. That's when I heard it, at the same moment as my mother.

"Oh, Mon Amour!" – both Gabin and Piaf rated "amour" – "but he makes Maria so happy!"

As other tables were as usual watching the goddess and her entourage, I rose without saying a word. My husband looked at my eyes and stood. We made our polite good nights and left before I could explode. The absolute coarseness of that French guttersnipe did not surprise me; unfortunately, neither did the basic nastiness of my mother. Neither did their love affair – the Lady and the Tramp.

My mother was very proud of being Piaf's "best friend," as she publicly put it. When Piaf married, it was Marlene who had her dress made for her, a copy of her own chiffon Dior, dressed her, hung a delicate Cartier cross around her little throat, and like the cavalier lover she was to most of her women, sent her into the arms of another. Later, when Piaf's pugilist lover was killed, it was Dietrich who calmed her grief-stricken Sparrow with comforting "amour."

Remarque announced he was thinking of getting married to – of all people – Paulette Goddard! My mother was appalled; I have to admit, so was I.

"What insanity! He is not really going to marry that Goddard woman, is he? Doesn't he know she only wants him for his paintings? I am going to talk to him," and she did. Boni asked my mother to marry him; if she refused, he was marrying Paulette, which he finally did. My mother's only comment:

"Now, just watch. Now – she'll try to kill him. He was a great writer, but about women – always so stupid!" and sweet Boni was no more.

When Remarque died in 1970, Dietrich declared, "Well! It took that terrible woman a few years, but she finally did it. Now she's as rich as Croesus and can rot in her luxury," and went into her room to mourn him as the rightful widow she believed herself to be.

Hemingway's masterpiece *The Old Man and the Sea* was published and my mother, who had fallen madly in love with it when he had sent her the first galleys, went about like a proud wife who had always known her husband had even deeper greatness than was realized by those not privileged to know the real inner man.

Thanks to Yul, I became involved in raising funds for the wonderful work done by the United Cerebral Palsy Organization. In the spring of 1953, when John Ringling North gave this charity the opening of the circus at Madison Square Garden, stars volunteered their services in everything from sweeping up after the elephants to flying through the air. Without jockeying for position, everyone joined in the common goal of raising money for the children afflicted with this devastating brain injury. My mother did not involve herself in charitable causes. I never knew her to make a donation to any charitable organization, and yet she was renowned for her limitless charity – another Dietrich myth that no one ever challenged. It is true that she was extremely generous, but only if it benefited her in some way: fur coats to maids, who then felt too overcome with gratitude to quit, no matter how she treated them; doctor and hospital bills paid for the children, wives, and husbands in her employ, acquaintances, and friends, who, then consumed by gratitude, could be counted on to keep their mouths shut about the intimate secret things they knew about their benefactress and be on call, day or night, to give service. Dietrich was ready to help anyone.

She used her money, her energies, her time, her fame, but never for the benefit of an organized charity. My mother demanded that her generosity be known by the individual recipients – in that way she could control them through their gratitude. All my life I heard my mother complain about those she helped, when they did not repay her generosity in ways she expected. It went something like this:

"Sweetheart. Can you believe it? The maid, just now, she can't come on Sunday! Because 'it's Easter' and she has to be with her child! Remember two years ago, when she told me all about that child of hers? How he limped and how I called all the doctors – remember when they said he had to have a special shoe? How I ordered it for her right away and how she thanked me, kissed my hands and cried? And, after all that, *now* she can't come because of some stupid holiday with that child! Ridiculous! You see how people are? You do everything for them and then they still do what *they* want!"

This extended all the way to ethnic levels:

"I gave up my country – my language – for them, and now, what do I get? The stores are closed for Yom Kippur!"

This time, knowing that cerebral palsy was Yul's favorite cause, I hoped to be able to persuade my mother to participate, particularly if she was offered a role in the circus that was unique, one that she would not have to share with any other celebrity. When we offered her the position of ringmaster, she immediately agreed and began designing her costume. Long before the era of "hot pants," Dietrich wore tiny velvet shorts above black silk tights, high-heeled boots, white tie, scarlet tailcoat, shiny top hat, and, cracking her whip, was a sensation. *Vogue* ran a full-page color photograph of her in her circus splendor, every newspaper proclaimed her the "star of the evening," and United Cerebral Palsy gained a lot of additional publicity. Ask Miss Dietrich what cerebral palsy is, and she would reply: "Oh, that's when I designed that beautiful ringmaster costume."

Eisenhower ran for president, and my mother's rage knew no bounds. When he was elected, she threatened to return her passport, but not her Medal of Freedom.

"That coward! *He* is going to lead a nation? The whole country has gone insane!" and went to call Hemingway.

I signed to star in what was to be the first TV adventure series in color to be filmed overseas. My husband would be the production designer, and our children would accompany us. My mother was furious. But, as Israel was to be our base of operations, she couldn't publicly show her disapproval; privately was another matter:

"All the Jews that didn't make it in Hollywood are there. What do you think you are going to be able to get done there? An American television show in the desert? It will be worse than what we went through in *The Garden of Allah!* And why must you schlep the children with you? They can stay here with me . . . and who will do your hair?"

Yul thought it a wonderful adventure and wished us well. So, on the 24th of May, 1953, we stepped into Pan Am's trusty Clipper and left for Gander, our first refueling stop on the long journey to Tel Aviv. My mother continued to fly to California for weekend meetings in Palm

Springs with "him." As I was away, I am not sure who this "him" is that her diary refers to. Knowing her, it could be anybody. Between lovers, she visited my father.

As our daily language was now English, even her letters to me acquired an American rhythm.

Angel,

I saw Papi. He is working terribly hard, much too hard I thought after the operation but he is stubborn, you know. Tami is nuttier than ever and I was crying into my beer driving home from the ranch because it still affects me to see the crazy be stronger than the sane. He had promised her that she did not have to cook in the beginning and they went with me where they always go for dinner, a lousy little joint with a loud jukebox. The food was so greasy that I had some cottage cheese instead and did not touch it. He ate all this terribly heavy greasy stuff and I asked him (I ask, you know, well trained as I am) if I should not cook Pot-au-Feu and bring it out, they could heat it for three days at least and he would have something good to eat and no work. I was told yes, I cooked a whole day, vegetables ready to eat, etc. When I arrived, Tami yelled she could not keep it all, she would still have to wash dishes even if she would only heat it, and I calmly packed everything together, washed the dishes after dinner and left too sad to say a gay good-bye. I never went out after that because I don't want to cause any trouble for him.

I could see my mother arriving at that little house, her limousine laden with enough expensive groceries to feed a family of twelve for a month. The chauffeur lugging the hotel-size kettles containing her famous pot-au-feu into Tami's tiny kitchen, throwing out whatever was in her refrigerator in order to make room for all the things the wife had brought, while Tami stood helplessly by. In one grandiose gesture that others would once again interpret as Dietrich's "wonderfully selfless generosity," she had invaded another woman's home, claiming her domain, belittling her ability to care for the man she loved, made her feel useless, poor, uncaring, and ungrateful, and to top it all off, my mother's pot-au-feu was so good, one even felt like a lousy cook. I knew exactly how Tami felt – I had been there myself. At least, I had a husband who made me feel wanted, even disliked my mother's cooking, whereas my father had probably given Tami hell for making trouble again and causing wonderful, generous Mutti to feel that her "great effort" was not appreciated.

We set up our house in the Sharon Hotel, between Tel Aviv and Haifa. What a country! Wild and serene, young and ancient, a land of contrasts – its life force guided in anticipation of a great dream yet to be fully realized. All pioneer countries have this sense of grabbing the future. Here, antiquity added its own dimension. Timelessness and newly born, the fire-brand cactus children and the sage survivors.

We ate kosher, learned the rules, customs of the ages. We didn't have to – we chose to. We wanted our young children to respect all religions by becoming involved, understanding their laws before making up their minds which one suited them, gave them the haven in which best to grow their own spirit.

The gentle young woman placed a dish before Michael, who, in his five-year-old treble, asked, intrigued:

"Sarah, why is your telephone number written on your arm?"

She looked at me, hesitant to give such a young child an explanation. I loved her for not being shocked or angry at his innocence.

"Tell him, Sarah. It is important for him to know."

And she did – simply, without rancor or personal anguish.

We looked for pebbles on the beach that day, a very serious, highly dedicated activity.

"Mommy, look – look! A pretty one, all shiny white with silver spots! I'm going to give it to Sarah, for her poor hurted arm!"

In New York, my mother wrote to me:

> I am writing an article for *Ladies' Home Journal* on: "How to Be Loved," for which I get 20,000. Yes! You read right, $20,000. Remarque was furious at the price. It did not help me that I pointed out that crap is better paid than good stuff, he was burning up.
>
> . . . I can see the men who claim to have been so miserable with me say: Why didn't she act like that with me? I give the women sugar too so that everybody is happy.
>
> Then I have signed to write a book on beauty for Doubleday. There Remarque was not so furious because it is about beauty. About love he felt the competition. Only I can write about love and the workings of it.

She worked on "How to Be Loved" during the hours she waited for Yul to call or appear at her door. She wrote of those emotions she wanted him to be aware of, then showed him her work in the hope that he would recognize all the feelings she was trying to communicate to him. Actually, most of the article was written to enchant Yul, and when he offered to help her, they spent some of the best times they had together collaborating.

For many sad reasons, our series collapsed without a single segment having been filmed. I cabled my mother that we were returning to New York.

August 13, '53

My love,

This is going to be one hell of a fast letter so that it gets there in case you leave.

The Las Vegas thing: I signed with the Sahara the biggest joint there. Not the Sands, the chicest joint there, where I stayed and went on with Tallu. She introduced me and I went out to see if I could get them to whistle. The Sands is a plush real night club that everybody prefers because it is small. They whistled all right, I sang three songs and then finished with Tallu with "May the Good Lord Bless and Keep You." But it proved to me that I was not nervous even without rehearsal, naturally discounting that it is easier to give a benefit always than performing for money.

The Sahara offered me $30,000 a week for 3 weeks against the highest price ever paid, $20,000 which Tallu got at the Sands. Also for the next year again. So I took it. December fifteenth I open, till Jan. 5 '54. Isn't it funny that I should have a year with big earnings and all outside of films? I am trying to contact Orson because I want to do the mind-reading act which I have completely forgotten. Danny Thomas is frantically searching his material to remember what he did with me. I thought after my songs it would be a good thing to get the audience to participate in the mind-reading. Then the chorus is going to do a Circus number with a clown act from Paris in it and Mitch is having a Circus song written. I will come into the dancers with a whip and finish my act with the Circus number so I can wear the costume from the Madison Square Garden evening. I only have to do 25 minutes, they beg you to be short so that the people go out and gamble. I could not say no to this fabulous offer. I am not scared either. I was so at home on the stage there that I am sure even when it is for real I won't shake like Van Johnson and Tallu did.

So I won't be home for Christmas.

The wandering Riva family headed home. Each of us a little wiser in a lot of things.

My mother's diary makes no mention of the Las Vegas deal. She recorded only those vital moments that were really important to her:

September 30
Here for lunch.

October 1
Here for same.

October 2
Here for same 12
After show to stay

October 3
Left 12:45

The next day, she records that Yul came back for "the same," which
I do not necessarily think was lunch, and that she went out with Otto
Preminger to the Stork Club that evening, and that Yul called her there
at two a.m., came over to the apartment, and stayed the night. How that
man managed to be the pivotal force of that exhausting musical astounds
me still.

She told me that Yul was against her idea of doing Orson's mind-
reading act, that he thought it would cheapen her to involve the audience
in such a way. I agreed and counseled her to either play against the Vegas
image or top it, but never to join it. She turned to Yul, saying:

"What is it that you two always agree? Just like that so important
charity thing of yours. But, you know, Maria is right, Dietrich must
be a *sensation* and that we can only do with what I wear."

She left for Hollywood to begin her first meetings with Jean Louis
at Columbia Pictures. She knew that only a Wardrobe Department of
a major studio was equipped to execute a costume worthy of Marlene
Dietrich's first appearance on a Vegas stage. Hollywood had cornered
the market in skilled beaders way back in the twenties, when Theda Bara
slithered across silent screens. Her first choice had been the wonderful
Irene, but as that was impossible, she had decided on Jean Louis, whose
work she admired. As he was Columbia Pictures' top designer, my
mother had to get permission from his boss to use him and the Studio's
workshop. It was sheer chance that at this time Harry Cohn, one of the
most feared and disliked of the movie moguls, was interested in hiring her
to star in the film version of *Pal Joey* that he was just beginning to develop,
or she might never have been allowed to make her famous dresses on
his lot. Years later, when Harry Cohn finally banned Dietrich from the
Columbia lot for disrupting the Studio's entire Wardrobe Department,
she loved to tell her many stories about him. How she had first approached
him in 1953, begging to be allowed to make her costumes and how he had
agreed only after demanding her sexual favors: "Right there, in his office,
he wanted it! In the daytime! In return for the services of his seamstresses!"
As Harry Cohn was despised by nearly everyone and a renowned lech, she
could get as raunchy as she wanted when telling her stories about him.
Yet her diaries make no reference to his demands, nor to her "shocked"

refusal. They do say that they discussed *Pal Joey* and that she dated him frequently over the next two years, until he dared to throw her off the lot. At which time, she told me that she asked Yul to get his gangster friends to intercede for her, or, if that didn't work, to beat him up in a dark alley. Dietrich loved this imagery of planned mayhem to one she considered her enemy. All who wrote books on her were wished this bloodied fate in shadowed alleys. I am extremely careful whenever I have to pass one!

Who finally did persuade Harry Cohn to change his mind and reopen the Columbia Studio facilities to Dietrich has always been an intriguing mystery. One version has Frank Costello the avenging angel, another had the Mafia threatening to set fire to the Studio, another that Rita Hayworth had been sent by Dietrich's supporters to Harry Cohn's office with orders to "soften him up"! Another that Hedda Hopper, with all the power of her position as the queen of the Hollywood gossip columnists, was willing and ready to divulge "all" she knew . . . if Harry insisted on being so mean to "Marlene."

During this time of upheaval, my mother notes in her diary:

Cohn here Talked left at 2:00 am

and shortly after:

Resumed fittings Columbia.

Dietrich didn't need gangsters to do her dirty work. But she so loved the idea of the underworld going to bat for her that she perpetuated many scenarios that showed her as being unjustly treated, only to be saved by "Dorothy di Frasso's boyfriend Bugsy Siegel's friends" and embellished such stories with her own inventiveness whenever she chose.

The basic design of that gold sequined dress that had served her so well during her "army days," that had called forth those wolf whistles from adoring GIs, was now pressed back into service. This time, the object was to entrance a civilian audience who had paid a huge fee for the privilege.

First, she and Jean Louis took Birannccini's "souffle," dyed it the color of Dietrich's skin, and constructed her foundation. Next, they covered her from neck to toe in the same diaphanous material, molding it to the foundation that formed her body. Only then could the work of "gilding the lily" begin.

My mother's stage career boasted many such works of art. Each dress cost thousands of dollars and, more important, thousands of hours of work. Hundreds of people labored to achieve their perfection. Each bead was placed by hand into its strategic position to form the intricate patterns, then sewn individually into place, only to be removed with trembling hands from the fragile material, to be repositioned for what was often the fiftieth time. Thousands upon thousands of beads were treated with this fanatic perfectionism, until Dietrich saw in her reflected image what she wanted the audience to see – the sublime woman, the perfect body, technically completely clothed, appearing naked to the human eye, yet remaining the untainted goddess.

Each year that Dietrich played Vegas, she strove for a new effect, hoping to recapture that stunned moment when the audience first saw her and gasped. And each time she achieved it. Over the years, she shimmered in gold, white, black bugle beads, sequins, mirrors, rhinestones, crystal tassels, balls, and fringes, trailed rivers of feathers behind her, enfolded herself in giant fox shawls, installed wind machines to blow masses of chiffon away from her body – so that she appeared as exposed, as magnificent as her favorite sculpture, the *Winged Victory of Samothrace*.

The wind effect she had used in *The Garden of Allah*, the chiffon shawl bordered in yards of fox had enveloped her in *Desire*, even the collar and sleeves of her justly famous swan coat were amazingly familiar in design to that swansdown jacket she wore in the boudoir scene in *The Scarlet Empress*. I am sure that my mother never realized that she was reinventing perfection from the past. Besides, it was all so perfect even the second time around, there was no reason to draw her attention to it.

By the time she designed her two masterpieces, her iridescent bugle-bead dress that we christened "the eel," because she looked like one swimming through clear water when she moved in it, and her swansdown coat, with its eight-foot circular train for which two thousand swans were said to have given the down off their breasts – willingly – she had outgrown Las Vegas, was performing her concerts in legitimate theaters.

In 1954, her second year in Las Vegas, when she achieved a one-minute change from her elaborate dress into her tails, it was not only to bask in the appreciation of such a metamorphosis, it also afforded her the opportunity to sing those songs whose lyrics she felt demanded a man's attitude. Though most songs written for men can be sung by substituting *she* for *he*, my mother was convinced that only male lyrics were truly worth singing. She believed that as men had their priorities right, only they could sing about love and its disenchantment with the proper authority. Women, being so unpredictable, were prone to emotional exaggeration and, therefore, could get boring singing about their loves. Dietrich, the woman who sat by the telephone all day mooning over her married lover while pining for her Frenchman, actually believed herself exempt from her critical judgment of all women.

I began choosing her material, structuring the emotional progression of her performances, giving her a dramatic format that she could handle and feel comfortable with. The opening segment of her show was easy, "glamour and sex," both visually and vocally, combined with her Dietrich standards from her films and records: "See What the Boys in the Back Room Will Have," "Johnny," "Laziest Gal in Town," and all the others. The applause would carry her to the wings. She would exit to shed her extravagant coat, in later years using this moment to also wash down her painkillers with champagne or scotch, and reappear, uncovered – divine fragility – to perform those songs that had a tragic impact, the Weltschmerz Dietrich knew how to communicate so very well. This was the hardest category for her to perform, but when she managed to sustain its dramatic impact without allowing herself to get maudlin with self-pity, she could be truly outstanding. "Go Away from My Window," "When the World Was Young," "Lili Marlene," and of course, "Where Have All the Flowers Gone?" She fought me often on my choices, especially with "Flowers." She absolutely refused to sing it, saying:

"All that toodle, toodle, toodle about where flowers have gone – it never ends! It's only good when the girls pick them!" When I explained to her that she should sing it with condemnation, that she should bring to it a hatred of war, she mumbled that, again, I was "asking a lot of her 'feeble' acting talent," but as I had been right about the other songs, she was willing to give "Flowers" a try. Occasionally, she found and fell in love with some awful songs, insisted on singing them – no matter what I said. As there were always more than enough idolizing fans in the audience who could be counted on to scream "bravo" if she did nothing but stand before them, she used their enthusiasm as proof positive that, despite my opinion, such songs as "Boomerang Baby" were after all just "perfect."

Once she was in her tails, I gave her material that she could relax with, could enjoy. She had fun with "Whoopee," indulged her favorite fantasy of the lonely lover in "One for My Baby," and explained love as she perceived it with "I've Grown Accustomed to Her Face" – Dietrich could always sing real love to a woman better than to a man. Sentimental love, *that* she did better as a woman. But these polished performances evolved over the years, when she performed her one-woman shows on concert stages and not in nightclubs.

Her first opening in Las Vegas in December of 1953 was a triumph, the "naked dress" – a sensation. Her diary is blank for the rest of that year. She was riding a new wave of success – no time, nor necessity, to record it.

Dietrich loved Las Vegas. She basked in the nightly adoration of her audiences and was proud that the elite group of Vegas entertainers accepted her as one of their own. Gone were the hours of waiting by the phone for Yul's calls, she had a job to do. As always, her entire energies were now marshaled toward her work. Only when her duty was done, her show over, did she allow herself to "play." During the years that she appeared there, Vegas was the entertainment capital of the world. In one night, one could see Dietrich's first show, run next door, catch Peggy Lee's, dash down the main drag to Tony Bennett's second show, Betty Hutton, Jimmy Durante, Lena Horne, Nat King Cole, Sophie Tucker, Louis Armstrong, Luis Prima, Noël Coward, Frankie Laine, Frank Sinatra, Rosemary Clooney, etc., etc. The celebrities at ringside often outshone the stars on the stage! My mother, who never wanted to be a part of the Hollywood community, who refused to fraternize with her fellow contract stars at Paramount, now experienced and welcomed, for the first time in her life, the warm feeling of belonging to this exclusive family of her peers. From all over the world, people flew into Vegas to catch Dietrich's act at the Sahara.

The night Harold Arlen came to see my mother's show, he fell madly in love with her and remained so till the day he died. In her nightly telephone calls to me, she described her first reaction on meeting this famous composer.

"I just stood there, in awe, in front of him. But you know he looks white! How can the man who wrote 'Stormy Weather' be white? He also wrote that Bluebird thing that Judy Garland insists on singing with all her blubbering, but – you know his hair is very kinky! I am going to ask Nat King Cole if Harold Arlen is black or white. He is also very ugly . . . but sweet." Arlen became my mother's first Vegas lover, and later, her ever devoted victim.

Always self-conscious of her lack of vocal range, she heard that a thing called cortisone was supposed to open the vocal cords and began swallowing this drug as though it were candy. This was long before cortisone was suspected to trigger certain forms of cancer. But even if she had known about these dangerous side effects, my mother would have continued taking it. She always believed that she was immune to all afflictions that mere humans are heir to.

Before the end of her Vegas engagement, Noël Coward called to tell her that when a Major Neville Willing announced himself, not to ignore his presence but to receive him, for he had had a most wonderful idea and could be trusted.

The major, a dapper little man, as elegant and spiffy as the nightclub he represented, offered to spread London at Dietrich's feet. A four-week engagement at the famous Café de Paris, throwing in the Oliver Messel suite at the Dorchester Hotel, and all the Rolls-Royces, complete with liveried chauffeurs, that she might desire. My mother, unimpressed, wondered why Noël had wasted her time. Then the major played his inspired trump card: He suggested that each night England's leading male actors would introduce the divine "Marlenaaa," that they might even be persuaded to write their own euphoric introductions of her. That did it! She accepted, but only after making quite sure that when the major said "leading actors," he had meant such luminaries as Laurence Olivier, Ralph Richardson, Michael Redgrave, Alec Guinness, Paul Scofield, and anyone else brilliant enough to warrant calling upon, reminding him that Noël had assured her that he was supposed to be "trustworthy."

My mother closed in Vegas, flew to Hollywood to repair and rebead the dresses she would need for London, then returned to New York.

We had gone to visit someone, maybe it was still Remarque at the Sherry Netherland, and as my mother had a fitting, we decided to walk the few blocks down Fifth Avenue to her tailor. Dietrich never strolled or window-shopped. Like most visibly famous people, she moved through a crowd rapidly, intent on reaching her destination before being recognized. Suddenly, her gloved fingers gripped my arm, and she jerked me into Tiffany. As my mother, besides never making such erratic gestures, loathed what she called "the most boring jewelry store in the world," I knew that something must be very wrong. Urgently, she whispered to me in German:

"My legs. I have pain in my legs. Pretend you want something, then we can lean on the counter as though we are looking," and pushed me against the glass showcase. One of those cool, polished Tiffany salesladies, her inner excitement veiled as she recognized her famous customer, brought forth her diamond wares for Dietrich's inspection. Taking her time, my mother examined each piece, murmuring such phrases as:

"Not bad stones, but the setting – really! Do men really buy this sort of thing for their women?" As she twisted a magnificent diamond solitaire, "Haven't you anything purer? Only the quality of a stone can excuse the vulgarity of such a size." Finally, my mother signaled me that the pain had subsided and we exited back onto Fifth Avenue, leaving a very disappointed Tiffany lady behind us. I hailed a taxi to take us to Knize, where my mother stood for the next two hours, ramrod still, while tailors worked on perfecting her tails. On the way back to her apartment and Yul's hoped-for call, I suggested that we pursue the cause of our morning's emergency by going to a doctor for a thorough check-up.

"No! Most doctors don't know what they are doing and the really great ones, you can't go to until you know what you have – because they are all 'specialists.' You see, my legs are fine now. You saw how I stood all that time at the fitting. But that was funny today . . . I mean 'ha-ha' funny, at Tiffany's. I wanted to tell that woman the story of Paulette Goddard on the train . . . remember? I told Boni but he wouldn't listen."

It was one of Dietrich's favorites, and as with all of her routines, needed to be heard in her unique cadence to do it justice.

"It was one of those terrible trips on the train, on the way to Hollywood, before we took airplanes. Paulette Goddard was on the train – I think it was when she was still married to Chaplin, or maybe after. She came to my drawing room and we talked. Now, you know me, I must have been *very* lonely to want to talk to Paulette Goddard! I think it was something that Papi had done or Chevalier or Jaray, or maybe it was later with Aherne or Jean. I can't remember, but it was someone, and I told her how he had treated me badly and she stood up, left, then came back schlepping a large jewelry case – a trunk! Like those that jewelers use when they come to your hotel to show you their whole store – They are made of ugly Moroccan leather and have drawers? Well, Goddard had one of those in *alligator*, and it was full! Nothing but diamonds! Like rocks! And she says to me, very serious, like a professor: 'Marlene, you have to get diamonds. Colored stones are worth nothing. Only pure white stones have lasting value. A man wants you? It's easy! You say no, right away. The next day, he sends you long-stemmed roses, you send them back. The next day, when his orchids arrive, you send them back. His little gifts, expensive perfume, handbags from Hermès, mink coats – things like that, you send everything back. Rubies and diamond clips – back, even emerald and diamond pins. When the first diamond bracelet arrives, it's usually small, so you send *it* back, but you call him and say thank you – sweetly. The next day, when the larger diamond bracelet arrives, you send that back, but now, you let him take you out to lunch – nothing else! The first diamond *ring* never is big – give it back, but say yes to dinner . . . go dancing. The only thing you have to always remember: *Never, ever* sleep with a man until he gives you a pure white stone of at least ten carats!'"

My mother always intoned this credo in a stage whisper, full of breathless admiration, then paused, adding:

"It's true! She really said all that to me. It must work! She has all those enormous diamonds. Terrible woman! But isn't it amazing how those women do it? Get away with it like that?"

The disabling pain, that was like a sudden cramp, came and went. Some days she could walk three whole blocks before having to stop. Some days, two. Other times, after only a few steps, she had to find some excuse to rest and wait out the seizure. She searched for a pattern that might give her a clue as to its origin. Were the legs bad when it was humid? About to storm? Too hot, too cold? Were they better in high heels, medium or low? She discovered that when she had had three glasses of champagne, her legs felt less constricted, and so, tried a couple of glasses at breakfast, and when that seemed to help, took to carrying champagne in a plastic bottle in her handbag. When the legs got better, she forgot for a while that they had ever bothered her, but still refilled her glass as well as her plastic bottle, just in case. She did not stop smoking. Those in her immediate circle were sworn to secrecy. She spoke of her pains to only those she trusted not to gossip and alert the press to what she perceived as a sudden flaw in the perfection of the Dietrich image. Goddesses who beget physical infirmities descend to the rank of lowly humans, and lose their right to deity.

She subscribed to medical journals, health-food publications, listened attentively to anyone who spoke of anything to do with pains of the lower regions of the body, asking what pills they had found that cured them – then ordered them from her trusted pharmacies around the world who supplied anything without prescription, just for the honor of serving Dietrich.

Over the years she swallowed enormous amounts of her favorite cortisone as well as Butazolidin, phenobarbital, codeine, belladonna, Nembutal, Seconal, Librium, and Darvon. Although my mother would swallow any pill she was given, she actually trusted medication by injection more. She now searched for a doctor who could be "trusted to say nothing," not insist on tests or examinations – just be willing to shoot magic potions into her behind that would do away with all her fears and woes. Reminding her of Tami's tragic history would have done no good; for my mother the thought of being like anyone else was beyond her comprehension. There was only one Dietrich.

"Sweetheart! Sweetheart!" she ran into my house, laughing: "I found him! He gave me one shot and, see – I ran in! He is wonderful! He just looked at me and said, 'All you need is vitamin B shots!' – and he is right! I feel wonderful. I told Yul he has to go there right away for energy."

Even my husband was persuaded to have a "magic" vitamin shot. It took three days to get him down off the wall! Yul was twirling his costar through that famous polka – like a whirling dervish – but my mother believed that she was cured, that all her troubles were over, at least, the physical ones.

Years later, this doctor was arrested for trafficking in amphetamines, but by that time, Dietrich had gone to so many doctors just like him that he no longer remained in her memory. When she boarded her plane on the 15th of June, she carried in her hand luggage the precious vials her "miracle" doctor had prepared for her to see her through the London engagement.

On the plane, she wrote to me, discussing her eventual departure from my life. Still distrusting planes, she was always very superstitious and full of last-minute thoughts whenever she flew, setting everything down on paper before the "final end" she was certain was about to happen. Once she landed safely, she sent the letter off anyway. No use wasting momentous thoughts that proved her eternal devotion just because she found herself still alive.

Angel,
I never knew fear of death before I had you. But I used to lie awake all night at the hospital already fearing the possibility of your being left without me. I am replaceable everywhere. In all categories. Except in one. And maybe that is what they say is Hell. Should one still know and be removed without power to protect?

Don't get too tired. You always needed sleep. You and Papi. Let the house go. The joy of a clean house is short. Here I sit with my nails broken, skin cracked on my fingers – I had joy cleaning your house – but I never took a minute away from the children because of the house. There I am again, "knowing the true values."

Massy

Ah! Those famous broken nails and roughened hands – they got a lot of mileage! Her stories of cleaning her daughter's house were famous and appeared in the press the world over. Ridicule by innuendo was her favorite game, and we all drew her fire. Some more than others. It was a lethal execution, devoutly to be escaped – whenever possible. The routine went something like this:

Scene

Manhattan
Elegant dinner party
Elegant people assembled in Elegant Town House
Living room
Famous World Star rushes in – stops – hesitates for an instant, until assembled guests notice her and respond to her magic aura
All heads turn upstage – toward her

"Marlene!" – the Russian-born hostess exclaims as she moves toward her in greeting.

Furs, white kid gloves are handed to hovering oriental servant as Marlene speaks: "Sweetheart! I rushed – I thought I would never finish and had to miss your wonderful Stroganoff! Maria called at four, the baby-sitter *again* – she always has such trouble with her baby-sitters – of course, I had to go and help her. So I run over to the house and my Michael is still asleep! He must have been fed a very late lunch – I was worried he was sick – sleeping *so* long in the afternoon? But Maria rushes out – No matter how big and pregnant she is, Bill *makes her work*. Don't ask me where she *has* to go – you know me, too well brought up to ask questions. Remember last week when I cleaned the nursery? All the walls and inside the drawers? The things I found! Well today – all afternoon – I washed all the floors! The entire house! That girl she has, that I found for her and pay, she uses a mop – one of those rag things Americans use! Ridiculous! They think that is cleaning? All they do is smear dirt around! So I did it correctly – on my knees with a scrub brush. You can't imagine the dirt! I'm sure they never clean – and I had to listen for the child, then the telephone rang and I have to answer it. Someone from CBS. I told them that Maria was out and I am washing the floor, so they hang up quickly. Finally, Maria comes back. She was at the supermarket – all this time? I don't know what she cooks for them – from a supermarket! Can't be any good – So I ordered six filet mignons and steak ground for steak tartare and a dozen lamb chops from my butcher the moment I got back to my apartment. Just had time to dress – but I couldn't fix my hands! Look at them! (She stretches her rough and reddened hands out toward the audience.) All my nails are broken! I had to use three new pairs of stockings – they tore every time I touched them with these hands . . . and you should see my knees!

My mother's repertoire included many such monologues. She performed them brilliantly, making every point. Her audiences sympathized, and condemned her verbal victims in absentia. She was a master at character assassination.

On her arrival in London, my mother called to tell me that Major Baby, her nickname for her new majordomo, had been true to his word, that the Messel suite was like a stage set too beautiful to live in, that all the great actors had agreed to introduce her, were writing their own elaborate introductions, that her feet were swollen, especially the left one but was sure that it was only because of the flying.

She had heard of a young man who was touted to be the best theater critic in England. Having read some of Kenneth Tynan's articles, she had asked to meet this young "genius," as she called him. She described their first meeting:

"I walked into that enormous Oliver Messel suite at the Dorchester and, suddenly, from behind the couch, pops up a white worm – like the ones you find in flour. And this white little thing turns out to be this 'brilliant' writer everyone respects! Well . . . I couldn't just throw him out, after saying to everybody how much I wanted to meet him, so I had to offer him a drink before asking him to leave . . . just to be polite. He was all nervous and shaking and I thought how sad – just another fan! Then we started to talk and he was wonderful! Brilliant! The things he said about Olivier . . . to die! It's so wonderful to finally find someone intelligent to talk to."

During her London engagement, she and Tynan became inseparable. When old lovers arrived, he delicately stepped back into the shadows, reappearing when the coast was clear. Kenneth Tynan wrote many things about my mother, always brilliant, always correct, always to the point, but nothing as true as my favorite: "She has sex without gender" – in my opinion, the best analysis of Dietrich's professional enigma.

FROM ITS OVAL SHAPE to its red velvet trappings, to its gold-leaf rococo plaster columns, the Café de Paris was the perfect cabaret for Dietrich. The place resembled one of those exaggerated sets that stars used to be photographed in front of for fan pictures in the old Studio days. Now, it suited the movie-queen image in the flesh that people had come to see. At midnight, on June the 21st, 1954, Noël Coward, with his famous haughty glance, surveyed the splendid audience before him, real royalty as well as those nearly royal due to fame and fortune, then spoke his party piece:

> We know God made trees, and the birds and the bees,
> We know God made trees, and the birds and the bees,
> and the sea for the fishes to swim in.
> We are also aware that He has quite a flair
> for creating exceptional women.
>
> When Eve said to Adam, "Stop calling me Madame"
> the world became far more exciting
> which turns to confusion, the modern delusion
> that sex is a question of lighting.
>
> For female allure, whether pure or impure
> has seldom reported a failure,
> as I know and you know, from Venus to Juno
> right down to La Dame aux Camélias.

This clamor it seems, is a substance of dreams
for the most imperceptive perceiver,
the Serpent of Nile could achieve with a smile
far quicker results than Geneva.

Now we all might enjoy, seeing Helen of Troy
as a gay cabaret entertainer,
but I doubt she could, be one quarter as good
as our legend'ry, lovely Marlenah.

At the top of the curved staircase, she moved into her spotlight, onto her mark. Stood very still, allowing the adulation to wash over her. Slowly, she began to descend the stairs that led down onto the small stage. Like the famous show girls of the Folies-Bergère, she moved, measured, regal; eyes front, never lowered to check the distance of a step. Her tight beaded dress caught the light, molding each leg from long thigh to satin shoe, all fluid movement. Suddenly she paused and, ever so slowly, leaned back against the white pillar, snuggled her body deeper into the fur of her voluminous coat, and surveyed her ecstatic audience through those amazing hooded eyes. The flicker of a teasing smile played momentarily around her mouth, then she continued her descent, while the orchestra struck the first notes of her opening number.

Everyone came to London that June to hear and applaud the "legendary, lovely Marlenah." Harold Arlen flew in; her diary records that he left after five days, was jealous of Tynan, but "at least" got something out of the trip by Oliver Messel agreeing to design the musical that Arlen was in the process of writing with Truman Capote, *The House of Flowers*.

The difference in time, her performance schedule, and Yul being only reachable in his dressing room made phoning practically impossible. So, they had worked out a letter system: He wrote on Tuesdays, Thursdays, and between shows on Saturdays, she on all the others.

My only love –
   This is my day for a letter, I guess I'd better type so that you can read. (I know that you can read it *quietly* and then tear it up.)
   They played the score of the *King* and the polka tore into my heart. I have never had the desire to openly belong to someone and rather laughed at the people who wished so much for it. But now I wish I could be yours, bright in the spotlight of everybody's eyes, and dance with you to that melody which will forever mean you. And I look at photographs of Sinatra and Ava and I feel really jealous because they made it after all. To think, that I ever would bother to look at photographs of those two, seems frightening. But there it is. Michael was there last night with Liz, sitting

rather stiffly in a corner and looking at me quite steadily and sadly, and I thought that that could happen to me, seeing you with another woman and I felt quite sick.

She told me she had to send her dresses and coats to the Queen's dressmaker, Norman Hartnell, to shorten the front by a quarter of an inch as she was having trouble maneuvering down that staircase. When I suggested that she should rest one hand on the curved banister for balance, she got angry and refused, saying that then the audience would immediately think she needed to steady herself like an "old lady." I knew the image of age was so repugnant to her that I did not insist, but on those nights when she called to tell me that her legs felt funny, "heavy, like sacks of flour," I had visions of her falling down those stairs.

On the 4th of July, 1954, she records that for her day off she flew to Paris at ten a.m., had lunch at Fouquet's in the rain, then dined with Noël and their special friends, Ginette and Paul-Emil Seidman, Vivien Leigh and her husband, and Peter Brook, the director. She stayed in Paris overnight, and the next day Gabin's niece took her to Le Bourget Airport in time to make her show in London and Tynan stayed with her that night until six a.m.

Those amphetamine-laced injections, plus my mother's astounding stamina, were obviously in full swing. On July 15th, she hit her right foot against the leg of the fruitwood piano, breaking two toes. That night she called, said she had to cut into one of her precious handmade shoes to relieve the painful pressure, a heralding of what would become routine in a few years.

When the Cavalier arrived in London, all of her English admirers were asked to withdraw until she could call them forth once more. So, for the three days he was there, he was happy, innocently believing that she was still his alone. The moment he left, Arlen returned, Christopher Fry came to lunch, Tynan for tea, a sexy new Swedish blonde to supper. After closing in London, she installed herself in the Hotel Palais-Royal in Paris, where Sam Spiegel and Chevalier awaited her. She made records, ordered clothes from the new collections, spent a weekend at Dior's country house with someone whose initials were G.P., and, hiding behind dark glasses, crept into a movie house to feast her soul watching Gabin's face in his latest film.

She accepted to sing at a gala in Monte Carlo and, having learned the value of being introduced by one as famous as, or, preferably, more famous than she, asked her "pal" Jean Cocteau to do the honors. She showed him what Noël had written about her and suggested that Cocteau might like to come up with something similar, or, if he felt like it, better? She didn't get Cocteau himself – he sent another pal of theirs, the pretty French actor Jean Marais, to speak his tribute for him. It was one of Cocteau's better efforts, and Dietrich was so impressed that she got Fry to translate it into English, later reprinting it often in her theater programs. Of course, brilliance written by an unknown would not have been acceptable. Dietrich was a real "celebrity" snob – funny, in one so famous.

On the 21st of August, looking very military and serious, she was photographed marching down the Champs-Elysées in the front rank of the American Legion in the Paris Liberation anniversary parade, wearing all her medals.

By September, she was in Hollywood to fit her new dresses for her Vegas engagement and to meet Yul. As usual, when she wasn't at the Beverly Hills Hotel or hadn't rented a secret house, she stayed with Billy Wilder and his wife, Audrey. They were good friends, listened to her endless yearnings, kept her secrets, could be trusted. This did not stop her from voicing her private opinion on their characters, habits, and life-style:

"All they do, those two, is sit in front of the television set! Billy even eats in front of it. They both sit there like Mister and Missus Glutz from the Bronx, little mennubles – eating their frozen dinners! Unbelievable! That's what happens to brilliant men when they marry low-class women! Sad!"

Yul was now on a grueling schedule of touring his play, juggling his performances to fit in hurried trips to Hollywood to confer with Cecil B. De Mille for his role of Ramses in *The Ten Commandments*. Reading his schedule and comparing it with the dates and notations in my mother's diary for this period of August to October 1954, I don't know how this man managed to be in six places at the same time and still give the glorious performances he did. Probably his supply of doctored "vitamins" had something to do with it!

MY ELDEST STARTED SCHOOL – real school, with teachers, friends, show-and-tell. He even had a real lunch box, with a picture of Howdy Doody. I loved it so, the homework, the school trips, the PTA, class projects, even gym! Couldn't wait to get up every morning, wanted to share it all – going to school through my child. Over the years, I drove my poor sons crazy, but they were kind and let me play – not minding the reputation of having a completely crazy mother who packed red lunch boxes on Valentine's Day, made green sandwiches in the shape of clovers for St. Patrick's, and miniature galleons for Columbus Day. Well, that's not entirely true, they minded – but not enough to spoil my fun. I even joined them in measles, chicken pox, and mumps – well, Japanese gardeners, servants, bodyguards, and Studio personnel don't give you those kinds of things, and I wanted a real childhood in all its aspects. By the time I was thirty-six, I too could boast, "I've had all my childhood diseases!"

In Hollywood my mother had her fittings, waited for that one phone call that would make her life worth living. Believing that Yul had heard rumors of "other" men and was angry, she wrote him:

> My love, I talked to you a couple of hours ago and feel sick with misery. What have I done to deserve this? I made my letter of last week funny because I thought it was better than to write you a weeping letter. But, funny or not, I made it clear that I had done nothing wrong. I am certain you believe me: That you are my only love and my only wish, that I don't look at any other man, let alone be interested in another man. Please don't throw me away – if you change your mind about us and end the love that you called "infinite," you must know that it will end my life. It cannot be that you want to do this without a reason, to me who loves you so much since so long.

She sent me a copy for my comments and suggestions of what she should do next.

On October 12th, she had an early morning rehearsal in Las Vegas, had a bad cold, then recorded her opening night as though it was nothing special. The next day, instead of the usual notation of wild success, she simply wrote: "Feel awful." The entire Las Vegas engagement was a repeat of this feeling of her being half alive while being the toast of the town. This shimmering, glorious image that stood so regally before her jubilant audiences each night wrote: "All days alike – dull."

Noël kept in touch. She sent his letters on to me. I had now graduated to the dubious position of being sent all the mail she received – my father got the carbons.

1/11/54
Noël Coward
17 Gerald Road
S.W.1

Darling.
The photograph is absolutely wonderful and the dress looks like a

dream and Oh, how I wish I could see you whirling on in that tiny hurricane.

I am having a lovely rich success at the *Café de Paris* and I got a beautiful laugh on the opening night by whispering "Hello" huskily through the mike and kicking an invisible cloak! I also leant against the piano with that imperious look and they cheered like anything.

I shall be in New York in the 1st week of December.

Kindly keep a lamp burning in the window and oblige.

Love, Love, Love, Love

                                                        Noël

I was doing a Cerebral Palsy Telethon, in Cleveland or Columbus I think. In those days, before Jerry Lewis mega-telethons, state organizations had to do their own to benefit local chapters. My mother was also in town, accompanying Harold Arlen on pre-Broadway tryouts of his new musical *House of Flowers*. After eighteen hours of continuous pleading on live television, I was groggy, but I stopped off at their hotel to say a fast hello before returning to New York.

I walked into Arlen's suite as Truman Capote, his Kewpie-doll face distraught, squeaked:

"Dear – Dear Marlene! Sweetie! – One simply cannot rhyme MOON and SOON – and EVER show one's face in public again!"

"Why not? Berlin would go crazy if he lost double *o*'s!" Pearl Bailey always cut to the bone. Everything that came her way was stripped of folderol, put into its proper place.

My mother, hand in trouser pocket, other holding her cigarette as in *Morocco*, very Tin Pan Alley Tunesmith, acknowledged my presence without breaking her stride or concentration:

"But Harold, sweetheart!" she crooned. "You don't want *that* kind of schmaltz – do you?"

"My love, his kind of schmaltz I have nothing but admiration for!" said Arlen with his usual humility.

"Me, too! Me, too!" Capote had a way of speaking that reminded one of an excited little girl clapping her hands at her own birthday party.

My mother gave him one of her "looks." Arlen's worker's hands skipped across the keyboard; it sounded like "Got the World on a String" played backwards.

I didn't want to interrupt all these creative geniuses, but I had a plane to catch, gave "Pearlie" a hug – I liked that big woman, big in stature, big in heart – kissed the sharp southern belle in man's disguise, my mother, the gentle man so full of magic, and left this odd quartet to their work in progress.

I don't care what the Broadway critics finally said – *House of Flowers* had true beauty. Like a perfect butterfly whose time was just too short to be fully appreciated.

CHRISTMAS WAS NEAR – my father wrote one of his rare letters:

9th December: 6 AM

Dearest Mutti,

I am so grateful to you for many things and I have been wanting to thank you for so long ago but you know how much I work! And in the evenings I am always so tired that I always mean to do it tomorrow. Now I am trying to write in the early morning hours, before starting work.

Well, your records are wonderful – out of this world, the introduction from Noël Coward. The Las Vegas photos great.

And now I would like to thank you for the money which helps me so, you just can't imagine how much! Every dollar counts now for me. And I could earn a lot of money – of course not like you as a star – but I have a sound business, i.e., a good clientele. I never have enough eggs to satisfy them, and therefore I have to buy eggs because I do not have the money to extend the layer-hen installation in order to have more hens. But I must say I now have 4000 hens – I had only 3000 when I took the farm over, with a production of 2100 eggs a day. The couple who is working with us has to go in January because I cannot afford to keep them – so that means even more work. Thank God I am healthy and can work. Tami works as I never would have expected, from dawn to sunset – we eat at home every day except one day when "the cook" gets "a free night" and then she goes out with me. Wednesday is the night out but we did not go out yesterday because of "bankruptcy."

I am not discouraged – I love my work, my life here, the animals – I realize I have achieved a lot, quite a lot and that I cannot be down now. It must go better. Things will go better.

Mutti, please get something for the boys for Christmas, a small gift from Papi! I am so sad that I cannot give any present to Maria and Bill – what can I do – one cannot pee against the wind!

I have to work now. I thank you again, dearest, for everything – I take you in my arms.

Papi

My father had become a pitiable man, possibly had always been, I, just too young and full of anger to recognize it. I never forgave him for what he did, allowed to be done, to Tami, but I learned to pity him for what he had allowed to be done to himself. Living with love makes nourishing ground for compassion. I even hoped I might, one day, think of my mother within the context of human frailty.

My mother called, read me my father's letter, adding this epitaph:

"How can Papi be 'happy'? Working like that – for what? What is he trying to accomplish? He doesn't *have* to work – and Tami? Works? Nebbish! I work enough for all of you. Like your Bill, working all the time – why? Even you, now the Big TV Star – why? I do Vegas for you, just for you, all of you, and still everybody wants to work? You're all nuts!" and hung up.

Hemingway was awarded the Nobel Prize in literature, and every parent in the world built a private shrine in their heart to Dr. Jonas Salk. I looked down at my sleeping children and cried, thanked God for him who had lifted the spector of polio from their lives.

1955 WAS A BUSY YEAR for my mother. She prepared and played a second engagement at the Café de Paris in London, triumphed again in Las Vegas, mourned Alexander Fleming, appeared in Michael Todd's *Around the World in* 80 *Days*, rented a secret California hideaway, where she kept house for Yul while he prepared for his role in De Mille's *Ten Commandments*. Repeatedly returned to New York, where she continued her old romance with the Cavalier, and indulged in numerous new ones, although her passionate involvement with Yul continued unabated.

Adlai Stevenson was only an interlude, as she explained it to me: "Such a brilliant man! How can a man who can write such beautiful speeches be so uninteresting? Remarque was difficult, but at least he could carry on a conversation! I had to say yes to Stevenson when he asked for 'it' – he was so shy and sweet, like a little boy!"

The physicist Oppenheimer apparently didn't ask for "it," and so was allowed to stay immersed in his brilliance and nuclear secrets, and escaped, although she often commented:

"Wonderful face . . . all those bones! Like me. Is his hair that short because he is radiated or because he likes it that way?"

The playwright William Saroyan did ask for "It" and was, of course, rewarded. One of the few civilian one-night stands in my mother's long history of bestowing herself for the enjoyment of others. Edward R. Murrow and Frank Sinatra lasted longer.

She met "E.M.," as she referred to Murrow in her diaries, on the 14th of January at a cocktail party she attended with Stevenson. By the 18th of February, they were lovers.

All her life, my mother was convinced that I would automatically agree with everything she did. After all, as she had been responsible for giving me her "superior intelligence," it was only natural that I would recognize and approve her judgment, opinion, and subsequent actions.

Since first hearing that deep, melancholy growl vividly recount the agonies of the London Blitz, Edward R. Murrow had been an idol of mine. His professional courage, his personal dedication to the principles he believed in, his deep love for his country, his hatred of McCarthy, and his crusade to expose this dangerous man's fanaticism made Murrow a very special man – a real live American hero.

When he became my mother's lover, I was shocked, but that reaction lasted only a second. Brilliant men infatuated with Dietrich were, after all, nothing new. The paradox of such beauty also being endowed with such polished intellect was, after all, an irresistible combination. Still, I was saddened that such a man as Murrow should be in need of casual companionship, no matter how seductive. But then Dietrich made bumbling adolescents out of many worldly, respected men – why not this one? So, Murrow began to appear, between meetings, conferences, rehearsals of his acclaimed television shows, to love my mother in the bed recently vacated by his friend Adlai Stevenson.

At first, she dedicated her energies to being wholly his, and in her usual style of possessive lover, wrote him longing letters, this time tinged with more Americanisms than those she wrote to Yul. The letters were secretly delivered to Murrow's headquarters at CBS by a trusted lackey of my mother's, hastily recruited as go-between, when I, for once, refused to play the role of courier. This did not exempt me from receiving a carbon copy and a Dietrich snarl:

"Oh! Suddenly you are so 'holier than thou'? Really – such 'goody-good' affectation."

My mother's need to continually prove to herself and others that she was more than just a movie star was so all-consuming, men of intellectual as well as international stature were vitally important to capture and hold. This did not stop her from making fun of him.

"Sweetheart! You should see Murrow. He walks around the apartment with nothing on except those underpants that flap – like the kind that old men wear, and with his cigarette, of course. He smokes even *during* – you know what I mean. But he is *so* brilliant – you just have to listen to what he is saying and try not to look down at those thin legs of his sticking out of those funny bloomers – otherwise, you have to laugh – and you know me, then I pee!"

Murrow was chastised for more than just his boxer shorts. She complained constantly of his penny-pinching. The day he gave her a pair of earrings, she strode through our front door, carrying the small jeweler's box.

"Now, you have to see these! Not to be believed! Little-itsy-bitsy-pearly-whirlies, all strung in a little row like five-and-ten-cent store! I said: 'You must be joking! I need a beautiful desk for this apartment – and you buy me dangling earrings?'"

The day he bought her that gorgeous antique desk she had picked out, they had dinner at our house. She was especially soft and beguiling that evening, while keeping a weather eye on the clock not to be late getting back to her apartment for Yul's call.

My mother considered my home a "safe house," a logical place to bring secret lovers. After all, as she had bought it, it was hers. During those hours that Yul was on stage and Murrow free from his many projects, they spent many evenings with us. It was difficult, at those times, to keep the Cavalier away, pretend that I didn't know where she was when Arlen or the others phoned, but lying to my mother's victims in order to spare them additional hurt was such second nature, I no longer questioned its justification.

Dietrich used her affair with Frank Sinatra as her private placebo against the loneliness of yearning for Yul, and later, out of superstition. She thought him romantic, gentle, and sweet. She explained to me that what she found most attractive about "Frankie" was his infinite tenderness. "He is the only really tender man I have ever known. He lets you sleep, he is so grateful – in a nice way, all cozy." In later years, she also loved him for his less gentle qualities. Whenever Dietrich saw another headline proclaiming that Sinatra had smashed some reporter's camera or face, she cheered: "Oh! How I love him! He hates them all – like I do! He wants to kill them too! What a wonderful man! You know, I only spent one night with him. . . ." Then there would follow the verbatim recitation of one of her lasting fantasies of the "only" night she had convinced herself she had spent in the arms of Frank Sinatra, and how to avoid detection, she left his house at the break of dawn to wander alone down amongst the honeysuckle in stocking feet searching for a cruising taxi that would carry her back to the Beverly Hills Hotel and safety. Actually, their first romantic encounter was way back in the early forties, and in her later diaries, "Frankie" reappears often.

In the autumn of '55, she was back in Hollywood, a guest of the Wilders in the throes of her usual suffering over Yul.

Sept 2
109 degrees
Nervous Stomach. Have too much to bear. Put on radio but music makes

me cry. Feel have lost "Him" forever. No use living. But have to get money Vegas first. Would be foolish anyway to kill myself in Wilder's house. Have to find out better way. Wish I could drink – but too hot and cannot breathe easily anyway. I ask nothing. He called at 4:30 said Wilder and Hayward told him I had taken Harold [Arlen] with me to London and how wonderful it was for Harold to have me. I did not cry. Did not behave badly, said how terrible London had been, how desperate I was and asked "You know how much I love you." He said no, so I told him and that if he was worried that he had made me suffer in these four years they were nothing compared to this summer. That I was sure he had had another woman, and that I nearly died those last days. He said he was going to San Francisco till Monday night "family business" and he would call when he came back. I said when will you call I want to be here. He said either Monday or Tuesday morning.

Betty Furness party.

Sat next to Frank, he talked of 1942. I was stunned.

That Sunday, she went to brunch at the Stewart Grangers', then:

Frank, Italian restaurant – here – Nice

September 5
Never moved waiting for phone
"He" called from airport
Called again 11:45 drunk –
Called again 12:30 – Talked hours. Angry because of Arlen. Could not argue.
He was too drunk. Don't know what to do.

September 6
Start dresses for Vegas
F. called 9 PM
Sweet and tender
Called again 12 AM

Billy Wilder and his wife must have been the perfect hosts – multiple lovers underfoot, phone calls at all hours, and – they kept having her back for more!

September 7
Frank called at 4 from rehearsal
Plans for Vegas

September 8
Left for Vegas 7:30 Together with Frank
To bed at 7 AM

September 9
Las Vegas
Sahara after noon while Frank rehearsed
F drunk but nice. To bed at 9 AM

The next day, she woke Sinatra at four as he had a five o'clock appointment and commented, as usual, that he was "sweet and tender"; then she went to the Sahara to try out the microphones for her next engagement there. Instead of staying at the Sahara, which would have been the normal thing for her to do, she was staying with Sinatra at his hotel. Yul called her that day and asked her to come back to L.A., using the word "home." She refused. She remained with "F."

September 11th
F To bed asleep in chair at 9:30 AM
Got up without kiss
Bad day did not behave as usual. I went to Sahara. F staying in sun with usual gang
Came home, talked to Harold. Asked him [F] in car to Dunes what was wrong. He said plans. TV show, picture – but he was different. Talked about Harold Arlen twice but I did not attach any importance. Up till 9 AM went to his room. He said "Go to bed" – I was thunderstruck. Left. Harold told me to leave and not wait till private plane with F at 4 PM. Left too miserable to think clearly. No word from him [F]. Fitting – Fainted.

"Miss Riva, I am so sorry but there is an urgent phone call for you downstairs."
I apologized, being the star of a show makes it a little easier to leave a full rehearsal, ran downstairs to the office, worried something had happened to the children:
"Sweetheart! I fainted! Today – at the Studio! Do you think I am pregnant?"
"Well, Massy – I don't really think that is possible – "
She interrupted me: "Why not? You know how I have always yearned for Yul's child – it has to be his, no one else in my life. What do you think? Should I call Carroll Righter?"
"Yes, good idea – you do that! He'll know!" I said and hung up on my fifty-four-year-old incorrigible.
On the 17th of September, she went to a party at Sidney Guilleroff's, got drunk, and flirted openly with Harold Arlen.

September 18th
Better day because if Harold the reason for "F" behavior there is hope that
"He" also could have thought the same.

The days were long. No calls from Yul, no calls from Sinatra. She
called me daily to ask for advice, forgetting it as soon as we hung up.

September 24th
Garland party. F came alone. Formal "Hello." Later I said, "How are you?"
Drunk! And he was more than I have ever seen. I took cigarette, he pulled
out lighter and said: "Like the lemon peel." All I could do was to put both
my hands around his and light the cigarette – "Lemon Peel" having been
our romantic word because I like his hands twisting it into my drink. It
was stunning again, coming again at this moment when he was so drunk
and like a stranger otherwise. He said formal good-bye after saying he
was going to Palm Springs. Horrible Sunday again because "lemon peel"
stirred everything up again. Why did he say it? And why did I not say
something?
    M. Rennie who took me to the party here afterwards scene jealous about
F. Wanted to stay – but no – Lonely day – Lonely day.

September 26th
God. I have to get down to work. Help from somewhere. Please! "He"
called – came. Is everything all right? Heard about Frankie. Said I could
do what I wanted to but don't "Bull shit me." I can do what *I* want?

She must have convinced Yul that she was his – and only his, for, on
September 27th through the first of October, her diary pages are blank
except for: "He came."
    She opened in Las Vegas and was an even greater sensation than she
had been the year before. How she found the time, not to mention the
energy, to fit in the next few weeks is beyond me.

October 19th
Came to L.A. two hours Beverly Hills Hotel.

Sometimes my mother could get very confusing. Did she dash so
gallantly from Las Vegas to a clandestine rendezvous in Beverly Hills
with Frankie? Michael? Arlen? Murrow? Yul? I suspect it was good old
Yul, for on November first, she notes once again:

To L.A. Beverly Hills bungalow
"He" came.

Two days later, she worked for Michael Todd. Her costars in that famous scene were David Niven, Cantinflas, George Raft, Red Skelton, and lo and behold, "tender" Frankie. She had been flirting outrageously with Michael Todd ever since they met, telling me he was the "sweetest," most "brilliant" man, and giggled when whispering in my ear the great secret she had discovered: that his real name was Goldenberg . . . "but he doesn't *look* Jewish. More like a Greek, and you know, he is much too passionate for just a 'Goldenberg'!" and was livid when Todd fell in love with Elizabeth Taylor. "That terrible woman again – who ruined Michael Wilding's whole life," but kept right on trying to get him for her own, switching to "bestest pal a man could ever have" when Taylor won out.

She looked absolutely stunning in her segment of *Around the World in 80 Days* and basked in the deserved admiration accorded her on the set. She molded herself into her "Goldenberg," reminisced with her old pal George Raft, ignored Cantinflas, rhapsodized over Danny Thomas to Red Skelton, rekindled tender Frankie's still smoldering embers, and tried to heat up David Niven.

In Alabama, a brave woman defied the racist law of that state by refusing to give up her bus seat to a white man and Dietrich flew to Vegas for Chevalier's opening night – then recorded clandestine meetings at various bungalows on the grounds of the Beverly Hills Hotel.

I signed to star in a touring company of *Tea and Sympathy*, a craziness only made possible by a husband who invented the term "supportive." Not to worry, he would look after our two children, see them to school, help with homework, be there for them – all would be well, I *had* to play this wonderful part that I would surely be brilliant in, and sent me on my way to Buffalo.

True, it was a part worth leaving your loved ones for – *if* acting was your world, in the marrow of your bones. After two months on the road, with four still to go, I knew what my marrow was full of: "Get me out of this – and Home!" But my run-of-the-play contract held me to our schedule.

THE SCRIPT OF *The Monte Carlo Story* was awful, but as Vittorio De Sica, the genius who had made *The Bicycle Thief*, was to be her costar

ABOVE: Harold Arlen, the composer, and her pal Noël Coward.
Everyone who adored her came to witness her triumphs.
BELOW: In her glitter dress, she sang to men; in her tails, to women.

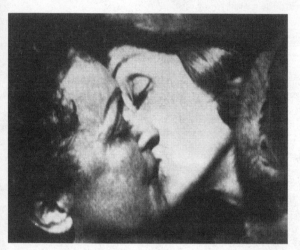

ABOVE: In Michael Todd's
Around the World in 80 Days,
she appeared with a number of
her pals and one who was far
more than just a pal.
LEFT: Dietrich thought Edith
Piaf was a lonely sparrow with
a busted wing. My opinion of
that corroded steel in "a little
black dress" is unprintable.
BELOW: This evening, my
husband and I must have
found a baby-sitter and played
"Dietrich's happy family."

ABOVE: Italy has a way of inspiring romance.
BELOW: But Vittorio De Sica, her costar in *The Monte Carlo Story*, filmed in Monaco and Rome in the summer of 1956, was not a candidate.

My sons, Peter and Michael, thought going out with their grandmother (Massy) meant "money is no object." Yelling for taxis was part of the fun.

and director, with Sam Taylor, a victim of the McCarthy witch hunt, as the official one, my mother agreed to do the film.

Once again, Harry Cohn was wined and dined, and Columbia Studios embarked on executing Dietrich's glamorous wardrobe for a film to be shot not on their lot, not even in the States, but in Monte Carlo and Rome! She had more than ten costumes to design with Jean Louis, then send the sketches with swatches of the various materials and colors to Italy for the producers' approval. She was so busy that the entries in her diary are preoccupied with preparations for the film. The usual "He came," "He called," "Here," are vague and unidentified – although on March 31, she records:

Left Vegas 5:45 A M. Home 7 A M. "He"

This could mean that it was Sinatra who came from Vegas or that she, who had been in Vegas with Sinatra, had flown to L.A. to be "home" when Yul appeared. Whoever it was stayed around for a week until the 9th of April, when my father was hospitalized with his first heart attack.

In Delaware, after much discussion, the producer allowed his wife, who was up on the part, to take over the lead so that I could fly to the bedside of my dying father. At least I thought he was dying after listening to my mother's frantic announcement over the telephone. As the final curtain came down on the third act, I walked off the stage, grabbed my coat and bag, was on my way to the airport and made the last plane with connections in New York to L.A. I remember thinking, Thank God it's a modern play – I would really look crazy doing this mad dash as Mary Queen of Scots!

Knowing that I had an hour's wait between planes in New York, Bill managed to bring the boys down to La Guardia despite the late hour for a fast kiss and a hug from their disappearing mother. The missing of each other was getting too hard. He didn't know it yet, but I was ready to give up the foolishness of so-called "fame" for something I should have known was far more valuable and rewarding.

Hours later, still dressed in the costume I had walked off the stage in, I entered my father's hospital room as he said: "Mutti, when you bring me my martini tomorrow, tell the hotel that the one today needed a little more vermouth, and don't forget, tomorrow *fresh* lemons and the correct melba toast for the caviar."

My mother whirled on hearing my laugh and shrieked: "Papilein – She is here! Look at her! Still in her makeup – straight from the stage!" and flung herself against me, sobbing – the "nearly-was widow"! Over her bowed head, my father and I looked at each other. With his index finger, he tapped his forehead, a gesture he often made when silently commenting on Tami's irrational behavior. I wondered where she had been hidden away during this time, when the world press was monitoring Dietrich in her role of "distraught wife at dying husband's bedside."

I told my father how happy I was to see him so far from death's door, then listened to my mother's grievances against the various private nurses assigned to her husband's case:

"Sweetheart! They are so rude. They behave as though they are doctors! And they are all black! Can you believe it! How can they allow those people to be nurses?"

While my mother was busy instructing the doctor in the latest techniques of coronary care, I went in search of Tami. I knew nothing and no one would pry her too far from my father's side. I finally found her in a waiting room on another floor – all alone, bony knees pressed tightly together, her gnarled hands fidgeting with the metal clasp of her worn handbag, her big eyes desperate, her frail body in its cheap summer housecoat, trembling in fear. She had accompanied the ambulance, come straight to the hospital as she was, stopping only to snatch her purse on the way. No one had bothered to tell her what had happened to my father. She believed him dead and was waiting for my mother to tell her so. She had been in that room, forgotten, since his arrival at the hospital ten hours earlier. She reminded me so of a wounded animal. I approached her cautiously:

"Tamilein – it's me, Kater. Papi is not dead. Do you hear me? Papi is not dead – Papi is alive."

"Oh, Kater! The truth? That's the truth? Kater, really," she pleaded.

I nodded my head, put my arms around her, and held her close – until the tears came and she allowed herself to believe me.

The next day, I rejoined my company. I arrived at the theater just in time to change my clothes and be discovered, serene, "terribly controlled" in a chintz-covered armchair, knitting, as the curtain rose on the first act.

Everybody lauded my mother's courage and superhuman stamina during her husband's illness. She fitted day and night, in between dashing to the hospital with her husband's lunch and dinner, supplied by the foremost restaurants of Beverly Hills – loaded with cholesterol. Tami was not allowed to visit. She was given strict orders to become invisible, remain at the "ranch," stay inside, and speak to no one. When my father left the hospital, my mother gave him back to Tami to take care of and flew to Paris to make hats and shoes. She arrived in Monte Carlo in time for the start of principal photography.

During the making of this film, she wrote me some wonderful letters, Dietrich at her best:

Hotel de Paris
Monte Carlo

June 10 '56

WELL, MY ANGEL – this is the first Sunday and no work. Have a cold and antibiotics keep me in shape to work. Voice doesn't matter which still seems funny. Entire film will be dubbed. Still, they fell into each other's arms when I played the first scene words and all. They are not used to that. They more or less mouth their lines like we do when we shoot a song and the soundtrack is playing. They do a silent picture and concentrate on the expression and the eyes and say the words rather tonelessly. I had a hard time playing to De Sica because there was no meaning to the lines. This all happened after they had just gotten over the shock that I was there in time, or there at all. The politeness is killing me. After the day's work, which was two lines at a time at the most and over my shoulder (I had to remind them gently that this was Cinemascope and I would be on the screen in full shots e.t.c.) I was kissed and hugged for performing molto bene bellissimo and: "How do you do it with all the expression in your eyes and in the voice." I should have been a silent Film Star or Italian to start with. They sure have an easy life. Also found out that Lollobrigida and Sophia Loren, Mangano, e.t.c. don't even dub themselves. They have other actresses dub for them. Their accents are too low-class for Rome consumption, also their acting talent when they speak.

The young girl in the film is called Trundy. Never made a film and looks not only 12 years old, but also has my color hair and complexion plus a few freckles. I thought they were kidding because in the script there is a lot of talk of her being 22, but to choose the same color hair for the other woman in the same film seems ridiculous. Everybody says it wasn't his fault and that's how it was until at midnight we saw the rushes in the local cinema and I saw her on the screen I finally said to Sam Taylor who takes director's credit on the screen, "I don't think it's funny anymore." He then asked *me* to put my foot down and ask the producer to change the girl. He said he couldn't do it. Well, you know that my hands are tied, because I can see the stories in print when the girl returns home: I was jealous, she looked too young, e.t.c.

De Sica gambles all night at the Casino and I see him only during the day when we work. He is charming, but a little stiff, very conscious of his profile, this being the first part of an elegant man and lover. His makeup is thick and pasty and I told them last night: that in America people will laugh at a man who looks made-up, men don't make up with grease in Hollywood. For color they have a water-soluble makeup which does not show, just for color sake. Sam Taylor said: "I know nothing about all these things." The little, very good cameraman was very sad and De Sica was still gambling and had not seen anything. I suggested they get another makeup man and make tests with De Sica before we get into the indoor scenes, which, by the way, will almost all be made here in the actual Hotel lobbies, restaurants, gambling rooms. There is very little left for studio work in Rome, which is very disturbing, because I looked forward to a dressing room and calm studio work instead of this location business where you have to change behind your retinue spreading their skirts. No mirror, no light, no place to stretch out or take your clothes off in this heat.

My wardrobe girl only speaks Italian and I understand everything she says but I still cannot speak it. Some words which don't make sense at all I have to ask for, like who can know that Left is sinistro, although Right is diritto, which makes sense. Pronto is the most important word on the set. And I run like the circus horse when I hear it.

The Hairdresser is very good and speaks French so we can communicate. Guilaroff will leave soon which I don't regret, but if I hadn't brought him I would have had more sleepless nights before I got here than I had.

My test was all right, they again fell into each other's arms about it, although they must have *known* that there was film in the camera when we made it! The eyes were not blue but some sort of mush and I told Peppino about the eye light we have and when I see my first rushes I will know more.

The Make-Up man is a little short fellow who speaks an Italian I can hardly understand and has hot, fat hands and they are *heavy*. He has already lost onto the floor, or they must have glued to his pants, 6 pairs of my precious eyelashes, but I always say: Non importa, non importa. (They say everything twice here) and he takes out another pair. Then he squooshes the liquid adhesive onto the band with a big squoosh which makes it get all over the lashes and sticks it onto my eyes, much too far into the corner, and I signal to put it further out. He then pulls on the band which by now is stuck to my lid and my lashes, presses it down on the outside and says: Va bene. I have slits for eyes and as I can still see the clock ticking away I say: Va bene too. When he is gone, I pull them off and get out another pair, because these being full of guck and he had them too long in his hot fat moist hands and the lashes are going every which way. I now get up an hour earlier and make-up myself. But he still insists on starting on the eyebrows and put his fist into my cheeks, twisting it while he sketches the eyebrows while I twist inside. He also loves to pat my face from the jaws up to the eyes using the same moist fingers from the darker color over the lighter highlights. I have stopped that with: Stop! which they *all* understand.

Yesterday the crew took me to St. Paul de Vence in a very fast Italian racing car for dinner. There I finally met Coxinelle, the young man who is a dead ringer for Marilyn Monroe, except he has a better voice. He sings in Juan-les-Pins and I must go one night, when I don't work in the morning. I naturally couldn't help looking at the beautiful décolleté of "her" evening dress and it was quite something. "Hitler should have had them for tonsils!" You should have seen the reaction of the Americans, Taylor and his society wife and Guilaroff (for more reasons than one)! We took a picture together, I will send it. Although I wish I could do one with me in tails that would be much more fun.

Grace has returned to the Castle we hear and Guilaroff claims he telephoned her, but I don't know if he just says that to impress me. He is like all MGM people devoted to her which is rather nice. I have a suite of rooms, if you could only get the kids into the air, even if it is not this air, which is not very bracing anyway.

I love you
Massy

Live television gave up, as it had to. America's different time zones were impossible to handle for sponsors and scripts alike. So, the drama shows and many other categories moved to Hollywood and on to film, and the studios that had so feared television, cried doom – predicted the death of Hollywood – suddenly had a brand-new industry where all their brilliant know-how could flourish anew.

I began having to commute from coast to coast. I never unpacked, I was like a visitor in my own home. No question of moving our family out to swimming-pool heaven, no matter how enticing. My husband's work was in New York, and I alone knew the hazards that such a move could create within a marriage. I had chosen to use my married name professionally for that reason – no "Mr. Manton" would stigmatize Bill, as had "Mr. Dietrich," my father. I was lucky that Riva went so very well with Maria. If your talent is such that it drives you beyond yourself, is a consuming need outside of your control, then all is fair in love and war. You really can't help yourself. But, my acting talent was not of the "glorious monster" type and therefore could be laid to rest quite easily without regret at something precious forfeited. I flew out to L.A., did one more big show – and quit. At the age of thirty-one, I had come to my senses. Thanks to Bill, our sons had weathered the motherless time extremely well, greeted my sudden reappearance with undramatic appreciation. My husband wasn't dramatic either, but appreciation? Wow! Was he appreciative!

My mother moved to Rome to shoot interiors. The film nearly finished, her letters were full of self-anger and depression:

September 10 '56

WELL? I'm on the homestretch – four more days and I am through. I hate
myself for having succumbed to fatigue and run-down nerves and spoiled
so many days for myself and work. But I just couldn't fight it alone. I felt
too lost and it shows. And this time it wasn't my perfectionism that made
me over-critical. I hardly bothered about the clothes. I just put them on and
forgot about them. That shows too. But that isn't bad. I wanted to play
this film lightly and fast and without a care. I thought it was the only way
possible to do this uninteresting part. I never thought that I would have to
fight for realism with Italian film-makers. But I had to fight every inch of
the way and was hampered enormously by the most old-fashioned camera
direction. But I am afraid I didn't fight hard enough. I got tired or because
it was hopeless to keep good humor around me and fight at the same time.
Not that they were not all charming. They just didn't know what I can do
if I don't feel harnessed. Besides this I had De Sica on one side who saw me
and the part one way and Taylor who saw me another way. De Sica says I
have the face of Duse and that he loves the melancholy which hangs over
me and Taylor wants the cynical "Femme du Monde." Both did not want
"love." Well, I hope I gave them both what they wanted. It is difficult for
me to forget completely what is being said to me just before the camera
starts to roll. And Taylor would always talk to me quickly just then.

One never has a chance to see all the rushes put together again and
again when one records directly. This way I see myself on the loops again
and again and every fault sticks out, every timing that is off, I have to
follow with my dubbing. It is like being put through torture to have to
do the same mistake over again, just because the lips move and you have
to go with it.

I am as thin as a herring and the cameraman instead of getting better
photographed me rather badly ever since we came into the studio. The
makeshift lighting in Monte Carlo became me much better. Also London
Technicolor found that our little cameraman is inexperienced and in order
to save money asked him for more and more light, and he complied without
telling me. I could not open my eyes anymore and he swore up and down
that I had the same amount as before. Only when I had to interrupt every
take because of tears rolling down my cheeks did he take some lights off.
I know enough about light not to confuse it with heat. If you saw the
rushes it looks like Nazi torture, a desperate face trying to keep the eyes
open and be funny and interrupting all the time saying I'm sorry I cannot
or "Excusate" or "je ne peux pas." I sit there with my hands over my face
and the camera keeps rolling and I try again and again and every time the
scene is over I hide my face in pain. It wasn't the pain that upset me so. It
was the knowledge that something was wrong, that it could not be good
on the screen. And I hated myself to be so well brought up that I could
not walk off the set and say: If you want me to act fix your lights so that
I can. The American cutter I forced onto them through Michael Todd's

help from United Artists is not first-class and not bright enough for the people here. He does not quite know what we are saying and he is cutting by the script I guess. I had so hoped he would give them a list of retakes to be able to speed up the picture which is very slow. But as we have no protection shots the best cutter cannot speed it. But I asked for a cutter with authority because my main reason for getting the cutter was to have someone other than me saying we needed added shots to be able to cut the picture for tempo. Even if De Sica dubs well, which I doubt, and could read some lines faster, we have no head of mine to insert to pull his lines over. This way he has to dub in the same slow tempo to match his lips. I have a terrible cold and could not dub today that's why I have time for this long letter. I am all packed; again I have put the unworn dresses back in the suitcases, again I have folded everything carefully to carry it back home. I never went out in Rome and in Monte Carlo I worked every night. Mostly I wore Blue Jeans. The fountains gush outside, it is still hot. I have seen Rome at night three times. I wished so much I could have left here not feeling like a "gutted chicken."

I salute you Americans.

Massy

Except for her middle-European sentimentality, Dietrich would have made a good director, perhaps even a better-than-good. What a shame she never took the time from "being in love" to concentrate on becoming one.

Somewhere, after this film, she got involved with an Italian actor, a cheap, very cheap version of Gabin. She always claimed their love was "pure," that he was impotent – then wondered out loud how his wife had managed to have so many children. Ensconced with her new heartthrob at the Hotel Raphael in Paris, at fifty-five she was in love again, and of course was convinced I would want to hear all about it.

Tuesday night
Sweet love,
It is 12:30 a.m. We came home from a dinner at his producer's house. He was beautiful, separated from me, opposite me and he dominated the conversation – brilliant and articulate.

. . . I could now come to him and he to me without hiding and only imagine to "Faire l'Amour" with me. I told him then that it wasn't only that that I had wanted – per se. I wanted him to attach me to him. Something physical, like you spit a dog in the mouth – so he stays – or sleeps in the same bed.

Her Hemingway-acquired truisms were always so fascinating!

That is what I had wanted. He said how terrible morning is, after a night of love and how wonderful his mornings are when he finds that I have put out the light and signs of love – like his clothes hung up and his socks gone – taken by me to wash. And I sat there and knew he was right but I knew also that I would forget his eyes which now seemed to be the only happiness I wanted to look into.

Page after page after page of subliminal love – until:

I will go to bed now. It is 2 a.m. No use sitting optimistically on the red couch in my gold dress. Should he wake up, he will not call. Such is not our relationship. He tells me often he woke up and read. I also wake up all the time since I am here. I don't read, though. His room is cozy. Mine isn't. I have no talent for that – I just have the longing.
    I kiss you.

For the first time, she had quite forgotten she was in Paris – and that this had always meant, Jean was near.

My mother returned to New York, found that I had decided to give up my successful career, and, to prove the point, was pregnant. She was not pleased.

As she had signed for another Vegas stint, she flew to Hollywood in November for the third and final fittings.

Michael Wilding, now free from his marriage to Elizabeth Taylor, came back into the fold. She planned to take him to the privacy of my father's "ranch," then noted in her diary that as Papi had friends visiting him, this was now out of the question. It made her angry. If she paid my father's bills, she felt it only just that she should be able to use his home to bring lovers to whenever she chose.

Yul was also in Hollywood, and so she began waiting for "Him" to call. When he didn't, she called me:

"Why doesn't he call me? I know he knows I am here! You think it is all because of that Swedish horse? How can an internationally known whore be allowed to star in films?" She was wildly jealous, certain that Yul was having an affair with his costar from *Anastasia*. Dietrich's hatred of Ingrid Bergman was born that winter. Years later, she would tell outrageous stories about anything connected with Bergman: How Rossellini had confided in her, told everyone how he would knock on her door, begging her to let him in so he could seek comfort in Dietrich's arms, there to unburden his soul by recounting Ingrid's many, many infidelities.

My father's friends finally left, and my mother was able to rendezvous with Michael Wilding at her husband's house in the Valley. She called me from there:

"Sweetheart. Tami cooked a wonderful dinner for all of us. She is so much better since they let her out of that place I found, but she is so tired all the time, I gave her all the Dexedrine I had. You should have seen how Michael ate! He is a new man, now that that awful woman that made his life so miserable is gone! Now, we have to get his children away from her! Here, he wants to tell you himself how happy he is," and she put Wilding on the phone, so that he could tell the daughter in his own words of his refound joy with the mother. Poor Michael, like Brian, he had manners and these calls embarrassed him so.

Quickly I whispered:

"Just say it, Michael, make her happy, keep the peace, but for God's sake, don't ever let her near your boys!"

She took the receiver back to inform me that Carroll Righter had said that, according to her stars, nothing would be resolved with Yul until the 2nd of December.

For eight hours a day, she fitted the new dresses for Las Vegas. Her diary is full of her usual astute observations of what is wrong with the cut, beading, placement of every stone and bauble and what must be done to correct it. Then, suddenly, all work is forgotten:

November 28th, 1956
"He" possible divorce. Am quite sick.

Sobbing uncontrollably, she called me. She was convinced that Yul was having an affair with Bergman, and now was getting a divorce for that "whore." I calmed her, reminding her that Yul and his wife, Virginia, had been on the verge of divorce many times. I knew my mother always hoped that when Yul actually decided to divorce, it would be because of his great love for her. She asked to talk to Bill. Perhaps, being a man, he could explain why after all these years that she had loved Yul, been faithful to him, "only him," he could now treat her so cruelly! Bill listened to these fantasies, mumbled something appropriate and noncommittal, and shaking his head in disbelief, handed me the receiver.

"Sweetheart! I told Bill. I will call the moment when I know more!"

She hung up, called one of her string of ever-obliging doctors, asked him to telephone her Beverly Hills drugstore to instruct them to deliver yet another hundred refill of Miss Dietrich's favorite amphetamines to her bungalow, then called Remarque to ask his opinion of Yul's strange behavior. When her blond movie-star lover of days gone by suddenly phoned that evening, she was still so miserable about Yul that she accepted Kirk's invitation for a cozy dinner at his beach house.

The next day, December 1st:

> Ordered *fur* sample for Vegas.
> Sick
> Called Doctor. Lie down. He comes at five.
> Says heart OK.
> Party for Hornblow.
> Tony Martin
> Home with Frank
> Finally, some love

> December 2nd
> Home at 3:30 PM
> F called at 9:30 PM
> Finally some sweetness
> Slept well and long

She had known when she moved to the Beverly Hills Hotel that Anatole Litvak, the director of Yul's film, and his wife, Sophie, lived in a bungalow across the walk from hers. She had even accepted Sophie's invitation to tea, a thing my mother never did, in the hope of seeing Yul or hearing news of him. My mother's private stake-out of the Litvak bungalow finally paid off:

> December 6th
> His car parked here. Caught him coming out of the Litvak bungalow, but he was with agent – so walked by, saying "Hello."
> Nothing all day. Home. Miserable.

> December 7th
> Decided accept 125,000 this year. Work Tropicana Vegas February
> Studio 2 PM First time black dress together
> No good. Looks like evening dress. Too even.
> Put extra fringe from samples on blouse to give accent.
> Home at 6, over to Litvak's. Stayed for dinner.
> Nothing.

> December 8th
> One o'clock. His car parked in front of my bungalow. Missed him going to Litvak. He came out with Litvak into car to lunch. Litvak came back on foot alone at three.

Separation notice in columns. What more can I suffer. Seeing him breaks me.

She went to see *Baby Doll* with the writer Charles Brackett. When she got home, recorded:

He stood in front of theater.
Saw me get out of car.

December 10
Did not send letter as planned. How can he believe that I am in despair if he sees me with Strange man, looking O.K.? called at 1:30 AM

December 12th
Feldman to screening *Anastasia*. "He" was there. Alone with De Mille. De Mille came to me at end. Kissed me, took me over to him, said I was the most wonderful woman, what he would not do for one kiss, etc. I shook hands and said:
   "You are wonderful in the film."
Then left, direct for home. Was so miserable that I could not whisper to him to call me.

She returned to New York to complicate our Christmas and tell us of all her despair at the cruelty of those she loved. It was time for United Cerebral Palsy's yearly telethon. That year I believed I had something very special to contribute – the image of a woman expecting a child, surrounded by children born impaired. I spoke of my belief that a whole and healthy child was the true miracle of birth, not the norm – but the glorious exception. I implored the parents who had been granted this gift to help us help those who strove against such terrible odds to achieve their own wondrous miracles.

My mother was furious: "How can you show yourself on television, with all those sick children? You are pregnant! All that sickness can mark the child! It's ridiculous, this obsession you have about those ugly, twisted children!" and she left for California, checking her handbag to make sure she had her favorite knockout drug for the plane.

She had found a sleeping pill in France. Actually, not a pill but a potent hypnotic in the form of a suppository. Dietrich preferred medication to enter her body through her rectum. It worked faster. She also mistrusted the ability of the stomach to know what was food and what was medicine, then have the intelligence to know where to send it.

Another advantage of suppositories was her belief that, due to the lack of space, one could not commit suicide inadvertently by shoving too many things "up there." Because this French medication worked so well, put her to sleep so quickly, she christened her suppositories with the name of the actor she considered the most boring man in Hollywood, Fernando Lamas.

The moment my mother arrived in Los Angeles, she called to tell me of the terrible thing that had happened to her on the plane, what Yul had done to her "in the air," then sat down to write Noël Coward the whole story from the beginning:

Last week in New York, I stood at the door when he came. I was not going to do one wrong thing. He came in smiling, bottle under his coat. He came into the bedroom and told me about Paris, the fog around the Eiffel Tower, the streets, the bridges and how he thought about me. I stood there thinking this is not a dream. He is really back and he loves me. Then the hurricane broke over me for three hours and I fell asleep, for the first time in two months to the day without torture and sleeping pills.

He woke at eleven, said he had an appointment at twelve. I made coffee as usual, gave him emperin as usual after a drinking night. He left as usual a little bit vague and at the door I said AS USUAL: When will I hear from you? and he said: "Later."

He did not call. Sinatra opened that night at the Copacabana. I went at midnight. He was there. I went home. He did not call. All day Friday I waited. As I had made plans to leave for California on Saturday (I open at the Sands on Feb. 13), I called him at 6 p.m. I said my name and he answered. I said I was leaving Saturday and he said he was on the same plane. He said I'll see you then. My heart stopped again. There was something wrong. I thought, maybe he hated himself for having come back and there would be scenes again and I said: Won't I see you before? and he said: "No, I have no time." I said I want you to know there will be no complications again, no scenes, no trouble ever, no questions. He said, "Thank you, ma'am." He said, "How did you like Sinatra?" (he saw me there and smiled to me very sweetly and intimately). I said: I thought it was terrible, Sinatra was drunk, had no voice, very unprofessional. He said, "I sat with him till 8 in the morning." Again I said: "Can't you phone me later tonight?" He said "No." I said: What is wrong? He said, "I want nothing anymore. I have no confidence in anyone or anything anymore. Not in you either. You asked for it."

I said: No confidence in me? He said, "Yes." I said: Don't you love me anymore? and he said, "You said you would not ask any more questions. I have to stop, someone is coming. See you tomorrow on the plane."

Horrible night. Wanted to cancel trip, but then thought I better go because if I don't go I will reproach myself and I went.

I was taken to the plane first. He came later. Walked by me and took a seat on the other side furthest away from me in the seat section in the back of the already made-up berths. The empty plane took off. He had three drinks and went to his berth without ever looking at me. Thank God I am German. Otherwise I would have jumped out of the plane.

I went to my berth. I took a Fernando Lamas but could not fall asleep. Dozed off and on. Then suddenly I FELT HIS HANDS ON ME AND HIS BODY FALLING HEAVILY ONTO ME. I did not know where I was only that he was there. I took his hand, heard the noise of the motors, knew he was in my berth on a plane and wanted to hide him and pull him in. He pulled himself up and half out and said something. I said: Come here! still half dazed. He started to crawl back to me, then he pulled back again and said, "No, there are too many people around." I let go of his hand. I opened my shade and saw it was light. I said I dreamt this. I looked through my curtains and saw his foot in the shoes I brought from Italy on the floor of the opposite berth. He sat again on his seat of the night before.

I went over to him and said: Good morning. He said, "Good morning. How did you sleep?" I took *Match* with his story in it so I could bend down, gave it to him.

If you are still with me after reading so far let me thank you.

Please write to me. I will be here at the Beverly Hills Hotel till February 8. I have to work which is the worst part of it all. Work usually helps unhappy people. But my kind of work cannot be done with unhappiness. A film would be different because one is being pushed and does not have to create everything alone.

I don't know how to do it yet. I have no "Lebensmut." And, without that it is difficult to exist, let alone go and dazzle the people in Vegas with a performance which is a fake anyway and took always work to put it over.

Now it becomes a mountain of silly, superficial exploits, which only my sense of humor of myself could surmount.

But where do I find that?

As long as I don't know what he feels I will have no rest.

If the jealousy angle is true then he must love me still. If not then why did he come back at all? Why did he call you? Why did he tell me he'd "missed me"? Why did he want me so badly?

How can one forget the one one loves when one has no pride at all and no way out like nervous breakdowns or trips around the world or jumping out of a window?

I love you and I wish I could behave in the proper fashion.

Noël replied immediately:

Firefly Hill
Port Maria
Jamaica B.W.I.

Oh, darling,

Your letter filled me with such a lot of emotions the predominant one being rage that you should allow yourself to be so humiliated and made so unhappy by a situation that really isn't worthy of you. I loathe to think of you apologizing and begging forgiveness and humbling yourself. I don't care if you did behave badly for a brief moment, considering all the devotion and loving you have given out during the last five years, you had a perfect right to. The only mistake was not to have behaved a great deal worse a long time ago. The aeroplane journey sounds a nightmare to me.

It is difficult for me to wag my finger at you from so very far away particularly as my heart aches for you but really darling you must pack up this nonsensical situation once and for all. It is really beneath your dignity, not your dignity as a famous artist and a glamorous star, but your dignity as a human, only too human, being. Curly is attractive, beguiling, tender and fascinating, but he is not the only man in the world who merits those delightful adjectives. . . . Do please try to work out for yourself a little personal philosophy and DO NOT, repeat DO NOT be so bloody vulnerable. To hell with God damned "L'Amour." It always causes far more trouble than it is worth. Don't run after it. Don't court it. Keep it waiting off stage until you're good and ready for it and even then treat it with the suspicious disdain that it deserves. . . . I am sick to death of you waiting about in empty houses and apartments with your ears strained for the telephone to ring. Snap out of it, girl! A very brilliant writer once said (Could it have been me?) "Life is for the living." Well that is all it is for, and living DOES NOT consist of staring in at other people's windows and waiting for crumbs to be thrown to you. You've carried on this hole in corner, overcharged, romantic, unrealistic nonsense long enough.

Stop it Stop it Stop it. Other people need you. . . . Stop wasting yourself on someone who only really says tender things to you when he's drunk. . . .

Unpack your sense of humor, and get on with living and ENJOY IT.

Incidentally, there is one fairly strong-minded type who will never let you down and who loves you very much indeed. Just try to guess who it is. X X X X. These are not romantic kisses. They are un-romantic. Loving "Goose-Es."
Your devoted "Fernando de Lamas"

She read me Noël's letter over the phone, then got angry when I said that I agreed with him wholeheartedly.

"Oh, you two Sagittarians! You two always agree! Neither of you can understand how one man can be a woman's whole life! Noël does it to boys in the ass – and you? You play house!" and she hung up on me.

On her arrival, Yul left Hollywood. "Frankie" was more than willing to lick her wounds. Two days later, she notes in her diary:

F.S. called at 1:30. Had just come from New York. I went there till Monday 5 A.M. Sweet and tender – hope it helps.

She hired a new accompanist. She was enchanted by his boyish charm and talent. He was handsome, vital, virile, and gifted. Strangely enough, they were never lovers, undoubtedly Burt Bacharach's sense of good taste. He did not believe in mixing work with pleasure.

Secretly, she did resent Burt's capacity to elude her famous charms and camouflaged this resentment by telling outrageous stories about his sexual escapades with others, always sounding like his private madam. Until Burt became famous in his own right and finally left her, those of her immediate entourage were told, innumerable times, of how she would case the Vegas chorines for likely candidates to share Burt's bed.

Dietrich's most tasteless story involving Bacharach was one of her lies she enjoyed telling the most. Of how she had first diagnosed his gonorrhea, then found ways to cure it for him. Her clutch of avid listeners at these times would gasp and gush:

"Marlenah! That's just too, too hilarious for words! Absolutely divine!" tears of derisive laughter running down their cheeks. By this time, Bill and I had usually left the scene, my mother's voice following us out:

"You see what I told you? About Maria? The manners? She was brought up with only the best manners! And now . . . where have they all gone?"

On the 13th of February, 1957, with Burt Bacharach at the piano, she opened in Vegas. Looking superb in her perfect diamond-fringe dress, she accepted her usual tumultuous accolade.

After closing in Vegas, she returned to Hollywood, flirted Paramount into copying her black wig from *Golden Earrings*, rummaged through the gypsy section of the Wardrobe Department, and appeared as the madam of a Mexican brothel for Orson Welles in his film *A Touch of Evil*. She had agreed to play the part as a favor to Orson, and when he told her that he had no money as usual, she did it for nothing. They shot her two short scenes in one night. The glowing reviews she received for her work in that film, the cult that regards that as probably her best acting since *The Blue Angel*, always amused her. I once asked Orson what had given him the idea of Dietrich for the madam of his brothel. He smiled that naughty "little boy" smile of his: "Never heard of type-casting?"

She returned to New York in the spring of '57, comforted Murrow, and made sure I could give birth. My third son was born physically handicapped. My mother was the first to be told that something was wrong. She took charge, ordered the doctors to say nothing to me, then in her best "Prussian officer" manner, announced to my anxious husband:

"Bill! We have a terrible tragedy! Maria's child is not perfect like the others! Is there something wrong in *your* family? No! No! You cannot see her now! They had to do a cesarean to get it out! *I* will tell you when you are allowed to see her!"

My loving husband never told me of this terrible moment. My outraged doctor and the shocked nurses did. My mother began sending cables, telephoning, alerting her private friends of the "tragedy" that had befallen her. Later she would embellish this by adding, "You know, Maria took that terrible pill when she was pregnant – that one . . . what is it called? – 'tha' – something . . . the one that makes babies with no arms and no legs . . . " Branding my child with a horrendous lie.

Billy Wilder and his superb timing – again came to my rescue. Three days later, my mother was forced to leave my bedside to prepare for her dual role in his film *Witness for the Prosecution*. Her parting words:

"You should have stopped after Michael. *He* is perfect. All this having children to–do is nothing but vanity. I told you – but you wouldn't listen. You had to do that 'cripple' telethon!," gave me a "sorrowing" embrace, pulled on her white kid gloves, and left.

Softly, Bill opened the door of my room, hesitant, face drawn, eyes haunted, so afraid it was he who had brought me this hurt – somehow. I reached out for him, we held each other, hard and close, more in apprehension than sorrow. Would we be able to help our child? Were we up to the task, were we good enough to do it right, was love enough to teach us the way? Then we squared our emotional shoulders and went to work, to be the very best parents we could be for our Paul.

This child was never given into Dietrich's care. What a cripple she would have made of that courageous little boy. By the time he did visit her alone, he was all of five, had conquered handicaps that doctors had deemed unconquerable, and even a Dietrich could not daunt him. She cooed, hovered, clucked, sighed, played the sacrificial nurse to the "afflicted," liked the connotation of complete dependence that she assumed he would be forced to exist under. As he said, when returning home that day:

"Massy was really silly, Mommy. She put on my shoes, cut all my food in little bits and got real mad because I didn't want her to feed me. I can do that now all by myself! I can, I learned it! Why was she so *mad?*"

I hugged him close. My lovely child, whose valiant battling spirit had conquered his physical destiny.

"Don't let her bother you, honey. Massy is not very bright about *really* important things."

He nodded his head – his "professor" nod he often used when contemplating anything he considered profound.

"Yes, Massy's *dumb!*" and went off to play with his favorite thing in all the big, big world – his little brother David.

Why did we keep it up? Why indeed. I think I so wanted to believe that a normal life was possible, I was blinded by my need to make it so. Bill inadvertently abetted my delusion – for him, "mothers" were people who belonged within a family unit. His world knew nothing of what my world knew too well and was afraid of. So I thought I could make it all "nice" by hiding all the ugliness from them, letting it corrode my spirit instead of theirs. I was conditioned to being ashamed of the "parent" Dietrich, they were not and should not be until they were old enough to judge for themselves. But they had to live with the backlash of my efforts and that was wrong. Being innocent spectators to fame and the adulation it begets, regardless of character content, being raised within the traditional boundaries of correct behavior, yet witnessing my mother's lack of any – and worse, seeing me condone such actions with what must have seemed to them as children, a suspect moral ease – harmed them. I should have cut – and cut deep – but did not. In subtle ways, it marked my children, for I notice the scars it left – even small, they should not have been inflicted at all. It is a crime I allowed, for which I am punished still and will be forever, and there is absolutely nothing I can do to make it right.

One of the tragedies of loving is the moment when "Kiss it and make it better" no longer works.

My mother was so busy making herself ugly for the cockney woman for *Witness for the Prosecution*, she didn't notice that I had ceased to call her, and when she called me, was too "busy" to talk. In July, when I notified her by telegram that we were moving to our little house on Long Island, she became so overly effusive, she must have been apprehensive. Her *professional* intelligence remained intact:

Saturday, July 13 '57

Oh my love,

What Joy your telegram is and what joy it gave my heart.

I have moved to a bungalow. This is my first morning at home and it is all too beautiful for me alone to have. But knowing you are at the seashore makes it less difficult to bear.

Everything is happening here. By now Laughton is co-directing me with Billy. He is a sly fox and Billy who is "in love" with him does not notice what he is doing. Through his advice I was made to yell in the first Courtroom scene which I think disastrous as I have no place to go.

But it was a beautiful foil for Laughton's long interrogation because he played it cynically sweet and led up to the end of his scene just yelling suddenly the word "Liar" after all the soft spoken proof of my lies. My yelling my answers made his sweet cynical attitude much more effective than if I had done it as I had thought of doing it. My: "No, I never loved him . . ." I wanted to say coldly which is emotional, and the spectators' reactions would have been the emotional impact against me, as they are supposed to be against me. And I always feel that people are more antagonistic toward cold and bitchy people than against anyone showing emotion.

But there were long conferences after every one of my takes, between Laughton and Billy and I just stood there and took it. I know that I have this terrible legend to overcome: that I am only interested in looks and have never acted before, and everything I would say would sound either that I did not want to distort the immobility of my face or that I knew I could not act emotional outbursts.

In the meantime Ty Power sits in the prisoner's box. He wears a beautiful tweed jacket, light in color, therefore more elegant than if the jacket were brown. His shirt is *immaculate*, cuffs freshly pressed. He wears *extra large* square *Hollywood* cuff links shining bright gold. He wears a beautiful wrist watch and a large signet ring on his little finger which has to be constantly rubbed with wax because the reflection hits the camera. His hair is brilliantined and *combed* before every take. He looks like Tyrone Power, American! When he has to bury his head in his hands out of despair about my bitchery he is very careful not to touch his hair. Like Claudette Colbert used to do because of the false bangs.

He looks as guilty as hell. None of the innocence and bewilderment the man should have so that you believe he is not guilty. None of the poor English appearance of the wrinkled cuffs and sleeves of a man who is in prison on top of that. They spray him with perspiration to make him look worried. When he makes a worried expression he looks quite guilty. But no one dares to say anything. I had gotten tiny pearl earrings from the dime store, and I was told they made me look too rich. I am photographed harshly so that nothing reminds anyone of my usual beauty, and there sits a Hollywood LEADINGMAN so out of character and his beautifully manicured hands with ring and cuff links and watch lie on the edge of the prisoner's box. I have not seen him in the witness box where he will stand in all his glory and say that he is out of a job since he lost his job, that although he is hard up he never got a chance from the old lady he is accused of having murdered. Well? One should laugh, I guess.

Now Laughton told me that he thought as I was so military in court as Mrs. Vole, I should go to the opposite and be fuzzy feminine as the Cockney woman. With a bee-stung mouth and flirtatious fiddling constantly with my hands on my clothes. When he showed it to me blinking with his little eyes and fiddling with his shirt I had to think of the joke about the analyst who tries to get the butterflies off himself that the patient says he feels on his own body.

We have also tested numerous scars. All of them too shocking to Hornblow. Until in the general discussion how wrong everything was, my makeup man said: "But I read in the script that the scar is the reason for this woman's hate and also that she shows the scar only for a flash. If it isn't horrible, why does she wear her hair hanging over it? She could put some pancake over it and cover it easily if it were just a red streak." "Ah," they said, "yes, that is true," and okayed the scar.

Billy has great trouble with the set as I anticipated. The Old Bailey is reproduced in solid wood to the specific measurements. As you know, photographically measurements mean nothing, with light you can give depth and space that is nonexistent, and can also crowd if you want to. But there they are, proud that they have the *real* thing. Except that it is new. That they have forgotten. The side ceiling, where the wood paneling stops is painted fresh and almost white, looking like a Hollywood set. The expert British Barrister we have on the set agreed with me that it is dirty up there from the years and even if they painted there each year it would never look like that. The leather on the benches is brand-new too.

On those benches sit the Hollywood extras. In their own clothes. Up-to-date hairdos, hats, jewelry à la Hollywood. Pretty faces. The men have white shirts that glare distractingly behind the actors' big printed ties. No narrow knots like the British are wearing, no middle-class English faces, all American, so wrong you cannot believe that nobody sees or objects to it. All that in the "true-to-life" Old Bailey set. No characters who go to murder trials but nice California good-looking ladies.

It is none of my business but these are the same people that judge me!

Una O'Connor played her scene exactly as she played it on the stage except she had trouble with the changed lines. She wore her same clothes and her long earrings dangled alongside of her face giving her sharp head turns a lot of life. She plays the old housekeeper of the murdered woman. There they had respect and let her do.

What else can I tell you? I have played whores all my life. And this one they don't even think I can contribute anything to.

Not that I feel they can spoil my performance altogether. I still will get Mrs. Vole on the screen, maybe not as perfect as I could have played her, but good enough.

As I have no other picture coming I find myself in that awful spot with interviewers: "What are you going to do afterwards?" All I can say is: "I go home."

> I kiss you with my heart,
> Massy

She kept her diary up to date:

Wednesday July 24th
Learning lines. Big end scene.
He called. I thought I was dreaming – Slightly drunk but not much. Enough to call me though.

Working hard and back still bad. One hour talk first time since January.

This reference to Yul's back pain may be the first indication of the virulent cancer that would destroy this talented man. On the 19th of August, she wrote:

Without brace first time. He said I came to tell you that I love you. He had three drinks when he said it. He was lying in bed when he said it.
    After saying good-bye at the door and decided to stay.

August 20th
Finished *Witness*.

August 22
Home all day waiting. Billy called, said I was wonderful in film. I Academy Award performance.
    Means nothing as *He* did not call.

September 4th
He came at 1:30 left at 4:30. Sweet, tender, looks wonderful (taking Ginseng). In bed an hour and a half. I should be happy.
    Difficult because it's love that matters, not the bed. Although that was always his sign of love.
    Dubbing Thursday Cockney woman.

September 13
Miserable. No call. Why?
To studio to see Billy. 3 PM
Chevalier
Ty Power

September 14
Dark bloodstain backache
No blood on Tampax at 9 PM put in at 12 noon
But still backache. Worried.

She had continued to record erratic staining in her yearly diaries and would continue to do so until 1964. She refused to go to a doctor.
    Tami took more and more refuge in the voices only she could hear. When they told her not to sleep, she sat for days, unmoving, eyes fixed, her frail body rigid in its suspended state. When her voices urged her to open her veins and she obeyed them, my father had her committed. It was the end of her long tortuous journey. I should have rushed to save her from

Witness for the Prosecution, with Charles Laughton and Tyrone Power, directed by Billy Wilder (BELOW). This is the only film I can remember my mother ever actually wanting to make. In it, she had a chance to play a dual role. I never thought she got away with the disguise, but she believed she did—one of the few times her sharp intelligence concerning film deserted her.

My mother wrote me enumerating all the faults of this famous court scene in *Witness for the Prosecution*. One must read her letter to appreciate her talent for criticism.

LEFT: Another Vegas, another see-through vision, another huge success, while yearning to be with her sexy "King of Siam" (BELOW).

that final anguish, but I was too engrossed with my own sorrow and fears to muster the strength to do battle for that sweet woman I loved. By the time my child had triumphed over his handicaps, it was much too late.

My mother summed it all up:

"Finally she is really crazy and put away! Now Papi can get some peace!"

His reaction was to continue his affair with Linda Darnell, begun before Tami's final collapse.

My mother returned to New York, and as her backache persisted, she resumed her daily doses of her favorite, cortisone. The moment it entered her bloodstream she felt really well. So well, in fact, that she recorded it in her diary. She also mentions that when she stopped it a week later, the numbness in her feet returned as well as the backache and so decided to continue taking cortisone on a regular basis.

When Michael Todd's plane crashed and he was killed, she went into mourning, ridiculing his real wife for doing so.

We campaigned for John Fitzgerald Kennedy, and I thought how this had been Big Joe's supposed destiny, not being shot down in a war, was glad that Jack had picked up the fallen torch, and wondered if he had really wanted to. Funny feeling to have a president who once made your knees woozy. I wished him well and wore my Kennedy button with "family" pride.

Gable died, and when I told my mother so had Henny Porten, the movie-star idol of her youth, she said, "Who? Never heard of her!"

Yul slowly began to fade from the pages of her diary. She had once said that if she could hate him, she could then stand the pain of losing him. With her Teutonic discipline, she was now true to her word. By the end of that year, the obsessive love that had so dominated her life for so many years, she had turned into an equally consuming hatred.

Unknown to my mother, Yul and I remained friends. I admired him for many reasons and always had a soft spot in my heart for Dietrich's victims.

THE WORLD

AS VON STERNBERG HAD ILLUMINATED, glorified what only his gifted
eye had seen, so now after a year of working with her, Burt Bacharach began
to mold, then hone Dietrich's talent to mesmerize a live audience vocally. He
rewrote all her orchestrations, trimmed her excessive use of violins, allowing
them only when their lilt would be most effective, injected American rhythm
into her old standards, then taught her how to sing "swing." He coached her,
directed her, treated her as a knowledgeable musician whose ability needed
only polishing to be recognized as laudable talent. As her confidence grew,
so did her ability to take command of a stage as a performer, not simply a
Hollywood glamour queen come to warble her ditties. From time to time,
as I found songs I knew were particularly suited to her philosophy of life and
loving, I discussed them with her, then sent the music to Burt to write his
orchestration, that is, if he agreed and approved of my choice. No one ever
was a better arranger for Dietrich's vocal capacity than Bacharach. By the
time she embarked on her first international tour in her one-woman show,
the Dietrich nightclub image had been replaced by a powerful performer,
in full command of her talent and, under the constant watchful eye of her
musical mentor, her material. All that was left over from her Las Vegas
days were the shimmering dresses and the extravaganza of the swansdown
coat. At sixty, she had found at last the lover she had been seeking since her
adolescence: one who worshiped without complaint, demanded nothing in
return, was grateful for all she might give, constant, welcomed the sweet
agonies of loving she offered, accepted her sorrows as his own, enjoyed
her with an exaltation devoid of all physical contact. This new lover
was completely hers to control, he was even punctual. As she had so
meticulously noted the minutes, the hours with Yul, she now recorded
the exact time her new and perfect love affair with her audience could begin
with "Curtain" – 8:30.

With Burt's talent protecting her, she began to tour the world. She triumphed on the concert stages of South America, Canada, Spain, Great Britain, the United States, Israel, France, Portugal, Italy, Australia, Mexico, Poland, Sweden, Germany, Holland, Russia, Belgium, Denmark, South Africa, and Japan. Knowing the people of Israel, I persuaded her not to cut her German songs from her repertoire as she had planned, but to sing them, and in the original language. She was hesitant about it. I said, "Believe me, do it," and she did, was loved and respected for her honesty.

She called me from Tel Aviv: "They loved me. They cried, kissed my hands. The theater was full – full! So many that did not get killed by the Nazis. Amazing!" and had a fast affair with one of Israel's more flamboyant politicians.

Brazil, too, offered more than just popular adulation:

> Hotel Jaragua
> São Paulo – Brazil

> It's autumn here – Beautiful!
> My love – quickly just so that you know. Great opening here. And Ricardo Fasanelli (the same FASAN – Goldfasan my sister used to call me "Golden Pheasant": the bird). Thirty years old. Basque and Italian ancestors intermarried . . . so out comes that delicately boned narrow body and face. . . . Giant black eyes very short-sighted, sometimes with horn-rimmed glasses. Baby-hair dark brown. Brilliant – and rubs his eyes with the fist like babies do. See what I mean? To die, no?
> I said at one point: "This is ridiculous – I promise you I will pull my net in." (We had just been talking about the ocean and fishermen and boats.) He said: "You do not make sense. You said you were in love with me and now you say: I promise to pull in my net. You couldn't do that if you are in love." Can you see how I greet all this with passionate delight? After all these years of emotional idiots? Maybe we should keep this the way it is, just loving each other's souls. Anyway I do no seducing or even suggesting anything else. But God, how he looks at me. It makes your teeth rattle.
> Kisses.

> Massy

When an egg was thrown at her during a performance in Germany, the audience nearly lynched the offender, then gave Dietrich a standing ovation for refusing to be driven off the stage by a "mere Nazi." One night, during her triumphal German tour, she fell off the stage into the darkened orchestra pit. My phone rang:

"Sweetheart – I fell!" Her frightened voice was barely audible.

"Where are you now?"

"In bed, in my hotel."

"Where did you hit when you fell?"

"Not my legs. Don't worry; only my left shoulder. It hurts but I tied my arm against my body with one of the men's ties and I finished the show. Thank god, I was already in the tails, so the dress didn't get torn when I fell."

"Now listen to me carefully. There is an American hospital near you in Wiesbaden. First thing in the morning, you go there and have them x-ray you – "

She interrupted:

"Oh! Nothing is broken! Just the stage was so dark, I didn't see the edge and suddenly disappeared from view. . . . Must have looked very funny to the audience."

"Don't try to get out of it. You go to Wiesbaden tomorrow for X rays. That's an order!"

On her return from the hospital, she called:

"I said to them, 'You see how my daughter is always right? She told me I had to come here and be x-rayed. She sits all the way back in New York and is the only one who knows that there is an American hospital in Wiesbaden.' You were right, as usual – they say my collarbone is broken, whatever that is, but I am just going to tie my arm to my side, like I did yesterday, and so, I can go on with the tour."

She did just that, and the added pathos of this indomitable soldier, gallantly performing despite her busted wing, endeared her even further to her German audience. I had a suspicion that too much champagne, and not just the darkened stage, had contributed to her fall. Her drinking had accelerated, not only before and after a performance, but during it as well. I knew the constant ache in her legs and back had become the perfect excuse to increase the intake of narcotics and alcohol she had been taking for years. Somehow, I had to get her to be examined by a reputable physician.

Again I was waiting for a baby. Again I spoke on television, again my mother accused me of putting my unborn child at risk. In the summer of '61, she was in Hollywood filming *Judgment at Nuremberg* but managed to fly back to New York in time to announce to my husband that I had given birth to another boy. She was genuinely surprised that this one was "unmarked by that telethon thing!"

By this time, my mother had decided which of my children were special enough, in her opinion, to be awarded her undying devotion.

She informed me Michael had inherited her "elegant, thin bones," and as his hair was also blond, she considered him her own. The fact that I had borne him was a mere happenstance, not worth a thought. Peter she tolerated – just. At the innocent age of two, he had looked at her one day and piped:

"Massy – you look old today," which put him out of the running for her favors for the rest of his life! He never rated porcelain bells, delicate silver sleighs, not even scampering Bambis. His Christmas "package codes" were always the least pretty, usually in shades of blah brown. Paul she had immediately adopted as her "serious cause," played "St. Bernadette to the afflicted," and would have wrapped him in emotional cotton had I let her. My new baby did not interest her in the least. He looked like my husband and screamed whenever she came near him. From birth, David was very intelligent.

She came to the hospital, cautioned me against having any *more* children, and returned to Hollywood, where she gave an amazing performance as the righteous wife of a condemned Nazi general. She never realized and would have been outraged if anyone had suggested such a thing, but the woman she portrayed so skillfully in *Judgment at Nuremberg* was a meticulous, brilliant recreation of her mother – masquerading as Tante Valli. How sad that her most vivid subconscious memory of her mother – should be one of stoic self-aggrandizing loyalty to duty – in a black velvet suit.

That summer, Hemingway committed suicide. My mother, in flowing black, took his letters out of their special strongbox, locked herself in her room, and played widow. Read his words over and over again, searching for a phrase, a thought, that might give her a clue as to – why. She never really came to terms with her friend's death nor ever forgave him for deserting her. Secretly, she blamed his wife:

"If *I* had been there with him, he would never have done it!"

Gary Cooper's death did not stir her to widowhood. She just went to his funeral and was photographed looking "stricken."

A wall went up – dividing Berlin and Germany; the *Tropic of Cancer* was finally allowed to be legally published in the United States, and Dietrich allowed herself to be examined by a competent physician.

The first X rays showed massive occlusions of the lower aorta. Because of this blockage of her main arterial branch, her legs were being literally starved of their normal blood supply. This accounted for the practically nonexistent pulse in both of her legs. Naturally, she refused to believe the diagnosis. In her view, only "old" people got advanced arteriosclerosis.

"That's what they told me my mother died of. You see how stupid they are? Of course, she had it because she was *old*!"

I persuaded her to consult the leading cardiologist of the day for a second opinion, and when he not only confirmed the original diagnosis but added the warning that if she did not have immediate attention, she faced the possibility of amputation of both limbs in the future, she refused to have anything more to do with any of them:

"Surgeons! All they want to do is cut. That's why they are surgeons. Ridiculous!"

For the next thirteen years, my mother played her own deadly version of Russian roulette with her body's circulatory system and nearly got away with it. Whenever she read or heard of anything that was touted to increase the flow of blood, she got it and took it, regardless of what it was or where it came from; found a weird little Frenchman who called himself a doctor by wearing a white smock, let him inject a secret potion into her groin with a horse syringe, for he had assured her that only his magic mixture could flush all the blockage from her arteries.

Her legs worsened, particularly the left one, which had the least pulse. The foot and ankle swelled, an ugliness she found abhorrent. So, once again, what she had done by chance for quite different reasons years before, now worked to her advantage and offered her the camouflage she needed. She resumed wearing her famous trousers. They hid the elastic stockings she was now forced to wear, and later, the bandages. For her tours, she invented tall boots, wore them with her new short-skirted Chanel suits, and set a fashion trend. For those times when she was forced to wear more elaborate clothes, she designed shoes that were elegant but did not attract the eye, then had them made in the same color as her stockings to further emphasize and enhance the illusion of the perfect unbroken leg and foot line.

When the first support tights came on the market, they were a real boon to her. She redesigned her foundation to include them. First, she eliminated the garter belt construction, substituted a row of eyes on which the tiny hooks sewn along the top band of the tights could be fastened around the waist, making them an integral part of the foundation design.

As the swellings were erratic and completely unpredictable, the left foot being sometimes two sizes larger than the right, boots and shoes had to be made in varying sizes. It was not unusual for Dietrich to pack eight pairs of identical boots in various graded sizes, repeated in twenty different designs and materials, before departing on one of her international tours.

Why the mystery? Why the desperate need to conceal the truth? Simple. She believed that no human flaw must ever be permitted to mar the perfection of the legend that was Marlene Dietrich and – history proved her right. But this game of hoodwinking the public produced a dangerous side effect – as long as she looked an unblemished Dietrich, she believed it herself.

In 1962, she narrated the *Black Fox*, gave this documentary on Hitler the prestige and impact it deserved, winning for it the Academy Award the following year. She again played Vegas, replaced her customary champagne with scotch when she learned that it opened veins, rekindled her affair with Michael Wilding so energetically that they broke the double bed in the guest room of the home of my friends. When she heard that Elizabeth Taylor was in need of a better bra to wear under her costumes in *Cleopatra*, she took Wilding with her for advice as to the correct size, scoured Hollywood for the perfect brassière, found it, and sent three dozen off to Rome. Had a fling with Eddie Fisher and observed, *now* she understood why Taylor had left him, was so "gaga" over Richard Burton.

By July she was back in New York to help us move to Europe. As our two eldest were scheduled to enter boarding school in Switzerland for their junior and senior high school years, and as Bill now had his own design business, we were "movable" and decided to set up camp near them with the two youngest.

While we drove through Switzerland looking for a town we could afford to settle in, my mother rented a little house near Geneva and took care of our year-old baby. I knew he was safe. He didn't cry anymore when she came near him – just gave a look of "don't you *dare* lay a finger on me." She wore her nurse's uniforms, starched and pristine, sterilized everything in sight, then received carefully screened friends to witness how superbly she was taking care of Maria's "neglected child." After many visits, Noël Coward had enough material to do a wonderfully amusing routine entitled "Visiting Marlenah's Nursery in Jussy."

I did love Noël. For some reason, I felt very maternal toward him. Always got the urge to reach out, put my arms around him whenever we met. I don't know why – just felt he was hurting inside that polished frame and needed comforting. For Dietrich, it was his style, brilliant success, and the "Noël Coward," as he lived his own creation of himself, that was her "chum." The sensitive, vulnerable, serious man, so easily lonely, hidden so well beneath the throwaway charm – him, she never took the time to find. And if she had? It would have confused her.

We returned to "Marlenah's nursery" to find my mother's sister in residence, utterly bewildered by all the rules of hygiene she was expected to adhere to and scared stiff that her adored Pussy Cat would once again be annoyed by her usual clumsiness. My Aunt Liesel welcomed my return

RIGHT: In her "lady" suit for *Judgment at Nuremberg,* looking like her mother. BELOW: She liked Spencer Tracy because Katharine Hepburn loved him, and was terribly jealous of the protection from scandal MGM accorded these two stars.

ABOVE: In *Touch of Evil* she played the bit part for nothing as a favor to her friend Orson Welles and was probably better than she had been since *The Blue Angel*.

BELOW: When we ran out of ideas for finales, we sometimes switched from black to white. In Rio de Janeiro, it looked great.

with sighs of relief, her little wren eyes brimming with tears of joy. I
should have known from past experience that once my mother had been
given authority over anyone, she assumed they were hers in perpetuity.
She greeted me with:

"David – walks! *I* taught him to walk!" as though God, nature, and his
age of thirteen months had absolutely nothing to do with it. From then
on, whenever she saw David, the first words out of her mouth were: "*Who
taught you to walk?*" said in a tone of military challenge, *daring* him to
give her a wrong answer. This can be a little embarrassing in the crowded
lobby of a Broadway opening night when you are twenty-five.

With my mother and her latest girlfriend, very smart in Chanel suits
and inherited wealth in residence, our first Christmas in our new home
near Geneva was a disaster. It was Europe – my mother's domain –
and French-speaking to boot! She ran everything. Me, my home, my
children, the village. When she tried to extend her field-marshal tactics
to my husband, he balked – "No way! New Year's Eve with those two
females is out!" – and I put in an SOS to Noël, fifty-some miles down
the road at Les Avants:

"Dear child! Simply send the German lady and her latest on to me!"
which we did and for which I thanked him with all my heart.

It was around this time that my mother invented her story of why
she suddenly stopped smoking. We all knew that the doctors had been
horrified at her continuing to smoke despite their warnings and that finally
she was frightened enough by the increasing leg cramps to stop. But the
gestures of smoking, the cigarette held so elegantly, the cupped hands
shielding an offered flame, the emphasis of cheekbones as she pulled the
smoke into her lungs with obvious pleasure, the pucker of her lips as she
exhaled, were so much a visual part of the Dietrich image, she knew the
press would notice their absence and want to know why. She told her
cover story so often, she finally believed it herself:

"Sweetheart! You know the year I stopped smoking – the legs,
always the legs! But you can't tell people that's why. So I said to
Noël, 'You should stop smoking too. You don't walk so well either
and we will tell them that we made a bet – whoever smokes loses.
That's fun, not something medical. We can play that very bon vivant,
à la man-of-the-world – you know, like: "Of course! I would *adore* a
cigarette! But I simply *can't*, I have a bet on with Marlenah!"'"

Years later, when Noël resumed smoking, she was furious and
called him:

"What about our bet?"

"What bet?"

"I have dreamt of a cigarette ever since you made that bet with me.

Not a day goes by that I don't *yearn* for a cigarette. I haven't slept one night since I gave up smoking!"

I could hear Noël chuckling all the way from Jamaica:

"My dearest Marlenah – it's been six years! You must be exhausted!"

My mother never appreciated sarcasm. Anyone daring to make fun of her was such an outrageous thought, that she never contemplated its possibility. But she had the last word:

"You see! Even without sleep, I have more discipline than you have. You lost our bet!" and slammed down the phone.

Near Montreux, just below where Noël had his Swiss home, a doctor, a pioneer in live-cell theory, ran his famous clinic. Although he boasted many cures for legitimate ills, the international fame of his treatment was perpetuated by those who spend their lives and fortunes searching for the fountain of youth. Patients checked into his elegant château on a Tuesday. The patient guest list was secret, and meticulously guarded. Wednesday they were tested and questioned:

> Memory flagging?
> Skin going to flab?
> Bones creaking?
> Perhaps a bored libido?

After these briefings, the patient returned to his lovely room to gaze out of French windows at fluffy pregnant sheep grazing contentedly on emerald green meadows. Thursday was slaughter day. The woolly sheep were cut open and their fetuses removed for their abundant supply of unused cells. A few very fresh brain cells for the memory. A half a teaspoon of bone cells for those creaking joints. A pinch of newborn liver cells to refresh that toxic one. A bit of this, a bit of that – put them all in a blender, mix until it looks like a rusty-colored malted, fill into enormous syringes, then shoot all those "miraculous" goodies into the willing and waiting behinds of the rich and desperate.

I always pooh-poohed the entire concept, but my mother took this cell treatment four different times, and knowing what she went through, what she was able to endure over the rest of her lifetime, I often wondered if that ghoulish intramuscular cocktail didn't have something to do with her amazing endurance. That incredible fortitude of hers just couldn't have been due to Prussian genes alone!

THE REST OF 1963, she toured the United States, performing in Washington, D.C., where she visited the charming son of her old boyfriend, Ambassador Kennedy.

September 6, 1963
Open Washington
Sold out

September 9
Women's Press Club. Walton drinks.
Visit Harriman.

September 10
With Walton Lunch White House.
Senator Pell
White House
Saw Jack 20 minutes
Show sold out.

September 11
Lunch Bobby at Bill Walton's
Schlesinger, Buckley (*Newsweek* and Mrs. B. Kennedy)
Wrote letter Papa Kennedy
White House drinks Jack
Jewish congregation to give me plaque. Had to cut White House visit short.
Not the first time the Jews interfered with my life.
Show at 10:30–250 sent away.

As we had rented our house in New York, my husband, when in America on business, stayed at my mother's apartment. He was there the day she returned from Washington. She came through the door, saw him, opened her large black crocodile handbag, extracted a pair of pink panties, and held them under his nose, saying:

"Smell! It is him! The President of the United States! He – was – wonderful!"

My husband moved to a hotel.

WE SETTLED IN LONDON for the young children's schooling, and, in order to be near us, my mother moved to Paris, where she rented an apartment opposite the Plaza Athénée.

Two of my mother's French "friends" died in October. To one, she had been a lover, to the other, a lifelong "pal." From both, Dietrich learned valuable lessons that enriched her stage career. Edith Piaf gave my mother her song "la Vie en rose" and taught her the art of economy of stage gestures. Jean Cocteau, the art of exaggeration to achieve the maximum theatrical effect on a large stage. My mother mourned Piaf like a husband his child bride, and took great comfort from the fact that her "little Sparrow" was buried wearing the gold cross she had given her on her wedding day. Cocteau's lyrical tribute to Dietrich she framed along with his picture and hung it next to Hemingway's.

She came over to London for the anniversary gala of the Battle of El Alamein. The Royal Albert Hall was jammed; many famous stars had agreed to appear to commemorate this great British victory against the "desert fox," the mighty Rommel. I dressed my mother in her golden sheath, walked her through the catacombs of that bastion of Victorian culture, sent her out onto its vast platform stage.

She stood in a single shaft of light, like a sword reflecting the rays of the sun, Excalibur made woman! Took a beat and began "Lili Marlene," and that giant domed concert hall took on a silence of such awe and respect, it vibrated like a living thing in that hushed air. The hall was filled with the veterans of that terrible desert war, and they accepted her as one of their own. She was quite magnificent that night and she knew it, but was angry we hadn't remembered her medals.

"Tonight, finally, I could have worn them – all of them!"

In November, my mother returned to appear at a royal command performance. As handmaiden conveniently in place, I took her through the rehearsals and dressed her. There were many famous stars who were scheduled to appear that night. We stood together backstage, waiting for our individual rehearsals to begin.

"Sweetheart – look. Look over there," she whispered. "What *are* those? They look like monkeys with all that hair! What are *they* doing backstage? All this big 'security' and *they* got in? Just look at them – how terrible!" and pointed to the Beatles.

"Massy, I think it would be a wonderful idea if Dietrich were photographed with them – "

"What? With those *monkeys?*"

"Yes – they are the new rage, kids adore them. It would create a big stir if Dietrich were seen accepting them! Trust me!"

She gave me one of her "the things I do for you" looks, and I walked over to John Lennon and said that Miss Dietrich had expressed the desire to meet the Beatles. When the photograph of The Legend and the soon-to-be ones hit every newspaper in the world, my mother was heard to exclaim:

"The Beatles? *You* don't know who the Beatles are? How is that possible? They are geniuses – they don't look it, but they are geniuses and so young! I asked them if I could have their autographs for Maria's children, and they said all they wanted was a picture taken with me – so of course I had to say yes!"

I WAS WORRYING where in London I was going to find real cranberry sauce for Thanksgiving dinner and Crisco for pies . . . and pumpkin? The TV was on. Suddenly – that pink suit . . . all I remember is that *pink* . . . scrambling out onto the back of the speeding car, reaching, a blur of bright color . . . over and over again, in slow motion, in speed, again and again, that pink haunted, became a part of our life – and I, so far from home, sat stunned, disbelieving, praying it was not true, knowing that it was, and . . . I saw him, tanned and lean, diving off the highest cliff, bowing in his white tuxedo jacket asking for a dance, laughing over tea, walking away so sure of himself toward that sexy convertible, so handsome, so wonderfully alive! He would be mourned by many, the great and small of many lands; I mourned him for the youth he wore so well.

My mother donned simple widow's black, her face a white mask of personal sorrow, sat erect, her voice hushed and reverent as she repeatedly told of their last romantic encounter.

By Christmas, a writer of children's books asked for "it," and helped ease her sorrow. They enjoyed each other so, this lady appeared often at our door during the holidays. My small children were oblivious. My older ones, home on vacation, asked a few pertinent questions and were given straight answers. They had observed enough of my mother's romantic entanglements, spent summer days with Yul, teas with Murrow, Christmas Eves with her real husband while the acting husband carved, to have no illusions about their grandmother's life-style.

Unfortunately, her lady author was killed in a plane crash soon after the New Year, and so, my mother went back into "widowhood" before she was completely through with the last one.

IN HER CRYSTAL DRESS, she stood before the velvet curtain, an incandescent diamond against the ruby-red curtain of the Queen's Theatre. She had made it. She had performed, been acclaimed on the same stage that had witnessed the brilliance of Olivier, Richardson, Gielgud, Ashcroft, and most of the great actors of England. It was her opening night in London and she had given the best performance of her life and knew it. We all did. The exuberant audience response merely confirmed this fact. The entire first London stage engagement was magical. She basked in being the toast of the town. London was at the feet of a Hollywood movie star who had stepped off her turf onto their hallowed boards and been accepted. She worked hard, played hard, slept little, was thin as a rail, at sixty-three – she had never looked better.

Only two things marred this successful time: the new pain in the region of her rectum, and the need to wear her trusty Tampax continuously to staunch the persistent pink staining. When she heard that an ailment called colitis could cause sharp pains similar to the ones she was experiencing and that a concoction known as slippery elm would cure it, we went shopping at London's health-food emporium and bought out the store. If slippery elm could cure "pains down there," why not find something to cure everything else that was bothering her? We returned to her Dorchester suite and set up "Dietrich's health clinic" in the spare bedroom. She particularly liked the idea that apple-cider vinegar, mixed with honey, was supposed to be the true elixir of life. She proceeded to mix half-gallon jugs immediately, and had them delivered to Burt's dressing room, along with his freshly laundered tuxedo shirts.

"Not that Burt needs any *more* energy, but you never know what he might pick up from those girls of his!"

Bill refused to partake, after he heard my mother exclaim in wonder how amazed she was that what she had been douching with all these years, she was now drinking!

She continued losing weight. We had to unpack the foundations marked "very tight." The thinner she got, the better she liked it, and in those incredible dresses, she did look divine.

The day after she closed in London, I took her to the great gynecologist Prof. de Watteville in Geneva. She was frightened and therefore full of fury. She called Noël:

"My private Gestapo, Maria, is dragging me to Geneva just so that her precious doctor can examine me. That's all she does – have me examined by strange men!"

After her initial consultation, she returned to Paris; I continued on to Gstaad to meet Bill and visit our boys' school in the Swiss mountains. I was so certain that my mother had cancer that I had arranged with the professor to secretly call me there the moment the results of the tests were in. He did, told me that she had cancer of the cervix.

My mother thought of cancer as a slow process of inner decay. I knew that she would never accept this process going on inside Dietrich. She, who was so proud to proclaim herself a soldier's daughter, always lacked the courage to face up to stark reality. If my mother had been told that she had cancer and that a hysterectomy was mandatory, she would have jumped out of the nearest window, German or no German discipline. So, the professor and I discussed alternatives. He was a wonderful man. He had many famous world beauties as patients and understood how vulnerable, how immature some of these women could be about their bodies. He suggested that it might be possible to do a series of radium implants; if, by some slim miracle, these radioactive packings resulted in checking the cancer, surgery might be avoided, for a while at least. We agreed to buy time. I suggested he tell my mother that the treatment he proposed was for a precancerous condition only and not in order to treat an already developed cancer. This script would be the only one she might accept. She was furious, balked, finally consented to being treated, but only if I accompanied her, stayed with her the full time.

In March, I flew from London to Geneva and met my mother as she arrived from Paris. She was so drunk, I had to help her into the waiting car. At the hospital, she gave orders that a cot be placed immediately in her room for me to sleep on. The nurses were alarmed and attempted to explain that if I were to stay in the room with her, I too would be exposed to radiation and any future children I might want could conceivably be at risk. My mother was not impressed.

"My daughter doesn't need any more children! And risk? She does that to them all by herself! She will stay here in this room with me!"

March 6, 1965
Curettage and first implant.

March 7
Taken out 3 P. M.

Before taking her back to Paris, I made her give me her solemn oath that she would return with me for her second treatment, scheduled for March 27th. I had to force her, but she went.

March 27
Second implant.

March 29
5:30 A. M. OUT.

As my mother was not allowed to have a telephone in her room, a nurse
came, conducted me to a glass-enclosed booth in the Victorian lobby of
the infirmary, to take my father's call from overseas. So I was alone when
I heard his voice telling me that Tami was dead. I remember the pretty
colors the sun made as it hit the cut-glass panels of the little booth; how
glad I was to be in a private place where I could cry. Sweet Tami – forgive
me. You should not have been left to die alone amongst mad strangers.

I returned to my mother's room. She was annoyed that I had been so
long on the phone. I gave her the news of Tami's death. She paused,
sighed, and said:

"Poor Papi! Anyway, it's good that he has that pretty Darnell woman
– so he's not alone," and that was Tami's epitaph from the lady who had
destroyed her life.

On the 24th of April, three and a half weeks after her last radium
implant, Marlene Dietrich opened her one-woman show in Johannesburg,
South Africa, to jubilant acclaim. While I glowed a little in the dark, my
mother, at sixty-four, had beaten cancer and didn't even know it!

By August, she was appearing in Edinburgh and became involved
with a gentleman she referred to as "P.D.," and, years later, as "that
sentimental old Jew I had in Edinburgh." Next, she toured Australia,
where she fell madly in love with a reporter, of all people, who looked like
a pugilist or a very, very, very poor man's version of Gabin – depending
on how much he had had to drink. As he had a wife and children, their
affair, which lasted for nearly two years, took on the intrigues of a French
bedroom farce.

She couldn't remain in Australia forever, so in the guise of helping
Dietrich write her memoirs, her new love persuaded his paper to give
him a leave of absence and followed his lady love to Paris. Although his
official address was the home of my mother's loyal friends, he secretly
lived with her in her apartment. To justify his remaining for longer and
longer periods, my mother devised a scheme of introducing him to other
famous people for the purpose of writing a series of profiles.

For the first time, Dietrich was willing to use her rather awesome
connections. She called everyone, telling them about this wonderful
young Australian writer she had found, who would be *so* grateful if they
granted him a moment of their precious time to write a piece about them.
While my mother was busy lining up the world's celebrities for her lover
to interview, our happy-go-lucky reporter lived the life of Riley.

Of course, she kept me informed. I was constantly amazed by my mother's absolute conviction that I would be intensely interested in everything concerning her. I was expected to listen to every detail of her life with him: his habits, his likes, his dislikes, his abilities both in and out of bed, his problems with his wife.

"You know, he is like a child! Excited to be in Paris. I don't think he has ever eaten such food," her voice dropped to a confidential whisper. "I don't think he comes from a very good family, so I am teaching him how one behaves in first-class restaurants."

All that restaurant-hopping must have caused her to gain some weight, for she complained: "You and your doctor fetish – I was so *wonderfully* thin in London! But *you* had to force me to go to that hospital in Geneva, and *now* – all my waistbands are too tight!"

She flew to London, with her Australian, and arrived at my house with him in tow. For some reason, this lover made my flesh crawl, an instantaneous reaction that interested me as much as it confused me. I had long ago stopped being affected one way or another by the array of flotsam my mother brought to my door – still, with this one, I balked. Somehow, I didn't want my children exposed to him – there was an aura of contagion about him.

On July 22nd, her brash Australian had the guts to write his own entry into my mother's "sacred" diary:

> *His*: Tonight she told me that men like I, know "Only about getting into bed and going 'Bam' – 'Bam' – and that's it." She added that we lack the imagination of men like another she mentioned. This, as someone said before, was the unkindest cut of all. I always thought going to bed with her a joy. Especially when it was not a fight night and, instead, we made love, sometimes – it seemed – forever. Those ruddy medicos tell us that women always get more out of that than we do. It appears that she is an exception. Or, does she want me to *think* that she is? I hope so. I love her.

Finally, he just had to return to his wife and job, but they made plans to meet secretly in Hollywood and, later, in Australia.

She returned to London for another triumph and arranged for her sister to fly in to witness it. In between sitting her down, making her listen to her "Pussy Cat's" many LPs for hours on end, Liesel was taken for slow walks, while being reminded to "take it easy" because of her varicose veins, her weight, her arthritis, her failing eyesight. "Oh, Lieselchen – be careful!" "Lieselchen, are you cold?" "Are you hungry?" "Are you tired?" "Are you all right?" – bounced about in such tones of speaking to the mentally afflicted. I cringed for my aunt, who didn't. She had been a victim so long, one couldn't victimize her.

While my aunt was in residence, I remember a bizarre family dinner in my mother's Dorchester suite. My clever husband had, once again, found something "urgent" to keep him from joining us. Bill had a way of doing that successfully that I envied. Over the lobster bisque, Michael and Peter, now seventeen and fifteen, asked Liesel what it had *really* been like to live in Germany during the Second World War. While my mother served our resplendent room-service banquet, hovering as usual over the table, anticipating her guests' slightest wish, completely oblivious to whatever was being said, we listened in growing amazement to her sister expound on the moral integrity of the German Reich. Assuredly, there had been some bad Nazis, but one could not deny that during their reign, Germany had regained its lost glory. We finished dinner, my sons took flight, slightly critical that I stayed. I couldn't blame them, yet I was sorry for this strange little woman, now so complex in her loyalties, who once had been so far-seeing, so politically astute. Somewhere she had lost her way or, more likely, the way had never been hers to lose.

A few years after that dinner, in yet another London hotel suite, my mother received a phone call informing her that Liesel had died. She turned to stone. I pried the receiver from her rigid hand, poured her a double scotch. She did not cry. From then on, whenever my mother referred to her sister, it was "Remember that day in London, when they called me and told me that Liesel was dead? I performed that night – I forget where I was playing, but I know I went on. I did my job! 'Do your duty,' my mother always told us. Poor Liesel, that terrible husband of hers, she wouldn't listen. She stayed because of her child. When I searched and found her in the concentration camp the day the British liberated Belsen, she wouldn't leave. All because of that son of hers! He was, of course, in the German army and she was frightened that if she moved he wouldn't know where to find her! So, I got Gavin and the British to find her a better apartment and got permission so that she could stay in Belsen and wait for her son."

Dietrich said these words to many people and never once did anyone challenge her, ask for explanations of the so obvious discrepancies. It is this nonchallenging, this automatic acceptance, without corroboration of utterances made by "living legends," and even nonliving ones, that angers me. People, and this includes those famous for their intellect, seem to have an inbuilt aversion to pick at surface gold, get down to those possible feet of clay. The fear of tumbling man-made gods is a really powerful phobia.

TWO HUNDRED THOUSAND U.S. TROOPS, under the guise of a nonaggression force, were now fighting in the jungles of Vietnam. The napalm bombing runs had begun.

My mother returned to California, secretly met up with her Aussie, took him onto the set of *Who's Afraid of Virginia Woolf?*, was ever so friendly with one of her pet hates, Elizabeth Taylor, and basked in the "looks" Richard Burton threw her way.

"Sweetheart! Oh, he is so beautiful! Those eyes! That voice! So Welsh! He *is* Welsh, right? I felt his eyes on me the whole time and had to pretend I didn't feel them, because everyone was watching. That Bitch – is even going to *act* in this picture because he is carrying her in the palm of his hands through the whole film with *his* talent. But, you should have seen them both – ever so jealous – because Burton couldn't keep his eyes off me. I wore my rain jacket, the shiny black one with the red lining, low heels – very simple, no big 'glamour.' I knew Taylor would do the "star" bit enough. Maybe that's what Burton liked? Wasn't he once a coal miner?"

IN 1967, DIETRICH CONQUERED BROADWAY. Although her producer had asked me to come to New York to fill my usual role of peacemaker between outrageously difficult star and the suffering minions, I couldn't. My husband was gravely ill. So I wasn't there for the nightly traffic jams, New York's finest on nervous horses trying to control the surging crowds blocking all of Forty-sixth Street, she – Chanel skirts hiked to her crotch – balanced on the top of cars, throwing autographed pictures like confetti to the screaming multitudes down below; nor when Dietrich accepted her special Tony Award for her one-woman show, broadcast live on national television. As she made her entrance, she stumbled, nearly fell, then slurred her thanks. Her words overlaid with that thick comic German accent that appeared in her speech whenever Dietrich was thoroughly soused. Those who called me in London to report my mother's shocking condition that night assured me that as she looked so absolutely fabulous, probably no one had even noticed. The next season, when Dietrich returned to Broadway, I was able to heed her producer's SOS and went to baby-sit his star. I arrived in New York, went straight to the theater, and was greeted with, "The witch is on her broomstick," and walked into a hornet's nest. The place was buzzing with fury and borderline mayhem.

"Well! Finally! The plane landed two hours ago! *Look* at this dressing room!" She stood aside for me to get a better view. In her honor, it had been painted, decorated, furnished – all new, all clean, and very un-Broadway. It is one of those affectations of the legitimate theater that dressing rooms have to be stark, ugly, with overtones of small-town morgue. This one was actually quite pretty.

"See? Garden furniture! Bent sticks and orange cushions? Not to be believed! And *dangerous* for the dresses!" Knowing she had a point about the rattan possibly catching the fine souffle, I didn't even try to cajole her into accepting the decor.

"Okay, Mass. Don't worry. This is easy to fix. You concentrate on the really important things, do your scheduled orchestra rehearsal – I'll do the dressing room."

A fast change in furniture is a bit harder to do, but we did it.

With the help of a courageous salesman, we collected floor models, stripped the French furniture department of Bloomingdale's, roped it to the roof of the gleaming limousine, stuffed the rest in the back, and two hours later, Dietrich had a gold-and-powder-blue "French château," instead of "Adirondacks porch". Her poor producer, when he got that bill, he flinched – but paid. One thing about Alexander Cohen, he always tried to make her happy, no matter what fortunes it cost him.

Next came the Flower Rooms. Just like the old days, when the trunks had their own allotted rooms in hotels, now our traveling florist shop and its special personnel had their own "dressing room." Having heard that the "cavalry" had arrived from London, they now descended on me like butterflies in heat.

"Mrs. Riva! Mrs. Riva! We haven't got our flower rooms yet! Where *shall* we put our boxes? And the pink ribbon they got for us – it won't *do!* It's all *wrong!* It's *synthetic* – not satin! And the pink is too *deep!* . . . Oh! It's all so disorganized – and tables? Where are our *tables?*" The Flower Boys always got very rattled as an opening night approached. One calmed them down with lots of soothing appreciation of their *tremendous* responsibilities, gave them the importance they craved, a strong cup of herbal tea, and then they were as good as new.

It was one of our best gimmicks; the organized running-down aisles of handsome young men, waving their lovely bouquets to present to their Queen. They were well rehearsed, their floral tributes in shades of complementary pinks, their attitude: "This is the first time I have *ever* done such a thing!" They did this act twice, once before "Honeysuckle Rose," so that Dietrich would just "happen" to have received a perfect nosegay trailing pink ribbons to swing in tempo to its jazzy rhythm, and at the end, in staggered runs, to lift, frame, prolong the homage to the vision so beautiful gathering up the many floral tributes offered by her young admirers. This also gave the audience the courage to join in the homage with their own posies. A lot of young men met on those euphoric sprints and remained friends forever.

I stood in back of the theater and watched my mother – star – on a Broadway stage. I who had seen her be superb, so many times, now saw her do a mediocre imitation of herself. The shimmering look, the incredible body, the pearl-pink skin, the golden hair, the military carriage, the hypnotic gaze from beneath those famous hooded lids – all was there, perfect and sublime, but the spirit was not. Vibrant energy had become diffused by spirits from a bottle, and her art lay heavy in the throes of mediocrity.

The audience went wild, gave her a standing ovation, the Flower Boys sprinted with their nosegays – still, her second Broadway triumph was more in memory of the first than its own.

I was never an audience fan of Dietrich's. Having been part of constructing the platform for her performances, I knew each transition, the split second of each gesture, every look, every pause and intonation. Being the innate, trainable soldier that she was, the structure of her performances never varied. Even when she was drunk, one could set one's stopwatch by when an arm would lift, a special pause would occur, a look punctuate a meaning of a lyric, a measured silence, a lowering of the head. With her amazing discipline, she Xeroxed her performance, night after night, year after year. It was this ironclad, unwavering construction that so depended on an inner vitality, a sudden burst of magical adrenaline, to bring it into glorious existence, make her come to life.

All great performers who go on forever live with this danger of becoming their own carbon copies. It is just that my mother started out as one, and so, to infuse it with ever new life became harder and harder as time passed. Finally, the drugs dulled even the spark of its ignition. As Dietrich believed her audience was there to only listen and worship, she didn't consider them having a life force of their own to contribute to her performance and, so, never called on it to help her when she needed it most. In this unawareness of her audience as possible energizing participants, she was forever the real Movie Star – remote, removed, up there looking down from above at those who had come to pay her homage. It made her later years as a performer terribly hard, and very lonely.

While I was still with her, she decided to fly my father, now infirm from long-term heart disease, in from L.A. to witness her Broadway triumph. The cuffs of his heavy silk shirts were frayed, the Knize suits hung on his old-man frame, his vicuña overcoat had thinned. His swollen legs made walking difficult; he used a cane to find his way, the splendid one my mother had bought for herself to wear with the broken ankle. He hadn't completely lost his air of elegance, only its polish of authority. He was a proud man – without pride.

Strange to have them together again. I tried to keep them both on their feet long enough to appear as a happy, healthy couple whenever they were seen in public by strangers. When the show closed, my father fled back to his ragged dogs and leftover chickens, I to my family in London; my mother continued on to San Francisco to be her own ageless, glamorous, living legend.

IN APRIL, Martin Luther King, Jr., was killed. In Europe, his murder hardly caused a ripple – it was an American, home-brewed tragedy. Two months later – "Oh, no! Not again!" our hearts cried as Bobby lay bleeding, life leaving him so quickly. That sharp mind, that daredevil spirit behind that organized intelligence, my octopus authority was no more.

My mother was back in Australia, performing in one town when her Australian was killed in a freak accident in another. She called me in despair. As he had a legitimate widow, Dietrich could not expose her sorrow publicly, nor her personal interest in his death, and gave me a list of telephone numbers to call for her in Australia in order to find out the details of the tragic accident, send the proper flowers to his funeral, and went into her room to mourn.

She closed in Australia and returned to Paris to be with her favorite Michael. My son was studying at the American College in Paris, and my mother threw off her widow's weeds and blossomed. Found, furnished, and fixed him a sumptuous bachelor pad, then never left him in peace long enough to enjoy it. She had her own key and entered whenever she felt like it, to clean, stock his refrigerator, and check his bed. On weekends, she took him to expensive restaurants, entered clinging to his handsome, tall frame, seated him next to her most aggressively homosexual friends and – waited. He came home to London for the Christmas holidays and asked my advice on how to make her stop.

So she was trying with her grandson what she hadn't accomplished with her daughter? I thought: She never gives up. I had suspected long ago that my mother had subconsciously wanted me to be initiated into a lesbian life-style, even maneuvered my sexual abuse in this manner, in the hope I would follow this path into maturity. No man could then have taken me from her. Certainly in later years, this would have served her well. Her daughter, unencumbered by husband and children, would have been available, by her side, ever the happy, willing companion, her lover, an

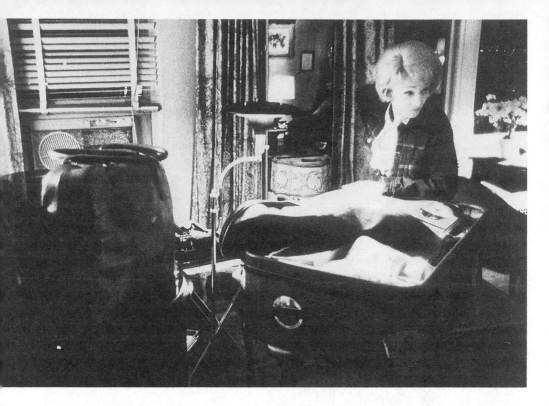

ABOVE: Packing—always packing.
BELOW: The golden years of success, acclaim, adulation, and wild applause.
She stood alone upon the stages of the world and let it wash over her.

ABOVE, LEFT:
She loved to lead Burt
Bacharach out before
the cheering audience
to acknowledge his
genius as her arranger
and conductor. His
being young *and* hand-
some was certainly a
plus.

ABOVE, RIGHT:
During one of her
Paris triumphs, Jean-
Pierre Aumont and
Jean Cocteau, old
nonlover pals, vied to
light her cigarettes.

RIGHT: On stage,
Maurice Chevalier was
allowed to show his
long, undying devotion.

Every night after the performances, the London bobbies lost their battles
with the surging crowd at the stage door.

ABOVE: Christmas together in London. David was a little shy of the lady by the tree, and she was miffed that Paul thanked his father for his present before opening hers.

RIGHT: The bugle-bead dress we christened "the eel" because my mother looked like one swimming through clear water wearing it. She loved being at her thinnest that winter of 1964. I worried about it.

BELOW: Her name in lights on the theater where England's greatest actors had performed. She was justly proud to have made it.

LEFT: My mother hid her pain.
My father could no longer hide
anything.
ABOVE: Her Broadway triumph
and its marquee, New York, 1967.
BELOW: Every night cheering
crowds blocked the streets.

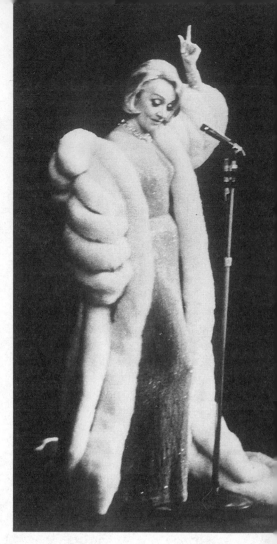

ABOVE, LEFT: Noël smiled when the cameras clicked but worried about her pill consumption.

ABOVE AND LEFT: The fabulous dress, the superbly tailored trousers hid what she needed to hide, and kept her secrets.

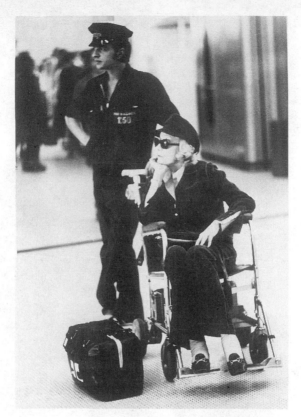

ABOVE: Wheelchairs at airports now often became a traumatic necessity.
BELOW: In Moscow with Bacharach, one of the last carefree tours before his own fame took him away from her and her accidents ended it all.

The enraptured audiences never knew what was happening to this icon glittering before them.

added handmaiden to fetch and carry. A truly contented *ménage à trois*. As Dietrich always proclaimed "all homosexuals *worship* their mothers," I figured, as she thought of Michael as hers, she was now, once again, investing in her future cosseting. As an added little love token she had given my son a "few," about a hundred, amphetamines – just to help him with his "so difficult" studies. It was one of the too few times I told her off. Shocked, outraged, stunned silence descended, and our Christmas was minus one legend, and, bliss!

JUDY LAY on a bathroom floor; she, who had died so long ago, was finally, officially, dead. I mourned my friend as one does a child who had a life to live and was not able to.

That summer, man invaded the moon.

My mother called: "Sweetheart, Papa Joe has died."

"I know."

"Remember Antibes? When he was Ambassador? You used to swim with his children. He was old then already, but sweet. Used to follow me around. Boni was jealous – Jo, too. I never hear from *her* anymore. Strange. Probably still on that island of hers with all her black people?"

In December, von Sternberg died in Hollywood. For the man who had given her professional immortality and loved her so, Dietrich did not play widow nor attend his funeral. The story most often told in reverent admiration is that Marlene Dietrich denied herself this last poignant farewell in order not to upstage her Svengali in his last moment of supreme importance. That after the ceremony, she appeared at his home wrapped in chinchilla, weeping, to console, give her loving support to his grieving widow.

Those of us who really knew Dietrich knew how frightened she was of all funerals, how she hated the press and the obvious, intimate questions they would certainly have focused on at this time, and knew, once again, she had instinctively chosen a path that the world would later interpret, laud, and recount as yet another example of Marlene's sublime thoughtfulness – while simply serving her own needs. Through the years, she continued to court Jo's widow as well as his son. Keeping the shine on the image never hurt – "You never know, said the widow . . ."

In the spring of 1970, Burt Bacharach received his first two Academy Awards. That definitely rated a phone call:

"Sweetheart. Now *you* know I love Burt, but 'Raindrops Keep

Falling . . .'? Where has he got them falling? On his head? Why? And it is such toodle-toodle – for *that*, he deserted me? For raindrops?" – and hung up.

In Paris, my mother had to have her shoes and boots enlarged, received daily injections into her groin by her quack, and prepared her first Japanese tour.

Remarque died – warranted two whole days of my mother's mourning routine, plus a letter to friends of mine.

> . . . I was alone when Remarque died. But I had known of his illness and, by chance, I tried to telephone him and he answered. I talked to him, sent him flowers every day and wires, all to arrive in the mornings because that bitch Goddard only came in the afternoon after her beauty sleep. Maria wrote to him and I also talked to Rudi on the phone and he sent a cable to him which he got during the few days when he was lucid, before he died.
>
> He had many strokes, but recovered and even wrote a letter to Maria, showing her how he had learned to write again. But then, life for him without his favorite, wine, was not good anymore. He loved to drink a lot – not for the effect but for the taste. Now the bitch has all the riches: van Goghs, Cézannes, Modiglianis, etc., etc. And the most beautiful carpets – all priceless. Maybe this is why she never allowed him to see me. Maybe she thought he would give me some of his treasures. It could not have been jealousy, because she never loved him. I could not go to the funeral last Sunday. If I survive Gabin, it will be the same thing. I could have had it all, the name and the money. But I said: "No." I couldn't do it to Rudi.

She emerged from her widowhood just long enough, to go right back in when De Gaulle died.

MY MOTHER WAS BACK in Paris the year the Duke of Windsor died. She called, laughing:

" 'David' is dead! Remember Clifton Webb always called him David? I once went to dinner at their château. What an evening! She sat there, 'ever so elegant skeleton,' and after dinner, clapped her hands – like calling a servant – and said in that affected American: 'David, go! Put on your kilts and do your dance for our guests!' and this man, who once was a king – goes! Comes back in full Scottish costume like some chorus boy from *Brigadoon* and does his little dance – on toes, skirts whirling – frightful! And those dogs! Did you ever see those ugly dogs they have?

They wheeze! Long things drip out of their pushed-in noses and their pop eyes water. . . . What a way to live! Terrible people! They deserved each other!"

Although my mother was in London when our son Peter was married, she did not attend the wedding. Practically impossible to explain to the bride's parents, as was our family's relief at having this beautiful day unmarred by the famous grandmother's presence. My mother's diary makes no reference to this marriage. Actually, as far as Dietrich's diaries are concerned, she has no grandchildren, she recorded none of their births, or later her great-grandchildren's.

For years, I had been trying to negotiate a television deal for Dietrich's one-woman show, but her demands, the special conditions she set down, were so outrageous, so unrealistic, that neither a network nor an independent producer could be persuaded to risk it. For an American TV special, my mother insisted that it be filmed in Europe, during an actual performance, and in a legitimate theater of her choice. She wanted Orson Welles to direct, Bacharach to conduct, her stage-lighting genius, Joe Davis, to light her, and for Dietrich to have full and unlimited artistic control over everything but the color of the toilet paper in the washrooms. My mother's prime objective for considering "a special" in the first place, besides the obvious money, was to record for posterity the tumultuous response to her performance. Believing that foreign audiences were much more prone to exuberant adulation, she absolutely refused to listen to our arguments that if she filmed in America, she would have the superb quality control of the entire television industry at her disposal. What my mother really wanted was to record her show in Soviet Russia. She believed that as artists in that country were so revered, applause from a Russian audience was the ultimate accolade. Copenhagen was her second choice, possibly Paris, Edinburgh, even Rio de Janeiro.

When I first discussed such a project with Orson in 1961, he fixed me with his shoe-button eyes, squeezed his soggy cigar; that wonderful voice rumbled up from its subterranean cave and said:

"Maria, if this should ever come to pass, I shall be out of town, conveniently very unavailable. You don't have to tell Marlene that now. You know how she is – this idea of hers may never get off the ground, but if it ever does, I want *you* to know that I shall be very, very far away."

Ten years later, the ever-courageous and willing Alexander Cohen took on the challenge and lived to regret it. After months of negotiations, trying to explain to my mother the astronomical complexities of shipping skilled American crews and their sophisticated equipment to foreign lands in order to film a television show best suited to a controlled soundstage in Burbank, California, Alex finally found an available theater in London that my mother was willing to approve, and the preparatory work could finally begin. Like an army preparing for battle, we marshaled our forces, each of us responsible for our own specialties – everyone geared toward one goal: to keep our star functioning and happy in order to capture her magnificent performance on film. While Alex negotiated with sponsors, unions, and the BBC, my job was to keep Dietrich cooperative, content, and, secretly, as sober as possible.

The Savoy Hotel was to be my mother's billet. This elegant establishment, with its beautiful river suites, the fast, silent, meticulous service of its staff, was my mother's favorite London hotel.

A Cinderella dream of a suite, its chandeliers ashimmer, awaited her. Everything ready, just waiting for our queen to grace its splendor with her presence, and I had two days before my mother's arrival to transform its beauty into Dietrich's "working headquarters." I was the best majordomo Dietrich ever had. Not only because I knew her better than anyone else, but because I believed that making enemies was not the way to achieve the cooperation and support of the people one needed. I knew my mother would be able to generate her own anger and dislike without any help from me.

I thought it was only fair that the Savoy Hotel should be warned, given basic instructions on how to face this imminent upheaval that would interfere not only with the smooth running of the entire hotel but intrude into the private lives of its staff as well. Being treated as slaves usually generates acute stress in normal human beings. I tried to set myself up as someone they could come to, commiserate with, relieve their stress. This time I was lucky. An eager, young assistant manager had been assigned to see to the special needs of Miss Dietrich. He was, even then, one of those rare people who know instinctively how to handle VIPs, solve their problems with the minimum of pompous fuss. Today, this likable man holds an exalted position within the great Ciga hotel chain and often has the charm to claim that what I taught him about handling Dietrich was a valuable lesson for a young man making his way up the management ladder.

"Mrs. Riva? May I introduce myself? I am Mr. Butavaba. May I be of service?"

"Mr. Butavaba and how! Have you about three hours to give me?"

Rather taken aback by my American exuberance, the small, rotund gentleman blushed:

"Certainly, madam."

"Wonderful! Come on. Let's go and inspect Miss Dietrich's suite and I will try to explain what we have to do to it," and I strode toward the discreet elevator of that Edwardian emporium. Mr. Butavaba, the tails of his staid morning coat flapping, rushed after me. We entered the suite and stood for a moment, appreciating its beauty. The dazzle of pinks, yellows, peach, lavender – flowers everywhere; the sparkle of everything, the brocade and lace framing the great views of the Thames embankment.

"How lovely you have made it all! Thank you. But, my mother is not a movie star in the style of Miss Elizabeth Taylor. I am going to be very honest with you, Mr. Butavaba. If we are going to work together, I have to trust you – I have a feeling I can. Now, let's start with the largest bathroom."

We opened a paneled door, two steps led up to a pink-tiled ballroom!

"Mr. Butavaba, please listen to me carefully. No one must know this. No one. You must give me your word. If ever Miss Dietrich should find out that I told you, she would kill me. My mother suffers from a circulatory problem of her legs. She must never injure them in any way. Anything that might cause her to trip, fall, stumble, even knock against her legs, is extremely dangerous. If she should ever receive even the slightest wound on any part of her feet or legs, her lack of circulation would make it impossible for the wound to heal. Gangrene would follow and, possibly, eventual amputation. Therefore, this suite must be made safe for her. Steps leading into a bathroom are out. She might forget they're there and trip. We will have to use this one only for 'hair washing' and the 'storage of supplies.' Show me what the other bathroom is like."

Not a ballroom, and with a window that let in daylight, but as it had no steps, it would have to do.

"Okay. We will need a curtain of heavy cloth to black out the window. Miss Dietrich always puts on her stage makeup in her hotel, never in her dressing room at the theater. I need an electrician to install a row of lights above the mirror, with mesh-covered bulbs to protect her face should one explode for any reason. This door has to be removed, so that she can exit and enter without difficulty. I need two tables along this wall for her makeup, a board over the top of the bathtub to make a counter for the wig stands, and a special outlet for her professional curling irons. Please have the chambermaid remove all the towels and, especially, all and any bathmats and throw rugs. Make sure that the housekeeper instructs the staff that this bathroom is not to be touched, or supplied with daily linen. Miss Dietrich uses her own makeup towels and will clean this area herself. In the other bathroom, we will always need at least twelve extra-large bath towels for when she washes her hair, but again, remember to caution the maids that no bathmats or scatter rugs are to be furnished to this suite. The special rubber mat for the inside of the bath, I have here in my bag. Make sure that the maids replace it securely each time they clean the tub. We don't need this chair in here – Miss Dietrich never sits when making up.

"Now, let's do the bedroom. . . . The hotel must have some blackout drapes that were used during the war. Please have them brought up and hung over Miss Dietrich's bedroom windows. As she prefers artificial light in her bedroom, we will be able to tape the edges of the curtains. Even the faintest crack of daylight wakes her instantly. I will also tape the edges of the carpets in the entire suite, to avoid her tripping anywhere where the joins may not be completely flush. Also, luminous cloth tape will be put down across every doorway. This is a precaution, so that if she gets up during the night, she can immediately see where to put her feet in the dark. You must impress on the entire staff that under no circumstance must these tapes be removed – ever."

The Savoy had a wonderful room-service system, a fully-fitted serving kitchen on each floor, presided over by its own room-service captain. He was my next target.

"Madam, this is Charles – he is in charge of this floor."

"Charles, let me be the first to offer you my condolences. These weeks are going to be murder. But, maybe I can give you a few tips that will make it a little easier for you and keep Miss Dietrich from being too irritated. First and foremost, when Miss Dietrich rings, grab your menu and run. Always react as though it were an emergency. By the way, Mr. Butavaba, you better tell that to the telephone girls – anytime they see any one of the phones from this suite light up on their switchboard, they must react as though it is a matter of life and death. I'll see them all individually myself later, but that is a cardinal rule for everyone. The faster one obeys Miss Dietrich, the easier it will be on everyone's nerves in the long run. Now, Charles – never expect to *serve* Miss Dietrich a meal. When admitted, simply roll the table into the room, arrange the order, do not wait for her to be seated, and never, ever expect her to sign a room-service check – simply bow and exit. Miss Dietrich is not an American and, therefore, dislikes glasses filled with ice water. Neither does she appreciate butter curls swimming in ice. Always see to it that there is an ample supply of seeded rye bread and pumpernickel in the bread basket. Never try to convince Miss Dietrich that the coffee is freshly brewed when it has been sitting for fifteen minutes waiting for her summons. Never, ever try to convince her of *anything*. Remember, she is always right – no matter how unjust it might seem to you and your staff. If she orders broccoli, and, for some inexplicable reason, they send up spinach and she commands you to explain this crime, you can only resort to one course of action that will get you out of the suite with your job intact: Bow, apologize profusely, and suggest that it must have been one of those very young apprentices who are being trained to be cooks by the great chefs of the Savoy kitchens and that you will report their negligent behavior immediately. This is the only scenario that Miss Dietrich would find engaging enough to forgive a mix-up from room service."

Next came the housekeeper, the doormen, bell boys, flower girls, and chauffeur. During the weeks that followed, I supported my little army with lavish tips and, much more important, gratitude.

Our star arrived weeks before rehearsals were to begin. New wigs had to be made, old ones redyed and shaped, and her private falls cleaned and set. I think it was Vivien Leigh who first introduced my mother to a genius wig-maker by the name of Stanley Hall. She had dinner with the Oliviers one night, and, knowing Vivien was going bald, was amazed by the beauty of her thick hair and asked her what pill she was taking. My mother told me later that Vivien laughed, gripped the bandeau encircling her head, removed it from her head with most of her "hair" attached to it. Wig-making has always been a special craft in England, where most actors wear wigs not only in period plays but in modern ones as well. Stanley Hall and his staff were so skilled, used such superb quality human hair, dyed and curled it with such expertise, that they made wigs and hairpieces that could be worn in life for daily wear. The design that my mother had seen close-up on Vivien Leigh and had been so impressed with, a short, bouncy, gleaming half-fall attached to a bandeau, became Dietrich's official hairdo from then on. She wore it for the rest of her life. My mother had dozens of them, dyed perfectly to match her own hair color in front. She covered the bandeaux in velvet to keep them from slipping, in colors to match her wardrobe, but mostly she preferred her favorite, the beige velvet ones; their color blended with the hair and camouflaged the line between her own hair and the false one.

How that TV special was ever completed was a miracle. Cohen did everything to please his star, gave in to her every whim, sometimes even to the detriment of his own investment. As she began to realize that something was not working for her, that perhaps she had been wrong to insist on filming in a real theater and in Europe, she panicked and, as usual, blamed everyone but herself, refused to listen to advice, and turned to her trusty bottle to escape having to face the truth. I searched for her scotch, hidden in the most outlandish places. Watered what I found, called for time-out when I thought she might pass out, and prayed that the visiting sponsor would not notice her condition.

As Dietrich's alcoholism was such a well-kept secret, the psychological adjustment that the entertainment industry usually makes unconsciously, before and during work involving a known alcoholic, was not in force for her. So her seemingly undisciplined, sloppy, and abusive behavior was observed and judged without the usual cushioning benefit of previous knowledge of her problem. After this fiasco, my mother gave out interviews, implying that her TV Special had been less than perfect due solely to the producer not living up to his promises, for which Alexander Cohen sued her for slander. In my opinion, he had ample justification to do so. Professional loyalty, although always associated with the Dietrich myth, was not one of my mother's strong suits. Whoever got to her first with an offer and worked her ego correctly could make a deal. She made out legal documents for sole representation as though they were postcards.

In later years, no one with any professional integrity would touch her with a ten-foot pole. You just couldn't trust her. Powers unto themselves are often treacherous.

To advertise her TV special, she returned to New York for a portrait sitting with Milton Greene. The famous pose of Dietrich enveloped in swan, just one leg showing as though completely naked underneath, was taken at this time. In glorious color and golden wig, one would never guess she is seventy-one, yet there is something terribly wrong. When I first saw it, I thought of my old San Francisco friend, she looks so much like a drag queen "doing a Dietrich," while doing one of her own. After she retouched the hell out of this picture, it looked even more unreal, except for that slightly swollen foot, *that* she couldn't completely erase.

Watergate. Nixon was reelected in a landslide. Only twenty-four thousand troops remained in Vietnam – the other forty-seven thousand had come home in shiny new boxes, while three hundred thousand more were strewn about in military hospitals, trying to mend more than just their physical wounds.

When my mother had flown back to Paris as Chevalier was dying, it was naturally assumed she was rushing to his bedside to bid him a last farewell, but her plane reservations had been made long before that date – it just worked out to her legend's advantage. Years later she made up a moving story to cover up Chevalier's adamant refusal to see her when she had arrived wan and beautiful at the hospital:

"When Chevalier was dying I flew all the way to Paris just to be with him. When I got to the hospital where he was – they told me that he had given strict orders that I was not to be admitted into his room! You know why? He didn't want me to see him like that. He loved me so – he gave up seeing me one last time – just so I wouldn't have to suffer. Wonderful man!"

She returned to tour the States, then the British Isles. Wheelchairs became a sometime necessity for arrivals and departures at airports; trying to avoid press photographers catching her in one, a constant nightmare. Noël died at his home in Jamaica. His famous friend blamed his smoking and lack of discipline.

"You see? After our bet I never smoked and I am still alive, but poor Noël couldn't stop. He was my friend. Now those two chorus boys of his will get those beautiful houses – everything! How awful! Now they will live like kings on Noël's money. Well, they stayed all those years with him, so maybe they earned it."

On the 17th of May, 1973, my mother and father celebrated their golden wedding anniversary – he wringing chicken necks in the San Fernando Valley, she lunching with her "latest" in Paris, very annoyed that a reporter had ferreted out the date, insisting that as I was only twenty-five, he got it all wrong anyway and planned to sue him.

On the 7th of November, at the Shady Grove Theater in Maryland, on the outskirts of Washington, D.C., my mother finished singing her third encore to jubilant applause. Being a theater in the round, the audience seated in a circle all around her, she had shifted her position at the microphone often to encompass every section of the full house. Now she turned her shimmering body, walked the few steps to the edge of the stage to salute the orchestra and her ever-attentive conductor below. She went into her famous bow, legs ramrod straight, her upper body bent down from the waist – so low that the top of her wig nearly touched the floor, her right arm stretched out in gallant tribute toward her conductor, Stan Freeman. Suddenly, she wavered and pitched from the stage into the orchestra pit. Freeman, seeing her begin to fall, jumped onto his piano stool, trying desperately to help her, but could not reach her in time. She lay amongst the music stands, ominously still. As anxious hands reached out for her, she snarled:

"Don't touch me! Clear the theater! Clear the theater!"

The sharp ring of the phone woke me. I grabbed the receiver to hear the alarmed voice of my mother's dresser:

"Maria – we are calling you from the dressing room. Something has happened. Here is your mother . . ."

I am instantly awake.

"Mass?"

I hear her breathing, trying to get out the words. I look at my clock, four-thirty a.m., London time. Must be eleven-thirty her time in Maryland, right after the performance.

"Okay. Mass? Take a deep breath – speak slowly – tell me what happened." I say it like a military command. It is the only way to make her function, come to attention.

"I fell," she whispers.

The fear and shock are alive in the room with me. I bark out my interrogation.

"Anything broken?"

"No."

Although I knew the wig would cushion her head in a fall, I still have to ask:

"Did you hit your head?"

"No."

"All right. Now . . . tell me, *did you hit your legs*?"

"Yes."

Oh, my god! I take a deep breath and continue: "Which leg?"

"The left one."

Jesus, the one with the least pulse.

"Tell me, slowly, exactly what happened."

The shock has softened her tone, she sounds like a little girl recounting an accident at school:

"You know – how I always bow at the end and present my conductor, how I reach out my hand toward him so that the audience understands? – Well, tonight, for some ridiculous reason, Stan Freeman thought I wanted to shake his hand and so he jumped up on the piano stool, grabs my hand, lost his balance and fell, pulling me down off the stage with him. The moment I hit the floor, I knew it wasn't bad – the dress was all right and the wig was still on. But you know the dress is too tight for me to get up, and I didn't want the audience to see me . . . so I lay still and yelled at the shocked musicians to leave me alone and to clear the theater. Then I felt a funny wetness on my leg and saw there was blood, and so I knew I would have to be carried back to the dressing room and *that* I couldn't let the audience see, so I stayed on the floor until everyone left and they got me out – All I kept saying was, 'Call my daughter – Call Maria'."

"I'm here. Now listen to me – carefully. Do *not* remove the tights – do *not* remove the elastic stocking underneath. Wrap a clean towel around the leg, leave it as it is and get to the Walter Reed Hospital. Do not let them touch your leg there before they know you have only peripheral circulation – "

She stops me: "We pulled off the tights already. We had to, they were full of blood and the stocking too."

Now I knew my mother was in bad trouble. By pulling the elastic stocking off the leg instead of cutting it off, precious skin had undoubtedly been removed. More in command of herself, she begins to argue:

"I can't go to a hospital. The photographers, the reporters . . ."

I'm already looking up the number for Pan Am. "Mass, I'm coming. If you won't go to a hospital, you must at least call a doctor. You must not get an infection. Do you hear me? You have to get the wound cleaned, bandaged, and get yourself medicated. Also you need a tetanus shot – the theater floor is dirty. Call Teddy Kennedy. He will know the best man in Washington."

"You're coming? When?"

"The earliest flight out of London is at ten this morning. I'll try to get on that one. I'll be there . . ." I looked at my clock – it is five a.m. "I'll be there about six tonight, your time. Now I want you to take two cubes of sugar and dissolve them under your tongue. Have them wrap you in a blanket, keep warm, go to the hotel, and don't put your leg up high."

"*Not* up high?" The way she said it, I knew that was exactly what she had done.

I got a reservation on the first plane out. As Bill was in New York on business, I called my married son who was living in London:

"Pete, forgive my calling so early – I need your help."

"Yes, Mom. Shoot!"

"She fell in Washington and opened the leg."

"Jesus!"

"I have to go . . . can you and Sandy take care of Paul and David?"

"Sure! We can come over right away, give them breakfast, and take them to school. Mom, everything will be taken care of at this end – just go!"

I arrived in Washington, D.C., late that afternoon, rushed into my mother's hotel suite, and found her bandaging her oozing leg, preparing to go to the theater for that night's performance. The wound was deep, the size of a man's fist. Because of the lack of blood supply, it had stopped bleeding almost immediately after the accident; for the same reason she felt no pain. At this point, the greatest danger was infection.

For me, Senator Kennedy has never changed from the little boy I knew as Teddy in those long gone summer days of 1938. Being helpful and conscientious was a very serious matter to him. One only had to say,

"Oh, Teddy, I forgot my book," and his chubby little legs would go into action, all the way up to the hotel from the sea. My mother had reached him – he had arranged for her immediate admittance to the great hospital in Bethesda. When she refused, gave her the name of a doctor in Washington who she could trust instead. He did not mention the personal tragedy that had struck his family. Within days, his son would lose his leg to bone cancer.

Of course I had to force my mother to see the doctor. As he didn't issue her orders nor prescribe "magic potions," she didn't like him. He was a good man and knew that without the proper blood supply the leg could not, would not, heal. As she refused to listen or even discuss the possibility of surgery, all he could do was try and protect her against the dangers of infection, giving her injections and antibiotics and routine dressings, in the hope of keeping the wound sterile until she came to her senses. None of this satisfied her, so she called Geneva, asked Prof. de Watteville what to do. He, knowing her *very* well, prescribed as many injections of new "miraculous" medications that he could think of. Most of them vitamins, concentrated proteins, and harmless hormones, and, as none of them would be available in America, a courier service was arranged. When he reminded her that she had too little circulation, she hung up on him. I insisted on canceling the rest of the Washington engagement.

Any inactivity drove my mother crazy. If I wouldn't "allow" her to go to work, she could at least be permitted to organize the suite to function as a first-aid station. Setting up a field hospital was right up her alley. As the suite boasted a pantry kitchen, she commandeered it, disinfected the walls and counters, then stocked it with every medical supply available in the District of Columbia. When she was through, we could have performed brain surgery in that kitchen. While my mother was busy and happy preparing her MASH unit, I took care of business. Although I had grave doubts that she would be able to continue her tour, open in Montreal by the 26th, I asked her personal musicians, those who traveled with her, to remain on standby and wait for my call. I phoned Bill in New York, Michael in Los Angeles, and my other children in London, bringing them all up to date. Typically, my mother had not asked about them.

The next day, a gaunt Stan Freeman accosted me in the hotel lobby. His bloodshot eyes searched my face, his voice pleaded:

"Maria! I didn't pull your mother off the stage! I swear it! She says I did – but I didn't! I would never hurt her. You must believe me!"

I tried to comfort him: "Stan, of course you didn't. You and I both know the real reason why my mother fell. I know it must be terrible for you – but Dietrich can tell any lie she wants to believe is the truth and the world will accept it as gospel. We're canceling the rest of the performances here in Washington. But keep yourself free. Knowing her, she just might make Montreal. Remember, when Dietrich has marked you the culprit, there is nothing we lesser mortals can do about it. Now you must get some sleep. Try to forget it. The people who love you will know what's the truth – that's all that really matters."

Brave speech, excellent advice, one I tried constantly to follow and often failed to do.

The wound remained open, slightly oozing precious protein. We became experts at changing the sterile dressings. The "medications" arrived from Switzerland, a nurse was hired to give daily injections. My mother felt well. Besides my constant presence, the actual rest was doing her good. We even celebrated Thanksgiving with room-service turkey:

"Well, because if *you* don't have your *precious* Thanksgiving, you will be impossible to live with – besides this American hotel probably has nothing else but that stupidity on the menu!"

Refusing to admit that her wound was not healing, she insisted on fulfilling her contract and continuing on to Montreal. I felt I had to accompany her at least as far as the next stop of her tour. I wanted to be there in case the injured leg gave her more trouble than she could handle. I was not sure that it would support her through the strain of an entire performance. During our hiatus in Washington, I had been watering her scotch and controlling the daily intake. Each time she put her half-filled glass down, the nearest flowers would receive another generous dose of J&B. She kept saying, "Why is my glass always empty?" but never caught on. I must say, the flowers did remarkably well on this diet of booze.

For the first time in years sober, she strode on stage, her swan's coat a huge marshmallow wave rolling behind her, and like the phoenix, the symbol of resurrection she so adored, she rose triumphant and gave a performance that, in my opinion, she never had nor could equal. No one who was privileged to witness her triumph that night in Montreal would have believed that under that lithe incandescent form oozed an open wound, swathed in wet gauze and thick bandages. For a full hour, she stood unwavering, immobile, sang encore after encore, bowed her famous low bow, finally begged her audience to stop, left the stage, and walked firmly to her dressing room. We had to strip her dress off in order to change the bandages. She had a second show to do. The next day, this review said it all. I don't believe in reprinting reviews, but this one Dietrich deserves to have recorded:

The Gazette, Montreal, Monday 26, 1973
– Dave Billington

When she was a teen-aged girl, the gassed and shell-shocked troops of Ypres and Vimy crouched in their slimy trenches. . . .

Twenty-five years later she was touring military bases crammed with the sons of many of those "war to end all wars" veterans. . . .

Twenty-five years later, on a concert stage in Montreal, Marlene Dietrich, Hemingway's Kraut, sings "Lili Marlene" for the umpteenth time in her life and a century of turmoil, hatred and hope clings to the changeless edges of a torn calendar caught on a blossoming thorn bush. . . .

She sings as the merciless white spotlight fails to find a flaw in the slightly sunken cheeks of the face which refuses to age. . . .

It's as if one were seeing this century personified. Past its prime and supposedly in its decline, but still proud with the hope in which any century (or person) begins life, she is still there, still alive and still refusing to yield. . . .

Perhaps it is stretching credulity too far to see Dietrich this way. After all she is only a human being, possessed of all the frailties implicit in that word; she is only a singer and actress of honestly average talents and skill. So why should she, above all others, be seen in other than this light? . . .

The lady herself provides the answer when she sings a simple children's "round" song first popularized by Pete Seeger – "Where Have All the Flowers Gone?" She provides it, not because she includes this antiwar plea in her repertoire, or even because of the passionate way she sings the song, but rather for one fleeting second of the splendid last verse. . . .

For more than an hour without break, without artificiality and without milking the audience for false sentimental appeal, Marlene Dietrich entertains – swinging from message, to love song, to vamp, to humor, in a perfect mixture which left the audience grinning like cats sated on Jersey cream. . . .

When it was over, the senseless calls for encores, echoing cheers and a mild (but fervid) attempt to rush the stage as if Dietrich were a talisman of immortality which must be touched.

The curtain closes and the lady disappears again into mythology, like a brief messenger from Olympus. . . .

And when it does this, the dimension which has made Dietrich more than just another phenomenon in a milieu which abounds in them, stands revealed. She ceases to be Marlene Dietrich, woman singer, actress and worshipped idol of an audience which would have given Freud a nightmare. . . .

She assumes the dimension of time given shape and substance. She seems to embody the whole century of Western man's worst and finest hours. For she was born when the century was born, and lived through and seen that century retreat from the greatest promise any century ever began with and yet still be unable to fully deny that promise. . . .

And she and the century are still there – perhaps tired, perhaps jaded and perhaps fading from hope but still there . . . and still able to ask with honest anger, "When will they ever learn?" . . .

Put aside symbolism, forget the phenomenon and just accept the fact that this was a consummate performance. The timing, the mixture of songs, the hand gestures, the lighting, the makeup – all of it a distillation of the elements which make audiences love great entertainers.

She had my admiration as well. Before returning to London, I tried to impress on her, once again, that although she had triumphed this time, it was madness to continue touring with an open wound. Only surgical intervention could effect a healing process, and I begged her to see the eminent heart surgeon Michael De Bakey, in Houston. Still heady after her triumphal resurrection, she hardly listened and complained about my continual prophecies of doom. I agreed with her – I was beginning to bore myself. I returned to London, my mother continued on to San Francisco, the next stop of her tour that was scheduled into the next year.

On January 10, 1974, my mother opened in Dallas. She was booked into the Fairmont Hotel for three weeks. She phoned and, on being questioned, admitted the wound was still open, its edges turning black. In London, I took matters into my own hands and dialed Dr. De Bakey's office in Houston. It was late afternoon, Texas time, and the great man answered the phone himself. For a moment, I was speechless, and rather scared by what I was about to attempt. I introduced myself as "the daughter of" and, as precise and to the point as possible, I launched into "the secret saga of Marlene Dietrich's famous legs." The eminent surgeon listened without comment.

"Please, Dr. De Bakey, if I can get my mother to fly from Dallas to Houston on Sunday, her day off, will you see her?"

"Of course, Mrs. Riva. Tell me the time and I shall arrange to be in my office here at the hospital."

"Oh, thank you, Doctor. Please, may I take one more minute of your time? If, when you see my mother, you decide she must have surgery, please – just look at her and say that if she doesn't, her leg will have to be amputated. This is the only way she will ever consent to an operation. You have to frighten her into it. Forgive me for assuming to tell you what to say – but I know my mother, she won't listen otherwise."

I gave him my London number, he promised to call me after he had seen her . . . now all I had to do was to get her to Houston to see him. She complained, argued, snarled, bitched – but she went. The moment she walked out of De Bakey's office, he called me:

"Maria, I didn't have to pretend at all. I told your mother that if she did not have immediate surgery, she could lose the leg. Because that's the truth. But she insisted she had a contract to fulfill first."

"Doctor, she will never do it unless I am there with her. She closes in Dallas in three days, on the 25th. Is it possible for you to schedule the operation around that time? Somehow, I'll get her to you."

On the 26th of January, 1974, Marlene Dietrich, known as Mrs. Rudolf Sieber, secretly checked into the Methodist Medical Center in Houston, Texas. I arrived from London the day after. Dr. De Bakey's staff was used to incognito VIPs. Their handling of my mother was a lesson in diplomacy. The doctor's personal assistant, complete with limousine, had greeted her plane and whisked the patient to a special suite in his famous hospital.

To determine the exact position and extent of the arterial blockage, first she had to go through a rather drastic procedure of an arteriogram done under full anesthesia. The moment she was wheeled out of the room, I began the search of her luggage for the pills and booze I knew she had stashed there. My mother was not beyond medicating herself in secret, swigging down a few shots of scotch the morning of surgery, the doctors none the wiser until their patient suddenly went into convulsions and cardiac arrest on the operating table. Despite her reputation of being a medical authority, her actual knowledge was appalling.

I dumped everything I found onto the bed. By the time I called the head nurse to verify what I had found and impound it, the bed was full. Although this type of raid was not unusual in order to protect a patient from themselves, I had not done one since my days when I looked after Tami. I was stunned by the quantity of my mother's stash, her true addict's inventiveness and duplicity. She always loved those tiny bottles of booze handed out on airlines and usually had a few dozen tucked away in her hand luggage. For this trip to the hospital, she had emptied their vodka and scotch contents into bottles marked "cleaning fluid," refilling the liquor bottles with the cleaning fluid. I shuddered at the thought of someone by chance drinking one of those. Skin lotions had done the same switch of identity, so had hair-setting lotion, mouth wash, and perfume. The most lethal hypnotics had become "European vitamins – special," her Fernando Lamases now were suppositories "for constipation." Those drugs impossible to camouflage because of their identifiable shapes and colors she had stuffed into sewing kits, dressing gown pockets, handbags, into the cardboard tubes of Tampax.

She was in an extremely agitated state when they brought her back to the room. By the evening, when the anesthesia had worn off, the first thing she asked for was her traveling bag. When I suggested that anything she wanted from that rather large and heavy satchel she could tell me and I would give it to her, she became furious, ordering me to do what I was told! Frantically, she searched the bag until, suddenly, it dawned on her that what she was seeking had been removed, surreptitiously, without her consent. From then on, I, the nurses, the state of Texas, were the Gestapo, and open war was declared on those who "keep me locked up in this concentration camp."

Dr. De Bakey is enormously proud of his personal battle against infection. His rules of hygiene, governing every aspect of his operating theater as well as his entire hospital, are strict, immovable, and border on the possessed. His victories over infections justify his fanaticism. His surgical patients were required, without exception, to take a shower, wash themselves with a special disinfectant solution in the early hours before surgery. I reinforced my identity of Gestapo agent when I woke my mother at five a.m. and informed her that she had to take a shower. Fear made her even more abusive than usual.

"I'm not dirty! Now you all think you have the right to tell me I have to *wash*? You're all Hitlers! You – *You* made me come here . . . You and your sick love of hospitals and doctors! I am not going to wash! Such ridiculous stupidity!"

It must have been a terrible time for her. Worse than any outsider could possibly comprehend. This woman, who reconstructed her aging body to suit an illusion of youth, who concealed the crepe-flesh of her hanging thighs in a thousand ways, who hid her thinning, wispy hair beneath golden wigs, who folded sagging breasts into gossamer harnesses, ever re-recreating the Venus the world wanted and expected Dietrich to be . . . was about to be laid bare. The legend exposed to the clinical gaze of many strangers. From that day on, there would exist in the world a group of people who had seen the real Dietrich, the seventy-three-year-old woman whose body bespoke her age even if her face lied. The major surgery she was facing did not frighten her as much as being discovered did.

Somehow, I got her into the shower. Knowing that she would be sedated before being taken down to surgery, I was still worried that they might not heed my advice – to do so as quickly as possible. I knew she could still change her mind and walk out of the hospital. It was five-thirty a.m., I was toweling her down, when she said:

"We are leaving! The leg will heal without all this to-do! You can make up a story, tell your precious De Bakey I'll come back after I finish the tour," and marched out of the bathroom in search of her clothes. I edged myself toward the bed and the nurse's call button. I needed help. Being forcibly deprived of her drug-alcohol fix, my mother was in the throes of acute withdrawal. She would have to be sedated quickly before she became too agitated, even violent. I pressed the bell without her seeing, then approached her cautiously – she was stark naked, trembling, her hands in spasm, hugging her waist.

"Easy, Mass. Easy – let me help you. We'll leave. I'll get your bra and panties but before you get dressed, remember? We have to put a dressing on the wound? Lie down on the bed for just a second, so I can bandage the leg."

Ten minutes later, my mother was being wheeled toward the elevators, a gentle smile curling her lips. She gazed benignly up at me beside her bed, sighed contentedly. A body that craved scotch was quite willing to accept a good hefty dose of Valium instead! I prayed she wouldn't remember how lovely she felt and get hooked on all the other narcotics her veins were about to sop up. I squeezed her hand, the elevator door closed. After all those years of worry and pain, finally a real doctor's skill could focus on saving Dietrich's famous legs. That morning, Dr. De Bakey successfully performed an arto right femoral, left iliac bypass, and a bilateral lumbar sympathectomy.

It is always so cold in intensive care. The machine breathed for her. My mother lay silent – for the first time since I had known her, utterly helpless – and I had the strangest sensation of feeling suddenly safe, unhurtable. I hadn't realized until that moment how much I still feared her. For one terrible moment . . . Then I turned and left her to the machines that would resurrect her.

During the early hours of January 30, the ring of the phone woke me. The agitated voice of the head nurse in intensive care:

"Mrs. Riva, I know it's three o'clock in the morning, and I am sorry to have to wake you, but it is your mother. No, no. Nothing to worry about. It's just that we are having trouble handling her. She's breathing on her own now and she keeps insisting we get you. She says she wants to see her daughter *right away*! We tried to reason with her but she is extremely agitated. We have put her in a section by herself."

"I'll be right there."

I entered the darkened unit. Still forms in long rows, monitors whined, singing their high tunes of hearts in transit, the monotone hiss of respirators, the soft squeak of rubber-soled shoes hurrying – machines and dedicated angels working to hold death at bay.

I entered my mother's secluded cubicle. She was yelling:

"You call yourself a nurse? I told you to *get my daughter*. *She* will tell De Bakey what you are doing to me. . . ." She was completely lucid, wide awake.

If her body hadn't been hooked up to the miracle machinery of modern medicine, no one would have believed that this woman had undergone major bypass surgery less than twenty-four hours before.

"Oh! You are *finally* here! I told them, 'Get my daughter.' They told me you were *sleeping* and I said to them, 'My daughter *sleeping*? She wouldn't sleep when her mother is in here! *Get* her!' I had to fight them – can you believe it? I lie here, I am the patient, and they *argue* with me? What a terrible place . . . they even dared to tell me to lower my voice, that they have other patients out there who are dying. The *great* De Bakey has patients who *die*? Since when?"

Intensive care nurses are always so happy when they can remove a patient's breathing tube. It is a moment when life again takes over from apparatus, and they wait for it with anxiety, dedication, and hope. With my mother, they now probably regretted having done so and felt guilty for wishing to put it back.

She gestured me to come closer, whispered: "They won't even give me an injection to sleep. Tell De Bakey, and tell him some young student is allowed to come in here to take my blood every two minutes. I call him 'Dracula.' He doesn't know what he's doing. Look at the blue marks he made on my arms. . . ." Suddenly, she froze, stared up at the soundproof ceiling: "Look – look," she hissed. "There they are! See? See them? They have cameras! They have cameras! See the reflection off their lenses? There are little men up there – with *cameras*. . . . Tell De Bakey!"

It is quite normal for patients to hallucinate after surgery, but they never remember those times – when the brain recovering from anesthesia emits disjointed thoughts. But my mother referred to this visit of mine often in the years to come, repeating the exact words she said to me. It was eerie. It gave my memory of that sparsely lit scene quite another dimension.

Three days after the operation, my mother was brought back to her room. Her usually icy legs were warm, their bluish whiteness replaced by a rosy hue. For the first time in fifteen years, both limbs registered a steady pulse. We celebrated – that is, everyone but Dietrich. Oh, it wasn't that she was displeased with the results, just enraged that no one would give her a proper drink. If it had not been for the anesthesia and the many drugs her system had been forced to absorb, my mother would have been pretty well dried out by this time. As it was, she was still irritable and unpredictable, going through the latter stages of withdrawal. To see her through this period, she was put on Thorazine, and heavenly bliss descended on our floor, the building, and the state of Texas. She was even heard to say "thank you" and "please." We looked at television together and laughed. My mother had turned into a human being, actually nice to be with. Until the day she received her new pharmaceutical encyclopedia, looked up Thorazine, and discovered that it was a medication used to calm patients in insane asylums. That finished Thorazine! She refused to take her medication from then on and the real Dietrich returned.

It was time to return to my family. I hugged Dr. De Bakey, thanked him for his kindness, infinite patience, and consummate skill. Kissed my mother and, in secret, the valiant nurses, wished them luck, strong nerves, and put my mother into their capable hands. We would be in constant touch by telephone. I was sure that the next operation, the skin-grafting, would be equally successful now that the leg had its sufficient blood supply. My mother had only to follow her doctor's advice, convalesce, hold on to her hard-gained sobriety, and all would be well.

On the 7th of February, with shaved skin from her thigh, the graft was performed and took on the first try. Once again, Dietrich was victorious – she would keep her leg.

Six weeks after the operations, my mother walked into her New York apartment, opened a bottle of scotch, and without a moment's hesitation, started down that familiar road that would lead, eventually, to her own destruction. By April first, after a traumatic fall, three consecutive full anesthesias, vascular surgery, and skin-graft surgery, Marlene Dietrich, at seventy-three, was back on tour.

M. DIETRICH 1974 Tour

New Orleans	Fairmont Hotel
4 3–13	
Los Angeles	Chandler Pavilion
4 15–16–17–18	
Washington	Kennedy Center Opera House
4 22–23–24–25	
Honolulu	Waikiki Sheraton Hotel
4 29–30	
5 1	
Phoenix, Ariz.	Pheonix Symphony Hall
5 16–17–18	
Toledo, Ohio	Masonic Temple
5 21–22–23–24	

St. Paul, Minn.   O'Shaughnessy Auditorium
5 25–26
Chicago, Ill.   Chicago Auditorium
5 28–29–30
Sacremento, Calif.   Music Circus
6 2–3–4–5–6–7–8–9
Mexico City   Fiesta Palace
6 11–23
Danbury, Conn.
7 10–24

She called me daily. Her legs, unaccustomed to the sudden rush of blood supply, were swollen, pulsed painfully. She drew pictures of what she called her "barrel leg," sending them to De Bakey. She was frightened that the "stitches" would rip and the Dacron "tubing" that he had spliced onto her arteries would tear loose. So, in a small drawstring bag, she carried a spare, an exact duplicate of what De Bakey had used – in case of such an emergency. Repair jobs had always been suspect; Dietrich hated them on her dresses, her costumes – it was only natural she would not trust them inside her body! Another worry plagued her: Since the time the catheter had been removed after the last operation, my mother at times could not control the flow of urine. With her amazing Spartan attitude, she decided to devise a way to overcome the possibility of leaving puddles in her wake. Sanitary napkins were the only logical protection that she could hide effectively under her stage dresses. They had another advantage; if anyone, like hotel maids, found them, they would automatically assume Dietrich still menstruated, not that she might have become incontinent. She suffered terribly under this new affliction; by its very connotation of old age it marred her own criteria of elegance and beauty. The fact that the more she drank the more she "dribbled," she refused to acknowledge. It was easier to blame De Bakey and wear two pads instead of one.

AFTER TWELVE YEARS in Europe, the Riva family was finally coming home. Paul pulled my arm: "Look! Mom! Look! Your Statue of Liberty!" and there she was, constant and true. This would be our first summer back in America. Oh, it was going to be wonderful! We rented a little house near good friends on Long Island, told the kids stories of when their big brothers had summered in the same place, fished for snappers, clammed, cooked real American steaks on a backyard barbecue, witnessed the workings of a true democracy – the impeachment proceedings of a president on national television.

On the 9th of August, a Capricorn president finally got the message and resigned, and the other Capricorn flew from Paris to Geneva for her annual checkup with Prof. de Watteville. As usual, my mother's Dutch courage routine was in effect. Back in Paris that night, she made a half-turn as she approached her bed and collapsed. The phone rang. I recognized the voice of one of the many young men my mother allowed to wait on her for the honor of serving their Queen.

"Maria, your mother fell. Something is very wrong. Here she is . . ."

Accidents sobered her fast: "Sweetheart, this whole thing is ridiculous. I just made a funny turn and fell – right here, in the bedroom – on the soft carpet. But when I tried to get up, I suddenly couldn't. Now you *know* that's stupid. The graft is okay, De Bakey's Dacron is okay, so *now* what?"

"Mass, listen to me carefully. Call Dr. Seidman, he's still in Paris. You must be x-rayed. Call him right now – I'll wait here. Have him call me."

While I waited, I called Prof. de Watteville at his home in Geneva, asked what had happened while she was with him that day. He informed me that he was extremely pleased, that he had found no sign of recurring cancer, that she had shown him the graft, and that in his opinion, it was a beautiful piece of work.

"Your mother is a truly amazing woman and an extremely lucky one, but I am very concerned about her drinking. I hesitated to mention it to her but felt that today it was necessary. Her reaction was most astounding. She insisted that as she hated the taste of all alcohol, she never drank anything more than an 'occasional' glass of champagne. But I must tell you, she was exceedingly drunk."

As its elevator was too elegantly small, my mother was taken by emergency stretcher down the back stairs of her Paris apartment. With her screaming directives, frightened to be discovered by lurking photographers, they took her through the subterranean garage to the American Hospital in Paris. After being x-rayed, she refused to remain there, insisted on being returned to her apartment. She had broken her hip.

She called to give me the news. By now, she was cold sober:

"Sweetheart – I can't stay in France. They kill people in France. London is out – the British press is vicious and since the Nazis killed all the Jews, there are no more good doctors in Germany. So maybe Sweden? Or America – again? Call De Bakey and ask," and hung up.

LEFT: The Living Legend at seventy-two. This photograph was universally acclaimed, yet if one looks at it long enough one begins to feel that something is terribly wrong with the beautiful lady.

BELOW: Los Angeles International Airport, 1975. This time we were caught by the press transporting Dietrich by stretcher.

ABOVE: My mother during one of the last visits to my father's "ranch."

BELOW: *Just a Gigolo*, the last film that she should not have had to make—the last costume that she should not have had to wear.

I called Dr. De Bakey and asked him for the best hip man in the world; without hesitation he said: "Frank Stinchfield," and gave me his New York number. I tracked him down at his home, introduced myself, and gave him my mother's full medical history. He was wonderfully kind, assuring me that there was a highly respected and skilled orthopedic surgeon in Paris that he could recommend. When I explained that under no circumstances would my mother consent to being treated in France, he said that if I could manage to have her flown to New York, he would make the necessary arrangements to have her admitted to Columbia-Presbyterian Hospital for hip surgery. I thanked him and promised to have her in New York within twenty-four hours.

First, I had to call my mother and convince her to be flown to New York. Second, I had to find someone trustworthy to accompany her stretcher from Paris. Third, I had to find an airline that would accommodate a stretcher and keep the entire procedure confidential. Fourth, hire an ambulance to meet the plane at Kennedy Airport. Fifth, organize my home so that I could leave for New York City. As the young man attending my mother held a British passport, which required him to have a visa before entering the United States, it would take too long for him to accompany her. Time was of the essence, not only because of the medical emergency, but because of the world press. The longer it took to get Dietrich from one country to another, the more time the press had to find out about this latest accident.

As I had to organize the New York end, I called an old flame of my mother's who held an American passport and was living in London, told her what had happened, asked for her help. She refused. Desperate, I called a friend I could trust, asked her if she would fly from her home in Canada to Paris, pick up my mother, and deliver her to me in New York. Her instantaneous "Of course," I shall be eternally grateful for.

I and the ambulance were waiting on the tarmac as my mother's plane landed at Kennedy Airport. The passengers disembarked, then we lifted our precious cargo off the plane. That the press of two countries did not get wind of all this was a real feat. A year later, we weren't so lucky, but this first time, as I climbed into the ambulance next to my mother's stretcher, I was jubilant.

"How is that for superb cloak-and-dagger? We made it! No reporters! The security system at the hospital is briefed, everything has been arranged. Stinchfield is the best in his field. We'll get through this too. New York is not Houston, but I think we'll get away with it. I have arranged to sleep in your room, as it takes two hours to get to our place out on Long Island. . . ." I kept up the chatter, trying to distract her. To be in an ambulance is a frightening experience for anyone. For one who was as petrified of cars as my mother, a really harrowing one. For her stretcher trip across the Atlantic, Dietrich had chosen to wear a candy-pink caftan; around her pale face she had draped a Chanel chiffon shawl of the same color. She looked vulnerable and absolutely gorgeous. Only the fear in her eyes marred the pretty picture she made. I held her hand and calmed her as best I could each time we hit another New York pothole. She was sure that every jar dislodged her broken hip even farther.

The next day, my mother was wheeled into yet another operating theater to undergo major surgery. Just five and a half months after the last one. When she regained consciousness, Dietrich's hip boasted a brand-new, man-made ball joint. She christened it "George." Much more intriguing to say, "You know, George feels funny inside me today," than "My prosthesis is bothering me." She had completely forgotten that this had also been one of Yul's code names – or had she?

While my husband kept the home fires burning and the kids teased him about his cooking, I concentrated on getting my mother back on her feet and walking. It was normal for her to feel fragile, breakable, petrified of testing the safety of that stainless steel inside her body. She refused all attempts to make her stand, canceling therapists right and left. Even when Dr. Stinchfield finally forced her out of bed, the moment he left the room she hoisted herself back into it. I mentioned that she was scheduled to open at the Grosvenor House in London on the 11th of September and casually asked if she wanted me to now cancel her contract. She lay there, just looking at me. I knew now she would get up and went to dial the therapist's extension.

Once again, my mother was being forced to undergo the stages of alcohol withdrawal and hated the whole world for its cruelty, especially the Columbia-Presbyterian Hospital staff. The one that received the most abuse was her young therapist. I remember that young girl's incredulous expression when my mother announced to her that it was a complete waste of her time to be forced to practice climbing stairs, informing her that Dietrich absolutely had no reason nor further need to do so – ever again. The mere idea that anyone had the power to eliminate stairs from their life was beyond the girl's comprehension. Privately, she asked me:

"Is your mother serious? Does she mean that? She is never, ever going to have to use stairs again?"

"Exactly. If my mother decides stairs are 'out,' they will cease to exist for her. You and I might have to maneuver such mundane obstacles, but Dietrich? She can change the world to suit herself!"

The steps leading up to the stage at the Grosvenor House were elimi-nated. Twenty-nine days after hip surgery, Richard Burton introduced

Marlene Dietrich to her glittering audience. She strode onto the stage, steady as a rock, without the slightest limp, bowed low into her famous bow, and triumphed once again.

She called me the moment she got back to her dressing room: "Sweetheart! The dribble wasn't too bad and the sound wasn't right for 'Where Have All the Flowers Gone?' because you weren't here to fix it. But De Bakey's Dacron held, the graft looks okay, the legs didn't swell too much after the flight from New York, and 'George' didn't snap out when I did the bow, and you'll be proud of me – I didn't limp."

I was, but I would have been even prouder if she hadn't slurred her *r*'s.

An hour later, she called back: "You know who insisted on seeing me? That little gnome – Princess Margaret. You know how I never let anyone come backstage and see me in the dress? Well, all this to-do with 'royal protocol,' I wasn't allowed to let a 'princess' wait! Big Deal! So I had to see her right away. Don't they have anyone who can tell them how to dress? You should have seen her. I hear she drinks – she looks puffy. Remember when Noël took me to dinner at her house? What is that palace where they live called? And how we were all taken on a 'grand' tour to see her new bathroom? All ruffles and ugly marble and solid gold rococo fittings and how I laughed that with all that to-do, in typical British fashion, the cold and hot water were *still* coming out of separate taps? I am going to take my Fernando Lamas now and go to sleep. Call Stinchfield and tell him I will send him the reviews in the morning."

By December she was touring Japan.

EARLY IN '75, she played a week's engagement at the Royal York in Toronto, and I flew up to see the show. She had asked me to check and fix the sound. I balanced the microphones, repositioned the speakers, stayed to dress her and see the show to double-check the system.

During the day, my mother had been particularly irritable and irritating. Using the imagined pain of her hip as an excuse, she had swallowed six of her new love, Darvon, with a fifth of scotch. By the time she stood waiting in the wings for her cue that night, she was a mess. Her eyes glazed, her wig off-center, her makeup sloppy, her lipstick smeared. She slumped, holding onto the weighted curtain for support. When her entrance music cued her onto the stage, she ambled, disinterested, and took up her position at the microphone. Her dulled glaze tried to focus on her audience. Despite the bright lights shining into her eyes, she could

distinguish the faces of those seated at their tables at the very perimeter
of the stage. I, standing at the back of the room, watched her anxiously,
expecting her to pass out any moment.

She missed a beat, hesitated over a lyric, and stopped cold. Her body
froze – a sudden stillness descended, and before my eyes, my mother
metamorphosed into vital, magnificent perfection. She sparkled! Teased!
Commanded! Enslaved! Became the "golden Venus" her audience had
come to worship. I had been witness to this startling transformation and
still couldn't believe my eyes. What had provoked it? I searched for a
possible clue among the faces at the ringside tables, and there he was –
Yul Brynner. It was the sight of his face that had galvanized my mother
into becoming "Dietrich."

Yul called her repeatedly that night. He was staying in the same hotel
and wanted to see her. At first, she made me tell him no, then decided
to tell him herself. She was not depressed. She obviously enjoyed
reawakening Yul's burning ardor, only to extinguish it. She felt on
top of the world.

She continued on to Dallas, Miami, Los Angeles, Cleveland, Phila-
delphia, Columbus, and Boston. Whenever I could, I flew to where she
was, listened to her suffering entourage, smoothed over irate hotel and
theater managers, checked the speakers, microphones, and consumption
of scotch. She always greeted me with heroic expectations – now everyone
would fall back into line, do as they were told, behave – Maria had come
to slay all her dragons.

As her drinking increased, her performances lost the crystal sharpness
of brilliance, dulled into "good" instead of "great," bookings into concert
halls waned. Anyway, she had played them all when truly magnificent,
so return engagements for a lesser impact became hard to find, and so
luxury hotel chains often took the place of legitimate theaters. These
were the hardest for her. She had outgrown those audiences that sit at
tables drinking, expecting a floor show. No matter how much it cost
them to see a legend in the flesh, these were not parishioners come into
an awesome temple, but merrymakers out for a good time expecting
their money's worth. I knew how difficult this "downscaling" was for
her and chose those times to appear, take up my old post of handmaiden,
and dress her.

As she lived in the hotel she worked for, she could prepare for the
performance in her suite. First the makeup – god, she was good at that!
When she was really drunk, she messed it up, but when even half sober,
one marveled at her skill and lightning speed. Now the wig. This one's
side wave was not correct, try another. No. 12A, marked "L.A. Chandler
Pavilion opening night" was finally chosen. Now the all-important tray

for the table that was always positioned stage right at the edge of the curtain – her safety net to exit to. Flashlight, hand mirror, comb, brush, lipstick, lip brush, Kleenex, pressed powder, Allenberry lozenges, glass of champagne, glass of scotch, four Darvon – individual capsules laid out ready to grab – three Dexedrine tablets in a row, one cortisone. All the essentials to get through yet another working night.

The foundation marked "No. 3 tight Denmark," then the golden dress. I took its heavy beaded coat down in the service elevator to the Cotillion Room, the Empire Room, or whatever name this particular hotel had chosen to impress its clientele with, then returned to take – her. The revealing dress hidden beneath a silk kimono, she stood waiting, breathing slow, body erect in gossamer harness of glowing armor. I was always so sorry for her when this moment came – the gladiator, ready to go into the arena, all alone. The tight dress, the distances, the alcohol-induced unsteadiness, the excuse of the hip, now made a wheelchair an acceptable convenience as long as no "strangers" saw her use one. I positioned it, she lowered herself carefully into it. The dress, always that worry for her dress. She adjusted the kimono, making sure that her revealing front was completely covered, reached out for her tray, positioned it securely on her lap, I made sure there was no one in the corridor, and we began our journey. Usually service elevators empty adjacent to hotel kitchens, and that is where we exited.

It was definitely Shrimps Casino tonight, with a faint overlay of broiled lamb chops. The cooks smiled at their nightly visitor, they all had received photographs especially dedicated to them and were her fans. Harried waiters, scurrying bus boys, acknowledged her glamorous presence as they weaved, avoiding her chariot. She was not disturbed at being seen by them, somehow she knew they wouldn't talk; besides, she always felt comfortable in kitchens. I pushed her wheelchair amidst the bustle, the pungent smells, and wondered if she too was remembering all those kitchens we had run through – laughing – young – so very long ago.

Her latest tour done, my mother returned to her Paris apartment. Paul graduated from high school and fell in love – with a Chevrolet; David was looking forward to getting back to our summer house and his special fishing cove. I had positioned a few loyal people in Paris who knew when to water my mother's scotch and keep an eye on her pill consumption. Darvon was now her daily favorite, she acquired hundreds of the red-and-gray capsules, ate them like candy, washing them down with her J&B. This, combined with her various sleeping pills, made up a really lethal combination. Everyone on my Paris surveillance team had their instructions and my telephone numbers in case of an emergency. I left for Long Island, convinced that this summer of '75 I would get to spend with my family.

On the 10th of August, my father suffered a massive stroke, was resuscitated by paramedics, then taken to Holy Cross Hospital in San Fernando Valley near his home. He was not expected to live. I called my mother, broke the news to her as gently as possible, said I was on my way to California. She cried – said she would remain in Paris until she heard from me.

My son Michael was waiting at the airport and drove me out to the Valley. My father was still alive. His right side paralyzed, speechless, but alive. I called my mother, gave her as much hope as I possibly could, minimizing my father's critical condition, trying to make it easier for her. Her only question: Were there reporters at the hospital already? When I said no, she was not convinced, saying that I should watch out for them, protect Papi from any publicity, to call her every half hour, that she would remain in Paris, sitting by the phone until I told her he was out of danger.

I was relieved. I had been worried how I was going to manage to keep her from rushing to her dying husband's bedside. Long ago, during one of those rare times when my father and I spoke to each other as friends, he had said to me:

"Kater, when I die, see to it that your mother does not stand looking down at my grave."

It was the least I was prepared to do for him.

Michael got me dimes for the pay phone, reminded me that there was a nine-hour difference between California and Paris, and left for a few hours' work.

As potential mourners, those who wait outside intensive care units develop a special kinship. They may never see each other again or know each other's names, but while they share their sad vigil, they bond.

We whispered hopeful platitudes to each other, needing to believe them, shared our prayers, coffee, and Kleenex. The long wait for life or death to flee had begun.

Every hour I was permitted five minutes to stand by my father's bed and witness his struggle. I held his good hand, repeated words I knew he couldn't comprehend, yet said them anyway:

"Papilein, I am here. It's Kater. I am here. You are safe – you are safe, I promise," and imagined it calmed him. After each viewing, I called Paris. As the hours dragged on, she became less emotional, more resigned to my father's critical condition, and began issuing orders. Her primary concern was his diaries. She was terrified they might fall into the wrong hands, be read, and all her secrets revealed. She ordered me to leave the hospital, go to my father's house, and remove the diaries to a safe place. I thought it a bit macabre to pick over the corpse before it actually was one, but assured her that I would see to it that the precious diaries were removed immediately, as ordered. I did nothing of the kind. I had more important things to worry about than my mother's reputation, her fear of being finally discovered the less-than-perfect "wife."

Nurses are always so concerned of possible bedside thefts; I was given my father's personal possessions for safekeeping, his wallet, his gold Patek Philippe wristwatch, and his teeth. I noticed that his large signet ring was missing. It and my father's hand had been inseparable. I remember how the square-cut emerald caught the light whenever he clenched his hand in anger. He would have liked to have been buried wearing it. Now the ring was gone and I wouldn't be able to, I thought, as though it mattered – as though he would ever know. Waiting for someone to die, one thinks such silly thoughts.

On my next call to my mother, I had nothing new to tell her, but she did. I was to see to it that my father's dogs were taken to the pound and gotten rid of. With true Germanic thoroughness, she was cleaning out her husband's home. I suppose, being so far away, having no actual control over events, she had to involve herself in something. Again, I assured her I would execute her orders immediately, but I had no intention of destroying what my father loved.

The doctors agreed and approved my request that my father be allowed to die in peace, not be subjected to further "heroic" methods of resuscitation. He was given extreme unction. We waited. The hours dragged on. My father continued his struggle, refused to die.

The Holy Cross is a wonderful hospital. Its staff skilled and dedicated angels, but for a seventy-eight-year-old stroke victim determined to remain alive against all odds, a more sophisticated, technically equipped institution was necessary. His doctors and I discussed the advisability of transferring him to the UCLA Medical Center in Westwood. We agreed that as he was fighting so hard to survive, he deserved to be given every chance to succeed. I began to make the complicated arrangements of transferring a critical patient from one hospital to another. Seven days after suffering a massive stroke, my father, hooked up to his life-support systems, was lifted into a private ambulance. No one really believed he would survive the long journey to UCLA. I rode with him. If he died on the way, Tami would want me there with him.

My father was still alive as our ambulance came to a screeching halt at the emergency entrance of UCLA. Expert hands lifted his stretcher and rushed him inside. While I handled the necessary paperwork, my father was being hooked up to IVs, monitoring devices in the intensive cardiac care unit on the fourth floor of one of the greatest medical centers in the world.

On the 22nd of August, twelve days after his stroke, my father resurrected himself, became aware that something was terribly wrong with Rudi Sieber. Now his real torture would begin – yet he must have wanted it, to fight so hard to reach this moment.

I called my mother with the incredible news. She refused to believe me. She had never fully comprehended the reason for my father's serious incapacities nor what had caused them. She was convinced that he had had "just" another heart attack, and could not understand how that could have paralyzed him, robbed him of speech and comprehension. As she was scheduled to begin rehearsals in Melbourne on the 26th, I suggested that she stop off in L.A. on her way to Australia, see her husband for herself, confer with his doctors. I felt it was time for her to take up some of a wife's responsibilities, besides paying for them.

I sat outside on the hospital steps, waiting for my mother's limousine. It was a cool, clear evening, the sky full of early stars, the air heavy with mock orange. The car swung into the driveway. Dietrich, looking every inch the breathtakingly beautiful, distraught wife, swept into her husband's special enclosure – and ICCU Four was never the same again. Although my father could not recognize her, she insisted that he did. The doctors were patient, drew her pictures indicating where the blood clots had lodged in his brain, where they had wrought their havoc. They tried to explain why her insistence that they operate "immediately" was impossible in her husband's case.

Lips tight, she waited for the doctors to leave, then fixed me with one of her looks: "*These* are the 'great' doctors you are so in love with? They are idiots! They say they can't operate on Papi because they don't know *how*. I talked to all the greatest doctors in Europe. They all tried to tell me that the Americans are the best brain specialists in the world! But nobody really knows anything. I should have taken Papi to Niehans to get fresh cells years ago."

She took a suite at the Beverly Wilshire for the night and was furious when I insisted on returning to my room near the hospital. The next day she got busy organizing her husband's future. First, she discovered that I had not killed off the dogs as ordered and was livid, then when I insisted that they be removed to a kennel instead of the pound, granted me their reprieve. With her beautiful eyes luminous with unshed tears, she informed the doctors that after she finished her Australian tour, she planned to return to California, rent a small house in Beverly Hills, and devote the rest of her life to pushing her husband's wheelchair in the sunshine. Her voice a soft caress of utter sincerity, she meant every word of it.

The listening male physicians melted, charmed by this so-beautiful woman's wifely devotion. There were many who, over the years, heard my mother pronounce those words, heard the plans she had for her crippled husband. Neither the doctors then, nor those who heard it later, ever challenged her idyllic script. No one ever said, "To devote your life to caring for your infirm husband is commendable – truly wonderful – but wouldn't it be better to dedicate yourself to his recovery? Help him to walk again? Help him to regain his pride, rather than pushing his wheelchair in the sun?" She left for Australia, I remained.

On the day my father was strong enough to be transferred to the neurological wing, I came to say good-bye. Hoping somehow my father would understand the meaning of my words, I tried to tell him how proud, how full of admiration I was that he wanted life, was willing to fight so hard for it, squeezed his good hand, touched his good cheek, and wished I could do more for him.

Back in New York, I kept a close check on his progress, calling my mother twice a day in Australia to give her the latest news. She was so convinced he would have to be institutionalized, she persisted in her obsession with the dogs. As she would pay for having them killed, "even buried," why did I continue to refuse to execute her orders? As for my father's house, it was to be stripped of his belongings, then sold.

Fortunately, my mother was so tied up with her tour, I was able to stall her. It was essential for my father's possible recovery, no matter how impractical it might seem, that his home, his possessions, his animals, all he treasured in his life, were kept safe for him to return to. It was the lodestone he needed to survive – he had no other.

Rumors of trouble began to filter back to me in New York. The Australian tour was going badly. I received a call from one of the irate producers – Miss Dietrich was complaining constantly about the sound, the lights, the orchestra, the audiences, the management. She was abusive, she was drunk, both on and off the stage. Her concerts were not sold out, the management was considering canceling the rest of the tour, I was asked if I would take on the task of preparing my mother for such an eventuality. I, and her faithful agent, negotiated a compromise. We would do our very best to persuade Miss Dietrich to consider terminating the tour, attempt to straighten out some of the more unpleasant disagreements if they, in turn, agreed to pay her contractual salary without any deductions. Fortunately, by now all they wanted was to get rid of her, cut their losses.

It was left to me to get Dietrich out of Australia as gracefully and as fast as possible.

"Mass? Listen. They say the ticket sales are not good at all. Oh! I agree with you. It is *their* fault entirely for not spending enough money for publicity. Yes, the ads are *much* too small but . . . they are willing to pay your full salary, even if you don't perform. So, why not take it easy. Take the money and get the hell out! Who needs all this hassle? With all these worries you have about Papi, you can just take the money, go back to California, and be with him!"

"What? He is in a hospital and I have a contract! I can't leave in the middle of a tour! They only say to *you* they will pay me, but you watch, the moment I left – Nothing!"

"I would insist that you were given a banker's draft before boarding the plane. That's the least of our worries."

"No! I have a *contract*! I go next to Canberra and then I open in Sydney. They are not going to get rid of me! How dare they! Don't you have anything more to do with gangsters like that!" and she slammed down the phone.

Filled with her usual Darvon, Dexamil, and scotch, Dietrich opened in Sydney on the 24th of September, 1975. Mike Gibson, of the *Daily Telegraph*, reviewed her performance that night correctly. Unfortunately, this one too she deserved:

> . . . A little old lady, bravely trying to play the part of a former movie queen called Marlene Dietrich, is tottering around the stage of Her Majesty's Theatre. When I say bravely I mean it. Without a doubt her show is the bravest, saddest, most bittersweet concert I have ever seen. . . .
>
> . . . With the aid of the best in lighting, cosmetics and modern-day underwear engineering, for more than an hour she defiantly stands there trying to recapture the magic of a woman who gave soldiers goose pimples in a war over 30 years ago.
>
> Her fans adore her.
>
> Like a wind-up doll, a camp impersonation of a German legend, she brazens her way through songs like "My Blue Heaven" and "You're the Cream in My Coffee." . . .
>
> She sways unsteadily as she shuffles her way offstage to take off her fur. . . .
>
> When it is over the applause from her fans is tremendous. The compulsory roses conveniently placed in front of the footlights fly through the air onto the stage.

Now you can see why the little old lady sings on. It can't just be money. She wouldn't try as hard as this. . . .

Hanging onto the red curtains for support, she takes bow after bow. She is still bowing, and waving, still breathing it all in as we leave.

When we get home the baby-sitter is watching the late-night movies on Channel 9.

It is called "Shanghai Express," it was made in 1932, and it starred Marlene Dietrich.

"Wasn't she marvelous," said the baby-sitter.

"Yes, she was," I replied.

Five days after this scathing review, my mother arrived at the theater for that evening's performance. My friend, that rescuing angel who had flown from Canada the year before, was in Sydney, had offered to "watch-dog" her for me, and help dress her. My mother was so drunk that she, together with the girlfriend of one of the musicians, tried desperately to sober her up in the dressing room with black coffee. Finally, they managed to zip her into the foundation and into the dress. Supporting their precious burden between them, they exited the dressing room as the first strains of Dietrich's overture came over the loudspeaker. They made their way to the wings and placed her by the curtain. She slumped and collapsed.

Her conductor, seeing Dietrich had missed her entrance cue, signaled the orchestra to repeat the overture while Dietrich was being carried away from the stage back to her dressing room. The shock of falling had sobered her sufficiently to realize that something was wrong with her left leg. It would not support her.

The performance had to be canceled, a crippled Dietrich had to be gotten out of the theater as fast as possible. But she absolutely refused to have fans waiting for her at the stage door see her close up in the stage dress and insisted on changing first. As she had to be held upright in order to remove the dress without tearing it, my mother locked her arms around the neck of the distraught producer, and just hung there, while the two women peeled off her costume and redressed her into her Chanel suit.

Back at her hotel, not knowing I had already been informed of this new accident and was in touch with Dr. Stinchfield, who was contacting doctors in Sydney, my mother forbade anyone to call me. With her usual luck, the international convention of orthopedic surgeons was taking place in Sydney that week. Within the hour, two leading physicians, resplendent in their tuxedos, came to my mother's suite. Though she believed that Dr. Stinchfield's hip joint was the culprit, it was obvious to the doctors that she had probably broken her thigh bone. They did not tell her this, preferring to wait for the X rays to corroborate their diagnosis. She refused to be taken to the hospital.

All that night, my mother lay in her bed, hardly daring to breathe. Early the next morning, she finally allowed herself to be smuggled out of the hotel into St. Vincent's Hospital. The X rays confirmed the doctors' suspicions. She had a broken femur of the left leg.

Alcoholics are always at risk, especially in the field of orthopedics. In order to protect them from the added danger of bone infection, tremors during traction, and other complications indigenous to their specific problem, it is essential that any surgeon be given the whole truth about a patient's alcoholism. I arranged for Dr. Stinchfield to confer with the Sydney doctors. But my mother absolutely refused to remain in Australia – where to take her?

Finally it was decided to place her into a protective body cast and fly her to the nearest medical center in California, into the care of the chief of orthopedics at UCLA, whom Dr. Stinchfield had recommended. After making the arrangements for her to be flown by stretcher from Australia, I flew to L.A. to prepare for her arrival, booked the ambulance to meet her flight, selected a room in UCLA's VIP Wilson Pavilion. Suddenly I realized that my mother and my father were about to sleep under the same roof! The thought of these two damaged people finally coming together this way saddened me.

I met my mother's plane on the tarmac and transferred her stretcher to the waiting ambulance. This time, the press caught us and snapped the only picture ever taken of Dietrich on a stretcher. Again I rode in the ambulance with her, holding her hand, trying to calm her fears. She was furious. I asked for her forgiveness, for I knew she held me responsible for the break in our usual tight security. Once installed in her new domain, across from the suite where John Wayne would die a few years later, my mother sent me out on all sorts of concocted errands so that she could unpack her little bottles and secrete them away in her night table, behind a stack of Kleenex.

More X rays, conferences, and discussions. In between, I visited my father. He was so proud of his latest feat: When the therapist placed a soft rubber ball into the palm of his once useless right hand, he had not only progressed to recognizing the touch of an object, but was able to actually curl three fingers around it! The day was not too far off when he might manage to give that little yellow ball a squeeze and know he was really alive!

The renowned surgeon, very handsome and "movie starish," flanked by his brilliant young assistants, leaned against the wall facing my mother's bed. Patiently, he tried to explain a relatively new, yet highly successful surgical procedure – the cementing of broken bones, as opposed to placing them in traction to wait for time and nature to heal the break. My mother was not impressed. She dismissed the three men as though they were bell boys, then ordered dinner for both of us.

"Did you see how young that doctor is? And those two on either side of him? Like little boys! Children like that can't know what they are doing . . . they are much too young! It's all too elegant here to be any good. Only in Hollywood would they have a hospital that looks like a movie set! You better take all my X rays back to New York, show them to Stinchfield. Explain to him what they want to do to me here and ask him what he thinks."

I kissed my father good-bye, told him to keep up the hard work, that he was terrific, and thought I saw a flicker of pleasure in his good eye. Before leaving them both, I asked my mother if she wanted to see him, and when her answer was a sharp "No," I wasn't surprised.

Dr. Stinchfield feared that further surgery might expose her to dangerous infection, and as she objected to remaining at UCLA, distrusted the doctors there, but he was still acceptable, it seemed the safest solution to fly her back to New York, install her in her old room at Columbia Presbyterian, and now that she had normal circulation, put her leg in traction.

On the 7th of October, I met my mother's plane at Kennedy Airport and helped transfer her stretcher to yet another waiting ambulance. She had been confined in a body cast since the 13th of September, flown from Australia to California and from there to New York, she was exhausted, scared, and, understandably, extremely cranky. She might have been worse, except that a very attractive blond, ex-army nurse had accompanied her – whose hand my mother held and patted until the doors of the ambulance shut behind us. I took her vacated hand; the potholes seemed to have increased since our last trip along this same route. As we rolled her stretcher into Columbia Presbyterian, I thought I felt the floor staff shudder.

It had been hours since her last drink on the plane. She was getting frantic and unmanageable. She slapped the first nurse who tried to sedate her, then tore the hypodermic out of the second one's hand and hurled it across the room. Finally we managed to put her under. The cast could be cut off, and the complicated procedure of placing and aligning her broken leg into traction could commence.

Normally, the time for such a break to heal in one of my mother's advanced age is from two to three months. It took my mother's alcoholic body four months to heal – until February of 1976. How she endured all those weeks, those screws through her flesh, her leg stretched, strung out, weighted, completely immobile, amazed me. It must have been torture. Granted, she was a terrible patient.

No one was allowed to enter her room without permission. She refused to allow any black or Puerto Rican maids to clean. The nurses were frantic, so were the poor maids, who feared for their jobs should any doctor report the deplorable condition of Miss Dietrich's room. I scrubbed the floor quickly whenever I could, and tried to coax my mother into more receptive and democratic attitudes, and continually apologized for her awful behavior. I had a refrigerator installed, where she stashed the hospital meals she ordered, then refused to eat.

"The food in this terrible, filthy hospital is not fit for human beings to eat! I had them put it all in the icebox for you to take home for dinner."

Sometimes I was able to get her to watch that "low-class form of entertainment," television. The night she saw a Robert Redford film for the first time, she fell madly in love with him. That helped. Now we had orders to bring her fan magazines, anything that mentioned him. I found a pillowcase with Redford's picture, she loved it – she could sleep with him and dream.

My friend, who, like St. Christopher, had brought my mother's stretcher safely over the seas, first from Paris, then from Sydney, who had valiantly struggled to sober her up, supported her, caught her as she collapsed, arranged X rays, doctors, packed up the dressing room, costumes, hotel suite, hid her as best she could from the Australian press, then accompanied her stretcher to L.A., was exhausted. Before flying home, she came to the hospital to say good-bye. As she entered my mother's room, she heard her say:

"You know why I fell? Why I have a broken leg? Just as I was going on the stage in Sydney, that friend of Maria's – tripped me!"

The enormity of my mother's lie stunned her so, she turned, left the room without uttering a sound, and never saw Dietrich again. She did write her a very detailed letter, in which she chronicled exactly the events leading up to the fatal Sydney fall, but my mother never recanted, nor ever modified her blatant lie, repeating it to everyone. Over the years, my friend's continued absence puzzled and irked her greatly. After all, she felt that as she had actually never blamed "that woman" for tripping her, causing her all that "agony and expense," why then did Maria's friend feel she had the right to be *so* offended? As usual, my mother simply refused to accept the truth – even when it was laid bare before her eyes.

Through Thanksgiving, Christmas, and New Year's, she gnashed her teeth: "Vacations! Everyone is on vacation! You ring the bell and nobody comes. You call the doctor's office and nobody answers. The whole world stops! What is this – this obsession with holidays? In every country, people find excuses to not work. *But* they want to get paid! If I see one more Santa Claus! . . . What has he got to do with somebody being born in a stable? That's what Christmas is, isn't it? Because someone was born in some stable?"

My mother was never too sure about the Bible. The Lutheran dogma of her childhood got mixed up with her agnostic sentiments, which, in turn, were confused by her superstitions. Actually, she was never too sure if she was an agnostic or an atheist. All she was really certain of was that God couldn't exist – for if He did, He would show Himself and do as He was told!

Angry that I wasn't with her constantly, that I was trimming a tree, cooking that awful thing known as turkey, spending time with my family, she took Polaroid pictures of her stretched leg with the pins through it and sent them to my sons as a Christmas greeting, inscribed: "No money – *this* Christmas!"

She phoned me incessantly, any hour of the day or night. The entries in her diary during this time have one recurring theme: "Haven't talked to Maria," "No one came," "No food," "All alone," and her perennial favorite: "No one called."

As my mother never recorded that she had called me ten times that day, any outsider reading her diary would be filled with justifiable outrage at her daughter's cruel neglect.

Finally, the traction could be removed and she was put back into a partial body cast. Because of her fragility, she remained in the cast even after I brought her home to her New York apartment. Her bed had been built up, the mattress reinforced, the bathroom transformed into her favorite first-aid station. The rented wheelchair, parked at the foot of her bed, she never used. She preferred staying in bed.

Although still partially paralyzed and speech-impaired, my father was declared strong enough to be brought back to his home. As he was being lifted from the car, his dogs swarmed around him, barking their joyous greeting. I was told that he cried when he saw them, knew he was home.

My mother decided that before returning to Paris, she would fly to California, make sure that her husband was being taken care of properly by all the people she was paying.

The day came when I took her to the hospital to have the cast cut off, then brought her home with a brand-new walker. Strangely enough, my mother did not shun this stark reminder of infirmity. She loved it. Suddenly, she had something to hold onto that moved with her, she could drink and still be mobile. She had no fear of being seen pushing her metal frame about. As she never went out on the street, had no need to enter a car to be taken to a theater to perform, her basic reasons for leaving her apartment were now nonexistent. Drunk, she shuffled, pushing her walker before her. Without its support, she couldn't walk, didn't even attempt to. We knew that she had to be weaned from this latest dependency.

As she refused to go outside for the prescribed therapy, Dr. Stinchfield arranged for therapists to come to her. These she either didn't like, objected to their touch, their manners, their looks, their age, certainly resented the truths they tried to make her understand. Instead of lengthening her shortened left leg through disciplined, conscientious therapy, she just built up her left shoe and fired the therapists for their obvious "stupidity."

For one so stoic, so enamored of military discipline, Dietrich's pathological refusal to follow the rules of systematic therapy astounded me each time anew.

Slowly I got her to let go of the walker, but only after she insisted one was sent ahead to my father's house and another to her Paris apartment. I phoned my father's doctor to warn him of my mother's impending arrival and the havoc she would accomplish. I was so sure she would maneuver my father's ultimate defeat by yet again belittling his accomplishments, destroying his hard-earned pride in himself. She had given me a very good idea of what she was capable of toward this struggling soul:

"Sweetheart. You won't believe this. I talked to Papi's two nurses today, and you know what they are doing? They are trying to teach Papi to speak! A waste of time! Why does he have to talk? I'm paying all those people just to take care of him so they should *know* what he wants! I said, 'All my husband needs to learn is "shit" and "fuck" – that's all that's important!' What other words does he need the way he lives now? And all that to-do . . . the Big excitement – that he can stand and 'diddle' in the *toilet*? Why? The moment I get out there, I will get him one of those wheelchairs that he can pee in while he sits. Then he can stay there, nice and comfortable all day, and pee without having to move. Why do they have to torture him? And why does he have to learn to walk? I *pay* people to *wheel* him! All idiots!"

My poor father, who for the first time in his ineffectual life had accepted the challenge to save himself, who had grasped a little pride by once again urinating as a man, not as a helpless infant, was about to be cut down by his loving, caring wife; I feared – this time for good.

On the 7th of April, having escaped the press from seeing her at the airport in a wheelchair, I put her on the plane for California. By the middle of May, after reorganizing my father's home, his therapy, his life, she was back in her Paris apartment. By the end of June, my father was dead.

I flew to California to bury him. My mother used the threat of the reporters she was convinced would gather around Dietrich's only husband's grave, as excuse to remain in Paris.

Amidst mahogany, walnut, satin, and brass, Michael helped me find the plain pine coffin I knew my father would have wanted. In one of his white silk monogrammed shirts, Hermès tie, Knize suit my mother and he had treasured so, my father was buried in the cemetery where Tami lay. I could let them rest together in the same place, but side by side? – *that* my heart refused to allow. I placed my cross on top of my father's coffin to help him on his long journey and turned away into the arms of my son to cry. The few friends present thought I was crying for the loss of a father. I was not. I was mourning the terrible waste of a man's life, for Tami's suffering, for his, for all the wasted years.

I received many suggestions for the wording on Rudolf Sieber's tombstone. Some were outrageous, some insulting to the man my father could have been, some simply banal. So I did what I thought he would have wanted. The husband of one of the world's great legendary women lies buried under a shady tree, his grave marked by a simple slab of Florentine marble in his favorite shade of green:

RUDI
1897–1976

It was time for me to leave. I went down the path to say good-bye to Tami. Looking down at that little piece of grass – it seemed impossible it could cover all the thousands of things that made up a human being. I spoke to her, asked her forgiveness, hoped she approved of what I had tried to do for Papi, because she loved him so.

Soon the telephone calls began: "Maria, how could you? Your poor mother called me. She told me how you did not let her come to Rudi's funeral. She was weeping. How could you do that to your mother? She said she was all packed, just sitting by the phone night and day, waiting for you to call! But you never did!"

I knew my mother had not wanted to be a witness to the actualities of her husband's death and was now simply assuaging her guilt, polishing her widow's image by laying the blame for her absence at her husband's grave on me. Besides, I had welcomed this need of hers to once again hide from reality. It had given me the chance to keep the promise I had made my father.

Dietrich lost two husbands that year. Soon after my father's death, Jean Gabin died. She was shattered, mourned him for years. It was not only his actual death that destroyed her so, it was also the realization that her long, secret dream of someday having Jean return to her was now at an end. Within weeks of each other, my mother lost the two men she loved the most – had betrayed the most.

They became her "ghosts." She looked for them – listened for their voices – complained when they didn't materialize, refused to give her signs of their comforting presence.

When Fritz Lang died, she celebrated; whenever someone else disappeared, she called me: "Did you hear Luchino Visconti died? Remember when he did that film where that bad actor he liked so, his boyfriend, played me in drag – in the *Blue Angel* costume? . . . And now with Howard Hughes dead, who is going to get all *those* millions? He used to chase me around Las Vegas, before he got that thing about living locked away with Kleenex boxes – and what is all this to-do suddenly in America, about a book about Negroes? I read something about it in *Newsweek* . . ."

"You mean *Roots*?"

"Yes – that's it! Who wants to read about them? It'll never sell," and hung up.

For the third time, she sold her unwritten autobiography to yet another American publisher. Refusing all help, advice, and counsel, she recounted her life as she believed she had lived it – pure, dedicated, a hymn to duty, honor, virtue, and motherhood.

In 1978, her agent brought me a deal for her to appear in a film being shot in Germany for worldwide distribution, to be called *Just a Gigolo*. The money offered her for a cameo role was exorbitant. Somehow, we had to find a way to get her to accept it. First, we had to get the producer to agree to shoot her sequence in Paris. In this way, she could be brought to the set directly from her apartment without the German press snapping too close at her heels. Secondly, her two scenes had to be filmed back to back. I knew that I could not keep her sober longer than two days. We also had to arrange that her main scene would be staged with her sitting, and her second scene, that required her walking into the set, be cut to only one step into frame. After long negotiations, two contracts were drawn, one my mother saw and finally signed – and the other she never knew existed. Knowing that only the need for money had made my mother agree to make the film, the contract stipulated that she be paid in installments: a large sum, on signing, to hold her locked into the deal; the next payment at the end of the first day of shooting, to ensure that she would not walk off the set; the final payment at the end of the second day, to make certain that she showed up. The private document stipulated that Maria Riva, daughter of Marlene Dietrich, had to be present and by her presence guarantee that Miss Dietrich would be in condition to perform her contractual duties.

So, they made the pilgrimage from Germany to France: the crew, the director, the cameraman, the actors. They built a duplicate of the set already standing on a German soundstage and waited for the great movie star to appear.

She chose a personal friend to design the costume for this film. It was this too personal relationship that I believe interfered with this costume designer's usual good taste. He is much too talented to have designed that hat, that awful patterned veil, that whole ghastly outfit all by himself. If von Sternberg had been there to photograph it, it might have worked. As it was, my mother looked like a female impersonator doing a rather tacky take-off on Dietrich. I arrived in Paris, saw this pathetic get-up that my mother had concocted to hide behind, finished, approved, and ready to shoot, and could do nothing to help her.

Once again I began watering her booze. My job was to keep Dietrich functioning for the next two days. As the first day of shooting dawned, I had grave doubts. She had decided to punish me. After all, I was responsible for forcing her to work, to be seen by a camera, to face a set full of "strangers" – this word was always synonymous with "enemies" to my mother. Worst of all, I had tried to take her scotch away from her!

I was so very sorry for her, but her lifelong refusal to listen to advice, her aversion to investments of all kinds, her extravagance, her romantic childlike belief that money would always be there for her, made it a dire necessity to provide her with the funds to continue living the only life she knew. The Impressionist paintings that she had once owned, then told everyone she gave to her daughter, making of her child a "billionaire," had mostly proved to be fakes, sold to pay the blackmailers who beat a steady path to my door.

It would have served nothing to tell my mother these sad truths. She so needed to believe that she alone had given her daughter life, love, and the means for the pursuit of grateful happiness.

We arrived at the French studio, our star intact. By the second day, my mother had found a breathless young thing and flirted her into smuggling a bottle of brandy into her portable dressing room. Before I found the bottle and could confiscate it, she had consumed half its contents. By the end of the day, she was too drunk to remember the lyrics of "Just a Gigolo." As I had done so often for her later stage performances, with a thick Magic Marker I printed the words out for her on large pieces of white cardboard and held them next to the camera for her to read.

I put her to bed that night. Nerves, exhaustion, and brandy had done their job. On returning home, she had been violently sick. Fearing that she might vomit in her sleep and choke, I stayed the night watching her. Well, we had done it! Pulled it off! She would get paid her full salary for the film. That would take care of the huge bills for a while, at least.

It might have been easier had she lived in New York, but she refused. Her fear of the American press was too deeply ingrained. She never forgot the reporters of the thirties, who had hounded her when von Sternberg's wife named Dietrich in her alienation-of-affection suit, the kidnapping threat, the years of fear of being discovered in the beds of so many lovers. In a way, I was relieved, as Europe regarded her as "holy royalty" – it was much easier to keep her secrets in Paris than in New York.

PARIS

SHE CONTINUED TO FALL. One night, she passed out in her bathroom, clutched the shower curtain as she fell, tore it from its rod – woke the next morning covered in pink plastic. Called me in complete confusion as to how this could have happened, insisting she must have been mugged by her maid who was then "so sorry" she had covered her with the curtain.

Once, on the way down, she hit her head on the edge of a marble table, got a huge shiner that spread down her face, that lasted for weeks – while I feared the phone call that might tell me the blood clot, formed when she hit her head, had traveled to . . . Each time the phone rang, I jumped!

"Sweetheart. It says in the paper that Charles Boyer died. Didn't I do a film with him?"

"Yes – *The Garden of Allah*."

"Oh, him! I thought *he* was dead long ago," and hung up.

In 1979, she passed out in her bedroom, woke, tried to get up and couldn't. Back down those stairs she was carried and x-rayed. She had a hairline fracture above her hip joint. Nothing too serious, no emergency flights, no dashing ambulances. With proper bed care it would heal by itself in less than four weeks. Refusing to be hospitalized, she insisted on being returned to her apartment and put herself to bed for the rest of her life. She had found the perfect solution. Now, when she passed out, she would already be lying down in a soft, safe place. Never once did the option of giving up drinking instead enter her mind.

She refused all efforts to help her. Fired legions of willing and concerned therapists, would not allow nurses nor trained companions near her. Only transients, who could be bought with huge tips to bring her the scotch she craved, were allowed admittance to her inner sanctum.

Like the organized German that she was, she assembled the necessities for her existence and created her own world. Her bed served as her headquarters. She needed only a very narrow strip of it on which to sleep in her drugged, unmoving stupor. On her left, her "office" – envelopes of all shapes and sizes, stationery, note pads, string, tape, photo-mailers, postal scales, sectioned trays of stamps, books, diaries, phone books, telephone, dozens of reading glasses, magnifying lenses, files, dictionaries, Kleenex boxes, rubber bands, paper clips, fan photos, towels, Handi Wipes, and her trusty six-shooter! Granted, it was plastic and unlethal, still it made a big enough bang to scare the hell out of the pigeons that loved to perch and coo outside her bedroom window.

At hand, her ever-ready, long-handled "pincher arms," that she used like a supermarket clerk to reach everything that lay beyond her inner perimeter.

On her right, against the wall, a table unit – its multilevels jammed with hundreds of pill containers, boxes, medicine bottles, jars, tubes, cases of suppositories – her private pharmacy. In front of this, low tables ran the length of the bed. These held second telephone, pencils, pens, markers, scissors by the dozen, dishes, cutlery, pepper mills, hot plate, drinking glasses, thermoses, dishes, cooking pots, frying pan, toothbrushes, plastic bowls, and clocks. Underneath stood her liquor supply, decanted by paid slaves into innocent-looking, tall, green, mineral-water bottles. Next to these, two small, lidded garbage cans, into which she poured her urine, after relieving herself into a Limoges pitcher. No common bedpans for Dietrich! Such an article had the connotation of "invalid," something she loathed. Next to the urine cans stood another receptacle, larger this time, on which perched an old metal casserole that had once belonged in my father's kitchen. Into this, my mother collected her bowel movements.

My mother's insistence on these macabre toilet maneuvers of hers resulted in constant little accidents. The sheepskins she lay upon and loved, since discovering them in the Sydney hospital, were badly soiled, as was her mattress, her sheets, gray and stained. She refused to allow anyone to touch her, change her bed, wash her. Everything stank. "When Maria comes, she will give me a bath," she loved to tell everyone, but when I arrived, ready to clean her, she found a thousand excuses to get out of it. When I insisted, she would say that she was not dirty enough yet, that the bed had just been "changed" for my arrival and that it wasn't necessary to go through all the trouble of moving everything away from the bed just so I could get close enough to "smear" her with soap. She knew that I was trained in giving bed baths, that I could change an entire bed without the patient having to move. Still, she shrank from being touched.

"Oh! If only I could have a real bath in a tub," she would rhapsodize. When I ordered a special sling chair and handrails to be installed in the bathroom that she had not been in for years, she canceled the orders.

Slowly, her beautiful legs lost their muscles and atrophied. Her unused feet developed a deformity known as drop foot. Her body took on some of the physical characteristics of a concentration camp victim. By now she had convinced herself that her bedridden state was not of her doing and searched medical books for any recognized disease that matched her "symptoms." Although this self-maneuvered return to the womb finally crippled her, its relative safety contributed to her eventual longevity.

I visited her often, while her diaries stated, "I never see Maria." Each time I would note "Maria here"; each time I returned, found it crossed out with her Magic Marker. We played our little games.

"Making order" was her favorite. I would bring drawers to her bed to sort out, discuss, label, then put back – while she made "important lists" so I would know where everything was. Nothing was thrown away. Everything was resorted, repacked, relabeled, to be gone through again the next time I appeared. A Balenciaga raincoat from the fifties was unearthed, originally of heavy rubberized material that, after thirty years, was stiff as a board, when bent snapped like peanut brittle. She examined it very carefully:

"This would be good . . . the worms could never get through *this*!" She was absolutely serious, refused to allow me to throw it out. "No, wrap it, then put it where you will know where to find it – to bury me in."

Throughout her life, my mother often spoke of her death. Not the actual occurrence but of its aftermath, the "disposal," resting place, and burial of her body. As with everything she dramatized, it could be lyrically romantic, macabre, or filled with her special brand of blackest humor. All were so much a part of the real Dietrich:

"I once found a beautiful little cemetery in the middle of a real French village, with poppy fields and cows, green benches in front of white cottages – just perfect, like a Monet. They even had a very good auberge that served a pot-au-feu almost as good as mine. With a restaurant so close, you could have gone there to eat lunch each time you visited my grave, but they said they had no room and that I wasn't French. The mayoress of the town said that if I bought land in the village, then I could be buried there, but as usual, I had no money, so . . . we will have to find another pretty village with a five-star restaurant that will bury me!"

Or:

"Sweetheart, I figured out how you can get my body out of this apartment after I am dead – without the reporters seeing you: You get one of those big, black, plastic garbage bags and you stuff me into it. You may have to break my arms and legs to fit me all in. Then, you get Peter – he is the strongest of your sons – to sling the bag over his shoulders and take the elevator all the way down to the basement garage. In the meantime, you go to Printemps and buy a big trunk, bring it back in a taxi, then put me in the garbage bag, into it. After that, you can take it to America, or some place. That's up to you."

She was deadly serious, but I just refused to take her ghoulish plan seriously, so attempted to laugh it off, saying: "Mass, what do you propose I do when I am asked to open that trunk in Customs?"

"Customs? Now they never open anything!"

"Maybe they don't with Marlene Dietrich, but with us lesser mortals, they certainly do!"

"Then, all you have to tell them is that you are doing what your mother *told* you to do!"

And then, there was Dietrich's world-famous monologue on her own funeral. She first invented it in the forties, polished and modified it, reassigned roles for new or departed lovers in the fifties and sixties, read other people's versions of it in their autobiographies and damned them to hell for their plagiarism in the seventies; finally, having fewer and fewer listeners, rarely performed it in the eighties. She had many versions, all unique in their own way, all pure Dietrich:

When I am dead, can you imagine the to-do? . . . The reporters! The photographers! The fans! De Gaulle will proclaim a national holiday. Not a hotel room to be had anywhere in Paris. Of course, Rudi is going to organize everything. He will *love* it! Nellie and Dot Pondel will arrive to get me ready, do the makeup and hair. They are both crying so hard, they can't see, and of course, don't know what to do anyway! All those years they were with me at Paramount, they never had to do anything because I did it all myself! Now, for once, I am not there to do it for them, and they stand sobbing, wondering how they are going to put on the false eyelashes and get the front of my hair right. The back doesn't matter because I am lying down.

Jean Louis has come all the way from Hollywood and is furious! He thought for once he would get the chance to put me into my foundation for the stage dress – now Rudi tells him that he will not allow his wife to be "seen like that!" and that I am going to wear "a simple black dress from Balenciaga" instead. Rudi says that only because he *knows* how I always wished I could get away with wearing just a little black dress on the stage . . . like Piaf.

De Gaulle wanted me to be buried next to the Unknown Soldier at the Arc de Triomphe and do the service at the Notre-Dame, but I said "No, I want it at the Madeleine." That is my favorite church in Paris and the chauffeurs can park their limousines in the square next door and go have a coffee at Fauchon while they wait.

We get one of those army wagons, like the one they had for Jack Kennedy when he was killed, with six black horses to pull the coffin, which is draped in a special tricolor, made by Dior.

The procession will start at the Place de la Concorde and make its way, slowly, up the Boulevard de la Madeleine – all the way to the church, with the whole Foreign Legion marching to the beat of a single drum. . . . Too bad Cooper is dead, he could wear his costume from *Morocco* and join them. . . . The crowds line the streets, silently weeping. The great dress houses of Paris have closed their doors so that the little shop girls, the fitters, can go to the parade and say their last tearful adieux to "Madame." From all over the world, the Queers have arrived. They push through the crowds, trying to get closer to those rugged, handsome Legionnaires. For the grand occasion, they have copied costumes from my films and all look like me in *Shanghai Express* in their feather boas and little veiled hats. . . . From his car, Noël takes one look and wishes he could mingle but knows he has to be on his best behavior – so doesn't stop. He has written a special tribute to "Marlenah," which, of course, he will recite at the church himself, but he is annoyed, because when he had dinner with Orson the night before, Orson told him that *he* was going to do a whole scene from *Macbeth* and that Cocteau told him *he* was reciting something too, *very* high class and – in French!

While I am being marched and mourned up the avenue, the invited guests start arriving at the church. Rudi stands in his special, newly made by Knize, dark suit, guarding the entrance. On a table in front of him are two boxes filled with carnations – one with white ones, one with red. As each guest enters the church, Rudi gives him, or her, a carnation to wear – *Red* for those who made it, *White* for those who *say* they slept with me but never did. Only he knows!

Inside, the church is crowded. The Reds on one side, the Whites on the other. They are all looking daggers at each other! You can imagine, everyone trying to see who has *red*, especially the women. . . . By the time Burt starts my overture, everyone is furious, madly jealous of each other, just like they always were when I was alive! Fairbanks arrives in a cutaway, bearing a letter from Buckingham Palace. . . . Remarque never makes it to the church – he is drunk somewhere and forgot the address. . . . Jean, smoking a Gauloise, leans against the side of the church – refuses to go inside. . . . All over Paris church bells begin to peal . . .

I once suggested that it might be a great touch to have the entire 82nd Airborne Division do a jump, wearing *their* carnations, with General Gavin leading the way. . . . My mother loved the idea so much, she immediately added it to her scenario.

BY 1982, my mother's legs were useless. She could no longer stand even if she had wanted to. With her usual fixed determination, she had accomplished what she had set out to do. She now had the perfect excuse to shut herself away from the world. Marlene Dietrich, without her beautiful legs? That was inconceivable . . . such a truth had to be kept hidden inside her bed, behind walls.

She started to cook odd bits of food on top of my father's lamp next to her bed. When that broke, she ordered an old-fashioned electric hot plate from her hardware store. Its plug joined the six others stuck into the various extension cords on the stained carpet next to the urine buckets. My imagination came up with horrific scenarios on that electrical madness of hers. I bought her a fire extinguisher and tried to teach her how to use it, wrote the directions in big black letters and pinned them to her mattress, but, knowing that if there was a fire, she would probably be too drunk to read or remember how to use it, I insisted that she at least learn to push her body down to the foot of the bed and slide herself into the wheelchair I had ordered to be positioned there permanently.

"Mass, in case of a fire, I want you to learn how to get out of here by yourself. As you refuse to have anyone sleep in, you must at least learn to get into the chair, wheel yourself to the front door and get out. You are not paralyzed! You can't just sit here and wait for someone to come up and get you."

"Ridiculous! How could there be a fire?"

"That hot plate next to your bed, that you love so, that you refuse to get rid of, for one."

"This little thing? I heat my sauerkraut all by myself. No one ever brings me anything to eat, so I *have* to cook for myself."

It was one of my mother's favorite fantasies, her being left to starve.

I cooked, fans prepared delicacies and sent them over on elegant trays, neighbors were willing to cater the famous star on their floor, her maid fretted that Madame would never allow her to cook, Berlin fans sent her packages of frankfurters that she loved to devour raw; Swedish fans, marinated herring. Her market bills ran to five hundred dollars a week, but Dietrich kept right on convincing everyone, including herself, that she had been abandoned, left to starve – alone!

Despite my mother's withdrawal from the outside world, her expenses remained the same. Now, instead of shoes, she bought Kleenex boxes. Even Howard Hughes would have been impressed by the hundreds stacked high against her bedroom wall. Money had to be found to pay the bills.

I had thought for a long time that as Dietrich was "common property," a term used for those famous enough to warrant losing the protection that normal beings are allowed to enjoy, that anyone not only could, but would, eventually film a documentary of her life. So why not have Dietrich do her own – keep the financial rewards for herself instead of letting others reap the benefits. As her appearing on camera was now impossible, the idea of letting Dietrich narrate her own documentary became an intriguing idea.

It took a long time to convince her, then find the right money, backers willing to go along with the concept of hearing Dietrich's eighty-year-old voice without seeing her eighty-year-old face. Finally, one day in 1982, she allowed herself to be lifted into that wheelchair, and, for the first time in more than three years, was wheeled into her living room and placed in a chair. Under the ruse that broken toes made it impossible for her to move, she remained seated, immobile, while recording a conversation with the director Maximilian Schell that was to serve as the dialogue for her own documentary.

By taping time, she was not as enamored of Schell as she had been in the beginning of negotiations. He had made the mistake of writing her that, to prepare for their auspicious "coming together," he was going off somewhere idyllic – to read Proust.

"What? He goes to read – what?"

"Well, it seems Mr. Schell thinks Proust is the perfect aura to prepare himself for coming to you." I tried to get him out of trouble. I needed him, and her full cooperation was not guaranteed because she had signed a contract that said so. Dietrich considered herself above such legal trifles.

"A Swiss! Typical! That sister of his is the same – a cutsie-poo mennuble. We have made a mistake with him! Proust? To talk to a movie star . . . he has to read *Proust*? What affected mishigas!"

If it hadn't been too late to change him, I'm sure she would have tried.

Fearing that I would somehow become involved in their dialogue, that Mr. Schell might be tempted to try and capitalize on having the famous mother *and* her "one and only" so close at hand, I asked my mother's agent to go to Paris and watch her for me while I stayed in Switzerland, played rear guard, and kept my fingers crossed. In order to make as much money on international sales as possible, and as both Schell and Dietrich were trilingual, the deal called for the first three days' conversation to be recorded in English, followed by the same amount of time on subsequent days in French and German. Again, to make certain that my mother cooperated, the contract stipulated that she was to be paid on a daily basis after each recording.

Despite the sincere effort of her agent, my mother was already high and aggressive on the morning of the first day, repeatedly switching back and forth from one language to another. That evening, after receiving the report of her condition, I called and tried, once more, to impress on her that as her largest market was America, the English version must be our main priority. Clear-headed as she always became around ten p.m., before turning to her Fernando Lamas and tranquilizers, she agreed, promising me to speak only in English for the next day's taping.

By eleven o'clock the next morning, all her good resolutions were swept away by the usual tide of scotch. Not only did she lapse into German constantly, she even indulged in rather coarse Berlin dialect, lied, argued, called everything "crap!" When asked about her sister, denied she ever had one. That shook Mr. Schell a bit.

Each day was a new disaster. We never did manage to get on tape what we had planned and hoped for. Maximilian Schell finally left Paris, a nervous wreck, without sufficient material, or so he thought, from which to fashion a documentary. Sometimes having nothing, being desperate, can create a climate in which pure inspiration can materialize. Although I never discussed it with Mr. Schell, I believe this is what happened. Finding himself without what he had come to Paris to get, Schell was forced to invent a whole new concept. What this very talented director finally came up with was marvelous. Better than anyone thought possible. New, inventive, far superior to the original format.

Knowing that my mother would be too frightened of having to hear what she had said, of what had been done to her life by "strangers" in an editing room, I flew to Paris, rented a VCR, and, holding her hand, showed her the tape of the rough cut of *Marlene*. My god, how she hated it! She was livid that I dared to think such "junk" was good, and besides, it had been *my* idea – the whole abortion! She ranted and raved, screamed abuse at the TV screen – kept asking me what she was saying:

"What? What? What did she say – that's not *my* voice! That's not *me*

talking! I never said that! Vulgar – vulgar! They must have faked my voice
. . . that's not me. We have to sue them!" She had become noticeably deaf,
but of course refused to admit to this sign of age. She kept complaining
that everyone whispered, that the world was full of mumblers, kept the
volume on her television set up so high that, in the summer, passersby
in the street below would look up at her open windows to see who was
shouting at them.

She spent the next six years hiring, firing, and arguing with German
lawyers. She was determined to stop the documentary from being shown,
later trying to send the producer to jail, or, better still, into "very dark
alleys." When her documentary won prizes at film festivals, she relented
a bit, suddenly got cozy-chummy with Schell, but it was a "seesaw"
relationship whenever she remembered Proust.

Time passed, more and more her bedroom took on the look of a
warehouse, everything was by dozens and gross. The Kleenex boxes
were joined by containers of glucose, crates of tea, and every liver cleanser
sold in Europe and points east. As she could hear well on the phone, those
bills ran into thousands. Besides calling me for hours at a time, when she
was feeling "mellow" she called fans. This fanatically private aristocrat
now babbled her secrets to complete strangers.

As she outlived more and more lovers and pals, she had them framed
and hung. I named it "the death wall" and watched fascinated as her
conquests were displayed like trophies. After a while, it got pretty
crowded up there. Just being dead did not automatically ensure you a
place of honor. First, you had to be famous, then dead, to get framed.

In the spring of 1983, my mother decided to acknowledge the hypertension I had suffered from for ten years. My usual flood of mail from
Paris contained a *Newsweek* article on hypertension and – three pounds of
salami. This was rapidly followed by – frankfurters, Chinese food high
in monosodium glutamate, cheese, and to top it off, a large container
of Coumadin, a highly dangerous blood thinner illegally obtained from
her druggist, a woman so infatuated that my mother could easily have
become the most successful drug dealer in France.

Dietrich played this form of lethal roulette constantly with people.
My mother, the postal pusher! When her one-time Swedish Blonde was
branded a drug user in the Swedish papers, Dietrich immediately began
making secret packages, disguised to hold the amphetamines hidden
inside. When I objected, she exclaimed:

"But she is my *friend*! And she'll get it anyway from those two fags
she lives with – so why can't I send it to her?"

"Conscience?" I ventured.

"Ridiculous! If it makes her happy – why can't she have what she wants?" and turned back to making her secret bundles. Mme Defarge of friendship. She was unstoppable. Her lethal packages to me were constant. It does give one a funny feeling when one day's post contains a morphine derivative for that "little twinge in your shoulder," cortisone for the "tiny pimple on your chin," handfuls of uppers just in case I might be "tired," downers in case I wanted to "rest" a bit, and for those in-between times? A year's supply of Valium!

When my grown sons, passing through Paris, asked if they could visit her, she always refused, making up ridiculous excuses, either that there were reporters lying in wait for them or she was just on her way to – Japan. Or, "Yes, of course they could come," then when they were announced from the lobby, forcing her concierge to blatantly lie, that "Madame was not at home."

In my family, being embarrassed by Dietrich's behavior was an inherited trait. Sometimes she wrote them scathing letters of personal criticism, then complained bitterly when they did not answer. After all, it was their "duty" to pay her court. When they wrote to her, she sent me their letters along with the fan mail – without comment. When she received pictures of their children, she sent those too, written across the back: "Who are these strange children?" When people would ask her about her grandsons, she would reply: "Maria's children? . . . I never hear from them!"

Although her liver must have been turning to stone, she thrived. Her constitution continually astounded me. One winter, she got bronchitis – called me, her cough deep, rumbling with thick catarrh. I went into my usual spiel about having a doctor look at her, that I knew she would reject, then told her which antibiotic to take from her night-table pharmacy and, passport in hand, waited for the call I was certain would come that my "eighty-something" bedridden mother had been rushed to the hospital with galloping pneumonia. Two days later, she was as right as rain, fit as a fiddle. Others lie in hospitals for just a few weeks and get bedsores – Dietrich was bedridden for more than ten years and got nothing more than itchy skin.

When she heard that David Niven was dying of motor-neuron disease, she decided that here, finally, was the suitable and sufficiently dramatic reason for *her* inability to walk and so convinced herself that she, too, had "Lou Gehrig's disease."

"You know, I have what David Niven has," she announced to everyone, and wrote him about their "mutual" affliction. David, with that infinite humanity of his, took the precious time from his own terrible tragedy to write her, tried to comfort her. Niven died, Dietrich lived on, ruling her world from her private bunker.

Slowly, she alienated the few friends who had hung on to their loyalty, their memory of her, until they too gave up to salvage what was left of their own nerves. She did not miss them. She had her fans, her battalion of infatuated lesbians and gays, and her gofers, the concierges of her building who, for exorbitant tips, fetched, did errands for her between their shifts of duty.

Despite all that liquor and the drugs, during those intervals when she was clearheaded, my mother retained the sharp mind that had enchanted and intrigued the world. Although her opinions reflected her age, her ego, her Teutonic background, her mind never lost its inquisitiveness. Hunched over, peering through her giant magnifying glass, she devoured the newspapers and journals of four countries, cutting out articles on any subject that she deemed worthy of her interest, scrawling her acidic comments along the margins, then sending them on to me – not for my opinion but my "education" and as proof of her "superior intelligence." She had something to say about everything, as always negative, critical, cruel, often ugly.

Stories on AIDS particularly fascinated her. As the majority of her fan mail came to her bed from homosexuals, she developed the theory that she might become contaminated by opening their letters. She sent me a poem she wrote on the subject, saying that I could make a lot of money from it after she was dead:

AIDS

My Mother
Died of
AIDS
She got it
From
The Mails
That's News!
She was hard
As nails
But AIDS

Was harder
Especially
By Mail!
She touched
No one
But Mails
And she got
AIDS,
My mother did!
Don't blow
A fuse –
That's News!

She wrote a lot of what she called "poems" in her last years. Setting down her thoughts always had kept her occupied. Some were satirically funny, some very sad, even frightening, but all, in whatever language, pure Dietrich vintage:

Isn't it strange:
The legs
That made
My rise to glory
Easy, NO?
Because
My downfall,
Into misery!
Queasy ? NO.

3 AM
April 9. 85

In later years, Dietrich wrote about herself at the drop of a franc, dollar, or mark. Making up stories around the real love of her life had always enticed her. She would call me, tell me the sum offered, read the questions asked for her to answer:

"Listen to this one: 'Who was the most difficult actor to work with?' Who? What shall I tell them? I make it all up anyway."

"Ray Milland?" I offer.

"Yes – good. Is he dead?"

"Yes."

"Then I can use him – easy! They also want to know who was the nicest one. . . ."

"Michael Wilding?"

"No – nobody knows who *he* is!"

"How about . . . Herbert Marshall?"

"Yes! They know who *he* is and he's dead too. Good. They ask about my stepfather, so I say, 'He was a shadowed figure and was killed in the war.' . . . I write fast – a whole block of paper in one morning. It's all made up, anyway – like when I talk to fans on the telephone – so it's real easy!"

Between writing stories to suit herself and reading the adoring fan mail, her day was filled with the legend of Dietrich. Her diaries, of course, had to remain sad, forlorn, long-suffering, and resigned to desertion – that too was part of the legend.

Her flirtations never stopped. At the age of eighty-five, my mother was given an award by the American Fashion Institute. Although my son David had been asked to accept it in her name, she refused, preferring to find someone who was famous, preferably renowned for their legs. Although she had never met him, she tracked down his private telephone number in New York City and called Mikhail Baryshnikov, asked him to accept the award for her, then proceeded to fall madly in love with him. For weeks after, she would phone me asking for love phrases in Russian so that she could sign off after their many marathon transatlantic phone calls with suitable passionate farewells in his mother tongue.

"Sweetheart, you should hear him! He is so wonderful! So soft, so lyrical, so romantic. But, you know, when I first phoned him I thought I had dialed a wrong number! A strange voice answered with a terrible American twang! But it was him. How is that possible? He is a Russian – how can he allow himself to sound so American? I told him he must get rid of that way of speaking right away. It doesn't suit him. It sounds so low-class! I told him, 'I used to be in love with Nureyev, but now I am in love with you! You are a much better dancer than he is and – you are a real *man*!' He wants to come here to see me. Of course, impossible . . . but it would be nice – after all the years of nothing, I should be nice and tight again 'down there,' don't you think? He would like that. Or just to sleep with him would be . . ." Her voice trailed off as her Fernando Lamas took effect. That was my usual cue to yell down the phone:

"Mass? Mass? Hang up the phone! Hang up – before you forget!"

When, in the summer of '87, her "two hours a day" maid went home to visit her parents in Portugal, my mother became frantic, asking the doormen and their wives to come in especially to empty her pails in the evening. When no one seemed overjoyed by this idea, she called me.

"Wouldn't you think that anyone can pick up a can of pee and throw it down the toilet? What is the big bit? You know, everybody should be *happy* that I *can* pee! Instead of saying 'how wonderful! Madame can pee!' they all behave as though I am asking them to do something unusual. I could be like Chevalier who died . . . remember? Because he *couldn't* pee. So they should all be *happy*! That I *can*, no?"

I had been trying for years to get her to agree to a regular nurse to look after her, but without success. Now I ventured, once again, to suggest that a trained professional could be the answer to all of her many physical discomforts. That made her furious:

"Give a stupid 'stranger' a key? Who has to be trained? That I have to teach where everything is? And, you know very well how I hate women. No! I have an idea. You know the man who is downstairs, who guards the garage at night? The one I gave a key to already, in case no one else can be reached during the night? He is the one who could come. He could come up every night and pour my pee out for me. He looks older than he is, but he is quite young and very sweet. I don't know why I asked him to come up here the other night but he came and we talked. He sat on the bed and showed me pictures from his wallet. He is a very nice man. He hugged me before he left and I hugged him. I'm sure he would come and empty my pee, if I asked him."

I too was sure that this beguiling garage attendant would appear nightly for his hundred-franc tip and a chance to get to know even better the famous recluse and wondered how much blackmail money I would wind up having to pay him in the not too distant future.

Being bedridden and persistently refusing to allow anyone to live with her, those that served her all had to have keys to be able to get into her apartment. I knew the ones who could be trusted and those who would stop at nothing to make their knowing her secrets a lucrative investment. One of my constant recurring nightmares was that when my mother died, I and the few I trusted would not be able to get to her apartment in time to prevent the vultures from gorging themselves on their publicity feast.

Baryshnikov bit the dust and another took his place – in spades! "He is a Doctor"; always intoned in that turn-of-the-century awe given to those who reached such pinnacles of respect and stature. He started out as just another infatuated fan. Seeing the mighty Dr. on his return address, she picked up the phone, dialed California, and full of booze and self-pity, flirted across the miles, until he caught fire, began writing her love letters, explicit, erotic, and very titillating. As with everything she received, she sent them on to me, proud, gloating a little to show off her ageless seductiveness. I read these tasteless outpourings to know just how far she was allowing this to go, how much she was telling him, and shuddered at the proof of what was developing. They kept on coming, sizzling hot and heavy. I began to wonder if maybe this poor man was one of those sexually aroused by corpses – then discarded this fleeting thought of necrophilia, knowing that like everyone else, he saw her in those frilly panties and garter belt, the eternal Dietrich identity. The references made in his letter to intimate moments involving her and Gabin, Remarque, and others especially worried me – for those were things he could never have known without first being told them.

"Sweetheart, my 'Doctor' – what do you think he wants from me? Something of mine – something, you know that I have worn on my body." She giggles. Eighty-seven-year-old recluses are supposed to cackle, not trill deliciously, but Dietrich does. "You know what I did? I called Dior and told them I was sending over my concierge to pick up panties – you know, those little itsy-bitsy ones, like chorus girls wear. He came back with a whole selection, but most of them were too big, but one pair was teensy-weensy and cute, so I sort of rubbed it – you know where – then also put perfume on it and sent it to him, express. Of course, you *know* what he is going to do with it when he gets it!" and hung up.

After a year of this running vulgarity, their routine changed. Now it was he who called her, every day on the dot of eight p.m., Paris time, even sending her checks which she endorsed without a moment's hesitation, sent on to her bank for deposit. I had visions of our "doctor" setting up his trusty tape recorder, dialing Marlene Dietrich's private number in Paris, letting her talk, ramble on, telling the most intimate times of her long life, then when she hung up, rewinding the cassette, placing the record of his latest conversation with the world's famous recluse amongst the others in his locked desk. In the not too distant future, should these juicy recordings in Dietrich's own voice come on the open market, those canceled checks of his, bearing Dietrich's endorsements, could easily be used to claim that he had paid her for recording their conversations and I? – Would spend the rest of *my* days looking for a lawyer who'd be willing to take the case.

I once ventured to suggest that those too, too intimate conversations could become very dangerous.

"What? He is a Doctor!" and hung up, highly offended. An unknown fan had become sacrosanct, untouchable. That he also supplied his lady-love with potent hypnotics had a lot to do with her devotion. He broke the law, the oath of his profession, sending an eighty-eight-year-old alcoholic legally restricted drugs without ever having met her, let alone having examined her, but that, of course, was not considered a yardstick by which to measure his impeccable conduct. His blissfully drugged recipient "trusted" her "pusher."

As time passed, and he reinforced his hold by the regularity of his nightly devotion, he was admitted further and further into her private realm. He was asked to call her accountants with instructions, discussed financial matters with her bank, contacted and gained entrance to famous acquaintances in her name, shopped for her, ferreted information, was given my sons' private phone numbers to contact if he wished, sent me dangerous mind-altering drugs on her instructions, was given my number without my permission – with orders to call me whenever he deemed it necessary.

This reprehensible behavior of hers was not due to extreme old age, senility, nor certifiable alcoholism – this was Dietrich as she always was. She never changed. She was a law unto herself, knew it, lived it, and the world condoned it. Had I been foolish enough to try to protect her, stop her madness by legitimate legal means, any judge would have simply remembered her in those famous panties – and – certified me instead!

FOR THE FOURTH TIME that day, she called: "Sweetheart – you will never guess who called me." Her voice was ever so "springtime young," it reminded me of those "young things picking wild strawberries"!

"Reagan?" (ever since receiving personal birthday greetings from the White House, he was definitely "in"), I asked obediently. I knew this game – "questions and answers" was one of her favorite pastimes.

"No – but I called Nancy. That picture of her in *Match*, she looks much too thin. I told her she looks *sick*. . . . She was sweet. I now have her private number. You haven't guessed."

"Burt?" Once a year he was overcome by nostalgia and phoned her, usually forgetting the difference in time and catching her just as her Fernando Lamases and Tuinal were taking effect, which made her ever so soft, dreamy, and gentle, which, in turn, charmed Burt anew.

"No, but I saw a picture of that terrible wife of his – she's Jewish!"

"Actually, Carole Bayer Sager is a magnificent lyricist – "

"Can't be. Well, who called?"

"Hepburn?" I knew she wouldn't have called, but my mother would appreciate my thinking she would.

"No, but I wish she would! Then I could tell her – how I love her! What a woman! All those years with Tracy and never a breath of scandal – but that was MGM. There they really protected their people. I hear she shakes all the time now – but still lets herself be seen, even does television! She must be rich – so why show herself like that? – So, who called me?"

"Sinatra?" I was running out of names and just took a stab.

"What? That old drunk? Hasn't got my number – anyway, if he called, I would do the 'maid.'" One of Dietrich's most persistent fantasies was that she could "do" accents, and constantly pretended to be Spanish or French maids who couldn't speak a word of English when answering her phone. She sounded exactly like Marlene Dietrich, trying to disguise her voice, but went right on believing she was another Meryl Streep – whose nose, whenever she saw a picture of her, irritated Dietrich enormously.

"I give up . . ."

"Kirk Douglas!"

"Kirk Douglas?"

"Yes! Out of the blue! How did he get my number? He was sweet. Told me he was writing a book – and I told him how I can't read anymore and we talked. . . . Nice man!"

When that book came out and Mr. Douglas recounted their telephone conversation, I walked into my mother's bunker and found her tearing his picture from his book jacket with a look that could curdle yogurt!

"Oh, there you are! That son-of-a-bitch talked about me in his filthy book, even my Fernando Lamases he mentions on the same page as Reagan! You can't talk about suppositories on the same page as a president! I cabled him. I told that bastard what I think of him!"

OVER THE YEARS, my husband knew he lived with a potential bomb in his head, suffered through brain surgery, subsequent stroke, emerged still a whole man through his magnificent courage and incredible will. At the age when boys think of who to ask to the high school prom, my youngest son faced the probability of cancer, endured the agony of major lung surgery, emerged to embrace his young life anew. My mother-in-law entered the long, tortuous road of senility and dementia within our home, et cetera, et cetera – as Yul would have said – and what was I most often asked? "How is your wonderful mother?" The one as healthy as a horse, except for what she alone had chosen to do to herself!

This powerful preoccupation the world has for the famous is a difficult yoke to live under. Those of us who carry it, due to birth, pay a price. Much less of a one, if the fame is earned through heroic or great intellectual achievement, but for those of us less privileged, who know that what is so revered is undeserving of canonization – until we learn that where fame and the power it engenders are concerned, fairness has no place – we scream into the void of non-acceptance and are driven mute by its very repetitive uselessness. Even death does not alter our condition.

Others bury their parents, mourn, for whatever reasons, confront their feelings anew in scattered moments; finding a forgotten letter, an old photograph, entering a newly empty room trigger emotions that with time are allowed to fade, eventually stay buried for good.

Our ghosts can never be laid to rest. They wander through countless laudatory tomes, photographic images, television screens, giant movie screens, their forms magnified a hundredfold – they breathe eternally! Alive forever. This continuous resurrection, this immortality constantly reconfirmed, is a haunting that invades our daily lives as when they lived. There is no escaping them, dead or alive. Dietrich is especially skilled at materializing. Looking for a picture frame anywhere in the world? Whose image will be looking at you from most of the models on display? Fancy card shops are one of her favorite places – there she sits in long racks, in multiple choice, or rolled up, poster size. Another poltergeist specialty is her voice, moaning through "la Vie en rose." It captures you in elevators, pursues you through supermarkets, airports, department stores, ricochets off tiles in fancy ladies' rooms, follows you through hotel lobbies in countries you wouldn't believe. Then there is the "Dietrich" type hat, the "Dietrich" type suit, the "Dietrich" type shoes – the "Dietrich" look. Never is there one day completely free of Marlene Dietrich. What is it like, to have a mother no one knows? Must be nice.

When I am with her, around ten in the evening, she hits a high and wants to "gab." I know I am not allowed to sit on her bed, position a chair near its edge and sit. She flips through the latest French *Vogue*:

"Look at this! They don't know *what* to do anymore! Ugly, ugly, ugly! Remember Travis? Nice man, always listened – had good ideas but, most of all, he listened. We used to work all night, just to get *one* look . . . the Review costume? And that wonderful hat! The hours we worked! But on the first sketches, didn't he have it different?"

"It was blue velvet, with ermine."

"Yes, yes . . . blue . . . not good, like for Jeanette MacDonald, so I made it dark green and — was right! Remember *Shanghai Express*, the cock-feather dress? How we worked and how Travis finally found the right feathers? How beautiful they were! What work! . . . And I made the shoes, like Chanel did years later. What a fake *that* woman was! Did one cut, repeated it a thousand times, and was called 'a great designer'! She was a decorator — not a designer. Like Schiaparelli . . . much *better* than her, but still a decorator. The gloves — did we put white on the inside for *them* or for the ones in *Desire*?"

"The black handbag for the cock-feather dress had a white Art Deco design, so you matched the idea in the gloves."

"Yes! We did a lot of that — as though it was really *that* important. No one really noticed, but we thought it *had* to be all — perfect. Now, they just throw things on actors and nobody cares. . . . All that work, the hours, the fittings . . ."

She sips her cold tea, swooshing it around her mouth before swallowing. Her tongue probes inside her cheek:

"Here, I lost another tooth — must be a cap? Can't be a real one . . . I used to chew hard lemon candy. Wish I had some of the real sour ones Papi always bought for me in Salzburg. Oh! Remember Salzburg? And how we used to buy out Lanz? . . . All those wonderful dirndls . . . wonder where *they* all are. . . . How we laughed!"

She is unaware she has switched to German. "Tami and I, we used to laugh and Papi scolded us because we always had to then pee! . . . Nice times . . . Remember the cow — Papi got because I told him I *had* to have a farmhouse with a real cow and red geraniums on the windows? He did it all! . . . Another life . . . I *had* to have an Austrian farmhouse with geraniums and a cow . . . then I never saw it — I was so in love with Jaray! The things he put up with! — Did you see that terrible picture of Garbo in the paper? Those bastards . . . they caught her. Did you see her hair? Ugly, ugly, and *long*, so old! Terrible! She used to count every piece of sugar to make sure the maid didn't steal. They never could do a long shot of her because of her big feet."

"I hear she has kidney disease . . . is going to Columbia Presbyterian for dialysis."

"*That* suits her! *That* goes with her character, smelly pee. She'll die of it, like Chevalier. Don't forget, you swore you will never let them take me — to put me in a hospital."

"Yes, Mass . . . I know."

"Remember! You swore on the *heads of your children*!"

She flicks the pages, continues in English, "Everywhere — braids! Big news! I wore braids in *Dishonored* and again in that stupid film, the one with that naked statue. . . ."

"Mass, you know that Brian died?"

"Who?"

"Brian Aherne," I yell. I keep forgetting she can't hear a normal tone.

"Oh? Didn't I make a film with him? Yes – he was in love with me! And came to Paris! A big 'romantic – coming to see me' and sat frozen through the whole dinner because Papi came with us. . . . He was *so* upset at the husband 'knowing' about us, he rushed right back to London. Typically British! . . . He used to write me long boring letters – and you liked him."

She takes another slug of tea, picks up the American *Vogue*. . . . "That Bergman daughter from Rossellini is everywhere! She must be *rich*! With those thick lips of hers, she looks like a Ubangi! . . . Look at this eye makeup. Clowns! Remember when I wanted dark eyes and put drops in my eyes and got blind as a bat! And Jo just gave them to me with his lights and was angry with me because I hadn't told him that I wanted 'Spanish' eyes? The things we did! And now they write books . . . and think they invented it all. Sweetheart, what was the name of Jack Gilbert's daughter – the one that wrote that terrible book about him and said I slept with her father?"

"Tinker."

"Yes . . . how you remember all those things! And who was the actor who talked to me first on the boat – in *Morocco*?"

"Adolphe Menjou."

"Terrible man . . . didn't he turn out to be a Nazi? Talking of Nazis, Jannings was one. He tried to choke me in *The Blue Angel*. He was furious, because Jo paid so much attention to me."

"I remember when we all looked for your costume through all the trunks and old hat boxes . . ."

"What? You weren't even born!"

"Yes, I was! In the Berlin apartment, with Tami, we all looked for cuffs. And . . ."

"Yes – yes! The cuffs! You *remember* that? I tell the 'Doctor' all the time – 'My daughter, she will know, I will ask her, she remembers *everything*!' *This* you won't remember. One day, the front office ordered a test for *Devil Is a Woman* and Travis got all hysterical because we had nothing designed yet . . ."

"And you made up a terrible costume, even used one of the piano shawls from the Colleen Moore house we rented."

"No, no, no – that *too* you remember? *That* memory you inherited from your father. He remembered everything too. You have Papi's diaries locked up?"

"Yes, Mass."

"I started a file marked 'precious' with rare photographs that I got from fans – important for when you write that book."

That is my cue to hand her the bulging file. I know she wants to show me. The pictures are well known, can be bought from any movie-fan outlet, but she thinks of them as "precious" because they are beautiful.

"Look, here is the beautiful one in the mink hat from *Scarlet Empress* and the banquet dress. Remember that terrible banquet? Me, in all those awful pearls, dying of the heat – and Jo's concentration camp sculptures. Long before we knew they would exist for real. . . . What was the name of the film where I wore that beautiful dress with the little fur cuffs?"

"Blonde Venus."

"Yes . . . and that wonderful hat we made for the whore scene . . . with the red cherries – same film?"

"Yes, Mass."

The heavy file slips from her hand, she is ready to let go, allow the sleeping pills to do their act of safe oblivion. I turn off the lights and go to my couch in the living room under the wall where Chevalier smirks, de Gaulle preens, Gabin broods, Cocteau poses, Coward mocks, Hemingway looks through you, Fleming sits atop his petri dish. It is three o'clock in the morning.

I have made the beef tea, Irish stew, boiled beef, and gallons of special chicken soup – all ordered and eagerly awaited when sober, that I know she will not eat, that will be given to the maid and doormen the moment I leave.

She wakes. It takes time to emerge from one tunnel, start on the scotch – and enter another. It is her daily journey, when the angry monster takes, once more, center stage and rules our day. As death sits nearer, her fear of being erased by it, overwhelms her. The fury it births invades everything. She hates life for being so fragile, unpredictable, capable of deserting her. How dare it not come into line – obey her command for immortality. Being immortal in the memory of others does not impress her in the least. Control is not ephemeral; control, and its henchman, power, is making people jump to execute one's orders. By renouncing all true friends and family, she faces her private hell alone, unaided by those who want so much to, and could, help ease her journey. The final rejection of life will not be my mother's death but her own casting out of all true love, and human need; she defies the God she has chosen to reject – to come and do His worst, over her dead body, if He dare!

MY TRAIN WAS LATE, taxis difficult to find on a rainy night. I let myself into her apartment, check if maybe she is still awake. She feels me, sits up, and rejects being taken over by the multiple doses of Tuinal and Serax. My mother can actually do that – command hypnotic drugs to halt their function inside her body. She puts her big pillow behind her back, wants to "talk." I bring my chair.

"Have you *seen* all those weeping pictures in the papers? It is really being overdone! And why wasn't she there to watch her husband race? All this Monaco to-do! It never ends! Now, instead of that terrible Stephanie, we are going to get nothing but the Royal Widow bit . . . with all those children . . . and – why was she in Paris? Buying dresses?"

"Mass, Princess Caroline didn't *know* her husband was going to be killed . . ."

"No, no, no – she's playing 'widow' *too* much. She *must* have a guilty conscience!" She pretends to look for something on the shelf by her shoulder, takes a fast slug of scotch from the shot glass hidden there. "Did you see what that terrible Bob Hope said in the paper? He isn't going to the desert in Arabia to entertain the soldiers – because *he* already has a desert in Palm Springs? Unbelievable! Terrible man! All those medals and big awards. For what? Schlepping chorines on generals' planes? Making sure he got photographed everywhere . . . ever so *brave*? Wasn't he once 'low-class English' . . . like Chaplin?"

I'm trying to keep a straight face – she's in form tonight!

"Yes, Mass."

"But *now* he's a 'big' American?"

"Yes."

Another fast slug. "Orson is dead, isn't he?"

"Yes, Mass . . ."

"With all that fat . . . no wonder. What was that film he made about Hearst, that made him famous?"

"*Citizen Kane.*"

"Yes, that was the one. . . . That terrible Hearst tried to stop the film. He threatened all the theater owners so they wouldn't show it. . . . And I was so in love with Jean at the time, I paid no attention. Isn't that terrible . . . that big Hearst scandal and I was so busy making pot-au-feu, I paid no attention to greatness! I would have gone to bed with him, but he only liked black hair. Oh, I got another one of those 'professor' books. Some American fan sent it. Again, full of 'deep' meanings. What Jo *really* meant with a 'shot,' what I *really* meant with a 'look'! The usual crap. Where do they *get* all these ideas? They all think they have discovered something new. All this 'to-do' about *deep* meanings and Freud. We made a film – then we did another. Now they all think it is *art*. Such stupidity! You get paid to make a film – if it makes money, you get to make another film. If it doesn't, you are suddenly not so la-di-da important. It's a business, not art."

She takes another fast sip. "You do your job – that's what you are here for . . . to do your job! If you can't do it right, you have no right to be paid the big salaries they pay. Does Lendl or that German horse – you know – the one who plays tennis and keeps mooning about her father? Do *they* get paid millions because they play tennis – *badly*? Of course not! But no one writes books about what they *really* meant to say with a forehand, or what *sexual meaning* was in a serve! So why do they always see big meanings in films? Why always with me? The reason I wore tails in *Morocco* was because Jo wanted to hide the legs, and I looked wonderful in them, and the Americans would be shocked! . . . That's why the next one, *Dishonored*, was never talked about – I did nothing shocking, except when I pierce the end of the chiffon scarf onto the tip of the sword. *That* is exciting and that's the only scene they remember and talk about! Meanings . . . meanings. Idiots! Just *work!* You must say *that* when you write your book. Teach them what was important! Today, I got a postcard from a fan, the one from *Scarlet Empress*, I put it in your file, the one in the white dress, with the ostrich feathers and that *beautiful* white wig. How they are all allowed to sell postcards of me and make money, I will never understand. . . . When I was in boarding school in Weimar, I went to a costume ball and wore a white wig. . . . Albert Lasky . . . he was the first who took – what *is* it, that they take?"

"Your virginity?" I venture.

She doesn't hear me, goes right on:

". . . took my 'innocence' away. . . . He was the conductor of the Weimar opera. I went to his house, took off all my clothes, sat on his sofa while he played the piano – but do you think I would take off that wig? . . . Even when we went to bed, I kept it on!"

"Made it more exciting?" I suggest.

"No! Nothing exciting! I just *loved* that wig!"

"But what about that violin teacher?"

"Oh! He was Weimar too. He wasn't so nice. . . . He took . . . whatever it's called, right there in the music room on the couch."

Her voice, a little sleepy, has slipped into German. "My mother put me in that school. She thought I couldn't get out – we had very strict hours," her face becomes still, thoughtful, her voice lowers, "she was a hard woman." She smooths the top edge of the sheet, as though embarrassed by this implied criticism.

"All day, I have had this song in my head – but I don't remember all the words." She hums a plaintive tune, sings the German words she

does remember, a sad little tale of wintertime and swallows . . . calling
farewell.

"Once, my mother moved us to where my father was. She would
walk us by the hospital, so my father could look down from his barred
window and see us. I always thought he had syphilis and it went into
his head."

She inspects her thumb. "Split nail – comes from opening all the
fan mail."

I hand her the nail file she likes, the one from *Foreign Affair*. "I never
felt anything – with any of them. I married Papi because he was beautiful
. . . but I never felt – anything. Then . . . I got pregnant . . ." Her sigh
is filled with regret.

" 'Fremdgehen,' that means – sleeping with your husband but also
sleeping with others." She twists the gold band on her finger. She has
begun wearing a wedding ring. I suspect her reason for wearing it. She
looks down and remarks: "I thought it looks better – when they find
me . . ."

Although she tells me it is her mother's, I know it is not. It is new.
Ever an eye on history, Dietrich will be found, the pure lady wife
true to her marriage vows, her diary by her side that says: "Have
not heard from Maria," "No food," "All alone." She has planned it
all. Planned it to the minutest detail, a superbly crafted script that the
world will believe. She is the true creator and curator of the Dietrich
legend.

Once again, I've come, have tried to get close enough to her to change
the dirty sheets, clean her – she screams invectives, her fury out of
proportion, raw. I stand there, helpless, and suddenly, I know! I know
her game that we have been playing. She wants it! She wants to be found
filthy, stench rising – it is her final self-crucifixion: the mother who was
left to die alone, neglected by the child she loved too well. A pitiable
creature thus discovered would never be branded a whore, especially if
she wears – a wedding ring. And such pity floods my soul – for this
once glorious creature, who lies in her hoarded filth doing penance, *still*
courting beatification.

Her eyes are closing, she is finally willing to let go, allow the pills to
take over and finish her day. She slides down, curls against the very edge
of the dilapidated mattress, murmurs:

"You're here . . . so I can sleep."

Her legs withered. Her hair, chopped short haphazardly in drunken frenzies with cuticle scissors, painted with dyes – iodized pink between dirty white blotches. Her earlobes have begun to hang low. The teeth, of which she is so proud because they are still "all hers," have blackened and cracked. Her left eye, dulled by a cataract she refuses to have treated. Her once translucent skin is parchment. She exudes an odor of booze and human decay.

Death sits like a Jabba on dirty sheets, and with it all, despite and through the decay, something remains . . . a faint glimmer, perhaps only a memory of what once was . . . *Beauty* . . . so enveloping . . . so enthralling . . . so perfect, that for more than fifty years, all women were judged by its standard, all men desired it.

Her snores are ragged, spittle trails from her furrowed lips. Like a fetus she lies, bony hands cradling a sunken cheek, her matchstick legs tucked high against her frail body, she lies – as though afraid to be born and face yet another day's survival.

I stand looking at this pathetic creature, who calls herself my mother, and feel sorry for both of us.

I make sure the fire extinguisher is by her side, the hot plate turned off, the water steaming in her thermoses, the pails, bowls, and pitchers ready for the morning. Crawl under the tables, haul out her bottles, take them to the kitchen, pour half their contents down the sink – funny how the smell of scotch turns my stomach – refill the bottles to their original marks with water, shake them, replace them into her hiding place. Even when I am not there with her, she hides her drinking from herself, the final delusion of a doomed alcoholic. I look once more to make sure she is still breathing, I leave – the door ajar as ordered.

The living room where no one lives – grimy drapes swagged in time, carpets threadbare, stained, cartons, packing boxes, files and more files, old suitcases, the big gray elephants of my childhood, all kept, all hoarded throughout the years, lists, lists and more lists hang from brittle Scotch tape amongst the Orders, Citations, Commendations, Awards, Decorations, ornate medals on wide faded ribbons, amongst the framed poster-size images of their once glorious owner – give the scene a sense of sepulchre in waiting.

I stand, looking at the organized deadness of her belongings, wish – oh, for so many things that should, could be different. Next time, I must – I will – try one more time to clean her, wean her off the bottle. Once more – Just once more – I must try . . . it is not right for her to die this way . . . I close the door. I am tired.

The Paris air is fresh and clean – it smells of soft rain and fallen leaves.

Across the street, the lights from the Plaza Athénée glisten upside down in the wet pavement. I stand – breathe deep – and, suddenly, I run. Like a child in anticipation, I run. I don't know why I suddenly need to hurry so – but I do. Life and love are waiting and I must get to them. Home! I'm going home.

November 1990.

SCHÖNEBERG 1901   PARIS 1992

MORTUARY SHADOWS – silent cold. I stand by the open coffin looking down. Carefully I place the small chamois bag containing her travel charms by her side. She has a long journey before her and might want them. How small she is, this power that controlled my life – Just a child in a white satin shroud – untried vulnerability – and the sorrow comes and I run out into the sunlight.

Dietrich had her funerals. No marching Legionnaires, no color-coded boutonnieres for long discarded lovers – the "husband who knew all" was long dead – as were the many loves. Still, her coffin draped in the flag of France rested before the heroic altar of her favorite, La Madeleine, her opulent wartime decorations displayed by her side and "shopgirls wept for Madame," as did the thousands who came to pay her homage.

Still one wish to fulfill:
    "Schöneberg – that's where my mother's grave is – Now, with the wall gone and Berlin normal again, one could go . . ." She leaves the thought suspended, a question half unanswerable.
    "Mass," I said without really thinking, "you could, you know, go back. We could do the black wig disguise bit, go by train . . . no one would catch us!"
    "NO! A wheelchair on a train? All that way? . . . And then in and out of taxis to go to the cemetery? No! Those sons of bitches would find out and catch us . . . No, too late, FINITO!" Again that tone of longing.
    Now she is safe. Shielded in her lead-lined box, no flashbulb can invade her face and now – now finally she can go home.

Before the journey, the tricolor is removed, her coffin redraped with the Stars and Stripes. This one act is for me – a selfish need to show the world, make the statement that Marlene Dietrich was an American citizen, regardless of her romantic attachments.

The coffin has been roped for passage, the Stars and Stripes lashed to its sides. Amidst the luggage of the living, it waits, a unique outline against the setting sun and, for me, it becomes the symbol of all the flag-draped coffins that have sat on lonely tarmacs waiting to be shipped back home – and I weep as they lift hers into the body of the plane.

Schöneberg, sun-dappled peace – in a country not known for it. An idyllic garden, as though conceived for just such a romantic girl's return. My mother sleeps beneath lilies of the valley – I walk the few steps separating her from her mother. I stand by my grandmother's grave and tears choke me. I have so much to tell her, and childhood words are not enough – to say it all – let her know I have brought her child, that was given me so long ago, back to her to love again – perhaps even forgive for the hurting of those who needed her so.

I only whisper: "Be good to her. She needs you to be good to her," and I cry – for all the lost love so unretrievable – and leave them to make their way together.

INDEX

Academy Awards 142, 698, 723
Aherne, Brian *149, 151*, 164–5, 181–4,
  186, 201, 209–10, 233–5, 246, 254–6,
  301, 337, 344, *367*, 372, 446–7, 458,
  496, 597, 786
Algiers 545
Allan, Elizabeth 353–4, 356, *370*, 613
'Allein in Einer Grossen Stadt' 207
American Fashion Institute 779
Anastasia 674, 677
Angel 436, 438, *439–40*, 454
Antibes 467, 469, 485, 723
Arden, Elizabeth 628
Arlen, Harold 632, 643, 650–1, 654, 656,
  659–61, *663*
Arliss, George 363
Armed Forces Radio 572
Armstrong, Louis *625*
Arnoldi, Miss 36, 39
Around the World in 80 Days 615, 656,
  662, *664*
Arthur, Jean 599
'Assez' 214
Astaire, Fred 427
Astor, Mary *369*
Atwill, Lionel 336
Augusta Victoria School for Girls 10–11
Aumont, Jean-Pierre 571, *716*
Aussig 250, 445
Australian tours 708, 714, 755–8

Bacharach, Burt 681, 693–4, 706, *716,
  721*, 723, 726, 771, 782

Bailey, Pearl 654
Bankhead, Tallulah 123, 133, 558–9,
  601, 638
Banton, Travis 86, 115–20, 162, 253,
  266–7, 314, 317–19, 386–8, 434, 438,
  439, 593, 784–5
Barrymore, Ethel 352
Barrymore, John 142, 352, 436
Barrymore, Lionel 352
Barthelmess, Richard 338–9, 349, 361,
  367, 370, 517
Baryshnikov, Mikhail 779
Beatles 704–5
Becky 55, 102–4, 106–7, 109, 163
Becky Sharp 387
Beery, Wallace 352
Bel Air 262
Belsen 534, 545, 576, 578, 710
Bennett, Constance 181
Bennett, Joan 359
Benny, Jack 534
Bergman, Ingrid 534, 674–5
Bergner, Elisabeth 269, 272, 447
Berlin 7, 14, 16, 21, 24, 39, 43, *46*, 52,
  187, 236, 563, *568–9*, 568, 573, 576
Berlin, Irving 352, 567
Berliner, Stephi 15
Berliner Theater 60
Beth 458
Beverly Hills 110, 112, 130, 362, 589
  Beverly Hills Hotel 495, 661–2, 676
  Beverly Wilshire Hotel 185, 454
  Bullock's Wilshire 130

Billington, Dave 736
Black Fox 698
Blonde Venus 132–3, 137, 141, 145, 153, 330, 787
Blue Angel, The 63, 67–9, 72–3, 74–9, 89, 93, 96, 103, 225, 476, 478, 786
Bogart, Humphrey 530
Boleslawski, Richard 395–401
'Boomerang Baby' 642
Borzage, Frank 373–4, 379, 384
Botchen, Paul 35
Bow, Clara 363
Boyer, Charles 328, 352, 388, 395, 397, 399, 767
Brackett, Charles 677
Bradley, Gen. Omar 555–6, 569
Brazil 694
Bremen, SS 79, 94, 97, 103–5, 152, 492
Brentwood 509
Brice, Fanny 314
Bridges 173
Brillantmont 419–23, 429, 452, 459–60, 480
Brook, Clive 115, 127, 129
Brook, Peter 651
Bruce, Virginia 376
Brynner, Rocky 619–20
Brynner, Yul 617–32, 623, 634–5, 637–40, 646, 650, 652–3, 656, 658–61, 667, 674–80, 686, 690, 691, 750
Bülow, Ulle von 23, 25
Burton, Richard 711, 748
Butavaba, Mr 726–8

Cabot, Bruce 508
Café Istanbul 629
Cagney, James 530
Camille 170
Camp Patrick Henry 561
Cantinflas 662
Capote, Truman 650, 654
Caroline, Princess 788
Caserta 561
Catalina 502
'Cavalier' 598–602, 604–6, 613, 617, 621, 629, 632, 651, 656, 658
CBS Television 614, 630
Chamberlain, Neville 477–9, 489
Chanel, Coco 211, 429, 785
Chaplin, Charlie 96, 363

Chatterton, Ruth 353, 357
Chevalier, Maurice 112–13, 122–3, 133–7, 141, 148–9, 181, 184–5, 193–4, 198, 374, 582, 600, 651, 662, 686, 716, 730–1, 780
Chicago 193
Clair, René 508, 512, 514
Cocteau, Jean 223, 231, 451–2, 651–2, 704, 716, 771
Cohen, Alexander 712, 725–6, 729–30
Cohen, Emanuel 227
Cohn, Harry 632, 639–40, 667
Colbert, Claudette 123–4, 293, 352
Cole, Nat King 642
Colette 425–6, 430, 433
Colman, Ronald 344, 352, 355–6, 363, 367, 535, 540–1
Columbia Presbyterian Hospital 747–8, 759
Columbia Studios 438, 515, 639–40, 667
Cook, Donald 558
Cooper, Gary 81, 91, 95, 284, 362, 376, 378, 381, 696, 771
Cornell, Katharine 337
Costello, Frank 640
Coward, Noël 223, 446–7, 472, 487, 501, 506–7, 513, 600, 627, 643–4, 649, 651, 653–4, 663, 678–80, 698, 701, 706, 720, 731, 749, 771
Coxinelle 671
Crawford, Broderick 501, 511
Crawford, Joan 129, 254, 288, 328, 352–3, 435, 438
Crosby, Bing 91, 114, 124, 269, 293, 303, 629

Daily Telegraph 756
Dalio 514
Dallas 757
Darnell, Linda 691, 708
Davies, Marion 270, 315–16
Davis, Bette 319, 438, 530
Davis, Joe 725
de Acosta, Mercedes 147, 154–60, 164, 168–9, 179, 181, 191, 238, 256–7, 286, 328, 411, 515
Death of a Salesman 608
De Bakey, Michael 737–43, 744, 747
De Gaulle, Charles 224, 508, 613, 724, 771
Del Rio, Dolores 270, 319, 331, 364, 369

de Mille, Cecil B. 365, 652, 677
Denham Studios 410
De Sica, Vittorio 662, *665*, 669–70, 672–3
Desire 365–6, 372–4, 379, *383*, 384, 404–5, 641
Dessau 21–3
Destry Rides Again 493, 496–9, *510*
Deutsches Theater 40, 45
Devil Is a Woman, The 221, 314, 317–19, 321, *322–3*, 330–6, 342, 344, 346–7, 361, 536, 786
de Watteville, Prof. 706, 734, 744
Dietrich, Elisabeth (Liesel) 6–7, 11, *12–13*, 17, 20, 24, *37*, 39, 55, 86, 138, 225–6, 235–7, 285–6, 448–9, 534, 545, 576, 578, 698, 709–10
Dietrich, Josephine 4–8, 10, *12–13*, 18–21, 24, 28–9, 34–5, *37*, 44–5, 53, 55, 68, 103, 225, 235–7, 442, 448, 534, 559, 563, 568, *571*, 575, 796
Dietrich, Louis Otto 3–7, 10, *12*, 16–17, 19–21
Dietrich, Otto 449
Dietrich, Gen. Sepp 553
di Frasso, Dorothy 344, 352, 362–4, *367*, 403, 430, 457, 640
DiMaggio, Jo 599, 604, 620
Dionne quintuplets 313–14
Dior 604–5, 613, 651, 771, 781
Dishonored 29, 93, *96*, 102, 118, 163, 786, 789
Don 621
Donat, Robert 408, 413, *415*
Dorsey, Tommy 530
Dos Passos, John 317
Douglas, Kirk 629, 632, 676, 783
Douglas, Melvyn 435
Douglas, Sharman 613
Dryden 388
Dunn, James 597
Dunne, Irene 435, 441
Durant, Will 473
Duvivier 514

Eden, Anthony 489
Edinburgh 708
Edington, Harry 160–2, 187, 361, 374, 384, 386, 436, 454
Edward VIII *see* Windsor, Duke of
Eisenhower, Dwight 555–6, 568, 635

Europa, SS 194–200
Evans, Edith 337

Fairbanks, Douglas 352
Fairbanks Jnr, Douglas 352, 771
'Falling in Love Again' 74, 90
Fasanelli, Ricardo 694
Faye, Alice 530
Feldman, Charles 489, 501, 515, 560, 603, 677
Felsing, Josephine *see* Dietrich, J.
Ferrer, Mel 626, 632
Firestone, Elizabeth 613
Fisher, Eddie 698
Fitzgerald, Scott 309
Flame of New Orleans, The 508, *512*
Fleming, Alexander 224, 606, 656
Follow the Boys 533
Fonda, Henry 352, 528
Fontaine, Joan 496
Foolish Notion 558
Ford, John 594
Fordham University 596–7, 599
Foreign Affair 172, 599–600, 602, *611*
Forst, Willi 58, 79, 104, 245
Francis, Kay 405
Freeman, Stan 731–2, 734
Front Page, The 559–60, 566
Fry, Christopher 651–2
Furness, Betty 659

Gabin, Jean 231, 309, 508–9, *512–13*, 514–15, 517–22, *523, 526*, 530–4, 541, 546, *549*, 558, 562–66, *571*, 574–5, 579–81, 583–4, *585*, 587–8, 592–4, 598, 604–5, 613, 632, 651, 724, 764, 771
Gable, Clark 246, 316, 352–3, 356, 362, *367*, 541, 691
Garbo, Greta 78, 93, 122, 128, 142, 154, 158–60, 169–70, 241, 269, 272, 318, 438, 499, 529, 785
Garden of Allah, The 347, 387–8, 393–6, *399–400*, 402, 411, 430, 641
Garfield, John 529
Garland, Judy 392, 499, 539–40, 632–3, 643, 661, 723
Garmes 142
Garnett, Tay *511*
Gavin, Gen. James M. 554, 563–4,

567–8, *570–1*, 574–5, 579–83, 605, 613, 710, 772
Gazette (Montreal) 736
Gaynor, Janet 142
George Heinrich 573
German tour 694–5
Gersdorf, Countess 27–8, 30, 32
Gershwin, George 352
Giacometti, Alberto 447
Gibbons, Cedric 364, *369*
Gibson, Mike 756
Gilbert, John 257, 344, 352, 356, 357–9, 361–2, 364–6, *369*, 372, 374–6, *380*
Gilbert, Tinker 366, 371–2, 786
Gloriapalast Theater 79
'Go Away from My Window' 642
Goddard, Paulette 534, 633–4, 645, 724
Goebbels, Joseph 345, 483
Golden Earrings 172, 589–92, *609*
Gone with the Wind 444, 450, 496, 499–500
Goodman, Benny 530
Grable, Betty 530
Grace, Princess 671
Granger, Stewart 659
Grant, Cary 132, *145*, 152, 265, 352, *370*, 434, 459
Graves, Robert 434, 507
Great War *see* World War I
Greene, Graham 430
Greene, Milton 188, 630, 730
Guilleroff, Sidney 459, 535–6, *537*, 540, 660, 670–1
Guinness, Alec 606

Hall, Stanley 729
Hank 379, 384
Hari, Mata 29
Harlow, Jean 123, 270, 316, 352, 445
Hartnell, Norman 651
Hathaway, Henry 384
Hays Office 365
Hayworth, Rita 530, 533, 640
Hearst, William Randolph 153, 315–16, 788
Hemingway, Ernest 223, 306–8, *418*, 449, 451, 456, 472, 486, 566, 575, 600, *609*, 635, 656, 696
    Across the River and into the Trees 608
    Old Man and the Sea, The 634
Hepburn, Audrey 170

Hepburn, Katharine 188, 438, 783
Herman, Woody 530
Hermès 221
Heston, Charlton 628
Hindenburg 402, 437
Hirsh, Herbert 22
Hitchcock, Alfred 603, 606, *611*, 615
Hitler, Adolf 466, 478, 559
    Mein Kampf 207, 413
Hollander, Adi 580
Hollander, Frederick 67, 206, 373, 490, 599
Hollywood Canteen 530
Hollywood Reporter 91, 266
Hollywood Victory Committee 518
Holy Cross Hospital 752–3
'Honeysuckle Rose' 712
Hope, Bob 594, 622, 788
Hopkins, Miriam 270, 372, 387
Hopper, Hedda 522, 527, 640
Horne, Lena 192
Horney, Karen: *The Neurotic Personality of Our Time* 555
Horton, Edward Everett 352
Hotel du Cap d'Antibes 467, *474*, 485
Hotel Imperial 356, 384
House of Flowers 650, 654
'How to Be Loved' 637
Howard, Leslie 431, 499, 533–4
Hugenberg, Mr 122
Hughes, Howard 764
Hume, Benita 540
Hutton, Barbara 459

I, Claudius 434
Ile de France, SS 306
Independent Theatre Owners of America 438
Irene 501, 535–6, 539, 543, 593, 639
Israel 635–7, 694
Italy 546–7
It's in the Air 58
Iturbi, José 313, 327–8, 357
'I've Grown Accustomed to Her Face' 642

Jaffe 287
Jane Eyre 628
Jannings, Emil 44, 60–2, 67, 69, *73*, 75, 79–80, 82, 447, 786
Jaray, Hans 241, 248, 251, 255,

271, 284, 286, 303, 305, 313, 785
Jo (The Pirate) 488–9, 496, 723
Johannesburg 708
'Johnny' 642
Johns, Glynis 613
Jones, Allen 561
Jones, Robert Edmond 597
Judgement at Nuremberg 695–6, 699
Just a Gigolo 746, 764–6

Karinska 536
Kaye, Danny 534
Kennedy, Bobby 470, 485–6, 714
Kennedy, Joe 470, 489, 570, 703, 723
Kennedy, John F. (Jack) 470, 473, 476, 484–5, 529, 691, 703, 705, 771
Kennedy, Teddy 470, 485, 733
Kennedy family 470–1, 476, 485
Kent, Duke & Duchess of 412
Kibbee, Guy 526
King, Martin Luther 714
King and I, The 617, 625, 632, 650
Kinsey report 607
Kismet 172, 535–41, 537–8
Knight Without Armour 410, 413, 415, 454, 483
Knize, House of 238–9, 644
Kohner: The Governess 29
Korda, Alexander 386, 405, 421, 433
Kreuder, Peter 206

Lackner, Hans-Heinz von 19
Ladies' Home Journal 637
Lady Is Willing, The 515–17, 525, 535
La Jolla 527–8
Lake, Veronica 530
Lamarr, Hedy 530
Lamas, Fernando 678
Lang, Fritz 344, 357, 361, 454, 515, 615, 764
La Quinta 520
Lasky, Albert 789
Lastfogel, Abe 534, 543
Las Vegas 625–6, 628, 638–9, 641–4, 652–3, 656, 661, 674, 681, 690, 698
Laughton, Charles 434, 683–4, 687
Lawrence, Gertrude 447, 621, 631–2
Lawton, Frank 356
'Laziest Gal in Town' 607, 642

Lee, Anna 501
Legion of Honor 608, 613
Leigh, Vivien 651, 729
Leisen, Mitchell 515, 589, 591, 614, 638
Lennon, John 704
Lifar, Serge 303
Life 602, 609, 624, 630–1
'Lili Marlene' 642, 704
Lillie, Beatrice 473, 487
Lindbergh, Charles 134–5
Lion, Margo 58
Litvak, Anatole 676
Lodge, John 292
Loesser, Frank 490
Lombard, Carole 123, 269–70, 348–9, 362, 365, 370, 435, 518
London 407–8, 426–7, 709, 717
    Café de Paris 644, 649, 654, 656
    Claridge's hotel 407, 605
    Connaught Hotel 188
    Grosvenor House 748
    Queen's Theatre 706
    Royal Albert Hall 704
    Savoy Hotel 407, 726–9
Long, Huey 366
Long Island 619, 631, 683, 743, 752
Losch, Eduard von 24, 26, 29
Louis, Jean 639–40, 667, 770
Lubitsch, Ernst 54, 288, 302, 314, 342, 345–6, 384–5
    directs Angel 430, 436, 438, 439
    produces Desire 355–6, 361, 364–6, 374
Lupino, Ida 518

McAuliffe, Gen. Anthony 553–4
McCarthy, Charlie 518
McCleery, Albert 596–7
McCrea, Joel 331, 336–7
MacDonald, Jeanette 133, 266, 352, 785
McLean, Evelyn Walsh 477
MacMurray, Fred 378, 516
Mamoulian, Rouben 149 157, 199, 246, 272
    directs Song of Songs 159–62, 173–7, 179–80, 183–4, 186
Manley, Nellie 91, 109, 127, 173, 292–3, 354, 375, 393, 400, 402, 441, 490, 587, 589, 770
Manpower 512, 514
'Man's in the Navy, The' 501, 511

Manton, Maria *see* Riva, Maria
Marais, Jean 652
March, Frederic 352
Margaret, Princess 749
Marie Antoinette 458–9
Marina, Duchess of Kent 409, 411–12, 427
Marlene 773–5
Marshall, George 490, 495, 498
Marshall, Herbert 132, 141, 435–6, 516, 779
Martin, Mary 612
Martin, Tony 676
Martin Beck Theatre 558
Martin Roumagnac 585, 586
Mary, Miss 570–1
Mata Hari 93
Matul, Tamara (Tami) 104, *147–8*, *151*, 181, 205, 220, 223, *242*, 303, 305–6, 311–12, *481–2*, 763
  death 708
  ill health 330–1, 340–1, 386, 424, 454, 457, 466, 488, 558, 583–4, 593–7, 600, 613, 636, 675, 686–91
  relations with Rudi 57, 86, 166–7, 350, 430–1, 495–6, 558, 616, 668
Mauban, Marie 580
Maugham, Somerset 471–2
Max, Uncle 25
Max Reinhardt Academy 39–40, 506, 529
Maxwell, Elsa 451, 472–3
Mayer, Louis B. 445, 459
Medal of Freedom 599
Meet Me in St. Louis 539
'Mein Blondes Baby' 207–8
Menjou, Adolphe 786
Mercury Theatre of the Air 533
Merkel, Una 498
Merman, Ethel 378
Messel, Oliver 650
Methodist Medical Center 738
MGM 534–5, 540
Midsummer Night's Dream 409
Milland, Ray 590, 592, 779
Miller, Glenn 530
Miller, Henry 542
Miller, Mitch 629
Milner, Victor 176
Mitterrand, President 613
Monte Carlo 651, 668–9

Monte Carlo Story, The 662, *665*, 669–70, 672–3
Montreal 735–6
Moontide 517
Moore, Colleen 263
Moore, Grace 374
Morgan, Michèle 508
Morgenthau, Henry 484
Morocco 81, 85, 89–90, 93, *95*, 100–2, 116, 118, 179, 330, 356, 786, 789
Mourning Becomes Electra 515
Murrow, Edward R. 223, 507–8, *623*, 632, 656–8

Nazis 206–7, 319–20, 534
Necklace 356
Negri, Pola 384
New York 83, 193, 307–9, 458
  Ambassador Hotel 193
  Broadway 711, 713, *719*
  El Morocco 633
  Plaza Hotel 600
  Radio City Music Hall 194
  Sherry Netherland Hotel 495, 600
  Waldorf-Astoria 308–9, 433
  World's Fair 495
Ninotchka 499
Niven, David 662, 776–7
No Highway in the Sky 613
Normandie, SS 402–5, 431, *440*, 441, 451, 458, 483, 518
North, John Ringling 634

Oberon, Merle 357, 433
O'Connor, Una 685
'One for My Baby' 642
O'Neill, Eugene: *A Moon for the Misbegotten* 596–7
Oppenheimer, J. Robert 656
Orry-Kelly 319, 435
Otto, Uncle 17–18

Paderewski, Ignacy 303
Pal Joey 639–40
Pallette, Eugene 352
Palm Springs 359–60
Paramount Studio 75–8, 89–90, 93, *98*, 111, 115, 122, 128, 132, 159–61, 226–7, 265, 297, 436, 438, 454, 456, 587

Paris 188, 203, 208–25, 227–35, 255,
301, 409, 413, 423, 429, 442–3, 460–3,
491–2, 556, 565, *586*, 604, 652, 704,
714, 767–92
  1937 Exposition 451
  American Hospital 744
  Belle Aurore 219–20
  Hotel George V 423
  Hotel Lancaster 442–3, 460, 484
  Hotel Palais-Royal 651
  Hotel Raphael 673
  Hotel Windsor 462
  Korniloff's 303, 580
  Little Hungary 216–19
  Maxim's 222–5
  Notre-Dame Cathedral 227–8
  Plaza Athénée 255, 301
Paris, SS 258–9
Parker, Dorothy 309
Parsons, Louella 176, 353, 385
Pasternak, Joseph 488–90, 496, 498, 501,
508, *512*
Patton, Gen. George S. 223, 552–3, *569*
Peer Gynt 596
Perry, Fred *148*, 155–6, 168, 181, 427
Philipe, Gérard 582
Photoplay 177
Piaf, Edith 584–7, 600, 606–7, 632–3, *664*,
704, 771
Picasso, Pablo 451
Pickford, Mary 240, 352
Picturegoer 397
Pierce, Jack 563
Pittsburgh 524
Plunkett, Walter 318
Polydor 133, 188
Pommer, Erich 66, 71
Pompidou, President 613
Pondel, Dot 126, 128, 173–5, 277,
324, 770
Porten, Henny 26–7, 29–31, 691
Porter, Cole 352, 434, 459, 607
Powell, William 352, 445
Power, Tyrone 337, 529, 629, 684,
686
Preminger, Otto 639
Princess Comes Across, The 435

Queen Elizabeth 594, 613
Queen Mary 490, 492–3

Raft, George 352, 378, 436, 514, 519,
522, 662
Rancho Notorious 615, 627
Rathbone, Basil 337, 352, 388
Raush, Otti 15
Reagan, Nancy 782
Redford, Robert 760
Reichsfilmblatt 82
Reinhardt, Max 40, 454, 506
Reisch, Walter 302
Reitz, Prof. 36, 39
Remarque, Erich Maria 206, 231, 464–7,
469–73, *474–5*, 477–8, 484, 486–8,
490–8, 502–3, 506–9, *524*, 560, 597,
600, 604–5, *612*, 629, 633–4, 637, 644,
656, 675, 724, 772
  All Quiet on the Western Front 464
  Arch of Triumph, The 469, 581
  Three Comrades 486
Rennie, Michael 632, 661
Renoir, Jean 514
Resi 74, 81, 83–6, 103–4, 106–7, 109,
193–4, 196
'Rhinoceros' 496, 500, 502, 504, 527–8
Ribbentrop, Joachim von 466
Richee, Eugene 188
Richepin, Jean 207
Richman, Harry 84
Richter, Anne Marie 15
Richthofen, Baron Manfred von 20
Riefenstahl, Leni 447
Righter, Carroll 516, 582, 594–5, 620,
660, 675
Riva, Maria *46, 51, 97–8, 144, 146–7, 149,*
242–3, 273, 416, 482, 610, 624, 664
  acting career 277–82, 388, 515, 518,
    522, 529, 558–9, 596, 614, 618–19,
    628, 630–1, 635, 654, 662, 671
  birth 53–4
  birth of children 599–600, 602, 608,
    613, 681–2, 695
  first marriage 526, 531, 555, 589
  kidnap attempt 135–6
  second marriage 597
  sexually abused 504
Riva, David 696, 701, *718*, 751, 779
Riva, Michael 602–3, 607, 637, 652, *666*,
696, 710, 714, 723, 752
Riva, Paul 682, 696, *718*, 751
Riva, Peter *666*, 696, 710, 725, 733

Riva, William (Bill) 596–8, 600, 602, *610*, 618, 635, 662, *664*, 667, 671, 682–3, 698, 710, *718*, 783
Riviera Country Club 324
RKO 627
Robin, Leo 329
Robinson, Edward G. 352, 514
Rogers, Ginger 352, 427, 530
Rogers, Will 360
Romero, Cesar 331, 336
Rooney, Mickey 568
Roosevelt, Franklin D. 559
Rosendorf, Margaret 26
Rossellini 674, 786
Rudi *see* Sieber, Rudolph

Sager, Carole Bayer 782
Salk, Dr Jonas 656
Salzburg 251–2, 443, 448, 785
San Fernando Valley 325, 616
San Francisco 737
Saroyan, William 656
Scarlet Empress, The 53, 226, 231, 266–9, 272, *273–6*, 277–9, 282–4, 286–92, 295–7, 299, 324, 641, 787, 789
Schell, Maximilian 773–5
Schiaparelli 429, 785
Schildkraut, Joseph 388
Schonbach, Erna 31
Schöneberg 5, 21, 795–6
Schulberg, B.P. 75, 87
Schultz, H. 14
Schupp, Erich 35
Schuricke, Fritzi 22–3
Screen Actors Guild 591
'See What the Boys in the Back Room Will Have' 496, 642
Seidman, Dr 744
Seidman, Ginette & Paul-Emil 651
Selznick, David 386–7, 395, 397–402, 430
Seven Sinners 501, *511*
Shady Grove Theater 734
Shanghai Express 98–9, 115, 117, 127, 132, 142, 179, 211, 771, 785
Shaw, George Bernard 447
Shearer, Norma 123, 458
Sheridan, Ann 530
Sieber, Anton & Rosa 250, 445, 572, 573–4, 577

Sieber, Maria Elizabeth *see* Riva, M.
Sieber, Rudolph (Rudi) 46–7, *50–1*, 52–4, 77, 85–6, 121–2, 124, 129–30, 141, *144, 146, 148–51*, 163, 210–11, 221, 234, *243*, 304, 319, 386, 405, *416, 482*, 496, 563, 593, *719*
death 763–4
health 239–40, 616–17, 667–8, 713–14, 752–5, 758, 761
marriage 44–5
relations with Tami 57, 166–7, 320, 341, 350, 414, 430–1, 558
small-holding 616–17, 655–6
Siegel, Bugsy 640
Simpson, Edward 595
Simpson, Wallis *see* Windsor, Duchess of
Sinatra, Frank 541, 632, 656, 658–62, 667, 676, 678, 680–1, 783
Skelton, Red 662
Smith, C. Aubrey 363
Snow White and the Seven Dwarfs 456
Song of Songs 149, 157, 160–3, 166, 170, 175–6, 178, 180–1, 184, 186, 189
South Pacific 608
Soviet Union 232, 725
Sperling, Hilde 31
Spiegel, Sam 632, 651
Spoliansky, Mischa 58, 60, 206, 606
Stage Fright 605–6, *611*
Stein, Gertrude 426, 452
Stevenson, Adlai 223, 632, 656–7
Stewart, Jimmy 488–90, 495, 497, *510*, 613
Stinchfield, Dr Frank 747–9, 757–9, 762
Streisand, Barbra 314–15
Strohman, D. 34
Stürmer, Der 483
Swanson, Gloria 352, 471
Switzerland 698–9, 706

Tamara (Tami) *see* Matul, T.
Tauber, Richard 58, 91, 454, 607
Taylor, Elizabeth 630, 650, 662, 674, 698, 711
Taylor, Sam 667, 669, 672
Tea and Sympathy 662
Ten Commandments, The 652, 656
Thalberg, Irving 154, 170, 427, 458
Theatre Guild 558, 596
Thimig, Helene 506

Thomas, Danny 543, 545, *549*, 638, 662
Threepenny Opera, The 59
Tiffany 644
Tilden, Bill 155
Todd, Michael 656, 662, 672, 691
Todd, Richard 606–7
Tone, Franchot 352
Tony Award 711
Touch of Evil 681, *700*
Tracy, Spencer 530, *699*
Trianon Palace Hotel 203
Trundy 669
Turner, Lana 530
TV Special 725–6, 729–30
Two Neckties 60
Tynan, Kenneth 648–51

UCCLA Medical Center 753, 758–9
Ufa 43, 60, 62–3, 76, 122, 153, 177, 488
United Cerebral Palsy Organization
    634–5, 654, 677
Universal 488–90, 517
USO 534, 541, 543–7, 552, 554, 559–60,
    563, 576

Valli, Tante 9–11, 18–20, 22
Velez, Lupe 91, 246
Venice 460, *461*, 465
'Vie en Rose, La' 607, 704
Vienna 57, 235–51, 305
Visconti, Luchino 764
Vogue 630, 635
von Sternberg, Joseph *96*, 100, 109–14,
    120–4, 134, *144, 146, 151*, 156, 158–9,
    174, 177–9, 189, 191, 245–7, 270, *322*,
    356, 387, 434, 460, *461*, 489, *612*
    death 302, 723
    directs *Blonde Venus* 132
    directs *Dishonored* 93
    directs *Morocco* 85–7, 89–93, 101
    directs *Shanghai Express* 115–16, 119,
        126, 128
    directs *The Blue Angel* 66–7, 69–77,
        72–3
    directs *The Devil Is a Woman* 316–17,
        333–6, 342–4, 347–8
    directs *The Scarlet Empress* 226–7,
        257–8, 263–4, 268, 277–9, 283, 288,
        291, 295–9
    first meeting with M. 61–3

von Sternberg, Mrs 107, 121, 723
Vye, Murvyn 592

Waldorf, Claire 573
Walter 546
Wanger, Walter 83
Warner, Ann *513*
Warner Brothers 514
Washington 703
Waxman 206
Wayne, John 501–2, *511*, 517, *524*,
    556, 758
Webb, Clifton 158, 318–19, 363, 409–12,
    417–18, 421, 426–7, 430, 433, 435–7,
    457, 724
Weimar 35, *37*, 39
Welles, Orson 223, 337, 479, 530, 533,
    638–9, 681, *700*, 725, 771, 788
West, Mae 132, 143, 152, 238, 265, 345–6,
    365, 377–8, *380*, 436
West, Vera 490
Westmore 324
'When the World Was Young' 642
'Where Have All the Flowers Gone'
    642, 736
'Whoopee' 642
Who's Afraid of Virginia Woolf? 711
Wilder, Billy 329, 590, 599,
    611, 630, 652, 658–9, 682–6,
    687
Wilding, Michael 605–7, *612*, 613–14,
    621, 630, 632, 650, 662, 674–5,
    698, 779
Willi, Uncle 17
William Morris Agency 534
Willing, Major Neville 643–4,
    648
Willys 319
Winchell, Walter *602*
Windsor, Duchess of 412–13, 445,
    724–5
Windsor, Duke of 412–13, 724–5
Wing, Toby 269
Witness for the Prosecution 682–6,
    687–9
Wizard of Oz, The 499
Women, The 529
Wong, Anna May 127, 436
World War I 16–21, 23, 25–7,
    29–33

World War II 490–2, 499–500, 506–8,
  514, 517, 521–2, 528, 530, 543–55,
  558, 561–2
Wyman, Jane 607
Wynne, Evie 547

Young, Loretta *369*, 379
Yuma 392–3

Zanuck 509, 532
Ziegfeld's *Follies* 314
Zukor, Adolph 282